CLASSIC
WALKS
of Australia

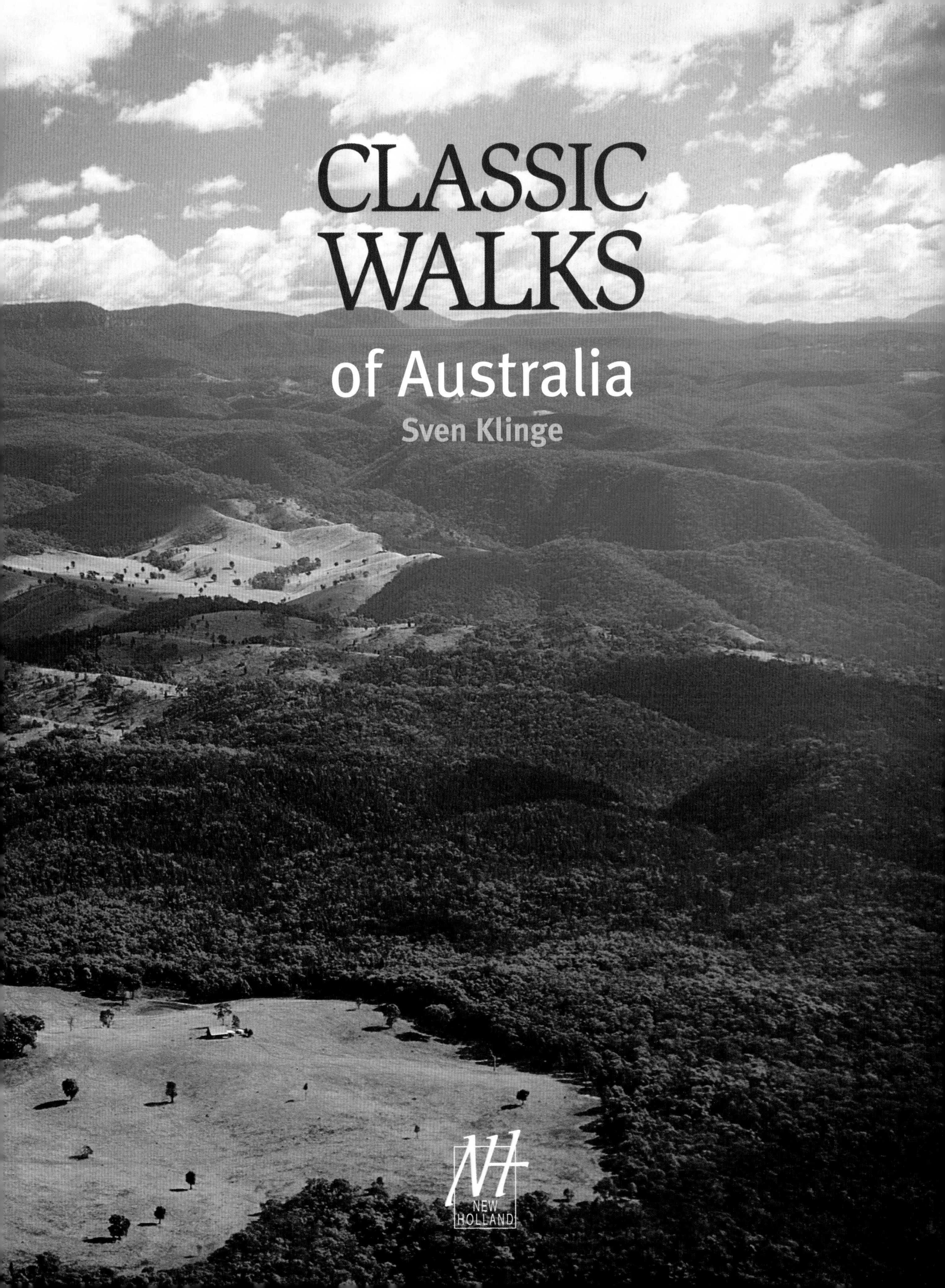

CLASSIC
WALKS
of Australia

Sven Klinge

NH
NEW
HOLLAND

For the bushwalking pioneers whose
passion and commitment were instrumental
in the formation of many of Australia's most
important national parks

First published in Australia in 2000 by
New Holland Publishers (Australia) Pty Ltd
Sydney • Auckland • London • Cape Town

14 Aquatic Drive Frenchs Forest NSW 2086 Australia
218 Lake Road Northcote Auckland New Zealand
24 Nutford Place London W1H 6DQ United Kingdom
80 McKenzie Street Cape Town 8001 South Africa

National Library of Australia
Cataloguing-in-Publication data:
Klinge, Sven, 1969- .
Classic Walks of Australia
Bibliography.
Includes index.
ISBN 1 86436 5498
Hiking – Australia – Guidebooks. 2. Australia – Guidebooks. I. Title.
796.510994

Publishing Manager: Anouska Good
Project Editor: Jennifer Lane
Copy Editors: Lynn Cole and Jennifer Lane
Designer, layout artist and typesetter: Anna Warren, Warren Ventures
Cover Designers: Peta Zoubakin and Nanette Backhouse
Maps: Guy Holt
Reproduction: Colour Symphony, Singapore
Printer: Kyodo Printing, Singapore

The author and publisher have made every effort to ensure that the information in this book was correct at the time of going to press and accept no responsibility for any errors that may have occurred. Transport services, park management, opening times, access routes, facilities, place names, amenities, official walk routes, track conditions, regulations and permit requirements can change over time so it is recommended that the reader call the relevant park management body, operator or service to confirm any information that may be required, prior to undertaking any of these walks.

Photographic credits

All photographs, including cover images by Sven Klinge with the exception of: Karin Klinge, inside back cover (author portrait); Frank Bichler pp 138, 261; Colin Campbell pp 14, 21, 30, 32; Carmen Frugone pp 61; Kay Gordon pp 43, 266, 272, 280, 316, 317, 318, 320, 325, 330, 333, 335; Gerd Klinge pp 119, 277; Karin Klinge pp 9, 64, 270, 322; New Holland Image Library pp 40; Dean Piggott pp 110; Noelene Proud pp 286, 295, 303; Kerrie Tambree pp 140; Tyrone Thomas pp 174, 186, 192, 200, 212, and Emma Vedris, image at far left on front cover and pp 309, 310.
The copyright for all photographs that appear in this book resides with the individual photographers.

Front cover (left to right): Natures Window in the Kalbarri National Park, WA; Majestic Blue Gum Forest in Blue Mountains National Park, NSW; subtropical forest on Lord Howe Island off the coast of NSW; Uluru, Kata Tjuta National Park, NT. Back cover (left to right): Looking over the Bunyeroo Creek Valley on the Heysen Trail in Flinders Ranges National Park, SA; The famous Cazneaux Tree at the entrance to Wilpena Pound in Flinders Ranges National Park, SA; The turquoise waters of Wineglass Bay in Freycinet National Park, TAS; Eurobin Creek, Mt Buffalo, in Alpine National Park, VIC. Image pp.ii, iii (title page): The Capertee Valley from Genowlan Point, Gardens of Stone National Park, NSW. Image p.18, Mulligan Falls in the south of Hinchinbrook Island, QLD; p.70, Crater Bluff from the Grand High Tops, Warrumbungle National Park, NSW; p.166, A gnarled snow gum glows red in the setting sun on the Brindabella Range near Bimberi Peak, ACT; p.174, Heavily eroded cliffs in the northern Grampians, VIC; p.222, Looking south from the Devils Kitchen along the coastal cliffs of the Tasman Peninsula, TAS; p.266, The arid Gammon Ranges, SA; p.286, The Pinnacles in Nambung National Park, WA; p.318, A termite mound in the Litchfield National Park, NT.

Contents

Publisher's Note

This book strives to present a comprehensive collection of the very best walks in Australia, but it is not a practical guide to camping, bushwalking and bushcraft. We recommend that all readers consult such a guide or handbook before undertaking any of the walks outlined in this book. *Don't Die in the Bush*, by Sven Klinge and Adrian Hart (New Holland, 2000), is a definitive guide of this kind, with a specific focus on equipment, techniques, health and safety, first aid, special clothing, food and energy requirements, navigation, bush skills and dangers.

It should be noted that the maps in this book have been designed only as simple visual guides to the area concerned and are not intended for use out in the bush. Every effort has been made to ensure the accuracy of the maps, which are based on the best source material available. However, this material varies widely from area to area and this variation will inevitably be reflected in the maps presented in this book.

Recent national park policy has begun to de-anglicise commonly used European place names and reinstate traditional Aboriginal place names. A famous example of this reversion has seen 'Ayers Rock' replaced with 'Uluru'. This book uses the names that were accepted and correct at the time of publication, but it is worth noting that common names will change as this process continues.

Any guidebook grows out of date with time, as new tracks are opened and old ones re-routed or closed altogether. Whenever you encounter a change that may affect the information in this book, the publishers would be grateful if you would advise them in writing; they will ensure that such details are incorporated in future editions.

While all care has been taken to ensure that information contained in this book is correct at the time of publication, neither the author, nor the cartographer, nor the publisher can accept any liability for accident, injury, damage or other misadventure incurred in relying on this book. We wish you safe and enjoyable bushwalking.

About the Author

Natures Window, Kalbarri National Park, Western Australia.

Sven Klinge began venturing into the Australian wilderness in the 1980s and quickly explored a host of national parks and state forests throughout eastern Australia. His first outdoor guidebook, *Cycling the Bush: 100 Rides in NSW*, was published when he was 19.

The other titles that comprise his *Cycling the Bush* series, including *The Best Rides in Australia*, form Australia's premier mountain biking guidebooks. A keen wilderness photographer, his landscape images have appeared in various books, advertisements and magazine articles.

While Sven has toured extensively throughout Australia, New Zealand and Europe, it is the great mountain wilderness world heritage areas of south-west Tasmania and Fiordland in New Zealand that particularly draw his attention. In addition to writing cycling books, Sven has also co-authored a major national walking title on Australia's mountains with Tyrone T. Thomas as well as a camping guide with Adrian Hart.

Educated at Sydney University, Sven currently works as an accountant, contract network administrator and freelance writer for professional legal journals.

The view north from Nina Peak to Ramsay Bay on tropical north Queensland's Hinchinbrook Island.

Acknowledgments

The author wishes to thank the following people, companies and organisations for their support in the publication of this book. New Holland Publishers for their advice and encouragement, Emma Vedris for her detailed illustrations and assistance with compiling transparencies and mapping, as well as proofreading; Noelene Proud, Kay Gordon, Colin J. Campbell, Tyrone T. Thomas, Gerd Klinge and Karin Klinge for contributing transparencies; Noelene Proud, Kay Gordon, Tim Sullivan and Peter Gibbes for their research. Thanks also to all my walking companions over the years who have all had to endure, patiently, my constant fiddling with the camera: Adrian, Andrea, Belinda, Bernarda, Bronwyn, Cam, Carmen, Caroline, Dean, Emma, Francis, Frank, Jason, Julie, Kalina, Kerrie, Linda, Matthew, Peta, Rupen, Sean and Tyrone. Many thanks go to my sponsors, PETZL, Berrivale Orchards, Mountain Designs, Cascade Designs, Paddy Pallin, Macpac Wilderness Equipment, Maxwell, Salomon, Kathmandu, High and Wild Mountain Adventures, Macson Trading and Adventure Designs.

Thanks to the many government departments that provided extensive material on national parks, vegetation, wildlife, historical information and walking track details: Adrian Goodrich (Department of Natural Resources and Environment, Victoria), Andrew Hanna (Land Information Centre, New South Wales), Graham Hudson and Danuta Gur (Queensland National Parks and Wildlife Service), Graham Stanton (SUNMAP/Department of Natural Resources, Queensland), Jennifer Fry (WHA Unit, Parks and Wildlife Service, Tasmania), John Giles (New South Wales National Parks and Wildlife Service), John Lane (Department of Environment and Natural Resources, South Australia), Kathryn van Akker (Environment ACT, Australian Capital Territory), Kate Booth (Namadgi National Park Visitors' Centre, Australian Capital Territory), Robert Avery (TASMAP, Tasmania), Toby Ware and Trent Vincent (Queensland National Parks and Wildlife Service), Elizabeth Stafford, Australian Bureau of Meteorology, Jon Guyver, Department of Land and Water Conservation, Tracey Orr (AUSLIG [Natmap/Ausmap] Canberra), and William Rogers (Department of Land Administration, Western Australia).

Much of the national parks information presented within was compiled from the plans of management, as well as numerous brochures, pamphlets, booklets and leaflets from the respective state national parks administration service.

Author's Preface

This is the book I've always wanted to write—an encyclopedic compilation listing Australia's very best walks. I can still recall being transfixed in a Sydney University bookshop in 1989, flicking through the pages of Robert Rankin's mesmerising photographs in his classic work *Wild Walks of Australia*. The majesty of the book's 25 depicted regions was awe-inspiring and, over the next few years, I set out to explore them myself, both as a walker and researcher. I quickly learnt that the bush isn't always as tranquil as

Empress Falls, Valley of the Waters, New South Wales.

calendars and posters might suggest. It can be a harsh, frightening place. White-knuckled terror gripped me as I descended from Federation Peak's dramatic near-vertical summit, realising that the placement of every footstep on the slippery wet quartzite was crucial. It didn't matter that help was days away—the 600m fall would ensure that rescuers had little to do. Being caught on Victoria's exposed Razorback ridge in the midst of a ferocious lightning storm was another memorable experience where adrenalin seemed to flow thicker than blood. There are times when it feels as though the wilderness is rejecting the intrusion of marauding humans. However, despite all this, or perhaps because of it, the bush never loses its astonishing beauty.

Other areas soon captivated me—the magnificent turquoise coral lagoon from Lord Howe Island's Mt Gower, the reflections in Lake Tali Karng on a windless day, the carpeted green hills from Bluff Knoll, and the towering sandstone canyons in the heart of the vast Wollemi National Park, to name just a few. Walking is, and will always be, the only way to see these places.

It is hoped that wilderness will always be a constant. Somehow it's reassuring to know that while we live and work in our airconditioned concrete boxes, it lies out there, timeless, reminding us of our origins and our fragility.

Introduction

Hiking. Tramping. Rambling. Trekking. Bushwalking. Whatever the term, the activity represents 'escape'. Where better to seek this escape than Australia? The variety in topography on this oldest of continents is astounding. The Great Divide spans 6000km of mountains containing ancient rainforests, dissected rocky plateaus, and an alpine zone larger than Switzerland's. Australia's low population density has left many rivers and lakes in pristine condition. Colourful sandstone gorges, carved out by ancient seasonal deluges, punctuate the empty interior. The bushwalkers of Australia have been blessed with many a lifetime of escape venues in this vast, empty, varied land.

The term 'bushwalking' does not only apply to eucalypt bush terrain. Coastal heath, sand dunes, alpine meadows and rocky plateaus are all 'bushwalking' environments.

Although bushwalking is a blanket term, the rewards can be quite different for each participant. A walker might focus on the wildlife, or the lure of swimming in a pristine river, or camping in a remote gorge, or the unique geological formations of the area or simply the light—to determine the optimal time of day to set up camera gear.

The bush offers many opportunities to improve fitness or survival skills, overcome personal challenges and obstacles and seek out historical, Aboriginal and cultural sites. Many people also find that social bonding is accelerated by the unique interaction that the natural environment allows. Others find the solitude a very comforting opportunity to focus inward. This collection of walks represents the widest possible variety of terrain to satisfy the most eclectic and discerning bushwalking tastes. See you out there!

The Australian Bush

The Australian wilderness has a deserved reputation for danger. What it doesn't have in large carnivorous animals, it makes up for in extreme isolation, the oldest and most inhospitable terrain, weather that knows no pattern and the world's most venomous snakes and spiders. 'Be prepared' is the scout's motto—'Be warned' is the Australian bushwalker's.

Weather can be unpredictable, with sudden and violent southerly busters reducing summertime temperatures from consistent 40°C maximums to less than 10°C in a matter of hours. Snow falls regularly around the Australian Alps in summer. Many other areas are prone to freak blizzard conditions—the Barrington Tops, the New England Tablelands, most of highland Tasmania and even Sydney's Blue Mountains. Cyclones in the tropical north cause mayhem between the months of November and April, yet more than 50 per cent of the country is classified as desert, with only the coastal ranges receiving reliable rainfalls.

The highly flammable eucalyptus trees that comprise a large proportion of Australian forests can also be dangerous: the oily leaf-litter can combust spontaneously when conditions are right, creating bushfires that have killed many a walker. Coastal mountains areas can suffer from lingering fog, making navigation skills essential. The sun itself is a potential menace, causing dehydration and heat exhaustion (hypothermia) with summer heat waves. The thinning ozone layer in the atmosphere above Australia increases the likelihood of severe sunburn and melanoma skin cancers. The wild, untamed terrain—cliffs, mountains, rivers, swamps, rainforest, desert plains and thick scrubs—also create their own unique risks.

Climate

The climate of the Australian continent falls into six major zones. These should be taken into consideration and walks undertaken during a season when surplus clothing and other equipment is not required.

Hot Humid Zone

This zone extends from the Kimberley to the Top End of the Northern Territory. Winter is the most comfortable time of year to be in this part of the country. Days are very warm and sunny; nights are warm, too. On average, rain falls only one day a month. Summer is sultry—hot and humid with rain and thunderstorms. Spring and autumn are also hot

Looking towards Mt Eliza from Lovers Bay, Lord Howe Island, New South Wales.

and rather humid. The 'build-up' to the monsoon season (November) is the least comfortable time of year; humidity and temperature is high without the benefit of cooling rain. Local folklore has it that November is the season for 'mango madness'—strange behaviour thought to be induced by climatic stress. The average sea surface temperature around Cairns is 28.1°C in summer and 22.6°C in winter.

Warm Humid Zone

This climate zone extends down the coasts of northern Australia and is best visited in winter, autumn or spring. Summer is very humid and very warm. In any part of the zone, winter is recommended for those planning a walking holiday. Brisbane, with an average of 24 dry days in July, is a typical example of this climate.

Hot Dry Zone with Warm Winter

The northern inland zone is best visited in winter, when warm days with endless sunshine are almost guaranteed. For example, in Longreach, in July, the maximum temperature averages about 23°C, with about 29 dry days and more than nine hours of sunshine each day. Heat stress and dehydration can be problems in the hotter months—if you plan to do strenuous walks, dawn is the best (coolest) time. In Longreach, the daily maximum temperature usually reaches around 37°C in January.

Hot Dry Zone with Cool Winter

This region covers the interior of Australia which is, again, best visited in winter, when warm, dry days are the norm. Winter nights can be very cold. Autumn and spring are good times to visit the southern parts of this zone. Wildflowers bloom in spring if rain has fallen. Again, heat stress and dehydration can be problems in the hotter months.

Temperate Zone (Warm Summer, Cool Winter)

The southern lowlands are suitable for exploring at any time of year. Autumn and spring are the most comfortable seasons in most parts, with summer the best time on the south coast of the continent. The weather is more changeable than in the tropics; cool cloudy days alternate with warmth and sunshine. Rainfalls do not usually last very long. Melbourne is an example of this climatic type.

Cool Temperate Zone (Mild to Warm Summer, Cold Winter)

The south-east highlands and Tasmania are usually very pleasant in summer, although summer snow can fall in much of the region. Wildflowers bloom during midsummer in the high country. Above the tree line, the summer sunshine is intense; walking and cycling trips might be best made in autumn. The higher mountains are usually suitable for cross-country skiing in winter and early spring, but snowfall varies greatly from year to year. Weather in the mountains is very changeable at any time of year. Low cloud rolling in over the snowfields may create a 'white-out', where the horizon vanishes, making navigation difficult. Thredbo is an example of this climate type.

Environmental hazards

For the well-prepared walker, there are relatively few dangers in the Australian bush. Far more injuries, accidents and deaths occur in day-to-day city life. Indeed, there is a far greater risk of being hurt at home or work than on a bush track. The crucial difference is that at home, resources and help are readily available if any misadventure occurs. Environmental hazards of the Australian bush include:

* temperature extremes
* bushfires
* cyclones and high winds
* thunderstorms and lightning
* floods
* desert
* cliffs.

Temperature Extremes

Although Australia is a warm country by world standards, the bush can become like a freezer in the winter months. In summer, southerly busters and thunderstorms can bring welcome, though sudden, drops in temperature, along with torrential rains, high winds, hail and lightning. Without southerly changes, summer temperatures can remain above 40°C for several days in a row—a heatwave.

By contrast, there are areas on Tasmania's south-west coast that can receive up to four months of continuous drizzly rain. Over Cape York, in Queensland, rainfall is regular in the wet season, but it is the sudden tropical deluge variety. Snowfalls across south-eastern Australia can, in extreme cases, extend as far up the Great Dividing Range as Brisbane. Light snow can also occur around Melbourne and on the Mt Lofty Ranges outside Adelaide. Even without this obvious white evidence, the bush can become bitterly cold, with maximum day temperatures rarely higher than 5°C.

Bushfires

Given the generous covering of flammable eucalypts and bush acacias in many of Australia's wilderness areas, the presence of hot and dry conditions also brings with it the risk of bushfire. When planning a trip, check the fire-danger status with the national parks authorities. Total fire bans may be in place making the lighting of any fire, even a match for a cigarette, illegal.

Wearing long clothes, particularly wool or cotton, offers the best protection from fires. A large clearing, ravine or gully can also be good shelter if you cannot outdistance or outskirt the fire. A car can be a safe refuge in smaller fires. Close the windows, doors and any ventilation system, duck down low and cover up. Don't try to escape on foot.

Cyclones and High Winds

Severe tropical cyclones, common to northern Australia between November and April, can reach speeds of more than 200kph. No walk should be maintained or even attempted if a cyclone warning is issued, because devastating winds and torrential flooding rains are likely.

Southerly busters are sudden wind squalls that replace hot north-westerly winds near the coast, bringing sudden temperature decreases of 10–15°C with wind speeds of up to 135km/h. Take care to avoid camping under trees with dead branches that may fall.

Thunderstorms and Lightning

Thunderstorms can develop from a type of cloud named cumulonimbus. This large cloud can punch upwards at heights greater than 10km; it is easily identified by its dark underbelly and bulging sides. There is as much energy as a small atomic bomb within such a cloud. Thunderstorm activity is most prominent in the tropical north of Australia and down along the Great Dividing Range from south-east Queensland, through New South Wales and the Victorian highlands. Thunderstorms can occur at any time of year, but they are more regular in hotter, unsettled conditions.

The major hazards of thunderstorms include large and sudden rainfall that can lead to flooding, lightning, high winds and in some particularly severe thunderstorms, hail. Lightning will seek the path of least resistance between the earth and the cloud, and this can include people. Avoid high earth points such as lone trees, boulders or the tops of hills and ranges. Keep low and minimise the contact points made by the body with the ground by sitting in a huddled position, knees up by the chin and heels close to the body.

Floods

River crossings can be hazardous at any time. If there has been recent heavy rain causing the water level to rise, such crossings can become extremely dangerous. The best way to cross a river or stream is to find a safe, shallow section and walk or wade from one side to the other. Be wary of:

- fast-moving, unclear water or deep water
- water with flotsam and debris in the current
- rolling boulders or slippery footings
- underwater snags, such as half-submerged trees or branches
- whirlpools or eddies where the current greets the sides of a bluff
- cold water temperatures, which can cause hypothermia or shock
- downstream rapids or falls.

Desert

As one of the driest continents on earth, Australia presents special risks, especially when you are walking through the arid or semi-arid regions across the centre of the country. While this isn't all desert, it shares similar traits: clear, wide skies, low average rainfall, sparse vegetation and extremes of temperature.

Maintaining an adequate water supply is the walker's chief concern in these parts. Keep plenty of water reserves on hand in containers and take note of resupply points on the map. Low water supplies can become polluted, so it pays to pack water purification systems or chlorine and iodine tablets as an additional precaution. The best times to visit deserts are in winter, when the heat is less fierce.

Although it doesn't rain in semi-arid areas very often, when it does it comes down by the bucketful. Dusty tracks and trails can become boggy very quickly and access can be cut for several days at a time. Because of the parched earth, rain can run off briskly, flowing into dry creek beds and causing flash floods.

Cliffs

The rugged cliffs, canyons and gorges that characterise Australia's mountain ranges, coastlines and outback regions offer some of the most breathtaking natural vistas in the world. The risk of falling is one of the most common dangers faced by bushwalkers. Most people experience a sense of vertigo as they approach a cliff-top and for this reason it is best to keep as close to the ground as possible when near the edge. If the urge to look over the edge is simply too great, then at least do it by lying down flat, keeping your stomach on the ground. Many cliffs, especially those along the Great Dividing Range, are made from sedimentary rocks that can crumble and shear from the effects of winds and rain. In fact, most accidents occur immediately after storms when erosion processes accelerate.

En route to The Knob, Para Wirra Recreation Park in the northern Adelaide Hills, South Australia.

Planning your walk

Day walks

Lazy car park-to-lookout strolls aside, a day walk can require almost as much preparation and fitness as an overnight walk. In southern Tasmania in late December, daylight can last more than 16 hours, allowing considerable distances to be traversed. The following is a broad checklist of gear one might pack for a typical day walk. Of course, the length of the walk, the experience of the walkers, the type of terrain and the weather forecast will determine the exact provisions needed.

Camera and film
Daypack: 20–50 L capacity
Firelighter
First-aid kit
Hat
High-carbohydrate snack food
Walking boots
Insect repellent
Detailed map and compass
Pocketknife
Sunglasses
Sunscreen
Toilet paper
Water—at least 3 L (more if hot weather is expected)
Waterproof jacket and warm jumper (especially if in mountainous country).

Overnight walks

Most Australian wilderness areas are large enough that many places cannot be accessed in one day. The distance may be small, but the terrain can be so rugged that progress is excruciatingly slow, requiring an overnight stay. On other occasions, or on longer walks, it may simply be pleasant to have a rest day along the way. The time immediately before, during and after sunset gives nature an ambience that day walkers miss out on. Silver leaves glow a brilliant red, the wind stops and the only sound audible is the crackling of logs in the campfire. Walkers need to carry their own sleeping gear and portable shelter. In addition to the list of gear for day walks, the following will also be needed:

Change of clothes
Cooking pots/billy
Cutlery
Ground sheet
Meals
Overnight pack: 60–70 L capacity (instead of day pack)
Personal toiletries
Scouring pad
Shelter
Sleeping bag
Sleeping mat
Stove and fuel
Torch/candles
Towel
Warm jumper.

Mt Bowen and The Thumb from Warrawilla Lagoon, Hinchinbrook Island, Queensland.

Expedition walks

When venturing into the most remote and inhospitable terrain, such as a traverse of the Western Arthur Range in south-west Tasmania, overnight walkers must be completely self-sufficient. Expedition walks are normally of long duration (up to two weeks) and often venture through trackless territory. In the event of an emergency, assistance can be as far as 100km away. Years of experience, a high level of fitness and excellent navigation skills are a prerequisite for undertaking these expedition-style walks. In addition to the two gear lists for day and overnight walks, the following may be needed for such expeditions:

Expedition pack: 70–80 L capacity (instead of day pack)
Contingency food provisions: usually enough spare food for 1–2 nights extra
Four-season tent
Gaiters
Gore-Tex over-trousers, gloves, balaclava
GPS Receiver
Inflatable sleeping mat
Space blanket
Thermal underwear
Windproof fleece jumper/jacket.

Author's Top Ten Day Walks

Bluff Knoll (WA)
Bungonia (NSW)
Carnarvon Gorge (QLD)
Cradle Mountain Circuit (TAS)
Eight Gorge Walk (NT)
Mt Buffalo (VIC)
Mt Feathertop (VIC)
Mt Gower (NSW)
St Marys Peak Circuit (SA)
Wollemi Creek Circuit (NSW)

Author's Top Ten Overnight Walks

Border Track (QLD)
Forest–Lakes Trail (QLD)
Jatbula (Edith Falls Walk) (NT)
Mt Jagungal Circuit (NSW)
Lake Tali Karng (VIC)
Murchison River (WA)
Overland Track (TAS)
Wilsons Promontory (Southern Circuit) (VIC)
Cape to Cape Walking Track (WA)
Wolgan River–Capertee River Circuit (NSW)

Author's Top Ten Expedition Walks

Thorsborne Trail (QLD)
Glen Davis—Culoul Range (NSW)
Bibbulmun Track (WA)
Howe Wilderness (NSW)
Western Arthurs Walk (TAS)
South Coast Track (TAS)

Ferns in the Dandenong Ranges, Victoria.

Federation Peak (TAS)
Larapinta Trail (NT)
Great North Walk (NSW)
Piccaninny Gorge (NT)

Maps

Information is power, as every media baron knows. Detailed maps are therefore the single most useful piece of equipment one can have when in the wilderness. All maps come in various scales relating map length to the corresponding distance on the ground. Choose the map (or maps) that best suit the purpose. The most useful scale is the 1:25 000 topographical (four centimetres on the map equals one kilometre). Where such coverage is not available, a 1:50 000 or even 1:100 000 scale can be used. Detailed information on the various state government mapping departments and their products is given in the Appendices. Good outlets for maps are national park visitors' centres and large camping/disposals retailers.

The First-aid Kit

A properly stocked first-aid kit is essential on any walking trip. Remember, if travelling far from townships, proper medical attention may be at least several hours away. A typical personal first-aid kit should contain the following items (more could be included for longer expeditions):

- sterilised bandages of widths between 5cm and 15cm
- large non-adhesive gauze dressings
- adhesive tape and packets of adhesive strips
- foil sheet for reflecting heat
- soluble aspirin and stronger pain-relief tablets
- antiseptic/disinfectant/alcohol
- maximum protection sunscreen
- relieving treatment; for example, solarcaine spray, calamine lotion
- bandaids (for blisters, cuts and open bites)
- aluminium sulphate (Stingoes) for the relief of stings
- cotton wool
- safety pins and tweezers
- small scissors (also found in many Swiss army knives).

Code of behaviour

To ensure that policy makers aren't forced to introduce increasingly draconian measures, it is imperative that all walkers follow the officially endorsed 'Bushwalking and Camping Code of Behaviour' reproduced below.

Be self-reliant

- Carry the things you need for comfort and safety. Take a lightweight tent or fly for shelter, or use a cave or rock overhang.
- Avoid huts unless weather conditions are really bad.
- Become proficient at bush navigation. If you need to build cairns, blaze trees, place tags, break off twigs, or tie knots in clumps of grass to mark your route, you are lacking in bush navigation skills. Only land management authorities may place permanent markers of any kind.

Tread softly

- Keep walking parties small; four to six people is ideal. In trackless country, spread your party out rather than walking in one another's footsteps and choose a different route each time you visit.
- Avoid crowded campsites during holiday periods.
- Use existing tracks; don't create new ones. On zigzag paths, don't cut corners as this damage leads to erosion.
- Walk on rocks where possible and avoid easily damaged places such as peat bogs, cushion moss and swamps, but also avoid fragile rock formations.
- Wade through waterlogged sections of tracks; don't create a network of new tracks around them.
- Except in really rough terrain, wear lightweight, soft-soled walking shoes or joggers rather than heavy boots.

Watch your safety

- Know what to do in emergencies. Rescue operations often cause serious damage so take care to avoid the need for them. Acquire knowledge of first aid so you know how to handle illness and injuries.
- Carry clothing and equipment to suit the worst possible conditions you are likely to encounter.
- Carry a mobile phone if you want to, but use it only for summoning aid in an emergency. Keep it switched off until needed or you may find the battery is flat.
- Watch for the health and safety of your group. Beware of fatigue or hypothermia/hyperthermia affecting your group.

Pack it in, pack it out

- Remove all your rubbish, including food scraps, paper, plastic, aluminium foil and empty containers. Don't carry glass bottles and jars, cans, drink cartons lined with aluminium foil and excess packaging. If you do, don't leave them in the bush. Remember, if you can carry a full container in, you can carry the empty one out.
- Don't burn or bury rubbish. Burning creates pollution and buried rubbish may be dug up and scattered by animals. Digging disturbs the soil, causes erosion and encourages weeds to grow. Carry a plastic bag for your rubbish. If you find litter left by irresponsible people along the track

Orchid Beach on Fraser Island, Queensland.

or around a campsite, please remove it. Show that you care for the environment, even if others don't.

Be hygienic

- Ensure that you are at least 100m away from campsites, streams and lakes when going to the toilet. Wait until you get out of sensitive areas such as caves and canyons before defecating or urinating.
- Bury all faeces and toilet paper at least 15cm deep. Carry a lightweight plastic trowel or a large aluminium tent peg to make digging easier. In snow, dig through the snow first, then dig a hole in the ground.
- Carry out things that won't easily decompose, such as used tampons, sanitary pads and condoms.

Keep water pure

- Washing dishes and bathing should be done at least 50m from streams as soap, detergents and food scraps are all harmful to aquatic life. Biodegradable organic soaps are preferable to commercial chemical-based varieties.
- Swim downstream from where you draw your drinking water.

Be VERY careful with fire

- Have a fire only when you are absolutely certain you can light it with safety. A fuel stove is preferable for cooking and thermal clothing is safer for warmth.
- Always use a fuel stove in places where even a tiny fire may cause permanent damage. Avoid lighting fires in rainforests and all alpine regions.
- Do not light fires in hot, summer conditions, in dry windy weather or in declared 'fuel stove only' areas or when there is a declared fire ban.
- Fire does not destroy aluminium foil, and plastics release toxic gases when burnt. Carry foil and plastics out in your pack with all your other rubbish, including your food scraps. Don't use your campfire as an incinerator.

Campfire techniques

- In popular campsites, light your fire on a patch of ground left bare by previous fires. Don't light it on fresh ground.

- Light your fire on bare soil or sand, well away from stumps, logs, living plants and river stones, which can explode when heated. Don't build a ring of stones around your campfire. This is an unnecessary and unsightly practice. Dismantle any old stone rings you find.
- Sweep away all leaves, grass and other flammable material for at least 2m around your campfire. Major bushfires have been caused by campers who failed to do this.
- Keep your fire small.Burn only dead wood that has fallen to the ground. Don't break limbs from trees or shrubs.
- Before leaving, douse your fire thoroughly with water, even if it appears to be out.
- Don't smother a fire by covering it with soil or sand as the coals will continue to smoulder for days. Only water will put a fire out with certainty.
- Feel the ground under the coals. If it is too hot to touch, the fire is not out. Douse it more.
- Scatter the cold charcoal and ashes well clear of your campsite then rake soil and leaves over the spot where your fire was. You should aim to remove all traces of it.

Choose campsites carefully
- Avoid overusing popular campsites. If possible, vary your route and find a site in a less frequented area.
- Camp at low-impact spots away from watercourses. Sand

Heritage Landing, on the bank of the Gordon River, shows the 'horizontal' scrub of Tasmania's south-western forests.

and hard surfaces are better than wet, soft, vegetated or boggy areas. With proper planning, you can use a pre-existing campsite rather than clearing a new one.
- Find an open space to erect your tent so that it is not necessary to clear vegetation. In difficult overgrown areas, trample undergrowth flat rather than pulling plants out of the ground. A trampled spot can recover. If you remove rocks to create a tent site, replace them before you leave.
- Use a waterproof groundsheet or tent with a sewn-in floor and you won't have to worry about surface run-off in wet weather. Do not dig drains around your tent. This practice causes environmental damage.
- Leave your campsite pristine. After a few days it should be impossible to see where you were camped.

Protect plants and animals
- Try not to disturb wildlife. You are the trespasser.
- Give snakes a wide berth and leave them alone. They have more right to be there than you do.
- Watch where you put your feet. Walk around delicate plants. Don't feed birds and animals around campsites or they may become pests. (Unnatural food can also be harmful to many species.)
- Avoid spreading 'dieback', a disease caused by a microscopic fungus (*Phytophthora cinnamomi*) that lives in the soil and attacks the roots of trees. Scrub your boots when entering a control area, and again when exiting. Clean tent pegs thoroughly before breaking camp.

Respect Aboriginal heritage
- Many places have great spiritual or cultural significance for Aboriginal people. Treat such places with consideration and real respect. Obtain permission from traditional landowners or the relevant land manager before visiting sensitive areas. Always leave Aboriginal relics as you find them. Don't touch paintings or rock engravings.

Etiquette
- Radios, CD-players and similar devices are out of place in the natural environment. Leave the electronics at home.
- Don't allow your behaviour and activities to offend others.
- Don't step over other people's uncovered food.
- Camp as far away from other groups as conditions allow. Don't use another group's campfire without permission.
- Leave gates and sliprails as you find them. When you open a gate, ensure the last person through knows it must be closed. Respect the rights of landowners and land managers. Don't enter private property without permission. In national parks, abide by the Plan of Management and encourage others to do so too.
- Do your share of getting firewood and water. When breaking camp, help to clean up the site.
- Offer to help others. This could be your leader, who may be carrying group items, someone in your group or another group you meet along the way. Some individuals may need help but will never ask for it. Volunteer it.
- Minimal Impact means leaving nothing and doing nothing that shows where you have been.

Walker Intention Form

When venturing out overnight, especially in difficult terrain, leave a copy of your itinerary with a reliable friend or relative. An 'overdue' time should also be included, beyond which time search and rescue authorities should be notified. This form is reproduced here with the kind permission of The Confederation of Bushwalking Clubs of New South Wales.

Walk Starts at:_____

Map: _____Grid Ref: _____

on _____ (Day) _____ (Date) at _____ hrs (Time)

Vehicle Registration Number: _____

Planned Overnight Camp Locations:

Day 1 - Map: _____ Grid Ref: _____

Day 2 - Map: _____ Grid Ref: _____

Day 3 - Map: _____ Grid Ref: _____

Day 4 - Map: _____ Grid Ref: _____

Day 5 - Map: _____ Grid Ref: _____

Day 6 - Map: _____ Grid Ref: _____

Walk Finishes at: _____

Map: _____ Grid Ref: _____

on _____ (Day) _____ (Date) at _____ hrs (Time)

Vehicle Registration Number: _____

Group experience: _____ experienced, _____ novices

Walkers who have first-aid certificates: _____

The group is carrying the following items:

[ ] Maps [ ] Compasses [ ] First-aid kits [ ] Extra food [ ] Water [ ] Warm clothing

[ ] Tents/shelter [ ] Sleeping bags [ ] Fire starters [ ] Mirrors [ ] Fuel stoves

[ ] Whistles [ ] UHF CB radio

[ ] Mobile Phone No. _____

Name: _____

Name: _____

Name: _____

Name: _____

INSTRUCTIONS

If the group has not returned or contacted you by _____(time) on _____ (day) _____ (date)

please contact _____by phoning _____

A guide to using this book

Order of appearance

The walk list commences with Queensland and moves clockwise around the country to end with the Northern Territory. Within each chapter the order of walks is loosely consistent with this pattern. This arrangement does not reflect a preference for any region in any way.

Key to Maps

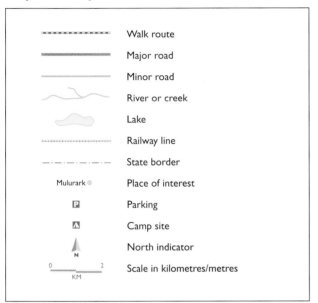

·▄·▄·▄·▄·▄·▄·▄·	Walk route
▬▬▬▬▬▬▬	Major road
▬▬▬▬▬▬▬	Minor road
∼∼∼∼	River or creek
⬭	Lake
+++++++++	Railway line
—··—··—··	State border
Mulurark ◉	Place of interest
℗	Parking
⛺	Camp site
⬆ N	North indicator
0 ⊢——⊣ 2 KM	Scale in kilometres/metres

Key to Track Index

Each walk begins with an index outlining the following important information points:

Walk Title: This is usually the official park title. Where none exists, or where the author's preferred route differs significantly from the officially endorsed route, a suitably descriptive name has been given.

Starting Point: Usually at the nearest car park or other public access area.

Destination: This is usually the end point, however, for round trips, the destination is the primary attraction along the route (usually about halfway).

Length: The quoted walk-lengths are all return distances and incorporate vertical changes in altitude as well as the horizontal. Some minor discrepancies to any walk may occur where a national parks authority has chosen to re-route sections of track for rehabilitation purposes.

Time: This is the estimated return time that will be required for a moderately fit person. The time can vary depending on track condition, equipment carried and the size of the walking party.

Options: Some walks present the opportunity to digress off the track and explore other attractions. Allow extra time for these options. If it is possible for the walk to commence at a different location, or for walkers to complete a shorter circuit, the information will be provided in this entry.

Attraction Rating: ★ ★ ★ ★ ★ This five-point scale grades the sensory quality of the walk. The more of these symbols, the greater the aesthetic character of its scenic attractions, and the variety in features, including vegetation, wildlife, geology and cultural points of interest. The walks awarded the highest rating signify the very best-of-the-best in the country and traverse the purest wilderness.

Fitness: ✖ ✖ ✖ ✖ ✖ A five-point scale also rates the walk from a fitness perspective. One symbol indicates a family-style walk for beginners, while five symbols represent a gruelling expedition with long, steep ascents. Heavy overnight packs will be required.

Maps: Detailed maps are essential for full-day walks and all extended overnight walks. Please consult the Appendices for information about purchasing topographical maps.

Access to Starting Point: Most of the starting points will need to be accessed by vehicle, although a few can be reached by public transport (indicated when applicable). A few walks are accessible only by 4WD or high-clearance vehicles (also indicated where applicable).

Facilities/Amenities: In some parks, authorities provide huts, firewood, toilets or other facilities for walkers, in order to minimise their impact when camping.

Recommended Equipment: This note provides pertinent information about additional equipment to take along. (For example, water purifiers, extra warm clothing, high-speed film for dark conditions, etc.)

Notes: This indicates whether permits are required, and whether walks are recommended only during certain seasons.

Further Information: This lists contact information for the local national park rangers' office or nearest visitors' centre. Particularly well-researched guidebooks of the area may be listed here too.

Walk Description: This book is not a detailed route guide and only general reference notes are given. Track notes are provided for a few select walks, however, especially if there is an absence of published information on that region.

'Remarkable Rocks', Kangaroo Island, South Australia.

Queensland

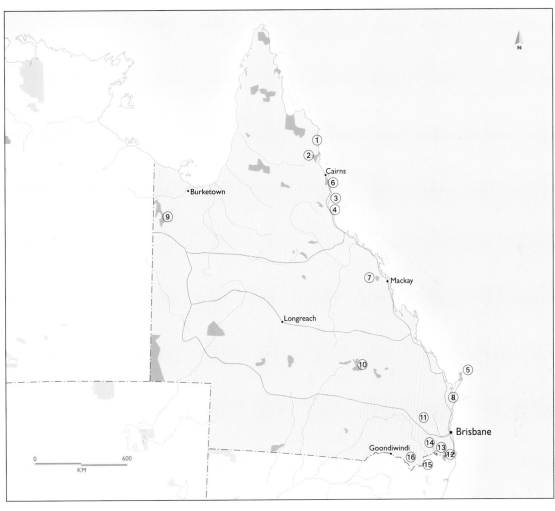

Introduction

Sparsely populated, much of Queensland is undeveloped and set aside in public reserves, ranging from state forests to World Heritage Areas. The state's first national park, Witches Falls, was established at Tamborine, south of Brisbane, in March 1908. Today, Queensland has 6 million hectares preserved in 220 national parks. The largest, Simpson Desert (1 012 000ha) is in far south-western Queensland. The smallest is Sarabah (1416ha) near Canungra in the Gold Coast hinterland.

Climate

The south of Queensland experiences some of the best weather in the country. Temperatures in Brisbane average in the low to mid-20s in summer with rainfall no higher than Sydney's; the least precipitation is in the late winter. In the tropics, rainfall is also strongly skewed to late summer, January–March, with relatively little falling in July and August. Many unsealed roads become impassable in the Wet season and there's the added danger of severe cyclones and flash-flooding. It is recommended that walkers undertake excursions to tropical Queensland in spring.

Transport

Because of the enormous distances, people visiting Queensland often fly. Cairns and Townsville are the two major coastal cities in the tropics. The railway system, primarily built for the transport of sugarcane, services only the coastal regions. Visitors to the interior must use the roads, either by private vehicle or by coach. A 4WD is handy in many of these regions. Passenger and vehicle ferries access various islands, such as Fraser and Moreton, and cross rivers in the Cape York area.

Accommodation

YHA Queensland organises cost-effective accommodation, catering and competitively priced excursions for groups. For further information contact:

YHA Travel and Membership Centre
154 Roma Street (opposite the Transit Centre)
Brisbane QLD 4000
Tel: (07) 3236 1680
Fax: (07) 3236 0647
e-mail: travel@yhaqld.org

The YHA's fully licensed travel agency can organise memberships, international/domestic air tickets, bus and rail passes, travel insurance, worldwide accommodation and IBN bookings, travel guides, package deals and member discounts. For further information and bookings contact:

Group Bookings Officer
YHA Queensland
GPO Box 1128, Brisbane QLD 4001
Tel: (07) 3236 4999
Fax: (07) 3236 1702
e-mail: yhaqld@yhaqld.org

The Brisbane YHA hostel can accommodate 160 people at:
92 Upper Roma St, Brisbane QLD 4000
Tel: (07) 3236 1004

Fax: (07) 3236 1947
e-mail: bnecity@yhaqld.org
Reception hours: 6.30am–10.30pm.

Maps

The main outlet for the state's official maps, SUNMAP (produced by the Department of Natural Resources) is at:
Landcentre
Corner Main and Vulture Streets
Woolloongabba (opposite the Gabba cricket ground)
Tel: (07) 3896 3251
Fax: (07) 3896 3562
The postal address is:
Landcentre
Locked Bag 40, Coorparoo QLD 4151

National Parks

The main Queensland National Parks and Wildlife Service Visitors' Centre is at:
Naturally Queensland Information Centre
Environmental Protection Agency
Ground floor, 160 Ann St, Brisbane QLD
Tel: (07) 3227 8197
Fax: (07) 3227 8749
Web site: www.env.qld.gov.au
The postal address is:
PO Box 155, Albert Street, Brisbane QLD 4002
Opening hours: 8.30am–5.00pm weekdays.

Permits and Fees

Camping is allowed in most national parks. Before camping in a national park or protected area, either in developed camping grounds or remote bush, you must have a permit and pay a small camping fee. The maximum length of stay is 22 days. (Shorter periods apply in some parks, such as Dunk Island.) At some parks, a 'self-serve' system operates. Here, you can obtain a camping permit by completing the form and depositing the camping fees in the box at the camping registration sign.

Some camping areas are heavily booked, especially during holidays and long weekends. You can sometimes book up to 12 months in advance. (At least six weeks' advance booking is recommended.) You must pay the total cost in advance. Check campsite availability before booking

The black, granity boulders of Black Mountain.

Looking over Marloo Bay to Sandy Cape, Fraser Island.

or include a self-addressed envelope with your written application for confirmation. You will be notified before the visit. If you cancel, contact the booking centre about a possible refund. Except in special circumstances, you must give two weeks' notice to obtain a refund.

The Queensland Department of Natural Resources, in conjunction with the Department of Environment, has produced an excellent publication, *Camping in Queensland*, that outlines all the major developed camping grounds throughout the state, including national parks, state forests and water reservoirs. Further information can be downloaded from the Queensland Department of Environment web site at www.env.qld.gov.au

Epic Walks

Most of the Bicentennial National Trail, which spans the continent, passes through Queensland. There are also three official constructed walks of several days' duration: the Cooloola, Forest–Lakes and Thorsborne trails.

Bicentennial National Trail

This mammoth trail of interconnected vehicle tracks and stock-routes extends 5530km from Cooktown to the outskirts of Melbourne, mainly along the western slopes of Great Dividing Range, between national parks and rural land. It is not ideal for quality bushwalking, so is not covered in this book. The trail is more practical for cyclists and equestrians, but walkers tackle some sections.

Cooloola Wilderness Trail

A 46km trail from Lake Cootharaba to the Rainbow Beach road via the Noosa River traversing a variety of sand-based environments in the Cooloola National Park, just south of Fraser Island. A car shuffle avoids backtracking.

Forest-Lakes Trail

Winding among the beautiful freshwater lakes on Fraser Island, this 38.1km trail begins and ends on Seventy-Five Mile Beach. To complete the circuit, you must walk 17km along a beach. There are plenty of campsites and side options through beautiful stands of satinay forest. Allow three to five days to walk the six sections. The Department of Environment has published a walking track guide.

Thorsborne Trail

This 32km trail on the southern part of Hinchinbrook Island, along its east coast, has both wilderness quality and variety. An off-track side option leads to the summit of the highest peak, Mt Bowen, which overlooks the island. This is tough country and only for the experienced.

Cape York

The Cape York Peninsula, one of the world's last wilderness frontiers, remains a vast landmass with few people and prolific wildlife. The gateways to this region are Cairns and Cooktown. The cape itself is home to the Injinoo Aborigines, who range from Shelburne Bay across to the west coast and all the way up to Pajinka at the very top of Cape York. These people know the land intimately and their naturalist knowledge has determined their survival in this harsh place. The Cape York landscape consists of rugged mountain ranges, rainforest, eucalypt and mangrove forests, woodlands, heathlands, grasslands, swamps and mighty rivers. Impassable in the monsoon season, (December–April) the area has extensive ancient culturally significant Aboriginal sites, such as rock art.

The cape presents a superb wilderness experience but has few modern amenities. Its enormous size (11 000 000ha) makes it one of the wildest unexplored wilderness areas in the world. All along the dramatic coast and through the rugged interior, you can still witness unique native flora and wildlife in its natural state. Fishermen can try to catch the elusive and prized barramundi. The most dangerous creature is the saltwater crocodile, found in freshwater creeks and lagoons anywhere on the Cape York Peninsula. Remember to camp at least 100m from waterways. Over the warmer months, deadly marine stingers infest the ocean.

Transport

By air

Cairns has an international airport, with domestic and general aviation terminals, and is served by major international, national and state air carriers. Overseas visitors can make Cairns their point of entry from New Zealand, Hong Kong, Japan, Korea, Taiwan, Papua New Guinea, Singapore, Indonesia, Malaysia, Thailand, Europe, the United Kingdom and the United States of America. Within Australia, Ansett, Qantas, Sunstate, Flight West Air Link and local charter companies provide regular flights from major southern cities and regional Queensland towns.

By rail

Two major train services run between Brisbane and Cairns. The Sunlander operates three times a week and The Queenslander once a week. First-class passengers have private, airconditioned accommodation and the trains have complete dining and refreshment services. A backpacker-style carriage option called the Spirit of the Tropics operates on this service. The journey takes about 32 hours to cover the 2000km distance. There are no rail services north of Cairns, though the major towns do have coach services.

Climate

The Cape York climate is typically tropical with a pronounced wet season from late December to mid April that sustains the island's lush vegetation and diverse wildlife. High humidity together with frequent heavy showers interspersed with long periods of sunshine is characteristic of the wet season. This means, however, that the water temperature is ideal for swimming. During and after a deluge, it is wise for walkers to check any exposed flesh for leeches as they are quite prevalent in the tropics. Insect repellent should be carried at all times.

Average Daytime Air and Water Temperatures

Month	Air	Water
	°C	°C
Jan	32	26
Feb	31	25
Mar	31	25
Apr	30	24
May	27	23
Jun	26	22
Jul	25	21
Aug	27	21
Sep	28	22
Oct	30	23
Nov	31	24
Dec	32	25

Mt Cook National Park

Located on the outskirts of Cooktown, the Mt Cook National Park was declared in 1998, and is centred on the massif of Mt Cook and its surrounding slopes. The park boundaries are enclosed between the Developmental road to the west, which links Cooktown with Cairns, and Quarantine Bay and the Coral Sea to the east. It protects a remnant of the old growth rainforests that once extended all the way down the Cape York Peninsula. In contrast to the larger Endeavour River National Park to the north of Cooktown, the Mt Cook National Park is quite small, being only 502ha in size. A year after the park was declared, a walking track to the summit of Mt Cook was constructed with the aid of local community

Commencing the ascent of tropical Mt Cook near Cooktown, Cape York.

groups. From the summit, fine views north along the coast can be obtained, especially over Finch Bay. Aboriginal guides can be hired for the climb by contacting the Gungarde Community Centre on (07) 4069 5412. There are no facilities beyond the car park.

Mt Cook Walk

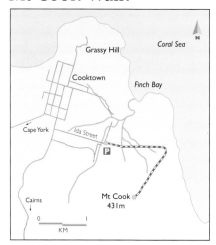

Starting Point: North Cooktown, Mt Cook National Park
Destination: The summit of Mt Cook (431m)
Summary: One of Queensland's most northerly formed walks, constructed in 1998/99
Attractions: Views over Finch Bay
Length: 8km
Time: 3.5 hours
Attraction Rating: ★ ★
Fitness: ◪◪
Height Variation: 350m
Maps: AUSLIG (Natmap/Ausmap)

Helenvale 1:100 000 topographical gives an overview of the area but is not necessary for the walk
Access to starting point: The walk starts just south of Cooktown and can be found by following the street signs from Ida Street
Facilities/Amenities: None
Recommended Equipment: Insect repellent
Further Information: Queensland National Parks and Wildlife Service
Charlotte St
PO Box 611
Cooktown QLD 4871
Tel: (07) 4069 5777
Fax: (07) 4069 5574

Walk Description:

Apart from Grassy Hill near the centre of Cooktown, Mt Cook offers the only other vantage point by which to view the mighty flood plain of the Endeavour River. Follow the signposts from the south of Cooktown to the walk start. Leave your vehicle at the rocky turning circle. The track is marked by a signpost and begins through dry scrub in a south-easterly direction. The dark vegetated summit of Mt Cook looms to the south. The track ascends a ridge to the east and then it's a steep climb to the rainforest-clad peak. Views to the south are very limited, but some reasonable views exist to the north, especially over Finch Bay, Cooktown and across to the Endeavour River National Park. Return via the same route.

Daintree National Park

Just an hour's drive north of Cairns, the Daintree National Park protects part of the largest tract of virgin rainforest in Australia. This lush, tropical vegetation is a remnant of the rainforests that once covered the earth's surface and has survived virtually unchanged for 100 million years. It contains several examples of the very first flowering plant species.

The lush Queensland Wet Tropic rainforests are the second-largest tract of virgin rainforest after the Amazon rainforest in South America, and are even older than the Amazon rainforest species. More than 150 species of trees, some individuals more than 3000 years old, grow here.

The Cape Tribulation section of Daintree National Park (16 959ha) stretches in a narrow strip from Daintree River north to Bloomfield River with the McDowall Range as its western boundary. The land slopes steeply up from the coast to the summit of Thornton Peak (1374m). The park boundary includes some flat land, most of which is freehold. A bushwalker's paradise, this region is well recognised for its superb wildlife and plant specimens. Eco-tourism thrives here with operators offering a range of package tours.

Kurranji, Aboriginal for cassowary, is the traditional name for Cape Tribulation. It is used by the Kuku Yalanji, the local Aboriginal tribe, who have inhabited this area for millennia. The headland was given its European name by Captain Cook, after his ship was holed on a reef in the area in 1770. His diary reads: '*I named... the north point Cape Tribulation because here began all our troubles.*'

A visit to Cape York allows visitors a rare chance to experience two of Australia's World Heritage sites: the Great Barrier Reef, listed in 1981, and Daintree National Park which, as part of the Wet Tropics area, was listed in 1988. The latter is one of only a few places worldwide to meet all four criteria for World Heritage listing, as it contains:

- continuing biological evolution
- exceptional beauty
- habitats for threatened species
- excellent examples of major stages in the earth's evolution.

Vegetation

The Cape Tribulation section of Daintree National Park contains a rich mosaic of vegetation ranging from coastal mangroves, swamps and rainforests to mountain rainforests and low plateau heathlands. The rainforests are of particular interest as scientists continue to discover new species, or creatures previously known only in the fossil record. These forests may well have been the evolutionary cradle for much of Australia's unique wildlife.

Wildlife

The rich and varied wildlife includes Bennett's tree kangaroo, found only in

Where the rainforest meets the reef. Looking south along Cape Tribulation Beach to Cape Tribulation.

this area. While visitors are unlikely to see this shy animal, they will probably see some beautiful birds— perhaps the wompoo pigeon, noisy pitta and white-tailed kingfisher on its summer visit from Papua New Guinea. There are also a number of casso- waries—giant flightless birds up to 2m tall—in the park. If you are lucky enough to see one, remember that cassowaries have powerful legs and horned heads and are potentially dangerous. You may also spot a lizard, Boyd's forest dragon, clinging to a branch as it watches for insects to devour. On Mt Thornton, a previously unknown rat was discovered recently. Estuarine crocodiles are present in most creeks and in the Daintree and Bloomfield rivers. From October to May, marine stingers make swimming in the sea dangerous.

Facilities

There is an official national park campground at Noah Beach, 8km south of Cape Tribulation, where toilets, water and a shower stand are provided. The necessary camping permit can be obtained from the ranger or from the self-registration stand at the campgrounds. Campfires are not permitted so bring a fuel stove. Four camping sites on Snapper Island have a toilet and BBQ. Permits must be obtained from the Cairns Regional Centre, the National Parks office in Mossman or the Madne Park office in Port Douglas. Several lodges offer up-market accommodation nearby.

Mossman River Circuit

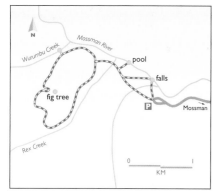

Starting Point: Mossman Gorge car park, Daintree National Park
Destination: Mossman River
Summary: A circuit tourist walk that

gives background information on the rainforest
Attractions: World Heritage rainforest including giant fig trees, waterfalls and pools.
Length: 3.2km
Time: 1 hour
Attraction Rating: ★
Fitness: ✖
Maps: AUSLIG (Natmap/Ausmap) Mossman 1:100 000 topographical gives a good overview of the area. The SUNMAP Mossman 1:50 000 topographical map gives a more detailed coverage of the Mossman Gorge vicinity.
Access to starting point: A 5km bitumen road allows access to Mossman Gorge from Mossman, just north of Port Douglas
Facilities/Amenities: Toilets and picnic tables are provided at the car park. Camping is not permitted here but accommodation is available in nearby towns.
Further Information: Queensland National Parks and Wildlife Service
Cnr Front and Johnston Sts
PO Box 251
Mossman QLD 4873
Tel: (07) 4098 2188
Fax: (07) 4098 2279

Walk Description:

This short track follows the bank of the Mossman River from the Mossman Gorge car park. Beyond the swinging bridge over Rex Creek, there is an easy 2.7km loop track through the rainforest. A number of signs give information on various trees and how they are used by forest animals and by the local Aborigines, the Kuku Yalanji.

Much of this 56 500ha section of Daintree National Park covers a rugged, uninhabited and largely inaccessible mountainous area on the eastern slopes of the Mt Carbine Tablelands. The national park is an area of very high rainfall that feeds the Daintree and Mossman rivers.

Several types of forest are found in this section of the park. These vary from the tall dense forests of the lowlands and fertile, sheltered river valleys, to more open forest up on the drier north-western slopes and stunted forests on the exposed mountain tops.

Although the term 'gorge' is something of an exaggeration, the pristine Mossman River has carved a steep-sided valley. The water here is untainted by topsoil run-off. The river is a focus point for the local wildlife. The brilliant blue Ulysses butterfly is a common sight. The green and black male Cairns birdwing (the female has no green) is Australia's largest butter-fly. At dusk, white-rumped swiftlets hunt insects over quiet pools.

In the water, the jungle perch (also known as the flagtail because of two prominent black spots on its tail) is quite distinctive. You might be lucky enough to see a platypus or a fresh-water turtle as it surfaces to breathe in the calmer parts of the river away from the cascades.

In the forest, intense competition for light between plants forces trees to stretch high on tall leafless trunks. Little light penetrates the canopy so, by contrast, vegetation on the forest floor is sparse. Various palms and ferns are among the few plants that can grow in such dim conditions. The competition has also forced many plants to evolve to the point of being dependent on others. These are the common parasites and epiphytes. The strangler fig starts life high on a branch and puts roots down to the ground. Gradually the roots join together around the trunk of the host tree, which eventually dies leaving the magnificent figs standing victor-ious on the forest floor.

Although rarely seen in the Mossman Gorge area, mammals in the park include tree-climbing kangaroos and musky rat-kangaroos (which are the smallest of the kangaroo family).

If you are a birdwatcher, you may be surprised to see some mountain species including the fern-wren and the grey-headed robin that have descended from nearby higher slopes. In summer, you also have a good chance of seeing the buff-breasted paradise kingfisher, a large, blue and buff bird with a striking red beak and spectacular long white tail. This bird migrates to Australia from Papua New Guinea to nest in termite mounds.

The most prominent of the reptiles is the Boyd's forest dragon, that can grow up to 45cm long.

Other walks in the Daintree National Park

Find out about the rainforest and mangroves along a short signed Marrdja botanical trail at Oliver Creek that leads to the confluence with Noah Creek just before Cape Tribulation. Another walk north of Mossman leads to the summit of the 439m Flat Peak. These walks are described in *50 Walks in North Queensland* by Tyrone Thomas.

Alternatively, the lazy can wander along one of the many white sandy beaches located between the warm water and the dense rainforest—an experience in itself. Be wary of crocodiles near river mouths and estuaries at all times, and of marine stingers in the sea. Many beaches have bottles of vinegar at prominent posts to neutralise stings. For the more adventurous, contact the Queensland National Parks and Wildlife Service office in Mossman which will be able to advise on possible long distance overnight walking destinations. There is no published information on extended expeditions as tracks are limited. Rainforest environments are not conducive to low-key tracks due to erosion of the soft wet soils, and the fact that trails can quickly overgrow. Furthermore the region is very remote so demand is limited. Park rangers find that the humid conditions and many insects also limit the numbers of overnight walkers.

Other walks on Cape York Peninsula

Black Mountain (Cooktown region)

Just north of Helenvale broods the mysterious Black Mountain, a giant 470m high peak comprised of massive dark granite boulders which are stained by algae. Eerie crevices and caverns separate the boulders and surveyors have found much of the interior of the mountain is hollow. Strange sounds emanate from the fissures as wind blows through. Local legend has it the mountain has claimed many lives that have been swallowed through the cracks. The ascent is fascinating but dangerous.

The most popular park on the peninsula is Lakefield National Park, one of the largest reserves in Australia. Consult the ranger station at New Laura for the latest conditions. To the north, Iron Range National Park offers remote walking opportunities.

The Islands

While Australia's perimeter is blessed with many islands, it is those of northern Queensland that attract the most attention. They are all part of the Great Barrier Reef, a 2000km-long marine park that stretches from Gladstone in Queensland's south to Papua New Guinea in the north. It's the world's largest expanse of coral and is still growing after 10 000 years.

A declared World Heritage Area, it protects 1500 varieties of fish, 400 types of hard and soft coral, 4000 mollusc species and six species of turtle.

The islands of the Great Barrier Reef, including Green, Dunk and Hinchinbrook, are Australia's premier island rainforest walking destinations. They offer a choice of leisure activities that ranges between leisure resort-based fun in the sun to extended wilderness walks. But the island getaways aren't all in the wet tropics. Moving south down the coast, there is Fraser Island, the world's largest sand island, with idyllic freshwater lakes, and Moreton Island, another sand island very close to Brisbane.

Dunk Island

Dunk Island is 7km east of the unspoiled Queensland coastal vacation resort village of Mission Beach, midway between Townsville and Cairns. Cardwell is some 36km to the south. It's part of the 'Family' group of islands and is regarded as the 'Father' of the group. Dunk Island is 6km long, 2km wide, and 75 per cent of its 970ha surface area is protected as national park. The highest peak is Mt Kootaloo (271m). About 13km of walking tracks encourage exploration of most of the island's many habitats. Other islands nearby are Bedarra, Kumboola and Mangum Gnackum.

Climate

Located in the tropics, Dunk Island experiences a high seasonal rainfall that peaks between January and March. Average maximum temperatures are in the mid-20s, even in winter, with the lowest rainfall from August to November.

Vegetation

Viewed from the reef, a mosaic of greens is apparent, revealing a pattern of vegetation dominated by rainforest species in gullies and on wetter slopes and eucalypt forest on drier ridges. The boundary between these forest types is never distinct. On much of the island, a relatively open forest of eucalypts is accompanied by an understorey of rainforest plants, including many palms and thick, looping, coiled lianas.

The early morning sun penetrates the rainforest canopy on Dunk Island.

Wildlife

The island's dense rainforest is home to a huge variety of wildlife, including 150 species of birds, and the beautiful electric blue Ulysses butterfly (also called the Mountain butterfly), is the island's famous emblem. With a wingspan of up to 10cm, this is one of the largest butterflies in Australia, and one of the most beautiful.

Access

An air service connects Dunk Island and the mainland, and a regular ferry service leaves from Clump Point jetty. Taxi boats are available from South Mission and Wongaling Beach. A boat ramp is at Mission Beach. Brammo Bay, on the northern end of Dunk Island, offers a protected anchorage in south-easterly winds.

Dunk Island Circuit

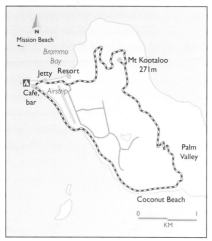

Starting Point: Dunk Island Resort, Brammo Bay

Destination: Mt Kootaloo, Palm Valley

Summary: A loop of the western half of the island

Attractions: Pleasant rainforest contrasting with empty beaches

Length: 10.4km

Time: Half a day

Options: Optional side trip to Muggy Muggy beach, 3km, 1 hour

Attraction Rating: ★ ★

Fitness: ◪

Maps: None needed, although SUNMAP produces a tourist and recreation map called Dunk Island National Park

Access to Starting Point: Mission Beach is just a two-hour drive (about 160km) from Cairns or a three-hour drive (about 230km) from Port Douglas, and a 15-minute (7km) boat transfer from Mission Beach to the island. Dunk Island is one of the very few Great Barrier Reef islands that has its own fully surfaced airstrip. It is serviced by Trans State Airlines with three return flights a day from Cairns using Twin Otter aircraft. The flight time from Cairns is about half an hour. The airstrip is between the jetty and the resort.

Facilities/Amenities: An island resort that suits most lifestyles, couples, honeymooners or families. It offers seclusion, peace and privacy along with a superb array of facilities, sports and activities. There are 148 rooms in four styles—Luxury Bayview Villas, deluxe Beachfront Units, and secluded Garden Cabanas and Banfield Units offering garden views. Camping is permitted for a maximum of three nights. Camping permits can be booked through the Dunk Island Resort on (07) 4068 8199.

Recommended Equipment: Sun block and swimming costume

Notes: Avoid the high-rainfall months December to April. Marine stingers may occur in surrounding waters from October to May; take adequate precautions when swimming.

Further Information:
Rainforest and Reef Centre
Bruce Highway
PO Box 74, Cardwell QLD 4849
Tel: (07) 4066 8601

Walk Description

From the back of the resort, signposts indicate the track to Mt Kootaloo. After crossing a swing bridge, there's a side option leading to Muggy Muggy Beach. Take the right option that ascends north and then south before joining another track that loops around the summit. Head left around the summit and right to climb it from the south-east.

At the top are views to the west and the remains of the World War II radar installation. From the summit, follow the ridge south for 2km to another lookout and then eventually to Coconut Beach via Palm Valley. Then to return, simply follow the beach back to the resort.

Hinchinbrook Island

This spectacular island ranks with Lord Howe as one of the most beautiful. About halfway between Townsville and Cairns, its natural habitat variety includes fragile heath vegetation on cloud-shrouded mountains, patches of lush rainforest that border the beaches, extensive eucalypt forest and a mangrove-fringed channel in the west. From any vantage point along the east coast, the walker is rewarded with sweeping bays, rocky headlands and craggy islets.

Protected as a national park since 1932, Hinchinbrook (39 900ha) lies within the Great Barrier Reef World Heritage Area. The island is separated from the mainland by the narrow Hinchinbrook Channel, which provides a safe haven for the unique dugong marine mammals and green sea turtles.

A small, exclusive resort featuring luxury tree-houses is on the far north tip of the island at Cape Richards. Unfortunately, at time of writing, a controversial development at Port Hinchinbrook is being constructed; this severely compromises the quality of the wilderness around Hinchinbrook Island and it's neighbouring islands.

Rising 1121m from the centre of the island is Mt Bowen massif, the largest in a chain of rugged granite mountains that form the north/south backbone of the island's southern half. To the north-west is a range of lesser peaks of older volcanic rocks. Similar in chemistry but finer grained than the granite, these peaks create an undulating skyline descending to the sandy beach of Hecate Point, 4km across the channel from Cardwell. The spectacular north face of Mt Bowen drops more than a kilometre in cliffs and forested rocky slopes almost to sea level. From here a narrow, 8km-long strip of sand stretches north to Cape Sandwich and Cape Richards.

Climate

The climate is very much tropical in nature with monthly rainfall as high as 500mm in January–March (with more than 15 raindays each) and as low as 30mm in July–September (with fewer than six raindays). Temperatures fluctuate little, however, with

Looking across Little Ramsay Bay to the ramparts of lofty Mt Bowen on the eastern side of Hinchinbrook Island.

maximums averaging in the low 30s in summer and mid-20s in winter.

The magnificent 32km Thorsborne Trail along Hinchinbrook Island's east coast is named after the late Arthur Thorsborne. Arthur and Margaret Thorsborne had a lifelong interest in nature conservation, and monitored the Torresian imperial pigeons that migrate to the island in summer to nest. They helped ban the shooting of the pigeons and in so doing, helped to save the species, which at the time was nearly extinct. A book about their experiences, *Hinchinbrook Island, the land that time forgot*, is still available from the resort.

Vegetation

On the sheltered western slopes and valleys, deeper soils support luxuriant growth. Dense rainforests of milky pine, figs, quandong, palms, vines and hundreds of other species grow between the mountain tops and the thick mangrove carpet growing in the channel. In places, the rainforest understorey comprises turpentine, pink bloodwood and red mahogany.

Closer to the exposed rocky pavements of the central mountain range, the vegetation changes to scrubs, heaths and stunted eucalypts. Black she-oak, turpentine and brush box grow on the shallow sandy soil overlying rock pavements, while heaths of banksias, tea-trees and grasstrees cover areas of soakage. In the deeper soils between boulders, stunted woodlands of eucalypts, banksias, wattles and she-oak can be found.

The exposed eastern slopes support woodlands dominated by swamp box and eucalypts, including white mahogany. Deeply dissecting these weather-worn slopes are numerous steep valleys.

Wildlife

Numerous birds and insects are active when flowers are in bloom in spring. The creeks, fringed by lush vegetation, act as corridors for wildlife. The forests have many animals in common with similar habitats on the adjacent mainland, but roughly 10 000 years of separation have brought about subtle but intriguing changes. Several species of possums of mainland forests are absent from Hinchinbrook. A small nocturnal native marsupial, similar in appearance to a rat, wreaks havoc if any food is left unattended overnight. Another threat is from crocodiles, especially at the North Zoe Creek ford.

Thorsborne Trail

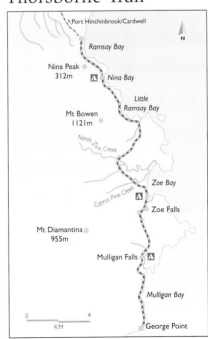

Starting Point: Ramsay Bay (north-east Hinchinbrook Island)

Destination: George Point (south-east Hinchinbrook Island)

Summary: An easy coastal walk down the eastern side of Hinchinbrook Island

South Zoe Creek, upstream from Zoe Falls, Hinchinbrook Island.

Attractions: Magnificent wild tropical island scenery, beach walking and beautiful secluded camping areas with rockpools fed by waterfalls. Zoe Falls are particularly photogenic.

Length: 32km

Time: 4–5 days

Options:

- The summit of Mt Bowen—allow a full day along Warrawilla Creek
- The summit of Mt Diamantina— allow a full day from Zoe Bay or Mulligan Falls
- Nina Peak—allow about 1.5 hours return from Thorsborne Trail near Ramsay Bay

- Sunken Reef Bay—allow 1 hour return from Thorsborne Trail

Attraction Rating: ★ ★ ★ ★ ★

Fitness: ✗ ✗ ✗

Maps: Cardwell 1:100 000 topographical or Hillock Point 1:50 000 topographical

Access to Starting Point: Domestic airlines fly to Cairns from where there is a bus to Cardwell. Transport is available through commercial water taxi services out of Port Hinchinbrook and Lucinda. Most walkers start at Ramsay Bay and walk south to George Point, but it's becoming increasingly popular to do the walk in reverse.

Facilities/Amenities: Six camping areas all with basic facilities; fresh water is fairly abundant near most of them, except in the middle of the dry season. The low-key resort at Cape Richards accommodates about 50 people. Note that there is no walking access from the resort or Macushla to the Thorsborne Trail, because of thick mangroves. There is a ferry.

Recommended Equipment: Fuel stove as no fires are allowed on the island. A lot of strong insect repellent is essential, as is sunblock.

Notes: Permits are needed for all camping. Book well in advance as the trail is popular in holiday periods. Only 40 people are permitted on the trail at any time. The largest group size is six. Large parties are advised to use the Macushla or Haven areas. Only two parties are allowed to Mt Bowen each month, so book ahead.

Beware of crocodiles in mangrove estuaries on the western side of the island. Also, ocean water may contain venomous marine stingers during the warmer months.

Further Information: For information and permits, contact the Queensland Department of Environment and Heritage at:

Rainforest and Reef Centre
Bruce Highway
PO Box 74, Cardwell QLD 4849
Tel: (07) 4066 8601

or

Ingham District Office
Canegrowers Building
11–13 Lannercost St
PO Box 1293, Ingham QLD 4850
Tel: (07) 4776 1700
(Monday–Friday)

Walk Description

Allow a minimum of three nights and four days to traverse the trail between Ramsay Bay and George Point, but a longer stay on the island is recommended, with a rest day either at Nina Beach or Zoe Bay. Plan to walk from Ramsay Bay to Little Ramsay Bay in one day, from Little Ramsay Bay to Zoe Bay in another day, and from Zoe Bay to Mulligan Falls on the third day.

The best time for walking is from April to September. At times work is carried out along the trail and parts of the old trail have been re-routed or are closed for revegetation. Walk the trail in either direction but it is commonly walked from Ramsay Bay south to George Point. Make prior arrangements with a boat operator to take you to Lucinda, thence a shuttle bus back to Port Hinchinbrook. Coloured triangular markers in both directions make navigation along the trail easy.

Day One
Ramsay Bay to Little Ramsay Bay (7km)
From the boardwalk where the ferry drops you off, walk south-east through mangroves to Ramsay Bay and south to the end of the beach. The Thorsborne Trail starts to the right of a large granite rock and follows a ridge across and down toward the northern end of Blacksand Beach. This section has recently been re-routed farther inland.

From Blacksand Beach, head immediately inland and steeply up. At the ridge crest, drop your packs for a steep ascent of Nina Peak. There are outstanding views on the approach and at the very top, especially toward the north and toward Mt Bowen. Try to climb early in the day to avoid the haze from sugarcane burning.

The Thorsborne Trail then descends to Nina Bay where seasonal water is generally available behind the small lagoon between January and August. Campsites and a toilet are provided; reliable fresh water can be found at the creek on the southern end of the beach and also about 100–200m along upstream. Watch for blue-spotted stingrays when swimming in Nina Bay.

At the southern end of Nina Bay, the trail crosses a rocky section toward the base of a small cliff. Climb this and proceed around the headland to Boulder Bay. Rock-hop around Boulder Bay to the base of the headland at the southern end.
Note: At very high tides, a detour through dense vegetation around the top of Nina headland may be necessary. At the southern end of Boulder Bay prominent rock cairns and triangles mark the trail, which proceeds south-easterly over the low ridge to the northern end of Little Ramsay Bay.

For fresh water, follow the creek up from the Warrawilla Lagoon a few hundred metres. The toilet here had burnt down in October 1999. It is from here that the most popular ascent of Mt Bowen commences. Consult the track notes at the end.

Day Two
Little Ramsay Bay to Zoe Bay (10.5km, 6 hours)
Walk south from Little Ramsay Bay. Cross a tidal creek and continue to the rocks at the end of the beach. Rock hop to the next small beach. At the end of this beach the trail leads to the upper edge of some rocks over to a larger sandy beach. From the other end of this beach the trail heads south-easterly via a small gully to the top of the ridge.

At this point, a signposted side path leads to Banksia Bay (600m return). The main Thorsborne Trail descends into Banksia Creek and heads upstream toward the base of a small waterfall, which may be dry.

Before the base of the waterfall, the trail branches away from the creek and heads south-east, passing over a saddle with limited northerly views. It descends via a dry rocky creek into a dark rainforest. The trail then turns south-westerly through open forest, rainforest and mangroves to North Zoe Creek. Signs warn that estuarine crocodiles can inhabit this area, so do be careful. This long section is time-consuming, but it's fairly flat.

From North Zoe Creek, the trail heads south again, crossing several smaller creeks—walkers will need to remove their boots. The most reliable fresh water is at Fan Palm Creek.

At Zoe Bay, the campsites are at the southern end of the beach, hidden in the forest. There are several marked sites and a toilet. Take care that native rats don't damage packs and tents in their attempts to get food. A metal box is provided for safe storage. Fallen coconuts usually have holes gnawed in them by the native rats.

Day Three
Zoe Bay to Mulligan Falls (7.5km)
The trail runs parallel with South Zoe Creek, then crosses it about 100m downstream from Zoe Falls. These falls and the resulting pool are one of the most picturesque sights on the island. Please note that camping is not permitted here. The eager fish can be fed by killing the freely available flies. Swimming is highly recommended.

The trail then continues up a steep slope onto the granite slabs above the falls. Some ropes/chains are installed for ease of climbing. Another attractive pool for swimming is at the top.

After following South Zoe Creek, the trail climbs a distinct spur to a granite rock pavement that marks the saddle. This point, 263m above the sea, is the highest part of the trail. Along this section the trail passes through the tall heath community typical of much of the mountainous part of Hinchinbrook Island. After crossing the saddle the trail traverses the steep forested slopes of the Sweetwater Creek catchment before climbing up into coastal she-oak, grasstree and shrubs. This section is fairly heavy going as it descends into several steep gullies that run perpendicular to the track.

The trail descends into the Diamantina Creek catchment and passes a signposted side track to Sunken Reef Bay. This side option takes about 30 minutes each way and there is an informal camping area at the beach. Water may be available up a small creek at the northern end, but should not be relied on. Seasonal water can be obtained from Diamantina Creek. No open fires are allowed.

Once on the Thorsborne Trail again, head south to Diamantina Creek. Be careful when crossing if it's swollen after heavy rain. Follow the markers diagonally across the creek. The trail continues up a short slope before descending a steep hillside to reach the base of Mulligan Falls. The camping area is about 100m from the falls. Another nice swimming pool here and, once again, take precautions against native rats. Either keep food in the tent, or use wire to suspend it from an overhanging branch. A better way is to hang the pack on a wire between two spinning plastic bottles.

The rock pavements above the falls are quite slippery and dangerous—heed the signs warning bushwalkers not to venture there.

Day Four
Mulligan Falls camp to George Point (7.5km, 2.5 hours)

If you intend to camp at George Point, collect fresh water before leaving Mulligan Falls. The trail continues a further 2.5km through rainforest and crosses five creeks. The last, Moth Creek, provides fresh water seasonally but should not be relied on. The trail then enters the northern end of Mulligan Bay beach, which is quite exposed to prevailing winds. A sign marks the track entrance about 300m south of Diamantina Creek inlet.

George Point, the southern end of the trail, is a 5km walk south along the beach. Two-thirds of the way along, Mulligan Creek flows into the bay. Cross this creek at low to half-tide; boots must be removed. There are good views of the two 900m peaks of Mt Diamantina and Mt Straloch.

Day Five
Mt Bowen (12km, 12 hours)

Much of the mountainous central spine of the island is covered with fragile heath vegetation. Walking in these areas is restricted, to protect the unspoiled nature of the mountains and in the interests of safety. A permit is required before any group sets off into the mountains, particularly Mt Bowen and Mt Diamantina. Walkers should be very experienced and some rock ledge negotiation is required. A topographical map and compass are essential. Allow at least one full day to access the top of Mt Bowen from Warrawilla Lagoon and return. Leave very early (at first light) and follow the creek upstream. This will involve easy but time-consuming boulder-hopping. It is imperative to note which branch to take when arriving at forks—these are marked by rock cairns. Some nice pools allow walkers a quick dip. Further on the flowing water dries up as the creek bed heads steeply upward. Keep on the creek bed to the saddle. From the narrow spine, head left up on to the rocky ridge crest where a pronounced track heads over several false bluffs to the summit, marked by a cairn.

There are great views in all directions, but midday can be hazy because of sugarcane burning on the mainland. Return via the same route and leave plenty of time to complete the trip in a day. Campsites are limited and it is recommended that you avoid carrying a heavy overnight pack.

Fraser Island

The largest sand island in the world, Fraser Island is famous for its pure freshwater lakes and surf beaches. Much of the sand that formed the island has come from the Blue Mountains sandstone plateau and northern Great Dividing Range. These have been eroded and drained out to sea, then carried up the coast by prevailing ocean currents. This process has taken about 800 000 years.

Three Aboriginal tribes occupied the island, the Badjala, Ngulungbara and Dulingbara, who referred to the island as *K'gari*, which translates as 'paradise'. Captain Cook saw these people in 1770, and estimated their numbers at 2000–3000.

The sunset from Sandy Cape Lighthouse, just south-west of Sandy Cape, on the northern shore of Fraser Island.

About 200km north of Brisbane, and only a couple of kilometres off the coast at Hervey Bay, Fraser Island has about 200 lakes and 40 of them are fresh-water. They are fed by the high rainfall (an average of about 1500mm a year). The island encompasses an amazing variety of landscapes: seemingly endless surf beaches, cliffs and gorges in all the colours of the rainbow, dense rainforests with trees up to 70m high, massive dunes, unbelievably clear freshwater lakes, picturesque winding streams, great basalt headlands and saltpans with dense mangrove forests.

The island is listed as a World Heritage Area, being of universal significance for its large, intact coastal dune system and its unique environments. This listing was the result of a protracted battle to save the island from sandmining and logging through the mid-20th century.

Despite being principally a 4WD destination, bushwalking is still a rewarding experience. The terrain is unusual and there is a wide range of camping opportunities. Avoid holiday periods so you're not competing with hordes of 4WD users for the best camping sites by the lakes.

Facts and Figures

Name: Fraser Island
Size: 165 280ha
Dimensions: 123km long, average of 14km wide; highest point is 235m
Reserve: Great Sandy National Park (74 900ha) enacted in 1974. Other reserves include a recreation area and state forest.
World Heritage Area: Enacted 1992
Visitors: 350 000 a year
Aboriginal Sites: Many midden piles have been found in this area.

The Lakes

Amazingly, each of Great Sandy's freshwater dune lakes is unique in shape and colour. More than 40 dune lakes occur here, which is over half the world's known total. Covering 200ha, Lake Boomanjin, found in the south of the island, is the world's largest perched lake. The Boomerang Lakes to the north of the island are the world's highest perched lakes at 130m above sea level.

Barrage Lakes

These form when a mobile sand dune dams a watercourse, usually in younger dunes close to the coast. Interested visitors can walk to Lake Wabby on Fraser Island; the best route is from the eastern beach, and walk or drive to Lake Freshwater in Cooloola.

Window Lakes

Occurring generally at low elevations, these lakes form where the ground surface drops below the watertable level and fills with groundwater. Some window lakes have been barraged by sand dunes. All the freshwater lakes are low in nutrients and support few plants and animals. Most lakes have only two or three species of fish.

Perched Lakes

These include Lake Birrabeen and Lake McKenzie on Fraser Island and Lake Poona in Cooloola to the south and are the region's most common type. They develop when a saucer-shaped 'hard pan' of organic debris, sand and peat forms in a depression between dunes. Water then collects, perched above the watertable.

Some animals, such as the region's unique 'acid' frogs, are specially adapted to living in the lakes' mildly acidic waters. The lakes contain three species of freshwater turtles. Park rangers advise against feeding turtles or fish, as any increase in food for one species alters the natural balance of life in the lake community.

The clear waters of lakes such as Fraser Island's famous Lake McKenzie and Cooloola's Lake Freshwater have percolated through sand over time, and minute quantities of aluminium and iron compounds have removed any organic compounds.

The tea-coloured waters of Fraser Island's Lake Boomanjin are stained by organic compounds from decaying vegetation, leached from soil. Great Sandy's lakes are popular recreation spots, but are vulnerable to damage. Most do not have streams flowing to or from them, so foreign materials are trapped. To protect the ecology, do not use soap, toothpaste or detergent, or urinate in or near lakes and streams and wear protective clothing rather than sunscreen in the water.

Climate

Fraser Island has a subtropical climate with temperatures moderated by proximity to the sea. Average coastal temperatures range from 22°C to 28°C in December and 14°C to 21°C in July, while it can be cooler inland. Annual rainfall varies across the island, from 1200mm on the coast to 1800mm inland. Wettest months are January to March (about 160mm rainfall per month) with drier months in winter to spring (54mm rainfall in September). Moderate winds predominate from the south-east—fierce storms often occur.

Vegetation

Plentiful water has given rise to exceptional rainforests, growing in sand and surviving on nutrients from the breakdown of other plants. Towering satinay and brush box are among the forest giants, some more than 1000 years old. The variety of vegetation is extraordinary, ranging from mangroves to kauri forests and wallum heathlands filled with wildflowers in early spring.

Wildlife

Some 25 species of mammals, including dingoes, possums, echidnas and wallabies, and 240 species of birds. Wild brumbies also roam free but numbers are declining. The most asked about mammals on the island are the dingoes (*Canis lupus*). Dingoes are wild dogs introduced to Australia from Asia at least 4000 years ago. They are closely related to domestic dogs but have some biological differences. For instance, dingoes breed once a year; dogs breed twice. Dingoes live in small groups in a home range (territory) and often howl in chorus. They live for about 10 years, start breeding at about two years and produce litters of up to six pups in spring.

About 170 wild dingoes live on Fraser Island. They are hunters and natural scavengers, eating anything from insects to wallabies, hunting alone or in packs. Because of the natural isolation of living on an island, these dingoes are believed to be among the purest strain in eastern Australia, having rarely interbred with

The sunset over Hervey Bay from Bowal Creek on the western side of Fraser Island.

domestic dogs. This is an important recognition for conservation purposes.

Many people believe that the dingoes are undernourished because they look thin, but a healthy dingo is naturally lean, like a greyhound. Like all scavengers, dingoes are always looking for food—in nature, smaller mammals and birds, but they prefer food that comes more easily from people and around campsites. Unfortunately, when it's easy for them to scavenge food, their hunting skills change. They lose their natural fear of humans and expect food from them. Dingoes then visit campsites, picnic areas, resorts and residential areas, follow people and tear open tents looking for food. Pups do not learn to hunt naturally and grow up without becoming wary of people. Some become aggressive, especially young males in the breeding season. There is a chance that they may bite or scratch visitors (particularly children) and may have to be killed by park rangers.

Access

From Brisbane, drive north to Rainbow Beach township via Gympie. For a more scenic route, travel by 4WD to Rainbow Beach along Cooloola's beach from Tewantin. From the north, drive south to Hervey Bay. Visitors can also travel by bus to Rainbow Beach or Hervey Bay, by aircraft to Hervey Bay, or by train to Maryborough, which is linked by bus to Hervey Bay.

From Rainbow Beach or Hervey Bay, you can travel to Fraser Island by vehicle barge, passenger launch, commercial tour or private boat.

Fraser Island's rough sandy forest tracks are suitable only for 4WD vehicles (these can be hired on the mainland and on Fraser Island at Eurong Beach, Happy Valley and Kingfisher Bay). Vehicles entering the island must be fully road-registered. Neither unregistered or recreational-registered vehicles are permitted. Vehicles with a low ground clearance may have difficulty on some inland tracks. Most forest tracks are not suitable for caravans. Campervans must be sturdy and have good clearance. Tracks are generally two-way and single lane; take care, drive safely, speed limit is 35km/h. Beaches may be inaccessible for at least two hours either side of high tide. Carry a tide chart. Entire sections of the western beach are inaccessible.

Facilities

Facilities include toilets, showers (20¢ coins required for hot water) and BBQs. For the island's protection, use established campgrounds where available (these are often full during school holidays). All serviced campgrounds have water suitable for drinking and a small supply of cut firewood (one armful per camp per day). Ensure that the RAM camping permit is prominently displayed on your tent. (RAM camping permits are not valid for the two private campgrounds, Cathedral Beach and Dilli Village.)

The public campgrounds are:

Lake Boomanjin: About 22 sites, set in open forest between the car park and the lake. Lake Boomanjin, the largest perched lake in the world, has water stained brown by vegetation. There are no rubbish facilities here so you must carry rubbish out with you.

Central Station: Day-picnic facilities,

a visitor information display, shelters and coin-operated gas BBQs are set in a forest clearing from the forestry era. An adjacent grassed campground of about 22 sites has easy access.

Lake McKenzie: A small campground with five marked sites for car-based campers in blackbutt forest near the lake. A popular area, it is usually full before midday. If full, camp at Central Station or the eastern beach; do not camp in non-designated sites or car parks. At the campground, avoid creating pathways or extending the edge of the campsite into the bush. Stay within barriers. There is a small campground for overnight walkers only. During peak holidays, day-visit car parks may be full around midday; access may be restricted between 11.00am and 2.00pm.

Dundubara: Close to the eastern beach, this camp area has about 90 sites, some in forest, others more open (a few are suitable for caravans). Picnic tables for day-visitor use.

Lake Allom: The campground, in a small rainforest clearing, has three sites and shares picnic tables with day visitors. Sheltered from strong winds but tends to be wetter than other areas. There are no showers. A bush track leads through the rainforest and around the lake where numerous freshwater tortoises live. Park authorities do advise against feeding or disturbing them.

Waddy Point: Set in coastal woodland with some understorey and ground cover, the campground and day-visit area is generally sheltered from southeast winds. There are 33 individual sites marked; do not extend them by trampling vegetation. A less formed camp area with 50 sites is on the nearby dune, among casuarina trees; use main area toilets. Group camping with seven sites.

Wathumba: This picturesque campground with views along Wathumba estuary and the Great Sandy Strait is the main formed campground on the west coast. There are 20 campsites in a grassed, open treed area. Nearby are extensive mangroves where sandflies and mosquitoes breed, especially in warmer wetter months, so insect repellent is essential. This site is popular with boat-users.

Beach camping: Undeveloped sites along the east coast are serviced by separate waste facilities at intervals along the beach for general rubbish and recyclable material. The west coast and the east coast north of Ngkala Rocks are not serviced so take all rubbish home or to a waste facility along the eastern coast. Store rubbish in a sealed container (preferably within a vehicle) to secure it from animals. Note that campsites are closed periodically for revegetation.

Further Reading: *Fighting for Fraser Island* by John Sinclair.

Further Information:

Queensland National Parks and Wildlife Service District Office
164 Richmond St
PO Box 219
Maryborough QLD 4650
Tel: (07) 4127 7100
To contact park rangers call:
Central Station   (07) 4127 9191
Dundubara   (07) 4127 9138
Eurong   (07) 4127 9128
Rainbow Beach   (07) 5486 3160
Waddy Point   (07) 4127 9190

....

Forest–Lakes Circuit

Starting Point: Dilli Village, Fraser Island

Destination: Eastern Beach

Summary: This walking track links together all of the most popular lakes on the southern half of the island. The beginning and end of the walk are separated by 16km of beach. To avoid walking along the beach, organise to be dropped off, or set up a car shuffle. Alternatively, walkers might try their luck at hitching a lift along the beach.

Attractions: Lake McKenzie, Lake Wabby, lakes, sand dunes, tall forest

Length: 38.1km, plus 16km beach walk

Time: 3–5 days

Options: 1-hour side trip to Pile Valley from Central Station

Attraction Rating: ★ ★ ★

Fitness: ◨◨

Maps: AUSLIG (Natmap/Ausmap) Wide Bay and Happy Valley 1:100 000 topographicals. The SUNMAP Tourist Map Fraser Island 1:125 000 also has the walking track marked on it.

Access to Starting Point: Access to Fraser Island is by vehicle barge, passenger ferries, private charter boats and aeroplane. The main access routes are Hervey Bay to Sandy Point, and Inskip Point to Hook Point. The Dillinghams road is a good quality access road from the west of the island. A 4WD is essential.

Facilities/Amenities: Vehicles need a Vehicle Access Permit (about $15.00). Most camping areas have toilets, showers, water, firewood, etc. Not all camping areas are open at the same time, because of rehabilitation work. A great resort, Kingfisher Bay, has recently been built on the west coast.

Recommended Equipment: Soft comfortable shoes, as the sand takes its toll on feet, ankles and calves

Notes: Camping permits must be tied to outside of tent

Further Information:

Queensland National Parks and Wildlife Service
Rainbow Beach Rd
PO Box 30
Rainbow Beach QLD 4581
Tel: (07) 5486 3160
(7.00am–4.00pm weekdays)
or Cnr Alice and Lennox Sts
PO Box 101
Maryborough QLD 4650
Tel: (07) 4123 7100
(8.00am–5.00pm weekdays)
Other permit offices are located at:
Marina Kiosk
Buccaneer Ave
Urangan (Boat Harbour) QLD 4655
Tel: (07) 4128 9800
(6.00–6.00pm daily)
River Heads General Store
9 Ariadne St

River Heads QLD 4655
Tel: (07) 4125 7133
(6.30am–6.00pm daily)

Get a low-cost brochure from any permit-issuing or national park visitors' centre. This describes the walks of the Forest–Lakes Walking Circuit and also gives detailed plant illustrations and descriptions and information about access routes to further points of interest.

Walk Description

The Forest Lakes Trail is divided into six sections that can be walked individually if desired. These are:
1. Dilli Village to Lake Boomanjin
2. Lake Boomanjin to Lake Benaroon (bushwalkers' camp)
3. Lake Benaroon (bushwalkers' camp) to Central Station
4. Central Station to Lake McKenzie
5. Lake McKenzie to Lake Wabby
6. Lake Wabby to Dilli Village

From Dilli Village (a private camping area), the walk route leads along the road heading west, and within 100m, turns right. This nature trail rises gradually, taking you to Lake Boomanjin via some sand dunes and varied forest types. If it is late in the day, you can camp here. The lake is about 70m above sea level and was the location for the Australian film, *Eliza Fraser*, in 1976. Walking tracks encircle the lake, and from its northern perimeter, the track continues to Lake Benaroon, crossing the main road on the way. The lakeshore is a good place to set up camp, as this is one of the less well-known camping areas on the island.

On the second day, continue north to Lake Birrabeen, another clear freshwater lake, but fed by the less appetising Lake Jennings to the north. Vegetation stains Lake Jennings a very dark brown. From Lake Jennings, the trail once again crosses the main road and heads north to Central Station. If progress has been good and it is relatively early in the day, drop packs and head east to Pile Valley to see a magnificent stand of satinay trees. The timber is unique to the area and its rot-resistant properties were sought after for ship building. Some of the harvested timber was even used to help build the Suez Canal in Egypt and Tilbury Docks in England.

Back at Central Station, head west through pleasant forest. Wanggoolba Creek is noted for its flow of crystal-clear water mainly localised from outflows of groundwater from the sandmass. The water here contrasts with the golden-brown, tannin-stained creeks and seepages, such as those into Lake Boomanjin. At Basin Lake, the trail turns north to the jewel of Fraser Island, Lake McKenzie (known as Wondunna Goong to the Aborigines). Spend the second night here. Once the site of an army training camp, it is one of the most beautiful camp retreats in the country. A swim in the lake is an absolute must.

Spend the third day following the main road that leads back to Central Station, but turning off east to Lake Wabby (at 11m, the deepest lake on the island) and then Eastern Beach (also known as Seventy-Five Mile Beach) just to the north of One Tree Rocks. Dilli Village lies 16km to the south—a long trudge, which can be avoided by having a car waiting at Lake Wabby or by hitching a lift with one of the 4WDs heading south.

Other walks on Fraser Island

Short and long day walks can be undertaken using various staging areas. Many of the walk distances and times can be halved if a second vehicle can be left at the destination. Information is readily available.

The Coast and Mountains

In this section are the pick of the coastal and mountain walks to be found between Cairns and Brisbane. The Great Dividing Range parallels Queensland's coast from Cape York to the New South Wales border.

Wooroonooran National Park

Wooroonooran is the largest rainforest park in Queensland at 79 800ha, and it contains the state's highest peaks: Mt Bellenden Ker (1582m) and Mt Bartle Frere (1622m). As well as rainforest, a diverse range of vegetation is protected in this large park, from lowland rainforest in the valleys to montane heaths on the mountaintops. Many fast-flowing rivers and waterfalls are also a feature. The Bellenden Ker Range is home to several plants and animals found only in this region.

The park lies within Queensland's Wet Tropics World Heritage Area, a 900,000ha strip between Townsville and Cooktown that was protected in 1988 for its outstanding natural value. There are two main sections in Wooroonooran National Park (formerly known as Bellenden Ker National Park)—the Josephine Falls Section and the Palmerston Section.

Climate

Summers are hot and wet, with temperatures reaching 37°C. Both sections of the park have an annual rainfall of at least 3,500mm, so it can be very wet, especially between November and March. Do not attempt to walk in the park after heavy rain, as the tracks will be slippery and creek crossings potentially dangerous. The winter dry season from June to September is generally the best time to go bushwalking here.

Vegetation

While the number of species of trees recorded is more than 500, this can be difficult to appreciate unless you pay more than casual attention to differences in leaves and bark. Other characteristics of this forest can be seen more easily. Well-developed buttressed roots and vines are common. Epiphytes, such as basket and bird's nest ferns, are abundant. Many tree species common here have clusters of flowers and fruit on the main stems and branches.

Wildlife

Much wildlife can be seen during the day if you walk quietly. The emerald dove (or green-winged pigeon), usually feeds on the forest floor. Higher in the canopy, the blood-red belly and bright green wings of the king parrot are exquisite. A microhylid frog is found only on the Bellenden Ker Range above 900m, while the Bartle Frere skink is restricted to exposed granite boulders at high altitudes. Few Australian mammals are active during the day but the musky rat-kangaroo, the smallest and most primitive of the kangaroo family, is an exception. Keep a special lookout for this small dark marsupial when you are walking on tracks through dense vegetation near creeks and rivers.

Josephine Falls Section

Mt Bartle Frere Walk

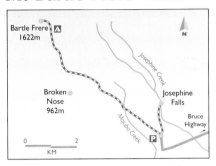

Starting Point: Josephine Falls car park, Wooroonooran National Park

Destination: The summit of Mt Bartle Frere, south peak (1622m)

Summary: A steep ascent of the highest mountain in northern Australia

Attractions: Magnificent rainforest, waterfalls, and superb views along walk and near summit

Length: 15km

Time: 1 day

Options: A 1.6km side trip at the base leads to Josephine Falls. It is also possible to camp near the summit with a permit. Another side option is to Broken Nose (962m), although this may be too much for a day walk. Most people backtrack on their return. If you wish to camp, obtain a camping permit from the office at the trackhead.

Attraction Rating: ★ ★ ★

Fitness: ☒☒☒☒☒

Maps: SUNMAP Bartle Frere 1:50 000 topographical

Access to Starting Point: From Cairns, head south along the Bruce Highway for 68km. Then take Lake Eacham Road right to Topaz Road. Proceed along Topaz Road past Butchers Creek and turn left onto a gravel road at Lamins Hill Lookout. Follow the signs on Gourka Road (also gravel) to the state forest boundary. A ranger's office lies at the end.

Facilities/Amenities: None. Campsites at Big Rock Camp (450m) and Upper Camp (1350m). Obtain permit from the office at the trackhead.

Recommended Equipment: Water containers, spare clothes. If you are camping, take a suitable sleeping bag.

Notes: Sudden weather changes can occur, so take extra clothing. Stinging trees also grow along the track. Brushing against the leaves can induce painful rashes. Views can be obscured by white-outs. August–September are the best months for climbing. Between January and April, it is often too wet. The temperature can drop below 0°C on the summit. If the upper mountain ridges cloud-in, as often happens, be especially careful to avoid getting lost. Fires are not permitted on the trail (in any case, the fallen wood is often too wet), so take a fuel stove if you wish to cook.

Further Information:
Josephine Falls Section
Wooroonooran National Park
(9.00am–5.00pm weekdays only)
PO Box 93, Miriwinni QLD 4871
Tel: (07) 4067 6304
Fax: (07) 4067 6443

Walk Description

The track is undeveloped but well marked. Keep to the route, as the

Bobbin Bobbin Falls on the less popular western approach to Mt Bartle Frere.

Josephine Falls at the eastern base of Mt Bartle Frere, is just a short stroll from the car park.

rainforest is dense and it's easy to get lost if you wander off the track. The terrain is mostly steep and rock-scrambling is often necessary. A spring flows from near the broad summit. The coast and Innisfail township are visible from the highest point and there is a view across the tableland from a sedge-covered clearing to the west.

Leave the optional walk to Josephine Falls until the end so that you have plenty of time to complete the summit ascent. People have died and been seriously injured at Josephine Falls, so be careful.

Other walks in Wooroonooran National Park
Bartle Frere Summit—western approach (15km, 10 hours)

Follow Lake Eacham Road to Topaz Road. Proceed along Topaz Road past Butchers Creek and turn left onto a gravel road to Lamins Hill Lookout. Follow the signs on Gourka Road (7km), taking good care because this

road can be slippery when wet. Conventional vehicles should be left at the end of Gourka Road at the national park boundary. The national park access track past this point is suitable only for 4WD vehicles.

A signpost 2km along the access track marks the start of the walking trail. Add this distance to the total if you intend walking to this point. Orange triangles mark the trail from the signpost to the summit. Do not stray from the marked trail as it is easy to get lost in the dense rainforest. Bobbin Bobbin Falls can be heard north of the trail at about 2km from the start of the walk. The falls are only 50m away from the trail and offer walkers the chance to take a break and fill their water bottles. The trail climbs sharply once past the falls.

On the long walk up the mountain, notice changes in the vegetation. Tall, large-leafed trees give way to a more stunted forest. Leaf size and tree trunk diameters decrease as altitude and exposure increase.

North West Peak, 5km from the start, marks the end of the steepest section. A short deviation to the south-west side of the trail reveals some small granite boulders. The view of the tableland from the top of these is spectacular.

The trail continues for another kilometre along the ridge to a group of large rocks. The view to the north from the top of these rocks overlooks Bellenden Ker and the Mulgrave River Valley. This excellent view is not possible from the Bartle Frere summit.

After leaving the lookout, the trail descends across two creeks. At the second crossing is a clearing suitable for camping and water is available year-round. The site is an ideal resting point before the final push to the summit some 750m away. The trail leaves the campsite, crosses the small creek and becomes a rock-scramble. It passes through and over numerous granite boulders to the summit.

If you are continuing to Josephine Falls, water is available most of the year from a spring at the remains of an old mine site at Top Eastern Camp. As you descend, the open grassland and low scrub of the ridges is replaced with rainforest.

Goldfield Trail
(19km, 7–9 hours)

This walk proceeds from The Boulders Scenic Reserve near Babinda to the Goldsborough Valley and follows the rough track made by gold prospectors in the 1930s as they rushed from the coast over a saddle in the Bellenden Ker Range to Mt Bartle Frere. The first section (11km) to the East Mulgrave River causeway is moderately steep in parts but not difficult. The second section (8km) follows a flat, former logging track to the Goldsborough Valley State Forest camping area. Visitors can choose to turn back at the East Mulgrave River and return to The Boulders or continue on to the Goldsborough camping area—both options take a similar time to complete. After heavy rain, it may be impossible to wade across the East Mulgrave River at the causeway.

Palmerston Section

Before European contact, this region was inhabited by the Mamu people. Their five clans were Waribara, Dulgubara, Bagirgabara, Mandubara, and Dyiribara. Each clan occupied an area of country with which it had close associations and spiritual ties. Wan and Dulgubara occupied the area in and near the Palmerston region. *Wan*, in the Mamu dialect, means 'gorge', and this clan group lived primarily in the steep escarpments along the North Johnstone and Beatrice rivers. *Dulgu* means 'thick scrub', and this group occupied the catchment areas of the South Johnstone River down to the present township of South Johnstone.

The names of many places are associated with stories. For example, Cowley Falls, on the eastern side of the Palmerston section, is known to the Wan and Dulgu people as *Gimbirr* or *Gumbay gumbay*, and was named after a story about a cyclone. (Cowley Falls is inaccessible for safety reasons.)

The park and highway closely follow the same route surveyed in 1882 by Christie Palmerston, a European prospector, bushman and explorer, commemorating his achievement. All previous attempts to find a practical route in the rough country had failed. Palmerston used Aboriginal guides to walk the 100km from Innisfail (then Geraldton) to Herberton, a mining town. He took 12 days. Today, the distance takes about 2 hours to drive.

Crawford's Lookout to falls and highway Walk (5km, 2.5 hours)

Follow this winding track down into the North Johnstone River Gorge, dropping 500m in 1.6km. Walk along Douglas Creek and Henrietta Creek to the falls. From the falls, take 10 flights of steps back to the highway. Arrange to be picked up there or return along a track beside the highway to the starting point (2km, 40 minutes).

Nandroya Falls Circuit
(7.2km, 3.5 hours)

Start at the camping area and climb the ridge between Henrietta and Douglas creeks before winding slowly down past Silver Creek Falls (10m) to Nandroya Falls (50m). (This 2km-walk takes 1–1½ hours.) Return along the main Nandroya Falls track or continue along the circuit track. Walk along Douglas Creek past large pools before skirting a steep hillside and rejoining the main track about 1km from the camping area.

Eungella National Park

Located on the Clarke Range between Bowen and Mackay, the 51 700ha Eungella (pronounced 'young-gella') National Park protects some rugged rainforest topography that peaks at Mt Dalrymple (1280m). The tops of the range are often shrouded in mist.

The name means 'Land of Cloud' to the Aboriginal tribe that occupied the area. The rainforests are a mixture of different rainforest communities representing latitudes to the south and north, as well as different altitudes. Elevated sections of the park include central Queensland's highest plateaus.

As well as the mountain peaks of the Clarke Range, the national park also protects the foothills, where lowland rainforest flourishes in tropical sun, and areas where open eucalypt forest has colonised drier parts.

Developed walking tracks lead to forests, granite cascades, waterfalls, lookouts and Aboriginal cultural sites. For the more adventurous, the park offers wilderness opportunities to the very fit, experienced and well prepared.

History

Eungella lies in the area of the Biria subgroup of the Aboriginal Birri Gubba language group, which extends from Townsville to north of Rockhampton. The Wiri, Gia and Juipera peoples are located in surrounding areas. Aboriginal relics can be found in dry forests near the park, where rock art also survives on sandstone surfaces. Inside the park, trees bear axe marks made by Aborigines. In the rainforest, evidence of Aboriginal occupation is less obvious. Moist air and efficient recycling processes work together to degrade artefacts quickly. Any art that was ever painted on the park's glassy granite surfaces is unlikely to have survived these moist conditions. On the 100m Sky Window circuit, one can learn more about Eungella's Aboriginal heritage.

Logging began on the Clarke Range around 1904, followed by the first road up the range in 1908. Dairy farming began here in the early 1930s.

Climate

Eungella has distinct wet and dry seasons. Average yearly rainfall at Broken River is about 2000mm, with more than two-thirds falling from December to March. Summers are warm, with average maximum temperatures up to 30°C in January. Winters are cold to warm. Frosts are common from May to September, with temperatures down to 14°C in August. September and October are ideal months to visit, with temperatures and rainfall being moderate. Slightly higher rainfalls in February and March offer a chance to see rainforest and fungi at their most lush, but leeches can be a pest in wet weather.

Vegetation

More than 1000 plant species, many rare or threatened, have been recorded here. Giant ferns and Mackay tulips up to 40m high grow among red cedars and palms of different varieties. Eungella is a living testament to past climate changes, which have profoundly affected Australia's forests. During cool, dry times, such as ice ages, rainforest survived only where moisture levels stayed high (for example, in deep gorges and on damp mountain tops).

Dry corridors of open forest have probably isolated Eungella rainforests for more than 30 000 years. Moisture-loving species, unable to cross these corridors, have evolved in isolation.

Wildlife

Eungella's endemic animals and plants are renowned among scientists and there are rare subspecies of more common animals. Birdlife here is exceptional and waterways support sizeable populations of platypus.

Access

Eungella is at the top of the Pioneer Valley, about 85km west of Mackay (975km north of Brisbane). To access the Broken River section from Mackay, follow Pioneer Valley Road up Clarke Range to the Eungella township (also known as Dalrymple Heights). Large caravans may have difficulty on this steep, winding road. From Eungella, follow the road that sweeps to the left and drive 6km to Broken River, site of the park headquarters, campgrounds, kiosk and facilities. Fern Flat campground is nearby.

Facilities

At both Broken River and Fern Flat camping areas the facilities include toilets, drinking water, showers, picnic tables, van sites. Take a fuel stove for cooking. No camping is permitted at Finch Hatton Gorge.

Remote bush camping is allowed in much of the park area. Dick's Tableland (15 000ha) in the centre of the Eungella National Park offers great wilderness opportunities for more-experienced overnight bushwalkers. Note that permits are necessary for all camping areas, however, and are available for a small fee. Book well in advance for long weekends and school holidays. Bookings can be made through the park office.

Clarke Range Track

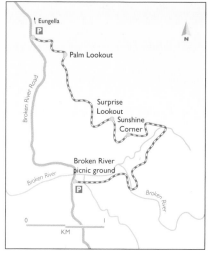

Starting Point: Broken River Road (south of Bevans Lookout), Eungella National Park

Destination: Broken River picnic area

Summary: This track passes through a variety of rainforest ecosystems in the heart of the southern section of the national park

Attractions: Rainforest vegetation, including piccabeen palms, views to the Pioneer Valley

Length: 8.3km (one way)

Time: Half a day

Options: This walk can be linked up with the Rainforest Discovery Walk. Either organise a car shuffle or backtrack via the walking track or the Broken River road.

Attraction Rating: ★ ★

Fitness: ☒ ☒

Maps: SUNMAP Eungella National Park Tourist and Recreation Map. A good overview is also provided by the AUSLIG (Natmap/Ausmap) Mirani 1:100 000 topographical but this isn't really detailed enough for walking navigation.

Access to Starting Point: The national park is situated 85km west of Mackay along the Mackay–Eungella road

Facilities/Amenities: Basic picnic and camping facilities at Fern Flat and Broken River

Recommended Equipment: Sturdy footwear

Further Information:
Eungella National Park
c/- Post Office
Dalrymple Heights QLD 4757
Tel: (07) 4958 4552

Walk Description

The start of the track is about 1km south of the Sky Window picnic area. You can join this track from the beginning or the end of the Palm Walk Track. There are two official lookouts with great views to Pioneer Valley along the way as you descend to Broken River via Sunshine Corner. (Views can be obscured by low cloud or mist.) Once you have forded the watercourse at Granite Bend, it is faster to take the right-hand branch of the Rainforest Discovery Walk to the camping area about 700m away.

Broken River Trail

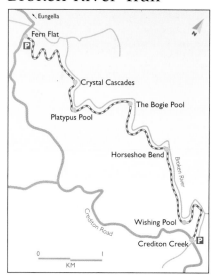

Starting Point: Broken River picnic and camping area, Eungella National Park

Destination: Crediton Creek

Summary: This track follows the southern bank of the Broken River to its confluence with Crediton Creek

Attractions: Numerous pools and cascades

Length: 8.4km (one way)

Time: Half a day

Options: Walkers can complete a circuit back to the Broken River picnic and camping area via Crediton Road, which roughly follows the southern perimeter of the national park

Attraction Rating: ★ ★

Fitness: ☒ ☒

Maps: SUNMAP Eungella National Park Tourist and Recreation Map. A good overview is provided by the AUSLIG (Natmap/Ausmap) Mirani 1:100 000 topographical but this isn't really useful for walking navigation.

Access to Starting Point: The national park is situated 85km west of Mackay along the Mackay–Eungella road

Facilities/Amenities: Basic picnic and camping facilities at Fern Flat and Broken River

Recommended Equipment: Tripod if photographing in overcast weather

Notes: No swimming is permitted in Broken River because of high bacterial levels. Water monitoring is carried out on a weekly basis.

Further Information:
Eungella National Park
c/- Post Office
Dalrymple Heights QLD 4757
Tel: (07) 4958 4552

Walk Description

The walk commences from the popular Broken River picnic and camping area, behind the Rainforest Discovery Walk and continues upstream past the Crystal Cascades, Platypus Pool and the Bogie Pool, following the Broken River past Horseshoe Bend, all the way to its confluence with Crediton Creek.

These tranquil pools are very picturesque and patient walkers might spot a tortoise or platypus feeding in the water. The bird noises in the Broken River valley usually come from whipbirds, scrub hens, golden whistlers and yellow robins.

Finch Hatton Gorge Falls Walk

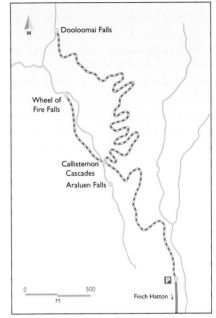

Starting Point: Finch Hatton Gorge picnic area, Eungella National Park

Destination: Dooloomai Falls

Summary: This track follows Finch Hatton Creek Gorge north, visiting various waterfalls along the way

Attractions: Araluen Falls, Callistemon Cascades, Wheel of Fire Falls, Dooloomai Falls, rainforest vegetation, rugged topography

Length: 9km

Time: Half a day

Attraction Rating: ★ ★ ★

Fitness: ⬕⬕

Maps: SUNMAP Eungella National Park Tourist and Recreation Map. A good overview is provided by the AUSLIG (Natmap/Ausmap) Mirani 1:100 000 topographical but this isn't really useful for walking navigation.

Access to Starting Point: To access the Finch Hatton Gorge section, take Pioneer Valley Road from Mackay through Marian. At the foot of the range, take the signposted turn-off 1km east of Finch Hatton Gorge township. Drive 12km along a narrow road to Finch Hatton Gorge picnic area. About 6km of the road is gravel and it may be closed in wet weather.

Facilities/Amenities: Basic picnic facilities at Finch Hatton Gorge

Recommended Equipment: Tripod if photographing in overcast weather

Notes: No camping is permitted at Finch Hatton Gorge

A grasstree on the Clarke Range Track, Eungella National Park.

Scenic views of lush rainforest from one of the many lookouts situated throughout Eungella National Park.

Further Information:

Eungella National Park
c/- Post Office
Dalrymple Heights QLD 4757
Tel: (07) 4958 4552

Walk Description

The waterfall track that departs north from the picnic area forks after 1.1km. The left branch descends to a large pool at Araluen Falls 400m later. The area is the only known habitat of the endemic Eungella day frog. Another branch continues north, fording Finch Hatton Creek and ending at the dramatic Wheel of Fire Falls. Giant flooded gum eucalypts, one of the world's largest tree species, can be found here. Some backtracking and climbing is required to access the track that leads north to the spectacular 60m Dooloomai Falls. From here the picnic area and car park are about an hour (3.6km) to the south.

Other walks in Eungella National Park

More information on several short walking tracks can be obtained from the park office. Many walking tracks start from along the road leading to Broken River. Wear sturdy shoes and check for leeches in wet weather.

Great Sandy National Park

Cooloola Section

Cooloola is a sand-based region like Fraser Island. In fact both of the two regions share the same national park. The 56 000ha Cooloola section of the 140 000ha Great Sandy National Park conserves the largest tract of natural land on Queensland's southern coast. The region is one of contrasts, from peaceful everglades and coastal wild-flower plains to the beach, bordered by dramatic coloured sand cliffs.

Dominated by sand, the landscape here comprises long beaches, high dunes and lakes centred on the upper catchment of the Noosa River. The vegetation that predominates in the Cooloola section includes woodlands of banksia and scribbly gum, shady blackbutt forests and rainforests with towering trees. The national park is a refuge for plants and animals whose habitats have greatly dwindled with expanding coastal development. A 4WD is the best way of accessing the park's attractions.

Facilities

Motels, caravan parks, camping areas, food and petrol are available at nearby Rainbow Beach and Boreen Point. Limited facilities also at the Noosa North Shore. Elanda Point has a private camping area 300m north of the national park office. A small kiosk has basic supplies, call (07) 5485 3165.

The Cooloola section of the Great Sandy National Park has the following limited campgrounds:

Harrys camping area: firewood supplied

Fig Tree Point camping area: firewood supplied

Noosa River camping area: three campsites; boil water; boat access only

Upper Noosa River: limited campsites; boil water; boat access only

Poverty Point camping area: 4WD access only

Day-use: Picnic facilities, toilets,

small BBQs and tables provided at Bymien and Freshwater picnic areas, and at Fig Tree Point and Harrys camping and day-use areas.

Cooloola Wilderness Trail Walk

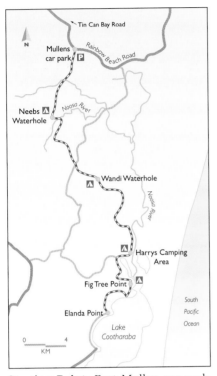

Starting Point: East Mullen car park, Great Sandy National Park
Destination: Elanda Camping Area
Summary: A one-way traverse of the heart of the region, keeping away from the coast and developed regions
Attractions: Wallum heath, rainforest, freshwater lakes, rich bird life. The route is of historical significance, being that taken by Eliza Fraser.
Length: 46.7km
Time: 3 days
Options: It's possible to exit early by leaving a 4WD vehicle on the Cooloola Way road. There is also a short side trip to Fig Tree Point but no fresh water is available there for campers (2km return).
Attraction Rating: ★ ★ ★
Fitness: ✗✗
Maps: There are no maps as such for the Wilderness Trail. The SUNMAP Cooloola Coast Tourist Map 1:100 000 is of some use and gives an overall view of the area. The more detailed maps are the SUNMAP Wolvi and Cooloola 1:50 000 topographicals.

Access to Starting Point: Turn right off the Bruce Highway just north of Cooroy. Once past the township of Pomona, head right onto Boreen Road to Lake Cootharaba.
Facilities/Amenities: Cooloola Wilderness Trail has two bush camping areas at Neebs Waterhole and Wandi Waterhole. There are no facilities here. The trail also intersects with a car-based campground at Harrys. For further information or to book sites, contact Kinaba Information Centre.
Recommended Equipment: A fuel stove is essential as fires are banned
Notes: Camping permits apply to all sites. Fees are small.
Further Information and Bookings:
> Rainbow Beach Rd
> PO Box 30
> Rainbow Beach QLD 4581
> Tel: (07) 5486 3160
> (7.00am–4.00pm weekdays)

or

> Great Sandy National Park
> Southern Cooloola
> Elanda, MS1537
> Tewantin QLD 4565
> Tel: (07) 5449 7364
> (9.00am–3.00pm weekdays)

The Kinaba Information Centre also puts out a sheet on the Cooloola Wilderness Trail. Tel: (07) 5449 7364.

Walk Description

This walk is fairly flat and easy and can be completed in as little as two days but it is recommended to take at least three days. It is best to walk south from East Mullen car park to Elanda Point, so as to finish at the lake. Another advantage is that in this direction it is all downhill. There is a long car shuffle involved so allow plenty of time to organise it.

The Cooloola Wilderness Trail can be divided into three sections. Aim to be at Wandi Waterhole on the first night (16.5km taking 4–5 hours). The second night's destination is Harrys hut (14.5km taking 3–4 hours). The final stretch to Elanda Point is then 15.7km, taking about 5 hours. The track is well marked. At Neebs Waterhole, cross the creek via a fallen tree. This is a good spot for lunch and a swim if the weather is appropriate. The Noosa River's far upper headwaters lie just to the west from here.

Farther south cross the sandy Cooloola Way. A track junction just over 4km from the road marks the turn-off to Wandi Waterhole, which is only a little out of the way. A welcome reward for the first day's effort will be a swim in one of the excellent secluded pools there.

The second day's walk toward Harrys camping area utilises old state forestry trails. The turn-offs are generally well signposted in this section. As you approach the camping area, the Cooloola Wilderness Trail parallels the Noosa River flood plain.

On the third day, the trail heads west, then south around Lake Como. From Fig Tree Point turn-off, it heads abruptly west to cross the Kin Kin Creek via a recently constructed bridge. Follow the dirt roads and you will soon come to the turn-off to Kinaba Information Centre on the left. The camping area at Elanda Point and National Park headquarters are only 2km farther along the trail.

Other walks in Great Sandy National Park (Cooloola)

As well as the walks outlined below, there are plenty of short walks. Distance and times given are return to the starting point. The SUNMAP Wide Bay 1:50 000 topographical and Wolvi and Cooloola 1:50 000 topographicals might be handy.

Freshwater Lake to Bymien Walk (14.6km, 5 hours)

Pass through scribbly gums, blackbutt and rainforest. Sidetrack to Poona Lake (2km return to main track) is through carrol (grey myrtle) understorey.

Telegraph Track (7km to Bymien)

From Rainbow Beach, follow the old telegraph line down to Bymien. Take a side track to Murrawar Lookout (2km return to main track) for a view of Double Island Point, Wide Bay Bar and Fraser Island.

Rainbow Beach Circuit (40km, 2 full days)

A long walk between Rainbow Beach and Double Island Point, combine Telegraph track to Bymien (7km) with Bymien to Poona Lake (2km) and Poona Lake to Freshwater Lake (5km).

Teewah Landing Track, (4km, 1.25 hours)

From Teewah Beach, walk through coastal heath and dune country to the eastern shore of Lake Cootharaba. A side track to Seawah Hill (4km return to main track) provides spectacular views of the river, lakes, ocean beach and Noosa.

Kinaba Track (11.4km, 3.5 hours)

Walk from Elanda Point private camping area to Kinaba Information Centre through grasslands, paperbark and palm wetlands (patches muddy after rain). Wear insect repellent.

Elanda Point to Fig Tree Point Walk (20.4km, 6 hours)

From Elanda Point private camping area, walk through open grassy areas, woodlands and forest to reach the remnant rainforests of Kin Kin Creek. Take the footbridge to Fig Tree Point.

Fig Tree Point to Harrys camping area Walk (15km, 5 hours)

Follow part of the Cooloola Wilderness Trail through open forest, eventually passing into closed forest. Parts of this track may be covered by water after rain.

Harrys camping area to campsite 3 Walk (12km, 4 hours)

Beginning on the opposite side of the river from Harrys camping area, this track connects campsites 1, 2 and 3. Note that there is no foot access across the river from Harrys camping area to the start of the walk.

Campsite 3 to Cooloola Sandpatch Walk (12km, 4 hours)

Follow the track along a low, sandy ridge with heath on either side. Climb through open blackbutt forest and grasstrees before emerging onto a huge natural sandblow with panoramic views. Carry drinking water.

Other walks Along Queensland's Coast and Mountains
Undara Lava Tubes

Located off the Kennedy Highway west of Cardwell, the underground volcanic caves of Undara are a remnant of a violent eruption that took place almost 200 000 years ago.

The longest cave is Bayliss, a chamber 1.4km long, 11m high and 20m wide.

Cape Hillsborough National Park

Just north of Mackay, a network of graded walking tracks allows access to the coast, where the rainforest contrasts with sandy beaches. The area attracts much wildlife and there are facilities for visitors. See *50 Walks in North Queensland* by Tyrone Thomas for notes on the 9km route.

Mt Archer Environment Park

Very close to Rockhampton, this short walking track leads through a eucalypt forest, then through rainforest and finally to the open flats of Moores Creeks and its tributaries.

Inland Parks

Much of central Queensland is uninteresting flat outback dominated by cattle ranches and vacant Crown Land, but this is sometimes interrupted to dramatic effect. Several remote inland national parks, such as White Mountains National Park and Blackdown Tableland, are set on spectacular rocky ranges. Generally, visitors must be well prepared and self-sufficient, as there are few facilities.

Lawn Hill National Park

Lawn Hill National Park is a 2800 square kilometre oasis in the desert. Within its boundaries is scenically spectacular terrain with the ineffable beauty of the rugged outback, yet with abundant water, too. There are also good examples of Aboriginal art. This park lies about 220km south-west of Burketown in the far north-west Gulf country of Queensland. Declared in 1985, it contains spectacular sandstone gorges with sheer 60m walls and crystal-clear pools.

History

The Waanyi people occupied this area for at least 17 000 years. Evidence of their culture can be seen in the art painted and etched in rock shelters within the park. There are two such areas open for viewing. The gorge also has a prolific selection of Aboriginal

middens and tool factories which can be viewed, but are definitely not to be collected. There is also spectacular scenery and wildlife.

In 1992, an immense fossil field on the ancient Riversleigh Plateau 75km to the south-east, was amalgamated into the national park. At the same time it was declared as a World Heritage Area, together with the Naracoorte fossil site 2000km away. Riversleigh is one of the richest and most exciting fossil fields in the world. Its deposits are a massive burial ground of prehistoric creatures, including giant pythons, carnivorous kangaroos, marsupial lions and huge flightless 'thunder birds'. At Naracoorte, Victoria Fossil Cave preserves a record of terrestrial vertebrate life spanning the past 170 000 years.

Climate

Despite the park being so far north, rainfall in the wet season is unreliable. Recent records indicate that the average is only about 500mm annually, most of which falls over the summer months. At the start of the wet season, continuous rain fills the creeks and black soils swell and close off the dry-season cracks. In 1991, the Gregory River rose to a peak of more than 15m with the bridge submerged for seven weeks of major flooding. Prolonged flooding is not an annual event, but the threat is real.

The dry-season rate of flow for Lawn Hill Creek is calculated at four million litres per hour. Queensland Water Resources Commission records show that on 9 January 1974, their tower on Lawn Hill Station measured 70 billion litres passing down Lawn Hill Creek! This produced a calculated 'record' flood height that peaked at 7m over the dry-season level.

Average flooding of Lawn Hill Creek sees the dry-season level rise by about 2m. At the 1m level, walking tracks to the Island Stack are impassable as they disappear into irregular opaque depths of flood water creating a true island. At Indarri, the natural tufa wall is submerged under a surging torrent and swimming or using a canoe become dangerous.

The deluge promotes flourishing plant life. Small, delicate annuals

Looking along Lawn Hill Creek from the top of Island Stack in the Lawn Hill National Park, central north Queensland.

appear from previously compacted soils and the landscape freshens with a new, luxuriant carpet of green. As the flood level recedes, silt coats all surfaces previously submerged and park authorities need to reconstruct the walking tracks. Another effect is that thousands of washed-up mussels become easy fodder for scavenging birds. By contrast, the dry season sees creeks become clear, with birdlife migrating elsewhere. Day temperatures during summer (October–April) may exceed 40°C, while mid-winter nights can be near freezing without the moderating proximity of the ocean. Walkers should pack warm sleeping bags at any time of the year.

Vegetation

The lush tropical vegetation includes Leichhardt trees, *Livinstona* palms, paperbarks, figs, pandanus and white cedar trees, remnants of the ancient rainforest that covered the gulf savanna millions of years ago.

Wildlife

Lawn Hill is where Queensland's first confirmed sighting of the rare rock hunting possum occurred. Other wildlife species include solitary wallaroos, insectivorous bats, the olivine python, fairy martins, water monitors, tortoises and an astonishing variety of exotic birdlife.

Access

Access by vehicle or plane during this season, December to March, is risky—4WDs are highly recommended. By road the park is about 400km northwest of Mt Isa and 220km south-west of Burketown. The last 280km from Mt Isa and the entire distance from Burketown are unsealed and can become impassable after rain. A dirt airstrip for light aircraft is at Adel's Grove. Arrange ground transport to the park in advance. Contact:

Adel's Grove at PMB 2,
Mt Isa QLD 4825.
Tel: (07) 4748 5502

Facilities

Rangers are stationed in the national park and a camping area with toilets and showers has been developed adjacent to Lawn Hill Creek. Camping permits are required and bookings should be made in writing to the ranger-in-charge or, with credit card, by phone. There is no guarantee that a campsite will be available if travellers arrive without a booking. Alternative camping may be available at Adel's Grove, 10km from the park. The nearest major centres for a full range of supplies and services are Burketown and Mt Isa. Fuel is available at Gregory Downs Hotel, 100km east of the park. Ice and minor supplies are available at Adel's Grove.

Collect firewood on the way into the park. Generators are not encouraged, but there is a special area set aside for camping with quiet generators (noise level up to 80dB at 2m); running times are restricted to hours negotiated with the ranger on site.

The Queensland National Parks and Wildlife Service has built some 20km of marked bushwalking tracks which provide access to the more spectacular viewing areas around the gorge area. There are five national park rangers resident in the park. The highland plains area, north-west of the gorge, is a wilderness beyond the end of all public roads. There are no facilities and no access.

Upper Gorge Circuit

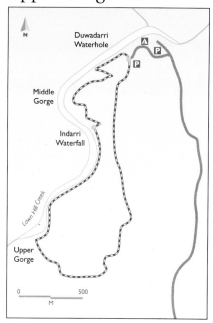

Starting Point: Lawn Hill camping area, Lawn Hill National Park
Destination: Upper Gorge (Jalyawala)
Summary: A day circuit incorporating all the easily accessible highlights of Lawn Hill Creek Gorge
Attractions: Indarri waterfall, Middle Gorge (Runnumu) and various vantage points
Length: 7km
Time: 2.5 hours
Options: Short options along the network of trails to various lookouts
Attraction Rating: ★ ★ ★
Fitness: ◪ ◪
Maps: SUNMAP Tourist Map Gulf Savannah 1:1 000 000
Access to Starting Point: 220km south-west of Burketown, 401km north-west of Cloncurry along the Wills Developmental road
Facilities/Amenities: No accommodation; self-sufficient camping only. Specific sites have been set aside for buses or large groups. Internal roads

are set out for easy caravan access and exit. The camping area is grassed. There are laundry tubs, showers, toilet facilities, BBQs, tables and hot water supplied by a 'donkey-boiler', which is a communal responsibility.
Recommended Equipment: Protective clothes for sun, insect repellent, swimming costume, water bottles
Further Information:
Lawn Hill National Park
PMB 12, Mt Isa QLD 4825
Tel: (07) 4748 5572
(3.00pm–4.00pm weekdays)

An excellent booklet, *Discover Lawn Hill National Park* by Cheryl O'Keefe, is available from the ranger's station.

Walk Description

From the camping area, go south along the track that parallels the Lawn Hill Creek gorge's eastern bank. A short steep rise across Mt Isa sandstone takes you to the top of the cliffs. Lawn Hill Gorge was formed by Lawn Hill Creek, which derives its continuous flow from numerous springs in the limestone plateau to the west. With abundant water and lush tropical vegetation the gorge is home to an amazing diversity of animals. A beautiful swimming spot is located at Indarri. It is quite safe if the gorge is not in flood. To the south, the view over the gorge can be admired before the track heads away from the water at Lawn Hill and circles back to the camping area across rocky terrain with views east to Constance Range.

Island Stack Circuit

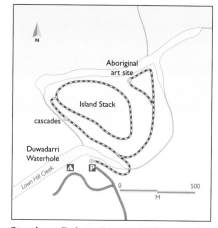

Starting Point: Lawn Hill camping area, Lawn Hill National Park

Destination: Lower Gorge (Luluwala)
Summary: A short circuit walk that accesses the cliff-lined top of an outcrop encircled by water
Attractions: Cascades, Aboriginal art site, plenty of views
Length: 6.5km
Time: 2.5 hours
Attraction Rating: ★ ★ ★
Fitness: ◪ ◪
Maps: SUNMAP Tourist Map Gulf Savannah
Access to Starting Point: 220km south-west of Burketown, 401km north-west of Cloncurry along the Wills Developmental road
Facilities/Amenities: Refer to the preceding walk
Further Information: Refer to the preceding walk

Walk Description

From the camping area, head downstream and ford the creek. Here the track branches left to the cascades and the ascent of Island Stack (Garra), and right alongside the old channels to the confluence of Widdallion Creek and Lawn Hill Creek to the Wild Dog Dreaming Aboriginal art site. Explore all three destinations, leaving the walk around the top of Island Stack to last. If it is early or late enough in the afternoon, photographers will find superb colours in the cliffs.

Carnarvon National Park

A walk through Carnarvon Gorge couldn't be more fascinating and varied if it were planned. The 314 500ha park is an awe-inspiring jewel in the great Queensland outback. Palm trees contrast with massive white sandstone cliffs and dozens of side gorges harbour natural amphitheatres, rare ferns, Aboriginal paintings, narrow canyons and picture-postcard waterfalls. The cliffs that dominate every section of the gorge were formed about 135–190 million years ago.

The road to the start of the gorge walk is well graded. Spend a fascinating day or two exploring the lower gorge near the car park and camping area. On the way is a swimming hole in Carnarvon Creek to keep in mind if the weather is warm.

The gorge forms only a small part of the park. The Queensland National Parks and Wildlife Service has been adding sections to the west and it now includes Mt Moffatt, Ka Ka Mundi, Salvator Rosa and Goodliffe. The floor of the main gorge, where Carnarvon Creek flows, is all that most of the 60 000 visitors a year see of the park. The remainder, part of the Consuelo Tableland and the Great Dividing Range, is largely inaccessible.

The spectacular scenery in this area has made it a popular destination for campers. Carnarvon Creek has gouged soft sandstone from the vertical white cliffs of the gorge over millions of years. The creek flows all year, giving life to many ferns, trees and shrubs. Narrow side gorges are shaded for most of the day, providing havens for ancient remnant rainforest, ferns and mosses. Above the cliffs is a dry, rugged environment where the forest is more open. More than 20km of walking tracks lead to places of interest, including Aboriginal art sites such as the Art Gallery and Cathedral Cave.

Facilities

Some basic food supplies, fuel and gas are available every day from the Oasis Lodge, 3km from the main camping ground. Firewood is not available in the park so bring a fuel stove. Creek water is not suitable for drinking. Bring water containers to carry tap water from the camping ground on walks. Bring extra food and suitable camping gear in case of wet weather. Private cabin-style accommodation is available at the Oasis tourist lodge adjacent to the national park.

Carnarvon Gorge Walk

Starting Point: Carnarvon Gorge campground, Carnarvon National Park
Destination: Big Bend camping area
Summary: Fascinating, action-packed walk through a cliff-lined gorge
Attractions: Lookouts, waterfalls, the Moss Garden, Ward's Canyon, the Amphitheatre and the Art Gallery
Length: 19.2km
Time: 1 full day or two half days if camping at Big Bend
Options: A 6.4km side trip to Boolimba Bluff (628m). If you stay

The famous Aboriginal Art Gallery in the Carnarvon National Park.

two days, do the walk to Battleship Spur in the morning on the second day, making the entire trip 29.6km. If you add the Boolimba Bluff option on the morning of the first day (overnight packs can be left at the car park), the entire distance is 36km. Boowinda Gorge is worth exploring if you take a rest day at Big Bend camping area. The return distance is 1.4km and takes about 45 minutes.

Attraction Rating: ★★★★★
Fitness: ▨▨
Maps: The Queensland Department of Environment and Heritage has produced a 1:50 000 scale vegetation-based colour map of the gorge and its surroundings. The AUSLIG (Natmap/Ausmap) Mt Howe 1:100 000 topographical gives an overview of the area. The Australian Geographic Society has also produced a Carnarvon National Park tourist map.

Access to Starting Point: One route is from Roma via Injune and Wysby, good bitumen for 170km and fair to rough unsealed road for 75km. The other is from Rolleston via Consuelo, 20km of good bitumen and unsealed road for 75km. After rain, unsealed

roads may become impassable.
Facilities/Amenities: An information centre, cold showers, toilets and a public telephone at the main camping ground. The less developed Big Bend bush camping area, 12km from the nearest car park, has only a toilet.
Recommended Equipment: Camera, tripod and sturdy walking boots
Notes: Write to the ranger at Carnarvon Gorge up to 12 months ahead for a permit. Applications must contain the relevant fee. Both camping areas may be booked out during school holidays. A maximum five-night stay applies during Queensland and New South Wales school holidays. The Big Bend campsite is restricted to 20 people a night.
Further Information:
The Ranger, Carnarvon Gorge
Carnarvon National Park
via Rolleston QLD 4702
Tel: (07) 4984 4505
Fax: (07) 4984 4519
or

Department of Environment
72 McDowell St
PO Box 981, Roma QLD 4455
Tel: (07) 4622 4266
Fax: (07) 4622 4151

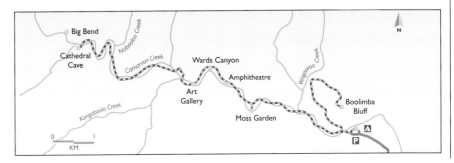

Walk Description

From the lookout on the right up on Boolimba Bluff you can survey the opening of Carnarvon Gorge and the flat tablelands beyond. Farther along is the Moss Garden, Ward's Canyon, the Amphitheatre and the famous Art Gallery. This important site has some 1300 engravings and 650 stencils along a 62m stretch of wall.

Close to the camping area, the Moss Garden is a photographer's dream, but a tripod is needed and exposure is difficult to estimate because of contrasting light. Wards Canyon, with its Freezer Chamber, is also photogenic, but sunlight penetrates to the bottom for only a few minutes each day. A rare species of fern found at the entrance here hasn't changed for about 300 million years. Only the widest lens will be able to capture the Amphitheatre properly.

As you continue up the walls get narrower, and the river begins to snake around dramatic headlands. The last attraction is Cathedral Cave, near the entrance to Boowinda Creek. From here it is only a short stroll up Carnarvon Creek to the remote Big Bend campground.

Battleship Spur Walk

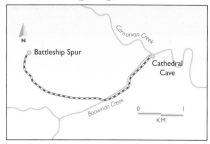

Starting Point: Big Bend camping area, Carnarvon National Park
Destination: Battleship Spur lookout
Summary: A difficult walk through rugged terrain to a prominent spur
Attractions: Outstanding views over the eastern part of the Carnarvon National Park
Length: 10.4km (return)
Time: 5 hours (return)
Options: A 4km, 2-hour walk continues up Carnarvon Creek to The Island, a sandstone formation in the middle of the gorge surrounded by a spotted gum forest.

Attraction Rating: ★ ★ ★
Fitness: ◪ ◪ ◪ ◪
Maps: As for preceding walk
Access to Starting Point: As for preceding walk
Facilities/Amenities: A toilet at Big Bend camping area; otherwise, none
Recommended Equipment: Complete self-sufficiency is essential. No water is available once you leave Carnarvon Creek so bring water containers.
Notes: The walk is best undertaken in winter as summer heat tends to create haze. The Big Bend campsite is restricted to 20 people per night.
Further Information:
  The Ranger, Carnarvon Gorge
  Carnarvon National Park
  via Rolleston QLD 4702
  Tel: (07) 4984 4505
  Fax: (07) 4984 4519
or
  Department of Environment
  72 McDowell St
  PO Box 981, Roma QLD 4455
  Tel: (07) 4622 4266
  Fax: (07) 4622 4151

Walk Description

Battleship Spur, a small spur projecting from the Great Dividing Range, commands magnificent views over the eastern end of the national park. The walk involves a steep climb and is strictly for experienced bushwalkers who are physically fit. The shortest route to Battleship Spur is via Boowinda Creek Gorge, up and out of the gorge, and then along the main ridge to the base of the spur.

An overnight camp at Big Bend campsite is recommended, leaving for the spur early the following morning. Average walking time from Big Bend to Battleship Spur Lookout is estimated at two to three hours. The walk is marked by a few very small red and yellow tags and a few yellow arrows have been placed on trees at appropriate places along the route.

Proceed to the entrance of Boowinda Creek Gorge, about 100m upstream from Cathedral Cave and about 400m downstream from Big Bend campsite. Walk up this gorge for about 1.5km (15–25 minutes' walk) keeping watch on the right-hand side for a tall cabbage tree palm on which is fastened a small red and yellow tag.

This palm is at the foot of a small, usually dry, rocky gully. It should take about 15 minutes to climb up this gully. Once on top, keep looking well ahead for the tags fastened to trees along the route. In many places a distinctive narrow bushwalkers' pad is discernible. The ridge becomes a narrow 'razorback' and at one place you will be confronted by a clump of crumbly looking rock that is too risky to climb. Go along a track on the left, marked by an arrow. After about 30m, another arrow shows you where to climb up to the top of the ridge again. It's about a 10m climb.

Proceed along the razorback now to its end at the base of Battleship Spur: an arrow points to the right and a narrow pad runs along the side for about 300m; then an arrow points upward for the last climb. Once on top of the spur, go to the right—it is a 500m walk out to the natural lookout and rock cairn. Return to the Big Bend camping area via the same route.

Other walks in Carnarvon National Park
Carnarvon Gorge section
This main section offers more short walks for visitors staying in the camping area or lodge.

Warrumbah Gorge Walk (4km, 1 hour)
The gorge is accessed from the Mickey Creek car park 2km west of Oasis Lodge. The track heads up Mickey and Warrumbah Creeks to a rocky pool.

Baloon Cave Walk (1.5km, 30 min)
The cave is accessed from behind Oasis Lodge—a short loop that leads back to the road.

Mt Moffatt section
Mt Moffatt's picturesque ranges have witnessed many changes and diverse land uses over the past 20 000 years and archaeological excavations have shown that Aborigines used its sandstone rock shelters for habitation for at least this long.

History
Little is known about the Aboriginal inhabitants, but it is believed there were two different groups, the Nun

The popular Moss Garden is the first feature on the Carnarvon Gorge Walk in Carnarvon National Park.

people on the lowland southern areas, and the Bidjara on the high northern areas. Boundaries were probably not static and ownership undoubtedly varied over the years.

The spectacular eroded sandstone landscape would have held a special significance for these people, but little cultural knowledge has survived to reveal its importance. Moondungera, the Rainbow Serpent, was said to be the creator of the Maranoa River, given this name by Mitchell during his expedition. During a severe drought, the Rainbow Serpent caused the big spring to form and flow out of the range, its water carving out the sandy winding river bed. It was from this that all the Maranoa people were said to have originated, from the kangaroo totemic ancestor.

The first known European visitor to reach the area was explorer Sir Thomas Mitchell. In June 1846, he trekked along the Chesterton Range area on Mt Moffatt's western side. The park's south-western section received closer investigation in June 1847,

when explorer Edmund Kennedy's expedition passed through in search of the supposed inland sea.

When the first settlers arrived cannot be determined with certainty, but the earliest recorded run appears to be one called Valentina, forming part of what is now Warrong Station, on Mt Moffatt's southern boundary. William Francis Kennedy, Tiereyboo Station (near present-day Condamine) applied for this and several other leases in November 1859, just days before Queensland became a colony on 10 December. Numerous owners used the marginal Mt Moffatt area for grazing until 1979 when it was declared a national park.

The Tombs Walk (1km, 30 min)

Aptly named, The Tombs are a dominant sandstone formation; the name also covers the famous art sites they contain. Numerous natural tunnels in this formation were once used as burial chambers by local Aborigines. Skeletons were wrapped and bound in ornately decorated bark cylinders.

Regrettably, by 1902 the site had been stripped of this material to such a degree that little evidence of this elaborate mortuary culture remains.

A large permanent waterhole that once existed on the river bend below the formation was significant for wildlife and Aborigines. This may account for the extent of occupation deposits that accompany the art in this site. Archaeological excavations have shown that these deposits extend 2m below the present floor level and cover a time span of at least 9400 years.

The dominant art style at this site is stencil art, but there are some obviously freehand red 'paw tracks' at the eastern end. A highlight is a large red stencilled human figure, the only known stencil of a standing adult in the park. A small number of child body stencils have been recorded in the eastern sector of the ranges, but as yet no other examples of adult stencils have been found. Some other stencils of interest here include a woomera or spear-thrower at the site's western

Carnarvon Creek begins near the Mahogany Forest on the Mt Moffatt tableland.

extremity, and a pair of grey kangaroo 'hoppers' in the central area. Stencils of full-length 'hoppers' are rare and may depict a sitting marsupial rather than one in motion as indicated by the 'half-hopper' stencils in Kenniff Cave (see below).

A number of small oval stencils to the lower right of the stencilled man are of a *Che-ka-ra*, or shell pendant, in which the string mounting hole can be seen. *Che-ka-ra* may have been traded from the Cape York area of north Queensland. The bright red contorted hand stencil on the central ceiling area is believed to be a 'signal stencil' signifying a spear-thrower.

Kenniff Cave (500m, 20 minutes)
Security fences aim to protect this important archaeological site from further vandalism. Visitors who want to inspect the cave must call at the Ranger Station to collect a key because the site is locked. Much of the Aboriginal culture has been lost in this area so please help to preserve what remains. Take great care when walking on the loose floor deposits as dust and oil damages the art; refrain from touching or brushing against the fragile art surfaces.

Professor John Mulvaney's archaeological excavations in the early 1960s revealed that traces of Aboriginal habitation at this site extended to a depth of 3.28m below floor level, and dated from some 19,500 years ago. This established Kenniff Cave as Australia's first verified Pleistocene site. The extensive site is dominated by stencil art, with only a scattering of faint freehand figures. The most obvious freehand motif is a red humanoid figure with outstretched arms and legs on the lower southwestern wall. Both poor lighting and damage from water seepage make the figure difficult to identify at times.

In the remaining stencil art you can see a comprehensive record of artefacts once in daily use. These include a variety of leaf boomerangs, a 'boomerang club', a narrow shield and hafted stone axes. Several pairs of wallaroo 'half-hoppers' are stencilled on lower wall areas and it is believed they represent animals in motion.

The cave perpetuates the name of the infamous Kenniff Brothers, the last of Australia's 'wild colonial boys', who lived near this cave at one time during their colourful career. Their horse-stealing and cattle-duffing came to an inglorious end in 1902 with the murder of Constable George Doyle and station manager Christian Dahlke. After a police hunt lasting for several months, the brothers were finally captured near Mitchell.

Further Information: New walks are currently being opened up in this area. For more details, contact:
Carnarvon National Park
Mt Moffatt
via Mitchell QLD 4465
Tel: (07) 4626 3581
Fax: (07) 4626 3581

Ka Ka Mundi section
When approaching the open plains toward Ka Ka Mundi, the white sandstone cliffs of the Great Dividing Range and steep slopes of the Wattle Tableland dominate the horizon. This remote section of Carnarvon National Park is named after Mt Ka Ka Mundi, rising 400m above the surrounding countryside. The word is derived from the Aboriginal *Ga Ga Moondee*.

More than 30km of sandstone escarpments and plateaus of the Great Dividing Range form the park's southern boundary. Several other peaks, such as Mt Mooloolong, lie along the western border with the Salvator Rosa section. Streams rising here flow north into the Nogoa River, across the agricultural plains of central Queensland and become the Fitzroy River, emptying into the Pacific Ocean near Rockhampton.

Geology
Sandstones of Ka Ka Mundi were laid down in freshwater lakes and streams during the Jurassic Age, about 180 million years ago. In more recent geological times lava covered the ranges. Erosion has removed most of the basalt cap, leaving only a few basalt outcrops, such as Mt Ka Ka Mundi. The prominent cliffs are the result of erosion along vertical weathering joints characteristic of precipice sandstone. To the west, in Salvator Rosa, boxvale sandstone landforms are more rounded because of different weathering patterns.

History
Mt Mooloolong was feared by the Aborigines and rarely visited—evil spirits were believed to live there. While the unusually shaped outcrops inspired many stories, little material evidence of the rich Aboriginal culture now remains.

A basalt-capped mountain northwest of Bunbuncundoo Springs is believed to have been the home of a mythological giant dingo. Healing powers were attributed to these springs and Aboriginal children with bone problems were bathed in the waters. The name Bunbuncundoo means 'skinny-legged children' in the language of the Bidjara people.

Old cattleyards near the springs are reminders of early European history. Ka Ka Mundi was lightly grazed for more than a century, but the area was preserved in 1974 in an effort to protect a representative sample of bonewood and brigalow scrubs. This region is very wild and remote and offers unique opportunities for pioneering bushwalkers to do some exploring. Destinations might include Fred Hill, Cave Gill, Goonganangie Springs, Den Spring and Mt Ka Ka Mundi.

Climate

A range of temperatures is common in the central highlands. Frosts occur regularly on winter mornings and temperatures can drop to 0°C. Summer days are usually very hot with many above 35°C. Most rain falls between December and March, and visitors can be stranded by impassable roads. Storms occur in any month.

Vegetation

The diversity of plant communities at Ka Ka Mundi is of particular botanical interest. Grey-green brigalow contrasts with the red clay soils on the undulating eastern plains. Bonewood and softwood scrubs also occur on clay soil. Other soil types support different vegetation—poplar box on clay barns, silver-leafed ironbark on sandy soils, while basalt-derived black soil supports grassy downs.

The Great Divide and range country is timbered with stunted eucalypts. Taller ironbarks and 'yellow jackets' have a shrubby acacia understorey. Along the main range, fire has resulted in the growth of acacia thickets. Elsewhere, the absence of fires has probably encouraged a complex mix of plant communities. Bottle trees overlook softwood vine scrubs on the northern face of the escarpment near creek headwaters. Many scrub plants are adapted from rainforest plants—reminders of a wetter past climate.

Wildlife

Several springs, such as Bunbuncundoo, seep from foothills and creek beds. These small oases, lush with tree ferns and coral ferns, attract many birds—king parrots, fig birds and wompoo pigeons. Wildlife can be difficult to spot in the dense timber and long grass. Red-necked and swamp wallabies may be glimpsed sheltering in thick understorey by day. After fires, fresh green pick will attract grey kangaroos. Stocky dark wallabies are usually seen around rocky ridges and sandstone outcrops. Koalas can sometimes be heard grunting along the escarpment, but they normally sleep by day in a tree fork.

Access

The Ka Ka Mundi section is about 120km or a three-hour drive southwest of Springsure. About 50km from Springsure along the Springsure–Tambo road, take the Buckland Loop road to the south. Follow the signed tracks past Petrona and Tanderra, through Yandaburra to the park boundary. Be careful if rain threatens; the road crosses black soil plains that become impassable even for 4WD vehicles. The same applies for the

Palms in Carnarvon Gorge, an oasis in the Queensland outback.

Salvator Rosa and Goodliffe sections to the west. Contact the ranger in Springsure or Emerald for the latest road conditions before visiting these areas of the Carnarvon National Park.

Facilities

No facilities are provided in this undeveloped section of the park. Most visitors use Bunbuncundoo Springs as a base. Be entirely self-sufficient and bring drinking water because feral animals, such as horses, pigs and cattle, roam the tops. The nearest fuel and food are at Springsure. There are bush camping areas at Bunbuncundoo Springs, where water is available. The wire grass flats are shaded by forest gum, Moreton Bay ash, dry rainforest species, such as *Alphitonia*, and a few bottle trees.

Walking Opportunities

A full-day circuit is possible from Bunbuncundoo Springs, walking west to Goonganangie Springs, then north to Three Monkeys, east to Red Hill and using the range to walk south of Packsaddle Springs and return to Bunbuncundoo Springs.

Further Information:
Department of Environment
PO Box 157, Springsure QLD 4722
Tel: (07) 4984 1716
Fax: (07) 4984 1173

Salvator Rosa and Goodliffe Sections

Located in the far west of Carnarvon National Park, 164km south-west of Springsure, this area is completely undeveloped and visitors need a 4WD vehicle to access the Nogoa River. The road can be impassable after rain. Like Ka Ka Mundi, some pioneering-style walking is possible in the cooler months between April and October. Despite the aridity, some 300 plant species have been recorded in the area.

Geology

Salvator Rosa and Goodliffe are at the western edge of the Central Queensland sandstone belt, formed when layers of sediment were deposited in a shallow inland sea. The coarse-grained sandstones of Salvator Rosa are very crumbly. Erosion has left many dramatic, interesting features

Looking over Lonesome National Park near Carnarvon Gorge.

that dominate the skyline including Spyglass Peak and The Sentinel.

The porous sandstones of the surrounding ranges capture much of the water that enters the Great Artesian Basin. The springs of Salvator Rosa occur where erosion has cut the overlying sandstone rocks down to aquifer level. In a 1950s report to Parliament on the springs of the Great Artesian Basin, geologist Dr F. Whitehouse stated that:

The most impressive group of such large springs is on Louisa Creek, near the head of the Nogoa River where there are many springs in a linear belt of five to six kilometres, three of which each flows at least 1 million litres per day.

History

The Nogoa River was a welcome relief in 1846 for Major Mitchell's party, which had travelled for weeks along the dry upper reaches of the Maranoa and Warrego rivers. These were also the first northerly flowing waters encountered in their search for a route to the Gulf of Carpentaria. The landscape apparently reminded Mitchell of the dramatic and haunting paintings of Salvator Rosa, a 17th-century artist from Naples, because many features now bear this name.

In his book *Expedition into the Interior of Tropical Australia*, Mitchell described his impressions:

...the hills overhanging it surpassed any I have ever seen in picturesque outline. Some resembled Gothic cathedrals in ruins, others forts. Other masses were perforated and being mixed and contrasted with the flowing outlines of evergreen woods and having a fine stream in the foreground, gave a charming appearance to the whole country. It was a discovery worthy of the toils of a pilgrimage...

The area so impressed Mitchell that he later returned to establish a base camp near the site now referred to as Major Mitchell Springs.

Unlike the Carnarvon Gorge and Mt Moffatt sections, evidence of Aboriginal occupation is scant in this westerly region. Mitchell's diary mentions encounters with Aboriginal tribes and evidence of their presence, such as the shells of large freshwater mussels near campfires. Mitchell also mentions seeing Aborigines with red-painted faces carrying mummy-like bundles. He may have witnessed part of a complex mortuary ceremony carried out by several Aboriginal tribes in the central highlands. These involved carrying preserved human remains for lengthy periods.

Mitchell describes fires started by Aborigines in bush around Major Mitchell Springs. These were probably started to flush out game such as grey kangaroos for hunting, and to ensure that after rain there was an abundance of fresh green grass on which such game could graze.

The 26 270ha Salvator Rosa section was gazetted in 1957; the 14 500ha Goodliffe section followed in 1998.

Vegetation

Eucalypt woodland and open forest cover most of this section of the park. Fringing forests of river red gum, poplar box and rough-barked apple line the Nogoa River and Louisa Creek. Open forests of silver-leaved ironbark on deeper alluvial soils gradually change to open woodlands of white cypress pine, smooth-barked apple and bloodwoods on the sandy ridges away from watercourses. Shallow soils on ridgetops support forests of gum-topped ironbark, while scattered black cypress pines can be found on exposed rock outcrops.

Wildflowers add colour to the landscape in spring. Large white flannel flowers and cream sprays of narrow-leaved *Logania* contrast with the red flowers hanging from the shrubby *Homoranthus*. Of more than 300 plant species recorded in the park, at least 10 are considered rare or threatened.

Wildlife

Many of the marsupials here are nocturnal or, like the kangaroo, drink and feed only at dusk or dawn, resting in the hottest part of the day to conserve their energy.

Maps

Consult the SUNMAP Amazing Central Queensland Tourist Map or RACQ QDM7 map for road details. Bush-walkers should carry the AUSLIG (Natmap/Ausmap) 1:100 000 Cungelella topographical map.

Access

Access to Salvator Rosa is from either Springsure or Tambo via unsealed roads that become impassable in wet weather. Nogoa River campsite can be reached by 2WD vehicle. The rest of Salvator Rosa is accessible only by 4WD vehicle or on foot.

From Springsure, head west along the Tambo Road for 114km to the Salvator Rosa turn-off. From Tambo, head north on the Alpha Road for 42km, then turn east toward Springsure. After 102km, turn south at the Salvator Rosa sign and travel for 50km via Cungelella to the boundary of the park. The Nogoa River campsite is another 4km. Respect the rights of property owners and leave all gates as you find them. Watch out for wildlife and livestock on roads, especially at night.

Facilities

Pit toilets are the only facilities provided at Nogoa River campsite on a broad sandy bank of the Nogoa River. Park authorities recommend that campers set up on the northern side of the river only and well away from the edge of the watercourse. Heavy storms in the upper catchment have been known to cause flooding. However, much of the river water originates from springs.

Further Information:

Department of the Environment
PO Box 157, Springsure QLD 4722
Tel: (07) 4984 1716
Fax: (07) 4984 1173

or

Roma District Office
Department of Environment
72 McDowall St
PO Box 981, Roma QLD 4455
Tel: (07) 4622 4266
Fax: (07) 4622 4151

Walking Opportunities

Nogoa River Walk (1km, 30 min)

This walk follows the northern bank upstream. River red gums and rough-barked apples with masses of creamy flowers line the riverbanks. In summer, honeyeaters feast on the nectar and, later in the year, king parrots seek out the seeds. Walkers may catch sight of a kingfisher, or hear a pheasant coucal calling from the swamp. Tiny finches and wrens dart about in the false bracken and climbing maidenhair ferns.

Pythagoras Rock and The Sentinel Walk (500m, 15 min)

A rough scramble up remnants of an eroded sandstone range near the Nogoa River campsite rewards viewers with some of the park's striking features, including Pythagoras Rock and The Sentinel. The ideal time to see these bluffs and spires is soon after sunrise, when the warm early morning light reflects off the cream-coloured sandstone.

Spyglass Peak Walk (1km, 30 min)

Impressive Spyglass Peak is so named because of the 10m-diameter hole near its summit. A rough walking trail leads from the road to its base. The sandstones of Salvator Rosa crumble easily so be careful when walking around sandstone outcrops. Plants seen along the trail include yellowjacket, the dominant eucalypt, with striking orange-yellow, 'bloodwood' bark. The *Astrotricha* shrub has large leaves with white, woolly undersides.

Trans-Carnarvon Traverse (about 200km, 2 weeks)

Ambitious walkers set up a car shuffle to do this walk from end to end, walking right through Goodliffe, Salvator Rosa, Ka Ka Mundi, Mt Moffatt and into the Carnarvon Gorge to emerge at the camping area. Food drops are necessary. Some diversion from the main range will be necessary to access water. The Carnarvon Station property to the south of Ka Ka Mundi is the most obvious place, as long as the property owners have agreed. Contact the ranger based at Carnarvon National Park for further details. As future additions augment the park, it may be possible to undertake longer, expedition walks.

Other walks in Central Queensland
Isla Gorge

This park, located 400km north-west of Brisbane, is a maze of sandstone gorges with high cliffs and weathered pinnacles. The nearest township is Biloela. Long overnight walks are possible through Kalloroo Creek, Budyi Creek and Hewitts Creek.

Snake Range

This small 3000ha national park between Springsure and Alpha is becoming an increasingly popular destination for walkers seeking complete remoteness and solitude. Some spectacularly rugged outback terrain, similar to Salvator Rosa, can be found within the protected area.

The South-east

Many national parks are concentrated in the south-east region where the Great Dividing Range lies quite close to the coast. Unlike parks of the tropics, not all vegetation consists of rainforest and the climate isn't subject to seasonal extremes. With Brisbane in the centre of this region, it comes as no surprise that the parks of the south-east are well used.

Bunya Mountains National Park

The Bunya Mountains form an isolated section of the Great Dividing Range about 150km from the coast. They rise abruptly from the surrounding country to an average of 975m, reaching more than 1100m at Mt Kiangarow and Mt Mowbullan.

Straddling much of the mountain range, Bunya Mountains National Park is best-known for its bunya pines, with their distinctive, dome-shaped crowns. But they're just one of many plants protected in the park's rainforests, eucalypt forests and woodlands. High-altitude grasslands include vegetation such as heathland and rare grass species, comprising an internationally significant ecosystem. Birdlife is abundant here, with parrots being popular visitors to picnic areas. Rare and threatened birds, reptiles and mammals are also found in the park.

Colourful Crimson Rosellas are common in the Bunya Mountains National Park.

Just 109km north of Toowoomba (90 minutes), or three to four hours from Brisbane, the 11 700ha Bunya Mountains National Park has bush-walking, camping, natural beauty and important heritage on offer.

History

Aboriginal occupation has been dated to about 30 000 years ago. About every three years, Aboriginal tribes gathered at the Bunya Mountains for tribal ceremonies, hunting, mock fighting, corroborees and feasting on the ripe crop of bunya pine 'nuts'. From the 1860s, timber cutters established sawmills to harvest the timber wealth of the Bunyas. The last sawmill on the mountain closed in 1945, but relics of the industry still remain. In 1908, 9303ha were gazetted as the Bunya Mountains National Park, the second national park declared in Queensland.

Climate

Bunya Mountains National Park has a mild climate with an annual rainfall of about 1050mm. Temperatures range between freezing and 30°C. The early morning and evening temperatures can often be quite low so be prepared with adequate warm clothing, even in summer.

Vegetation

The distinctive, dome-shaped crown of the bunya pine emerges above the tall, moist rainforest along the crest of the range. In dry rainforest at lower elevations, bunya pine is replaced by its relative, the hoop pine, which produces giant cones weighing 6–7kg.

Internationally important natural grasslands containing a number of rare grass species adjoin the rainforest. These probably formed during a cooler and drier climatic period that caused the forests to recede and allowed the grasses to dominate. The national park also protects open eucalypt forests, woodlands and other dry rainforest communities. Vine thickets dominated by bottle trees or brigalow and belah can be found on the western slopes. In the north of the park walkers will notice thickets of very tall grasstrees.

Wildlife

The Bunya Mountains are home to many species of birds. Brilliantly coloured king parrots and crimson rosellas are commonly seen around the picnic areas. Red-necked wallabies often feed in grassy areas. Swamp wallabies and red-necked pademelons prefer the cover of the rainforest but can be seen along the road edge. Spotlighting at night may reveal many animals, including the mountain brushtail possum and the smaller Bunya Mountains ringtail possum. Walkers should beware of a scrub tick that is common in the area.

Access

The park can be reached from Dalby, Toowoomba, Kingaroy or Nanango. From Toowoomba, drive 44km to Jondaryan and take the Bunya Mountains turn-off. Travel a further 65km through Maclagan. Some sections of the road are gravel. From Dalby, travel 25km to Kaimkillenbun and then 30km to Bunya Mountains via Yamsion. From Kingaroy, take the road to Kumbia and the Bunya Mountains. The park is located 56km from Kingaroy via this route. From Nanango, take the road to Maidenwell and turn right. This 55km route is gravel in parts. All routes to the Bunya Mountains are steep; caravans and trailers are certainly not recommended. Note that no fuel is available on the mountain.

Facilities

Camping areas are at Dandabah, Westcott and Burtons Well. Dandabah has toilets and hot showers. Westcott has pit toilets and no showers. Burtons Well has toilets and boil-your-own-water showers.

For school holidays and long weekends, you should aim to book up to 12 months ahead. Write or telephone the ranger for a camping permit. A small fee must be paid by cheque or credit card at this time. If no booking has been made, obtain a permit before camping (if there are vacancies) from the office between 2.00pm and 4.00pm daily, or from the self-registration station at the camping area.

Westcott Plains Track Walk

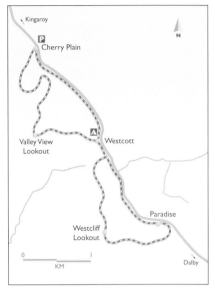

Starting Point: Paradise car park, Bunya Mountains National Park
Destination: Cherry Plain picnic area
Summary: By combining the Westcliff and Westcott Plains tracks, it is possible to complete an interesting tour of the clifftops on the west of the range
Attractions: Westcliff Lookout, Koondai Lookout, Valley View Lookout
Length: 11.3km, including 3.3km road walking to return
Time: Half a day
Options: Ambitious walkers can make a day walk by continuing on Cherry Plain track to Burtons Well
Attraction Rating: ★ ★
Fitness: ☒ ☒
Maps: AUSLIG (Natmap/Ausmap) Kingaroy 1:100 000 topographical gives a good overview. Other maps are the Mowbullan 1:50 000 topographical and the Queensland Forest Service's Bunya Mountains 1:25 000 map.
Access to Starting Point: See access notes in previous column
Facilities/Amenities: Basic picnic facilities at Cherry Plain picnic area and Westcott camping area
Notes: Set up a car shuffle to avoid the 3.3km, 1-hour walk back along the Bunya Mountains road
Further Information:
Bunya Mountains National Park
MS 501, Dalby QLD 4405
Tel: (07) 4668 3127
(2.00pm–4.00pm daily)
Fax: (07) 4668 3116

Walk Description

This walk explores the top of the western escarpment of the Bunya Range. The walk is basically in three stages, starting with the Westcliff Track to Westcott camping area. Follow the Koondai Lookout circuit downhill to the Koondai Lookout and up to Valley View Lookout, which surveys the Darling Downs region. Follow the Westcott Plain track through grassy 'balds' and rainforest to the Cherry Plain picnic area. From here it's about an hour's walk south, along the Bunya Mountain road back to the Paradise car park.

Barker Creek and Lookout Circuit

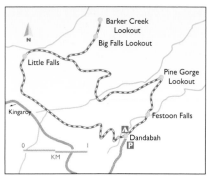

Starting Point: Dandabah camping area, Bunya Mountains National Park

Destination: Barker Creek Lookout, Paradise Falls

Summary: The best walk in the park as it contains the most varied scenery

Attractions: Waterfalls and lookouts

Length: 14.4km

Time: 1 day

Attraction Rating: ★ ★ ★

Fitness: ✗✗

Maps: AUSLIG (Natmap/Ausmap) Kingaroy 1:100 000 topographical gives a good overview. Other maps are the Mowbullan 1:50 000 topographical and the Queensland Forest Service's Bunya Mountains 1:25 000 map.

Access to Starting Point: See Access, page 54

Facilities/Amenities: All facilities, information, kiosk, showers, toilets and accommodation at camping area

Recommended Equipment: Tripod for waterfall photography. Take warm clothes as a precaution against sudden temperature drops.

Notes: Start early—there's a lot to see

Further Information:

Bunya Mountains National Park
MS 501, Dalby QLD 4405
Tel: (07) 4668 3127
(2.00pm–4.00pm daily)
Fax: (07) 4668 3116

Walk Description

This walk on the eastern side of the range is the longest and most varied in the park. It combines four smaller walks into a circuit that requires no road walking or backtracking to return to the starting point. From Dandabah camping area, head along the Bunya Bunya Track, through rainforest, and Barker Creek Track to Paradise Falls and Little Falls. The track then swings east to Big Falls and a turn-off to Big Falls Lookout and Barker Creek Lookout. These are the real highlights of the day's walk. From the Barker Creek Lookout junction, turn left to access Tim Shea Falls where the Scenic Track branches off to Pine Gorge lookout. From here it is only a little over 1km back to Dandabah camping area.

Other walks in Bunya Mountains National Park

Use combinations of the previous walks to make shorter or longer walks, from a 500m stroll to a 30km overnight walk. National park rangers sometimes organise activities during school holidays or on busy long weekends. Visit the Information Centre to obtain a guide to activities. Members of the Bunya Mountains Natural History Association voluntarily assist rangers in providing activities. Enquire at the National Parks and Wildlife Service headquarters at Dandabah camping area. If you plan to walk or camp in the state forest, contact:

Yarraman Forest Service
PO Box 21, Yarraman QLD 4314

Lamington National Park

This park contains a series of densely forested valleys and ranges rising to more than 1100m on the crest of the McPherson Range, which marks the Queensland–New South Wales border and also the rim of the Mt Warning caldera. The park lies on the southern side of the Scenic Rim, a chain of mountains stretching from the Gold Coast hinterland to Mt Mistake. The 20 500ha area is made up of two main sections: Binna Burra in the east and Green Mountains to the west.

Climate

Be prepared for extremes in weather conditions. Summer storms occur frequently and can cause a sudden drop in temperature. Summer days may be quite hot with temperatures exceeding 30°C, followed by cool nights. Winter days are often fine but chilly, around 12°C, with evening temperatures falling to near freezing. Warm clothing, raincoats, a first-aid kit and sturdy boots as well as food, a compass and a torch are essential, even for day walks. Most rainfall occurs from November to March, but torrential downpours and storms may occur at any time of the year. After rain, tracks can become slippery. Don't attempt creek crossings when creeks are in flood. Advise a relative or friend of the proposed route and destination, especially if you are walking away from tracks.

Vegetation

In 1994, Lamington National Park was listed as part of the Central Eastern Rainforest Reserves (Australia) World Heritage Area. The listing includes the most extensive areas of subtropical rainforest in the world, most of the world's warm temperate rainforest and nearly all of the Antarctic beech cool temperate rainforest.

Wildlife

Most mammals here are nocturnal but at Green Mountains and Binna Burra the red-shouldered pademelon, a rainforest wallaby, can be seen feeding in the late afternoon. Mammals include the dingo, tiger cat, water rat, bush rat, ringtail possum, short-eared brushtail possum, pygmy possum, short-nosed and long-tailed bandicoots, flying 'squirrel' (phalanger) and echidna. Snakes, some of which are aggressive if disturbed, include carpet snake, tiger snake, red-bellied black snake, green tree snake. Lizards include the land mullet, lace monitor, tree goanna, eastern water dragon, water skink, pink-tongued lizard, soft-scaled gecko and rainforest dragon.

The many bird species include the Albert lyrebird, scrub turkey, satin bowerbird, regent bowerbird, several species of pigeons, rufous scrub bird, logrunner, whipbird, noisy pitta, paradise riflebird and the green catbird. There are three whistlers—rufous, olive and golden, and three thrushes—grey, rufous and Australian. Both little black and little pied cormorants visit the lower creeks. Birds of prey include 35 perching birds such as the Australian kestrel. Many of the country's 70 species of honeyeaters frequent the park.

In *Birds of O'Reilly's*, the Green Mountains Natural History Association has published a list of 216 bird species sighted in the Green Mountains section of Lamington National Park and along Canungra Creek to Mundoolan Lagoon.

Facilities

Lamington National Park has an extensive network of developed walking tracks, designed to access the area's highlights while avoiding backtracking. Circuit walks range from short strolls to intense overnight expeditions and therefore cater for most people's ability. Walking track guides with maps and details of the track system are available from the information/orientation offices at Binna Burra and Green Mountains.

Overnight campers must contact the national park ranger in advance to secure a permit, to check on conditions and to complete a bushwalker safety form. Camping permit fees apply, with a maximum of six people per site. Always practise minimal-impact bushwalking ethics, especially by using fuel stoves rather than open fires. Remote camping is not allowed between 1 December and 31 January. Sites include Point Lookout, Rat-a-tat Hut and Tweed Trig. Complete self-sufficiency is essential. In June 1999, a party of bushwalkers had to be rescued when one member suffered hypothermia, so take care.

Fires are banned in the park, except where BBQ facilities are provided. Gathering firewood leads to trampling around campsites, removes vital habitat for insects, reptiles and small mammals and interferes with normal recycling of nutrients.

Binna Burra Section

Find out about the park at the Information Centre on the right-hand side of the road. Nearby is a small picnic area with toilets. Walking tracks to the caves, Illinbah and Gwongoorool leave from here, while the Lower Bellbird circuit has its lower entrance 500m down the road.

Travel a further 1.2km and you will reach a fork in the road. Walking tracks leave from both left and right sides of the road. From here, turn

An Antarctic beech near the Border Track, Lamington National Park.

sharp right to reach the lodge. The main track entrance and picnic area, as well as a private kiosk, camping area and telephone, are at the end of the road. Unleaded petrol (but not diesel) is available at the lodge.

Lamington is popular for day visits, so expect crowded conditions in the picnic areas during weekends and holiday seasons. Come prepared with your own fuel stove and seating. Accommodation is available nearby at O'Reilly's Rainforest Guesthouse, on private land adjoining the park. A nearby kiosk sells meals and some basic supplies.

Lamington National Park has nearly 160km of graded track walks in some of the best rainforests in south-east Queensland. But although they are graded, some tracks cross creeks and have slippery and rocky sections to negotiate.

Access

Binna Burra Section is 35km (50 minutes) by bitumen road from Nerang. From Brisbane, travel via Nerang or 107km via Canungra. Roads are narrow and winding in places, and used extensively by wildlife and pedestrians, especially between the Binna Burra Information Centre and the end of the road.

Ships Stern Circuit

Starting Point: Binna Burra, Lamington National Park
Destination: Kooloobanoo Point
Summary: An interesting and varied

full-day circuit walk in the far north-eastern section of the park with very little backtracking

Attractions: Dense beech tree rainforest, spectacular lookouts over Nerang Valley and pretty waterfalls
Length: 19km
Time: 1 day
Options: Many options to lengthen the walk, based on the Border Track
Attraction Rating: ★ ★ ★ ★
Fitness: ◪ ◪ ◪
Maps: SUNMAP Beechmont 1:25 000 topographical
Access to Starting Point: See access notes in previous column
Facilities/Amenities: None en route. Accommodation at Binna Burra Lodge, tel: (07) 5533 3622
Recommended Equipment: Rain jacket, tripod for photographing falls
Further Information:

The Ranger
Lamington National Park
Binna Burra section
via Nerang QLD 4211
Tel: (07) 5533 3584
(1.00pm–3.30pm weekdays)

or

The Ranger
Lamington National Park
Green Mountains section
Via Canungra QLD 4275
Tel: (07) 5544 0634
(1.00pm–3.30pm weekdays)

An excellent publication on the area is *History of Lamington National Park* by J. Keith Jarrott.

Walk Description

Starting 300m back from the end of the Binna Burra road, the Ship's Stern Circuit descends into Kurraragin Valley (Nixon Creek). Lower Ballunjui Falls, reached by a short side track, are 5.3km from Binna Burra.

As it winds up the hill and along Ship's Stern Range, the track passes through open forest with wildflowers. Lookouts provide views into Numinbah Valley and Kurraragin Valley. Continue through open forest and rainforest (with a possible sidetrack to Upper Ballunjui Falls, which is not linked by track with Lower Ballunjui Falls). Join Border Track to return to Binna Burra. A side option is the short Rainforest Circuit, passing through majestic stands of beech trees.

Coomera Circuit

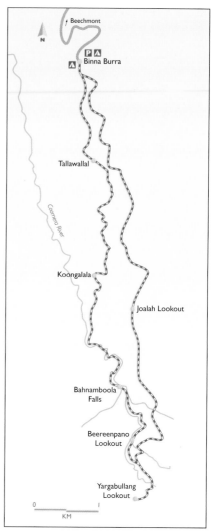

Starting Point: Binna Burra, Lamington National Park
Destination: Yargabullang Lookout
Summary: A spectacular, but long, walk along the Beechmont Range, meeting with the McPherson Range for views into New South Wales. Only a little backtracking is required.
Attractions: Antarctic beech rainforest, many waterfalls and lookouts over spine of the McPherson Range
Length: 21.6km
Time: 1 full day
Options: This is a figure-eight loop that can be done any number of ways. Various other tracks branch off the Border Track allowing for short or long extensions.
Attraction Rating: ★ ★ ★ ★
Fitness: ◪ ◪ ◪ ◪
Maps: SUNMAP Beechmont and Tyalgum 1:25 000 topographicals
Access to Starting Point: See Access in introduction, at far left

Recommended Equipment: Rain coat, tripod for photographing falls

Notes: Leave early—there are many attractions on this long walk

Further Information: As for Ships Stern Circuit details on opposite page

Walk Description

Centred on the crest of the Beechmont Range, this scenic circuit leaves the Border Track 1.9km from the park entrance and passes through rainforest and giant brush box forest. Coomera Falls Lookout, 5.4km from the track entrance, provides a view of Coomera Falls (64m) and Yarribilgong Falls. The track crosses the sparkling creek a number a times as it winds up the gorge before rejoining the Border Track.

Before returning to Binna Burra, continue south to the New South Wales border, where a number of lookouts allow you to survey the Oxley River valley. Creek crossings can be hazardous after rain and should not be attempted when the river is in flood.

The White Caves (Talangai), near Binna Burra, Lamington National Park.

Border Track Link Walk

Starting Point: Binna Burra, Lamington National Park

Destination: Green Mountains

Summary: One of the best walks in Queensland, and one of the best rainforest walks in the country

Attractions: Magical Antarctic beech forest, numerous lookouts on the McPherson Range

Length: 21.4km (one-way)

Time: 7 hours

Options: Numerous tracks branch off the Border Track allowing for short or long extensions. To save a little bit of effort, do the walk in the opposite direction, so you are descending more than you're climbing.

Attraction Rating: ★ ★ ★ ★ ★

Fitness: ☒ ☒ ☒

Maps: SUNMAP Beechmont and Tyalgum 1:25 000 topographicals

Access to Starting Point: See access notes in introduction, page 56

Facilities/Amenities: None en route

Recommended Equipment: Rain jacket, tripod for photographing falls, waterproof boots

Notes: Set up a car shuffle so that you have transport waiting at the exit

Further Information: As for Ships Stern Circuit details on opposite page

Walk Description

The Border Track is the backbone of the park system, connecting Binna Burra and Green Mountains. This is a full-day walk (21km one-way) passing through rainforest and patches of Antarctic beech (*Nothofagus moorei*). This species is an interesting tree, and not only from an aesthetic point of view. It has close relatives in South America and New Zealand, and fossils have been found in Antarctica. As its seeds are not suitable for dispersal across oceans, many scientists accept this as part of the evidence that these continents and Australia were once linked but have since drifted apart.

Many tracks lead from the Border Track to places of particular interest. Parallel to one section of the Border Track on the Green Mountains side is the Pensioner Track, an easier walk, but no shorter. The lookouts along the McPherson Range traverse offer spectacular views of the Lamington wilderness, Mt Warning and the Tweed Range.

Other walks in the Binna Burra region of Lamington National Park

Mt Hobwee Circuit (18.2km, 6 hours)
After leaving the Border Track 5.4km from Burra, this circuit winds through rainforest to the summit of Mt Hobwee (1140m), continues to Dacelo Lookout and then rejoins the Border Track to return to Binna Burra.

Lower Bellbird Circuit (12km, 4 hours)
This track branches off the main Ship's Stern Circuit and passes through a patch of dry rainforest below Bellbird Lookout to emerge at the Egg Rock clearing. The circuit then returns via the Binna Burra road or by the Caves Track (which adds 1.6km to the walk).

Daves Creek Circuit (12km, 4 hours)
To see a fascinating variety of forest and heath, branch off the Border Track 2.3km from the entrance and descend through the head of Nixons Creek out into Daves Creek country. The track passes through rainforest, very tall eucalypt forest and montane heath. Numinbah Lookout is a good place for a rest.

Araucaria Lookout Walk (17.8km, 6 hours)
This side track branches off the Mt Hobwee Circuit, passes Orchid Bower and ends at Araucaria Lookout, where tall hoop pines grow. The return trip is 5.2km from the Mt Hobwee Track.

Wagawn Walk (18km, 6 hours)
This track branches off the Mt Hobwee Circuit 2km from the Border Track junction and leads to the Warumblebah, Junimbabah and Garragoolba lookouts. Wagawn is 3.4km (return) from the Mt Hobwee Circuit junction. A track also leads along Mt Wagawn to Bushrangers Cave.

Mt Merino Track (23.8km, 8 hours)
Mt Merino (1160m) is halfway between the two accommodation houses along the Border Track. A short loop track off the Border Track leads to a lookout with spectacular views into New South Wales over the Tweed and Limpinwood valleys. Some of the largest Antarctic beech trees in the national park can be found here, their trunks and branches covered in moss. Listen for the loud calls of the rare rufous scrub-bird, whose ecological niche is this cool temperate rainforest.

Blue Pool Walk, (9.8km, 3 hours)
The Blue Pool Track branches off the Border Track 250m from the park entrance. As you steadily descend, you will pass some large rainforest trees, including red cedars. Few large red cedars, prized for their beautiful timber, remain outside the park. You may also see Christmas orchids along this track. In season, their fragile white flowers brighten the rainforest floor. The track finally reaches Blue Pool (Yerralahla) on West Canungra Creek, a popular swimming spot. Large eels live here and you may see a platypus. The spectacular Stairway Falls are 1.7km farther downstream. The creek flows over what appear to be stairs before plunging into a refreshingly cool pool.

Toolona Creek Circuit (17.4km, 6 hours)
The Toolona Creek Track branches from the Box Forest Circuit near Elebana Falls then follows Toolona Creek up a gorge and past its headwaters to emerge on the Border Track near Wanungara Lookout. Numerous waterfalls and cascades can be seen along the way. In many of the pools the blue Lamington spiny crayfish lives. The return trip is via the Border Track passing Toolona and Bithongabel lookouts. Many outstanding clumps of Antarctic beech (*Nothofagus moorei*) are seen near the lookouts.

Box Forest Circuit (10.6km, 3 hours)
This track branches from the Border Track 1.6km from the park entrance. It leads down through rainforest past impressive stands of smooth pink-barked brush box before reaching Picnic Rock and Elebana Falls on Canungra Creek. There is a swimming hole below Sunshine Falls about 100m upstream from Picnic Rock. The track continues down the valley before climbing the opposite side.

Green Mountains District
Being somewhat more developed than Binna Burra, Green Mountain attracts large numbers of visitors, especially on weekends and during school holidays. O'Reilly's and the road to it can be quite busy, especially on Sundays.

A national park campground with facilities is 500m from the ranger park headquarters. No provision is made for caravans. Campsites must be pre-booked through the park office, preferably three to four weeks in advance for weekends. For campsites during school holidays and public holidays, bookings should be made six to eight weeks in advance. A small camping fee applies. Toilets and hot showers are provided. Bring a gas or fuel stove as no open fires are allowed in the campground. Petrol and general supplies can be bought at Canungra and there is a public telephone at the bus turnaround.

An Orientation Centre provides detailed information on walking tracks and other general park information. The camping registration area is in the visitors' centre. If it is not staffed, a self-registration system still allows campers to pay. Formed tracks, mostly passing through subtropical rainforest, allow walkers to reach gorges, waterfalls and lookouts.

Access

Green Mountains Section is 115km from Brisbane via Canungra, or 70km from the Gold Coast via Nerang and Canungra. The bitumen road is winding and often narrow; drive with great care. The final ascent into the national park is not recommended for vehicles towing caravans.

Canungra Creek Circuit

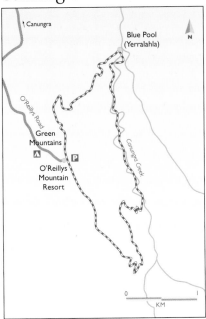

Starting Point: Green Mountains, Lamington National Park
Destination: Canungra Creek
Summary: This walks links up several tracks and visits numerous waterfalls
Attractions: Bunyip Falls, Blue Pool, Elabana Falls
Length: 13.9km
Time: 1 day
Options: Many side options, including Stairway Falls and Toolona Falls
Attraction Rating: ★ ★ ★
Fitness: ✗ ✗ ✗
Maps: SUNMAP Beechmont 1:25 000 topographical
Access to Starting Point: See Access in introduction to Green Mountains section on opposite page
Facilities/Amenities: None en route
Recommended Equipment: Rain jacket, tripod for photographing falls, waterproof boots
Further Information: As for Ships Stern Circuit details, page 56

Walk Description

From O'Reilly's Mountain Resort, this track joins the Box Forest Circuit and the Blue Pool (Yerralahla) Track to complete the round trip. The track follows the Canungra Creek for most of its length, crossing it several times. Birdlife is plentiful along the way including the spine-tailed log-runner and Australian ground thrush which may be seen foraging for insects in the leaf litter on the forest floor.

Albert River Circuit

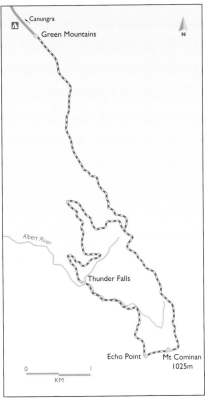

Starting Point: O'Reilly's Mountain Resort, Green Mountains, adjoining Lamington National Park
Destination: Echo Point
Summary: A long day walk that traverses the Border Track between Green Mountains and Mt Bithongabel
Attractions: Several lookouts along the route, including Cominan and Valley of Echoes; Lightning Falls, Thunder Falls and Bithongabel Falls
Length: 20.6km
Time: 1 full day
Options: The easier Pensioner Track can be used to vary the return route
Attraction Rating: ★ ★ ★ ★
Fitness: ✗ ✗ ✗ ✗
Maps: SUNMAP Beechmont and

A gigantic strangler fig tree chokes its host.

Tyalgum 1:25 000 topographical
Access to Starting Point: See Access in introduction to Green Mountains section
Facilities/Amenities: None en route
Recommended Equipment: Rain jacket, tripod for photographing falls, waterproof boots
Further Information:
The Ranger
Lamington National Park
Green Mountains
via Canungra QLD 4275
Tel: (07) 5544 0634

Walk Description

The left branch of the Albert River can be accessed from a pleasant circuit track that branches right off the Border Track about 5km from the walk start. This track winds down to the river where Lightning Falls and Thunder Falls can be viewed. The track turns upstream, then north along the ridge that forms the border between Queensland and New South Wales. Echo Point and Cominan Lookout provide excellent views over the McPherson Range escarpment. Beech orchids flower along this section in late winter to early spring. Simply follow the Border Track back to return to Green Mountains.

Other walks in the Green Mountains region of Lamington National Park

Morans Falls Track (6km, 2 hours)

This track leaves 800m from the ranger station and winds down through rainforest to Morans Falls, with a spectacular drop of 80m. A lookout provides an excellent view of the falls and the Albert River Valley. A picnic area is at the top of the falls.

Python Rock (5km, 2 hours) and West Cliff Track (7.4km, 2.5 hours)

A variety of forests and spectacular lookouts make these walks interesting. Leave the main road 800m from the ranger station. The track continues for 800m through rainforest before branching. From Python Rock, 300m farther on one branch, you can see Morans Falls, Castle Crag and the Lost World. This track is sealed and suitable for wheelchairs. On the other branch, walk 1.2km to West Cliff, overlooking Stockyard Creek Valley.

Box Forest Circuit (10km, 3 hours)

After leaving the Border Track 1.6km from the entrance, the Box Forest Track leads down through rainforest and impressive brush box trees before it reaches Picnic Rock and Elabana Falls on Canungra Creek. It continues down the valley before climbing the opposite side.

Toolona Creek Circuit (17.4km, 6 hours)

The Toolona Creek Circuit branches from the Box Forest Circuit near Elabana Falls, then follows Toolona Creek past its headwaters to emerge on the Border Track near Wanungara Lookout. Many waterfalls and cascades are seen along the way. Return trip is by the Border Track passing Toolona and Bithongabel lookouts.

Blue Pool and Stairway Falls Track (9.8km, 4 hours)

The Blue Pool Track branches off the Border Track about 300m from the entrance. As it descends, it passes some large rainforest trees, including red cedars, before reaching Blue Pool (Yerralahla) on West Canungra Creek.

The pool is a popular swimming spot. Another 1.7km downstream are the spectacular Stairway Falls.

Balancing Rock/Castle Crag/Morans Falls Walk (6km, 2.5 hours)

Balancing Rock is a formation that lies on the ridge leading out to Castle Crag, just before the razorback. Good views along the entire ridge. Castle Crag is a razorback ridge leading out to a spectacular lookout. The Castle Crag pad is narrow and exposed, not a graded track walk. There's no climbing involved, but the route requires a head for heights. You can combine Balancing Rock and Castle Crag with Moonlight Crag and Lyre Bird Lookout for an interesting day walk.

The track out to Castle Crag starts above Morans Falls and follows a 4WD track to Balancing Rock. You pass a campsite five minutes before Balancing Rock. From here it is easy to follow a pad out to Castle Crag.

Beyond the Lost World

An ambitious self-sufficient walker with an overnight pack can explore the wilderness to the west of Green Mountains. A trail continues along the border to Echo Point, Point Lookout and the Tweed Trig. Areas of interest are the Lamington Plateau, Black Snake Ridge and the right branch of the Albert River valley. The access is difficult to the western side of the park as many of the routes cross through private property. Furthermore, because of the soft terrain, dense vegetation and high rainfall, tracks quickly get overgrown and it is easy to become lost. Expert navigation skills are essential. Consult the SUNMAP Tyalgum, Lamington, and Cougal 1:25 000 topographical maps.

Mt Barney National Park

Ascending Mt Barney is one of the classic climbs in Australia. Its sheer mass, combined with a tremendous height gain, utilising ridge crests that often border on rock-climbing, secure its place as a top walking venue. Add to this the magnificent views, the potential for high-altitude camping, and the possibility of a round trip, and you have a challenge for even the most demanding bushwalker.

The mountain is made up of volcanic granophyre rock, which intruded through sandstone about 25 million years ago. There are actually several peaks and the whole mountain is considered a massif. The two highest summits are East Peak (1351m) and West Peak (1359m). East Peak offers the more dramatic views and is the objective of most walkers. The tops are mainly grassy, rocky, open eucalypt forest, but there is also rainforest in sheltered gullies and ravines. Six main ridges approach Mt Barney's two summits, some quite difficult. They are Logans Ridge, South-East Ridge, South Ridge, Midget Ridge, Leaning Ridge and Eagles Ridge, as well as a host of creeks, gullies and gorges between the ridges. The best suggestion is to climb via the closest route to the Yellow Pinch camping ground and to descend via the easiest, most popular route, the South Ridge (or Peasants Ridge).

South-East Ridge is a spectacular approach direct to East Peak. There are great views along the rocky knife-edge, but a few tricky sections involve some rock-scrambling. For most walkers, the effort involved will be more than adequate without attempting other, harder and longer climbs on which fatalities have occurred.

The South Route, used for the descent, is fairly straightforward, offering a fast, easy exit from the Mt Barney complex. While it is recommended to do the walk in a day with a light pack after an early start, it is also good to take two days, allowing one to camp in the pleasant saddle between the two main peaks with the opportunity to witness a spectacular sunrise over cloud-filled valleys. This involves a hefty 1200m climb with overnight packs—not for the faint-hearted. Ropes for pack-hauling are recommended for this option.

Great care is required on Mt Barney in fog. The Mt Lindesay topographical map is poor, with most contour lines around the summit not being depicted. To make matters worse, the actual walking tracks and ridge names have not been included. Water is usually available at the saddle, but it

The view from the summit of Mt Barney—one of the most spectacular walks in Australia.

is wise to carry plenty of fluid for the climb—at least five litres per person per day. Do not attempt the ascent on a hot day. Ensure also that you leave early, well before 9.00am (earlier in winter). It is disconcerting for experienced bushwalkers to see amateurs still ascending late in the afternoon.

History

On a cold August morning in 1828, the Commandant of the Brisbane settlement, Captain Patrick Logan, and botanists Alan Cunningham and Charles Fraser set out from their camp to climb Mt Barney. This was the first recorded ascent of the mountain. Fraser's journal graphically recounts the climb, describing the perils the group encountered. Logan was the only one to reach the summit; both Cunningham and Fraser turned back after finding the ascent too difficult.

Mt Barney National Park, with many rare plant species, is important for nature conservation. It has special significance for Yugambeh Aborigines.

Vegetation

Most of the national park consists of open eucalypt forest, with some beautiful grassy slopes and lower country bearing tall, spreading gums, boxes and native apples. Creeks with cascades, deep pools and shallow sections flow through the park and are lined with river she-oaks, red-flowering bottlebrushes, golden silky oaks and patches of gallery rainforest. Rarely seen platypus swim in the lower reaches of the creeks and nest in their banks.

Higher rocky slopes and depressions support patches of heath, some of which have spectacular wildflower displays in spring. Vegetation of special significance includes Antarctic beech forest on Mt Ballow, low closed forest (rainforest) on Mt Barney, heath on Mt Maroon and tall banksia forests on Mt Lindesay.

Wildlife

The steep rock-covered slopes of Mt Barney are the habitat of brushtail rock wallabies. Higher up, vantage points provide nesting sites for birds of prey. Kangaroos and wallabies are very common, as are many species of birds such as kingfishers, robins and honeyeaters.

Mt Barney Walk

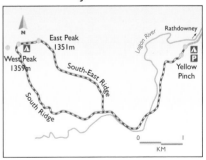

Starting Point: Yellow Pinch campground, Mt Barney National Park
Destination: West Peak, the summit of Mt Barney (1359m)
Summary: A spectacular climb using the South-East Ridge for the ascent and the South Ridge for the descent

Attractions: Outstanding views, great variety in vegetation due to significant altitudinal variation.

Length: 16km

Time: 1 day

Attraction Rating: ★ ★ ★ ★ ★

Fitness: ✗ ✗ ✗ ✗

Maps: SUNMAP Mt Lindesay 1:25 000 topographical

Access to Starting Point: Follow the Mt Lindesay Highway 1km south from Rathdowney, then turn west along the Rathdowney–Boonah road for 7km and along the Upper Logan road south-east to Yellow Pinch camp and picnic area, about 19.5km from Rathdowney. A barrier here prevents further vehicle access.

If you have a 4WD, cross the narrow gully and camp on the grass flats opposite. Don't use the nearby private Mt Barney Lodge as the free council camping ground is closer to the walk start and offers the beautiful Logan River for swimming. To access an attractive pool from the Yellow Pinch campground, cross the gully and follow a faint vehicle track to the right and down a small rocky trench.

Facilities/Amenities: Campground at Yellow Pinch has BBQs and toilets

Recommended Equipment: Water, insect repellent

Notes: If planning to use the East-West Saddle camping area, be aware that it is closed from 1 December to 31 January each year. Likewise, the small East Peak camping area can be closed at times during vegetation rehabilitation work.

Further Information:

Mt Barney National Park
Old Coulson School, Coulson
MS342, Boonah QLD 4310
Tel: (07) 5463 5041
(7.00am–3.30pm weekdays)

Walk Description

To access Mt Barney, set off along the road south over the Yellow Pinch ridge from the gate. A signpost here warns that physical fitness and navigational skills are needed to tackle the summit where rapid temperature and climatic changes can occur. Once over the ridge, continue south along the open Logan River flats to a gate. There are good views of the Mt Barney massif with its imposing 300m cliffs near the summit of East Peak. The vehicle track continues, crossing the Logan River via a causeway and entering the

Mt Barney National Park and the pleasant forest of the Cronan Creek valley. Plenty of numbered, cleared campsites are located on the left as the trail ascends.

About 800m later, a faint right-fork vehicle track climbs to South-East Ridge above a prominent saddle. The turn-off is not signposted and is quite derelict. A fallen log bars the way. The vehicle track rises steeply, being largely washed-out. It leads to the very crest of the ridge and heads up along it to the north before petering out into a bushwalking track.

The track is quite distinct, rising very steeply and generally keeping right of any rock outcrops barring the ridge. When possible, it ascends to the top of these rock platforms for fantastic views south to Mt Ernest and Mt Lindesay. There are a few minor saddles and some boulder-hopping before the ridge rises even more steeply. At one point you must descend into a small gully. The summit is obscured by more rock outcrops. Go around these, either to the left or the right.

The ridge becomes narrower after two minor ridges join up from either

Sunlight penetrates the leaf canopy in the rainforest at Cunningham's Gap, Main Range National Park.

side (at about 1000m elevation), the vegetation becomes increasingly wind-pruned and the dramatic drop to the right becomes quite acute. Some tricky scrambles are encountered in some shallow chimneys but there are generally plenty of hand holds from bushes, roots and rocks. Sometimes the track is only metres from a massive drop on the right. Good photographs of Mt Barney's dark cliffs can be captured here.

Once at the top of the ridge, head right and descend. The prominent West Peak with its sloping rockface dominates the view. The more rounded, gentler East Peak is to the right through some thick shrub and across a tiny camp clearing. A small trigonometrical survey marker is cemented in the rock at the highest point. There are superb unobscured views in all directions. Logans Ridge, Eagles Ridge, West Peak and Mt Lindesay are all highly photogenic as is the wild terrain of the surrounding foothills of Mt Barney. White-outs often occur here, even in otherwise sunny weather. Proceed along the track that descends north-west to the 'Rum Jungle' rainforest pocket at the saddle between West and East peaks. Some scrambling down the rock gullies is required before the track becomes distinguishable again at the upper Barney Gorge Creek. There is normally clean water here. Mt Barney National Park is a fuel-stove-only area. No wood fires are permitted.

At the old hut site in an open grassy clearing, the track crosses the creek and rises briefly, passing into rainforest before coming to the East-West Saddle camp clearing. The South Ridge Track is on the left of the clearing. It rises at first, before coming to a junction. Fluorescent neon orange and green arrows mark the way down. There are many confusing turn-offs before the ridge becomes well defined and easy to follow.

Some further rock-scrambling is encountered but this is not as difficult as the ascent. On one section about halfway down, a steep rock ramp must be negotiated; this can prove slippery after rain. Another section involves a mildly sloping face with no more than a crack for support.

The vegetation becomes pleasant near the bottom of the ridge. The track heads left, crossing a perennial creek to enter dense rainforest before emerging onto an old vehicle track. This is easy to follow as it winds down Mezzanine Spur to meet the main road to Yellow Pinch at a signpost noting the start of South Ridge. Head left and shortly you come full circle to meet up again with the South-East Ridge turn-off. Simply retrace the morning's route to the Yellow Pinch campground. By this time, the mighty east face of Mt Barney will now be in shadow.

Do not delay departure from the summit beyond lunchtime. The steep descent translates into slow progress for many walkers and will tax bones, knees and feet. A swim in the Logan River at the end will be welcome if the weather is hot.

Other walks in Mt Barney National Park

Various other approaches can be used to reach the two summits, including ridges and creeks. The advantage is that ambitious, experienced walkers can plan many more circuits using one of the many approaches up and another down. Some of the bases of these ridges, however, require quite a bit of walking to get to from the nearest vehicle access and there are no formed tracks. Furthermore, the walking often borders on rock climbing or abseiling, with progress so slow that an overnight trip is entailed. The ridges approaches are:

    Eagles Ridge
    Leaning Ridge
    Logans Ridge
    Midget Ridge
The creek approaches are:
    Barney Gorge
    Egan Creek
    Rocky Creek
Ropes are a prerequisite, especially on Logans Ridge and Leaning Ridge.

Main Range National Park

The park is a succession of impressive peaks, escarpments and ridges to the south-west of Brisbane. Encompassing 18 400ha, it extends from Mt Mistake in the north to Wilsons Peak on the Queensland–New South Wales border and west to Queen Mary Falls. This is the western part of the 'Scenic Rim', a spectacular arc of mountains that stretches from here to Springbrook in an almost continuous belt of national parks and state forests. The park comprises several sections: Mt Mistake, Cunninghams Gap, Spicers Gap, Mt Roberts and Queen Mary Falls.

A mosaic of vegetation types occurs within the park boundaries. Rainforests grow in moist or sheltered locations, open eucalypt forest on the high rocky ridges and drier slopes, and mountain heath vegetation grows on the cliffs and rocky outcrops.

These diverse habitats shelter much wildlife, including the seldom-seen Albert's lyrebird, eastern bristlebird and black-breasted button quail. Populations of these birds and other wildlife have been threatened by land clearing and fire. A restricted plant species, the giant spear lily, also occurs in the park, especially on the flanks of Mt Cordeaux. Forests, rugged landscape and breathtaking views have established Main Range as a popular bushwalking destination.

History

Allan Cunningham was the first European to discover Cunninghams Gap. On 25 August 1828, he named the guardian peaks of the gap as Mt Mitchell (after Sir Thomas Mitchell, Surveyor-General) and Mt Cordeaux (after William Cordeaux, Mitchell's assistant). Later, as a result of strong representation by local people, Cunninghams Gap was reserved as a national park on 3 July 1909.

A road was built through Cunninghams Gap in the 1920s and sealed in the 1940s. Walking tracks were built in the park from the late 1930s to the late 1950s. In the 1960s and 1970s, a number of other national parks were reserved along the Main Range. In August 1980, the parks were amalgamated to form Main Range National Park. Finally, in December 1994, the World Heritage Committee officially declared the Central Eastern Australian Rainforest Reserves World Heritage Area over the Scenic Rim (including Main Range, Mt Barney,

Lamington and Springbrook national parks) and the rainforests of northern New South Wales.

World Heritage status is a prestigious international recognition of the important conservation values of this area, especially its unique geology, subtropical and cool temperate rainforests and rare wildlife. Further additions to the national park are occurring as a result of this listing.

Facilities

Camping in developed campgrounds and wild bush-camping are both permitted. A permit (for which a small fee is charged) is required to camp in the national park. Camper self-registration stands are located at Cunninghams Gap and Spicers Gap camping areas. Advance bookings should be made for long weekends, large groups and all camping sites. Bookings are accepted only when accompanied by the appropriate fee.

Limited bush campsites, reached only by walking, are available in the national park. Group size is limited. Bushwalkers intending to bush-camp are required to fill in a bush safety and camping application form available from the Main Range National Parks and Wildlife Service headquarters. Bookings are necessary four to six weeks in advance.

Cunninghams Gap section

Cunninghams Gap (754m) contains extensive walking tracks, camping and picnic areas and the park headquarters, located on the western side of Cunninghams Gap.

The main campground is 3.5km west of the gap in open forest on the banks of West Gap Creek adjacent to the Cunningham Highway, opposite the national park headquarters. No bins are provided; visitors are asked to carry their rubbish out with them. The Main Range picnic area, 2km west of the gap, is home to a colony of bellbirds.

There is a car parking area beside the Cunningham Highway at the top of the crest of Cunninghams Gap. All walking tracks begin at this point, except for the track to Sylvesters Lookout. A monument to Allan Cunningham stands beside the car park.

Mt Mistake section

This section (5560ha) comprises the northern portion of the park. Some logging took place in the open forests and rainforests here until the 1960s, While there is no vehicle access to the park, there are several unmarked bushwalking trails. Contact the Main Range National Park staff before visiting Mt Mistake. This section of the park remains undeveloped.

Mt Roberts section

Located at the park's southern boundary, this section is undeveloped and access is limited. Mt Superbus (1375m) is the highest mountain peak in south-east Queensland. Limited bush campsites are available in remote areas of the park.

Access

Main Range National Park is 116km south-west of Brisbane and 50km east of Warwick. The Cunningham Highway crosses the park at Cunninghams Gap. Access to the Mt Mistake section is via Goomburra State Forest Park. Turn off the highway at Gladfield and follow the signs to Goomburra State Forest. The Mt Roberts section can be reached via the Killarney–Boonah road, 50km south-west of Boonah.

Gap Creek Falls Walk

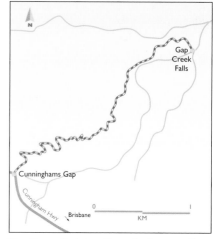

Starting Point: Cunninghams Gap, Main Range National Park
Destination: Gap Creek Falls
Summary: A zigzag trail descends into the Gap Creek valley near the eastern perimeter of the national park
Attractions: Gap Creek Falls
Length: 9.4km
Time: 5 hours
Options: The short Rainforest Circuit can be incorporated for some variety and to minimise backtracking
Attraction Rating: ★ ★ ★
Fitness: ◪ ◪ ◪
Maps: SUNMAP Cunninghams Gap 1:25 000 topographical

Koalas sleep for up to 20 hours a day.

Access to Starting Point: Follow the Cunningham Highway 116km south-west from Brisbane. The track leaves right from the very crest, about 15.5km from Maryvale.

Facilities/Amenities: Picnic area at the crest

Recommended Equipment: Sturdy footwear, tripod for photographing falls

Further Information:
Main Range National Park
MS 394, Warwick QLD 4370
Tel: (07) 4666 1133
Fax: (07) 4666 12 97

Walk Description

The best time to see the falls is soon after rain; there is little water over the 100m drop in dry weather. The trail, mostly through open eucalypt forest, starts at the crest car park via the stairs leading to the Fassifern Valley lookout. Descend the ridge below Mt Cordeaux to the top of the falls. The return trip is all uphill and can be very tiring in hot weather. This trail requires a high level of fitness and is not recommended for the very old or very young. Take full water bottles.

Bare Rock Walk

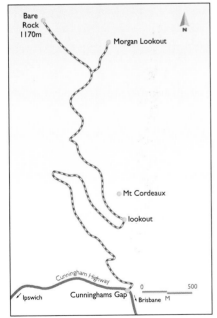

Starting Point: Cunninghams Gap, Main Range National Park

Destination: Bare Rock (1170m)

Summary: The best day walk in the Cunninghams Gap section of the Main Range National Park; spectacular lookouts, rainforest

Attractions: Rainforest, Morgan Lookout, and views to the dramatic peak of Mt Cordeaux from the north

Length: 12.4km

Time: 4 hours

Options: The short Rainforest Circuit can be incorporated for some variety and to minimise backtracking

Attraction Rating: ★ ★ ★ ★

Fitness: ◪ ◪ ◪

Maps: SUNMAP Cunninghams Gap 1:25 000 topographical

Access to Starting Point: Follow the Cunningham Highway 116km south-west from Brisbane. The track leaves right from the very crest, about 15.5km from Maryvale.

Facilities/Amenities: Picnic area at the crest at Cunninghams Gap

Recommended Equipment: Sturdy footwear

Further Information: As for previous walk

Walk Description

Detouring west of the peak of Mt Cordeaux, this track crosses a rocky saddle north of the peak and re-enters rainforest. Two varieties of tree fern grow near the track and lyrebirds can be heard in winter. Morgans Lookout, 2.4km past Mt Cordeaux, overlooks the northern section of the park. The track to Bare Rock veers west off Morgans Lookout track and can be reached after a brief scramble up a rocky outcrop. Being just above the canopy, the lookout provides a fascinating panorama over the escarpment of the Scenic Rim.

Mt Mitchell Walk

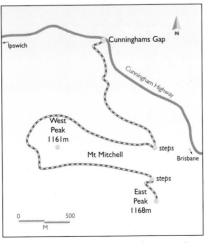

Starting Point: Cunninghams Gap,

Main Range National Park

Destination: The east peak summit of Mt Mitchell (Cooyinnirra)

Summary: A good-quality medium-distance track

Attractions: Outstanding views over the southern end of the Main Range National Park, rainforest

Length: 10.2km

Time: 3 hours

Attraction Rating: ★ ★ ★

Fitness: ◪ ◪ ◪

Maps: SUNMAP Cunninghams Gap 1:25 000 topographical

Access to Starting Point: Follow the Cunningham Highway 116km south-west from Brisbane. The track leaves right from the very crest, about 15.5km from Maryvale.

Facilities/Amenities: Picnic area at the crest

Recommended Equipment: Sturdy footwear

Further Information: As for previous walk

Walk Description

A graded walking track to the twin peaks of Mt Mitchell begins on the southern side of the highway. Rainforest and open eucalypt forest will be encountered on this track, which ends on a knife-edge ridge above a sheer cliff on the east peak of Mt Mitchell (1168m). This peak is known as 'Cooyinnirra' to Aboriginal people. Care must be taken at the cliff-edge as there are no fences.

Other walks in the Main Range National Park
Palm Grove Walk
(4.4km, 2 hours)
This easy walk from Cunninghams Gap takes in Fassifern Lookout and an outstanding grove of picabeen palms.

Box Forest Track
(8.4km, 2.5 hours)
This easy walk along West Gap Creek links the crest with the picnic and camping areas. Passing through rainforest and open forest, the track is named after the brush box trees that line the creek. Birdlife is plentiful along the way. Return to the starting point via the Box Forest Track or arrange to be picked up at either end of the track.

Girraween National Park

Surprisingly, Girraween means the 'place of flowers', despite the national park's main feature being spectacular rounded granite outcrops upon which are towered precariously stacked boulders called tors. The park lies at the very northern end of the New England Tableland on the New South Wales border and has an average elevation of 900m. It shares a boundary with Bald Rock National Park across the border, a park also dominated by granite. Eucalypt forests and heathlands support a diverse range of birds, including the rare turquoise parrot and superb lyrebird. More than 146 bird species have been recorded. At night, possums, gliders, spotted-tailed quolls and kangaroos are active. In spring, an array of wildflowers is on display.

There are 17km of walking tracks within the park, most of which begin from the visitors' centre at the end of Pyramids Road. The tracks range from a 1km return walk to the Granite Arch to a 10.4km return walk to Mt Norman. A guidebook with a map and a description of the walks is available at the park.

Climate

Because of the park's high altitude, be prepared for cold changes in any season. Winters are usually dry and cold with frosty nights reaching a minimum of −8°C. Summer days are warm (25–30°C) with cool nights. The average annual rainfall is 850mm, most of which falls between November and March.

Facilities

Two camping areas, Castle Rock and Bald Rock Creek, have hot showers, toilets, picnic tables, firewood and fireplaces (not every table at the campsite has a fireplace). Caravan sites are not powered and generators are not permitted. As in all Queensland national parks, all campers require permits. Prepaid bookings are required for peak visitor periods and can be made up to 12 months in advance. Camping applications containing fee payment, details of party size, proposed dates and other relevant information should be sent to Girraween National Park. The park is very popular, particularly during school holidays and long weekends. After peak times, park authorities may close a campsite for revegetation.

Remote camping is permitted along firebreaks at least 1km from walking tracks and the two camping areas. Fuel stoves are essential—no fires are permitted on overnight walks. Once again, camping permits are required and an itinerary of the proposed walk route must be left with the park ranger at the visitors' centre. A large, open, grassy picnic area is located on the southern bank of Bald Rock Creek next to the visitors' centre. There are fireplaces, picnic tables and septic toilets. The visitors' centre, with coin-operated STD public telephone, is usually open between 2.00pm and 4.00pm weekdays, and may open earlier on the weekend. It may be open at other times, park duties permitting.

Kookaburras at Castle Rock, Girraween National Park.

The Mt Norman day-use area, accessible from Wallangarra, has a toilet, but no camping is permitted. Rubbish bins are not provided nor is rubbish collected in the national park. You must carry out your own.

Basic food supplies are available at Wyberba. Fuel and food are available at Ballandean, Wallangarra and Stanthorpe. Chlorine-treated creek water is on tap in the picnic and camping areas, but campers and walkers may wish to boil it before drinking.

Access

Girraween is about 260km by road south-west of Brisbane. To reach the park, turn off the New England Highway 26km south of Stanthorpe or 11km north of Wallangarra. The winding bitumen road continues 9km east through the Wyberba Valley to the park information centre. The road from Stanthorpe to Girraween via Eukey and Storm King Dam has some sections of gravel.

The Pyramids Walk

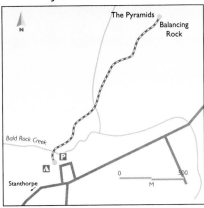

Starting Point: Girraween Visitors' Centre (Bald Rock Creek picnic area), Girraween National Park
Destination: The Pyramids
Summary: A short, easy walk to one of the most outstanding geological features in the national park. Only the southern pyramid (1080m) is scaled.
Attractions: Granite outcrops, views from first Pyramid, Granite Arch
Length: 3.5km
Time: 1.5 hours
Options: On the return, walk the Junction Track westward to where Ramsay Creek flows into Bald Rock Creek. There are some rapids here. This distance is an additional 4.4km

and takes about 1.5 hours.
Attraction Rating: ★ ★
Fitness: ✖
Maps: Hema Maps Girraween and Bald Rock National Parks 1:33 000; LIC Wallangarra 1:50 000 topographical
Access to Starting Point: See introduction
Facilities/Amenities: See introduction
Recommended Equipment: Sturdy shoes, hats and sunscreen; take a first-aid kit and drinking water
Notes: Granite rocks can be slippery, especially when wet
Further Information:
Girraween National Park Ranger
PO Box 731, Ballandean QLD 4382
Tel: (07) 4684 5157
Fax: (07) 4684 5123

Walk Description

From the picnic area, follow the signs across Bald Rock Creek veering right almost immediately. You can see the destination for almost the entire route. Do the Granite Arch loop either on the way there or on the return. The climb up the first Pyramid is steep in places but generally of fairly easy grade. The granite rock offers good grip in dry weather but when wet it can be alarmingly slippery. Rock-climbing skills and experience are necessary to climb the second Pyramid. The way up is at the back of the granite dome. There is a chimney to climb and a jump across a deep split in the rock. A belay rope is recommended for safety.

Mt Norman Walk

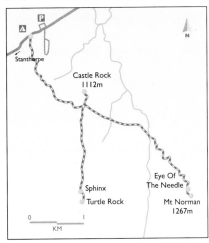

Starting Point: Castle Rock campground, Girraween National Park
Destination: Mt Norman (1267m)

Summary: One of the longest day walks possible in the national park
Attractions: View from the summit of Mt Norman, The Eye of the Needle
Length: 10.4km
Time: 3 hours
Options: An 800m side trip leads to Castle Rock (1112m). A longer side trip leads to the Sphinx and Turtle Rock—allow about 1.5 hours for this option. Walkers wanting an overnight experience away from the car should continue from Mt Norman all the way to Bald Rock in New South Wales. Consult the ranger for more details. A more direct route to Mt Norman is possible from the sandy Mt Norman day-use area located at the end of the Mt Norman road. This distance is 4km return and takes about 1.5 hours.
Attraction Rating: ★ ★ ★
Fitness: ✖ ✖
Maps: Hema Maps Girraween and Bald Rock National Parks 1:33 000; LIC Wallangarra 1:50 000 topographical
Access to Starting Point: See introduction
Facilities/Amenities: None en route
Recommended Equipment: Sturdy shoes, hats and sunscreen; take a first-aid kit and drinking water
Notes: Granite rocks can be slippery, especially when wet
Further Information: As per details for The Pyramids Walk

Walk Description

From Castle Rock camping area, the track passes south and then south-east to various interesting geological features, such as Castle Rock with good views, the Sphinx and Turtle Rock, the granite boulders of the Eye of the Needle and Mt Norman.

The Eye of the Needle calls for some climbing experience, while Mt Norman has a difficult 6m chimney to negotiate to access the top. Both are not too dangerous for experienced walkers but inexperienced people should take extra care. Return by the same route.

Other walks in Girraween National Park

Several other good walks are possible throughout the Girraween National Park for walkers with an inclination to explore less-frequented areas. Some destinations include Underground Creek, Dr Roberts Waterhole, the Aztec Temple and The Valley of the Winds. This last destination, just to the south-west of Mt Norman at the end of a ridge, is most fascinating—a hidden gorge with fragile vegetation.

Sundown National Park

Sundown National Park lies together with a Queensland National Parks and Wildlife Service management area along the New South Wales border about 250km south-west of Brisbane. The area includes Sundown National Park and Sundown Resources Reserve and covers about 16 000ha of high rugged country with sharply defined ridges and panoramic views. Peaks rise to more than 1 000m with most of the area averaging from 600–800m. Sundown is bisected by the Severn River and crossed by many creeks, some with spectacular steep-sided gorges. The integrity of the wilderness of the park is maintained by zealously keeping development restricted to an absolute minimum.

Geology

Locals refer to the Sundown National Park region as 'traprock' country. The hard dense rock was formed from ancient marine sediments deformed by heat and pressure. Intense minor faulting, folding and weathering has resulted in the existing layered rocks forming steep ridges and gorges leading down to the Severn River.

Intrusions of granite occur at Jibbinbar Mountain in the north-west and the deeply eroded Red Rock Gorge. Two roughly parallel granite dykes run through the area. One forms Rats Castle, a local landmark, and can be traced through the park and across the road near the southern entrance. Sundown's landscape and vegetation contrast sharply with the granite tors and valleys of the adjacent Granite Belt and Girraween National Park to the east. The two parks offer visitors interesting and different experiences.

History

Sundown was once part of Glenlyon, Nundubbermere and Ballandean rural stations. Around 1900, some parts of the stations were subdivided into smaller leasehold blocks. Much of the area was cleared for grazing, but although fine-grade wool was produced, the properties were not economic. Some reminders of early farming, including salt-troughs and yards, can be seen. Open areas remain from the extensive early clearing.

Mineral deposits, primarily tin, copper and arsenic, were mined sporadically at Sundown from the 1870s. Remains of mining activity can be seen from the main access track. While rich pockets of ore occurred, the deposits were usually of low grade, and although more than 70 men were employed for a short time, the mines were never a financial success. Old surface diggings can be inspected throughout the Red Rock area. The area around the Sundown mines and treatment plant is contaminated and, accordingly, public access is restricted to the 4WD track.

Vegetation

The vegetation gradually changes from the northern to the southern end of the national park, reflecting differences in climate and soil type. Eucalypt forests of stringybark, yellow box, brown box and Tenterfield woollybutt dominate the higher northern slopes. Caleys and silver-leaved ironbarks, tumbledown gum, white box and cypress pine form the southern woodlands. Kurrajongs, red ash and larger waffles are present with an understorey of hop bush, dead finish and peach bush.

In the steep-sided gorges, dry vine scrubs occur, as well as figs, stinging trees and numerous other vines. Wilga and native willow, species associated with the drier inland, occur at the southern end. Several ground orchids, including the donkey, waxlip, greenhood and hyacinth, flower in spring. King and cymbidium orchids may also be seen. River red gum, river oak, tea-tree and bottlebrush grow along the Severn River.

Wildlife

More than 130 species of birds have been recorded within the national park boundaries. While some birds live throughout the area, many have special, localised habitat needs. Satin bowerbirds, superb lyrebirds, scarlet and rose robins are present in the northern parts of the park, while spiny-cheeked and striped honey-eaters, red-capped robins and spotted bowerbirds, white-face and red-winged parrots live in the drier southern areas. Black duck, wood duck, herons, cormorants and tiny azure kingfishers feed along the river.

Wallaroos are common in the steep rocky country while grey kangaroos prefer less sloping habitats. Other macropods include the red-necked, swamp and pretty-faced wallabies. Marsupial mice, gliders and possums can also be seen.

Red Rock Gorge Walk

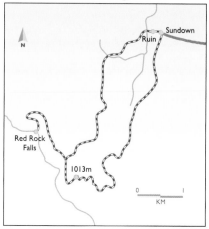

Starting Point: Sundown homestead, adjoining Sundown National Park
Destination: Red Rock Falls, Mt Lofty
Summary: A circuit walk using old 4WD trails to access Red Rock Gorge
Attractions: Red Rock Falls, Mt Lofty summit
Length: 16km
Time: One full day
Attraction Rating: ★ ★
Fitness: ✕ ✕
Maps: SUNMAP Sundown National Park 1:50 000 and the Wallangarra 1:50 000 topographical
Access to Starting Point: Follow Currs Road and then Sundown Road from Ballandean (just north of the border via the New England Highway). Sundown Road eventually leads to the park's eastern boundary, accessing the old Sundown homestead site. A high-clearance vehicle is highly

Moist sheltered habitats support vegetation such as tree ferns in the deep gullies and canyons of Sundown National Park.

recommended. A rough 4WD track at the park entrance continues to campsites along the river.

Bushwalkers usually leave vehicles just inside the park boundary at the start of the 4WD track. To the north, a rough shire road leads off from Nundubbermere Road to a reserve above Nundubbermere Falls on the Severn River. Take care when fording. Conventional vehicles can reach the Broadwater camping area and Severn River at the southern end of the park via 75km of bitumen from Stanthorpe and 4km of graded gravel surface.

Facilities/Amenities: No facilities at walk start. Broadwater camping area next to the Severn River has individual sites with fireplaces or BBQs. Pit toilets, firewood and facilities for hot bush showers are provided. Bush camping is permitted elsewhere, the most popular area being the banks by the river. Pit toilets and some mowed sites are available to

4WD campers at Burrow's Waterhole. Larger waterholes are suitable for swimming and canoeing. Be careful when entering waterholes as there may be hidden submerged obstructions.

No food or petrol supplies are available after you leave the New England Highway. A small general store at Glenlyon Dam provides basic supplies and fuel.

Recommended Equipment: Water

Notes: The best months for walking are May to September when nights can be cold with frosts, but are usually followed by warm, clear days. Summer temperatures can reach 40°C and conditions can be humid and uncomfortable.

Further Information:

The Ranger
Sundown National Park
via Glenlyon Dam Rd
MS312, via Stanthorpe QLD 4380
Tel: (07) 4737 5235
Fax: (07) 4639 4524

Walk Description

From the homestead, head across Back Creek and up onto a ridge heading south-west, then south along an old dirt track. After 4km, you reach a junction with another road. Turn right here and follow the track to the end. Continue north across open forested country for 1km to Mt Lofty, one of the highest peaks in the park, offering views over the north-east part.

Backtrack to the end of the road and follow a small walking track that leads south-west along the rim of the gorge to the waterfall. There are excellent views here—especially if it is early in the morning with the sun on the cliffs opposite. To return to the walk start, backtrack to the junction of 4WD tracks and head right (south) past a knoll where you should turn left onto another trail leading east then north-east to arrive back at the homestead ruins.

New South Wales

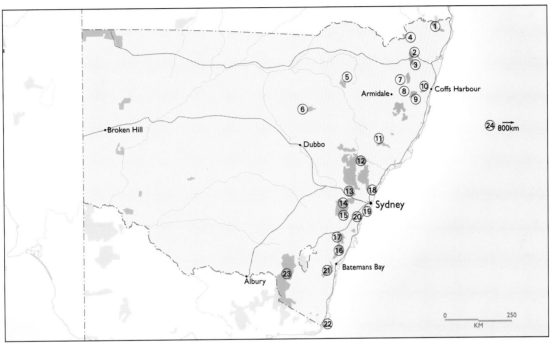

Granite tors abound in the Cathedral Rock National Park, located on the New England tableland.

Introduction

In no other state is there more variety than New South Wales. Australia's most populous state has an astonishing range of geographical environments within its borders. Surrounded by water to the east and three states in other directions, New South Wales occupies about 10 per cent of Australia's landmass. Mt Warning, near the Queensland border, is the first point on the mainland to be graced by the rising winter sun. This volcanic peak is surrounded by lush rainforest parks that have been declared World Heritage Areas for their age and diversity of species. The Great Dividing Range parallels the coast to the Victorian border. Cape Howe, the very southern point of the state, is the first point on mainland Australia to receive the summer sun.

Most of the population lives in the narrow corridor between the coast and the range. About one-third of the coast is protected in reserves, comprising coastal ranges, sand dunes, beaches, peninsulas, lakes and estuaries. Virtually all the state's major national parks are in the mountains, but even so, there's an enormous variety of terrain. The gently sloping ancient highlands in the south contain Australia's highest mountain. The rugged valleys of the Deua and Wadbilliga rivers and the spectacular Budawang escarpment are nearby. The central part of the Great Dividing Range contains sandstone mesa formations, the cliff-lined gorges of the Blue Mountains and the maze of steep canyons and ravines of Wollemi. These contrast with the lofty alpine plateau of the Barrington Tops and the rainforests of the New England Tableland.

To the west lie the wheat belt and the volcanic parks of the Warrumbungles and Mt Kaputar, regions of dramatic geological interest. Beyond is the desert where Australia's oldest World Heritage Area is located. Kinchega National Park, near Broken Hill, embodies a series of dry lakes with impressive anthropological sites. Underground, New South Wales boasts some of the most extensive cave systems in Australia, while off-shore Lord Howe Island is one of the country's true idyllic paradise getaways.

Walkers can also feast on a host of Aboriginal, historical and cultural attractions. Cave paintings, pioneering monuments and colonial buildings are all evidence of the land's rich past. The struggle to tame it is the cornerstone of Australia's conservation history. New South Wales has the second-oldest national park in the world. The Royal National Park, in Sydney's south, was declared in 1879, only seven years after Yellowstone in the USA, and was the first reserve to be officially called 'national park'. Furthermore, the state's percentage of preserved land is the highest on the mainland. International visitors are often surprised that Sydney is encircled by national parks. The city's four million residents have more recreation space than just about any other city in the world. (This can be a hazard too, as the great bushfires of January 1994 showed.)

The best bushwalking in the state is found, undoubtedly, in the Blue Mountains, 60km west of Sydney's Central Business District. A terrific freeway and railway line provide fast, direct access to the central plateau of the mountains, allowing walkers to set off north or south for their adventures. The epic scale of the Blue Mountains allows novices to undertake short day walks around the small towns of the Blue Mountains, while experienced adventurers can embark on two-week expeditions down the spine of the mountains, camping at lakes, rivers, caving resorts and mining ghost towns.

In all, New South Wales offers bushwalkers opportunities for limitless exploration of spectacular scenery. The climate is largely mild, access to staging areas is generally good, and there is accommodation to suit every taste.

Climate

Being close to the coast, Sydney has a generally mild climate. Temperatures seldom exceed 30°C in summer with average maximums of about 27°C, although during hot dry conditions, temperatures can climb above 40°C. Such afternoons are often followed by a thunderstorm, sometimes with hailstones. In April 1999, Sydney's inner suburbs were hit by a brief but intense storm with hail the size of cricket balls causing considerable damage.

In winter, the average minimum is about 13°C during July and August, the two coldest months. Rainfall is distributed fairly evenly throughout the year, with the first half receiving slightly more, about 100mm a month. Rainfall on the coast increases as you move north and south from Sydney, where the proximity of the coastal ranges causes moist sea air to mix with colder air pushed into higher altitudes. The resulting condensation causes fog and usually settled-in rain. Enthusiasts of the Budawang Ranges near Ulladulla will be accustomed to these conditions.

The upper Blue Mountains, centred on Katoomba and Wentworth Falls, also receives a lot of rain, but summer conditions on the plateau tops can be extremely hot, and walking should be avoided. Snow can fall in winter months and has fallen as late as November. Snow can also fall on the New England Tableland and the Barrington Tops, as well as the central townships of Bathurst, Oberon, Orange and Wellington.

The far north of the state, around Lismore and Murwillumbah, receives the most rain and late autumn to early spring are the best times to visit. The south coast is also notorious for the likelihood of long periods of precipitation and the countryside is distinctly greener than the central to mid-north coast. Generally dry conditions prevail west of the Great Dividing Range, so it's a safe bet for a holiday. To the south, Kosciuszko can get freak blizzard conditions and even snowfalls at times throughout summer, so walkers should be prepared for all conditions.

Transport

To New South Wales

Mascot Airport in Sydney is the main gateway for international and national visitors to New South Wales. Daily train and coach services to Central Station run from Brisbane, Adelaide and Melbourne.

Within New South Wales

City The metropolitan State Rail Authority's CityRail network services most areas of Sydney. The main lines are Hornsby, Epping, Carlingford, Hornsby, Eastern Suburbs (Bondi Junction), Sutherland, Cronulla, Campbelltown, Bankstown, Richmond and Emu Plains. Off-peak rates (out of business hours on weekdays) are quite cheap.

Country In the late 1980s, there was an unfortunate trend by the state government to close many of the inter-city railway services. The main CityRail and CountryLink lines that extend to or past the electrification limits are:

- Blue Mountains Line (Lithgow is the terminal station)
  No reservations needed until Lithgow
  Rail continues to Bathurst, Dubbo, and Broken Hill
  Bus services to Mudgee
- Newcastle line (Dungog, Scone)
- Wollongong line (Bomaderry–Nowra is the terminal station)
- Goulburn line (Campbelltown, Mittagong, Moss Vale)
  No reservations needed until Goulburn
  Bus services to Thirlmere and Hilltop
  Extended services include Armidale, Dubbo, Canberra, Cooma and the Far North Coast. Occasional CityRail and CountryLink services involve buses.

Accommodation

There has been feverish activity throughout the late 1990s in constructing accommodation and facilities in Sydney for the 2000 Olympic Games and the city caters for all budgets. The YHA Membership and Travel Centre and State Office is at:

    422 Kent Street, Sydney (just near Town Hall Station
    and the Queen Victoria Building)
    Tel: (02) 9261 1111
    Fax: (02) 9261 1969
    e-mail: yha@yhansw.org.au
Their postal address is:
    GPO Box 5276, Sydney NSW 2001
    Opening Hours: weekdays 9.00am–5.00pm
    Thursday 9.00am–6.00pm
    Saturday 10.00am–2.00pm
New memberships and renewals are available on the spot, by fax or by mail. Membership is available at most hostels or at Membership Issuing Agencies (MIAs) in most regions.

Maps

The Land Information Centre (LIC) is the state government's official supplier of maps. The LIC headquarters and mail-order department is located at Bathurst:

    Map Sales counter
    Panorama Ave
    PO Box 143, Bathurst NSW 2795
There is also an office in Sydney:
    Department of Lands
    33 Bridge St, Sydney NSW 2000
Almost all walking areas between, and including, the Great Dividing Range and the coast are covered in a useful 1:25 000 topographical scale. Only Kosciuszko National Park and the far south-east are covered in the less-detailed 1:50 000 topographical scale.

The LIC also has a web site with a unique and popular aerial photography service. You can look at aerial photos of all the national parks along the Great Dividing Range in considerable detail. Often details such as fire trails can be made out. Unfortunately, you can't save or print the pictures, but it can be a useful planning utility. The web site is www.lic.gov.au

National Parks

New South Wales has the oldest, most diverse, and one of most extensive national park systems in Australia. Despite the term national, the parks are entirely state-managed. The national park concept was first introduced with the establishment of the Royal National Park in 1879. National parks in New South Wales were managed by trusts until the *National Parks and Wildlife Act 1967* transferred their management to the National Parks and Wildlife Service.

For the purposes of preparing management plans, the New South Wales National Parks and Wildlife Service has adopted the International Union for the Conservation of Nature and Natural Resources (IUCN) Guidelines for Protected Area Management Categories which, in 1994, defined a national park as:

A natural area of land and/or sea, designated to
(a) protect the ecological integrity of one or more
ecosystems for present and future generations,

Lake Burragorang from Kings Tableland.

(b) exclude exploitation or occupation inimical to the purposes or designation of the area, and
(c) provide a foundation for spiritual, educational, recreational and visitor opportunities, all of which must be environmentally and culturally compatible.

National parks are reserved under the *National Parks and Wildlife Act 1974* and are one part of a system of reserves managed by the New South Wales National Parks and Wildlife Service. Other types of reserves managed by the service include nature reserves and historic sites.

The management of a national park aims to minimise environmental disturbance. Further to these aims, recent policy decisions have favoured a concentration of visitor facilities in just one or two specific areas within the park, while leaving the remainder in as pristine a condition as possible. In these wilder areas, roads have been rehabilitated by planting seedlings on them, while existing building sites have been dismantled.

Wilderness

Wilderness areas are a subset of national parks and, once again, New South Wales has been a leader in implementing and recognising this type of reserve classification. Wilderness, by definition, is a large area of land which, together with its native plant and animal communities and the ecosystems of which they are a part, is in an essentially natural state. Wilderness areas represent the most intact and undisturbed expanses of Australia's remaining natural landscapes. They include vast red deserts and dry sandy riverbeds, river valleys and flood-prone wetlands, extensive inland plains, rugged mountains cloaked in tall gum forests, jagged coastlines, snow-covered alpine areas and misty rainforest gullies. Wilderness is a scarce and diminishing resource. Only four or five per cent of land in New South Wales could still be called wilderness, but only a quarter of this has been legally declared as wilderness.

Wilderness protects landscapes, plants and animals and allows the natural processes of evolution to continue with minimal interference. This means that the biodiversity, or the total variety of life, in these different environments is conserved as a single functioning natural system. Wilderness areas protect already rare and threatened plants and animals, and play an important role in making it less likely that other species will become endangered. These large natural areas provide clean air and water. They are also a storehouse of genetic material from which future generations may obtain new food crops, drugs, clothing and other valuable natural products.

Importantly, and unlike many other land uses, wilderness areas do not close off any land-use options for future generations. As a conservation land use protecting whole ecosystems, wilderness reserves also provide a comparison with areas that have been changed by modern technological land uses and myriad other demands placed on the landscape. As such they have significant scientific value. Cultural values are also protected, and wilderness areas can provide a reminder of the Aboriginal landscape of Australia that retains immense cultural significance to the present day. Wilderness provides a place of inspiration,

Jerusalem Creek Falls, Barrington Tops National Park.

renewal or recreation far from the bustle and pressures of modern life. It is part of the national identity—even now, the 'bush' and the 'outback' landscapes so typified by wilderness retain a central place in Australian culture.

The *Wilderness Act 1987*, administered by the New South Wales National Parks and Wildlife Service, provides for the identification, declaration and proper management of wilderness areas. Under the legislation, any area in New South Wales can be proposed as wilderness by any person or group. The proposed area is then assessed for its wilderness qualities by the New South Wales National Parks and Wildlife Service. If the area is found to meet the criteria for wilderness, as defined under the Act, the service identifies it as wilderness. This wilderness assessment report is placed on public exhibition and comments from the community are invited. The New South Wales National Parks and Wildlife Service provides advice on the identified area and issues raised during the public consultation period to the Minister for the Environment. After considering all relevant issues, the government may declare all or part of the area as wilderness. Once declared, the wilderness area is managed to protect its wilderness values. Pest animal control, weed control and bushfire management are all important parts of this management.

In wilderness areas people are only occasional, and respectful, visitors. To ensure that these scarce and valuable areas remain largely unaltered by human activity into the distant future, the New South Wales National Parks and Wildlife Service recommends that visitors appreciate the solitude and inspiration that wilderness offers from the margins of these areas. Numerous locations on the edges of wilderness areas offer stunning views or short walks and other visitor facilities, and are readily accessible to people of all ages and fitness levels. Visitors venturing into these areas must be thoroughly prepared, self-reliant and adhere strictly to the principles of minimal-impact wilderness recreation. Generally, access within a wilderness area is only by foot. To protect wilderness values, vehicles and horses are not permitted. Vehicle access is allowed only for essential management purposes and in emergencies, such as firefighting and search and rescue. Declared wilderness areas occur within the following New South Wales reserves (listed by geographical location from north to south):

Border Ranges National Park
Limpinwood Nature Reserve
Washpool National Park
Gibraltar Range National Park
Nymboida National Park
Guy Fawkes River National Park
Guy Fawkes River Nature Reserve
Mt Kaputar National Park
New England National Park
Oxley Wild Rivers National Park
Werrikimbe National Park
Willi Willi National Park
Barrington Tops National Park
Mt Royal National Park
Wollemi National Park
Blue Mountains National Park
Kanangra–Boyd National Park
Nattai National Park
Morton National Park
Budawang National Park
Deua National Park
Wadbilliga National Park
Kosciuszko National Park
Bimberi Nature Reserve
Scabby Range Nature Reserve
Nadgee Nature Reserve
South East Forest National Park
Mootwingee National Park

Fees

Most of the 350 parks and reserves in New South Wales have free entry, but some, designated 'Popular Parks', charge a small daily fee per vehicle.

Further information

New South Wales National Parks and Wildlife Service
Level 1, 43 Bridge St
PO Box 1967
Hurstville NSW 2220
Tel: 1300 361 967
or (02) 9585 6333 (9.00am–3.00pm)
Fax: (02) 9585 6527
e-mail:
feedback@npws.nsw.gov.au
web site: www.npws.gov.au

Epic Walks

New South Wales contains several lengthy official walks, some of which transcend state boundaries to the north and south. These are:

Australian Alps Walking Trail

This is a spectacular high-altitude walking trail that follows the spine of the Great Dividing Range from Walhalla (south of Baw Baw National Park) in Victoria through New South Wales to the Namadgi National Park Visitors' Centre in the Australian Capital Territory. The 655km trail winds, almost exclusively, through the Alpine, Kosciuszko and Namadgi national parks. The total walking time for the entire walk would be about eight weeks, requiring much planning and many stops to replenish food supplies. Most walkers explore only parts of the trail at a time, usually in conjunction with other trails so that circuits can be completed.

An extension of the Victorian Alpine Walking Track, the AAWT passes through New South Wales and the Australian Capital Territory. For many years bushwalking enthusiasts from the Federation of Victorian Walking Clubs and various government agencies promoted the concept of a long-distance walking track from Walhalla to Canberra. The VAWT, developed in the 1970s, was the first stage in the dream.

The AAWT generally follows ridges and high plains through some of the highest country in Australia above the tree line and following the spine of the Great Dividing Range. It also passes through magnificent stands of mountain ash forest, giving excellent variety in a remote natural setting. The track is distinctively marked at

The Carabeen rainforest walk in the Werrikimbe National Park.

track and road intersections for its entire length. It incorporates well-maintained walking tracks, barely visible footpads, grassy fire-access trails and 4WD vehicle tracks.

The track passes through five wilderness areas: Razor/Viking, Cobberas, Pilot, Jagungal and Bimberi. The boundaries of these areas are shown by Wilderness Entry signs and there are no AAWT markers within these areas. Here walkers should be prepared for remote-area navigation and be completely self-sufficient.

Weather conditions in the mountains are colder, wetter and much less predictable than at lower altitudes. During winter and spring, snow can cover long sections of the track. In summer, thunderstorms are common. Number quotas apply along sections of the track, for example in the upper Cotter River region, east of Bimberi Peak. Fuel-stove-only areas exist in Baw Baw National Park, Alpine National Park, at Mt Bogong, in Kosciuszko National Park (NSW) above the tree line (about 1700m altitude), and in the Bimberi Wilderness (ACT) where camping permits must also be obtained.

Bicentennial National Trail

This mammoth trail of interconnected vehicle tracks and stockroutes extends from Cooktown in Queensland to the outskirts of Melbourne, some 5530km, principally following the western slopes of the Great Dividing Range, weaving between national parks and rural land. Because of its route and construction, it is not ideally suited to quality bushwalking and therefore is not covered in this book. The trail is more practical for equestrians and cyclists, although walkers tackle some of it in sections.

Great North Walk

This 250km, two-week trek from Sydney to Newcastle starts right on the urban Sydney Harbour foreshore. Opened in 1988, the track has been very popular as it is cleverly routed to pass through bushland almost all the way, despite being largely surrounded by residential development. The track is managed by the Department of Conservation and Land Management, which has now produced a Discovery Kit with detailed information on the walk. Like most other epic walks, there are abundant shorter options for walkers not wishing to commit to two full weeks of walking. One example is the side branch that passes through Paxton to the Hunter Valley vineyards.

Hume and Hovell Walking Track

The development of this historical track was the principal contribution to the 1988 Bicentennial celebrations by the former Department of Lands. The historic track is now managed by the Department of Conservation and Land Management and primarily passes through Crown Land and state forests from Gunning to Albury.

The route follows, as closely as possible, that taken by explorers Hamilton Hume and William Hovell when they made the first European overland expedition from Sydney to Melbourne in the summer of 1824. While the full 372km takes up to 20 days to complete, it is also possible to do a number of short day walks using the track, such as to Cribbs Bridge and The Hole, which was formerly known as Goobarragandra Station. As the Hume and Hovell Walking Track only skirts around the northern boundary of the Kosciuszko National Park, this book will not feature any walks based on it. For further information on the walk, consult *The Hume and Hovell Walking Track Guidebook* by Harry Hill.

Royal National Park Coast Walk

The coast from Bundeena to Otford is dominated by dramatic cliff-lined headlands interrupted by secluded beaches. At 32km, it's Sydney's most accessible major bushwalk and can be done in one long or two shorter days.

Six Foot Track

The western Blue Mountains is the scene of this 42km walk from Explorers Tree (near Katoomba) to Jenolan Caves. Although the walk is mostly completed in two to three days, runners in a cross-country event held in March each year try to break the 200-minute mark. Jim Smith has written an excellent publication, *From Katoomba to Jenolan Caves—The Six

Myall Lakes National Park is at the end of the Tops to Myalls Heritage Trail.

Foot Track*, compiling the history of the historic route.

Tops to Myalls Heritage Trail

A 220km trail that connects two great national parks just north of Sydney allows walkers from the Barrington Tops to access the coast, primarily through forest. It takes 10–14 days to walk and can be broken up into smaller segments.

Wilderness Coast—Mallacoota (Vic) to Pambula (NSW)

Beautiful Croajingolong National Park and Nadgee Nature Reserve are two of the least known coastal parks located between Melbourne and Sydney. The 51km walk can be done in stages. The area around Cape Howe has beautiful wild coves and lagoons. A boat is needed to cross Mallacoota Inlet.

The Northern Rainforests

The north-east corner of New South Wales is noted for its rich volcanic soils, warm temperatures and high rainfall, an ideal recipe for rainforests. Walkers here have several mountainous national parks to choose from. On one hand, close to civilisation, a series of small reserves such as the Border Ranges, where you can undertake many short family strolls. On the other hand, large remote parks have extensive wilderness regions where

overnight backpacking is essential. This section of the country attracts alternative lifestylers, who place the emphasis on arts, crafts, cottage industry and self-sufficiency.

Mt Warning National Park

About 23 million years ago, one of the world's largest-ever shield volcanos was active in the region of what is now the border of northern New South Wales and Queensland. Covering an area of over 4000 square kilometres, it reached from Beenleigh and Mt Tamborine in the north to Coraki in the south. Westward it extended to Kyogle and to the east its remnants occur as reefs in the Pacific Ocean. The Tweed River and other streams eroded the central crater (caldera), leaving a core island of harder volcanic rock, now called Mt Warning. The original mountain once stood more than 2000m above sea level, about the height of Mt Kosciuszko today. This has been slowly eroded to just 1157m, but it still permits an outstanding panorama over the far north-eastern corner of the state.

The flanks of the old mountain's basaltic dome remain along the state border in the form of the McPherson and Tweed ranges, but erosion has created great low-angle spurs called 'planeze', interspersed with deep gorges. Such dramatic features as The Pinnacle mark the rim of the eroded crater, where the softer surface rocks have given way. The erosed caldera is about 30km in diameter. For walkers, the main challenge is ascending the summit of the ancient volcanic plug.

Geology

Mt Warning was formed by massive outpourings of lava, layer after layer. The height of the volcano alone was sufficient to trap moisture-laden air from the coast. Over millennia a multitude of small streams produced by this trapped moisture carved out a unique and curious landform. Harder rocks, such as the rhyolite cliffs of the caldera rim and the rocks of the central chamber, resisted erosion. Only these are left standing.

History

Mt Warning itself was the original volcano's magma chamber. Composed of hard rocks that cooled underground, this massif resisted the erosion that carved the surrounding caldera down to bedrock. It stands as the dominant feature in the district's landscape and can be easily recognised from the coast around Cape Byron, Australia's most easterly point. Mt Warning remains significant to Aborigines, who call it 'Wollumbin' meaning 'fighting chief of the mountains'. They believe that lightning and thunder observed on the mountain were warring warriors and that landslides were wounds obtained in battle.

The mountain made its first appearance in recorded history when Captain Cook named it to warn future seafarers of the offshore reefs he had encountered on 16 May 1770. Ironically, these reefs were remnants of that same volcano. Reserved for public recreation in 1928, Mt Warning was dedicated as a national park in 1966. Inclusion in the UNESCO World Heritage Listings in 1986, along with other New South Wales rainforest national parks, ensures its protection for all future generations. The national park now covers 2380ha.

Vegetation

Fertile volcanic soils, high humidity and rainfall of Mt Warning provided sanctuary from advancing aridity. The ancient forest that occurs here is a window into the past. Among the many tree species are giant stinging trees, figs, booyongs, carbeens, brush box and flame trees. Many threatened plant species are found here. Winding up from the Breakfast Creek parking area is the Mt Warning Summit Track, which passes through a variety of vegetation communities including subtropical and temperate rainforest, wet sclerophyll forest and heath.

Wildlife

A variety of birds, mammals and reptiles may be seen en route to the summit or on the short Lyrebird Walk near Breakfast Creek. More than 100 species of birds have been recorded, including the endangered rufous scrub bird, wompoo pigeon, marbled frogmouth and Albert's lyrebird.

Access

To reach Mt Warning National Park in far north-eastern New South Wales, leave the Pacific Highway at Murwillumbah and follow the Kyogle Road west for 12km. Turn onto Mt Warning Road and proceed a further 6km to the Breakfast Creek picnic area at the park entrance. All turn-offs are signposted.

The short (15-minute) Lyrebird Walk leads from the car park to an elevated platform in the palms where you can sit and experience the serenity of the rainforest. Walkers are advised to keep to the formed tracks, as it is very easy to become lost in the rainforest. Taking shortcuts from the tracks can cause severe erosion in this fragile and precipitous park. Camping is not permitted, particularly on the summit. Picnic facilities are provided for day use and commercial camping facilities are provided on nearby properties. Bush-camping facilities are provided by the Forestry Commission of New South Wales at the Mebbin Forest Camp, to the west.

Facilities

Because thousands of visitors climb to the top each year, the impact on the small summit area has forced authorities to prohibit camping anywhere in the national park. There are no toilets or garbage bins on the mountain after Breakfast Creek, factors that should be considered before your walk.

Mt Warning Walk

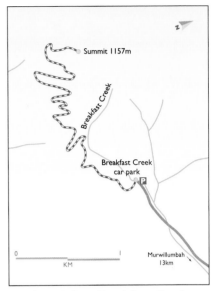

Starting Point: Breakfast Creek car park, Mt Warning National Park
Destination: Summit of Mt Warning (1157m)
Summary: An excellent steep climb to access superb views over the Tweed River valley
Attractions: Changing vegetation, a challenging climb, fascinating views
Length: 8.8km
Time: 4 hours
Attraction Rating: ★ ★ ★ ★
Fitness: ✗ ✗ ✗
Maps: LIC (CMA) Burringbar 1:25 000 topographical
Access to Starting Point: Leave the Pacific Highway at Murwillumbah and follow the Kyogle Road west for 12km. Turn onto Mt Warning Road and travel 5km to the Korrumbyn Creek picnic area at the park entrance. All turn-offs are signposted. Proceed another 1.5km along the road to the Breakfast Creek parking area at the base of the mountain.
Facilities/Amenities: Toilets available only at the start of the walk. Camping and fires are not permitted within Mt Warning National Park. Facilities for BBQs are provided at Korrumbyn Creek picnic area, 1.5km down the road from Breakfast Creek parking area.
Recommended Equipment: Suitable footwear, water and garbage containers
Notes: A warning—do not undertake the walk after 2.00pm in winter; you can become lost in the dark on the return journey. Be aware that the temperature drops rapidly as you ascend.

Further Information:
Suite 9, Colonial Arcade
75 Main St, Alstonville NSW 2477
Tel: (02) 6628 1177
Fax: (02) 6628 3937

Walk Description

Follow a well-graded track that leads from the car park to the summit. It starts behind an informative data wall at the top of the car park. These information panels explain the origin and importance of Mt Warning. A number of plant labels can be seen along the route of the climb. The path is easy at first, but rises constantly. The last short steep ascent above 1000m elevation has a chain to assist you to scale the sloping rocks. Even without the chain, there are many handholds. Seats by the track, progress distance markers and information plaques help to make the walk enjoyable. Rainforest is abundant, confined to the igneous rock areas of the main peak and associated peaks where soil depth and moisture are adequate.

The first section is comprised of many short steps. Right near the start is a massive flooded gum (*Eucalyptus grandis*). The track then becomes covered with roots and increasingly rocky as you gain altitude.

The upper rockfaces feature shrubby and grassy plants, such as tussock grass, grasstree, blunt-leaf mountain wattle, tea-tree and broad-leafed cassinia. There are good views once leaving behind the thick rainforest canopy on the upper reaches, but only at the summit can you see the spectacular 360-degree view of the erosion crater walls that border the enormous bowl of the caldera. Cape Byron, the Border Ranges, Surfers Paradise, Mt Lindesay and Focal Peak near Mt Barney are all in view. In the foreground lie the Tweed River and Murwillumbah.

Four viewing decks on the summit divide up the panoramas, and plaques illustrate and name the features to be seen. Walkers often attempt the peak as early as 3.00am to catch the first rays of sunrise. Avoid the summit during storms because it attracts frequent lightning strikes. Seek shelter under the larger platforms if lightning is close. There are no branch tracks along the route of the climb, so walkers must ascend and descend via the same route. Have lunch on the top before descending.

Washpool National Park

The 51 737ha Washpool National Park protects a wilderness area with World Heritage rainforests on the eastern escarpment of the New England Tableland adjoining Gibraltar Range National Park. Visitor facilities are focused on Coombadjha Creek (800m) on the southern edge of the vast rainforest wilderness, which stretches 22km to the north. The 3000ha Willowie Scrub to the north of the park is the largest undisturbed rainforest area in New South Wales, containing the largest intact stand of coachwood in the world. Giant trees, such as tallow wood, red cedar, and blue gum and pristine rivers are some of the attractions.

Vegetation

The Washpool forests are diverse, alternating between rainforest and wet eucalypt forest. In season, the rainforest canopy is rosy with coachwood fruit. The park also contains a mix of old growth and new young rainforests. On the drier slopes down Washpool Creek is dry rainforest composed of shatterwood, red cedar and flame trees. The boulder-strewn creeks are laced with king ferns.

Wildlife

Despite the thick canopy, the undergrowth is fairly sparse and walkers can usually catch sight of mammals, such as the long-nosed potoroo, rufous rat-kangaroo or parma wallaby.

Facilities

Picnic or camp overnight at Coombadjha in rainforest surrounds. The self-guiding Coombadjha Nature Stroll is a great way to experience the rainforest and its diversity of lifeforms for the first time. The Coombadjha area is well suited to rainforest studies by educational groups or interested amateurs. Facilities include BBQs, camping and picnic areas, toilets and wheelchair access.

Washpool Rainforest Circuit

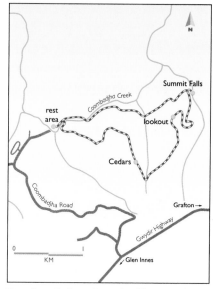

Starting Point: Coombadjha rest area, Washpool National Park
Destination: Summit Falls
Summary: A medium-length loop centred on Coombadjha Creek
Attractions: Red cedars, Summit Falls, lookout, rainforest understorey
Length: 8km
Time: 3 hours
Options: None
Attraction Rating: ★ ★ ★
Fitness: ☒ ☒ ☒
Maps: LIC (CMA) Coombadjha 1:25 000 topographical
Access to Starting Point: All-weather access to Coombadjha Creek is via Coombadjha Road off the Gwydir Highway 88km west of Grafton. From inland, take the Gwydir Highway east from Glen Innes. Parking for caravans and coaches.
Facilities/Amenities: Picnic facilities at walk start
Recommended Equipment: Tripod for photographing within the dark rainforest; take swimming gear
Notes: Washpool Rainforest Circuit is not depicted on topographical map

Further Information:
68 Church St, Glen Innes NSW 2370
Tel: (02) 6732 5133
Fax: (02) 6732 5130

Walk Description

This signposted track runs parallel to Coombadjha Creek, crosses it, and climbs through the rainforest to the eucalypts. Listen for the song of

The pristine Coombadjha Creek in Washpool National Park—some of the purest water in all of eastern Australia.

bellbirds. Onward the track climbs, predominantly to the west, to a small turn-off to Summit Falls, then through drier eucalypt forest on the ridge-side, past a small lookout. It reverts to rainforest again as it enters Coombadjha Creek valley. Along the way are two giant red cedars. This species was the 'red gold' so eagerly sought by pioneers who made the first inroads into these virgin forests. This tree is one of the few deciduous native species and for this reason it was easily spotted by cedar-getters during spring when it came into new leaf. The new leaves show a dark red crown that makes a vivid contrast with the surrounding forest from a considerable distance.

Other walks in Washpool National Park

As well as the short Coombadjha Nature Stroll (1.1km, 30 minutes), you can take longer overnight walks following the old logging roads deep into the northern part of the park,

especially along the western boundary, but consult the ranger before you leave. Many of the trails marked on the topographical map are overgrown and it's easy to get lost in such remote wild country.

Gibraltar Range National Park

Like Washpool, this park is roughly halfway between Glen Innes and Grafton, part of a plateau more than 1200m above sea level. It features fascinating geology, a skyline studded with huge granite outcrops such as Old Mans Hat, Anvil Rock and The Needles. It's well worth the walk to The Haystacks or to Coonarma Rocks.

Facts and Figures

Name: Gibraltar Range National Park
Size: 21 618ha
Enactment: Public Recreation
  Reserve, March 1963
  National Park, 1967
  World Heritage Area, 1986

Visitors: About 5000 annually
Aboriginal Sites: Bora grounds, sacred ceremonial sites, fascinating stone arrangements, axe-grinding grooves, and art sites are examples of previous occupation by three tribes: the Badjalong, the Jukambol and the Kumbaingiri.
Vegetation: Gibraltar Range has a diverse variety of plant communities, including heathland, swamp, dry sclerophyll and rainforests. Among notable plants are large grasstrees, waratahs (found here at their northernmost limit), giant elkhorns and orchids.
Wildlife: Some 34 species of mammals, 225 bird species, 19 frog species and 248 moth and butterfly species. The park is renowned for the rare occurrence of the tiger cat. The wallabies around Mulligans Hut are quite tame.
Camping: Primitive camping allowed anywhere off trails. Mulligans Hut rest area provides basic facilities.
Adjoining Parks: Washpool National

Park lies to the north and the Gibraltar Range State Forest lies to the south and west.

Further Information: Visitors' centre at the entrance to the park at the start of Mulligans Road. The district office is in Glen Innes.

Vegetation

This park is quite famous for its wildflowers, especially the Christmas bells and waratah in late summer. Among the eucalypts and the yellow green of the summer grass, big red waratahs come into view. They differ from their southern cousins, and have grown here, and only here, for millennia. Grasstrees also dominate the landscape. In spring, the sub-alpine mountain heath swarms with mountain birds, eager for flower-honey. On the highest peaks, snow gums and peppermints grow. Below them on the slopes, dry eucalypt forest predominates.

Facilities

These include picnic and camping areas, BBQs, toilets, showers and visitor information. Mulligans Hut rest area is a very pleasant grassy camping ground by Little Dandahra Creek where walking tracks allow visitors to explore the creeks and dramatic granite crags. There's a visitors' centre at Dandahra picnic area on the Gwydir Highway.

Gibraltar Range Highlights Walk

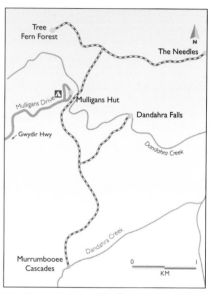

Starting Point: Mulligans Hut rest area

Destination: Each of the attractions

Summary: Several walking tracks leave from Mulligans Hut rest area to all the major highlights

Attractions: The Needles, Tree Fern Forest, Dandahra Falls, Murrumbooee Cascades

Length: 18km

Time: 1 day

Options: The track passes through Mulligans Hut rest area halfway through, so the walk can be broken up into two smaller half-day sections

Attraction Rating: ★ ★ ★ ★

Fitness: ⬛⬛⬛

Maps: LIC (CMA) Cangai 1:25 000 topographical

Access to Starting Point: All-weather access via the Gwydir Highway, 92km west of Grafton

Facilities/Amenities: Picnic and camping facilities at Mulligans Hut, none on walks

Notes: Not all the walking tracks are marked on the topographical map

Further Information:
   68 Church St, Glen Innes NSW 2370
   Tel: (02) 6732 5133
   Fax: (02) 6732 5130

The tree fern forest near Mulligans Hut in the Gibraltar Range National Park.

Walk Description

From Mulligans Hut camping ground, cross Little Dandahra Creek (water is drinkable) and walk up through eucalypt forest until you come to a 4WD track. On the way are some fine specimens of grasstrees. To see The Needles, head right—the turn-off is signposted. The 4WD track soon deteriorates into a walking trail through thick undergrowth and takes you over a crest to the viewing area. This is rather obscure and the best vantage point entails a scramble. The pointed rock stacks are reminders of the park's volcanic origins.

Return to the junction with the walking track that leads to Mulligans Hut, and walk straight ahead. Soon the vegetation closes in and within 400m you come to Twin Bridges, which is simply a couple of old planks over the infant Richardsons Creek. There is a lovely and unusually dense concentration of ferns in this vicinity with more than 20 species recorded at this one spot.

The trail climbs steadily and steeply for 2km from here, and the surface can be quite muddy after rain. A turn-off left leads down to the Tree Fern Forest, dominated by four species. There are many mature specimens and some are quite tall.

Return to Mulligans Hut and take the track south through dense rainforest to the Murrumbooee Cascades. On the return route, take a side option that descends steeply to Dandahra Falls. Access the top of the falls here, and it's also possible to jump across the rock platforms to the eastern side of the creek. This is truly wild country. Return to Mulligans Hut via the same route.

Other walks in Gibraltar Range National Park
Dandahra Crags Walk (6km, 2 hours)

Starting from Mulligans Drive, 3.4km south of the Gwydir Highway, this circuit passes over geologically fascinating terrain with many quartzite and granite boulder formations. The track curves around Mt Mistake and Cardinals Gap before returning to Mulligans Drive via Surveyors Creek.

Anvil Rock Walk, (4km, 2 hours)

Also starting from Mulligans Drive, just 100m farther than the Dandahra Crags turn-off, this short work leads to another fascinating natural rock sculpture to the south.

Overnight Walks

A 120km week-long walk on the edge of wilderness leads through several national parks and state forests on the edge of the New England escarpment. Consult the rangers' office in Glen Innes for more details.

Other walks in the Northern Rainforests
Border Ranges National Park

Border Ranges National Park protects a 31 683ha area centred on a range covered with rainforest. To the north, the park shares a boundary with Lamington National Park in Queensland. Its main tourist feature is the 60km Tweed Range Scenic Drive, which winds across the Wiangaree plateau. Several short walks emanate from this tourist drive. From Lismore or Murwillumbah, the Tweed Range tourist drive can be accessed via Mt Lion or Barkers Vale.

Surrounding the Antarctic Beech and Bar Mountain picnic areas are Antarctic beeches, with their massive trunks caked in lichens and mosses. At these high altitudes, they are also often cloaked in mist, which makes them eminently photogenic. These ancient trees have strong connections to the Gondwana super-continent and live for many thousands of years.

Great views over the pristine rainforest of Gradys Creek to Lamington National Park are another feature of the Antarctic Beech picnic area. Bar Mountain (1140m) is the highest point in the Border Ranges. Look down at the long drop to Collin's Creek Falls from the roadside nearby.

The view from Blackbutts Lookout is stunning: Mt Warning, the Tweed Valley and the rim of the amphitheatre are spread out before you. The lookout takes its name from the New England blackbutts, a type of eucalypt that grows here.

The walk along the southern bank of Brindle Creek offers something totally different. Dwarfed by the rainforest-clad mountains, this ferny, lily lined creek with its waterside walk epitomises the lushness of northern rainforests. The eastern end of the track starts at Tweed Valley Lookout.

At the other end, you can extend the walk by continuing to the giant red cedar. The Cedar Loop section passes through lush rainforest and is usually possible even in the wettest weather. Allow half a day to explore the Brindle Creek and Cedar Loop walks from the Tweed Valley Lookout. Consult the LIC (CMA) Brays Creek 1:25 000 topographical for details.

The Pinnacle is a spear of rock jutting from the edge of the escarpment with long drops all around. Because of its prominence, it offers the most spectacular views of the rim. Reaching The Pinnacle itself is only for the experienced.

Camping is allowed at Forest Top and Sheepstation Creek. The Forest Top rest area is, as the name implies, on the mountaintop beside the road. A great half-day downhill walk leads from here through rainforest to Sheepstation Creek. Set up a car shuffle to avoid a return uphill slog. Sheepstation Creek rest area is at the base of the mountain among open eucalypt forest. Facilities include BBQs, toilets, camping and picnic areas.

Mann River Nature Reserve

A walking track from the Town of Mitchell camping area follows the Mann River through stands of river oaks. The highest point in the nature reserve, Tommys Rock Lookout (1015m), can be reached by walking up the southern side the valley. From here you can walk all the way to the southern boundary of the nature reserve via Surveyors Creek.

Inland Parks
Bald Rock National Park

The park entrance is 29km north-east of Tenterfield, along the Mt Lindesay Highway on the Northern Tablelands. While the park is small (5451ha), it protects an awesome natural feature, Bald Rock. This spectacular granite dome is 750m long, 500m wide and

The massive granite dome of Bald Rock, near the Queensland border.

rises 200m above the surrounding bushland. It is the largest exposed granite rock in Australia. Most people who visit Bald Rock note similarities with Uluru (Ayers Rock). The summit (1277m above sea level) is an easy walk from the car park. Strictly speaking, Bald Rock does not consist of granite, being classified as Stanthorpe Adamellite from the Lower Triassic age. It shows marked phases in mineralogy and texture. Resultant soils are generally poor and sandy.

Together with the adjoining Girraween National Park in Queensland and Boonoo Boonoo National Park to the east, the region preserves land with magnificent recreational potential and great conservation value. Two walking trails lead to the summit of the rock and visitors energetic enough to climb this structure will be rewarded with spectacular 360-degree views of the Tweed coast, Girraween National Park and Mt Mackenzie to the south. Another walking trail leads to another large boulder, South Bald Rock, passing through pleasant bush with native wildlife along the way.

Vegetation

Run-off from the large surface area of Bald Rock gives rise to relatively high moisture levels in the area immediately around its base. This area is termed wet sclerophyll forest whereas most of the remaining land is dry sclerophyll forest. In addition, there are heaths on the rock and swamps in low-lying gullies.

Facilities

The picnic area has tables and BBQs, two pit toilets, a camping area and visitor information. A creek on the northern side of the picnic area has water. The camping area can get very cold at night, while during the day, like most of the granite belt, it can get quite hot.

South Bald Rock Walk

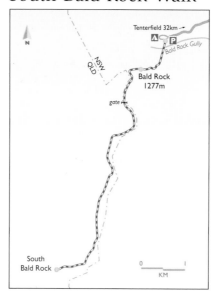

Starting Point: Bald Rock picnic area, Bald Rock National Park
Destination: South Bald Rock

Summary: A great walk that takes in the best features of this granite region
Attractions: Bald Rock, South Bald Rock
Length: 11km
Time: 4 hours
Attraction Rating: ★ ★ ★
Fitness: ◪ ◪ ◪
Maps: LIC (CMA) Bookookoorara and Boonoo Boonoo 1:25 000 topographical or Heam Maps Girraween and Bald Rocks National Parks 1:33 000
Access to Starting Point: A 6km sign-posted gravel access road runs from the Mt Lindesay Highway to the camping ground adjacent to Bald Rock. From New South Wales, the closest town is Tenterfield; from Queensland, the closest is Stanthorpe.
Facilities/Amenities: Picnic facilities, toilets and rubbish pits are provided; fresh creek water; short-term camping is allowed at the rest area
Recommended Equipment: Shoes with good grip
Notes: The granite can be slippery when wet
Further Information:
68 Church St, Glen Innes NSW 2370
Tel: (02) 6732 5133
Fax: (02) 6732 5130

Walk Description

It is only a short, steep climb, 2km return, via the Bungoona Walk or the Direct Route from the base of the rock. The walking tracks are marked with white paint on the rock leading to the summit of Bald Rock (1277m).

The climb rewards the walker with extensive panoramic views over a granite outcrop-dotted landscape. Highlights include the volcanic plugs of the Tweed Valley. Photographers love the curved sloping foreground with dark bands in the granite in superb contrast with the mountains on the horizon.

From the trig-point on the summit, walk south to the saddle and continue down to the flat bushland. Once at the bottom, turn west-south-west and walk 1km to the border road. Follow this fire trail south to the base of South Bald Rock and climb from its western side near Racecourse Creek. Although it doesn't have the grandiose dimensions of Bald Rock, it is said by many to be even more fascinating.

Other walks in Bald Rock National Park

Several overnight walking options are possible by setting up a car shuffle between Girraween National Park and Bald Rock National Park.

Good campsites can be found at Racecourse Creek, near South Bald Rock, Racecourse Creek before Billy Goat Hill, and Paling Yard Creek. Water can sometimes be a problem in the area, but Racecourse Creek near South Bald Rock usually has water year-round, even in dry conditions. Consult *120 Walks in New South Wales* by Tyrone Thomas for a description of an extended circuit through both parks.

Mt Kaputar National Park

Volcanic activity about 17–20 million years ago formed the unusually shaped peaks and domes that are the main attraction of the park. The lava shield was once about 700m thick, but much of this has been eroded. Columnar jointing, created in rare cooling conditions, is evident in formations like giant pipes of a church organ. The classic example of these can be seen at Sawn Rocks in the north of the park. Farther south lies Yulludunida Crater, a huge curved dyke 150m high that attracts many tourists.

Much of the park is wilderness and inaccessible by vehicle. Fortunately, the highest peaks can be reached directly along the main road. A number of other trails then branch off south and east and all the best parts can be explored on day trips.

Facts and Figures

Name: Mt Kaputar National Park
Size: 36 817ha
Enactment: Public Reserve, 1925 National Park, 1967
Visitors: Numbers unknown, mostly bushwalkers
Vegetation: Mainly dry eucalypt
Wildlife: 104 species of birds have been recorded, kangaroos are quite tame and regularly inspect camping sites; also native to the park are koalas, echidnas, bats, and the magnificent wedge-tailed eagle; unfortunately, feral animals (pigs,

rabbits, and especially goats) are becoming a problem
Aboriginal Sites: The Kamilaroi people who first inhabited the Nandewar Range and adjacent plains left only a dozen small sites within the park boundaries.
Camping: Dawsons Spring and Bark Hut are the only developed sites (fees and permits required); two cabins for rent; amenities block at Dawsons Spring.

Scutts Hut Walk

Starting Point: Bark Hut camping area, Mt Kaputar National Park
Destination: Scutts Hut, Kurrawonga Falls
Summary: The longest walk in the Kaputar National Park. It leads south and downhill to Jokers Spring.
Attractions: Kurrawonga Falls, wilderness atmosphere in the southern half of the national park
Length: 19km
Time: 1 full day
Options: Camp down by Scutts Hut, breaking the walk into two days
Attraction Rating: ★ ★ ★ ★
Fitness: ◪ ◪ ◪ ◪
Maps: LIC (CMA) Kaputar 1:25 000 topographical
Access to Starting Point: Bark Hut is 6.1km by road from Dawsons Spring
Facilities/Amenities: None en route
Recommended Equipment: Complete self-sufficiency
Notes: Contact the ranger before setting out

Further Information:
Level 1, 65 Maitland St
Narrabri NSW 2390
Tel: (02) 6799 1740
Fax: (02) 6792 1133

Walk Description

Head south from Bark Hut along the Jokers Spring fire trail (marked on the map as Scutts Track) passing Euglah Spring, Euglah Rock and Euglah Cave. About 2.2km past Jokers Spring, a very steep (signposted) track leads down to Scutts Hut, an historic stockmen's shelter. Follow Horse Arm Creek another 2km downstream to Kurrawonga Falls and Gorge. Alternatively, take a poorly marked route from Scutts Hut across the hills to the west of the creek. Carry drinking water.

Other walks in Mt Kaputar National Park
Kaputar Plateau Walk (6.1km, 4 hours)

This track starts 4.1km along the road from Dawsons Spring and weaves down to meet the road again near Bark Hut. It also connects with the walk to Scutts Hut. The fire trail covers a wide range of terrain and vegetation with many scenic view-

Volcanic outcrop of Mt Ningadhun, Mt Kaputar National Park.

points. Allow an extra 45 minutes if walking the full loop via the main road, rather than returning by car.

Mt Coryah Walk (4km, 3 hours)

This hard walk begins at Coryah Gap, 7.8km down the road. It's well graded but climbs steeply past basalt cliffs and through grasstrees. There are excellent views over surrounding peaks on the way up to the summit (1405m). This is one of the better walks in the national park.

Warrumbungle National Park

The volcanic hotspot that formed the Nandewar Range and Mt Kaputar also formed the Warrumbungle Ranges about 13–15 million years ago. Erosion has resulted in the distinctive domes and spires seen in this park. The volcanic trachyte (a rock like basalt) is not the only rock in the park—sediments of a similar age to the sandstones of the Sydney Basin, including coal, have been found beneath the volcanic layer.

The Warrumbungles (Aboriginal for 'jump-up' mountains) would be by far the most frequently visited national park west of Lithgow. For years, The Breadknife and Crater Bluff have had cameras pointed at them and the walking tracks are very well defined. (Some are even concreted.) The walking is relatively easy and camping facilities include showers and laundry at Camp Blackman. A caravan site is also available, as well as numerous hotels and motels between Coonabarabran and the park.

The main attraction is the geology. In addition, the park is one of the few areas where wild kangaroos and emus are tame enough to approach humans and will actually eat out of their hands. The vegetation is fairly dry.

Facts and Figures

Name: Warrumbungle National Park
Size: 22 945ha
Enactment: State Reserve, 1953
　National Park, 1967
Visitors: More than 150 000 a year
Vegetation: More than 530 species of
　plants are known from the park, in
　a variety of communities, including

dry eucalypt woodland, heath and damper forms of forest. The central area was cleared of forest many years ago for grazing and is still mainly grassland.

Wildlife: 12 mammal species, 46 reptile species, 170 species of birds

Aboriginal Sites: Kamilaroi people, though there is limited evidence, possibly due to their dispersed occupation. The mountainous area was probably not very productive.

Camping: A variety of camping is permitted in the park, though sites are mainly restricted to the central area. Check in at the visitors' centre to obtain camping permits and information on current conditions. Pre-cut firewood is available from the side of the road just before Camp Blackman on the other side of Mopra Creek. There are several remote bush-camping sites are on the Grand High Tops and to the south at Gunneemooroo Camp.

Further Information: The visitors' centre and rangers station is just 10 minutes from the entrance at Camp Elongery:
56 Cassius St
Coonabarabran NSW 2357
Tel:　(02) 6842 1311
Fax:　(02) 6842 2124
or

Warrumbungle Visitors' Centre
Tel:　(02) 6825 4364
Fax:　(02) 6825 4334

Geology

The spectacular towers of rock pinnacles were formed by a process that went something like this… An upwelling of magma occurred through a break in the crust. A cinder-flow cone then developed and later became a composite volcano, with several points of outflow. Other cones developed along a fault line in the crust. Swarms of dykes developed. The old trellised drainage pattern became deranged and watercourses were disconnected from their water sources. Flows of lava dammed many valleys and in some of the warm lakes great quantities of diatoms (unicellular algae) flourished. The great effusive pile of volcanic debris grew and from it a typical radial drainage pattern evolved. The course of the

Castlereagh River was diverted into a new sweeping course to encircle the mound of debris.

A new landform known as a caldera developed after a cataclysmic explosion or perhaps because the whole crown of the volcano collapsed into the vacant recess below and formed a lake. A small eruptive cone within the caldera became an island in the lake until the confining wall was breached by erosion and the lake was drained. Lavas such as basalt filled old valleys to great depths with only a relatively shallow capping across old sandstone tops. Erosion etched out the less-protected sandstone so that what was once a valley is now a ridge. Volcanic activity by this time had ceased.

As the landscape weathered, the central neck and radial dykes, because their 'roots' are so deep, persist as 'spires' and 'walls', such as the famous Breadknife formation. Basalt-capped mesas are the last remaining evidence of the vast area once covered by flow materials. Stream action has transported the results of the previous mountain-building and deposited it as mud across flood plains to the west.

Of all the features, the most dramatic are the spires of Crater Bluff, Belougery Spire and Needle Mountain, Tonduron Spire and Mopra Rock. These pinnacles of trachyte mark the centre of ancient volcanic activity. Trachyte is a viscous lava with a high proportion of silica, which causes the rock to harden quickly, plugging up the throats of the volcanoes. As the plug is harder than the cone, the cone erodes more quickly and over time the plug is left standing. These plugs do not necessarily mean that the centre of the volcanic activity was at that point. It would probably be more correct to assume that they are but part of a region of volcanic activity.

The Breadknife is the cast of a great crack (dyke) in the volcanic ash of the cone of Crater Bluff. Being of harder, more dense material, it has withstood weathering longer than the cone so only the dyke stands as a reminder of past land levels.

Mt Exmouth is a different shape to all the others. Its 1206m summit is square-topped with obvious horizontal layers of fragmentary rock interspersed with tuffaceous material and flows of andesite and basalt. Mt Exmouth is a mountain of debris with flows sandwiched between.

History

Aboriginal sites up to 5000 years old have been identified, but most of the occupation in the core of the park seems to be 1000 to 2000 years old. The earlier period is well represented around the margins of the ranges. Explorer John Oxley and his party were the first Europeans to marvel at the grandeur of the Warrumbungles in 1818. The National Park and Primitive Areas Council (New South Wales) advocated the creation of a national park as part of its national campaign. The design was formally placed with the Department of Lands, Sydney, on 1 July 1937 and A.J. Pincham donated a large tract of land toward the establishment of the park.

Vegetation

Warrumbungle National Park contains a wide range of plant life supported by the rich volcanic soils. Most noticeable are various eucalypt species, such as the white gum, white box, red stringybark and grasstrees that dominate the Grand High Tops. Only a small amount of soil covers the many tops in the range, and only a few plants, such as mallee, can stand up to such conditions. Another hardy species, kurrajong, grows on the higher slopes.

Two species of trigger plant can be found in the damper areas of the park. Unable to self-pollinate, the trigger plant has evolved a special mechanism for the task. Each flower has a long column that is normally tucked behind the petals. When an insect alights at the centre of the flower, it triggers off the column, which swings gently over the face of the flower, lightly dusting the insect with pollen. The insect visits the next plant, accidentally pollinating it by brushing pollen onto the flower's sticky stigma.

Ferns, mosses and liverworts are common in these areas as are 28 species of wattle. Mid-August is the best time to see these flowers in full bloom, especially in the lower sandstone areas.

Wildlife

Wildlife observed within the park include the eastern grey kangaroo, wallaroo, yellow-footed marsupial mouse, rock-wallaby, spiny anteater, brushtail possum, ring-tailed possum, squirrel glider, greater glider and feather-tail glider. The koala can be found in woodlands, especially in the western creek flats. Red-necked wallabies and swamp wallabies are also present but not common.

Most of the animals are nocturnal, so late at night or early in the morning is the best time to observe them. To observe glider possums, look for a series of large, weatherbeaten trees with many hollows for 'nests' during the day and quietly take up a position nearby during the dark hours.

Access

The most direct way to get to the Breadknife in the Warrumbungles from Sydney is via Lithgow, Dunedoo, Mendooran and Coonabarabran, a total of 485km by road.

The Breadknife—the remnant of a volcanic vent, Warrumbungle National Park.

Grand High Tops Walk

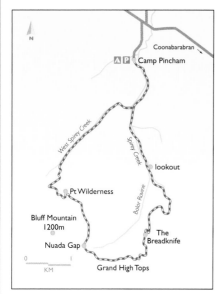

Starting Point: Camp Pincham, Warrumbungle National Park

Destination: Grand High Tops

Summary: This well-graded walk tours the best highlights in the southeast part of the park

Attractions: Belougery Spire, The Breadknife, views to Crater Bluff

Length: 14.5km

Time: 1 day

Options: If you leave early enough, there is time to do Goulds Circuit or ascend Bluff Mountain (1200m)

Attraction Rating: ★ ★ ★ ★ ★

Fitness: ◪ ◪ ◪

Maps: LIC (CMA) Warrumbungle National Park 1:30 000 topographical Tourist Map

Access to Starting Point: Camp Pincham is south of Camp Blackman off the John Renshaw Parkway

Facilities/Amenities: None en route

Recommended Equipment: Sturdy shoes with good grip, water

Notes: Make sure the car is securely locked when you are walking in the park because theft is a problem

Further Information: See Facts and Figures

Walk Description

Three things make this walk unique: The Breadknife, Belougery Spire and the unsurpassable view to the south of the park past Crater Bluff. It is illegal to climb The Breadknife itself. All along the walk, Belougery Spire dominates the eastern horizon. From the Grand High Tops, the track continues west toward Bluff Mountain. Descend to Camp Pincham via Dows High Tops and Ogma Saddle. Navigation is not difficult as all trails are well marked and there is not much rock-scrambling.

Mt Exmouth Walk

Starting Point: Camp Wambelong, Warrumbungle National Park

Destination: Mt Exmouth (1206m)

Summary: The direct approach to the highest point in the national park. The return route is a simple backtrack.

Attractions: Views from the summit of Mt Exmouth

Length: 20km

Time: 1 day

Options: The summit of Mt Exmouth can also be approached via Western High Tops from Camp Pincham. This would also be a full day's walk.

Attraction Rating: ★ ★ ★

Fitness: ◪ ◪ ◪ ◪

Maps: LIC (CMA) Warrumbungle National Park 1:30 000 topographical Tourist Map

Access to Starting Point: Private transport to Wambelong Camp on John Renshaw Parkway via Coonabarabran

Facilities/Amenities: Shelter, tank water and pit toilets at Burbie Camp along the way

Recommended Equipment: Plenty of water

Notes: Mt Exmouth is also known by its Aboriginal name, Wambelong Mountain

Further Information: Refer to Facts and figures, page 84

Walk Description

Mt Exmouth, at 1206m, is the highest peak in the national park and from its summit there are views over the entire area. Bring a packed lunch and a water bottle or two because it is very dry on top.

From Camp Wambelong, follow the Burbie Spur Trail south. It starts very flat as it parallels a dry creek bed on the left to a turning circle and the start of the walking track to Belougery Split Rock. From here on, the fire trail begins to rise, deteriorating slightly as it passes through dry eucalypt bush. A good downhill leads to a flat grassy open section where it's easy walking before a non-stop uphill. As the vehicle track meets the beginning of the slope, the surface becomes very rocky. There are occasional half-obscured views to the east during the ascent.

There is a brief interruption from the grinding uphill at Burbie Camp. A barrier here prevents further travel by any vehicle. Distances are also given to various points of interest accessed from this road. Burbie Camp is a wide, flat, open camping area with a large water tank amid trees on the far side and so makes a good place for a break. There are pit toilets.

A walking track leads up to Wambelong Mountain, but you should keep to the trail where the barrier is. The track still climbs, with gradients varying between steep and very steep. To the south, the bulk of Mt Exmouth dominates the horizon. The final slog to Danu Saddle is painful, rocky and slippery. From the prominent crest, there are good views to the south of the park. The road continues here to Gunneemooroo Camp and is quite rough. Walking tracks lead to the left and right of the saddle. The left track, near an unusual volcanic vent formation, leads to the Grand High Tops. Take note of how large Bluff Mountain looks now. At the top of Mt Exmouth, it will appear quite small.

Take the right track as it zigzags up an initial crest to a spur on Mt Exmouth. As you get higher the views get better. The track passes through pine-dominated woodland and contours to the south of the second tier of

Looking toward Bluff Mountain from Mt Exmouth, Warrumbungle National Park.

cliffs, where grasstrees take over as the dominant plant. There are some tricky sections over ledges before the track climbs again to attain the top of the plateau from behind. Simply walk west along the rocky top to the height marker for panoramic views.

From here, the Grand High Tops area looks very insignificant. Looking east, a line of high rocky outcrops stretches out from the vicinity of Bluff Mountain. Another leads to Belougery Rock from Belougery Spire. These are probably the remnants of old flows or of a fissure. Bluff Mountain and Belougery Split Rock mark places where great masses of trachytic materials welled to the surface. The northern face of Bluff Mountain shows some well-defined cooling prisms. Looking west, you can see to the beginning of the great flat bleak interior of the continent. Retrace your route to Camp Wambelong. If you have started sufficiently early, it is possible to return via Bluff Mountain by walking east from Danu Saddle.

Gunneemooroo Camp Walk

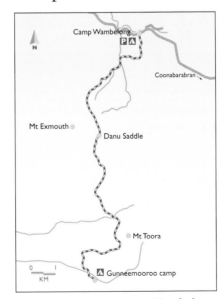

Starting Point: Camp Wambelong, Warrumbungle National Park
Destination: Gunneemooroo Camp
Summary: The longest walk in the park, taking backpackers to the remote south, not often seen by visitors

Attractions: Tonduron Spire, Danu Saddle, remote wilderness camping with few visitors
Length: 39km
Time: 2 days
Options: This walk can also start from Camp Pincham, where all the main features of the Grand High Tops, Bluff Mountain and Mt Exmouth can be explored. Returning via Burbie Camp would make this a three-day option. Alternatively, a long car shuffle could place a car near the park boundary at Gunneemooroo, so walkers don't have to backtrack.
Attraction Rating: ★ ★ ★ ★
Fitness: ▢ ▢ ▢
Maps: LIC (CMA) Warrumbungles National Park 1:30 000 topographical Tourist Map
Access to Starting Point: Private transport to Wambelong Camp on John Renshaw Parkway via Coonabarabran
Facilities/Amenities: Shelter, tank water and pit toilets at Burbie Camp along the way. Toilets are provided at Gunneemooroo Camp.

Recommended Equipment: Plenty of drinking water

Notes: Complete self-sufficiency is essential

Further Information: See details in the Grand High Tops Walk section

Walk Description

From Camp Wambelong, follow the previous walk's tracknotes to Danu Saddle via Burbie Camp. Continue down the other side, skirting the base of Bluff Mountain and ending up in the Tonderburine Creek valley. Few people venture this far, so there is plenty of wildlife here. It is possible to explore the upper Tonderburine Creek valley using disused tracks. Why not have a rest day here before retracing your route to Camp Wambelong?

Other walks in the Warrumbungle National Park

Belougery Split Rock (4.5km, 3 hours)

This circuit begins and ends at Camp Wambelong. It investigates another prominent geological feature just to the south of Canyon Camp on the John Renshaw Parkway. Great views are obtainable here. Wear sturdy boots.

Bluff Mountain Walk (16.6km, half a day)

Most commonly accessed from Camp Pincham via Ogma Saddle, this long walk climbs to the top of one of the park's most dramatic mountains, with its massive north face a popular venue for rock climbers and abseilers.

Warrumbungle Range Circuit (18km, 1 day)

This northern circuit from Camp Blackman uses fire trails closed to vehicles to access the slopes of the Warrumbungle Range, including Mt Bregon and Mt Aranon. Mountain bikes might suit this route better.

Gould's Circuit (5.7km, 3 hours)

This walk starts from Camp Pincham and passes through various plant communities. Not as many outstanding features on this walk as on the Grand High Tops, but ambitious walkers sometimes do this on their way up to The Breadknife.

Belougery Spire, en route to the Grand High Tops, Warrumbungle National Park.

Bress Peak (5.5km, 3 hours)

The summit of this small peak gives magnificent views over the Grand High Tops area. This is the closest lookout to the central part of the ancient volcano. Quite steep in some sections, but well worth the climb.

Other walks in the Inland Parks

To the north of Griffith lies the 8358ha Cocoparra National Park with two good short circuit walks. The first is to Woolshed Bluff (6km) from The Pines picnic area. The second is a 2.5km loop around Jacks Creek. Refer to *120 Walks in New South Wales* by Tyrone Thomas and consult the Griffith National Parks and Wildlife Service District Office for more details at:

105 Banna Ave
Griffith NSW 2680
Tel: (02) 6962 7755
Fax: (02) 6962 5480

New South Wales also has several superb desert parks, such as Sturt National Park (340 000ha), Mungo National Park and Kinchega National Park. However, walking here is not recommended because of the lack of shade and water, the hot dry climate and the vast, largely featureless terrain. Park authorities have concentrated on establishing 4WD touring circuits that visit significant features.

The one exception is the 68 912ha Mutawintji National Park (formerly known as Mootwingee), which lies 130km north-east of Broken Hill. Walkers here have a range of options from the Homestead Creek camping area, the longest being an 8km circuit along the Bynguano Range and through Homestead Gorge. Contact the ranger at Broken Hill for more details. The address is:

National Parks and Wildlife
Service District Office
Western Region
183 Argent St
Broken Hill NSW 2880
Tel: (08) 8087 1466
Fax: (08) 8088 3034

The New England Tableland

The New England Tableland covers a large portion of north-eastern New South Wales. It is quite high, peaking at 1600m, and some regions become snowbound in winter. The eastern edge drops away in a dramatic escarpment where rivers tumble down on their way to the coast. The terrain is rugged and wild, and overnight walks call for experience and complete self-sufficiency. Rainforest dominates the vegetation with stands of Antarctic beeches. There are some very good day walks, most within a few hours' drive from the major coastal holiday townships of Coffs Harbour and Port Macquarie. The climate is mild in summer, because of the high altitude, but come well prepared for extremely cold walking conditions in winter. The principal reserves in the New England Tablelands include:

Guy Fawkes River National Park
Cathedral Rock National Park
New England National Park
Dorrigo National Park
Oxley Wild Rivers National Park

Guy Fawkes River National Park

Dedicated in 1972, Guy Fawkes River National Park (63 395ha) covers the entire central and lower catchment of this river. This dramatic valley serves as a structural boundary between the Dorrigo plateau to the east and the New England Tableland to the west. Surrounded by thousands of hectares of state forest in all directions, this is one of the most remote national parks in the Great Dividing Range.

Vegetation

The vegetation is mainly dry sclerophyll forest with wet sclerophyll forest in areas with better soils. Characteristic species include messmate, New England blackbutt and narrow-leaved stringybark, growing to 25–40m with a sparse ground cover. Dry sclerophyll forest trees average 18–30m tall with moderate ground cover; principal species include grey gum and grey ironbark. Woodland on high exposed country has a scattering of snow gums. Rainforest with rare and much sought-after red cedar also occurs.

Wildlife

An abundance of wildlife includes black-tailed phascogale, greater glider or flying phalanger, red-legged pademelon, black-tailed or swamp wallaby and wallaroo. Bird species include painted quail, wonga pigeon, noisy pitta, spine-tailed logrunner, red-wattle bird, yellow-faced honey-eater and pied currawong. The common black snake and diamond python have both been noted here.

Lucifers Thumb Walk

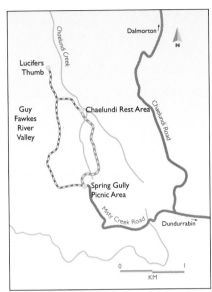

Starting Point: Chaelundi rest area, Guy Fawkes River National Park
Destination: Chaelundi Bluff
Summary: A circuit of Lucifers Thumb peninsula, which juts into the Guy Fawkes River valley
Attractions: Views, Chaelundi Falls
Length: 13km
Time: 4 hours
Options: Jordans Trail down to Guy Fawkes River. This is a 10km option involving regaining 640m of altitude; it is best to camp overnight near the confluence with Housewater Creek.
Attraction Rating: ★ ★ ★
Fitness: ☒ ☒ ☒
Maps: LIC (CMA) Chaelundi 1:25 000 topographical
Access to Starting Point: The park is

100km north-east of Armidale, accessible via Hernani from the Armidale –Grafton road. Follow Hardens Road, Chaelundi Road, then Misty Creek Road. Allow plenty of driving time as the roads are unsealed and not very well graded so progress is slow.
Facilities/Amenities: Basic camping facilities are provided at the Chaelundi rest area: tables, toilets and BBQs
Recommended Equipment: Water
Notes: The walking track is not depicted on the topographical map
Further Information:
Dorrigo Rainforest Centre
Cnr Dome Rd and Lyrebird Lane
Dorrigo NSW 2453
Tel: (02) 6657 2309
Fax: (02) 6657 2145

Walk Description

From the rest area, take the walking track north to Chaelundi Falls and then Lucifers Thumb Track to Chaelundi Bluff, where there are great views north to the Guy Fawkes River gorge more than half a kilometre below. Backtrack south and then keep to the edge of the valley following the rim all the way to Spring Gully picnic area. It's fairly flat along this section, with only a small rise at the end. From Spring Gully, follow the road back to the Chaelundi rest area.

Other walks in Guy Fawkes River National Park
Ebor Falls

It's possible to find your own route

Ebor Falls are a spectacular multi-level drop in the Guy Fawkes River gorge.

down the steep sides of the gorge to access the very top of the falls. Some scrambling is required. Allow 20–30 minutes for the climb back up again.

Overnight walks

The Guy Fawkes River itself is the principal destination of overnight walkers. There are few tracks and good navigation skills are essential to distinguish the many spurs and tributaries. Alternatively, walk along the Guy Fawkes River between two access points. You'll need the Guy Fawkes River, Chaelundi and Marengo 1:25 000 topographical maps to plan such an expedition. Nearby, the Mt Hyland Nature Reserve offers a 3km loop track through temperate rainforest to the summit of Mt Hyland.

Cathedral Rock National Park

The main attractions in this 6529ha park are the gigantic tors, similar to those in Gibraltar Range National Park. The Barokee and Native Dog Creek rest areas and their associated swamp plains and boulder-strewn grasslands make pleasantly green scenery on some of the highest land north of the Kosciuszko main range.

Geology

The granite in the park was formed about 230 million years ago when it crystallised from molten rock deep in the earth. As it cooled, cracks (joints) formed. The rocks that originally covered the granite were eroded away and the granite is now at ground level. Weathering of the granite extended well below the surface, following joint lines. In some areas all the granite was broken down, but in others, blocks of rock remain. The greater the weathering, the smaller and more rounded these blocks became. Some are now like marbles.

Vegetation

Despite being a swamp with poor drainage, the water at Barokee is very clean and fresh. The sphagnum bogs and peat swamps around the area are quite unusual and make interesting study for the botanist. The area contains ground orchids, lilies, mint

Ascending Woolpack Rocks, Cathedral Rock National Park.

bushes, bottlebrushes and heath. The many creeks in the area are bordered with patches of low heath shrubs that contrast with the taller eucalypt trees. As you walk through the forest, notice the patches of tussocky snow grass, a fine curly grass which, along with the snow gums, indicates how cold this area can be. In spring and summer it's a different story, with multitudes of colourful wildflowers, particularly in the heath and swamps.

There are several vegetation types. Most of the park is eucalypt forest, the most common trees being broad-leaved and wattle-leaved peppermint and mountain gum with small areas of manna gum, messmate and New England blackbutt in some valleys.

Wildlife

The park is a refuge for eagles and yellow-tailed cockatoos. Near the main camping area at Barokee, you will often see grey kangaroos and swamp wallabies grazing at dusk.

Access

The park is 70km east of Armidale on the New England Tableland. The nearest township is Ebor, situated on the Armidale–Grafton road.

Facilities

Amenities at Barokee and Native Dog Creek rest areas include BBQs, tables, running water nearby and toilets. Short-term camping is allowed and

reservations are not necessary. Both experience frosts and snow in winter. The area at Native Dog Creek is more spacious than Barokee, so this is the best site for caravans. A short walking track leads to water in Native Dog Creek, but the creek may run dry in late winter and spring.

Woolpack Rocks Walk

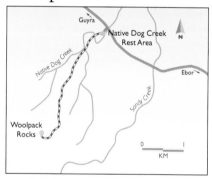

Starting Point: Native Dog Creek rest area, Cathedral Rock National Park

Destination: The summit of Woolpack Rocks

Summary: A return track to a prominent rock outcrop with views

Attractions: Views from a boulder-strewn landscape

Length: 7.4km

Time: Half a day

Options: An extended walk through to Cathedral Rock

Attraction Rating: ★ ★ ★

Fitness: ☒☒

Maps: LIC (CMA) Ebor and Hyatts Flat 1:25 000 topographicals (Maiden

Creek covers many of the views overlooked from the tor). Walking tracks are not marked on the map.

Access to Starting Point: From Ebor (on the Armidale–Grafton road), head west. Turn on to the Ebor–Guyra road and drive for 10km before taking the signposted turn-off on the left to Native Dog Creek rest area.

Facilities/Amenities: Firewood, BBQs and pit toilets at the Native Dog Creek rest area

Recommended Equipment: Windproof jackets for cold, windy days

Notes: Beware of swooping magpies in spring

Further Information:
Dorrigo Rainforest Centre
Cnr Dome Rd and Lyrebird Lane
Dorrigo NSW 2453
Tel: (02) 6657 2309
Fax: (02) 6657 2145

Walk Description

The walking track is well signposted and basically skirts the base of Woolpack Rocks, ascending the boulders from the south. It gets very windy on top because of its exposure to south-westerly winds. The boulders are pink Adamellite granite formed by weathering and often arranged in lines running north-west to south-east because of the vertical jointing of volcanic dykes. Some of the tors are up to 30m high.

There are superb views from the top of some gigantic granite tors. You can see the coast, much of the Armidale district and the New England escarpment. Campsites are scattered throughout the Native Dog Creek rest area. In winter this area often receives snow because of its high altitude. Return via the same route.

···

Cathedral Rock Walk

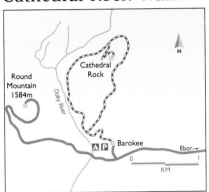

Starting Point: Barokee rest area (also called Snowy Creek picnic area)

Destination: The summit of Cathedral Rock

Summary: This short circuit climbs a large rounded rock outcrop. Some scrambling is necessary.

Attractions: Southerly views to the New England escarpment

Length: 5.8km

Time: 2.5 hours

Options: An extension to Woolpack Rocks. This entails a car shuffle.

Attraction Rating: ★ ★ ★

Fitness: ✖ ✖

Maps: LIC (CMA) Ebor and Hyatts

Flat 1:25 000 topographicals (Maiden Creek covers many of the views overlooked from the tor). Walking tracks are not marked on the map.

Access to Starting Point: From the Armidale–Grafton road, a signposted narrow 8km gravel road leads to Barokee rest area. A rough dirt road leads up a hill through grazing land. It is 3km to the entrance of the national park and another 5km to the actual starting point of the walk at the Barokee rest area. The Round Mountain Road goes on but a locked gate prevents access to Round Mountain. The Civil Aviation Authority, which owns the land, installed a microwave/radar rotating dish in the late 1960s.

Facilities/Amenities: Secluded campsites are set amid tall banksias and eucalypts. The camping ground is not very large. Water is available from a small stream running through nearby heath-covered wetland or swamp.

Recommended Equipment: Camera

Notes: Some rock-scrambling is required, using an installed chain

Further Information:
Dorrigo Rainforest Centre
Cnr Dome Rd and Lyrebird Lane
Dorrigo NSW 2453
Tel: (02) 6657 2309
Fax: (02) 6657 2145

Walk Description

From the summit of Cathedral Top you can see the coast, much of the Armidale district and the New England escarpment. Cathedral Rock National Park (6529ha) contains the highest point north of the Alps. Wallabies are everywhere, especially in the early or late hours near the swamp at the base of Cathedral Rock.

The start of the walking track is well marked; walk clockwise. The track heads out across the swamp and up into a gully between Cathedral Rock and Round Mountain. Ignore a track to the right as this is where you come out on the return. Along the way are gigantic boulders that have crashed down from the top. About halfway around the mountain, a signposted trail heads up to the rock stack itself about 400m away. It involves some scrambling. The last section is entirely over rock where you have to crawl under and over

Near Round Mountain, Cathedral Rock National Park.

rock. A chain provides assistance up a small steep slope. At the top is an amazing display of wildflowers on the southern end. You can't get to the very top because of the sheer roundness of the highest boulders but they make an interesting foreground for anyone willing to drag a camera up there. Another rock stack is visible across the gully opposite, while to the south-east it is not unusual to see clouds scraping the ground near the Point Lookout area. Although Cathedral Rock is higher, it is also much drier because it doesn't sit on the edge of the escarpment.

The weathered pink Adamellite granite boulders are often arranged in lines, running north-west to south-east because of the vertical jointing of volcanic dykes. Some of the tors are 30m high. The trail returns to Barokee rest area around the mountain, passing more giant boulders.

Other walks in Cathedral Rock National Park
Traverse (12km, 4 hours)
Set up a car shuffle, or arrange to be picked up at one of the rest areas, if you wish to make a day trip of a full traverse of the park. A link track connects Cathedral Rock and Woolpack Rocks. Alternatively, walk back to the starting point after camping overnight at the other end.

New England National Park

New England is usually approached from Armidale or the coast where tourists can inspect Point Lookout and walk to the base of the cliffs through magical beech rainforest that could have come straight from the pages of a fantasy novel. Nevertheless, few people venture into the landscape they view from Point Lookout. Several trails extend from the ridge (1563m high) down to the Georges River through the extensive Styx River State Forest. This area, administered by the forestry commission, is larger than some national parks. On the way, take a side trip to Wrights Plateau and the wild cascades that make up the headwaters of Five Day Creek. Ideally, travel to New England with another

party in a second car and set up a car shuffle before setting off.

The park is best suited to overnight walks with the main access to the southern end by the Macleay River road (Kempsey–Armidale road) allowing walkers to descend into the the valley. The closest public transport is the railway to Armidale, Kempsey or Coffs Harbour.

The park is notorious for its misty weather. In fact, there's a one-in-three chance that Point Lookout will be in a 'white-out', increasing to one in two in the summer months, especially in the mornings. Don't despair if this happens, because conditions for photography in the beech rainforest just below become perfect. Take plenty of film and a tripod.

The only major trail into the heart of the park starts from near the park entrance and extends down past the base of Wrights Plateau to Killiekrankie Mountain and out through Horseshoe Road.

Facts and Figures
Name: New England National Park
Size: 55 989ha
Enactment: State Reserve, 1931
    National Park, 24 May 1935
    Significant additions, 1940
    World Heritage Area, 1986
Visitors: About 77 000 a year, mostly casual tourists to Point Lookout
Vegetation: More than 500 species in 11 communities, determined by the soils, aspect, climate and exposure. Rainforest and wet sclerophyll are the most common vegetation forms in the park. The three quite distinct types of rainforest that are found here include subtropical rainforest, warm temperate rainforest and cool temperate rainforest. A distinct division of flora types occurs at 1200m where the communities change from beech trees to snow gums. Heathlands are restricted, but rich in species. Weeds, mainly lantana, pose a few problems.
Wildlife: Because of the rugged wilderness nature of the park, very little is known about the wildlife that inhabits the area. So far 113 species of birds have been recorded and some 30 species of animals. Not many of the likely reptile and

insect species have been recorded. Rare species include the sphagnum frog, found in the higher swamps.
Aboriginal Sites: At present, little is known. The Aborigines who lived in the area were mobile, using the freshwater streams as transitional base-camps on journeys from the coast and the tablelands.
Camping: Camping is permitted anywhere off roads and permits are not required. Several excellent cabins are available at a price, but bookings are required well in advance. The Thungutti Camping Ground is the main developed area for visitors and can be used as a base camp for walking tours. It comes with showers and toilets. Sites are secluded and bookings are not necessary.
Adjoining Parks: Numerous state forests surround the southern perimeter of the park, including Nulla Five Day, Styx River and Lower Creek. Also adjacent are nature reserves such as Georges Creek and Serpentine. Nearby lies the large Guy Fawkes River National Park and its associated state forests. To the north and west lies the striking Cathedral Rock and Oxley Wild Rivers national parks respectively.
Further Reading: *A history of the establishment and administration of New England National Park* by Howard Stanley
Map: The Armidale and District Tourist Map 1:150 000 topographical gives a good overview of the New England National Park and adjacent state forests

Geology
The precipitous cliffs at the edge of the plateau are the result of at least five basalt lava flows from the Ebor volcano, which formed a rim more than 300m thick. Active until about 18 million years ago, this massive volcano was centred on The Crescent, a semi-circular ridge in the Bellinger Valley, visible from Point Lookout. Below the basalt lies sedimentary rock almost 500 million years old, which has been carved into a multitude of virtually inaccessible peaks and ridges that are now densely forested.

Looking east over an escarpment towards the coast from the lofty Point Lookout in the New England National Park.

History

The first European account of this area came from surveyor Clement Hodgkinson, who explored the Bellinger Valley in 1841. Cedar-getters and farmers soon moved in but the rugged upper catchment remained untouched. In the late 1920s, local grazier Phillip Wright, together with other far-sighted New Englanders, began a campaign to preserve the area as a national park. Nearly 17 000ha were declared a reserve in 1931 and officially opened in 1935.

Before the National Parks and Wildlife Service was established in 1967, the management of national parks was in the hands of individual trusts which were, in turn, responsible to the Parks and Reserves Branch of the Department of Lands. At this time there was considered to be no difference between a national park and a camping ground or recreational reserve. Fauna protection was under the control of the Fauna Protection Panel within the Chief Secretary's Department. The protection of native plants was the responsibility of local government and, later, the Fauna Protection Panel.

Vegetation

New England National Park contains a rich flora of about 500 species in a variety of communities. These occur in a clearly defined pattern according to altitude, topography, soil type and degree of exposure to wind. The high, cold windswept plateau at Point Lookout has practically no species in common with the warm, sheltered, subtropical eastern margins. Cold-tolerant open woodland of snow gum and tussocky snow grass dominates the high-altitude country around Point Lookout. Open sclerophyll forest of other eucalypts, particularly brown barrel, messmate and stringybark, is found in areas above 1200m. Over the edge of the escarpment, cool temperate rainforests of ancient Antarctic beech stand festooned with hanging moss.

In the lower, warmer parts of the park, sheltered valleys are occupied by subtropical rainforest of booyong, yellow carbeen and red cedar trees. Eucalypt forests containing Sydney blue gum, brush box and tallowwood grow on the ridges and spurs. Areas of heath, swamp and mallee complete the diversity.

Wildlife

The richness and variety of animal life in the park reflects its wide range of habitats. Both of Australia's famous 'living fossils', the egg-laying platypus and echidna, occur in the park. There is a variety of marsupials too, including kangaroos, several species of gliders, possums and the native quoll.

More than 100 species of birds have been recorded, many of which arrive to breed in the summer or visit seasonally when rainforest trees fruit. Most commonly seen are white-throated tree creepers, rufous fantails and pied currawongs in the open forests, while flowering banksias attract lewins, honeyeaters and eastern spinebills. In the rainforests the beautiful superb lyrebird reigns supreme, scratching among the moist leaf litter for food. Perhaps the national park's strangest resident is *Peripatus*, a 'missing link' between worms and insects. It looks like a velvety caterpillar with slug-like feelers.

Facilities

Accommodation for caravans and car-camping is just outside the park in the Thungutti campground. Toms Cabin, the Residence and the Chalet at Banksia Point require bookings, which can be made up to six months ahead. For more information, phone the Dorrigo District Office. Facilities include beds, stoves, gas lights, hot water and, perhaps best of all, four walls. Below the ridgeline, primitive camping is available anywhere in the national park. One of the most popular sites is at Platypus Creek. The grassy flats by the Styx River to the south are perfect for car-campers.

Point Lookout Circuit

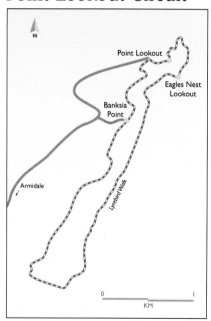

Starting Point: Point Lookout, New England National Park
Destination: Lyrebird Track
Summary: A loop encompassing both the Eagles Nest and the Lyrebird Track
Attractions: Antarctic beeches, views, moss-covered boulders, a range of vegetation environments
Length: 9km

Time: Half a day
Options: Several extensions can be done along the walking tracks below Point Lookout escarpment, including exiting at Banksia Point or at the ranger's residence
Attraction Rating: ★ ★ ★
Fitness: ◪ ◪ ◪
Maps: LIC (CMA) Ebor and Hyatts Flat 1:25 000 topographicals
Access to Starting Point: Point Lookout is at the far end of Point Lookout Road in the New England National Park, 85km east of Armidale. The best access is from the Grafton–Armidale road. The turn-off is signposted just to the west of Ebor.
Facilities/Amenities: Picnic shelters at Point Lookout
Recommended Equipment: Tripod for photographing beech trees
Notes: This walk can be done in either direction. The track is often wet and muddy so waterproof shoes with quite good tread are recommended. Be prepared with extra clothes as the region is notorious for experiencing four seasons in a day.
Further Information: Contact Dorrigo National Parks and Wildlife Service District Office

> Dorrigo Rainforest Centre
> Cnr Dome Rd and Lyrebird Lane
> Dorrigo NSW 2453
> Tel: (02) 6657 2309
> Fax: (02) 6657 2145

Walk Description

From Point Lookout, take the signposted Eagles Nest Circuit left to descend through the cliffs to their base. You travel underneath Point Lookout until you come to Eagles Nest Lookout. Continue walking south via the Lyrebird Track underneath the wet cliffs to the saddle between Wrights Lookout and the main plateau on the Robinsons Knob road. Moss-covered boulders and dripping waterfalls along the way evoke the enchanted forests of Tolkien's *Lord of the Rings*.

Return to Point Lookout along the top of the cliffs, passing through Banksia Point and experiencing heath and open snow gum woodland. The subalpine vegetation found above the escarpment contrasts starkly against the temperate rainforest shadowed under towering basalt cliffs.

Weeping Rock and the Rainbow Spray are permanent watercourses that tumble over the scarp in a spectacular display. In winter, they are frozen. More details on this walk is available in the 'Eagles Nest Nature Track' and 'Lyrebird Walk' leaflets.

Wright Plateau and the Cascades Walk

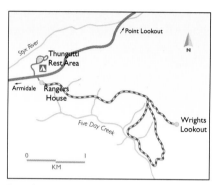

Starting Point: Thungutti camping area/ranger's residence, New England National Park
Destination: Five Day Creek
Summary: An excursion into wilder parts beyond the escarpment
Attractions: Great views from the end of Wrights Plateau; numerous photogenic cascades on Five Day Creek
Length: 9km
Time: Half a day
Options: If you leave early enough, you could also do a loop walk all the way to Point Lookout and back, thereby exploring all the attractions in the main escarpment area
Attraction Rating: ★ ★ ★ ★
Fitness: ◪ ◪ ◪
Maps: LIC (CMA) Hyatts Flat 1:25 000 topographical
Access to Starting Point: Thungutti camping area is on Point Lookout Road at the entrance of the park
Facilities/Amenities: None en route; the Thungutti camping area has BBQs, toilets and showers
Recommended Equipment: Water containers—Five Day Creek water is drinkable
Notes: Watch for snakes on this route
Further Information:

> Dorrigo Rainforest Centre
> Cnr Dome Rd and Lyrebird Lane
> Dorrigo NSW 2453
> Tel: (02) 6657 2309
> Fax: (02) 6657 2145

Walk Description

From the Ranger's Residence, opposite Thungutti camping area, head east down Robinsons Knob Trail. Note that no vehicles are permitted on this route. The road descends to a saddle. From here, a walking track heads right down to Five Mile Creek, while another branches off up the back of Wrights Plateau. Do the plateau first if the weather is warm. Some minor scrambling is necessary on both routes. Wrights Lookout, a prominent windswept plateau of trachyte rock, juts from near the escarpment to afford commanding views over New England National Park, especially down the Bellinger River valley. The 300m-thick basalt was formed about 40 million years ago from volcanic origin. Stunted open heath grows on the flat top, the most successful community to colonise the area to date.

Do the Cascades loop in a clockwise direction to get maximum traction for the descent. In warm weather, you can cool off in some of the pools.

Platypus Creek Walk

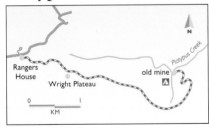

Starting Point: Thungutti camping area/ ranger's residence, New England National Park
Destination: Platypus Creek (downstream from Antimony Gully)
Summary: A walk along Robinsons Knob Trail on the Macleay Range to access a remote gully in the heart of New England National Park
Attractions: Historic antimony mining site, remote wilderness camping
Length: 26km
Time: 2 days
Options: On the way down to the campsite, drop the overnight packs and explore the summit of Wrights Plateau. If time is available, also do the Cascades Loop.
Attraction Rating: ★ ★ ★
Fitness: ◪ ◪ ◪ ◪

Maps: LIC (CMA) Hyatts Flat 1:25 000 topographical
Access to Starting Point: Thungutti camping area is on Point Lookout Road at the entrance of the park
Facilities/Amenities: None en route; the Thungutti camping area has BBQs, toilets and showers
Recommended Equipment: Camping gear for full self-sufficiency
Notes: Consult the ranger before embarking on this route

Further Information:

Dorrigo Rainforest Centre
Cnr Dome Rd and Lyrebird Lane
Dorrigo NSW 2453
Tel: (02) 6657 2309
Fax: (02) 6657 2145

Walk Description

Walk down Robinsons Knob Trail from the ranger's residence, past Wrights Plateau. The trail descends steadily and there may be some fallen

Antarctic beeches on the Lyrebird Track, New England National Park.

logs to negotiate. The trail follows the spine of the ridge, which soon becomes quite prominent. As you approach the turn-off to Grasstree Ridge on the left (north), the ground becomes undulating. Descending Grasstree Ridge, you pass Callans Rocks on the right. The trail then veers left off the centre of the ridge. An old overgrown vehicle track then leads left, zigzagging down to Platypus Creek at the old antimony mine site. Antimony is a brittle, lustrous metallic element used primarily in medicines. It is also found at Port Davey in south-west Tasmania. Mining by Hobart and Pearson started in 1934 after the construction of an access road. The operation proved uneconomic and ceased in 1956.

Other walks in New England National Park

As well as several short easy walks, the park provides experienced walkers with some outstanding overnight wilderness walks. By selecting suitable routes from the escarpment via ridge tops to the valley floors an exciting, strenuous, yet satisfying excursion is assured. If you prefer an extended walk on a more defined route, follow the fire trails from the park entrance to Robinsons Knob, or Diamond Flat, or the Bellinger River. It is vital to have topographical maps. Set up a car shuffle to avoid backtracking up to the escarpment again.

Another beautiful area for exploration is the 29 000ha Styx River State Forest to the south of Point Lookout.

Dorrigo National Park

This 7885ha park protects the rugged escarpment of the Dorrigo Plateau and the mountain range stretching toward the coast. The edge of the escarpment is steep and abrupt and humid coastal air masses are forced to drop their precipitation as they pass up and over the escarpment, giving the area a high but seasonal rainfall.

Numerous creeks spring from the gullies of the forested escarpment to form the headwaters of the Rosewood River (the north branch of the Bellinger River). In their steep descent to the coastal plain near Coffs Harbour,

these watercourses fall from an altitude of nearly 920m to about 100m above sea level. Farther to the east, the national park covers the catchment area of the Never Never River, which rises on the plateau and drops over the escarpment at Gleniffer Falls, the highest falls in the park.

Geology

The basalt of the Dorrigo Plateau is a remnant of the 18-million-year-old Ebor volcano. The combination of the rapidly changing altitude, a variety of soils and high rainfall has produced a rich variety of plant and animal life.

History

Until the 1830s the Dorrigo Plateau was the territory of the Gumbaingerri Aborigines. Thereafter, timber-getters exploited the thick rainforest for cedar and the Dorrigo Scrub was eventually cleared to make way for an expanding dairy industry. In 1902, parts of what is now known as Dorrigo National Park were dedicated for public recreation and the preservation of native flora. This long history of concern has ensured the continuing protection of a remnant of the original Dorrigo scrub, as well as a major part of the remnant subtropical rainforest of the Upper Bellinger River.

Climate

The area has a very high rainfall (2500mm per annum), which falls mainly in summer.

Vegetation

The forest of Dorrigo National Park falls into three major types: subtropical rainforest, warm temperate rainforest and wet eucalypt forest. The subtropical rainforest found along the Wonga Walk Track includes many different large trees, such as booyongs, yellow carbeens, giant stinging trees, red cedars and strangler figs. Many trees have buttressed roots, and thick twisted vines, epiphytes and ferns are common. Characteristic features of subtropical rainforest are the variety of tree species and several canopy layers.

Warm temperate rainforest, found around the Never Never picnic area, has many coachwood, hoop pines and sassafras trees, and an abundance of

ferns, mosses, orchids and fungi. While subtropical rainforest has many layers, warm temperate rainforest is less complex. Most of the orchids flower in spring and the spectacular flame trees can be seen in November and December.

Wet sclerophyll forest can be seen on the ridges sloping down into the Bellinger Valley. The darker green canopy of the rainforest in the gullies is in sharp contrast with the grey-green crowns of wet sclerophyll forest on the drier, more-exposed ridges.

Wildlife

Dorrigo National Park offers habitats to a wide selection of wildlife. More than 120 bird species have been observed, including the lyrebird, brush turkey and pitta. In the picnic areas you will see currawongs, honeyeaters and brush turkeys, but most others will be seen deeper in the forest along the tracks.

Many of the mammals are nocturnal, but visitors may glimpse a swamp wallaby, red-necked pademelon, brushtail possum, brushtail phascogale, tiger cat or one of several species of gliding possums. The most abundant animal life in the rainforest is in the leaf litter on the forest floor. Old leaves and logs are broken down and returned to the soil by a host of small snails, beetles and other insects.

Access

The park is about 4km east of Dorrigo and 60km west of Coffs Harbour on the Dorrigo–Bellingen road.

Facilities

For day visitors, there are two staging areas from which to explore the park. The Glade and Never Never picnic areas have BBQs, wood, tables, toilets, water and shelter sheds. Camping at the picnic grounds is not permitted. For those with limited time there are views of the Bellinger Valley from the Glade picnic area and the Satinbird Stroll nearby. This graded walking track takes 15 minutes and leads directly into rainforest.

To challenge the keen bushwalker, there are longer walks in the Killungoondie/Never Never River area of the park. Bush-camping is permitted for those undertaking overnight stays.

Wonga Walk

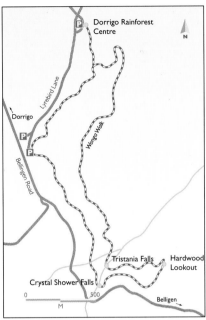

Starting Point: Dorrigo Rainforest Centre, Dorrigo National Park
Destination: Crystal Shower Falls
Summary: An excellent circuit through rainforest with many highlights
Attractions: Hardwood Lookout, Crystal Shower Falls, Tristania Falls, 'Walk with the Birds' raised walkway
Length: 6.6km (including the 'Walk with the Birds' option)
Time: 2.5 hours
Options: Take a short stroll along the Skywalk before embarking
Attraction Rating: ★ ★ ★ ★
Fitness: ⊠ ⊠
Maps: LIC (CMA) Darkwood and Dorrigo 1:25 000 topographicals
Access to Starting Point: The Rainforest Centre car park is just east of Dorrigo
Facilities/Amenities: Picnic area at The Glade along the route. A full visitors' information centre is at the start, with a range of brochures and leaflets for surrounding New England Tableland national parks.
Recommended Equipment: Walking boots with good tread as sections of the walk are wet
Notes: Crystal Shower Falls are particularly photogenic and you can access an overhang behind them. This area of the national park is very popular with tourists and can get crowded in peak holiday seasons.
Further Information:
Dorrigo Rainforest Centre
Cnr Dome Rd and Lyrebird Lane
Dorrigo NSW 2453
Tel: (02) 6657 2309
Fax: (02) 6657 2145

Walk Description

This walk follows the Lyrebird Link Track to connect with the Wonga Walk Circuit. This is, in effect, a long ramp. You can go in either direction, but for a more comfortable uphill gradient on the return route, head right, keeping to the high ground en route to the 'Walk with the Birds' raised walkway. This allows visitors to climb gently to the height of the canopy. Information plaques describe unique features of the rainforest. You can avoid crowds at The Glade picnic area by using the short Satinbird Stroll to head south below the rim of the escarpment to the very attractive Crystal Shower Falls. The track then heads down to Hardwood Lookout and more falls before doubling back north to join up with the Lyrebird Link ramp again.

Cedar Falls Circuit

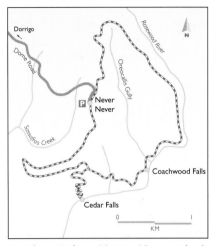

Starting Point: Never Never picnic area, Dorrigo National Park
Destination: Cedar Falls
Summary: A circuit centred on the Rosewood River valley and taking in several attractive waterfalls
Attractions: Coachwood Falls and Cedar Falls
Length: 8.2km
Time: 3 hours
Options: Either set up a car shuffle or walk along Dome Road to extend the walk. Follow the Blackbutt Track to Endiandra Creek and Callicoma Falls. Another short side option goes to Casuarina Falls.
Attraction Rating: ★ ★ ★
Fitness: ⊠ ⊠ ⊠
Maps: LIC (CMA) Brooklana 1:25 000 topographical
Access to Starting Point: The Never Never picnic area is accessed by travelling the length of Dome Road. Turn off the Dorrigo–Bellingen Road at the same park entrance as the Rainforest Centre.
Facilities/Amenities: BBQs, wood, tables, toilets, water and shelter shed. Camping is not permitted.
Recommended Equipment: Tripod for photographing waterfalls in overcast weather

The Dorrigo rainforest canopy from the Skywalk, Dorrigo National Park.

Further Information:
> Dorrigo Rainforest Centre
> Cnr Dome Rd and Lyrebird Lane
> Dorrigo NSW 2453
> Tel: (02) 6657 2309
> Fax: (02) 6657 2145

Walk Description

This section of parkland was formerly known as Never Never State Forest. Early in 1973, about 1650ha was revoked from the state forest and added to the park in order to include all the headwaters of Rosewood Creek within the park boundary. Never Never picnic area has been constructed in a section of the Dorrigo National Park that provides access to many interesting features of the damp east coast forests and rugged escarpment landform. The picnic area is designed for day visitors wishing to picnic or walk on the tracks.

The two dominant features of this section of the park are the forest itself, with its many associated plant communities, and crystal-clear streams with rainforest growing right to the water's edge. There are excellent views along many sections of the 13km of tracks. To reach Cedar Falls, follow Rosewood Creek Track in an anti-clockwise direction as the signposts indicate. These are the most spectacular falls in the park, named after the large cedars growing at their base. Although the track is well formed the final section is quite steep.

Other walks in the Dorrigo National Park

Casuarina Falls Walk (4.8km, 1.5 hours)

The name Casuarina is taken from the forest oaks growing in the vicinity. Follow Blackbutt Track to this drop. The track goes over the top of the Casuarina Falls, which can even be seen Dorrigo Mountain Road during periods of heavy rainfall.

Blackbutt Track (6.4km, 2.5 hours one way)

Blackbutt Track connects the Never Never picnic area to the park entrance on Dome Road. The rugged beauty of the park as seen from the top of Casuarina Falls gives way to the stillness of the crystal pools along Endiandra Creek. Other features of this track are the large blackbutt tree and blackbutt log about 1.75km past Casuarina Falls. The Callicoma Falls are in a beautiful section of rainforest toward the end of the track.

Other walks on the New England Tableland

Oxley Wild Rivers National Park has a multitude of cascading waterfalls, plunging from around a gorge rim and flowing south as wild rivers. Wollomombi Falls are Australia's highest, plunging almost 300m to the floor of a dramatic steep-sided gorge. They are accessed from the Armidale–Grafton road about 40m east of Armidale.

The Wollomombi River gorge is narrow and deep, with steep V-shaped valleys. Actively eroding slopes nurture no trees and are bare, jagged slides. Dry rainforest clings to the dizzy heights. The rim is cloaked in open woodland with brittle gums, stringybarks and blackbutts. Clumps of snow grass are tied to small flowering shrubs by twiners, creating natural clearings. A track leads away from the Wollomombi Falls car park around the rim to various vantage points, then winds down ridges into the gorge.

To the south, Apsley, Tia and Dangars falls dive into ravines to flow down long valleys with deep pools. Canoes, kayaks and li-los are often carried in by visitors eager to explore the surrounds. The more adventurous are tempted by the white water. In all, 13 major tableland rivers flow through the gorge system, to be drawn down into the wilderness.

Facilities at the 117 349ha Oxley Wild Rivers National Park include BBQs, toilets, caravan sites, visitor information, wheelchair access and picnic areas. Walkers should consult the Rowleys Creek, Kunderang, Tia, Apsley, Green Gully and Kangaroo Flat topographical maps for walk ideas. For information contact the Armidale National Parks and Wildlife Service District Office at:
> 87 Faulkner St
> Armidale NSW 2350
> Tel: (02) 6773 7211
> Fax: (02) 6771 1894

The Hunter Valley Region

Barrington Tops National Park

Snow often falls on this beautiful national park within an hour's drive from Newcastle. The peaks, rising to 1586m, are among the highest outside Kosciuszko National Park, and the forests are among the oldest and most lush. Before the Barrington Tops were formed, the region north-west of Newcastle was composed chiefly of sedimentary rocks, such as limestone and mudstone. Then volcanic rock rich in quartz was forced up through jointing and folded in the original

Wollomombi Falls, Australia's highest, in the Oxley Wild Rivers National Park.

The view east from Gloucester Tops, Barrington Tops National Park.

layer to form a lofty range. This was subsequently eroded away leaving only a small residual area of some 300 square kilometres. Volcanic basalt flows occurred about 50 million years ago, although much of the basalt has been worn down by rivers. Little evidence now remains of the original limestone and even less of the basalt. Limestone is confined to the spurs and rim walls around the plateau, while basalt is evident on isolated caps.

There was once an active logging industry and literally hundreds of mountain trails now exist throughout the upper Barrington and Gloucester River areas. Most of these are well graded and open to 4WD vehicles through summer. Public transport is limited to Dungog and Gloucester, which are unfortunately at an altitude of only 100–200m, leaving a long climb for anyone intending to camp on the tops. Alternatively, drive to the Polblue rest area in the centre of the park where some fine circuits begin.

Because of the park's popularity, especially during holidays, walkers will have to contend with the many other users of the park: 4WD owners, canoeists, mountain bike cyclists and equestrians. Visitors in school holidays, especially during good weather, will find the lower Barrington Tops bustling with sightseers.

Dungog is three hours' drive from Sydney and the national park just another hour to the north. From there, you can drive to the tops, amid snow gums, beeches and rainforest. Any number of days can be spent exploring the mountains before descending again to civilisation.

Facts and Figures

Name: Barrington Tops National Park
Size: 62 449ha (85 per cent of which is wilderness)
Enactment: 1969 (since 1986, much of the park has been declared a World Heritage Area)
Visitors: 250 000 per year
Vegetation: Most notable trees are the ancient and beautiful Antarctic beech trees, found in the highest rainforests. The Barrington and Gloucester Tops areas have diverse plant communities. The range of species includes subtropical rainforests, eucalypt forests and woodlands, and the largest areas of peat swamps to be found outside of the Kosciuszko National Park. An introduced species, the bright yellow scotch broom, has become quite a major pest in the northern half of the plateau.
Wildlife: Kangaroos, platypuses, bandicoots, gliders, possums, bats, koalas and a large variety of aquatic wildlife, rare invertebrates and many hundreds of species of birds. Brumbies also live within the park and adjacent state forests.
Aboriginal Sites: Apparently limited pre-European use of the park. Little evidence of permanent occupation.
Camping: A number of developed campsites provided around the Allyn River in the south, on the Gloucester River in the east, and the Polblue Swamp area in the north. Permits are not required for primitive bush-camping.
Adjoining Parks: Adjoining the south-west boundary of the park is the wild Mt Royal National Park, while to the north lies Woko National Park. Large and numerous state forests, including the Avon River, Chichester, Stewarts Brook, Masseys Creek and Barrington Tops state forests, make up an area twice the size of the national park itself.
Further Information: Gloucester ranger's office, (02) 6558 1478
Or: 22–24 Bourke St
Raymond Terrace NSW 2324
Tel: (02) 4987 3108
Fax: (02) 4983 1031

Barrington Tops Circuit

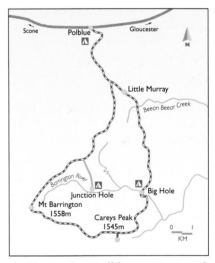

Starting Point: Polblue campground, Barrington Tops National Park
Destination: Careys Peak (1545m)
Summary: This circuit links all the best attractions on the fascinating Barrington Tops plateau
Attractions: Views over the Hunter Valley from Careys Peak, The Big Hole, the Barrington River
Length: Total distance is 53km
Day 1: Polblue camping area to The Big Hole via Careys Peak, 35km
Day 2: The Big Hole to Polblue camping area via Beean Beean Plain, 18km
Time: 2 days (maybe spend an extra day by The Big Hole)

Options: If you start this circuit walk from Lagoon Pinch in the Chichester State Forest to the south, a much larger height gain is involved. Several short cuts can be taken on this route. For example, you can cut across the Barrington Tops plateau from Junction Hole camping area using a walking track over Aeroplane Hill (not marked on the topographical map). Walkers who prefer to use walking tracks rather than fire trails may prefer this, but it means sacrificing the lookout at Mt Barrington.

Attraction Rating: ★★★★★
Fitness: ☒☒☒
Maps: LIC (CMA) Moonan Brook and Barrington Tops 1:25 000 topographicals. Also useful is the Barrington Tops and Gloucester Districts Tourist Map 1:100 000 topographical.
Access to Starting Point: Use private transport to the Polblue camping area via the Barrington Tops Forest Road linking Scone with Gloucester. From Sydney, go through Newcastle to Gloucester. The total drive takes 4–5 hours from the metropolitan area.

Two ways lead from Gloucester to the national park. The short one simply goes north through flat, uneventful agricultural land. The road, first called Barrington Road, passes through the town of Barrington, crosses Barrington River before entering Barrington Tops State Forest, where it becomes Barrington Tops Forest Road to Barrington Tops National Park.

A better road, which gives almost total relief from the word 'Barrington' and, incidentally, passes through some lovely countryside, is the Gloucester Tops–Rawson Vale road. Turn left 9km before Gloucester on Bucketts Way and drive upstream alongside the river for about 45 minutes. Turn right up onto the Rawson Vale Road, which climbs to a crest where a spectacular valley panorama is spread before you. Cross the Kerripit River and turn left soon after. The road follows the Cobark River for several kilometres before climbing steadily to a ridge about 1500m above sea level. This road is another 200–300m higher than the tallest peaks in the Blue Mountains. The Polblue camping area is close to the road on the left in the Stewarts Brook State Forest. This area is on the western edge of the Devils Hole Wilderness Area, some 2330ha of the rugged catchment area of the upper Moppy River.

Facilities/Amenities: Picnic and car-camping facilities at Polblue include water, cooking shelters, fireplaces and toilets
Recommended Equipment: Overnight camping gear, warm clothes
Notes: Temperatures can get very cold at any time of the year. This trek can also be done in the opposite (clockwise) direction if you wish to have the shorter day first.
Further Information:
22–24 Bourke St
Raymond Terrace NSW 2324
Tel: (02) 4987 3108
Fax: (02) 4983 1031

Walk Description

This is the best easy walk in the park and one of the best in the state. There are none of the big uphills that characterise the Barrington Tops, but it covers the most visually attractive scenery, including features of interest

On the approach to Gloucester Tops in the Barrington Tops National Park.

such as spectacular lookouts, the highest peak, swimming holes, good-quality walking tracks, beech trees and subalpine vegetation.

The circuit basically goes around the western and southern edges of the plateau before cutting in by an alpine plain to The Big Hole. Along the way is Careys Peak, where a short track leads to the summit with impressive views over the upper Allyn River.

On the first day of walking, go back up to the main road, turn left and take the first track on the left. This is the Polblue Trail, which connects with the Barrington Trail at a T-intersection at the base of Mt Polblue (1577m) on the edge of the park. Turn right and head south-east down a long slope to the Little Murray picnic area. The track is well graded and good progress can be made. You are now inside the national park. Turn right where the trail heads around two large round mountains that mark the Mt Royal Range. Brumlow Top (1586m) is the highest peak in the entire Barrington Tops area although it resembles a wooded hill. There are some pleasant stream crossings along the way, ideal for rest breaks. The yellow-leafed weed, scotch broom, predominates in the undergrowth throughout summer, and actually looks quite attractive.

Ignore the turn-off to Junction Pool and keep right, following the Barrington Trail along the Mt Royal Range. You can make a minor detour up to the summit of Mt Barrington (1555m) where there are reasonable western views. The Middle Ridge Trail is used by many 4WD enthusiasts to access the national park.

The trail swings to the east, always following the rim of the escarpment. It is now called the Careys Peak Trail and is very easy and pleasant walking to a spur just before Careys Peak. The trail deteriorates here and it's a steep short uphill slog to the grassy clearing on the right. An old hut marks a clearing on the very southerly edge of the plateau. A walking track on the western end climbs for 200m to the top of the lookout. A fence prevents sightseers falling down the steep slope. To the right is the stark, dark green to light green line between dense moist beech rainforest and dry

eucalypt bush on the plateau. The prevailing winds are from the south-west and drop most of their moisture on their way up the slopes.

Most of the Hunter Valley can be seen from this lookout. At night, even the lights of Sydney and Newcastle are visible. On a clear day, you can see as far south as Gospers Mountain in the Wollemi National Park, but usually warm days produce haze, which limits views. Even worse are frequent white-outs, especially in the early morning. This is a perfect place for lunch, but there is no water. Keep an eye out for snakes around here.

Head back out to the Careys Peak Trail and continue east to a turn-off. A gate on the right bars vehicle access to The Corker and the Wombat Creek camping area. A sign tells you that The Big Hole is to the left. On the way is Black Swamp, an open alpine plain surrounded by white eucalypts. Just before you cross a creek that flows out of the swamp, there's an informal picnic and camping area on the right-hand side. After the creek, it's a bit of an uphill before more pleasant level walking. The trail then drops into the Barrington River valley and it's down-hill all the way to The Big Hole, one of the very best camping sites in Australia. The grassy open area is separated from the end of the trail by a barrier. The hole itself is a very deep wide bend in the river, set in pleasant open woodland with plenty of shade.

If the campsite is crowded, there's another place slightly downstream from the boulders at the end of the road. This is a much smaller clearing with a rough walking track that takes you around some rapids directly to The Big Hole. The water is chilly but well worth the effort. Here you can swim in a large pool on top of a plateau more than a kilometre higher than the rest of the Hunter Valley area. A rare species of native pepper, found nowhere else in the state, occurs here among the snow gums.

Spend one or more lazy days here. Exit the area via Bobs Crossing upstream and then the Watergauge Trail up to Beean Beean Plain rejoining the Barrington Trail. A lot of scotch broom and snow gums grow in this section, and the level Beean

Beean Plain itself must be one of the best subalpine walking environments in New South Wales.

To complete the round trip head right after the large uphill to Mt Polblue emerging onto the Barrington Tops Forest Road to the east of the Polblue camping area. This minimises any backtracking.

Other walks in Barrington Tops National Park

As well as the well-known Link Track Walk, there are countless opportunities for short and long walks in the park and its adjoining state forests. Car shuffles can be set up to exploit the height differentials and allow walkers the luxury of descending more than 1000m from the tops to pick-up points in the foothills.

Rocky Crossing Walk (8km, 4 hours)

Walk starts from the Barrington Guest House on the Williams River and heads north up the left bank with several highlights along the way—a natural slippery dip, Lion Rock and the Pool of Reflections. The track links up with Fern Tree Creek Walking Track.

Overnight Walks

If you set up a car shuffle, it's possible to connect the Barrington Tops Circuit and the Link Track with the Mt Nelson Trail so as to exit the plateau to the east via Gloucestor Fall, and finish at Chichester. Allow at least four days for this walk.

The Sandstone Parks

This section outlines some superb walks through this large wilderness area. Four major national parks, state recreation areas and several state forests make up well over a million hectares of eucalypt forest covering the rugged Great Dividing Range. Large tracts of this region are among the highest quality wilderness in the country. The parks are centrally located and easily accessible from Newcastle, Sydney and Wollongong. Public transport allows you to leave the car at home when visiting the main plateau of the Blue Mountains between Mt Victoria and Glenbrook.

Wollemi National Park

Wollemi National Park was declared to protect 492 531ha of a rugged dissected plateau on the north-west fringe of the Sydney Basin. The second-largest in New South Wales, the park is part of a large system of interconnected sandstone landscapes surrounding the Sydney metropolitan area. Wollemi National Park extends from the Singleton–Windsor road west to Rylstone and Kandos, north to Bylong, Denman and Bulga, and south to Bilpin and Kurrajong Heights.

The national park is contiguous with other major conservation areas, including Blue Mountains National Park to the south, Goulburn River National Park to the north, Gardens of Stone National Park in the west, and Yengo National Park and Parr State Recreation Area in the east. Important values of the national park include its spectacular wild and rugged scenery, its geological heritage, its diversity of natural environments, and the occurrence of many threatened native plant and animal species.

Wollemi National Park offers some excellent walking opportunities. The wilderness zone within it is part of a greater area known as the 'Wollemi Wilderness', the largest wilderness declaration in New South Wales. Its size and rugged terrain present outstanding opportunities for the conservation of plant and animal communities in their natural state and the maintenance of natural ecological processes with little or no human interference. Additionally, many of the catchments within the park are both large and pristine. The Colo River valley is one of the largest sandstone canyon systems in Australia and has been identified as one of a number of wild and scenic rivers in New South Wales. The large relatively undisturbed catchment areas of the park provide an extremely important control mechanism for flood mitigation, water supply and water quality maintenance in the Hunter River and Hawkesbury–Nepean catchments. Recent, rigorous endeavours by park authorities has led to the reduction of willow trees from the headwaters of Capertee River, a tributary of the Colo River.

Facts and Figures

Name: Wollemi National Park

Size: 492 531ha (361 000ha gazetted as wilderness)

Enactment: National Park, April 1979 Wilderness areas declared 1999

Visitors: Most visit Newnes, Dunns Swamp, Glow Worm Tunnel, and Wheeney Creek. Other popular areas are Bob Turners Track, Canoe Creek and Glen Davis.

Vegetation: More than 700 species in diverse communities, such as rainforest, heath, swamp and mallee, including 40 rare and endangered plant species and the Wollemi pine (*Wollemia nobilis*)

Wildlife: Dingoes, the eastern grey kangaroo, the red-necked wallaby, numerous nocturnal animals, many endangered species, however feral animals are increasing in numbers

Aboriginal Sites: More than 120 sites have been recorded in the area

Camping: Anywhere—no permits are required. There are official camping areas at Dunns Swamp (formerly known as Kandos Weir), Newnes and Wheeney Creek.

Adjoining Parks: Blue Mountains National Park, Yengo National Park, Goulburn River National Park, Gardens of Stone National Park, Pantoneys Crown Nature Reserve, Parr State Recreation Area, and numerous state forests, including Newnes, Bylong, Ben Bullen, Putty, Coricudgy, Comleroy and Nullo Mountain

Further Information: Blue Mountains National Parks and Wildlife Service District Office The Heritage Centre Govetts Leap Rd Blackheath NSW 2785 Tel:　(02) 4787 8877 Fax:　(02) 4787 8514 Local offices are also at: Upper Hunter–Mudgee Shop 479 Church St Mudgee NSW 2850 Tel:　(02) 6372 7199 Fax:　(02) 6372 7850 and Upper Hunter–Bulga 2156 Putty Rd, Bulga NSW 2330 Tel:　(02) 6574 5275 Fax:　(02) 6574 5274

The Richmond office, which administers the south-eastern part of the national park, can be contacted on (02) 4588 5247.

Further reading: *Wild Places*, by Peter Prineas and Henry Gold, for good background information on Wollemi National Park

Geology

The park's dissected plateau has large volcanic basalt caps on many of the peaks. Some of these peaks, most notably Mt Coricudgy (1257m) and Mt Monundilia (1108m), support pleasant rainforest on top. Nutrient-rich basalt outcrops occur as pockets throughout the area. These support plant communities that are different from the surrounding sandstone areas and provide a more diverse range of species and habitats within the park, albeit in small and mostly disturbed areas. Accordingly, these are sites of considerable conservation interest.

History

More than 120 Aboriginal sites have been recorded here, representing only a small proportion of what could be expected after 12000 years of occupation. A study of these sites is being undertaken to help explain their contemporary significance and earlier traditional functions.

The western border was quickly surveyed and settled by 1840, with farmers making full use of the rich alluvial soils along the Cudgegong and Capertee valleys. In the Wolgan and Baerami valleys, a new resource was discovered: oil shale. By the start of the 20th century, mine shafts were sunk, refineries built and railway tracks laid through the mountains.

Vegetation

The internationally famous Wollemi pine (*Wollemia nobilis*) was discovered by David Noble in the remote Jurassic Canyon in the west of the park. The pine is a very significant species, being a remnant of the pre-flowering Gondwana era (60–200 million years ago) and a previously unknown genus of gymnosperm (cone plant). Wollemi National Park's range of topography, altitude, aspect, fire regime and microclimates has resulted in diverse habitats for native vegetation. For example, the Illawarra and Singleton Coal Measures, which outcrop in the northern escarpment areas of the park, produce deep clay barns that are an important habitat for conserving poorly represented yellow box and ironbark woodland communities. These, in turn, support the threatened regent honeyeater.

The Mellong Swamp on the eastern edge supports a unique assemblage of plants and communities and is, therefore, of great geomorphological and botanical interest. The swamps are important for the conservation of reptiles and invertebrates. Mellong Swamp communities are small areas that are not well conserved in other nearby conservation regions. Wollemi National Park also contains elements of subtropical rainforest at Wheeney Creek, near its south-westernmost point on the coast of New South Wales.

Wildlife

Animal inventories for the Blue Mountains plateau currently record 46 mammals, 235 birds, 55 butterflies, 58 reptiles and 32 amphibians within the park or in close proximity. A number of threatened mammal and bird species have been recorded, such as the brushtail rock wallaby, koala, yellow-bellied glider, broad-headed snake, brushtail phascogale, tiger quoll, turquoise parrot, glossy black cockatoo, and powerful owl.

Facilities

Recreation use is largely unsophisticated and self-reliant, but a small number of sites on the edge of the park, such as at Dunns Swamp, the Colo River area, Wheeney Creek and Newnes, are more developed. The south-eastern section of the park, near the Colo River in particular, is conveniently close to Sydney's north-west.

Activities

Although officially designated a wilderness area, excellent walking is available. The most approachable part is north of Lithgow, about 3 hours from Sydney along the scenic Bells Line of Road. Places to see include the magical Glow Worm Tunnel, the abandoned mining towns of Glen Davis and Newnes and a belt of deep, narrow canyons—many yet to be explored. The park is also popular for horse-riding. Canoeists frequently use the rivers and sometimes this is the only way to get into otherwise inaccessible areas. A canoe trip through the rugged Colo River gorge in the southern part of the park is some 70km long and takes about a week. This sport also comes with its dangers, however: rain upstream can quickly turn the Colo River into a swirling mass of 150 Grade 6 rapids that would almost certainly result in death or at the very least, destruction of the canoe.

Gospers Mountain Walk

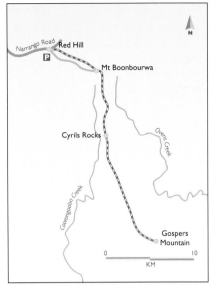

Starting Point: Red Hill, Wollemi National Park
Destination: The summit of Gospers Mountain (847m)
Summary: A long, arduous overnight walk into the heart of the central-western region of the national park. The route goes via Mt Darcy, Wollemi Range and the Army Road.
Attractions: Wild sandstone country, panoramic views over scenic Wollemi National Park
Length: Total distance is 76km
Day 1: Red Hill to Rollen Creek, 8km
Day 2: Rollen Creek to Gospers Mountain, 30km
Day 3: Gospers Mountain to Red Hill, 38km
Time: 3 days
Options: You can continue to Wirraba Trig, or to the Capertee River gorge
Attraction Rating: ★ ★ ★ ★
Fitness: ☒ ☒ ☒ ☒
Maps: LIC (CMA) Coorongooba and Gospers Mountain 1:25 000 topographicals. To access the starting area by car, use the LIC (CMA) Wollemi National Park 1:150 000 Tourist Map.
Access to Starting Point: Take Narrango Road from Rylstone to Red Hill. From Sydney, head to Richmond and Lithgow via the Bells Line of Road, then take Mudgee Road and the turn-off to Kandos and then Rylstone. Travelling time is about 4–5 hours.
Facilities/Amenities: None
Recommended Equipment: Complete self-sufficiency is essential in some wild terrain. Provision for at least 6

Taking a break crossing the Wollemi National Park from west to east.

Dunns Swamp (Kandos Weir) in the Rhylstone area of Wollemi National Park.

litres of water per person for the round trip, especially in hot weather. **Notes:** Do not attempt this walk in summer as there is no water en route

Further Information:
> Shop 479 Church St
> Mudgee NSW 2850
> Tel: (02) 6372 7199
> Fax: (02) 6372 7850

Walk Description

This walk penetrates deep into one of the wildest and most inaccessible areas in the state. No vehicles are permitted along the Army Road. In fact, landowners have recently locked gates along the road, making it easier for park authorities to rehabilitate sections near the Gospers Airstrip.

The object of this walk is to camp on top of Gospers Mountain, a bald basalt-capped residual, and enjoy 360-degree panoramas to the coast, north to the Barrington Tops, and south to the Bells Line of Road ridge. In the foreground is the endless maze of gorges and canyons that make up much of the park. At night the steelworks of Newcastle are clearly visible along with a few million stars.

Walk along the sandy Army Road south-east, then east. The next 8km are quite flat but unfortunately sand causes problems. Ignore the first turn-off on the right. Soon you come to another gate that is usually closed. This is not marked on the map, but after passing through it you are into the Coricudgy State Forest. Ignore the

well-signposted Glen Alice Trail on the right; another sign pointing left confirms that you're on the Army Road.

Continue on to the base of Mt Darcy, where the trail suddenly climbs steeply to the left. Instead, head right behind the signpost on a short trail that climbs slightly and comes out at a beautiful grassy clearing. For wilderness enthusiasts, natural bush clearings can be better campsites than developed camping grounds and this is a fine example. Water may be obtainable from a track that climbs to the north up the slope of Mt Darcy. This is the very upper catchment of Rollen Creek, which eventually flows into the Cudgegong River and then into South Australia via Bourke. Believe it or not, the low hills less than 1km to the south form part of the Great Dividing Range. Water falling on the other side of them flows into the Capertee River, thence the Pacific Ocean via the Hawkesbury River.

Next day, rise early, because what lies ahead is a long trek into the wilderness. Backtrack to the signposted Mt Darcy ascent (Army Road) and begin the gruelling climb up to the 1,079m peak. The road here is quite rocky, making the footing slippery. Continue up the slope as it bends south-east and then north. Then just when you thought it couldn't get any steeper, it does.

The vegetation changes on top, becoming more moist. Despite being on the highest point of the trip, the

views are not that great. The road curves around to the right of the summit and you see a height indicator by a grassy clearing on the left—a good place for a rest. The road continues to climb slightly before accessing the centre of the ridge down to a saddle between Mt Darcy and Mt Duran Duran. The walking is quite pleasant here, marred only by the occasional cesspit. Limited views of cleared agricultural land to the north.

Suddenly, the road heads right and plunges down a 300m hill into the Wollemi National Park, passing some formerly private land on the right. The trail is very steep and constant braking pressure is required. Quite dramatically the green vegetation is left behind and you are among very dry Aussie bush, dominated by heath and sandstone. Travel south along the approximate centre of a ridge that rises and falls considerably, slowing progress. Fortunately, there is not too much sand on the track. Sometimes there are reasonable views, mainly to the east, of domes and pagodas. This is truly desolate country, unsuitable for any commercial activity. Its only inherent value is as pure wilderness.

If it is a cloudless day, you'll need a lot of water along this section for there is little cover. Cyrils Rocks is a nice place for lunch. There are taller trees and a prominent sandstone monolith. Don't bother climbing it for the views are limited by trees on top. The road momentarily branches in two here. The easier option is to head right. The trail gets quite rough after this before improving as it passes through pleasant open woodland.

Continue south to the top of the ridge once more where it is easy walking to a deep saddle. Walk up the other side and around the base of three knolls, the highest of which is 812m. There is a short steep climb to the top, leaving the open stunted vegetation behind. A level track leads south through pleasant bush until the turn-off to Gospers Airstrip (rehabilitated) at the Geebung Ground. To the left lies Mt Wirraba and Putty Road, accessible through private property on the eastern side of the park.

Head right, then left again soon. Gospers Mountain is not visible at this stage, being shielded by a knoll to its west. The trail contours around this knoll to a saddle between the two peaks. A rough trail heads right to the Capertee River gorge.

With Gospers Mountain looming ahead, the trail heads east and approaches the summit to the north. A Sydney Catchment Authority rain-gauge and an old shed containing an old tractor are evidence of former land use. A steep track heads straight up to the trig marker. Camp wherever you want, the most obvious place being right by the trig survey marker (847m). The summit is bare, covered only by grassy tussocks, so it can get windy, but the views are superb. Besides the cleared land in the fore-ground, try to spot anything man-made within the panorama around you. To the south-west is the Capertee River gorge, claimed as the second largest in the world after the Grand Canyon. Within its walls is the historic town of Glen Davis. The last of the great bushfires of early January 1994 started near Gospers Mountain area and spread all the way to Putty Road. Gospers Mountain, originally called Mt Uraterer, was settled in 1877 by the Gosper family, who grazed cattle there. Robert Gosper remained, living like a hermit, when the rest of the family moved away.

Retrace your route to Red Hill. This is a long way, so leave very early. The route could be broken in two by camping at Rollen Creek again.

Pantoneys Crown Walk

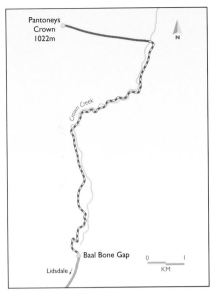

Starting Point: Baal Bone Gap, Ben Bullen State Forest
Destination: The summit of Panto-neys Crown (1022m)
Summary: A difficult walk to the top of a narrow, prominent rock outcrop
Attractions: Spectacular views over the upper Capertee Valley
Length: 24km
Time: 1 long day (9 hours), or 2 days if camping on the summit
Attraction Rating: ★ ★ ★ ★
Fitness: ◪ ◪ ◪ ◪
Maps: LIC (CMA) Ben Bullen 1:25 000 topographical. Cullen Bullen 1:25 000 or Wollemi National Park 1:150 000 map are useful for vehicle access to Baal Bone Gap.
Access to Starting Point: Access is

through a network of state forestry trails north of Lithgow. A 4WD or sedan with good clearance will be an advantage here as the trails can be rough. Take the Great Western Highway north and turn onto Mudgee Road. After you pass the power station to Lidsdale, turn right to Newnes. All turn-offs are signposted. Just before you get to Wolgan Gap, turn left onto an unmarked vehicle track through a gate and follow the upper Coxs River through rural land to the Great Dividing Range. Head left at a T-intersection where the trail passes through dry sclerophyll state forest north. Ignore a minor turn-off on the right. The track descends steeply to a short incline to pass a camp clearing on the right and emerge on the Baal Bone Gap road. Turn right here where there's a short rise to the Pressure Reducing Station and the locked gate on the top of the cliffs. There is plenty of room to park the car. Pantoneys Crown is clearly visible from here, dominating the valley.
Facilities/Amenities: None
Recommended Equipment: Plenty of water
Notes: This walk is actually within the Pantoneys Crown Nature Reserve, not the Wollemi National Park, although the summit looks across the Capertee Valley to the Gardens of Stone and Wollemi National Park
Further Information:
  Shop 479 Church St
  Mudgee NSW 2850
  Tel: (02) 6372 7199
  Fax: (02) 6372 7850

Walk Description

Pantoneys Crown is an isolated 1km-long plateau in the outer reaches of the vast Capertee River gorge. Its prominence from any vantage point in the area makes it an alluring goal for experienced walkers. Only 150m wide and shaped like a cliff-lined fortress, it offers commanding views over Glen Davis, Airly Turret and the western boundary of the Wollemi National Park. Numerous wedge-tailed eagles soar from their nests on the summit.

The walk is strenuous, with two major climbs, one to the summit and one to return to the vehicle at day's end. In addition, the cliffs surrounding

Rest break at Genowlan Point near Airly Turret, overlooking Capertee Valley.

Walking down the Capertee River gorge near Myril Creek.

the crown are largely unbroken and only at each end are they low enough to allow bushwalkers access to scramble to the top. Those uncomfortable on vertical rock ledges will not be able to complete the walk. There is no formal walking trail from Crown Creek to the plateau, so good navigation skills are necessary.

Leave early if driving from Sydney, or stay at a guesthouse at Capertee the night before the walk. Bruce Jeffries, a property owner on the escarpment just below Pearsons Lookout south of Capertee, has a superb guesthouse that walkers can use as a central base from which to explore the western part of the park. Phone (02) 6359 0194 for details.

Walk down the road through the cliff pass, descending into the Crown Creek valley and quickly losing more than 300m in altitude. You enter immediately into the Pantoneys Crown Nature Reserve. It is flat easy walking, and crosses the creek occasionally, which can be dry after periods of drought. The hills on either side obstruct the view of Pantoneys Crown until you leave the road to climb. At a locked gate and a signpost, you leave the nature reserve.

The valley opens up and passes through old cleared pastoral land, and you eventually see the top of

Pantoneys Crown on the left (west). Here you are almost flush with the northern end of it. Leave the road, cross the eroded Crown Creek bed and head for a steep spur on the other side. Follow animal tracks gradually up the spur to reach the rocky volcanic crest. It's then a matter of heading for the northern end along the ridge by the path of least resistance. The ridge becomes indistinct and you must use a visual bearing to stay oriented. Some scrub-bashing near the base of the cliffs is necessary, as you must cross some shallow gullies. As you near the northern end, a faint walking track becomes more defined.

There is a pass through the rocks here and some scrambling is required to attain a ledge about halfway up with great views over the Capertee Valley. This is a good spot for a break. To reach the very top of the plateau, head west initially, traversing before climbing steeply again to reach the base of more cliffs. The path is now indistinct because of rock ledges. Go right a few metres and then climb up a ledge, heading left to a small slanting chimney. The rock becomes steeper at the top. This is the most difficult section. The rock is the iron-based pagoda terrace formation common in the area and the little handholds and footholds here can easily break away. This wall is only about 7m high and is the last obstacle to the summit. On top, you then gain great views to the west. Take some time to explore the dry plateau top. People camping here are sometimes rewarded with early morning low cloud over the Capertee Valley. At the southern end of the crown are pagoda stone formations where wedge-tailed eagle nests are common.

Return to the car park via the same route, taking care to keep due east when heading down to the road from the base of the cliffs. A maze of gullies and ridges will no doubt confuse but the vegetation is sparse and as long as you keep going east, you have to intercept the north/south road by Crown Creek. The final ascent of Baal Bone Gap will be gruelling, especially if you have an overnight pack.

Wolgan River–Capertee River Circuit

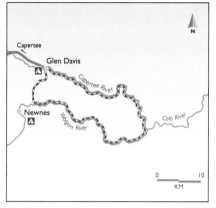

Starting Point: Newnes, Wollemi National Park
Destination: Colo River
Summary: Mainly river walking, exploring both the lower Wolgan and Capertee gorges, but there is one high-level traverse over the Pipeline Track involving a significant gain in altitude
Attractions: Spectacular wild gorge country, the Pipeline Track, clifftop views, historic ruins
Length: 68km
Time: 4–6 days
Options: Set up a car shuffle to avoid a climb over the Pipeline Track back to Newnes. If only one car is being used, walk in an anti-clockwise direction so that the hardest walking is left until the pack is relatively empty.
Attraction Rating: ★ ★ ★ ★ ★
Fitness: ◼ ◼ ◼ ◼
Maps: LIC (CMA) Mt Morgan, Gospers Mountain and Ben Bullen 1:25 000 topographicals. The Wollemi National Park 1:150 000 topographical is useful for road access to Newnes.
Access to Starting Point: Newnes is accessed via Lithgow and Lidsdale
Facilities/Amenities: Car-camping area at Newnes. Water is available from a camping ground at Glen Davis. Toilets are provided too, but otherwise there are no facilities. Campsites can be found anywhere, preferably at the confluence with freshwater creeks that flow into the valleys.
Recommended Equipment: Sandals for river walking, water purifier
Notes: Learn to identify quicksand as there are pockets along the lower Capertee that significantly slow down progress. Beware of red-bellied black snakes in the lower Wolgan River

regions. If camping by the lower Capertee River, boil all water or use purification tablets. Preferably fill water containers at side creeks, such as Gospers Creek and Freshwater Creek. The owner's permission at 'The Poplars', Glen Davis, must be obtained before passing through.

Further Information:

Shop 479 Church St
Mudgee NSW 2850
Tel: (02) 6372 7199
Fax: (02) 6372 7850

Walk Description

For total wilderness atmosphere, there are few places that compare with the lower Wolgan and Capertee valleys. Despite walking along the banks of rivers, the views to the cliffs on either side are awe-inspiring at every step. There are some gorgeous camp clearings, the best being at:

- The confluence of Rocky Creek and the Wolgan River (good site)
- The confluence of Deanes Creek and Rocky Creek (off the route) (excellent site)
- Wolgan River just upstream from its confluence with Annie Rowan Creek (excellent flat grassy area)
- The confluence of Annie Rowan Creek and Wolgan River (good site)
- The confluence of Wolgan River and Capertee River (average site)
- Capertee River downstream from its confluence with Gospers Creek (excellent site with large pool)
- Capertee River just upstream from its confluence with Dingo Creek (excellent site with picturesque swimming hole)
- Capertee River at its confluence with Freshwater Creek (good site with pool).

From Newnes, cross the river and head downstream on the old fire trail that follows the southern bank. The river is normally quite shallow with a sandy bottom and there are very few pools. You soon come to the historic ruins of the mine shafts and oil shale processing plant. When camping in the Wolgan or Capertee valleys, you will notice light oily black rocks on the ground. If you throw these on the fire, they burn quite brightly.

When you've finished exploring the ruins, continue downstream where the trail follows the river to Rocky Creek. Some height gains will be necessary to overcome spurs—these will be gruelling with a fully laden pack. The old abandoned fire trail continues almost to the junction with the Capertee River, although the topographical map depicts it petering out before Rocky Creek. At this point, there's a large wash-out to be negotiated. Head right (west) briefly to rejoin the trail.

After Rocky Creek, the old trail fords the river and passes through pleasant bushland along the northern bank. At one section it becomes completely overgrown—if in doubt stay close to the river. The trail becomes more prominent and fords the river at a great flat grassy clearing ideal for camping, although there is no fresh water or swimming hole.

From here the trail rises sharply and passes over another spur to descend into the Annie Rowan Creek valley. This was also formerly private property, but not much is left except long grass. Beware of red-bellied black snakes in this whole region. They are quite common but, fortunately, they are timid and move away when approached. Goannas are also common.

The trail continues across the deep gully of Annie Rowan Creek a few hundred metres south-west of the Wolgan River. Here the gorge starts to close in. It is faster to travel along the old trail than the riverbed as there is a lot of quicksand to negotiate. The trail eventually peters out and soon you come to the confluence with the Capertee River gorge. This is a deeper watercourse, although it too can be flat, shallow and sandy at times. This is the start of the mighty Colo River that drains the entire southern half of the Wollemi National Park.

Turn left up the Capertee River, following the gorge as it winds north. There is a lot of quicksand here and walkers might find it easier to stay on the banks. There are occasional nice pools should you fancy a swim.

Progress is slow through this completely trackless territory. The scenery is spectacular, but few people have seen it. When the river is in flood, kayakers, rafters and li-loers use the water, although passage is quite dangerous over the many rapids. There are also numerous block-ups to negotiate. Sandals may be handy for walking in the water, where possible.

When the gorge heads west at the confluence with Myril Creek, you join the road again. A particularly nice campsite is between Myril Creek and Dingo Creek. Plan to arrive at Glen Davis early in the morning after camping at the confluence with Freshwater Creek. There is a sandy bank on the northern side of a deep pool. Cross some old private property and head over a steep spur where the road leads across a paddock down toward Goorangooba Creek.

Traverse more private property at 'The Poplars' and leave the national

Deanes Lookout in the Wolgan Valley, Wollemi National Park.

Tough terrain in the upper Rocky Creek valley, Wollemi National Park.

park at Glen Davis. There are some more industrial ruins here from the oil shale refining days. Take the Pipeline Track up Green Gully to the clifftops to regain the Wolgan Valley—terrific views from the top. Allow a full day to cross over from one gorge to the next.

Glen Davis to Culoul Range Walk

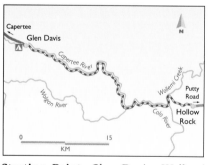

Starting Point: Glen Davis, Wollemi National Park
Destination: Hollow Rock (Culoul Range)
Summary: A full traverse of Wollemi National Park from west to east, following the lower Capertee River gorge and the Colo River to its confluence with Wollemi Creek
Attractions: Spectacular cliff-lined gorges, views from Culoul Range
Length: 49km
Time: 5–7 days
Options: This walk could also start from Newnes
Attraction Rating: ★ ★ ★ ★ ★

Fitness: ☒ ☒ ☒
Maps: LIC (CMA) Mt Morgan, Gospers Mountain and Six Brothers 1:25 000 topographicals
Access to Starting Point: The easiest access to the area is from Glen Davis via Lithgow and Capertee. Park at the well-developed camping ground.
Facilities/Amenities: Car-camping facilities, including an amenities block, toilets, BBQs, bins and tables, are provided at Glen Davis. Otherwise, it's all remote bush-camping by the rivers. Good campsites can be found anywhere, preferably at the confluence with freshwater creeks.
Recommended Equipment: Sandals for river walking
Notes: Leave the car at the end of Culoul Range Road, accessible from the Putty Road north of Lithgow. This access track is signposted with a very small sign. Access in dry weather only. When camping on the lower Capertee River, boil all water or use purification tablets. Preferably fill water containers at the side creeks, such as Gospers Creek and Freshwater Creek. Obtain the owner's permission at 'The Poplars', Glen Davis, before passing through. Learn to identify quicksand as there are pockets of it along the lower Capertee.
Further Information:
Shop 479 Church St
Mudgee NSW 2850
Tel: (02) 6372 7199
Fax: (02) 6372 7850

Walk Description

This walk crosses through Wollemi National Park via the only practical route: following the Capertee River, Colo River and Wollemi Creek watercourses. Glen Davis is an historic mining town set in a very rugged gorge of the Capertee River. The Australian film *The Chain Reaction* was shot on location at Glen Davis using the ghost town and industrial ruins as backdrop.

Since the entire trail is alongside a river, there are no great uphills or downhills and all the way are views up to the spectacular cliffs that line this majestic valley. Good camping areas are at:

• Capertee River at its confluence with Freshwater Creek (good site with pool)
• Capertee River just downstream from its confluence with Myril Creek (excellent site with picturesque swimming hole)
• Capertee River downstream from its confluence with Gospers Creek (excellent site with large pool)
• Colo River just upstream from its confluence with Girribung Creek (where it turns from south to east)
• Wollemi Creek just upstream from its confluence with the Colo River (several options).

Continue through the valley to Glen Davis. Signs at the large white gate warn against trespassing, but with permission from the owners, who live in a large old estate house behind you, walk straight through the property before heading briefly left and then right onto a concrete road that leads due west down the gorge. This road passes through derelict refinery ruins—a ghost complex with towering orange cliffs in the background. At the end of this tarmac is a giant black slagheap. If you can manage the slippery scramble to the top, you'll be rewarded with fine views over the Capertee Valley backed by Mt Gundangaroo (789m). This is a perfect place for photographs. It is difficult to know what is the main attraction. Certainly the derelict industrial complex and mining town is a central feature but so is the steep gorge in which Glen Davis is located.

As you round the northern side of the slagheap, the bush closes in and you are soon in the Wollemi National Park. Continue east parallel with the Capertee River to the left. The walking is quite easy, the surface being dominated by black oil shale. Collect a few samples for the night's campfire. It burns brighter than wood.

You soon come to a gate signposted as Goorangooba Station. Pass through a large cleared area where some horses roam. It seems that no-one lives here permanently. Sometimes the army uses this valley for field training. To the left, Goorangooba Creek gorge joins with the Capertee. Some of the cliffs visible here are massive. Old farm tracks head down to the water.

Keep right, passing some fences and walking uphill to the south-eastern corner of the cleared area. The trail continues to climb quite steeply. Sandstone rocks dominate the surface. After the short climb, the track contours over a spur past some huge boulders before descending to the river again. There are some great grassy clearings here—some showing evidence of campfires. There is also a large pool farther along, just before a block-up that makes an ideal place for lunch and a swim. When the trail crosses Freshwater Creek, fill up the water bottles. Numerous pools can be found along this section.

If you left early enough, the first night's camp could be 1km downstream of Myril Creek by a beautiful open pool. Do not rely on water in Myril Creek as it can be dry. Wild cattle roam this area. The trail peters out to the west of Myril Creek but it's fairly easy going through open woodland on the southern bank. Then the river flattens out and it can be faster to walk on the wide sand bed. Once the gorge turns north-east at the confluence with Myril Creek, watch out for the camping spot.

Try to get as far down the gorge as possible each day if you plan to complete the walk in five days. If you push on at a leisurely pace there shouldn't be too much pressure about getting up early or walking until dusk. Remember progress can be slow in negotiating the many obstacles of this trackless terrain, such as boulder block-ups, thick undergrowth and patches of deep quicksand. Sandals might be good for walking in the river.

The terrain changes once more when the Wolgan River meets the Capertee River and the Colo River officially begins. The riverbed becomes very flat here and the sides of the gorge are extremely steep. The walking is fairly easy here, except for the wet parts. Walkers in the 1930s experienced a different riverbed when they were exploring this region. Alex Colley recalls that there was a lot of tangled undergrowth to negotiate. This has since been covered with sand as a result of all the tree-clearing in the upper Capertee Valley. Despite this, bushwalkers then made the journey from Glen Davis to Kurrajong in about 12 days.

At this stage you are in the deepest part of the wilderness and it is more than a day's walk to civilisation in any direction. Continuing east, the Colo River gorge starts to curve significantly before joining Wollemi Creek in a gigantic amphitheatre. As you head left up Wollemi Creek, several changes occur: there's not as much sand, the pools are deep and the water dark. A lot of boulder-hopping will be necessary. You might have to carry your backpack through deep pools to access the other side of the prominent hairpin bend.

At about grid reference 696244 on the Six Brothers topographical map, a walking track heads up the steep slope to the Culoul Range. It starts opposite a notably large beach just downstream from a long deep pool with rock ledges on the northern bank. Rock cairns mark the way, with a particularly large one sitting on top of boulders at the start. The spot might be difficult to find if you don't know what you're looking for. When organising the car shuffle, it might be a good idea to spend a day exploring the route from the end of Culoul Range Road to Wollemi Creek. Some tracknotes on this area are given in the Wollemi Creek Circuit walk in this book. The Six Brothers topographical map is essential here, although the walking track isn't marked. Once on it, the exit track is fairly easy to follow as it weaves up steeply between rock ledges to attain a sharp crest before traversing east. Some tricky ledge-scrambling is then necessary as you approach the top, and you will have to haul the packs separately. Once over the rim, a faint pad contours right to a rock platform with superb views over Wollemi Creek's hairpin bend and the confluence with the Colo River.

From here, it takes about 1.5 hours to reach the car near Hollow Rock. A cairned route leads back to the old Culoul Range fire trail and then to Hollow Rock.

Glow Worm Tunnel Circuit

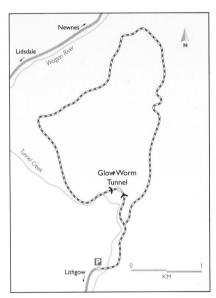

Starting Point: Glow Worm Tunnel Road (at vehicle barrier), Wollemi National Park

Destination: Glow Worm Tunnel

Summary: A circuit encompassing the tunnel and base of the cliffs lining the Wolgan Valley, returning via Old Coach Road

Attractions: Views, fern gullies, glow-worms, pagoda rock formations

Length: 7.5km

Time: 3 hours

Options: This loop can also commence at the Wolgan River. Access from the Wolgan Valley Road is via the concrete ford (about 7km back from Newnes camping area).

Attraction Rating: ★★★

Fitness: ☒☒

Maps: LIC (CMA) Ben Bullen and Cullen Bullen 1:25 000 topographicals

The glow worms that inhabit an old railway tunnel are a popular attraction in the Wollemi National Park.

Access to Starting Point: Turn off the Bells Line of Road at Clarence (Zigzag Railway) and follow the gravel road through Newnes State Forest for 34km. Glow Worm Tunnel parking area is 3km past the junction of the Glow Worm Tunnel Road and Old Coach Road. It is a 5km walk to the Glow Worm Tunnel along the original railway formation. Alternatively, drive to the vehicle barrier and walk 1km to the tunnel. The railway formation is narrow and there is limited parking beyond the car parking area at the Wollemi National Park boundary.

Facilities/Amenities: None

Recommended Equipment: A torch is essential in the tunnel area

Notes: Do not shine a torch on the glow worms themselves

Further Information:
Blue Mountains National Parks
and Wildlife Service District Office
The Heritage Centre
Govett's Leap Rd
Blackheath NSW 2785
Tel: (02) 4787 8877
Fax: (02) 4787 8514

Walk Description

From the vehicle barrier, walk north along the historic Glow Worm Tunnel, then continue along the Wolgan Valley Railway at the base of the cliffs as far as the Old Coach Road and return via this and the Pagoda Track. Large sections of the road have been washed away down the embankment of Tunnel Creek. There is some dramatic country here, as the track crosses an old reservoir. The final approach to the tunnel is flat and surrounded by thousands of ferns. The narrow shallow canyon is a perfect backdrop for photographers.

The Glow Worm Tunnel was built by the Commonwealth Oil Corporation Limited as part of an 83km railway link between Newnes Junction and the Wolgan Valley mines at Newnes. The development of Newnes in the Wolgan Valley centred on the shale oil mining complex established in 1906. Because the only access to the Wolgan Valley in 1897 was via the present Lidsdale road, the company engaged Mr Henry Dean to survey and construct a railway.

In November 1907, a single-track railway from Newnes Junction at Clarence to Newnes in the Wolgan Valley was completed. The difference in elevation from Newnes Junction to Newnes is more than 700m, so to facilitate this drop, tight curves and grades of 1:25 were constructed. Two tunnels also had to be built; Number 2 Tunnel, called 'Bell's Grotto', is the longer of the two. By 1912, the company had gone into liquidation. The rails were dismantled during World War II, cut up and used for beach defences in Europe.

The mouth of the tunnel is a great site as you approach it, a dark hole through the ferns, reminiscent of an Indiana Jones movie. The tunnel is curved, so have a torch ready and walk in about 200m, where it becomes pitch black and there is no light visible from either end. Allow about 10 minutes for your eyes to adjust so you can fully appreciate the spectacle. Even though you are inside a mountain, it looks as if you are staring at a cloudless night sky with myriad blue-white stars.

The glow-worms are harmless, about 2–3cm long with a luminous bulb on one end. Close inspection reveals that they attach themselves to the walls and ceiling in spun silk cocoons. They belong to the order of flies (diptera) and their scientific name is *Arachnocampa richardsae*. Glow-worm flies are known as fungus gnats. The cocoons and webs contain minute droplets of a sticky silky substance used to trap small insects such as mosquitoes. The glow, formerly called bioluminescence, is the result of a chemical reaction between the glow-worm's waste products and oxygen. The glow comes from the enlarged tips on the insect's four excretory outlets. The more oxygen supplied to these outlets, the brighter they glow. Shining torches directly on them will make their light go out.

From the larval stage, the insect changes into a pupa. When about to pupate, the larvae shrink in size, become translucent and shed their skin. Adults emerge after 12 days and can glow until they mate. Three weeks after the eggs are laid, the larvae hatch and the process starts over again. Both male and female larvae glow. Adults can also glow, but once the egg-laying starts, females seldom do.

A pretty little grotto lies just on the other side of the tunnel. There aren't as many ferns here but the place is very sheltered. Bring your own water because the stream here is saturated with rust from the remains of the railway. A short walking track heads upstream to the left. The area here is quite picturesque, but very sensitive because of soft wet soils.

When you've finished exploring the grotto, head right along the base of the cliffs where is it level walking all the way around the mountain. Eventually you come to the signposted intersection with Coach Road. Turn right and climb south up to the top of the plateau. There are extensive views along here, especially from the top of the many rock outcrops. Be careful when climbing these, as the thin protruding layers are brittle. Take the

Pagoda walking track to descend to the Glow Worm Tunnel Road shortly before the vehicle barrier.

Wollemi Creek Circuit

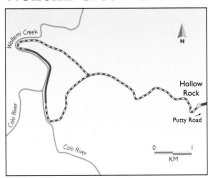

Starting Point: Hollow Rock (Culoul Range), Wollemi National Park
Destination: The confluence of the Colo River and Wollemi Creek
Summary: A loop through some wild terrain for experienced walkers only
Attractions: Magnificent cliff-lined gorge country, beautiful swimming holes, trackless terrain where few people have ventured
Length: 12km
Time: 1 full day
Options: The walk can also be done in reverse, although the exit point may be hard to find. Another route lies up Boorai Ridge to the south.
Attraction Rating: ★ ★ ★ ★
Fitness: ◪ ◪ ◪ ◪
Maps: LIC (CMA) Six Brothers 1:25 000 topographical
Access to Starting Point: Travel north along Putty Road from Windsor. Turn left 19km north of Colo Heights, on a dry-weather 2WD dirt road signposted as Culoul Range. Be careful not to take the Grassy Hill track to the south. A turning circle and barrier are located at Hollow Rock.
Facilities/Amenities: A picnic table is located along the Glow Worm Tunnel Road. Nearest shops are in Lithgow.
Recommended Equipment: Map and compass are absolutely essential in this trackless terrain. A GPS receiver might also be handy. A 20–30m length of rope could help in negotiating the many ledges on the approach and exit from the gorges. Sandals might allow more comfortable river walking.
Notes: This walk is for the very experienced only. It is easy to get lost in such remote country.

Further Information:
National Parks and Wildlife Service
2156 Putty Rd
Bulga NSW 2330
Tel: (02) 6574 5275
Fax: (02) 6574 5274
Contact the Richmond office, which administers the south-eastern part of the national park, on (02) 4588 5247.

Walk Description
At the Hollow Rock car park at Culoul Range, a sign says 'Wollemi Creek— Experienced Walkers Only'. This is a confusing piece of information as the fire trail that continues actually leads to clifftops over the Colo River, well to the south of Wollemi Creek. Before starting this tough walk, head up to Hollow Rock to survey the daunting terrain you are about to go through.

From the barrier, continue down the trail as it descends and curves around Hollow Rock. As it straightens out and starts to climb, curving very gently to the left, watch out for an overgrown trail on the right. A large log has been placed across the track. This is the route to Wollemi Creek, which you will be using to return to Hollow Rock.

Continue left on the main graded fire trail, which eventually ends at a clearing that serves as a makeshift helicopter landing pad. This section of the trail is not marked on the topographical map. At this point, the route to the Colo River enters completely trackless terrain. Continue on the ridge and head left down a small gully. This eventually turns into a major watercourse that effectively acts as a ramp allowing access to the Colo River. The boulders are mossy and slippery and call for extreme care.

As you descend, the creek bed gets steeper and progress gets slower. At the very end, some massive boulders must be negotiated and a rope might come in handy. It should take about two hours from Hollow Rock to reach the Colo River. Note this point if you need to come up this way again. Once on the Colo River bed, there are some sandy beaches and pools to relax.

Leave the gorge via Wollemi Creek. Simply head upstream to the spectacular open amphitheatre confluence between Wollemi Creek and the Colo

By the Colo River at the end of the T3 walking track, Wollemi National Park.

River. In the mid-1990s, a hermit was found dead here after breaking a leg. He had written 'HELP' in the sand so aircraft might be able to spot him but given the remoteness of the area, this was a forlorn hope.

As you head left up Wollemi Creek, several changes occur: there's not as much sand, the pools are deep and the water dark. A lot of boulder-hopping will be necessary. You might have to carry your backpack through deep pools to access the other side of the prominent hairpin bend.

At about grid reference 696244 on the Six Brothers topographical map, a walking track heads up the steep slope to the Culoul Range. It starts opposite a notably large beach just downstream from a long deep pool with rock ledges on the northern bank. Rock cairns mark the way, with a particularly large one sitting on top of the boulders at the bottom.

The spot might be difficult to find if you don't know what you're looking for. Some ledge-scrambling is once again necessary near the top and packs will have to be handled separately. At the top of the rim, a track leads right to a rock platform with superb views over Wollemi Creek's hairpin bend and the confluence with the Colo River. From here, it takes about 1.5 hours to reach the car near Hollow Rock. A cairned route leads back to the old fire trail for the return walk.

Canoe Creek Circuit

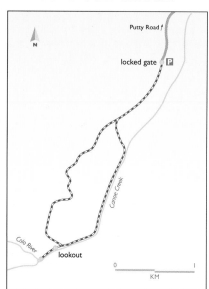

Starting Point: A locked gate on the Alidade Hill fire trail, Wollemi National Park
Destination: Colo River
Summary: A loop through spectacular gorge scenery to access a beautiful swimming spot
Attractions: Views, a prominent hairpin bend in Colo River, a large beach
Length: 7km
Time: Half a day
Options: The route can also be done in an anti-clockwise direction. In summer, walkers may wish to camp on the prominent beach on the inside of the rim, while in winter the rock ledges on the rim of the gorge may be more suitable as camping areas.
Attraction Rating: ★ ★ ★ ★

Fitness: ❌ ❌ ❌
Maps: LIC (CMA) Colo Heights 1:25 000 topographical
Access to Starting Point: Drive north along Putty Road from Windsor and turn left 16km after Colo Heights at a low-key signposted turn-off called Grassy Hill
Facilities/Amenities: None
Recommended Equipment: Swimming gear
Notes: This place is popular on summer holiday weekends, so avoid such times if you seek peace and quiet
Further Information:
National Parks and Wildlife Service
2156 Putty Rd
Bulga NSW 2330
Tel: (02) 6574 5275
Fax: (02) 6574 5274
Contact the Richmond office, which administers the south-eastern part of the park, on (02) 4588 5247.

Walk Description

A locked gate on the Alidade Hill fire trail blocks further vehicle access about 7.5km from Putty Road. From here, walk south along the road until you come to a large clearing. A small 4WD track drops down steeply to the left but soon peters out. Follow the Canoe Creek Valley for an hour until you come to the confluence with the Colo River. Just before this, the trail heads up slightly and you can follow a walking track to a small rock platform overlooking the hairpin with its magnificent beach. This is the place Total Environment Centre director Milo Dunphy, son of famous conservationist, Myles Dunphy, took Premier Neville Wran to in 1979 just after the government committed to declaring the Wollemi National Park.

The beach by the river is a great place to relax for a few hours in the hottest part of the day. Fresh water is available from Canoe Creek just upstream from the confluence.

To return to the car, head back up Canoe Creek for 300m before turning left up the steep side to regain the fire trail at the top. The path is well trodden and relatively easy to follow. Once reaching the fire trail, head right and follow the road as it contours around the side of a hill, back to the locked gate and car park.

The Lower Colo River Walk

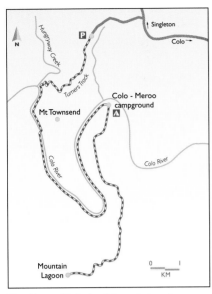

Starting Point: Mountain Lagoon, Wollemi National Park

Destination: Bob Turners Track

Summary: An easy river walk along the lower Colo River, using a car shuffle to avoid backtracking

Attractions: A spectacular cliff-lined gorge, swimming holes, wilderness atmosphere close to Sydney

Length: 19km

Time: 1 full day or 2 half days

Options: A shorter alternative is to exit at the confluence of Tootie Creek and the Colo River, using the T3 walking track to form a circuit back to the starting point and avoiding the need for a car shuffle

Attraction Rating: ★ ★ ★

Fitness: ◨ ◨

Maps: LIC (CMA) Colo Heights and Mountain Lagoon 1:25000 topographicals

Access to Starting Point: Mountain Lagoon is accessed by travelling to Richmond and then the Bells Line of Road. At Bilpin, a signposted right turn leads to Mountain Lagoon via Mountain Lagoon Road. At Mountain Lagoon, take Sams Way around the lagoon and a fire trail to the north leading to Gospers Ridge. Here there's a locked gate up a slope to the right. Bob Turners Track is accessed by travelling up Putty Road from Windsor to Colo Heights and turning left on the signposted track.

Facilities/Amenities: Camping area with toilets at Colo–Meroo. There are plenty of bush-camping sites, with a particularly nice one at the Hungry-way Creek junction.

Recommended Equipment: Sandals for river walking

Notes: Bob Turners Track and the T3 walking tracks are not marked on the topographical. The walk is taken in this direction because there's a 300m difference in altitude between start and end points.

Further Information:

Bulga National Parks and Wildlife Service office

2156 Putty Rd, Bulga NSW 2330

Tel: (02) 6574 5275

Fax: (02) 6574 5274

Contact the Richmond office, which administers the south-eastern part of the park, on (02) 4588 5247.

Walk Description

A simple walk along Gospers Ridge and then Mailes Ridge to the Meroo Trig and descend to the Colo River at the camping area. This is the most easterly section of the Colo River gorge that's protected in the Wollemi National Park. Head upstream to Tootie Creek and exit at Hungryway Creek on the Bob Turners Track.

Other walks in Wollemi National Park

This great national park contains virtually unlimited opportunities for walking, especially for those with a sense of adventure. Trackless regions for overnight exploration exist in the spectacular Widden Valley which is dominated by Wedding Cake Mountain, the canyons near Nullo Mountain, the Wollangambe wilderness, and the ridges north of the Mt Darcy and Tootie areas. Popular areas for shorter day walks include Deep Pass on the Newnes plateau, Dunns Swamp, Upper Colo and Wheeney Creek.

Since much of Wollemi National Park is dissected by sheer cliffs and steep narrow canyons, rope skills for climbing and descending are essential on pioneering expeditions. Remote destinations worth investigating are:

- Upper Wirraba Creek to a highly unusual cone-shaped knoll that sits in the middle of the valley
- A traverse of Wollemi Creek from Putty Road or Hunter Range

- The junction of the Colo River and Wollangambe River from Putty Road, using an unnamed creek to descend to the Colo River from the end of the ridge track
- Mt Coricudgy as a staging area for walks radiating along ridges or through remote canyons.

Walkers should be adept navigators and take into account safety issues and the potential for very slow progress when planning trips.

To the north, Goulburn River National Park adjoins Wollemi in the Hunter Valley. This 70 161ha national park is the northernmost limit of the sandstone and some walking opportunities extend from the Springvale to Merriwa road and along the Goulburn River itself. Consult the Mt Misery and Killoe topographical maps at:

National Parks and Wildlife Service

Shop 479, Church St

Mudgee NSW 2850

Tel: (02) 6372 7199

Fax: (02) 6372 7850

Blue Mountains National Park

Those who walk the length of Narrow Neck will pass a small track on the right toward the end called Dunphys Pass. It was named after the extraordinary man whose vision it was to protect the Blue Mountains from logging, mining, commercialisation, agriculture, urbanisation and other forms of development. Myles Dunphy (1891–1985) had to wait almost 30 years after he formally proposed the idea and by then the first advances of civilisation were already in evidence.

Today, the mining towns are ghost towns, agricultural land is slowly being rehabilitated, mine shafts are closed and the coal and shale railway lines have been dismantled. There are thousands of hectares of untouched land, the closest true wilderness areas to Sydney. Whatever you wish for in a walk, every degree of difficulty, you can find here.

The beauty of the Blue Mountains is that it is the only place in New South Wales where you can catch a train up to 1000m above sea level and walk all the way down to another train station just 30m in altitude. If you prefer to see some landscape you can take it easy and stick mainly to the flat plateaus and clifftops around Katoomba, Leura and Blackheath. On the other hand, you can drop down into the valleys, camp by a river and walk down to the plain where you can catch a train home again.

The walks in this section are by no means a comprehensive list of the trails available for exploring. Get some experience, then buy some maps and design your own walks. The state forests on the western boundaries and Kanangra–Boyd National Park are criss-crossed by hundreds of kilometres of disused trails offering many opportunities for adventure.

Facts and Figures

Name: Blue Mountains National Park
Size: 24 7156ha
Enactment: 1959
Visitors: More than 4 million a year
Aboriginal Sites: More than 100 dating back 22 000 years
Vegetation: Well over 10 000 species in 40 separate communities
Wildlife: 27 marsupial species, 2 monotremes, 17 other mammal species, 98 types of reptiles and more than 200 bird species have been recorded
Camping: There is an official car-camping ground at Euroka Clearing (fees apply). Car-camping also at Murphys Glen, Woodford and Ingar from Wentworth Falls. Elsewhere bush-camping is permitted in most places. There are no fees or permits required for this park.
Adjoining Parks: Kanangra–Boyd National Park, Wollemi National Park, Nattai National Park, Burragorang State Recreation Area, Thirlmere Lakes National Park, Bents Basin State Recreation Area, Abercrombie River National Park, Gulguer Nature Reserve and many state forests on western perimeter
Further Information:
The Heritage Centre
Govett's Leap Rd
Blackheath NSW 2785
Tel: (02) 4787 8877
The visitors' centre is managed by the National Parks and Wildlife Service, and is open from 9.00am to 4.30pm

daily. The centre has an educational display on the wildlife, Aboriginal and European history and geology of the Blue Mountains. In the shop, you can buy maps, brochures, books and gifts. Bookings for the 'Discovery: walks, talks and tours' program are also taken here.

Other National Parks and Wildlife Service visitors' centres with shops and tours are located at:
- Hartley Historic Site
  Hartley NSW 2790
  Tel: (02) 6355 2117 (open from 10.00am–1.00pm and 2.00pm–5.00pm daily, except Wednesday)
- Bowmans Cottage
  370 Windsor Rd
  Richmond NSW 2753
  Tel: (02) 4588 5247, (open from 9.00am–12.30pm and 1.30pm–5.00pm weekdays
- National Parks Shop
  38 Ross St, Oberon NSW 2787
  Tel: (02) 6336 1972 (open from 9.00am–4.30pm weekdays)

Caving permits are available from the National Parks and Wildlife Service by phoning (02) 6336 1972 (Oberon office). Enquire about four weeks before the expedition.

Two Blue Mountains Tourism Authority visitors' centres are at Glenbrook and Katoomba. The Glenbrook centre is on the Great Western Highway next to the Glenbrook cinema; the Katoomba office is at Echo Point. These offices are more able to give information on accommodation and transport than on walking trails. Call (02) 4739 6266 for more details.

Further Reading: For background information on the Blue Mountains National Park, read *Wild Places* by Peter Prineas and Henry Gold. For the lower Blue Mountains, *A History of the Blue Labyrinth*, by Bruce Cameron. Two great books on the fascinating early bushwalking and conservation history of the Blue Mountains are *Myles and Milo* by Peter Meredith and *Myles Dunphy, Selected Writings*.

Geology

The rich history of this land deserves to be told. Before there were even mountains in the area, rivers deposited sand up to 1km thick. The lower half of this sand was com-

pressed into sandstone that was subsequently uplifted about a million years ago. Rivers flowing down on either side of the central plateau (where the train and highway now are) formed spectacular gorges, especially where the uplift was most pronounced, in the west.

The Blue Mountains area is part of a larger geological unit known as the Sydney Basin, which probably extends from the continental shelf in the east, west to Kanangra Walls and Lithgow, north to the Hunter Valley area and south to Batemans Bay. During the Permian and Triassic periods (about 280–190 million years ago) sediments were laid down into the slowly subsiding basin. Early in the Tertiary Period (about 70 million years ago) the relatively flat surface of the basin rose gently and slowly from a hinge line at the Lapstone Monocline, west of the Nepean River, to the level of the plateau. As the land rose, the gradient of existing steams increased, which developed their erosive force.

This, combined with the erosion of softer bands under the sandstone, resulted in the formation of the vertical sandstone cliffs and talus slopes of rock fragments so typical of the upper Blue Mountains area. Devonian rocks at the bottom of Jamison Valley have been dated at around 400 million years old. The sandstone of the upper Blue Mountains generally belongs to the Narrabeen Group. This rock has a strong vertical jointing characteristic seen in the cliffs and waterfalls.

History

Two tribes lived here for at least 20 000 years. Many examples of their culture have survived: archaeological deposits, engravings, stencils, rock paintings, grinding grooves and stone arrangements. Only a fraction is formally documented. There have been unconfirmed reports of hundreds of sites throughout the park, especially in the central portion around the Jamison and Burragorang valleys.

This area, along with the land to the west, was first occupied by the Gandangara tribe. Farther south, along the Kowmung and around present-day Yerrandrie, was the territory of the Duruk tribe. Displaced

The spectacular view from Govett's Leap at Blackheath, one of the best lookouts in the Blue Mountains.

by the encroachment of European civilisation, both tribes died out.

It took Europeans 25 years to conquer the Blue Mountains. Stories of what was on the other side were intriguing: inland seas, China, the coast. As settlers began to establish farms along the Nepean River, the pressure for a way across grew. Numerous attempts were made: in 1793, William Patterson explored the lower Grose River but had to give up because of slow progress. In the same year that he was stranded in the present day Royal National Park, George Bass made his way toward Kanangra Walls via the Burragorang Valley but also had to turn back because of sheer cliffs. Another explorer, Francis Barrallier, almost made it via the same route but was forced to return for the same reason.

In 1813, Blaxland, Lawson and Wentworth tried a new strategy, working their way in a predominantly west-north-west direction along the ridges instead on walking along valleys. They almost reached the site of Lithgow. The same year, George Evans followed the route and ended up where Bathurst now stands. On the other side of the mountains they found millions of hectares of fertile agricultural land.

One century later, when the Royal and Ku-ring-gai Chase national parks were established as reserved land, Myles Dunphy saw the threat posed by progress and proceeded with his famous campaign to save the Blue Mountains. After three years of very extensive exploration of the southern wilderness, he formed the Mountain Trails Club in 1914, one of the first bushwalking clubs in Australia. Much of the land from Jenolan Caves to the Burragorang Valley was investigated and documented in sketchmaps and notes. After World War I, the proposal for a national park was first discussed at one of the club's meetings. Ten years later, with strong support from other bushwalking groups, a formal submission was made to the Surveyor-General in 1932. Earlier collaboration among various clubs had succeeded in saving the Blue Gum Forest from two Bilpin farmers who had started ring-barking it. The going price was £150 for the lot.

It took another 20 years for the state government to submit to pressure from the public and enact the proposal. Ironically, the commercial sector was the most persuasive, seeing potential profits in the tourist trade.

The national park grew in stages. A decade later the south-west extension was added and 20 years on the Nattai Wilderness area was added in the south-east. Today, there is more than 1 000 000ha of continuous bushland from the Hunter Valley to Mittagong in what is already one of the world's great park complexes.

Climate

Temperatures can become extreme in the Blue Mountains because of their range of altitudes. While Katoomba is generally 5–10°C cooler than Sydney's Cumberland Basin, summer heatwaves from December to February can make bushwalking unbearable.

Taking a break on the way to the Grose River from Mt Victoria.

In winter, it can snow as far down the mountains as Springwood. Roads become blocked, especially around Blackheath and Mt Wilson. It has even snowed in November. At the other extreme, devastating bushfires are a threat in summer. Every few years undergrowth builds up to such an extent that in any drought year it is likely to blaze. The cycle seems to repeat itself every 10–15 years.

Rainfall is not too seasonal, but thunderstorms often occur in late summer. The storm fronts sweep up the range from the south-west. Hail is also common during late afternoon storms. Waterways can be impassable after a deluge so check the forecast before any extended expedition.

Vegetation

A number of vegetation communities are evident in the Blue Mountains. The two most common types are the dry and wet sclerophyll (hard-leaved) forests. These are dominated by the eucalypts that give the Blue Mountains their name. The oil in the leaves evaporates, creating a thick blue haze that hovers above the canopy. Stunted heaths dominate the more exposed plateau tops and pockets of rainforest remain in the cool deep gullies, with swamps where drainage is poor.

Swamps on the ridges of the Blue Mountains are known as 'hanging swamps' because they are elevated and 'hang' above streams and water-falls, often right to the edge of the cliff line. A typical hanging swamp associated with a dry sclerophyll forest significantly reduces erosion and provides a good storage soak. Vegetation in the forest protects soil from the erosive impact of falling rain. Litter on the soil minimises erosion by running water and reduces moisture loss by evaporation.

Access

The Blue Mountains are best accessed by car via the Great Western Highway from Sydney. Take the M4 motorway to Emu Plains. To the north, the Bells Line of Road connects Richmond with Lithgow. The two popular vehicle entry places are at Glenbrook and Blackheath. The southern part of the park can be accessed from Mittagong via the Wombeyan Caves Road.

Conveniently, a rail line goes right along the plateau, parallel with the Great Western Highway as far as Mt Victoria. Bushwalkers alight at Blackheath, Katoomba, Wentworth Falls, Springwood and Glenbrook.

Facilities

Car-based camping at Euroka Clearing at Glenbrook, Murphys Glen at Woodford (fuel-stove-only area), Ingar at Wentworth Falls and Perrys Lookdown at Blackheath (walk in from cars). More information on these sites is available in the leaflets. Bush-camping virtually anywhere outside the Sydney Catchment Authority exclusion zone around Lake Burragorang. There's a popular developed site in the Blue Gum Forest in the middle of the upper Grose Gorge.

There is also a wide choice of accommodation, from luxury resorts, grand old hotels, historic guesthouses, motels, lodges, self-contained cottages, holiday cabins and caravan parks.

A number of areas in the park have barrier-free access, including the Govett's Leap Lookout area, which has parking nearby. The Heritage Centre at Blackheath has toilets and a sales and display area.

Lake Burragorang

Generally, walkers are permitted in any area in the national park. The only exception is the 3km restricted-access zone that constitutes the Lake Burragorang Catchment Area, the source of Sydney's drinking water. The Warragamba Dam is managed by the recently established Sydney Catchment Authority based at Penrith. All queries regarding permission for access should be first directed here.

Sydney Catchment Authority
311 High St, Penrith NSW 2750
Tel: (02) 4732 3600

Grose Gorge (Victoria Falls–Lockleys Pylon) Walk

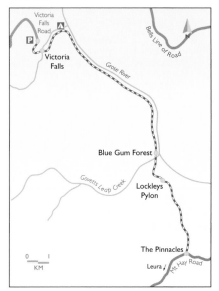

Starting Point: Victoria Falls car park, Blue Mountains National Park
Destination: Lockleys Pylon car park

Summary: A walk through the length of a most spectacular gorge

Attractions: Views, waterfalls, Blue Gum Forest, spectacular cliffs, swimming pools

Length: 19km

Time: 1 full day

Options: It's possible to break up the walk into two half days by camping at Acacia Flat near the Blue Gum Forest

Attraction Rating: ★ ★ ★ ★ ★

Fitness: ☒ ☒ ☒ ☒

Maps: LIC (CMA) Katoomba and Mt Wilson 1:25 000 topographicals

Access to Starting Point: Mt Victoria is on the Great Western Highway 20km north of Katoomba. The Victoria Falls turn-off is signposted just south of Mt Victoria near the bridge that crosses the railway line. To access the Lockleys Pylon end of the walk, drive to Leura and take the Mt Hay Road to the north. It leaves the Great Western Highway close to an overhead footbridge near the turn-off to Leura.

Facilities/Amenities: Basic camping facilities at Acacia Flat

Recommended Equipment: Strong sturdy shoes as there are two cliff passes to negotiate. Plenty of water as the Grose River is not drinkable. If camping at Acacia Flat, remember that it is a fuel-stove-only area. No camping allowed in Blue Gum Forest.

Notes: Set up a car shuffle between Leura and Mt Victoria. Leave early as the final climb out of the gorge takes some time and is extremely gruelling.

Further Information:
The Heritage Centre
Govett's Leap Rd
Blackheath NSW 2785
Tel: (02) 4787 8877
Fax: (02) 4787 8514

An informative booklet, *Walking Tracks in the Grose Valley*, is available from the Heritage Centre. This gives information of geological and botanical interest about the walk.

Walk Description

This walk is an excellent introduction to majestic Grose Gorge. By parking cars at either end of the main gorge, you can avoid backtracking. The gorge is a classic bottleneck valley that is wider and deeper in its upper section than in its lower reaches. Similar examples include the Wolgan and Capertee River valleys.

From Mt Victoria, head down the steep cliff pass to Victoria Falls. There are some lovely pools for a swim here if the weather is hot. A tripod will be necessary for photographs. The track continues to the Grose River and then downstream. There's a small camping area just upstream at Burra Korain and more good swimming pools near the confluence with Pierces Creek. All around are 300m-high cliffs.

Continue downstream through the beautiful Blue Gum Forest, which is an excellent spot for lunch and photographs. A sign on a tree details the conservation campaign that saved the forest from a farmer's grazing plans. The story is also told in *The Edge*, an IMAX film screened at Katoomba.

The start of the Lockleys Pylon track may be difficult to find as it is one of the more minor routes from the gorge. Ford the river at the junction with Govett's Creek and head for the narrow spur to the left. The track soon becomes evident. When approaching Lockleys Pylon, you will wonder how the walking track negotiates the sheer cliffs of Du Faur Buttress ahead. It's a gruelling ascent of more than 600m. Once on top, there are terrific views over the cliffs of the gorge. The walk to the car at Mt Hay Road is largely through open heathland. Just before the end you will pass some rocky outcrops, The Pinnacles, on the left.

Grose Gorge (Evans Lookout to Pierces Pass) Walk

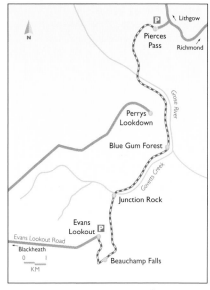

Starting Point: Evans Lookout, Blue Mountains National Park

Destination: Pierces Pass car park

Summary: Walk passes through some superb gorge scenery

Attractions: Waterfalls, views, Blue Gum Forest, swimming, gorge scenery

Length: 18km

Time: 1 full day

Options: It's possible to break up the walk into two half days by camping at Acacia Flat near the Blue Gum Forest

Attraction Rating: ★ ★ ★ ★

Fitness: ☒ ☒ ☒ ☒

Maps: LIC (CMA) Katoomba and Mt

Sunlight on a fern deep in the Grand Canyon, Blue Mountains National Park.

Wilson 1:25 000 topographicals

Access to Starting Point: To reach Evans Lookout, turn off the Great Western Highway just 2km south of Blackheath. Pierces Pass is accessed from the Bells Line of Road either from Richmond or Lithgow.

Facilities/Amenities: Basic camping facilities at Acacia Flat

Recommended Equipment: You will need strong, sturdy shoes. Take plenty of water as the Grose River is not drinkable. If you camp at Acacia Flat, remember that it is a fuel-stove-only area. No camping is allowed in the Blue Gum Forest.

Notes: Leave very early, allowing an hour to organise the car shuffle

Further Information:

The Heritage Centre
Govett's Leap Rd
Blackheath NSW 2785
Tel: (02) 4787 8877
Fax: (02) 4787 8514

Consult *Walking Tracks in the Grose Valley*, available from the Heritage Centre. This gives information of geological and botanical interest.

Walk Description

Similar in scope to the previous walk, but exploiting a slight height differential by starting at Evans Lookout. Although you could start at Pierces Pass, the climb up to Evans Lookout is more intense, so it is recommended to walk up the gorge, instead of down it.

There are spectacular views from Evans Lookout over Govett's Creek Gorge and the first part of the walk. Head down to the opening of the Grand Canyon, past Beauchamp Falls. The Rodriguez Track descends along cascades all the way to the floor of the valley. Continue north to Junction Rock and then down Govett's Creek to its confluence with the Grose River, walking high up on the left bank. The track is pretty well defined and reasonably popular. The scenic Blue Gum Forest is a delightful place to stop for lunch.

Exit by heading up the Grose River gorge and using the Hungerfords Track which climbs steeply to reach the Pierces Pass car park. There are four alternative exit routes—Govett's Leap, Victoria Falls, Perrys Lookdown and Pierces Pass.

Grand Canyon Circuit

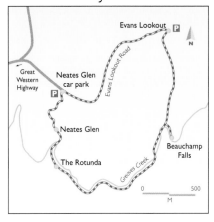

Starting Point: Neates Glen, Blue Mountains National Park

Destination: The Grand Canyon

Summary: This circuit allows walkers to experience a deep, narrow picturesque canyon

Attractions: Rainforest, moss-covered boulders and cliffs, lovely views, Beauchamp Falls

Length: 7km

Time: Half a day

Options: This walk can be done in either direction

Attraction Rating: ★★★★

Fitness: ◪◪◪

Maps: LIC (CMA) Katoomba 1:25 000 topographical

Access to Starting Point: Neates Glen is on the Evans Lookout Road just south of Blackheath

Facilities/Amenities: Picnic facilities and toilets at Evans Lookout

Recommended Equipment: Sturdy shoes with good tread as some sections of the walk are through wet terrain and over slippery rocks

Notes: Carry water as Greaves Creek is not safe to drink

Further Information:

The Heritage Centre
Govett's Leap Rd
Blackheath NSW 2785
Tel: (02) 4787 8877
Fax: (02) 4787 8514

An informative booklet on the walk is available from the Heritage Centre and gives background information of geological and botanical interest about the walk.

Walk Description

A fascinating short circuit walk with the bonus of a lot of attractions in a very short distance.

From the Neates Glen car park, head to the bottom of the Grand Canyon, passing some miniature waterfalls along the way. Once you reach the creek, walk downstream, crossing a couple of times. There are some great views up to the narrow cliffs and you also pass through a tunnel.

When you come to the exit track to Evans Lookout, don't turn left just yet, but continue down on the eastern bank of Greaves Creek to see the lovely Beauchamp Falls. Backtrack to the turn-off and head up the steep rocky staircase to the lookout. Your reward is a dramatic vista from Evans Lookout over the Grose River gorge. To get back to the Neates Glen car park, just head west along Evans Lookout Road for 1.4km.

Mt Banks Circuit

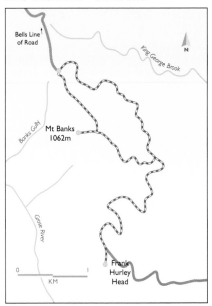

Starting Point: Mt Banks picnic area car park, Blue Mountains National Park

Destination: The summit of Mt Banks (1062m) and Frank Hurley Head

Summary: A loop that ascends the summit of one of the most prominent basalt caps in the upper Blue Mountains. At 500m, the cliffs here are among the highest on the continent.

Attractions: Dramatic views up and down the Grose River gorge

Length: 14km

Time: Half a day

Options: This walk can be done in either direction

Attraction Rating: ★★★

Fitness: ◪◪

Maps: LIC (CMA) Mt Wilson 1:25 000 topographical

Access to Starting Point: Mt Banks is on Bells Line of Road 4km east of the Mt Wilson turn-off near Bell

Facilities/Amenities: Water tank, fireplaces, picnic tables and toilets

Recommended Equipment: Water as there is no water at all along the way

Notes: Gusts of wind and crumbling edges are common in this region, so be very careful near cliff edges

Further Information:

The Heritage Centre
Govett's Leap Rd
Blackheath NSW 2785
Tel: (02) 4787 8877
Fax: (02) 4787 8514

Walk Description

Mt Banks (formerly known as Mt King George) is cut by 500m cliffs. Imagine what an early explorer, George Caley, must have felt after he had travelled for a week to get here on his quest to find a way over the mountains. A sign at the start of the walk reads:

Mount King George. George Caley (1770–1829) was a botanist explorer who, with companions, travelled via Kurrajong and ascended the mount on 15 November 1804. He named it Mount Banks after Sir Joseph Banks. There ended his heroic attempts to cross the Blue Mountains.

The story is tragic. Caley's party walked from Mt Tomah and camped at the base of Mt Banks. Next morning, he climbed to the summit and saw for the first time the impenetrable gorge of the Grose Valley. Finding no way around it, he had to turn back to Parramatta. You can relive his ascent by means of a small walking trail that climbs to the summit from the car park. An old fire trail down the other side of the basalt cap gives access to more outstanding panoramas from the top of Banks Wall. Together with Govett's Leap and Kanangra Walls, this ranks as one of the great views in the Blue Mountains.

Mt Banks rises above the plateau because of its erosion-resistant basalt cap and the twin-humped summit is easily recognised from any vantage point in the Sydney metropolitan area. Abseiling and rock climbing used to be popular here before the National Parks and Wildlife Service removed all the anchor points in the massive cliff.

In January 1994, much of this area was burnt out by savage bushfires and severe back-burning. Occasional glimpses of the cliffs that line Grose River gorge along this section sometimes distract drivers so that they miss the Bells Line of Road. The turn-off to Mt Banks is signposted. If you are travelling from Sydney, it's on the left side of a long sweeping right-hand curve. If you come to Pierces Pass or Mt Wilson, you've gone too far. The small dirt 2WD road winds south and Mt Banks looms ahead, dominating the horizon. On the left is a pleasant developed picnic area; on the right is a large rock with the commemorative plaque quoted above. Between the plaque and the cleared picnic ground, a locked gate bars motorised transport.

Simply head up the walking track to the summit, dominated by wet sclerophyll forest. You can see most of the route and destination from the car park. There are a few old picnic tables in grassy clearings on top. From the trig point on the first of the two humps, a very small footpad leads down a steep rocky slope to a narrow ridge. Notice that the rocks here are of volcanic origin, not sandstone.

The vegetation changes once more, reverting to traditional dry eucalypt bush as you walk along the centre of the spur to prominent rock outcrops and unusual weathered sandstone formations. Mt Banks is one of the first peaks in the Blue Mountains to receive sunlight at dawn. Watching the sun hit the cliffs over a mist-covered Grose River will inspire any camper who has spent the night here.

Backtrack to the summit and follow an old vehicle track down the southern side to join a fire trail. Follow this out to the top of Banks Wall and climb Frank Hurley Head. Directly opposite is Perrys Lookdown, accessible from Blackheath. The Grose River gorge recedes majestically into the distance with the towering 300m cliffs on either side creating an impassable barrier. Directly below is beautiful Blue Gum Forest, a popular walking destination.

Backtrack to the car park following the predominantly descending fire trail around the eastern base of the mountain. It's in fairly poor condition, the surface being roughened by many large sharp rocks. The vegetation is often low, dry and stunted allowing expansive views to the east. There are many popular walks departing from here to several canyons in a labyrinth of ravines based on the tributaries of Carmarthen Brook.

Morning sunlight on the golden sandstone cliffs of the Grose River Gorge.

Hanging Rock Walk

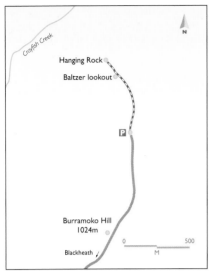

Starting Point: Baltzer Lookout car park, Blue Mountains National Park
Destination: Hanging Rock
Summary: A short walk and scramble to an awe-inspiring narrow sandstone cliff protruding into the Grose Gorge
Attractions: Views both ways along the gorge
Length: 1.1km
Time: 2 hours
Attraction Rating: ★ ★ ★ ★
Fitness: ◪
Maps: LIC (CMA) Mt Wilson 1:25 000 topographical (but walking track is not shown)
Access to Starting Point: Baltzer Lookout is accessible by 4WD or mountain bike from the Great Western Highway just north of Blackheath. It's signposted as Ridgewell Road. The dirt access road is rough in places and cess-pits form after rain.
Facilities/Amenities: None
Recommended Equipment: Sturdy shoes with good tread and a camera.
Notes: Gusts of wind and crumbing edges are common in this region, so be very careful near cliff edges
Further Information:
The Heritage Centre
Govett's Leap Rd
Blackheath NSW 2785
Tel: (02) 4787 8877
Fax: (02) 4787 8514

Walk Description

From the end of the road, head up the short track to a terrific open lookout with a more than 180-degree vista up and down the Grose Gorge. The view right (east) to Mt Banks is particularly good. The cliff here is several hundred metres high. Head left down a slope and follow a faint walking track to another prominent outcrop. Be very careful, as there are no fence railings. Turn left down a slippery rocky slope to another clifftop. The Hanging Rock formation before you becomes more and more spectacular as you approach it. It's barely attached to the main cliff and one day will collapse in a pile of rubble in the Grose Gorge below.

There are anchor points for sports rock climbers and abseilers here. A faint walking track continues along the cliff to Burramoko Head. The brave jump across onto Hanging Rock and see how far out on the narrow 'diving board' they can stand. The sense of vertigo is extreme. Retrace your route back to the car.

Mt Solitary Circuit

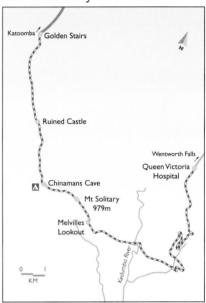

Starting Point: (Golden Stairs car park) Narrowneck, Blue Mountains National Park
Destination: Queen Victoria Hospital, Kings Tableland
Summary: A walk through the Jamison Valley over Mt Solitary (979m)
Attractions: Views over the Katoomba skyline
Length: Total distance is 22km
Day 1: Camping in Chinamans Gully, 8km
Day 2: Wentworth Falls, 14km
Time: 2 days
Options: Choose either to climb the Ruined Castle or skirt the northern flank. The distances are similar, but the ascent of the Ruined Castle is harder and more time-consuming. You will be rewarded with great views.
Attraction Rating: ★ ★ ★
Fitness: ◪ ◪ ◪ ◪
Maps: LIC (CMA) Katoomba and Jamison 1:25 000 topographicals
Access to Starting Point: Drive from Katoomba via Cliff Drive. The turn-off is signposted as Glenraphael Road. Walkers unable to set up a car shuffle can catch a cab or walk from the Katoomba railway station, 4.7km and

Dramatic Hanging Rock, upper Grose Gorge, Blue Mountains National Park.

about 1.5 hours. Access Kings Tableland by turning off the Great Western Highway at the signpost just east of Wentworth Falls. A garden nursery is on the corner. Follow this road to the Queen Victoria Hospital and park as close to the locked gate at Kedumba Pass as possible.

Facilities/Amenities: None. A nice camp clearing in Chinamans Gully on Mt Solitary. If camping out of holiday season times, use one of the rock overhangs for shelter instead of a tent.

Recommended Equipment: Overnight camping gear. Salt to combat leeches can also be handy.

Notes: The descent off the eastern end of the Mt Solitary plateau involves some ledge negotiation. Those unsure over rocks may want to take a length of rope to make pack-hauling easier and to offer some protection. Beware of leeches around Cedar Gap. Do not drink from the Kedumba River.

Further Information:

The Heritage Centre
Govett's Leap Rd
Blackheath NSW 2785
Tel: (02) 4787 8877
Fax: (02) 4787 8514

Detailed tracknotes of this walk are given in the book *Bushwalks in the Sydney Region—Volume 2* by the National Parks Association.

Walk Description

The object of this walk is to camp on Mt Solitary plateau. Mt Solitary, the central feature, is visible from literally hundreds of lookouts from Wentworth Falls to Katoomba. From the Golden Stairs car park, walk down to Federal Pass and on to the Ruined Castle, a rocky outcrop on top of the prominent ridge connecting Mt Solitary to Narrowneck. Climb the rock outcrops if it is still early. Swooping magpies may be a nuisance here in spring, but not at other times of year. Sometimes water can be obtained along the track that skirts the northern flank of Mt Solitary, after rain.

From the Ruined Castle head south through Cedar Gap to the knife-edge spur of Mt Solitary. Some wet forest is encountered along the way and leeches can be a problem. Reliable water can be found along a 300m side track to the right of the main spur just

before the main part of the ascent. Some rock-scrambling will be necessary to reach the top along the centre of the Koorowall spur. There are outstanding views from here to the north, west and south.

Once on top, continue east to Chinamans Gully for the night's camp. Most people camp under the overhangs, but these can be all taken on summer weekends. For more views, follow the creek to either side of the plateau. From Melvilles Lookout, Lake Burragorang can be seen in the distance. This is the source of Sydney's drinking water.

Leave early next day and head east along the plateau, keeping to the northern cliffs. The descent to Solitary Pass is difficult through the broken cliffs and the trail is faint in places but as long as you keep descending through the eucalypt woodland in a true south-easterly direction, you are bound to come to the fire trail near Sugarloaf Creek. Head left and walk through the old Kedumba homestead and up Kedumba Pass to Queen Victoria Hospital. This last section is a long, tiring road-bash, but there are westerly views near the top of the cliff and it's a good place to watch the sunset.

Katoomba cliffs and falls Circuit

Starting Point: Leura Cascades car park, Blue Mountains National Park
Destination: Scenic Railway
Summary: Using the many walking

Cascades below Beauchamp Falls, Blue Mountains National Park.

trails, including Federal Pass and Dardanelles Pass, a cliff-base traverse of the best of the Katoomba and Leura scenery, taking in literally dozens of highlights, including the Three Sisters, and numerous waterfalls

Attractions: Bridal Veil Falls, Linda Falls, many other lovely falls, grottos, rockpools and spectacular lookouts

Length: 14km

Time: 1 full day

Options: Numerous options to add or subtract on this walk. Once, you could start at the Fork and View Restaurant at Leura, using the Fern Bower to descend to the Leura Forest, but this has been closed for some time.

Attraction Rating: ★ ★ ★ ★

Fitness: ◪ ◪ ◪

Maps: LIC (CMA) Katoomba 1:25 000 topographical

Access to Starting Point: By car to Narrowneck Peninsula

Facilities/Amenities: Several picnic areas with tables along the Prince Henry cliff walk. Kiosk and food outlet at the Scenic Railway.

Recommended Equipment: Camera, tripod for waterfalls, warm jumper

Notes: Leave very early in summer if you wish to complete the entire walk and the many little side options to lookouts. In winter (with fewer daylight hours) it's a good idea to make the day less rushed by shortening the walk.

Further Information:

The Heritage Centre
Govett's Leap Rd
Blackheath NSW 2785
Tel: (02) 4787 8877
Fax: (02) 4787 8514

Two informative booklets, *Bushwalking in the Katoomba and Leura Area* and *Echo Point and the Three Sisters*, are available from the National Parks shop at the Heritage Centre.

Walk Description

Being close to amenities, the cliffs of Leura and Katoomba are a drawcard for weekend visitors and international tourists. But you can still enjoy these attractions and avoid the crowds by undertaking an ambitious circuit from Leura Cascades down to the Leura Forest. Follow the base of the cliffs via Dardanelles Pass all the way to the Scenic Railway and catch the train up to the clifftops. Follow the Prince Henry cliff walk back to Leura Cascades via a series of lookouts. The tracks are well graded and signposted, so detailed navigation instructions are unnecessary. If the Scenic Railway is full or closed, you can always walk up the Furber Steps.

The National Pass Circuit

Starting Point: Wentworth Falls car park, Blue Mountains National Park
Destination: The Valley of the Waters
Summary: The scenic National Pass Trail traverses a mid-cliff route viewing waterfalls and cascades
Attractions: Majestic waterfalls and spectacular views
Length: 5km
Time: 2 hours
Options: Return via Wentworth Pass at the base of the cliffs but this is a lot

harder and longer. There are several options to extend the walk. For example, you can do a secondary loop at the Valley of the Waters via the Nature Track. The Weeping Rock circuit is another additional loop at the start of the walk.

Attraction Rating: ★ ★ ★ ★ ★
Fitness: ✗ ✗
Maps: LIC (CMA) Katoomba 1:25 000 topographical
Access to Starting Point: Wentworth Falls car park is right at the end of Falls Road. Turn south opposite the Blue Mountains Grammar School just west of Wentworth Falls railway station. Or catch the train to Wentworth Falls and follow the Darwin Walk to the start of the National Pass walk.
Facilities/Amenities: Picnic area at Wentworth Falls. A short side option to the Conservation Hut at the Valley of the Waters. A café sells selected hot and cold foods and drinks.
Recommended Equipment: Sturdy footwear as the track is wet and slippery in places; tripod
Notes: While the walk can be done in either direction, clockwise is recommended so you can view the Jamison Valley as you walk

Further Information:

The Heritage Centre
Govett's Leap Rd
Blackheath NSW 2785
Tel: (02) 4787 8877
Fax: (02) 4787 8514

An informative booklet entitled *Bushwalking in the Wentworth Falls Area* is available from the Heritage Centre. The Conservation Hut at the end of Fletcher Road also has some information about the area.

Walk Description

The major part of the route is along a broad cliff ledge, allowing great views

over the Jamison Valley. At either end are waterfalls that will delight photographers. From the car park at the end of Falls Road, head along Sir Henry Burrell Drive, then down a walking track signposted to Wentworth Falls.

The track descends via stairs and crosses a creek with a small cascade upstream. Then continue on through a particularly dramatic section as the track climbs down steep steps on an open cliff face to access the main Wentworth Falls. Tall people will have to stoop in some sections. The track crosses Jamison Creek and heads up to the mid-cliff pass that makes this track unique. Go west to the Valley of the Waters where you climb through a gully punctuated with magnificent waterfalls and cascades. There are some staircases and ladders to assist walkers here. Near the top, a walking track branches right. This is the Overcliff Track and it leads back to the car park via the Den Fenella Track, which serves as a shortcut. A lookout allows a last look over the valley.

The Lower Grose River Walk

Starting Point: Faulconbridge Ridge, Blue Mountains National Park
Destination: Vale Lookout
Summary: A wild river walk through trackless terrain close to Sydney
Attractions: Rugged river scenery
Length: 15km
Time: 2 days
Options: Do a 4km side option to Wentworth Cave, or explore the area around Burralow Creek
Attraction Rating: ★ ★ ★
Fitness: ✗ ✗ ✗ ✗

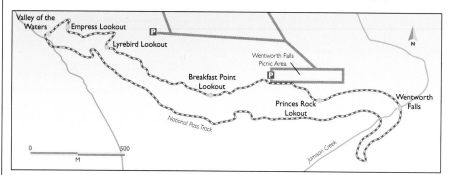

The view over the lower Grose River from Vale Lookout, near the eastern boundary of the Blue Mountains National Park.

Maps: LIC (CMA) Springwood and Kurrajong 1:25 000 topographicals

Access to Starting Point: Set up a car shuffle for this walk. To reach Faulconbridge Ridge, turn off the Great Western Highway at Faulconbridge onto Grose Road. Kept left and you soon enter the national park. Ever since the bushfires in 1994, a gate near the entrance has been locked. The road deteriorates (but is beyond the capabilities of most 2WD sedans anyway) as it climbs a short steep hill. Park the first car here. Drive the second car to Vale Lookout via North Richmond. Cross the Hawkesbury River and turn left on Grose Vale Road and follow Cabbage Tree Road to the end. Park at the top, marked on the topographical map as Vale Lookout. If the road is too rough, park at the junction with the fire trail on the left side just before the steep rise.

Facilities/Amenities: None

Recommended Equipment: You will need overnight camping gear. A water-purification system will also be handy as small freshwater tributaries of the Grose River are unreliable.

Notes: Lots of boulder-scrambling along the Grose River and no track, making progress slow

Further Information:

The Heritage Centre
Govett's Leap Rd
Blackheath NSW 2785
Tel: (02) 4787 8877
Fax: (02) 4787 8514

or

The Glenbrook National Parks and Wildlife Service Visitors' Centre
Bruce Rd, Glenbrook NSW 2773
Tel: (02) 4739 2950

or

Richmond National Parks and Wildlife Service office
Bowmans Cottage
370 Windsor Rd
Richmond NSW 2753
Tel: (02) 4588 5247
Fax: (02) 4588 5335

Walk Description

While most walkers in the Blue Mountains are familiar with the upper Grose Gorge, relatively few venture to the lower reaches of the valley. The object is to camp by one of the many splendid dark pools there. Walk north from the barrier along the flat Grose Road fire trail which follows Faulconbridge Ridge to Faulconbridge Point. There are some great views up and down the gorge here. Double back for 1km and head down the Grose River walking track to the river. Near the end, some ledges must be negotiated and overnight backpacks must be passed down separately.

At the bottom is a nice camping area, and if you plan to take three days for this walk you can certainly stay here. It should have taken 2–3 hours to get here from the barrier.

To exit the gorge, continue downstream below the cliffs of Grose Head South. There are lots of block-ups here so you must frequently ford the river. Some of the pools are very deep and thick undergrowth on the steep banks also slows progress. About 400m past Cabbage Tree Creek, a track (marked on the map) leads up a steep gully. Use the rope/chain/wire to access a sandy fire trail and vehicle-turning circle. You cannot access this directly from the northern bank because of rock ledges. Walk along the southern bank of Grose River until the first opportunity to cross, then backtrack and scramble up the gully. Once you're at the turning circle, a rough walking track proceeds north-west up the hill, keeping fairly close to the top of the rim. This allows direct access to Vale Lookout, where you will be rewarded with a dramatic view of the lower Grose River.

If you are unsure of the exit route out of the Grose River valley, a second option is to continue downstream for 1.2km on the southern bank, then cross and take an old 4WD trail up to the main Cabbage Tree Road.

Other walks in the Blue Mountains National Park

A complete listing of all walks in the Blue Mountains National Park would take several volumes. A good start has been the relevant chapters contained in the two-volume *Bushwalks in the Sydney Region*. Tyrone Thomas' *120 Walks in New South Wales* also lists a number of short walks here, as does Neil Paton's *Walks in the Blue Mountains National Park*. For those wishing to try mountain biking, Sven Klinge's *Cycling the Bush: 100 Rides in New South Wales* is the definitive reference guide to off-road cycling here.

Kanangra–Boyd National Park

Kanangra Walls, a classic wilderness terrain, has long been a favourite with Sydney bushwalkers. The park is 180km west of Sydney, just 20 min-utes by car from Jenolan Caves, and the views from the famous lookout rank with the best in the state. In fact, Kanangra is derived from the Abor-iginal words for 'beautiful view'. Walking is mainly limited to the plateau as there are few tracks in the narrow valleys. Self-sufficiency is essential because of the isolation and difficulty of access. Due to the sheer distance, walks from Blackheath or Katoomba entail overnight camping. Alternatively, take private transport to the car park at Kanangra Walls and explore the plateau by a combination of driving and walking.

Facts and Figures

Name: Kanangra–Boyd National Park
Size: 68 644ha
Enactment:
    Kanangra Tourist Resort, 1891
    Kanangra–Boyd National Park, 1972
    Significant additions (94 00ha), 1977
    Wilderness declarations, 1999
Visitors: Unknown
Vegetation: Snow gums and mountain gums are among the hundreds of species that grow on the slopes of the Boyd Plateau. In the valleys, cool rainforest provides a pleasant alternative to the dry heath and swamp on the tops.
Wildlife: Sugar gliders, wombats, wallabies, pademelon, water rats, koalas and over 100 species of birds have been observed here

The massive cliffs of Kanangra Walls, Kanangra–Boyd National Park.

Aboriginal Sites: No detailed survey conducted. The Gandangara tribes left some evidence of occupation: rock art and axe-grinding grooves.

Camping: Anywhere, but at least 800m from the main road. A formal site 8km from the Boyd River lookout.

Adjoining Parks: Blue Mountains National Park, Abercrombie River National Park, Jenolan and Gurnang state forests and the Lake Burragorang catchment area

Further Information:
The Heritage Centre
Govett's Leap Rd
Blackheath NSW 2785
Tel: (02) 4787 8877
Fax: (02) 4787 8514
or
Oberon Visitors' Centre
38 Ross St, Oberon NSW 2787
Tel: (02) 6336 1972
Fax: (02) 6336 2122

Geology

The view from the main lookout is dominated by the walls: sheer gold-banded cliffs. On the left are the heavily folded Thurat Spires made from extremely tilted white Devonian sandstone some 350 million years old. The place is a geologist's paradise in the sheer variety of unusual formations created by complex uplifting and erosion of shale, volcanic basalt, quartzite and other metamorphic rocks, coal seams and granite.

Climate

The climate of the Kanangra–Boyd Plateau is cool and moist, with cold winters that bring snow contrasting with scorching hot summers with temperatures in the high 30s. Electrical storms in summer can ignite dry undergrowth, causing bushfires.

Vegetation

Wet sclerophyll forest covers most of the Boyd Plateau. The remainder is mallee, heath, swamps, montane and dry forest communities. The first community walkers experience when setting out over Seymour Top is heath, where typically dense stands of Blue Mountains mallee may dominate, together with dwarf she-oak, heath banksia, silver-leaf banksia and sedges. The forest communities on the

exposed edges of the plateau are dominated by populations of silvertop ash and stringybark eucalypts, with understoreys of acacia. The forest floor is home to vanilla plant and spikey mat-rush. At the Boyd River camping area, walkers will find mountain gum, snow gum and alpine snow grass. Nutrient-rich, granite-derived soils support this important plant community. Brown barrell, a species favoured by the forest industry, was heavily logged from 1945 until the national park declaration. Other species in the northern part of the plateau include hickory wattle and mountain silver wattle. Ferns grow in the shaded glens at the bottom of the deep gorges, and stands of soft tree ferns are common.

Wildlife

The park contains habitats of quite a few rare and endangered species. The broad-headed snake, a venomous nocturnal creature, is one example. It lives on exposed rock-strewn ridges and its numbers have been in decline because of loss of habitat and hunting by feral cats and foxes.

The brushtail rock wallaby was once abundant and widespread in the mountainous country of eastern Australia, but is now restricted to a few isolated cliffs throughout its former range. Numbers of this species are now critically low, and the Kanangra Walls region provides the rocky ledges and crevices necessary for its survival. The brushtail rock wallaby is small, weighing no more than 7.5kg, and is easily identified. It has a thick chocolate-brown coat with

a white stripe on its cheek, a rufous tinge on the flank, a brownish-yellow belly and sometimes a white chest blaze, as well as a thick almost black untapered (brushy) tail. Red-bellied black snakes, while quite prevalent, are, fortunately, shy, but be alert in high grass and when stepping over rocks and logs. Always wear high closed-in boots as a precaution.

Access

Most people approach the area either by walking the Six Foot Track to the Jenolan Caves, or by driving to Kanangra Walls via Oberon or Jenolan Caves. There's a pleasant camping area at the Boyd River, 8km from the end of the road.

The Six Foot Track Walk

Starting Point: Explorers Tree, Great Western Highway, Katoomba
Destination: Jenolan Caves
Summary: Pleasant developed walk in the western part of the Blue Mountains
Attractions: Nellies Glen, Megalong Valley, Coxs River, wild terrain
Length: 42km
Time: 3 days (marathon runners can complete the journey in several hours)
Options: You can also start at the Old Ford Reserve in the Megalong Valley, turning it into a two-day walk
Attraction Rating: ★ ★ ★
Fitness: ◪◪◪◪
Maps: LIC (CMA) Jenolan, Hampton and Katoomba 1:25 000 topographicals
Access to Starting Point: Travel to Katoomba by rail or on the Great Western Highway from Sydney via Penrith or from Lithgow. To reach the

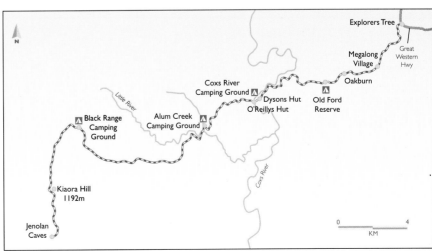

Jenolan Caves, head south from Hartley between Mt Victoria and Lithgow. Coach services, such as Aussie Tours, operate both ways daily between Katoomba and Jenolan Caves. Bookings: ph: (02) 4782 1866.

Facilities/Amenities: Camp facilities at Old Ford Reserve; other bush-camping grounds by the Coxs River, Alum Creek and on Black Range. Luxury accommodation is available from the Jenolan Caves Guest House.

Recommended Equipment: Overnight camping gear

Notes: Walk from east to west to take advantage of the substantial height difference between the two end points. The trail is easy to follow because it has been extensively marked by the Orange Lands Office.

Further Information:
Oberon Visitors' Centre
38 Ross St, Oberon NSW 2787
Tel: (02) 6336 1972
Fax: (02) 6336 2122

The Department of Land and Water Conservation has published an information brochure with a good map overview of the walk. Enquiries about accommodation and transport can be made at the Tourist Information Centres at Glenbrook, Katoomba and Jenolan Caves. For more information on the history of the track, consult Jim Smith's book *From Katoomba to Jenolan Caves: The Six Foot Track*.

Walk Description

The Six Foot Track begins at the Explorers Tree on the Great Western Highway just west of Katoomba and before Medlow Bath. The signposted tree was marked by the Blaxland, Lawson and Wentworth party on the first crossing of the mountains in 1813. The route is down Nellies Glen and through Megalong Valley to Coxs River, over Mini Mini Range to Little River, up the Black Range and down the Binoomea Ridge to Jenolan Caves.

The track was built in 1884 at the instigation of New South Wales Premier Alexander Stuart as a six-foot wide horse-riding or bridle track from Katoomba to Jenolan Caves. It halved the travelling time to the caves. Today it has been superseded by a standard fire trail for much of its way and so is the perfect trail for novice walkers to

have an overnight bushwalking experience. Several types of terrain and reserve classifications are encountered: state forest, national park and private property.

If you camp at Old Ford Reserve, the best places are on the north-eastern side of the ford, but it can be crowded on weekends. More-secluded places are on the north-western side, where there are good swimming holes in Megalong Creek. Firewood can be a problem so carry a fuel stove.

At the Jenolan Caves end of the walk, you can do several short day walks taking Carlotta and McKeowns tracks to the north of the Grand Arch. Harrys River Walk heads down the Jenolan River.

Upper Kowmung River Circuit

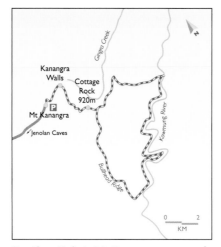

Starting Point: Mt Kanangra car park, Kanangra-Boyd National Park
Destination: Kowmung River
Summary: A loop walk on the pristine Kowmung River, descending Bullhead Ridge and ascending Roots Ridge
Attractions: Views and several fantastic swimming holes
Length: 34km
Time: 3–4 days (including a rest day)
Options: The walk can also be done in reverse (a clockwise direction)
Attraction Rating: ★ ★ ★ ★ ★
Fitness: ▨ ▨ ▨ ▨
Maps: LIC (CMA) Kanangra and Yerrandrie 1:25 000 topographicals. The Gangerang sketch map by Myles Dunphy is handy for this entire area.
Access to Starting Point: Drive to Mt Kanangra by a wide dirt road south of

Jenolan Caves. Allow 3–4 hours to the staging area from Sydney.

Facilities/Amenities: Camping area with pit toilets, firewood and water at Boyd River Crossing, 8km from the walk start. Otherwise, there are no facilities along the walk itself.

Recommended Equipment: Complete self-sufficiency for overnight camping

Notes: Red-bellied black snakes are common. If walking in mid-summer, leave Roots Ridge very early in the morning as it's a long gruelling climb back up to Maxwell Top.

Further Information:
Oberon Visitors' Centre
38 Ross St, Oberon NSW 2787
Tel: (02) 6336 1972
Fax: (02) 6336 2122

Walk Description

From the Kanangra Walls car park, a well-constructed walkway leads directly to the lookout. Keep left at the first fork and the rock platform is on the right, marked by a small warning sign. At sunset, when the west-facing cliffs glow bright gold, there are few better places to be. What impresses most are not the cliffs themselves, but the way they contrast with the extreme folding of the Thurat Spires on the left. The gigantic convoluted pile of ridges at the far end of the gorge is Mt Cloudmaker.

To inspect a large overhang called Dance Floor Cave, head back to the track junction and then left on the walking track that winds down into a gap between two plateaus. Some large twisted eucalypts obscure more views of the gorge. At the lowest point, just before it climbs again onto Seymour Top, a track leads through the trees to the right. The Dance Floor Cave is about 50m farther along. Located here is an open concrete cylinder which captures and stores dripping water that seeps through the rock, but don't rely on this for your water.

Continue up to Seymour Top where there are views to Kanangra Falls on the other side of the gorge. The track passes through thick low heath where small watercourses have formed ruts in the soil. Some platforms on top allow access to the very edge of the cliffs, where the unusual white strata of Thurat Spires can be studied.

The track generally heads northeast along the plateau top, over a narrow neck to Maxwell Top. Turn right here and head south through tall heath. The track is reasonably well defined despite a couple of minor forks that parallel each other before joining up again. The track descends easily through the cliffs then contours around the base of Murrarang Top. There are some great views south here. The Coal Seam Cave has long been a favourite refuge for walkers. This is the start of Gingra Range, which slopes all the way down to the Kowmung River.

After you go around Cottage Rock on its northern flank, head right at the next knoll and down a spur that becomes Bullhead Ridge. Climb over Bullhead Mountain and drop steeply down to the river via Cambage Spire and Sullen Tor. Some sections here are extremely steep and slippery because of loose rock. Some rock-scrambling and pack-hauling is also necessary at Cambage Spire, but there are plenty of handholds. You reach the Kowmung River near its confluence with Christys Creek and there's a grassy camping site on the other side. If there is enough time, head downstream for several hours where the swimming pools are significantly deeper.

Camp wherever you like and spend a day down here. There are many camping spots between Sunrise Bluffs and Roots Ridge. A short cut goes over Bullhead Buttress saddle, but with all the scrambling and scrub-bashing involved, is it worth the effort?

When it's time to leave, rise early to avoid climbing Roots Ridge in the hottest part of the day. Allow at least 4–5 hours for the climb up to Maxwell Top. The topography of the land, with its prominent spurs and ridges, makes navigation simple. The walking becomes significantly easier once you're over First Top Mountain.

Mt Cloudmaker Walk

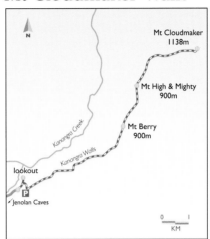

Starting Point: Kanangra Walls, Kanangra-Boyd National Park

Destination: To the summit of Mt Cloudmaker (1138m)

Summary: A traverse along a rollercoaster ridgeline to the summit of this prominent peak

Attractions: Views over the dramatic Kanangra Creek gorge and Lake Burragorang Valley

Length: 28km

Time: 2 days (14km each). Very fit parties could complete the return walk in a day if they leave early enough.

Options: An extension to the Ti Willa Plateau is possible

Attraction Rating: ★ ★ ★

Fitness: ◪ ◪ ◪ ◪

Maps: LIC (CMA) Kanangra 1:25 000 topographical. The Gangerang sketch map by Myles Dunphy is handy for this entire area.

Access to Starting Point: Drive to Kanangra Walls by a wide dirt road south of Jenolan Caves. Allow 3–4 hours to the staging area from Sydney.

Facilities/Amenities: Camping area with pit toilets, firewood and water at Boyd River Crossing, 8km from the walk start. Otherwise, there are no facilities along the walk itself.

Recommended Equipment: Camping gear for complete self-sufficiency. Plenty of water.

Notes: There is no water along the way, although Dex Creek north of the summit can have water after rain

Further Information:
Oberon Visitors' Centre
38 Ross St, Oberon NSW 2787
Tel: (02) 6336 1972
Fax: (02) 6336 2122
Consult *Kanangra–Boyd National Park Walking Track and Visitor Guide*, available from information and visitors' centres at Blackheath, Jenolan Caves and Oberon, for a small cost.

Walk Description

While Mt Cloudmaker's summit is no higher than the Boyd Plateau, its isolation and central location make it a challenge for wilderness enthusiasts. The walk can be completed in one long, tiring day but it is better to camp at the informal bush clearing by Dex Creek on the northern side of the summit. Access by private vehicle is either through Oberon or Jenolan Caves from Mt Victoria. There are small informal car-camp clearings on the first part of the Boyd Range Track. Because of the distance from Sydney, most walkers camp at the Boyd River rest area before setting out early next day for Mt Cloudmaker. This gigantic mountain is really a series of knolls

Looking over Megalong Valley en route from Kanangra–Boyd National Park.

and peaks seemingly locked in a struggle to get on top of one another.

Follow the description of the Upper Kowmung Circuit Walk to the cliff edge on Seymour Top where Thurat Spires can be seen. The track generally heads north-east along the plateau top, over a narrow neck, to Brennan Top. Because the heath is stunted, there are great views east to the Burragorang Valley. The track descends a cliff pass onto the Gangerang Range, passing beneath Crafts Wall.

From here, follow the ridge crest over Mt Berry and down to the deep saddle of Gabes Gap, the lowest point of the journey. It's a roller-coaster walk as you attain Mt High and Mighty and then Mt Stormbreaker before climbing onto the Cloudmaker complex itself by way of four small rocky knolls, Rip, Rack, Roar and Rumble. A cairn, trig and visitor book mark the summit but views are mainly obscured. From here, follow the ridge north-east and north to Dex Creek camp clearing. Don't go farther north as the tracks disappear and many parties have been lost trying to reach Coxs River down the wrong spur.

Next day, retrace your steps southwest over Gangerang Range back to the Kanangra Road car park to enjoy a spectacular sunset over the Walls.

Colong Caves Walk

Starting Point: Batsh Camp, Kanangra-Boyd National Park
Destination: Colong Caves on Cave Creek
Summary: A short, interesting walk in a remote part of Kanangra–Boyd National Park along the Uni Rover Trail to the entrance of Colong Caves
Attractions: Wild creek bed, karst area, Colong Cave entrance arch
Length: 8km

Time: Half a day
Attraction Rating: ★ ★ ★
Fitness: ◪ ◪ ◪
Maps: LIC (CMA) Bindook 1:25 000 topographical. The Gangerang sketch map by Myles Dunphy is handy for this entire area.
Access to Starting Point: To reach Batsh Camp, follow the Yerrandrie Road via Shooters Hill Road. Consult the LIC (CMA) Blue Mountains 1:150 000 topographical Tourist Map for directions.
Facilities/Amenities: None
Recommended Equipment: Torch for looking at the cave interior
Notes: No camping is allowed in the caves area and permits are required to enter the cave
Further Information:
    Oberon Visitors' Centre
    38 Ross St
    Oberon NSW 2787
    Tel: (02) 6336 1972
    Fax: (02) 6336 2122

Walk Description

From Batsh Camp on Black Swamp Creek, head along the Uni Rover Trail to Mt Moogan and descend steeply to Caves Creek via Moogan Spur. The area is mainly limestone and the creek is sometimes subterranean. Head upstream for 300m and climb the right (west) bank to the cave entrance. Several limestone formations can be seen here. Return via the same route.

Other walks in the Kanangra–Boyd National Park

There are two main focal points for walkers in the Kanangra Walls area. The first is the Kowmung River, where a host of minor tracks lead down spurs from Gingra Range. Brumby Ridge and Hughes Ridge can also be used as well as Roots Ridge and Bullhead Ridge to tailor walking circuits to individual wishes. To the south, the Uni Rover Trail leads across the Boyd Range and Lannigans Spur for 15km to the upper Kowmung River.

The second point is the Mt Cloudmaker massif, where tracks radiate outwards. Access the Kowmung River valley via Ti Willa Top, Hundred Man Cave and Compagnoni Pass, or proceed north over Mt Moorilla and Mt Amarina along Strongleg Ridge to reach the Coxs River. Take great care in navigation here. Stories of walkers getting lost north of Mt Cloudmaker are common, because of the maze of similar-looking ridges. Attractions near Mt Cloudmaker include Crafts Wall and Pages Pinnacle, worth inspecting in their own right for magnificent views from the top.

Other interesting day-walk destinations include the spectacular country between Yerrandrie and Mt Colong. Colong Gap, Yerrandrie Peak and Church Creek Caves all different and worth visiting. Accommodation is available in the old Yerrandrie township, now privately owned.

From Yerrandrie, the Scotts Main Range fire trail allows walkers to use several ridges to approach Kowmung River from the east. Options include Armours Ridge, Dennis Ridge (Kiaramba Spring) and Bran Jan Hill.

From the Kanangra Walls car park, a short tourist walk leads down to Kanangra Brook and Kalang Falls. It's a rare treat to swim in nice small pools, see waterfalls and yet still be so high up over a gorge. Be careful on the treacherous rocks when exploring in the Kalang Falls vicinity. To the north, it is possible to walk to Mt Thurat, opposite Kanangra Walls.

Christys Creek winds through the wildest terrain in the Blue Mountains. There are numerous waterfalls and rockpools, but a rope is often necessary to negotiate the length of this watercourse. Other rugged overnight walk opportunities are possible at the bottom end of Kanangra Creek.

Several adventurous epic walks are also possible. For example, use a 4WD to access the Tuglow Caves and Dingo Dell region via the Kowmung River fire trail 5km west of the Boyd River camping area. From here, walk downstream all the way to the confluence of the Kowmung and Coxs rivers, leaving the park either via Green Gully (also called 'Carlons Farm' or 'Packsaddlers'), or via the Narrowneck Peninsula. A track has been made at the base of Mt Cookem, so that walkers can avoid the Waterboard Road. This walk takes about a week. For a half-day walk from the upper Kowmung River to Morong Falls, use the Shooters Hill topographical map.

Nattai National Park

The attractive and little-known Nattai River flows from Mittagong north into Lake Burragorang and, unlike many watercourses in sandstone country, has wide, flat grassy banks, ideal for camping. The 47 612ha Nattai National Park, declared in April 1992, was the last major part of Myles Dunphy's 1934 proposal. It can be accessed by driving along the Picton to Mittagong road, south of Penrith. From Sydney, take the F5 freeway toward Mittagong and take the Picton, Bargo or Hilltop exit. Follow the signs to Hilltop, then turn right after crossing the old railway line and continue on Wattle Ridge Road to a car park. Leave the car before the gate between the Camelot property and Point Hill (666m). Except for holiday periods, the area is not crowded.

Middle Nattai River Circuit

Starting Point: Wattle Hill Ridge Road, Nattai National Park
Destination: Nattai River (McArthurs Flat, Emmetts Flat)
Summary: The loop uses Starlights Trail to descend to the river and Troys Creek fire trail and Nattai Road to return to the car
Attractions: Wild river, gorge scenery close to Sydney, swimming holes
Length: 19km
Time: 1 full day
Attraction Rating: ★ ★ ★ ★
Fitness: ☒ ☒ ☒ ☒
Maps: LIC (CMA) Hilltop 1:25 000 topographical

Access to Starting Point: Access Hilltop from the Picton to Mittagong road, then follow Wattle Ridge Road to a vehicle barrier car park near the 'Camelot' homestead
Facilities/Amenities: None. A beautiful grassy clearing on the northern bank of the river is an ideal campsite.
Recommended Equipment: Water, as the Nattai River is not drinkable
Further Information: To contact Nattai National Park ranger's office, call:
Tel: (02) 4659 6133
or   (02) 9542 0666

Walk Description

From the vehicle barrier, just east of the pluviometer (marked on the topographical map), walk along the road toward Point Hill. A signposted turn-off leads south and then west before turning into a walking trail. This trail descends along the southern bank of Coastes Creek and is well defined. There are some good views just before the final zigzagging descent. Once at the bottom, spend a couple of hours in the idyllic pool. Lots of goannas here.

The Nattai River, Nattai National Park, south-eastern Blue Mountains.

To exit the Nattai River valley, head downstream and ford Troys Creek (usually fairly dry) to reach Emmetts Flat and its ruins. An old fire trail (not marked on the topographical map) climbs north to the top of the plateau via a winding cliff pass. More views, looking up Nattai Creek valley. The fire trail reaches a T-junction with another minor trail. Head right and right again onto the graded Nattai Road, then walk south-east along the flat sandy road back to the car park.

Upper Nattai River Walk

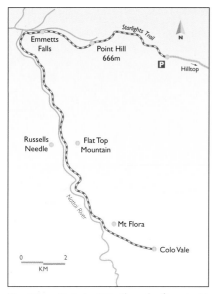

Starting Point: Westbreak fire trail, Colo Vale, Nattai National Park
Destination: Starlights Trail, Hilltop
Summary: A walk through largely trackless terrain of the wild and remote upper Nattai River valley
Attractions: Beautiful pools, gorge scenery
Length: 24km
Time: 1 full day (or 2 half days)
Options: Camp in any number of riverside sites, one of the best being McArthurs Flat or Starlights Hollow
Attraction Rating: ★ ★ ★
Fitness: ☒ ☒ ☒ ☒
Maps: LIC (CMA) Mittagong and Hilltop 1:25 000 topographicals
Access to Starting Point: To access Westbreak fire trail, drive to Colo Vale on the Picton to Mittagong road. Continue north-west from Colo Vale on Colo Road and turn left opposite a quarry pit onto Westbreak fire trail.

There is a private property here called 'Avalon'. You can drive all the way to the unofficial lookout at the end of the ridge, but the road is rough and overgrown in some places and a 4WD or other high-clearance vehicle is recommended. Access to Hilltop is from the Picton to Mittagong road, then Wattle Ridge Road to a vehicle barrier car park near the 'Camelot' homestead.
Facilities/Amenities: None. Numerous wild bush-camp settings along the Nattai River.
Recommended Equipment: As stinging nettles are a problem, wear gaiters for protection and carry a small bottle of vinegar or 'Stingoes' (aluminium sulphate)
Notes: Set up a car shuffle to avoid backtracking. All gates should be left as found. If you plan to do the walk in one day, leave very early.
Further Information: To contact Nattai National Park ranger's office, call:

    Tel: (02) 4659 6133
    or   (02) 9542 0666

Walk Description

From Westbreak fire trail, head down a break in the rock ledges (called Craigs Pass) to an open paddock with electricity lines running through it. This is the Stockyard Creek valley. Don't cross this watercourse until you descend to the Nattai River. From here, head downstream to the north. This section is called Blatchs Pass and continual fording is necessary to find the best route. Attractions along the way include the Russells Needle rock outcrop and Rocky Waterholes Creek.

Exit the valley by the Starlights Trail up the Coates Creek valley to Point Hill then the Wattle Ridge Road car park near 'Camelot' homestead. Allow about 2 hours from McArthurs Flat to the car park.

Other walks in Nattai National Park

Beloon Pass is the primary access route between the Kanangra–Boyd and Blue Mountains national parks to the west and the Nattai National Park to the east. As well as the 3-day Lower Nattai River Circuit, some epic walks from Kanangra Walls or even from Blackheath or Katoomba are possible, exiting at Hilltop or Mittagong along

the Ensign Barrallier Walk. The top of Beloon Pass is great in its own right, giving walkers an overview of a remote and little-known section of the lower Wollondilly River valley. Consult *Mittagong Nattai—Walking Tracks for the Southern Highlands* by Robert Sloss for more information on the entire Nattai National Park area.

Morton National Park

Incredibly scenic Morton National Park is divided into three general sections: basically, the northern and southern ends with a core of the inaccessible wilderness between them. The Shoalhaven River cuts a dramatic 500m gorge through the north of the national park and its tributaries have also cut deep, narrow canyons where swimming or canoeing are popular pastimes. Nearby, the Bungonia Caves provide an interesting display of limestone sculptures. Farther east lies Bundanoon's Glow Worm Glen.

Facts and Figures

Name: Morton National Park
Size: 170 462ha (including Budawang National Park)
Enactment:
    Morton Primitive Area, 1938
    National Park declaration, 1967
    Major extensions, 1970
    Budawang National Park, 1981
    Plan of Management, 1998
    Wilderness declarations, 1999
Visitors: In the north, many casual sightseers frequent Fitzroy Falls, Bungonia Caves and Tallowa Dam. In the south, visitors are restricted by the wilderness nature of the Budawang mountains. Experienced walkers and clubs are the main users of this end of the park. The one exception is Pigeon House Mountain, a popular lookout for coastal holiday-makers.
Vegetation: With great variation in altitude and habitats, Morton National Park's vegetation is very diverse. The tablelands have a thin cover of heath, while rainforest, forests, swamps and woodlands also occur within the park.
Wildlife: Dingoes, brumbies, grey kangaroos, native mice, pygmy possums, koalas, gliders, dragons, and pythons, among others.

Aboriginal Sites: There is an interesting, well-preserved bora ground on Quiltys Mountain in the mid-south. Humans have occupied the region for about 20 000 years. In the heart of the Clyde Valley, carbon dating has found remains about 3500 years old. Sharpening grooves and cave paintings have also been found.

Adjoining Parks: Budawang National Park to the south, together with several state forests that include Macdonald, Croobyar, Yadboro, Flat Rock, Clyde, Currawan and Monga. To the west, various plots of freehold, leasehold and Crown Land separate the national park from the more built-up areas of Braidwood and Goulburn.

Further Reading: Two excellent and comprehensive booklets have been published by the Budawang Committee covering the Morton National Park, Bungonia State Recreation Area and Budawang National Park. These are *Fitzroy Falls and Beyond* and *Pigeon House and Beyond*.

Further Information:
Fitzroy Falls Visitors' Centre
Morton National Park
Nowra Rd, Fitzroy Falls NSW 2577
Tel: (02) 4887 7270
Fax: (02) 4887 7203
or
Nowra National Parks and Wildlife
Service District Office
55 Graham St, Nowra NSW 2541
Tel: (02) 4423 2170
Fax: (02) 4423 3122

Geology

Like the Blue Mountains and Wollemi, Morton National Park is dominated mainly by sandstone. Erosion of this sedimentary rock has formed steep-sided valleys and gorges, creating a spectacular landscape. There are double-cliffed gorges up to 500m deep within the national park. The main sources of erosion are the waters of the Shoalhaven, Kangaroo, Endrick and Clyde rivers. The sandstone overlies older sedimentary and metamorphic rock, some of which is more than 500 million years old. The unusual dendritic-shaped erosion pattern of the metamorphic rocks has created

extremely rugged terrain, which is typically tough going for walkers. Whereas experienced fit walkers can sometimes maintain an average of 4–5km/h in other national parks, the average in most parts of Morton is only 1–2km/h.

History

When Europeans first began to explore the region, they encountered Aboriginal tribes speaking five different languages or dialects. Within a relatively short period of European settlement, populations of Aborigines

were much reduced and the tribes were scattered about the tablelands, Kangaroo Valley and around the Shoalhaven River. In 1882 the Aborigines Protection Board began to force the remainder into missions.

Research, yet to be finished, has uncovered significant archaeological records. Aborigines seem to have been seasonal visitors. Some groups restricted their seasonal forays to the hinterland areas and met with coastal people only for special occasions. The area was also used as a route for interaction between coast and inland

One of the lovely pools of Ettrema Creek in Morton National Park.

Aborigines for trading and ceremonial occasions. Site distribution has been found to be associated with corridors of relatively easy access along ridges through forested areas where resources were plentiful, and along major watercourses.

Several hundred Aboriginal sites have been recorded in the national park. These consist of rock shelters with occupational deposits, wall art and axe-grinding grooves. They occur in areas of sandstone outcrops on cliff-rimmed hills and plateau surfaces in the Nowra sandstone and massive sandstones of the Snapper Point formation, especially along creek lines and in rock shelves above the cliffs. In the art sites are paintings, drawings and some stencils. Only one ochre quarry has so far been recorded.

Rare stone arrangements occur on the rocky summits of hills and on promontories above cliffs. Most are of deep spiritual significance to the indigenous population. One example is the Quiltys Mountain bora ground.

European contact dates from the naming of Pigeon House Mountain by Captain James Cook in 1770 when he was sailing north along the coast. The dramatic beauty of the area was recognised soon after European settlement. The first reserve was established in 1824 at Bundanoon, a significant milestone in Australia's conservation history. In the 1860s, trails were built to the many lookouts at Bundanoon, Fitzroy Falls and Manning Lookout.

Resorts developed in the highlands adjacent to Morton National Park from the 1870s with the coming of the railway and there was a rapid rise in tourism in the 1880s when bicycling became popular. The first guidebook to the northern escarpment area was published in 1904. Today there are dozens of such publications.

Climate

The climate of the park is broadly humid temperate, but this is greatly influenced by local variations in topography. There is a radical temperature difference between the high plateau and range areas, where snow occasionally falls in winter, and the much warmer gorge and valley floors. Precipitation in the eastern part is more than double that on the western edge, because it is closer to the coast. Rainfall is also fairly high on the Hawkesbury Sandstone plateau at the northern end and on the Budawang Ranges in the south, compounded by orographic effects.

Vegetation

Despite the sandy soil on the plateau being relatively infertile, a variety of tree species grow there, including black ash, red bloodwood, scribbly gum, turpentine and Sydney peppermint. In sections of the dissected plateau where drainage is poor, the vegetation is predominantly shrubby and herbaceous and heath communities are very common.

A diverse array of wildflowers includes the Christmas bell and trigger plant. Under the major cliff lines, in shaded conditions, the rainforest is mixed with tall open forest, dominated by giant turpentine trees. In places like The Vines, near the upper Endrick River valley, the soil is a rich dark brown and more fertile. There are substantial portions of complete rainforest canopy in these areas. The lower slopes of the valleys support tall, shrubby forests with species similar to those of the plateau rim. Dead tree heads are a mute testimony to earlier destructive wild fires. Rare and endangered plants occurring in Morton National Park include Ettrema mallee, Budawang ash and pigeon house ash.

Wildlife

The variety in topography and vegetation has produced habitats for many animal species ranging from grey kangaroo, red-necked wallabies, swamp wallabies, reptiles and a particularly varied bird life. There are large birds of prey such as wedge-tailed eagles and whistling eagles, while lyrebirds and several species of parrots live in the forests. Two threatened bird species, the eastern bristlebird and the swamp parrot, are found in the heath communities.

Access

Fitzroy Falls are on the Moss Vale to Nowra Road about 19km south-east of Moss Vale. Gambells Rest is adjacent to Bundanoon. Tianjara Falls are reached by way of the Nowra to Braidwood road, 41km west of Nowra. Access to Pigeon House Mountain and the southern sections of the park is signposted on the Princes Highway, 16km from Ulladulla.

Facilities

In the south, no facilities are provided and, apart from Monolith Valley, camping is permitted almost anywhere. In the north there are several developed camping areas: Fitzroy Falls and Gambells Rest, Bundanoon (bookings essential). Both allow for car-camping. There's also a developed campsite at Bungonia Caves in the Bungonia State Recreation Area near Goulburn. To the west, Wog Wog Camping Area on the Nerriga–Sassafras Road allows walkers access to the Budawangs via Mt Corang.

Fitzroy Falls Walk

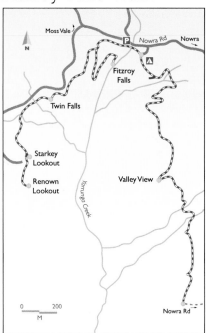

Starting Point: Fitzroy Falls Visitors' Centre, Morton National Park
Destination: Renown Lookout, East rim, West rim and valley floor
Summary: A walk along the rim of two escarpments, each with a number of lookouts
Attractions: Views, waterfalls, pools
Length: 9.5km
Time: 3 hours
Attraction Rating: ★ ★ ★
Fitness: ✗ ✗ ✗

Maps: LIC (CMA) Bundanoon 1:25 000 topographical

Access to Starting Point: Fitzroy Falls Visitors' Centre is 17km east of Moss Vale on the road to Robertson in the southern highlands, 155km south-west of Sydney

Facilities/Amenities: Full day/picnic and overnight facilities at Fitzroy Falls

Recommended Equipment: Camera

Notes: Children should only do the Valley Walk accompanied by adults

Further Information:

Fitzroy Falls Visitors' Centre
Morton National Park
Nowra Rd, Fitzroy Falls NSW 2577
Tel: (02) 4887 7270
Fax: (02) 4887 7203

Walk Description

Although the west rim is the better of the two for walking, start the day by walking the east rim. A brochure available from the visitors' centre highlights the wildflowers and other vegetation you might see. The half a dozen lookouts along the way and the eastern rim offer excellent views down Yarrunga Creek to the Mt Carrialoo plateau. Backtrack to Fitzroy Falls and descend by the Valley Walk to Yarrunga Creek and a 7m ladder near the bottom. Note how the vegetation changes in the cool spray from the falls. Once you've climbed back to the top, walk along the western rim to Renown Lookout for spectacular views back to both Fitzroy and Lady Hordern falls.

Shoalhaven River Walk

Starting Point: Badgerys Creek Lookout, Morton National Park

Destination: Long Point Lookout

Summary: Descend the deep gorge of Shoalhaven River at one vantage point and climb out at another

Attractions: Expansive views and wonderfully wild river scenery

Length: 16km

Time: 1 long day or 2 half days

Options: You can also exit the gorge at Bungonia using the White Track to the lookdown car park. This makes the walk about 2km longer.

Attraction Rating: ★ ★ ★ ★

Fitness: ◪ ◪ ◪ ◪

Maps: LIC (CMA) Caoura 1:25 000 topographical

Access to Starting Point: Badgerys Creek lookout is signposted and accessible from the Caoura Ridge Road, 8km south of Tallong. Long Point is accessible from the Wingello Road, 5.8km south of Tallong. The NRMA Map 'Southern Highlands' gives a good overview of road access.

The Fitzroy Falls, at the very northern end of Morton National Park.

Facilities/Amenities: Basic picnic facilities at each of the lookouts. Along the Shoalhaven River there are no facilities but plenty of pleasant places to camp. A particularly nice one is on the northern bank of Louise Reach, just west of the Barbers Creek confluence.

Recommended Equipment: Shoes with very good tread as the descent is extremely steep

Notes: Complete self-sufficiency is essential. Water from the Shoalhaven River is not drinkable.

Further Information:

Fitzroy Falls Visitors' Centre
Morton National Park
Nowra Rd, Fitzroy Falls NSW 2577
Tel: (02) 4887 7270
Fax: (02) 4887 7203

Walk Description

The Shoalhaven River gorge is one of the deepest and most rugged on the east coast of Australia. Looking at the Caoura topographical map you'll notice a thick blood-red mass of topographical lines that show its stark contrast with the flat surrounding plateau. Set up a car shuffle—the distances between the lookouts by road is only about 16km. Head down to the Shoalhaven River from Badgerys Point, taking great care on the slippery surface. The track drops almost 500m in 2.5km, a one-in-five gradient, but at times it's a lot steeper.

At the bottom, head upstream. You'll have to ford the river a few times, depending on its level, and possibly get your feet wet. It can be nice to spend the hottest part of the day in one of the many pools. The section of the Shoalhaven River below Rainbow Saddle is especially deep and swimmable. Generally the bottom of the gorge is open, sparse and rocky and can get very hot in mid-summer.

Leave several hours for the massive ascent to Long Point, but at the same time try to avoid climbing in the middle of the day. If you camp at the bottom, why not have a rest day on the second day? Leave the overnight packs and tent behind and explore downstream to Bungonia Gorge. It's easy walking on the northern bank through pleasant casuarina oaks.

Bungonia State Recreation Area

Bungonia State Recreation Area is 3973ha and forms an extension to the Morton National Park. People have been visiting the caves since the 19th century, but today, you need a permit from the ranger. The area is one of three important recreational caving areas in Australia, the others being Wee Jasper and the Cape Naturaliste to Cape Leeuwin region of Western Australia. It has a large number and variety of caves with few restrictions on access. The deep shafts, including one unbroken drop of 47m, make the caves especially attractive to the sporting caver. The entrances are scattered around the recreation area; some are only small holes in the ground, while others are gaping entrances in the sides of hills. Some are named (e.g. Hogans, Fossil, Drum), but most are just numbered.

The scenery here is outstanding, the most prominent features being the dramatic gorges of Bungonia Creek and the Shoalhaven River, up to 400m

Possibility Point juts out over the dramatic Ettrema Gorge in central Morton National Park.

deep in the plateau. Tributary creeks fall steeply into the gorges forming numerous waterfalls and deep plunge pools. Other interesting features include limestone cliffs, scree slopes, limestone depressions and sinkholes, and rock outcrops.

Geology

The Bungonia caves tend to be deeper and more vertically developed than other cave areas of eastern Australia. Odyssey Cave, at 147.8m, is the second deepest on the Australian mainland. The Bungonia caves have unusually high concentrations of 'foul air' (carbon dioxide), primarily attributed to the large amounts of organic matter washed into the caves during heavy rain and poor ventilation.

The Bungonia limestone contains many fossil beds recording a diverse wildlife, including corals, brachiopods, cephalopods, trilobites and gastropods. Graptolite fossils have been found in the Adaminaby Group and Tertiary leaf impressions have been recorded in sandstone in the area. There are indications that Scuttle Cave and other caves nearby may be prolific sites for vertebrate subfossils. This fossil record makes Bungonia a most important geological site.

History

The many campsites on the plateau section of Bungonia Recreation Area indicate frequent use of rock outcrops for manufacturing Aboriginal tools. At least one cave at Bungonia was used as a burial site.

Bungonia Canyon lies close to the early land route to southern New South Wales and was settled by Europeans as soon as graziers were permitted to take their cattle beyond the County of Cumberland. In earlier times, the caves attracted many visitors. Remains of fossicking and mining during the late 19th and early 20th centuries are scattered through the recreation area, including remnants of a village built by miners. This is known as the Depression Village and probably dates from the 1920s but possibly from the 1890s. There are few other examples of such villages.

About 50 000 people visit Bungonia each year, but few venture farther

than the lookdown and so miss out on one of the most interesting day circuits in New South Wales.

Vegetation

The variety of geology and landform in Bungonia is reflected in the range of vegetation associations. Galleries of dry rainforest occur along some creeks, along with threatened plants.

Wildlife

Drum and Grill caves are maternity sites for a vulnerable population of up to 15 000 bent-wing bats and are the only such sites for this species known between Kempsey and Wee Jasper. Chalk Cave is a wintering site for bats. One of the more significant marsupials in the state recreation area is the koala. Some rare species of cave invertebrates appear to be endemic to the Bungonia caves, including a silverfish, an anemone, two beetles, a pseudoscorpion and a spider.

Bungonia Canyon Circuit

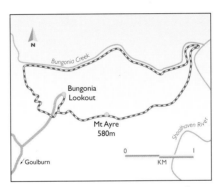

Starting Point: Bungonia Lookout, Bungonia State Recreation Reserve
Destination: Shoalhaven River, Bungonia Canyon
Summary: Because of its great depth and steep sides, Bungonia Canyon is a fine example of a limestone gorge. This circuit walk takes in the canyon, via the Red Track, and the Shoalhaven River, via the White Track, before returning to the car park.
Attractions: Rugged scenery, lookouts, narrow canyon and deep gorge
Length: 9.8km
Time: 1 day
Options: This walk can also be done in reverse or shortened by descending to Bungonia Creek by the Red Track.

You can camp where Bungonia Creek joins the Shoalhaven River.
Attraction Rating: ★ ★ ★ ★ ★
Fitness: ☒ ☒ ☒ ☒
Maps: LIC (CMA) Bungonia 1:25 000 topographical
Access to Starting Point: Bungonia State Recreation Area is 190km south-west of Sydney and 35km east of Goulburn. Simply follow the entrance road to the end.
Facilities/Amenities: Picnic and overnight camping facilities at Bungonia
Recommended Equipment: Sturdy shoes with good tread
Notes: Clear the area if you hear sirens signalling explosives activity in the quarry on the northern bank of Bungonia Creek. Signs at the bottom indicate frequency and duration of signals and what they represent.
Further Information:
> The National Parks and Wildlife Service Ranger
> Bungonia State Recreation Area
> Bungonia NSW 2580
> Tel: (02) 4844 4341
> or (02) 4844 4277

Walk Description

From Bungonia Lookout, head down the White Track to the Shoalhaven River. The track is well marked, especially the first 1.5km to Mt Ayre. There are some great views before the very steep descent from the end of the ridge. The rock here is quite loose and treacherous.

Once at the bottom, why not swim in the Shoalhaven River? Then head up Bungonia Creek to the canyon where massive limestone boulders slow your progress. The entrance to the canyon has a 300m cliff on the left side known as Troy Walls. It is difficult to follow the track as you scramble over and under the giant light grey boulders. In addition your hands will get very white.

Finally, you emerge from the boulders onto a pebble-strewn floor and you are into the canyon. Where has the creek gone? It's now subterranean, surfacing only during particularly protracted rain. It can rise suddenly though. The canyon walls are very narrow and because of their alignment, sunlight rarely reaches the bottom. With all the rock here, it's now hard to figure out why the Aborigines called this creek *bungonia* meaning 'sandy creek'.

On the other side, the creek re-appears and the track heads up a gully on the left, climbing steeply via the Efflux (Red) Track and a rocky slope to the top. It's then easy walking east back to the car park through open woodland. Once you've rested after the climb, spend the rest of the day exploring the other lookouts. Adams Lookout has very good views over a western amphitheatre with some waterfalls. A Yellow Track, leaving from the camping area, leads to Jerrara Falls, while the Green Track connects Adams Lookout with Bungonia Lookout. An Orange Track leads south past some large cave entrances to a lookout over the Shoalhaven River gorge.

An extended 2–3 day walk option in the south of the area is to walk to the Shoalhaven River using the Trestle Track to its confluence with Tolwong Creek. From here, walkers can climb up the remote and wild eastern side of the river to investigate the old mine workings. Campsites abound upstream and the topography of the Shoalhaven Gorge is spectacular here.

Return to Bungonia via the White Track. Consult the ranger at the Bungonia State Recreation Area Visitors' Centre for more information or read *Fitzroy Falls and Beyond*, a useful guide written and published by the Budawang Committee.

Ettrema Gorge Circuit

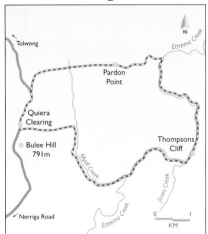

Starting Point: Quiera Clearing, Bungonia State Recreation Reserve

Walkers must camp overnight in trackless country to see remote Ettrema Gorge.

Destination: Ettrema Creek

Summary: A circuit strictly for fit, experienced walkers, using Myall Creek to descend into the gorge and Transportation Spur to climb out of it

Attractions: Incredibly rugged gorge scenery, views, waterfalls, trackless wilderness atmosphere

Length: 15.7km

Time: 2 days (3 with a rest day)

Options: There are two ways to descend into Ettrema. The navigation-ally easier but technically more difficult route is via the length of Myall Creek. The second route is via Jingles Pass just to the north of Myall Creek. A third rest day in the bottom can be spent exploring upstream into Sentry Box Canyon.

Attraction Rating: ★ ★ ★ ★ ★

Fitness: ◼ ◼ ◼ ◼

Maps: LIC (CMA) Touga 1:25 000 topographical

Access to Starting Point: To access Quiera Clearing, turn north from the Nowra to Nerriga road onto Tolwong Road. Drive for 14km along this unsealed road and park the car at the southern boundary of the clearing. The Nerriga topographical map is useful for car access.

Facilities/Amenities: None

Recommended Equipment: Complete self-sufficiency, including a well-stocked first-aid kit. Map and compass are essential, as well as expert navigation skills.

Notes: The route is not marked on the map. The bottom of the gorge is infested with red-bellied black snakes so wear tough gaiters for protection. Take a 20–30m rope for pack-hauling and protection from a fall on the last tricky descent from Myall Creek. Do not drink from Jones Creek as it is contaminated with arsenic from the old mine workings.

Further Information:

Fitzroy Falls Visitors' Centre
Morton National Park
Nowra Rd, Fitzroy Falls NSW 2577
Tel: (02) 4887 7270
Fax: (02) 4887 7203

or

Nowra National Parks and Wildlife Service District Office
55 Graham St, Nowra NSW 2541
Tel: (02) 4423 2170
Fax: (02) 4423 3122

Detailed track notes can be found in *Fitzroy Falls and Beyond*.

Walk Description

There are no tracks in the Ettrema region, the wildest and least fre-quented part of Morton National Park. While walkers enjoy a rare pure wilderness experience, they have to be experienced, fit and self-sufficient to cope with this dynamic and hostile terrain. There are deep ravines through the sandstone plateau. Allow time for slow progress when descend-ing and ascending. The last section from Pardon Point to the Tolwong Road through rough thick scrub is also slow going. From Quiera Clear-ing, walk east along a broad open spur and drop down into the Myall Creek gully. The walking is initially easy as you head south through patches of bracken fern. The cliffs steadily get higher, but a break on the left where a creek enters offers a technically easier approach to Ettrema Creek. To take this option, leave Myall Creek only about 350m after you entered it and follow the small unnamed creek up to the plateau top where you cut through swampy terrain to the ramp that is Jingles Pass, marked on the topographical map. The other option is to continue along Myall Creek, although it gets significantly steeper as you descend. There are several pools along the way and great views down the creek. Take great care on the very slippery rocks. There are two main waterfalls to negotiate. You can use a large tree branch on the right-hand side to get around the first.

The steep rocky terrain gives way to a broader flatter section as the creek swings east. To access the knife-edged ridge on the right, scramble up a low wall for your first glimpse of Ettrema Creek. There's an unusual and quite photogenic rocky knoll opposite the gorge.

Continue down Myall Creek as it swings north-east. The large 15m–20m waterfall with steep sides is a major obstacle. The only practical thing is to follow the northern (left) bank until you can find a place to scramble down. Take care as the rocks embedded in the ground here are very loose and cannot be relied on as hand or footholds. Use a 30m rope around a tree trunk to help, especially with the packs. You can't roll the packs down, because they will end up in the large pool at the base of the waterfall.

From the bottom, it's a short walk over a rocky bed to the confluence. The alternative route from Jingles Pass meets up near here. The first practical campsites are at the confluence and a few minutes downstream on the western bank. The second place is a wide open grassy area, but there is no swimming pool.

If there is enough time, make the confluence of Ettrema Creek and Jones Creek your destination. The rock strata in Thomsons Cliff opposite is quite spectacular. Beware of red-bellied black snakes among the river rocks along the entire length of the Ettrema Creek.

Spend the next day walking downstream to the base of Transportation Spur. There are several pleasant pools along the way and walkers will have to ford Ettrema Creek many times as it winds north. It's not practical to access the spur directly from the creek bed as it ends in a large ledge dominated by fig roots. The best access point is the unnamed creek that flows just north of Transportation Spur (not Gallows Gully). Follow it for 500m to the confluence of two tributaries and ascend very steeply to the left to reach the crest of Transportation Spur. There's some incredibly rugged terrain here and you sometimes need to climb the slopes on all fours. The going is easier once you reach the top and head west to Pardon Point.

At the base of the cliff pass, go round to the right and scramble over some ledges to the top. This is not as technically difficult as the Myall Creek descent. Once you are on the flat rocky clifftops at Pardon Point, there are great views to the north down the Ettrema Creek gorge. This is one of the highlights of the journey.

By contrast, the next hour or two is through thick scrub to Tolwong Road. Take a bearing due west and follow it, or follow the sun which will be in the west anyway, by the path of least resistance. Although it's not far, it's quite time-consuming, so make sure you don't run out of daylight. Head south once you reach the road and approach Quiera Clearing from the north to complete an eventful circuit.

Northern Budawang Circuit

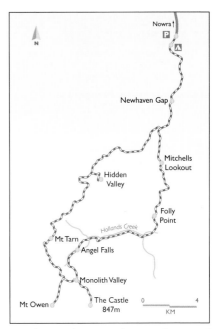

Starting Point: Newhaven Gap road vehicle barrier, Bungonia State Recreation Reserve
Destination: the Monolith Valley and Hollands Gorge

En route to Monolith Valley, Budawang Range, Morton National Park.

On the tail of The Castle, Budawang Range, Morton National Park.

CLASSIC WALKS OF AUSTRALIA

Summary: A rugged 5-day circuit through magnificent wild terrain

Attractions: Mt Owen, The Castle, Hidden Valley, Hollands Creek gorge, Folly Point, Monolith Valley, natural arch, rockpools, wilderness

Length: 64.5km

Time: 5 days (some parties might find 6 days a more comfortable pace)

Options: You can also start the central circuit of Hollands Creek gorge and Monolith Valley from Wog Wog camping area in the west of the park. While it takes longer, it avoids the road-bash from Newhaven Gap. A two-hour side option from The Vines leads to the bora ground up on Quiltys Mountain.

Attraction Rating: ★ ★ ★ ★ ★

Fitness: ◼ ◼ ◼ ◼ ◼

Maps: LIC (CMA) Tianjara, Endrick, and Corang 1:25 000 topographicals. The Budawang Committee Northern Budawang Ranges 1:50 000 Sketch Map also helps with tracks not marked on the topographical maps.

Access to Starting Point: To access Newhaven Gap Road, turn left off the Nowra to Nerriga road at Sassafras. The turn-off is 8km west of Tianjara Falls and the vehicle barrier is 3.6km along this road at the park entrance.

Facilities/Amenities: Walk-in camping area with toilets and tank water 600m south of the vehicle barrier

Recommended Equipment: Camera and plenty of film

Notes: The walk is hard going and there is nowhere to swim or wash

until day four. No camping is permitted in the Monolith Valley itself.

Further Information:

Fitzroy Falls Visitors' Centre
Morton National Park
Nowra Rd, Fitzroy Falls NSW 2577
Tel: (02) 4887 7270
Fax: (02) 4887 7203
or

Nowra National Parks and Wildlife
Service District Office
55 Graham St, Nowra NSW 2541
Tel: (02) 4423 2170
Fax: (02) 4423 3122

Detailed track notes can be found in the Budawang Committee's *Pigeon House and Beyond,* and *70 Walks in Southern New South Wales and A.C.T.* by Tyrone Thomas.

Walk Description

Every day of this walk is packed with features that will delight even the most blasé bushwalker. Experience, fitness and good navigation skills are necessary as much of it is remote and trackless. The sandstone country is very broken, nothing like the cliffs or flat ground territory around Katoomba and Blackheath. The only downside is that there is a vehicle barrier 7km before the traditional staging area at Newhaven Gap.

From Newhaven Gap, head to The Vines through a second barrier. Where you cross Camping Rock Creek, there is a small pool to dip in just downstream. At The Vines, the vegetation suddenly becomes lush as the soil

changes from a sandstone to a basalt base. A side walk at a crest leads up Quiltys Mountain to an Aboriginal bora ground, represented by a circular stone formation.

Head left, following an overgrown vehicle track. The vegetation continues to be predominantly rainforest. When you are at the closest point to the marked Hidden Valley, look for a bit of clearing with a fallen log with 'HV' carved in it. Leave your overnight packs here. A small faint track leads east on a very indistinct spur to the entrance, dominated by many rock stacks. It's about 3km return to the valley. Once inside the cliff-lined valley, turn south and follow trampled walking tracks up a cliff to overlook the valley from the top of the southern rim. Because it is such a unique and fragile landscape, the National Parks and Wildlife Service is considering restricting camping in the valley.

Backtrack to the packs and head south-west to Styles Creek for the first night's camp. The vegetation is quite open here, in contrast to the last section. There are several flat clearings by the eroded stream.

Next day, head south following Styles Creek upstream and turn left at a track leading toward the Pagoda Rocks. This gets you around the swampy ground in the middle of an expansive open amphitheatre. The track eventually curves 180 degrees to approach Mt Haughton, where there are some reasonable views looking back over the territory you have just traversed. The walk then follows the base of the southern cliffs where there are several rock overhangs, water drips and ferny glens.

Climb up a ridge to Mt Tarn and go south-west across the flat plateau. The tracks through heath and button grass are sometimes easy to follow but side branches can be misleading. Cross a deep, narrow gully before descending into another smaller gully via a waterfall that is usually dry. The pass is not technically difficult. From the base of the Mt Tarn plateau, head west along the bottom of the cliffs to attain a forested ridge that is your exit ramp to another open plain. This is the upper headwaters of the Corang

River and there's a very small pool by the campsite. The Wog Wog Track from the west enters the region here. Continue to the south-east, where you skirt Bibbenluke Mountain to a ridge that connects with Mt Cole. There are several large cave overhangs. Make camp here for your second night.

Leave very early next day and head south along the base of the cliffs to a narrow ravine that separates Mt Cole and Mt Owen. Climb this, keeping to the right. There are some tricky sections here and you'll have to haul packs separately. Once on top, drop the packs and head south to the end of Mt Owen for superb views over the coast, The Castle, Budawang National Park and the state forests in the Batemans Bay hinterland.

Return to the packs and follow the rock cairns east, descending steeply via rock shelves and tree roots to the Monolith Valley amphitheatre. Navigation can be difficult here and walkers should stay alert. If you are caught in one of the frequent white-outs, stop and wait for it to clear.

At Monolith Valley, have lunch by the small stream that runs through the centre by the bridge, then head out to Nibelung Pass via a chain to climb The Castle. Along the way is a wonderland of striking domes. The route follows the base of Mt Nibelung south to Meakins Pass. There is a lot of sword grass in this area and a large boulder marks a camp clearing. Leave the packs here and follow the eastern cliffs of The Castle for 10–15 minutes.

Just after a large rock overhang, you reach the start of the climb marked by white arrows pointing up. Almost straightaway you have to scramble over two large rocks to follow the arrows around the 'tail' of The Castle. The final ascent is on the western side with fantastic views of hundreds of unusually-shaped domes on the side of Mt Mooryan. Good opportunities for photos here and on one section, Byangee Walls, Pigeon House Mountain and the coast provide a spectacular backdrop to the rugged cliff of The Castle. (This shot has become rather clichéd.)

The ascent involves one particularly tricky part with a steep wall to the left of a chimney. Climbing up is not so difficult if you have good tread on your shoes, but getting down again can be a problem if the rock is wet. The installed ropes will help. This is the most exposed section of the climb. Above this ledge, it's an easy walk south along the flat top of The Castle. A walking track leads through low scrub and interconnecting rock platforms to the southern tip where there are expansive views over vast state forests to distant Deua National Park. There is usually a visitors' book in the large rock cairn near the end on the left. Descend by the same route, taking care on the steep ledge, and return to your packs. Set up camp at Meakins Pass. If the weather looks ominous, campers often use one of the rock overhangs at the base of The Castle or Mt Nibelung.

On the fourth day, head back into the Monolith Valley and north to the Seven Gods Pinnacles. Along the way are narrow ravines involving rock-scrambling and vines to assist walkers in climbing out. There's a natural arch here too, with a tree growing through it. Head to the very western cliff of Dojon Mountain and follow a faint track around the base for 300m, then down toward Angel Creek. It is a very steep descent and some ledges must be negotiated at the bottom.

Follow Angel Creek downstream. Progress will be slow over the slippery boulders. Look out for spider webs.

Follow the creek for only about 1km until it plunges over a great abyss. Climb up the northern (left) bank to the base of the cliffs and traverse around them for 500m to find the top of a pronounced spur. This then descends extremely steeply toward the junction of Angel and Hollands creeks. From here it is easy going along Hollands Creek, changing banks occasionally.

There are some very pleasant swimming pools along here. Camp where you please, but one good place is just north-east of the confluence with Camping Rock Creek. This may not be immediately obvious, so make sure you are on the northern side of Hollands Creek before turning left up the eastern bank of Camping Rock Creek. The pleasant camp clearing is quite large and flat.

On the fifth day, head along the eastern bank of Camping Rock Creek. A well-defined walking track then rises steeply. Fill water bottles before climbing rapidly up to Watsons Pass and Folly Point. The climb is relentless and walkers must navigate very carefully. The track through the tall eucalypt forest can be hard to follow as there are many rock outcrops to weave between. Metal markers on tree trunks guide the way. Two sets of cliffs must be negotiated, one at the head of a gully and the second by means of rock-scrambling up a chimney. Chains and pegs are installed.

At the top of Folly Point, walkers are confronted by a labyrinth of rock outcrops. There are great views south to The Castle and Shrouded Gods Mountain. A plaque commemorates the discovery of Watsons Pass, named after Colin Watson, one of the founders of the Budawang Committee.

Cross a gully before you head north through bush to Mitchell Lookout. There are occasional views to the east as the faint track sometimes follows the top of the cliffs. Otherwise it is a fairly uneventful section to Newhaven Gap and the hard slog along the road back to the vehicle barrier. There is water at the camping area on the right, just before the final uphill.

The Castle Walk

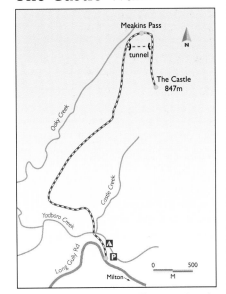

Starting Point: Yadboro Creek, Bungonia State Recreation Reserve
Destination: The summit of The Castle, Mt Owen (847m)

Early morning on the summit of Mt Owen, looking toward Pigeon House Mountain.

Summary: A dramatic two-tier cliff-lined plateau resembling a prominent fortress is the destination of this spectacular walk

Attractions: Views over the upper Clyde River gorge

Length: 12km

Time: 1 day

Attraction Rating: ★ ★ ★ ★ ★

Fitness: ◪ ◪ ◪ ◪

Maps: LIC (CMA) Corang 1:25 000 topographical. Budawang Committee Northern Budawang Ranges 1:50 000 Sketch Map also can be useful.

Access to Starting Point: Best access to Yadboro Creek is from Milton or Ulladulla on the New South Wales south coast. Turn off Princes Highway and follow the signposts to Pigeon House Mountain then continue along Yadboro Road to the Clyde River. Take the Western Distributor to the camping area at Yadboro Creek in the Yadboro State Forest.

Facilities/Amenities: Basic car-camping facilities at Yadboro by the Clyde River and Yadboro Creek

Recommended Equipment: Self-supporting tent for rock-ledge camping

Notes: No camping is allowed in the Monolith Valley

Further Information:

Fitzroy Falls Visitors' Centre
Morton National Park
Nowra Rd, Fitzroy Falls NSW 2577
Tel: (02) 4887 7270
Fax: (02) 4887 7203
or

Nowra National Parks and Wildlife Service District Office
55 Graham St, Nowra NSW 2541
Tel: (02) 4423 2170
Fax: (02) 4423 3122

Detailed track notes can be found in the Budawang Committee's *Pigeon House and Beyond.*

Walk Description

The Castle remained unclimbed until 1947. Several attempts were made throughout the early part of the 20th century but its double layer of sheer cliffs seemed to many unconquerable. Thanks to pioneers of the 1950s, it is now almost a Sunday stroll to the summit, taking a good five to six hours. For campers, additional days can be spent exploring the fascinating and eerie Monolith Valley, a wonderland of domes, moss-covered walls, narrow chasms, and pockets of rainforest set in an art gallery of natural rock sculptures. From the car park, a signpost points the way to The Castle and Monolith Valley walking tracks. Be wary of red-bellied black snakes in the area during summer.

The first problem is to ford the Yadboro Creek, which can flood after rain preventing walkers from crossing. In dry periods, you can cross via stepping stones without getting your feet wet. A good track then leads up Kalianna Ridge through pleasant forest to a rocky bluff. It is overgrown at first because of the sheltered nature of the terrain, but it opens up as you gain altitude. The conglomerate at the end of the ridge can easily be climbed and a rope has been installed for convenience. At the base of the bluff is the Morton National Park entry sign, marking the southern boundary of this great national park. Once on top, enjoy the view over the Budawang foothills, especially east to Pigeon House Mountain.

The easy part is now over, and it's tough walking following the base of the western cliffs along a small rocky track. You pass several overhangs and water is available from a pool surrounded by gigantic boulders. Almost an hour farther on, climb a short steep slope to a large conglomerate overhang. The track contours around and a short footpad detour on the left leads out to some rock platforms where there are superb views over the Oakey Creek valley, up to Mt Owen and the Yadboro State Forest. From this point, the track immediately ascends along a muddy creek. Close to the top is a junction marked by three arrows on the rock. The track forks between a 'T' for tunnel and 'MV' for Monolith Valley. The slope between the two cliffs has been badly eroded by walkers and the NPWS has installed wooden steps to help stabilise the track.

Follow the tunnel track directly up to the base of the second cliff and turn right. White chalked arrows lead to the tunnel itself and some scrambling is involved in negotiating more large boulders. Keep an eye out for arrows. The narrow chasm that leads into the tunnel gets smaller and you have to crawl. However, there is plenty of light from gaps in the roof. Descend over some ledges onto the forest-covered eastern side of The Castle. Turn right and follow a good track south along the base of the second-tier cliffs. Just after a large rock overhang, you reach the start of the climb marked by white arrows pointing up. Almost straightaway you have to scramble over two large rocks to follow the arrows around the 'tail' of The Castle. The final ascent is on the western side with fantastic views of hundreds of unusually shaped domes on the side of Mt Mooryan.

The ascent involves one particularly tricky part with a steep wall to the left of a chimney. Climbing up is not so difficult if you have good tread on your shoes, but getting down again can be a problem if the rock is wet. The installed ropes will help. This is the most exposed section of the climb.

Above this ledge, it's an easy walk south along the flat top of The Castle. A walking track leads through low scrub and interconnecting rock platforms to the southern tip where there are expansive views over vast state forests to distant Deua National Park. There is usually a visitors' book in the large rock cairn near the end on the left.

Descend by the same route taking care on the steep ledge and Kalianna Bluff at the bottom of the first set of cliffs. To avoid passing through the tail on the descent, head north along the base of the second cliffs. Pass the tunnel and continue to Meakins Pass (named after Reg Meakins whose life ambition was fulfilled when he made the first recorded ascent of The Castle). At the pass, a signpost points the way to Junction Rock, rejoining with the original ascent track.

Mt Owen Walk

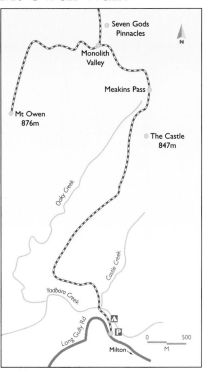

Starting Point: Yadboro Creek, Bungonia State Recreation Reserve
Destination: Mt Owen
Summary: The mecca of bushwalking in New South Wales, approaching from the south via Kalianna Bluff
Attractions: Sunrise from the end of Mt Owen, exploring Monolith Valley
Length: 17km
Time: 2–3 days
Attraction Rating: ★ ★ ★ ★ ★

Fitness: ☒☒☒☒☒
Maps: LIC (CMA) Corang 1:25 000 topographical. Budawang Committee Northern Budawang Ranges 1:50 000 Sketch Map also can be useful.
Access to Starting Point: Best access to Yadboro Creek is from Milton or Ulladulla on the south coast. Turn off Princes Highway and follow the signposts to Pigeon House Mountain. Continue along Yadboro Road to the Clyde River. The Western Distributor will take you to the camping area at Yadboro Creek.
Facilities/Amenities: There are basic car-camping facilities at Yadboro by the Clyde River and Yadboro Creek
Recommended Equipment: Self-supporting tent for rock-ledge camping
Notes: No camping is allowed in the Monolith Valley
Further Information:
Fitzroy Falls Visitors' Centre
Morton National Park
Nowra Rd, Fitzroy Falls NSW 2577
Tel: (02) 4887 7270
Fax: (02) 4887 7203
or
Nowra National Parks and Wildlife Service District Office
55 Graham St, Nowra NSW 2541
Tel: (02) 4423 2170
Fax: (02) 4423 3122
Detailed track notes can be found in the Budawang Committee's *Pigeon House and Beyond.*

Walk Description

Twin of the famous Castle, Mt Owen is slightly higher and is less frequently visited but presents a more interesting walk as you must pass through the fantastic hanging Monolith Valley.

Follow the notes for the Castle Walk above to where the track forks between a 'T' for tunnel and 'MV' for Monolith Valley. Head left, traversing up the slope through steadily thicker vegetation and larger boulders to Meakins Pass (named after Reg Meakins who made the first recorded ascent of The Castle). There is a large rock overhang here and a makeshift camping area. The pass is another junction, with walking tracks leading right to The Castle and left to Monolith Valley. Head left again, gradually ascending north-west up to the base of Mt Nibelung. The route continues right under impressive cliff overhangs, passing a small waterfall (which may be dry) and another campsite. Shortly, 400m from the pass, you enter a big ravine. There is a stream and cascade and the track divides below the ravine. Climb the left fork pad up through the ravine into wild, rocky terrain. A few steep sections must be negotiated before you reach Nibelung Pass about 1km from Meakins Pass. A steel chain allows access to rock platforms and the mysterious Monolith Valley. Walking is easier on the rock and there are many sights. During low cloud, the mist creates an eerie effect as it swirls and eddies around the domes. The pad at first leads gently down an open, broad valley before turning west into a really rugged ravine. It crosses a bridge over a small pleasant stream. This has been used as a campsite in the past, but camping and fires are now strictly prohibited in the Monolith Valley. Drop the packs and do a bit of exploring.

Head north (right) up an absolutely fascinating ravine just east of Mt Cole. Moss covers very high vertical walls and there is a natural arch. Once through this chasm, walk along a small valley between Mt Cole and seven unusual rock stacks called the Seven Gods Pinnacles. You ascend into normal forest, then out onto open rock platforms. Here are great views over Holland Creek gorge and Dojon Mountain. Return to the packs.

Walking access to Mt Owen is on the left (west) of the bridge to an impressive open amphitheatre. The signposted start of the Mt Owen climb is on the right. The tracks are vague at this point and there are many false leads. People often have to turn back because they become confused in the maze of rocky canyons. Immediately climb up a steep slope to a saddle. Scramble down to a rocky creek on the right. Cross over and a root-dominated climb takes you up to the base of rocks. The trail splits here; keep right as it ascends around the corner to some rock ledges. Access to the top is aided by vines and roots, offering excellent foot and handholds. You'll probably have to haul overnight packs manually up the many ledges.

The vegetation changes dramatically on top, becoming immediately drier. Head up to the base of giant rocky spurs, keeping right. The track enters a gully between two rock spurs and disappears. Continue up to the very top, where it's a short scramble to the rock platforms.

The worst part is over. Now it's a matter of following rock cairns over rock platforms to the back of Mt Owen, almost to Mt Cole. Here the trail swings left and it's easy walking south over more rock platforms connected by muddy grass and heath-enclosed footpads. At the end, sign the visitors' book and enjoy outstanding views to the coast and the Budawang National Park. There is no wood or water here so campers have to be totally self-sufficient. There is barely enough room for one or two tents, and peg-less self-supporting dome tents are preferable. Enjoy the sunset from this vantage point and, in the morning, the sunrise over the mist-filled valleys is simply awesome. Return to the car via the same route. If you have the time and inclination, drop the packs at Meakins Pass and climb The Castle.

Pigeon House Mountain Walk

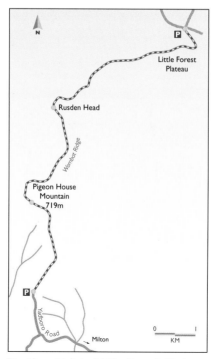

Starting Point: Little Forest Plateau, Bungonia State Recreation Reserve

Destination: Pigeon House Mountain (719m)

Summary: A traverse of Wombat Ridge from Rusden Head to approach Pigeon House Mountain from the north then descend to the car park on the southern side

Attractions: Views from Rusden Head and the summit of Pigeon House, overlooking the upper Clyde River Gorge

Length: 19km

Time: 1 long day

Options: An overnight walk is possible by camping in Pigeon House Creek Gorge, but this is very rugged terrain. Ropes are highly recommended for descending to this creek.

Attraction Rating: ★ ★ ★ ★

Fitness: ☒ ☒ ☒

Maps: LIC (CMA) Milton 1:25 000 topographical. Northern Budawang Ranges Sketch Map produced by the Budawang Committee is also useful.

Access to Starting Point: To access Little Forest Plateau, turn off the Princes Highway onto Pointer Gap Road just north of Milton. Watch out for wombats at night. You can also travel south in a 4WD along the Tianjara Plateau from the Nowra to Nerriga Road. To access the Pigeon House car park, turn off the Princes Highway from Milton or Ulladulla and follow signs along Yadboro Road. The Tabourie topographical may be useful.

Facilities/Amenities: Very basic picnic facilities at Porters Creek Dam (fireplace and tables) and at the Pigeon House car park

Recommended Equipment: Self-supporting tent for rock-ledge camping, compass and maps, long trousers, water for two days

Recommended Equipment: Water

Notes: The major part of this walk is along abandoned fire trails so walking is relatively fast

Further Information:

Fitzroy Falls Visitors' Centre
Morton National Park
Nowra Rd, Fitzroy Falls NSW 2577
Tel: (02) 4887 7270
Fax: (02) 4887 7203
or

Nowra National Parks and Wildlife Service District Office
55 Graham St, Nowra NSW 2541
Tel: (02) 4423 2170
Fax: (02) 4423 3122

Detailed track notes can be found in the Budawang Committee's *Pigeon House and Beyond*

Walk Description

This prominent peak is often mistaken for a volcanic plug, but it is just a sandstone outcrop. It was first sighted by Europeans in 1770 when Captain Cook noted in his diary 'a remarkable peaked hill which resembled a square dovehouse with a dome on top and for that reason I called it Pigeon House'. Rather than use the tourist approach from the car park to the south of the summit, approach the peak from the north and then descend to the car park. Naturally, this will involve a car shuffle. The walk follows part of the epic Two Rivers Walk route, connecting the Shoalhaven and Clyde rivers.

The car park is just south of the prominent bend in the road connecting Pointer Gap with Porters Creek Dam. Signposts give details of a short nature trail from here. Head south-south-east along the walking track and join up with a fire trail to Rusden Head. There can be boggy sections after rain along here because of poor drainage on the button-grass plains and heath. The fire trail heads west before swinging south where the terrain gets rockier. At Rusden Head, enjoy the views before going left along the clifftop to a break in the cliffs. A rope has been installed here for safety. The trail heads steeply down through thick forest. It is important to keep to the centre of the prominent spur if you lose the trail.

Once the ground levels out, join the Wombat Ridge fire trail, which proceeds south through tall forest. This section will take several hours. At the junction, go right toward Pigeon House, which now dominates the horizon. A small faint walking path heads up the side around the cliff and then climbs it via ladders.

The views from the stone-capped summit rank among the best in the state. To the north and south are nothing but unblemished mountains. The rugged Clyde River Gorge dominates the view. At the end of Byangee Walls the legendary Castle beckons to anyone with a sense of adventure. Descend to the car park using the well-maintained track.

Other walks in the Sandstone Parks

There are a number of smaller national parks in the sandstone region around Sydney. These include Cattai National Park, Scheyville National Park and Dharawal State Recreation Area. However, none of these have any developed extended walks. Several other national parks dispersed around the sandstone regions do have significant walking opportunities. These are Budderoo National Park, Barren Grounds Nature Reserve, Macquarie Pass National Park and Bents Basin State Recreation Area.

Budderoo National Park

At 5846ha, this park covers most of a sandstone plateau isolated by steep cliffs of the Kangaroo Valley and coastal escarpment. Exposed heaths and eucalypt forests cover the plateau, while important pockets of rainforest lie in the shelter of the cliffs.

Looking from Kalianna Bluff to Pigeon House, Yadboro State Forest.

Walking Opportunities: A popular walk is along the raised walkway to Minnamurra Falls, but this is really something of a tourist path. More challenging walks can be found around the Carrington Falls area, walking down the Kangaroo River via Missingham Steps. Some great views from here. An even less-frequented walk is to Gerringong Falls from the runway on the Budderoo plateau.

Facilities: The Minnamurra Rainforest Area is very well developed with a visitors' centre exhibition, picnic facilities and kiosk. At Carrington Falls, camping is permitted only in the designated area.

Access: The national park is 110km south of Sydney, 25km south-east of Mittagong and 60km north of Nowra on the eastern edge of the southern highlands escarpment.

To reach Minnamurra, take the Jamberoo Rd from Kiama and follow the signposts some 3km to the rainforest area. Note that a small park entry fee applies for vehicles and camping is not permitted.

To reach Carrington Falls, turn off the Jamberoo–Robertson road about 8km east of Robertson where the access road is signposted. Follow the unsealed road to a Y-intersection. The right fork leads to one of the picnic areas, while the left fork continues to a bridge, after which take the right turn to another picnic area called Thomas Place.

Further Information:
Nowra National Parks and Wildlife Service District Office
24 Berry St
PO Box 707, Nowra NSW 2540
Tel: (02) 4423 2170
or
Minnamurra Rainforest Centre
Budderoo National Park
Minnamurra Falls Road
via Jamberoo NSW 2533
Tel: (02) 4236 0469

Barren Grounds Nature Reserve

This 2024ha reserve lies to the immediate south-east of Budderoo National Park and is accessible via the Jamberoo–Robertson road. The reserve was originally gazetted as a Faunal Reserve in 1956 to protect the habitat of the rare ground parrot and the eastern bristlebird. A picnic area and associated walking tracks are located immediately inside the reserve entrance, 5km east of the Carrington Falls turn-off. The main walking destination in the reserve is Drawing Room Rocks, a round trip of 3.4km.

Macquarie Pass National Park

Topped by a rim of impressive cliffs, the 1064ha Macquarie Pass National Park preserves a section of the Illawarra escarpment. Its steep, densely timbered ridges and rainforest gullies contain interesting historical features, including the Nurrewin homestead, built around 1900. The principal stream that drains the national park is the Macquarie Rivulet. Its headwaters are on the plateau outside the south-western boundary of the park, after which it tumbles over waterfalls and rapids within the park and leaves via gentler flats on the eastern boundary.

Geology: The cliffs of the steep escarpment are of Hawkesbury sandstone. Other less conspicuous geological formations support the diverse plant communities of the area. Under the sandstone there are seams of Illawarra coal and laterite, and under the lower sections of the park, strata formed by volcanic activity 230–280 million years ago.

Vegetation: This area was once a source of red cedar, and there is now some regrowth of this fine tree. Due to the shelter offered by the Illawarra escarpment, much of the vegetation in the park is lush subtropical rainforest, especially along watercourses.

Wildlife: In the moist woodland, swamp wallabies, wombats, bandicoots, lyrebirds and satin bowerbirds abound. Small native fish and eels swim in the creeks and many reptiles may be seen during the warmer months when they are most active.

Walking Opportunities: Several short tracks and branch tracks through tall open forest provide walkers with the opportunity to explore. The Macquarie Rivulet is the main destination for longer walks. Use Clover Hill Road to reach numerous waterfalls, including Clover Falls, Mulangong Falls and Rainbow Falls.

Facilities: Picnic area at the foot of Macquarie Pass on the northern side of the road. Camping is permitted only if the site is at least one kilometre from any road, picnic area or other public facility. There are two areas within the park where visitors can leave the highway and take a walk in the forest: the Cascades Rainforest Walk and the Glenview Track.

Access: About 130km south of Sydney, Macquarie Pass National Park is on the Illawarra escarpment between Robertson on the Southern Tablelands and Albion Park on the south coast. Access is by the Illawarra Highway, which traverses the national park, or from the Mt Murray railway

Macquarie Rivulet, Macquarie Pass National Park in the southern highlands.

station on the Moss Vale–Unanderra line. The nearest towns are Robertson, about 7km to the south-west, and Albion Park, 10km to the east.

Bents Basin State Recreation Area

Although not a national park, Bents Basin State Recreation Area is a very scenic and secluded green 'oasis' that has long been popular with locals. It is surrounded on three sides by the Nepean River. The preserved area (48ha) was named after Justice Ellis Bent who had leased the area from the Crown. Bents Basin is a natural geological feature at the juncture of Cumberland Plain and the Blue Mountains escarpment. Gazetted as a State Recreation Area in 1980, the area now receives more than 70 000 visitors a year.

Walking Opportunities: A short track leads from Bents Basin Road car park to Caleys Lookout on the western bank above the basin. Allow 15 minutes to complete the basic walk. There are lots of unofficial walking tracks that lead upstream on both sides of the Nepean River. Excellent swimming opportunities here, too.

Access: This recreation area is on the Nepean River 25km south of Penrith and 14km south of Wallacia. The main access is via Wolstenholme Avenue, off Greendale Road. There is a second entrance via Bents Basin Road leading from the Wallacia–Silverdale road.

Facilities: The Richard S. Venables Education Centre features displays and a film on the significance of the area: its unique wildlife, superb scenery, fascinating history and its importance to the Aboriginal culture of the Gandangara tribe. The centre makes an ideal venue for school field studies and community groups and can be hired for private functions. The kiosk offers a range of takeaways as well as camping supplies. Staff will also cater for functions and school camps. The kiosk is open weekends, public holidays and during school holidays. Bents Basin Recreation Area is open seven days a week, but check closing hours because the entrance gates are locked at night. A small fee is charged for vehicle entry.

Further Information:
Bents Basin SRA office
Wolstenholme Ave
Greendale NSW
PO Box 12, Wallacia NSW 2750
Tel: (02) 4774 8662

Around Sydney

Few cities in the world have so many large areas of reserved land so close to their metropolitan area. No fewer than 15 national parks and other reserves are easily accessible from Sydney by a short drive or public transport. Sydney Harbour National Park, near the centre of the city, can be accessed by ferry. The two principal reserves, Ku-ring-gai Chase National Park to the north of Sydney and Royal National Park to the south, are well used and the National Parks and Wildlife Service takes special measures to accommodate the large numbers of people yet minimise their impact on the environment. These include requiring camping permits, closing tracks and charging entrance fees.

Trains run close to most of Sydney's perimeter parks, so day walks linking railway stations are possible, avoiding the inconvenience of car shuffles and backtracking. Some parks near the coast are relatively flat, which makes walking easy and makes them excellent training grounds for the young or inexperienced walker. Yet they are also rugged and challenging enough to prepare any walker for the more demanding and larger parks of the Great Dividing Range.

Another advantage of the parks near Sydney is that they offer fine facilities. Roads are well signposted, tracks are regularly graded, and picnic spots and camping places, complete with fireplaces, tables and toilets, are everywhere. The best time to walk on the plateau tops is between April and October when it is cool and dry, with the added advantage of spectacular wildflower displays. In these months, also, the threat of bushfires is lower. The ocean-based national parks are best visited in summer, when the sea moderates Sydney's extreme summer heat—a blessing for all walkers. Always be wary of rips when swimming at deserted beaches.

The Hawkesbury Region

....
The Great North Walk

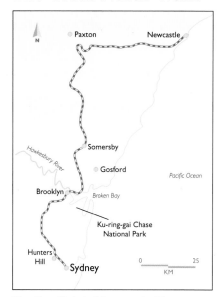

Starting Point: Macquarie Place, near Circular Quay, Sydney Cove
Destination: Newcastle
Summary: An epic walk through bushland along fire trails that connect suburbs and towns. The track passes through some good natural scenery, even within the cities.
Attractions: These include Sydney Harbour, Lake Macquarie and the Newcastle coastline, a section through Hunters Hill and another passing through magnificent Lane Cove River bushland. The historic Benowie section goes to Berowra Waters and the Hawkesbury River. The Great North Walk also passes through Brisbane Water National Park and an impressive network of state forests.
Length: 250km
Time: 2 weeks
Options: Walkers can start from many places on the outskirts of Sydney. One possibility is from the Cumberland State Forest. The walk can finish at Paxton in the Hunter Valley, rather than pushing on to Newcastle.
Attraction Rating: ★ ★ ★ ★
Fitness: ◪ ◪ ◪ ◪
Maps: The Department of Land and Water Conservation's *Discovery Kit* booklets contain the relevant topographical coverage for the route. This saves a lot of money as about 11 topographical maps are involved.

Looking toward Garie Beach on the Coast Walk, Royal National Park.

Access to Starting Point: Walk to the obelisk at Macquarie Place from Wynyard or Circular Quay railway stations. You then catch a ferry to the Valentia Street Wharf where the walking really starts.

Facilities/Amenities: Campsites are provided along the route. In some areas shops and comfortable accommodation are never far away. In more remote sections a tent is essential.

Recommended Equipment: Overnight packs, the information kit, and ferry timetables

Notes: Food can be bought along the way, so it is never necessary to carry more than about three days' supply.

There are several costs involved in a complete traverse of this walk. In addition to the train fare back from Newcastle, two ferry trips are required to cross Sydney Harbour and the Hawkesbury River.

Further Information:
The Department of Land and Water Conservation
23–33 Bridge St
Sydney NSW 2000
Tel: (02) 9228 6111
or
The Department of Land and Water Conservation
District Office, Level 9
2–10 Wentworth St

Parramatta NSW 2150
Tel: (02) 9895 7503
or
The Department of Land and Water Conservation
District Office
Cnr Newcastle Road and Bank St
East Maitland NSW 2323
Tel: (02) 4934 2280

Walk Description

This epic walk was one of the lasting monuments of the Bicentennial year of 1988. There six main sections: Lane Cove Valley, Benowie, Hawkesbury, Cedar Brush, Watagan and Yuerlarbah. The walk is well covered in the *Discovery Kit* booklets produced by the Department of Land and Water Conservation. The booklets come in a packaged bundle and cost about $10.00 —good value considering you then don't need to buy topographical maps.

Royal National Park

The area known today as the Royal National Park is a significant part of Sydney's heritage, a glimpse into the past. Being only 30km from Sydney, its history has been interwoven with the state's capital since the late 18th century. Before Europeans settled Australia, the land was occupied by the Dharawal tribe, who used the sandstone caves for shelter and fished the coast, estuaries and inland streams. Most of the adjoining Heathcote National Park was burny out by severe bushfires in January, 1993.

Facts and Figures

Name: Royal National Park
Size: 15 080ha
Enactment: 26 April 1879 (the world's first named 'national park')
Visitors: More than 1.5 million a year
Vegetation: The park environment alternates between coastal heath, woodlands, and rainforest. On the plateau tops alone, there are 700 species of flowering plants.
Wildlife: Swamp wallabies, koalas, rat kangaroos, gliders, echidnas, New Holland mice, numerous ground-dwelling animals, ringtailed possums, Javan Rusa deer; more than 200 species of birds.
Aboriginal Sites: The Dharawal tribe left many remains: rock engravings,

axe-grinding grooves, charcoal drawings, and hand stencils. All sites are protected.

Camping: Developed camping ground at Bonnie Vale. Bush-camping is permitted anywhere else with a free permit.

Adjoining Parks: Heathcote National Park, Garrawarra State Recreation Area

Further Information:
National Parks and Wildlife
Service District Office
Royal National Park
Farnell Ave, Audley NSW 2232
Tel: (02) 9542 0648
Fax: (02) 9542 1420

The Coast Walk

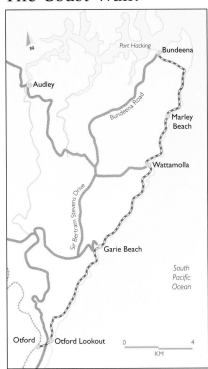

Starting Point: Otford railway station
Destination: Bundeena ferry wharf
Summary: A fantastic walk along the entire coast of Royal National Park. One of the best coastal walks possible in New South Wales.
Attractions: Sea cliffs, views, pockets of palms and rainforest, rock platforms, many secluded beaches
Length: 27km
Time: 1 long day, or 2 half days
Options: This walk can also be done from north to south, but this involves walking up rather than down. It can also be completed in three stages with Garie Beach and Wattamolla as access

points and setting up car shuffles.
Attraction Rating: ★ ★ ★ ★ ★
Fitness: ◪ ◪ ◪
Maps: LIC (CMA) Royal National Park 1:30 000 topographical
Access to Starting Point: Take a train to Otford station (via Sutherland) in the morning and catch the Bundeena ferry to Cronulla. To check ferry times, call Cronulla National Park Ferry Cruises on (02) 9523 2990.
Facilities/Amenities: Campgrounds at Burning Palms, Curracurrang, Deer Pool, Little Marley Beach and Marley Beach. Shops at Otford and Bundeena and a kiosk, open on weekends, at Garie Beach.
Recommended Equipment: Swimming gear. In summer, sunscreen is important as there are many sections of the track with no shade.
Notes: A permit is required if you plan to camp. Contact Audley Visitors' Centre for bookings. The warmer months are the best time to visit.
Further Information:
National Parks and Wildlife
Service District Office
Royal National Park
Farnell Ave, Audley NSW 2232
Tel: (02) 9542 0648
Fax: (02) 9542 1420
Consult *Coastal Walking Tracks*, a NPWS brochure.

Walk Description

If you want to do this classic walk in one day, leave very early, arriving at Otford no later than 8.00am and check the time when the last ferry is due to leave from Bundeena. You may prefer to camp overnight at one of many secluded bush clearings along the way so you can take your time and swim at some of the beautiful beaches.

From Otford railway station, head up to Otford Gap where Otford Lookout allows superb views over the sea cliffs toward Port Kembla. Head along the cliff track where paragliders often make use of the updrafts from the ocean. You can either walk down to Werong Beach or continue along the cliff track, turning off to the right to go to Palm Jungle. Both tracks end up at the same place at Werong Point. Be advised that Werrong Beach (also called the Hell Hole) is an authorised nude bathing area.

It is then fairly easy walking north to Burning Palms, along one of the more scenic sections of the track. This is a very good swimming spot, but don't venture too far out as there are no patrols to monitor for rips.

Continue north following the coast. The section between Garie Beach and Wattamolla is along clifftops with no ocean access. At Wattamolla, the Coast Track goes inland around Wattamolla Creek. Little Marley Beach is another good swimming place and has a great campsite among trees. The track leaves the coast south of the Waterrun, cutting north to Bundeena.

Other walks in the Royal National Park

Contact Audley Visitors' Centre for information and a list of guidebooks to the multitude of walking options in the park. The National Parks Association has produced two books with detailed notes: *Bushwalks in the Sydney Region,* Volumes 1 and 2.

Heathcote National Park

Heathcote National Park is the Royal National Park's kid sister, a 2250ha triangle bordered by the Woronora Catchment Area to the south, Holsworthy Field Firing Range to the north and Royal National Park to the east.

Geology

Like much of the Sydney basin, the landscape is a dissected Hawkesbury sandstone plateau. Heathcote Creek is a good example of the deep dissection. The sandstone was deposited some 200 million years ago, and periodic uplifting began about 94 million years ago. Each period of uplift has caused streams to erode deeper into the ancient plateau surfaces. Heathcote Creek cascades and tumbles via a number of rock pools down to the Woronora River.

Access

For private transport, the Woronora Dam Road allows vehicles to the dam as well as to Sarahs Knob. From Waterfall railway station, access to the park is from Warabin Street; from Heathcote railway station, use Oliver

Street. Access by foot or mountain bike also via the Pipeline Track that connects Woronora Dam Road with Heathcote Road.

Facilities

A very nice bush-camping area at Kingfisher Pool and other pools along Heathcote Creek and at Girronba Creek about 2km north of Sarahs Knob. Picnic facilities at Sarahs Knob.

Heathcote Creek Circuit

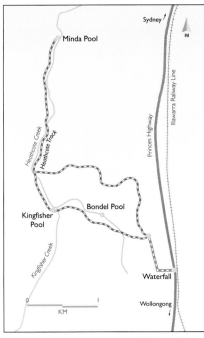

Starting Point: Waterfall Railway Station

Destination: Minda Pool, Heathcote National Park

Summary: A scenic walk down the Heathcote Creek valley, through pleasant forest, passing many secluded pools ideal for swimming

Attractions: The Kingfisher Pool and Bondel Pool

Length: 13km

Time: 4.5 hours

Options: Many informal walking tracks lead to various attractions in the Heathcote Creek valley. A variation on the walk is to descend via the Bullawarring Track to Kingfisher Pool and then walk to Minda Pool, returning via Avarco Gully to the Mooray Track. A short 30-minute side option leads south from Kingfisher Pool to Yelgun Cave.

Attraction Rating: ★ ★ ★

Fitness: ◪◪◪

Maps: LIC (CMA) Royal National Park 1:30 000 topographical. The Appin and Campbelltown 1:25 000 topographical maps could come in handy.

Access to Starting Point: Waterfall railway station is on the Illawarra line via Sutherland

Facilities/Amenities: Shops at Waterfall, camping area at Karloo Pool

Notes: To camp overnight, get a permit from the Audley office

Further Information:

National Parks and Wildlife Service District Office
Royal National Park
Farnell Ave, Audley NSW 2232
Tel: (02) 9542 0648
Fax: (02) 9542 1420

Walk Description

From the western side of Waterfall railway station, head down Kooraban Street and turn right at Warabin Street. Follow this north to the end where it turns into the Mooray Track. Follow this down the Mooray Gully to Myunga Pool and walk north along Heathcote Creek to Minda Pool for lunch and a swim. Backtrack to Myunga Pool, then take the Bullawarring Track to Kingfisher Pool, Bondel Pool and Yellow Pool, before returning to Waterfall railway station via the Mooray Track. These pools will be a welcome relief on a hot afternoon. Of all these pools, Kingfisher is the loveliest. Since it is only about 2km from Bondel Pool to Waterfall railway station, you can plan your exit to maximise swimming time.

Other walks in Heathcote National Park

The Bullawarring Track continues to follow the Heathcote Creek valley all the way to the Pipeline Track from where it is possible to walk to Heathcote railway station, completing an 11km traverse. Another popular swimming place is Lake Eckersley with the nearby Dingo Cave. This is commonly accessed via the Pipeline Track from Heathcote Road.

Other walks in the Sydney Area

Australia's largest city is blessed with dozens of national parks and reserves, all within an hour or two of the CBD.

Kingfisher Pool in Heathcote National Park—one of the many good pools for swimming in the park.

Most walks are less than a day and public transport can be used to and from starting and finishing points.

Metropolitan area

Close to the heart of the city lies the Sydney Harbour National Park (393ha) on the foreshores of Port Jackson, where several short harbourside walks are possible. Access points are at North Head from Manly, Dobroyd Head from Balgowlah Heights, Bradleys Head from Mosman and Taronga Park Zoo, and South Head from Vaucluse.

In Georges River National Park (324ha) near Picnic Point, the 2km Ridge Track connects Morgans Creek with Cattle Duffers Flat. The Yeramba Lagoon Walk is another short path. The Basin, a destination in the nearby Basin Reserve, is accessible from the Georges River Road via Kentlyn. Other walks include a circuit of Manly Dam, a section of the Great Northern Walk through the Lane Cove National Park (372ha), and exploration of the Garigal National Park (2203ha) via Middle Harbour Creek and Deep Creek. To the north, Barenjoey Head offers a small circuit from Palm Beach to the lighthouse with views over the mouth of the Hawkesbury River.

Broken Bay

By far the greatest concentration of walks occurs around Broken Bay, which is lined with several reserves. One of the most popular with bush-walkers is Bouddi National Park (1216ha). There are lots of great circuit day walks, based on Little Beach, Maitland Bay, Putty Beach and Box Head. The main access route is through Gosford.

Longer, more remote walks can be undertaken in nearby Brisbane Water National Park (11 376ha). Opportunities include following a section of the Great North Walk, circuits based on Piles Creek, Mooney Mooney Creek and Patonga. Consult the National Parks and Wildlife Service office below for more details.

Central Coast—Gosford
Suites 36–38, 207 Albany St
Gosford NSW 2250
Tel: (02) 4324 4911
Fax: (02) 4324 7747

Hawkesbury River

On the southern side of the Hawkes-bury River, the Marramarra National Park allows adventurous walkers to access several watercourses from the Old Northern Road. On the northern bank, Dharug National Park (5991ha) features convict history and remote wilderness opportunities.

There is a ranger's depot at Hazel Dell, roughly between Wisemans Ferry and the Mill Creek camping area. Several trails are possible from this place. The most common is a nature circuit based on Biamea Creek. The walking trail starts at the picnic ground (500m north of the Mill Creek camping ground past a helicopter landing pad). The track leads east at the far side of the grassy cleared area. Follow the creek for several kilometres before ascending to a ridge and back down a hanging valley to the base of some cliffs. It is not marked on the Gunderman topographical map, but it's well defined and regularly up-graded. Allow about three hours for this 7.5km hike through hilly terrain. Longer extensions lead from this track to Matthews Ridge. The vegetation along Biamea Creek includes sassafras and epiphytes, but most characteristic of the area are the grasstrees.

The South Coast
Deua National Park

This wild and remote national park, a five-hour drive from Sydney, is still largely unknown. Within its boundaries lie the Bendethera Caves, Hanging Rock, the Big Hole, Marble Arch, pristine catchment areas, a river that rivals the Kowmung for beauty and the impressive Wyanbene Cave. Most are accessible by a short walk from a fire trail.

Like the Budawang Ranges, the national park is primarily a wilderness area so walkers should be experienced with minimal-impact bush-camping techniques. In places such as these, you must be fully self-sufficient and trips of up to one-week duration are necessary to see the main features. This is enjoyable but tiring, with a lot of climbing involved.

Access is via the Princes Highway to Moruya, about 20 minutes south of Batemans Bay. Walk at any time of the year, but be prepared for rapid changes of weather when cold winds from the Alps mix with moist coastal air.

Facts and Figures

Name: Deua National Park
Size: 82 926ha
Enactment: February 1979
Visitors: Fewer than 10 000 a year, most of whom travel along the Deua River road to Araluen. The upper Deua River valley is popular with 4WD users, and Bendethera Caves attract cavers.
Vegetation: Mainly wet and dry sclerophyll forest, depending on altitude and proximity to water. The rare leaning *Eucalyptus fraxinoides* grows in isolated patches.
Wildlife: More than 90 species of birds, and hundreds of mammals, reptiles and invertebrate species
Aboriginal Sites: No survey yet conducted. Because of the area's rich wildlife, many examples of past occupation are expected.
Facilities: Since the entire area is a designated wilderness zone, no facilities are provided, except at the car-camping grounds at the Deua River on the Araluen to Moruya Road, and at Bendethera on the upper Deua. Facilities include toilets, information boards, and fireplaces. Bush-camping is allowed anywhere.
Adjoining Parks: Wadbilliga National Park as well as numerous state forests around the perimeter: Buckenbowra, Wandera, Dampier and Tallaganda. These 'buffers' make up an area twice as large as the park itself.
Further Information:
Cnr Field St and Princes Hwy
Narooma NSW 2546
Tel: (02) 4476 2888
Fax: (02) 4476 2757

Bendethera Caves Walk

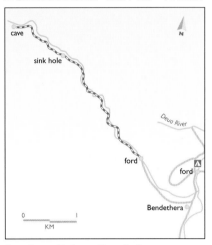

Starting Point: Bendethera, upper Deua River, Deua National Park
Destination: Bendethera Cave
Summary: A walk along an over-grown fire trail through pleasant forest to a cave entrance, where a self-guided tour can be undertaken
Attractions: A large limestone cavern with impressive formations
Length: 7km
Time: 3 hours (including cave tour)
Attraction Rating: ★ ★ ★
Fitness: ◪ ◪ ◪
Maps: LIC (CMA) Snowball 1:25 000 topographical
Access to Starting Point: The only access is by 4WD vehicle from Moruya. From the main street (Princes Highway), turn west onto Campbell Street and follow this to a left turn into Wamban Road just before the Deua Diver (called the Moruya River at this stage). Do not cross the river. Wamban Road soon turns into Little Sugarloaf Road. It is unsealed and

The Deua River is one of the most pristine watercourses in Australia.

ascends 1000m before a steep descent into the upper Deua River valley via the Dampier Mountain fire trail. The valley can also be approached from Krawaree Road in the west via Dampier Trig, also strictly 4WD access. The start of the walking track is signposted near the old yards and ruins at the Bendethera homestead.

Facilities/Amenities: Toilets, fireplaces (some firewood is provided)

Recommended Equipment: Torches (at least two) with spare batteries.

Notes: Claustrophobic people may be uncomfortable with the tight squeezes necessary to reach the main chamber. This limestone karst region was discovered in 1875; by 1890, through the efforts of Benjamin George, a 1180ha reserve had been established.

Further Information:

Cnr Field St and Princess Hwy
Narooma NSW 2546
Tel: (02) 4476 2888
Fax: (02) 4476 2757

Walk Description

A sign in the car park gives information about the rare Bendethera wattle, an unusual silver-blue tree. There are many creek crossings as you head up the Little Con Creek gully, before turning right. After some pleasant flat sections, there's a final very steep uphill to the cave entrance, which looks like something out of an Indiana Jones movie. Another nearby cave is the 59m deep Windlass.

Let your eyes adjust to the light. The track through the cave keeps to the left and two chains are installed through tricky sections. Tiny bats will zoom in and out of your torch beam, but they're nothing to worry about. At the end is a large cavern, but the best attractions are some gigantic columns and stalagmites. The return walk should take about an hour. Why not spend the afternoon exploring the many trails in the valley, to the north and south? If you take a swim, watch out for the huge long-legged spiders that hunt on the river rocks. The most gorgeous pool in the valley by far is located just 200 metres downstream from the site of the old Bendethera homestead. The quartzite walls of this pool enclose the river with a bathtub-like formation. The water is quite deep here with many good ledges to dive from. An idyllic camping area can be found nearby.

Mother Woila Circuit

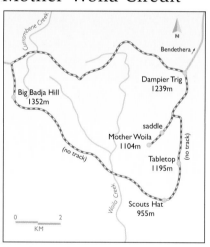

Starting Point: Dampier Trig, Deua National Park

Destination: Mother Woila (1104m)

Summary: An extremely wild circuit through harsh, trackless terrain

Attractions: Pure wilderness, rugged scenery, pristine watercourses. Prominent features include Tabletop, Scouts Hat, Woila Clearing and Big Badja Hill.

Length: 48.6km

Time: 4 days

Options: Walkers can exit Woila Creek valley via Euranbene Mountain

Attraction Rating: ★ ★ ★

Fitness: ☒ ☒ ☒ ☒ ☒

Maps: LIC (CMA) Badja and Snowball 1:25 000 topographicals

Access to Starting Point: To access Dampier Trig, drive south from Braidwood along the Krawaree Road, then east from Pikes Saddle, one of the high points along the main vehicle access route to the Bendethera region. This main access road has been re-routed recently.

Facilities/Amenities: None. Complete self-sufficiency is essential.

Recommended Equipment: Map and compass are essential. Because of the confusing nature of the terrain and poor visibility on many of the thickly forested slopes, a GPS system will aid navigation. Also, plenty of water for an overnight stay, at least 7 litres per person. Gaiters to protect you from stinging nettles. A self-supporting tent for high-level ridge sites would allow for a greater variety of options.

Notes: Mid-summer is too hot for this walk, so do it at a cooler time. You must be experienced in trackless terrain, confident on exposed rock, adept at orienteering and fully equipped. The final day can be made shorter by leaving a vehicle at the Badja fire trail turn-off near Pikes Saddle.

Further Information:

Cnr Field St and Princes Hwy
Narooma NSW 2546
Tel: (02) 4476 2888
Fax: (02) 4476 2757

There are articles on Mother Woila in *WILD* magazine, Issue 66 (Spring, 1997) and Issue 46 (Spring, 1992).

Walk Description

The objective of this walk is to camp in a saddle near Mother Woila and return down the beautiful Woila Creek, traversing some very exposed high-level ridges on the way. Mother Woila is not marked on the Badja topographical map, but its grid reference is 387099. The upper Woila Creek region has gained a reputation as one of the most inaccessible in New South Wales. Average walking progress is very slow because of the rugged terrain, massive height variations and thick vegetation.

Park at Dampier Trig and walk south along the watershed, keeping the rim of the eastern escarpment to your left for easier navigation. Then

head south-west onto a razorback spur that descends to a prominent saddle at the base of Mother Woila's eastern cliffs. Camping opportunities are limited and there is no water unless you are prepared to descend steeply into surrounding gullies. Unless you have a spare day, it is not really worth the effort to climb the mountain, as thick vegetation obstructs views.

Return up to the Deua–Woila divide, then head south to Tabletop, via the knife-edged ridge composed of very exposed granite. Make camp on the second night on top of Tabletop. If it has been raining recently, water can be found near the south-eastern edge of the plateau.

On the third day, head over Scouts Hat along another prominent razorback ridge. Some sidling to get around vertical sections will be necessary. On the western side, drop down to the grassy Woila Clearing amid pleasant open forest and reliable water. This is a sanctuary in such difficult terrain.

The next day involves a long steep ascent of Big Badja Hill on the Great Dividing Range. This is one of the highest peaks in the area and, because of its central location, offers commanding views east to the ocean and south-west to the Alps. Navigation skills will be required on this section because of the confusion of ridges and spurs and limited views.

The going gets much easier once you attain the trig point at Big Badja Hill, where it is then a mere matter of following the road back to Dampier Trig to the east. If possible, use a car shuffle to avoid this section as you will, no doubt, be exhausted.

Other walks in the Deua National Park

There are great opportunities for truly wild remote pioneering walking in Deua National Park. There are few tracks of any description here and plenty of water in the valleys.

Follow either the Shoalhaven or Deua rivers from its source to civilisation. They both start in the south of the park and have fire trails along their watersheds for ease of access. Other than that, it's trackless walking, camping by remote pools lined with river oaks.

Just a short drive south of Berlang camping area on the Krawaree Road is the entrance to Wyanbene Caves, with one of the longest river caves in the state. The main cave is almost 2km long and 112m deep. One large cavern is open to the general public. It is a water cave and involves some wading to get from cavern to cavern—definitely not recommended for claustrophobic people. Permits are required for the deeper parts of the cave.

Nadgee Nature Reserve

Located in the far south-eastern corner of NSW, the 20 671ha Nadgee Nature Reserve is the state's largest coastal wilderness area. It provides habitat protection for plants and animals as well as conserving the catchment area of the Nadgee and Little River systems and Nadgee Lake. The climate is very variable—it can be raining here while East Gippsland and the rest of the south coast are bathed in sunlight, or vice versa. Permits are required for camping and overnight bushwalking. Make bookings or get permits from the Merimbula office.

Vegetation

Dry open forest areas occur widely throughout Nadgee, with patches of rainforest in the upper Nadgee/ Battery Creek catchments and low shrubby heaths at Mt Nadgee and along the coastline.

Wildlife

Wildlife includes ground parrots, little terns, eastern bristlebirds, potoroos, pygmy possums and dingoes.

Access

Drive south via a rough sandy track from Womboyn (4WD may be needed in its latter sections).

Facilities

A small parking area at Baycliff with short sandy paths to Wonboyn Lake and Wonboyn Beach. Limited facilities at Newtons Beach. Walking tracks using old fire trails extend from the Merrica River crossing southwards from Nadgee Lake to Croajingolong National Park in Victoria.

Nadgee Beach Walk

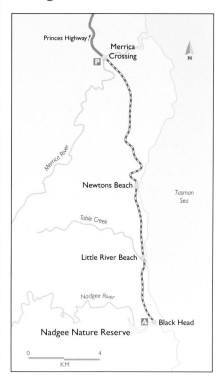

Starting Point: Merrica Crossing (ranger's residence), Nadgee Nature Reserve

Destination: Black Head, Nadgee Beach

Summary: A magnificent walk down the coast taking in outstanding coves with turquoise water

Attractions: Little Creek

Length: 42km

Time: 4 days

Day 1: Merrica Crossing to Little Creek, 16km

Day 2: Little Creek to Nadgee Beach, 5km

Day 3: Nadgee Beach to Newtons Beach, 10km

Day 4: Newtons Beach to Merrica Crossing, 11km

Options: Camp either on the Nadgee River (inland of Nadgee Beach) or at a very pleasant shady spot just to the north of Nadgee Beach. By increasing the pace, fit parties could actually do this walk in two days, while other people may want to extend the estimated four days with rest days at Little Creek or to explore farther south to Nadgee Lake and Cape Howe.

Attraction Rating: ★ ★ ★ ★

Fitness: ⊠ ⊠ ⊠

Maps: LIC (CMA) Narrabarba and Nadgee 1:25 000 topographicals

Access to Starting Point: The reserve is 500km south of Sydney, 40km north of Genoa in Victoria and 35km south of Eden. To reach Merrica Crossing, turn off the Princes Highway onto the Womboyn Lake Road, then right onto the Mountain Road, then Newtons Road, which provides 2WD access in dry weather. Turn-offs from the Princes Highway are signposted.

Facilities/Amenities: Harrys Hut on the Nadgee River provides emergency accommodation, but it is better to camp in a tent because of the wildlife living in the hut.

Recommended Equipment: Sandals for beach walking, sunscreen and swimming gear. Bring large water containers, which can be filled on the second night at Nadgee River.

Notes: A mountain bike would speed up the first stage to Newtons Beach, but it would have to be pushed uphill on the return trip

Further Information:

Cnr Merimbula Drive and Sapphire Coast Drive

PO Box 656, Merimbula NSW 2548

Tel: (02) 6495 4130

Fax: (02) 6495 4137

Newtons Beach, Nadgee Nature Reserve. This reserve is the largest coastal wilderness in New South Wales.

Walk Description

This great, relaxing four-day trip takes in some of the most exquisite coastal scenery in south-eastern Australia, beautiful coves and inlets to camp by, rivers, beaches and shaded grassy clearings. Each day's distances have been kept short to maximise time at the beaches, and every night is spent at a different place. Unfortunately, the walk begins with an 11km road-bash from Merrica Crossing to Newtons Beach. Have a swim if the weather is hot. The grassy field here will be your campsite on the third night, so you might like to save weight by leaving some food behind. Cans are best as wildlife can't spoil them.

Head south to Little Creek. The old fire trail is a little rocky and there are occasional views across the heath. Little Creek is a great place to swim with a choice of protected venues. Bring drinking water, as there is none in the vicinity.

On the second day, cross the beach and continue south to Nadgee River. Be careful with the tracks here, as there is a slight deviation from what is depicted on the topographical maps. If the weather is good, you can camp just north of Nadgee Beach via Impressa Moor. Alternatively, head inland to Palmers Crossing on the Nadgee River. Once again the track is aligned differently to the map. In reality, the track heads up the northern bank of the river through rainforest before fording a tangle of fallen logs and small pools. Good-quality fresh water is obtainable here. If it's early, you could leave your overnight packs at Harrys Hut and continue south back to the coast at Nadgee Lake. There is no fresh water there.

On day three, backtrack to Newtons Beach, then walk out on the final day. This will leave plenty of time for the drive back to Sydney, Melbourne or Canberra.

Other walks in Nadgee Nature Reserve

Most walks here follow the coast. From Nadgee Beach, continue south to Nadgee Lake and Cape Howe. Just before Cape Howe are some delightful beaches, with good camping spots inland by Nadgee Lake. Beyond Cape Howe is the great Howe wilderness. The coastal terrain changes remarkably and becomes characterised by long open beaches punctuated by small rocky headlands.

Walkers can complete circuits by returning to Merrica Crossing via the Dalight Ridge and Table Ridge fire trails but this involves long periods of tedious road walking without water.

To do the full-length coast walk, start from Mallacoota because Mallacoota Inlet is a major obstacle. Private boat operators will ferry walkers across the inlet and drop them behind Big Beach. See the Nadgee Wilderness Walk in the Croajingolong section of the Victorian chapter of this book for more details.

The Snowy Mountains
Kosciuszko National Park

Although the Kosciuszko National Park contains the highest mountains in the country, walking is fairly easy as gradients are gentle and the staging areas are also high. Most of the peaks on the Main Range are accessible by foot, including a trail to the summit of Mt Kosciuszko itself. Because of its remote locality and its huge size, the park is well suited for overnight expeditions. Many forms of overnight accommodation are available, from primitive huts and youth hostels to expensive hotels, so rough camping is not always necessary. Prices are reduced by many lodges during summer, as the owners try to generate a more stable cash flow rather than relying just on the ski season. Thredbo has led the way and now caters extremely well for summer visitors with a whole range of activities: bushwalking, horse-riding, mountain-bike riding, gold fossicking, tennis, swimming, fishing, even oriental meditation. Bookings here and for other resorts are just as necessary as they are in winter.

Late summer is the ideal time to go, but the park is notorious for its 'killer' flies, so take plenty of insect repellent. A greater degree of map-reading skill is also required as the LIC (CMA) hasn't produced a 1:25 000 topographical series for the region. This means that the less detailed 1:50 000 scale maps are the best available.

The authorities have traditionally been very relaxed about the heavy recreational use of the park and it is only now that stricter rules are in force. The soil and vegetation are very fragile and easily subjected to erosion. The hundreds of fire trails and service roads that exist within the national park are all open to walkers, and camping is permitted in most places off the roads. Herds of brumbies and many old stockmen's huts scattered throughout the national park help generate an atmosphere of timelessness. Twisted snow gums and graceful mountain ashes set among this large tract of wilderness make this national park one of the best loved. Overnight walkers should fill out a route form at the visitors centre.

Facts and Figures

Name: Kosciuszko National Park
Size: 649 378ha
Enactment: State Park, 1944
National Park, 1967
World Heritage Listing, 1977
Visitors: 2.5 million a year (most of whom are skiers)
Vegetation: The variety of plants in the park is enormous, with the area divided into four zones related to altitude. Snow gums and other eucalypts dominate, while shrubs and herbs add colour to the alpine meadows above the tree line (1850m).
Wildlife: At least 202 species of birds, 21 species of reptiles, 35 species of mammals and more than 300 types of invertebrates. Feral animals include cats, dogs, rabbits, foxes, pigs, trout and brumbies.
Aboriginal Sites: Little evidence of Aboriginal occupation, but they visited the area in summer mainly to feast on Bogong moths.
Camping: Campers are asked to register at the visitors' centre at Sawpit Creek on their way into the park, or at the various rangers' stations on other access routes. Camping is not permitted in resort areas (e.g. Perisher, Thredbo). No permits or fees are required.

Adjoining Parks: Alpine National Park in Victoria, Namadgi National Park in the Australian Capital Territory. Numerous state forests on the western flank.

Further Information:

Snowy Region Visitors' Centre
Kosciuszko Road
Jindabyne NSW 2627
Tel: (02) 6450 5600

Telephone number for other rangers' officers are:

Khancoban: (02) 6076 9373
Perisher: (02) 6457 5214
Tumut: (02) 6947 1849
Yarrangobilly: (02) 6454 9597

Cooleman Caves Walk

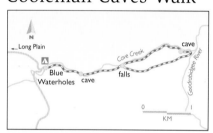

Starting Point: Blue Waterholes campground, Kosciuszko National Park

Destination: Goodrabigbee River

Summary: Spectacular walk through a limestone gorge

Attractions: Cave entrances, waterfall, cascades, a steep canyon and the Goodradigbee River

Length: 7km

Time: 5.5 hours

Options: If the weather is too cold to swim, walkers can turn back at the waterfall

Attraction Rating: ★ ★ ★ ★

Fitness: ☒ ☒ ☒ ☒

Maps: LIC (CMA) Rules Point and Peppercorn 1:25 000 topographicals. Caves Creek is inconveniently right on the boundary of the two maps.

Access to Starting Point: To access Blue Waterholes, drive over the Brindabella Range from Canberra to Long Plain. The road is unsealed. From the Snowy Mountains Highway, drive north of Kiandra or south from Tumut and turn onto Long Plain Road. The Blue Waterholes turn-off is signposted about 17km from the Snowy Mountains Highway.

Facilities/Amenities: Basic camping facilities at Blue Waterholes include pit toilets and BBQs. Another camping area on the main access road at Cooleman Mountain while Long Plain Hut toward Yarrangobilly Caves offers a simple roof over your head if the weather suddenly becomes inclement.

Recommended Equipment: A torch (preferably waterproof) and gear that can get wet because of the considerable swimming involved

Notes: This walk is best done in midsummer because of the altitude and swimming required for crossing waterways. Note that Long Plain Road is closed between June and October. Walk in the middle of the day when the sun is on the floor of the canyon.

Further Information:

Snowy Region Visitors' Centre
Kosciuszko Road
Jindabyne NSW 2627
Tel: (02) 6450 5600

Walk Description

An interesting walk route that explores the main section of the scenic Clarke Gorge, one of the few limestone canyons in Australia. From the camping area, follow a flat walking

Cooleman Caves at Blue Waterholes, Kosciuszko National Park.

track downstream and turn right into the cliff-lined gorge. The walking track ends at some waterfalls on Cave Creek. Some fording is necessary. The caves, 96 in all, were discovered in 1922 and range in length from just a few metres to 784m. The most interesting are the Murray, River, Easter, Cooleman and Barber caves.

To explore Barber Cave, take a torch and climb up a slope to the right. While this used to be a popular one for casual cavers, the National Parks and Wildlife Service now advises that only members of speleological societies should proceed past the entrance chamber. This is to reduce the risk of damage to cave formations.

At the waterfall, descend into the ravine and follow the watercourse to the Goodradigbee River. Progress will be very slow over the large slippery boulders and you must often swim from pool to pool in the cold water. Once you reach the confluence, head to the right up the spur, following the southern rim of the gorge back to the waterfall before descending again to the track. From here, retrace your steps to Blue Waterholes camping area.

Mt Jagungal Circuit

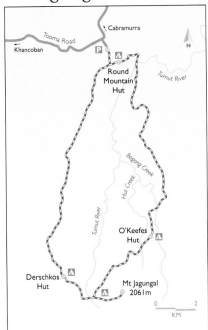

Starting Point: Round Mountain Hut, Kosciuszko National Park
Destination: The summit of Mt Jagungal (2061m)
Summary: A long walk along old fire trails to the peak. Use the Farm Ridge and Grey Mare fire trails to approach Mt Jagungal, and the Round Mountain fire trail to return to the car park.
Attractions: Views of the mainly alpine plains as well as 360-degree views from the summit
Length: 42.6km
Time: 2–3 days
Options: Several approaches can be used to access Mt Jagungal, including the Hell Hole Creek fire trail from the west. For notes on an approach from the south via Valentines Hut and the Grey Mare fire trail, consult Tyrone Thomas and Sven Klinge's *Australian Mountains: The Best 100 Walks.*
Attraction Rating: ★ ★ ★ ★
Fitness: ◪ ◪ ◪ ◪
Maps: LIC (CMA) Khancoban 1:50 000 topographical
Access to Starting Point: Round Mountain car park is just off Tooma Road to the east of Tooma Reservoir. Approach from the west through Khancoban and from the east through Cabramurra. Allow plenty of time for the winding roads. A good overnight spot close to the car park is Bradleys Hut, just north on Tooma Road.
Facilities/Amenities: Camp clearing at the base of Mt Jagungal, clean water
Recommended Equipment: Warm, windproof clothes as the summit can attract snow at any time of the year
Notes: The walk can be completed comfortably by fit parties in two full days; others may wish to spend three days, using the second to walk to the summit, without having to pack up camp. A mountain bike makes the approach and return a lot faster—it is possible to do it in one day using only the Round Mountain fire trail where good speed can be maintained.
Further Information:
Snowy Region Visitors' Centre
Kosciuszko Road
Jindabyne NSW 2627
Tel: (02) 6450 5600

Walk Description

Walk south from Tooma Road and turn left to descend steeply into the Tumut River valley. Ford the river and head up Farm Ridge. Wild pigs commonly churn up the grassy tussocks by feeding here. It's pleasant walking all the way with the dark massif of Mt Jagungal on the horizon. Turn right onto Grey Mare fire trail and past O'Keefes Hut, one of the larger huts in the highlands, with three rooms and four bunks. Follow Grey Mare fire trail to the western base of Mt Jagungal. The camping area and start of the walking trail is at grid reference 232982 on the Khancoban topographical map. The small stream here is the very upper headwaters of the Tumut River. The distance covered on the first day is 20.6km.

Depending on how much daylight is left, you may want to climb the mountain now or early next morning. Allow about three hours for the return walk and take warm clothing. With the wind-chill factor, air temperatures rarely climb above freezing. The track crosses the stream and proceeds up to the south-east. Frequent use has made it fairly easy to follow. After ascending through the snow gum forest, you suddenly emerge into open grassland; some minor rock-scrambling takes you to a broad spur, where the track turns north (left). It's easy to make your way up through the final rocky obstacle to the summit. The best approach to the peak, also known as Big Bogong, is from the south-east. Snowdrifts may lie in shady areas.

A concrete column marks the highest point and the view is unobscured. Particularly prominent is the main range and Gungartan to the south, the Munyang Range to the east and Tabletop Mountain in the north. The colourful rock that characterises the summit comes from ancient lava flows throughout the region. The eastern flank contains wide-open slopes with many species of alpine grasses. Return to camp the same way.

On the final day, head west on the Grey Mare fire trail, then north along the Toolong Range. This is quite a long haul with some tedious walking along the flat sections on the Round Mountain fire trail. Leafless snow gums line much of the way, creating an eerie atmosphere when the sun is low. From certain vantage points, it is possible to look back and see the bulk of Mt Jagungal dominate all the surroundings. If you opt to ride a mountain bike here, the last section is the most rideable.

Valentine Hut Walk

Starting Point: Guthega Power Station

Destination: Valentine Falls

Summary: A great walk to the beautiful Geehi River valley using service roads and negotiable routes

Attractions: Gungartun, Valentine Falls, alpine meadows, open views

Length: 54km

Time: 3 days

Attraction Rating: ★ ★ ★

Fitness: ◪ ◪ ◪ ◪

Maps: LIC (CMA) Mount Kosciuszko and Khancoban 1:25 000 topographicals

Access to Starting Point: Drive from Jindabyne and turn right 23km later to Island Bend in the Snowy River valley. Turn-offs are signposted. From Sydney, Canberra or Melbourne, car-camp the first night at Island Bend on the Snowy River. There's a car park at the Guthega Power Station.

Facilities/Amenities: A well-serviced hut on Valentine River can be used, but it may be occupied already

Recommended Equipment: Warm, windproof clothing, and four-season tent and sleeping bag

Notes: Complete self-sufficiency is essential in such remote terrain. Blizzards can occur at any time of the year. Vehicles need an entry permit, obtainable from Sawpit Creek.

Further Information:

Snowy Region Visitors' Centre

Kosciuszko Road
Jindabyne NSW 2627
Tel: (02) 6450 5600

Walk Description

The Guthega Power Station pumps water from the Snowy River up over the Great Dividing Range to Geehi Reservoir. From the car park here, follow the Australian Alps Walking Track, which crosses the Munyang River and heads steeply up Disappointment Spur. It meets up with the main service road 2.5km south of Schlink Pass. Continue north, climbing to the 1800m pass through some open hills topped by piles of rocks, evidence of the area's glacial origins. To the right is massive Gungartan pinnacle—climb this on the last day on the return to Guthega Power Station.

At the crest of prominent Schlink Pass, you are on the Great Diving Range. From here, water flows south into the Snowy River and eventually into Victoria, or north into the Murray River and heads for South Australia.

Once over the crest of Schlink Pass, you descend through an almost identical valley where the well-graded road curves in and out of side gullies. The ubiquitous powerlines are a reminder of the industrialisation of this national park. On the left is the 'Schlink Hilton', a large hut with a wooden floor and toilets, making it among the more luxurious accommodations in the area. Half of the building is closed off and reserved for SMA workers. Access for the public is around the back.

Continue north to the inconspicuous turn-off onto the Valentine fire trail, (really just two overgrown tire tracks meandering north to Valentine Creek). Traverse a small, pretty valley and proceed up a steep hill through a magnificent patch of pure white snow gums. A makeshift bridge marks the crossing of Duck Creek and from here it is only a short distance to Valentine Hut. Despite its small size, the hut is in better condition than the 'Schlink Hilton', with a potbelly stove, furniture, bunks and a visitors' book. Pre-cut wood and a toilet are out the back. Because of its good condition, the hut is well frequented and it is rare indeed that you will find it vacant. It was built by the SMA, but is now owned by the National Parks and Wildlife Service and is maintained by both the Coast and Mountain Walkers and the Kosciuszko Huts Association. Many other huts in the area are serviced by these volunteer organisations.

If there is no room in the hut, camp on the grassy clearings down the slope by Valentine Creek. Large swimming holes are about 100m downstream among some cascades.

On the second day, leave your camp set-up and follow the road across Valentine Creek and up and around through open and relatively flat country. There are good views south-west to the main range, and every now and then the massive bulk of Mt Jagungal looms over the gentle hills in the foreground. On the way down the slope to Back Flat Creek are views across the valley to Valentine Falls on the far left. This is the Geehi Valley where gold was once mined. Grey Mare Hut, built in 1949, has iron walls and a wooden floor. Inside are benches, a table and six bunks. Like Valentine Hut, it is heavily used and attracts house rats that live off campers' foodscraps.

Once you arrive at Back Flat Creek, leave the Valentine fire trail and head downstream to the confluence of Geehi River and Valentine Creek. Head up Valentine Creek to the magnificent falls and climb up the southern embankment by a faint walking trail. Continue on the northern bank back to Valentine Hut and camping spot.

On the third day, retrace your steps to Schlink Pass. Before descending to Guthega Power Station, drop the overnight packs and head steeply up through the thick vegetation to the Gungartan summit. At 1940m, the vegetation gives way to open rocky terrain. Simply head to the highest peak for terrific views to Mt Jagungal to the north and the main range to south-west. Return to the packs and then down to Guthega Power Station.

As an alternative to backtracking along the Australian Alps Walking Track, walkers may use the Snowy Mountains Authority service road. This will be easier on the feet after such a strenuous walk.

Main Range Circuit

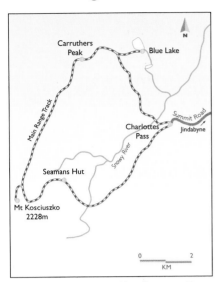

Starting Point: Charlottes Pass, Kosciuszko National Park

Destination: Mt Kosciuszko (2228m)

Summary: This walk is a high-level alpine circuit that passes over several peaks and visits several lakes, returning via the Mt Kosciuszko Road

Attractions: Blue Lake, Club Lake, Lake Albina, summit of Mt Kosciuszko, views from several other peaks

Length: 24.5km

Time: 1 long day or 2 half days, camping at Wilkinsons Creek below Mueller Peak

Options: The circuit can also be approached from Thredbo via the Crackenback chairlift. Possible walk extensions include climbing several other peaks such as Mt Twynam (2196m) and North Rams Head (2177m). This would make a 39km round trip.

Attraction Rating: ★ ★ ★ ★ ★

Fitness: ✖ ✖ ✖

Maps: LIC (CMA) Mount Kosciuszko 1:50 000 topographical

Access to Starting Point: Charlottes Pass lies at the end of Summit Road from Jindabyne via the Perisher–Smiggin Holes skifields

Facilities/Amenities: None

Recommended Equipment: Warm, windproof clothing, good-quality tent if camping

Notes: No camping is permitted at Blue Lake or its catchment area, or by any of the other alpine lakes, due to the sensitive soils and vegetation around the shores. Vehicles need an entry permit, obtainable from Sawpit Creek.

Further Information:
Snowy Region Visitors' Centre
Kosciuszko Road
Jindabyne NSW 2627
Tel: (02) 6450 5600

Walk Description

This is a fairly long and tiring walk, involving a few minor rock-scrambles. Furthermore, the ridge is exposed to the elements and blizzards can occur at any time of the year. Walkers must be prepared for all conditions.

From the Charlottes Pass car park, head down a steep brick-surfaced trail to the Snowy River and up the other side. The road then climbs steeply up toward Mt Twynam. There's one downhill, where the road suddenly changes to dirt and rock before a steep paved ascent to Blue Lake lookout. The lake, a large glacial pool, is an excellent spot to have a rest. It is possible to swim here in summer as the water temperature remains constant.

Between December and March, many species of wildflowers (such as gentians) bloom in abundance here. The tracks are strictly for walking and were built by the Soil Conservation Foundation in the 1950s and '60s. Much of the initial erosion has been halted by seeding and mulching the immediate track borders with straw.

Head back up to the path once you've been down to Blue Lake, and turn left at the saddle to climb over Carruthers Peak (2140m). You are now on the main ridge, which you can follow all the way to Mt Kosciuszko. Along the way are views over Lake Albina, particularly from Northcote Pass. On clear summer days there will be many people on the summit, mainly walkers from Thredbo who use the metal grid from the top of the Crackenback chairlift.

The rock here is not the coarse-grained granite so common in the Snowy Mountains but a metamorphosed sedimentary rock resembling slate. The landscape is very bare with piles of granite boulders or tors dominating the summits of all the visible peaks. These rocks were exposed by a 'periglacial' erosion in which the original covering of the mountains was removed by saturation from snow and melting ice. Even in summer, snowdrifts remain in the shadows. The landscape shows the only evidence of glacial activity on mainland Australia (there is some more in Tasmania).

The entire highlands where uplifted in stages about 12 million years ago, with the greatest rise occurring very recently: only two million years ago. Since then, periodic ice ages saw glaciers carve out mountainsides, creating hollows called carries and depositing rocks into large piles called moraines. You can explore the beautiful Blue Lake, a good example of this

Snowdrifts on Mt Jagungal, Kosciuszko National Park.

activity, in the afternoon if you have enough daylight left. Once you've reached the summit of Mt Kosciuszko, head down and follow the Summit Road back to Charlottes Pass. The large granodiorite boulders strewn all around this region were deposited some 20 000 years ago during the Pleistocene ice age.

Along the way is Seamans Hut, built as a memorial to Laurie Seaman who died of hypothermia nearby in 1928. It offers good shelter from sudden weather changes and has saved the lives of many a walker visiting the main Range.

Mt Kosciuszko Walk

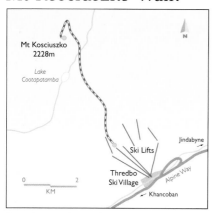

Starting Point: Thredbo Ski Village
Destination: The summit of Mt Kosciuszko (2228m)
Summary: A short walk to Australia's highest peak, using Crackenback chairlift to save walking distance
Attractions: Views over a glaciated landscape
Length: 12.2km
Time: 4 hours
Attraction Rating: ★ ★ ★ ★
Fitness: ⚅⚅
Maps: LIC (CMA) Mount Kosciuszko 1:50 000 topographical
Access to Starting Point: Drive to Thredbo via the Alpine Way from Jindabyne (from the east) or Khancoban (from the west)
Facilities/Amenities: None
Recommended Equipment: Warm, windproof clothing
Notes: Do not leave if the weather is deteriorating. People have died on the exposed ridges of the Ramshead Range. Private cars need entry permits obtainable from the rangers' stations at Sawpit Creek or Thredbo.

Further Information:
Snowy Region Visitors' Centre
Kosciuszko Road
Jindabyne NSW 2627
Tel: (02) 6450 5600

Walk Description

The best reason for walking up Mt Kosciuszko is the scenery. The large white patch on the Mt Kosciuszko 1:50 000 topographical map follows the 1800m contour line around its circumference, indicating that no trees grow past this point. This walk, entirely above the tree line, is the easiest approach to the summit.

Take Crackenback chairlift from Thredbo Village to the top (Eagles Nest). (Check the closing time of the chairlift.) From this point, follow a paved path out of the Basin. The footbridge crosses Ramshead Creek and you start on the metal walkway in the Back Basin. To the west, the large pile of granite boulders is the edge of the Ramshead Range. Follow the metal walkway to Kosciuszko Lookout (2000m). It is then downhill into the headwaters of the Snowy River and up and through the saddle to Rawsons Pass. From the saddle you can see Lake Cootapatamba on your left, the highest of mainland Australia's five glacial lakes. This name means 'the place where eagles drink' in the language of local Aborigines.

Follow the walking track to Rawson Pass (2100m) where it meets with Old Summit Road. When climbing Mt Kosciuszko, refrain from climbing straight up the eastern face. This area is undergoing revegetation under the care of the National Parks and Wildlife Service. Instead, keep on the road as it circles around the peak. From the top are panoramic views. To the west, 1500m below, lies the Murray River in a deep valley. Return to Thredbo via the same route.

Instead of taking the chairlift back, walkers may opt to follow one of the many pleasant and well-graded walking tracks down the mountain. Information leaflets from the park office near Sawpit Creek give information on highlights along the way. An interlocking network of tracks leads to interesting destinations around the Thredbo Village.

Pilot Wilderness Walk

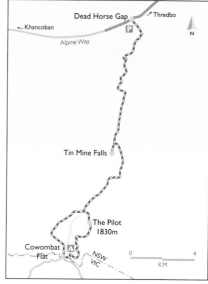

Starting Point: Dead Horse Gap, Snowy Mountains
Destination: Cowombat Flat
Summary: A long alpine walk over the Great Dividing Range to the Victorian border in the south of Kosciuszko National Park
Attractions: The summit of The Pilot (1830m), waterfalls, the very upper headwaters of the Murray River, old stockmen's huts, remote wilderness atmosphere
Length: Total distance is 89km
Day 1: Dead Horse Gap to Carters Hut, 24.5km, 9 hours
Day 2: Carters Hut to Cowombat Flat, 19km, 8 hours
Day 3: Cowombat Flat to Carters Hut, 18.5km, 7 hours
Day 4: Carters Hut to Dead Horse Gap, 27km, 9 hours
Time: 4 days
Options: Eliminate backtracking by walking through to Victoria, coming out at Black Mountain Road, but this would entail a lengthy car shuffle
Attraction Rating: ★ ★ ★ ★ ★
Fitness: ⚅⚅⚅⚅
Maps: LIC (CMA) Thredbo and Suggan Buggan 1:50 000 topographical maps
Access to Starting Point: You will need a private car to drive to Dead Horse Gap along the Alpine Way from Khancoban or Thredbo. The car park is 4.3km west of Thredbo ski village. Just before you cross the Thredbo River (also known as Crackenback River), there is a large car park that

Heading toward Round Mountain in the central Kosciuszko National Park.

marks the start of the Cascades Trail.

Facilities/Amenities: Several stockmen's huts, including Carters Hut and Cascades Hut

Recommended Equipment: Warm, windproof clothing, fuel stove, four-season tent, equipment for complete self-sufficiency

Notes: The use of a mountain bike would reduce travelling times along the fire trails

Further Information:

Snowy Region Visitors' Centre
Kosciuszko Road
Jindabyne NSW 2627
Tel: (02) 6450 5600

Walk Description

The Pilot Wilderness in southern Kosciuszko National Park is dominated by The Pilot, well above the tree line. From its bald peak, it commands outstanding views south to the Victorian Alps and north to Ramshead Range. The Pilot Wilderness is more susceptible than other areas to sudden weather changes. Snow and frosts in summer are common, so you should bring a waterproof jacket and at least one fleece jumper. Down sleeping bags are also highly recommended. Another factor to consider is the presence of tiger snakes in the southern region. If walking, wear gaiters and thick long pants. The trip is only suited to the warmer months as the entire district is quite snowbound in winter. Alpine plants dominate the whole region.

People often wonder about the name, Dead Horse Gap. Apparently 17 horses were killed in a snowdrift here. There is a gate at the very beginning not marked on the map. To the right of the gate is a Backcountry Register, in which you should leave details of your route. Note the stream flow pattern at Dead Horse Gap with the aid of a map. The headwaters of the Thredbo River flow north-west to near the gap where once they flowed across the gap and down Dead Horse Creek to the Murray River. Erosion has now re-routed the Thredbo River and Bogong Creek eastward to Thredbo.

On the first day, head 2km up the Cascade Trail following the Thredbo River to a bridge. Snow gums and alpine herbs are on the mountainsides and snow grass grows on the river flats where cold air in the hollows stops tree growth for a 180m climb over 2km onto the Great Dividing Range. In warmer months the wildflowers are spectacular here.

From the crest, descend Bobs Ridge 2km through snow gums and alpine ash to a hairpin bend. Another 1.2km down the trail and 320m lower than the crest, cross Cascade Creek and follow the trail close to the creek for 800m. It is then only 200m through snow gums on a side track left to Cascade Hut. This was built in the 1930s by Harry Nankervis, who leased the surrounding area for high-country summer cattle-grazing. For 40 years the hut deteriorated until the Illawarra Alpine Club restored the interior to its present condition. Just behind the hut is a small walking pad to a creek where a pipe enables you to retrieve water easily. Within the hut itself are usually emergency food rations and precut firewood for the open fire. There is a wooden platform, raised above the dirt floor, which serves as a makeshift bunk. The toilet is outside. Being 8.2km from Dead Horse Gap, the hut is a convenient spot for lunch.

From the hut, continue on the trail predominantly south through snow gum country for the next 12km. Ahead, the granite-covered Pilot dominates the horizon. At 12km there is a minor track off to the right known as Ash fire trail. Note the location as you return to this spot on the fourth day for a side trip to Tin Mine Falls.

For the next 1km the trail swings east then south-east to join Tin Mine fire trail. Keep going south for 3.5km and end the day at Tin Mine Huts (Carters Hut). This last section is across quite flat alpine country with snow grass clearings and, in summer, many wildflowers. Camp near the hut or perhaps use it for the night. Replace the firewood and leave the hut clean.

Charlie Carter's hut was built in the inter-war years and served the miners and brumby runners. It is generally in good condition with bunks, a fireplace and a toilet. Carter was the last true hermit of the Snowy Mountains, catching brumbies for a living.

On the second day, the trail forks into the Cowombat (also called Quambat) and Ingeegoodbee fire trails. Take the right fork west past the old tin mine. After crossing the bridge over Tin Mine Creek, the trail climbs to a saddle and another junction 8km from Carters Hut. East of this junction is Little Pilot peak (1680m).

The climb to The Pilot is moderately easy, through open snow gums for 2km and taking about an hour. There is no formal track but the route is easy to follow. Climb east up a spur crest gaining 180m to Little Pilot then turn south down to and across a saddle and more steeply up to The Pilot itself another 1km on. The rocky summit is marked by a massive stone cairn and a trig marker surrounded by low stunted heath and snow gums. On top there are rewarding panoramic views of Ramshead and the Main Range to the north while the Cobberas dominates the view to the south. After lunch, continue south along the ridge-top and descend from the crest of the main southern spine of the mountain. There is no track but progress is fairly easy. The crest arcs westward so that when you are about 2km south of The Pilot's top, you should be descending west and meet the Cowombat fire

The subtropical forest on Lord Howe Island is dominated by Kentia palms.

trail within another 1.5km. Turn left (south) at the fire trail and follow it for 5.5km, mostly downhill, into Cowombat Flat to camp. Drinking water is available from the Murray River and if you are quiet you have a very good chance of seeing the herds of brumbies that populate this region.

Spend next morning on a short side trip to investigate the wreckage of a plane that crashed here in 1954. Despite being marked on the LIC tpographical map as the 'Southern Cloud', it was, in fact, an RAAF C-41

Dakota (the military equivalent of a DC-3). Most of the wreckage remains have been souvenired over the past few decades. Pieces of fuselage were once used to construct a makeshift hut nearby. To the east is Forest Hill and a Control Point that marks the switch from the irregular Murray River state border to the straight line direct to the coast at Cape Howe.

After the side trip, leave camp early for much of this day will be spent on the trail back to Tin Mine, initially by a another route. Riders and walkers have the same route and camp intentions. From Cowombat Flat campsite, turn north and head up a fire trail to the scenic Cowombat Ridge. The going gets steep and you gain nearly 400m to an easy walk along the ridge crest north-east back to the Cowombat fire trail. Some 800m short of the Cowombat fire trail, veer right to avoid the Murray River fire trail. It is 9.5km via this ridge route, the same as if you had retraced the Cowombat fire trail. You then back-track 8km to Tin Mine to camp.

On the fourth and last day, retrace the first day's route back to Dead Horse Gap, but 4.5km after setting off, take the side trip option to Tin Mine Falls just 2.5km return south-south-west from the Ash fire trail turn-off. There is no defined track and the falls may be difficult to find. They are spec-tacular even if you can only view them from a side-on vantage.

The Islands
Lord Howe Island National Park

Beautiful Lord Howe Island is sur-rounded by the world's most souther-ly coral reef. It is the warm eastern Australian sea current that makes it possible for the beautiful coral reef to flourish so far south.

On the 11km long, 1300ha island is lush subtropical vegetation, several exquisite beaches and two gigantic cloud-topped mountains. The entire island is classified as World Heritage, so development is restricted to ensure that scenic and ecological values are preserved. Officially part of New South Wales, it is not regarded as an 'exotic' location for Australian holiday makers, so the island has remained a relatively obscure tourist destination. While the 300 residents enjoy the income generated by visitors, the actual tourist industry is limited by a special act of parliament. There are no casinos, luxury resorts, advertising, or multistoreyed buildings of any kind, so it remains a natural paradise. Tourist numbers are limited and no camping is allowed on the island, so book your accommodation before you fly.

The island lies about 800km north-east of Sydney and 800km south-east of Brisbane, being roughly east of Port Macquarie. It is surrounded by more than 25 other islets that share the same submarine ridge.

The island's rugged topography means that only about 8km of shoreline is accessible. Almost every vantage point is dominated by two summits, Mt Lidgbird (777m) and Mt Gower (875m). Their bulk takes up the entire southern half of the island. The north part is wild, with the rest being Crown Land with perpetual leases. Another glorious feature of the island is a vast sheltered lagoon lined by a long beach that ranges in depth from one to two metres.

Contact: Lord Howe Island Board
Tel: (02) 6563 2066

Climate

Lord Howe Island's maritime climate means that frosts do not occur. The seas are warm and there is moderately heavy rainfall spread throughout the year, but heavier in winter. Winter rain and winds cause a definite tourist off-season and some accommodation closes during June to August. February is the driest month with average minimum temperatures of 23°C.

Vegetation and Wildlife

The island boasts 600 plant species, one-third of them endemic. The most famous species is the kentia palm (*Howea fosteriana*), very popular as an indoor plant. Around the island are some 500 fish species, 10 of which are endemic, and 60 coral species living in the lagoon, reef and surrounding sea. In addition, 130 species of birds call the island home—large gannets, sooty terns, masked boobies, provi-dence petrels, shearwaters, red-tailed tropicbirds and the rare Lord Howe Island woodhen. Fortunately for the walker, there are no snakes on the island. Introduced rats are common and have become a pest.

Access, Facilities and Costs

Unlike most places in this book, walking on Lord Howe Island involves a good deal of expense for transport and accommodation. Ask your travel agent about flight and accommodation packages. Prices are expensive comp-ared with equivalent packages to Townsville or Cairns as the short island runway prevents larger planes operating. Accommodation includes self-contained apartments or full-board guesthouse accommodation, but no motels. Only islanders are permitted to camp and only at North Beach and on the eastern slopes of Mt Gower when they are collecting palm seeds for export. In special cases, visitors may camp on North Beach if they hire an island guide.

There are excellent restaurants and four general stores on the island, but merchandise, again, is costly. The usual mode of transport is by bicycle. Walkers can reach most parts of the island and return in a day on an extensive network of walking tracks. The island has a small hospital but limited search and rescue services so take extra safety measures.

Take a torch, as there is very little street lighting. Glass-bottom boat trips are available to see the reef. Snorkel-ling gear can be hired, as well as sea kayaks. The island has a museum outlining its interesting history during the whaling days. There is a departure tax at the airport (currently $20.00).

Mt Gower Walk

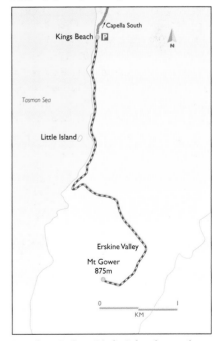

Starting Point: Little Island, southern end of Lagoon Road, Lord Howe Island National Park
Destination: Mt Gower summit (875m)
Summary: A steep, often exposed

The turquoise waters of Lord Howe Island's Lagoon from Mt Gower.

route through rainforest

Attractions: Mt Gower, the highest peak on Lord Howe Island, offers outstanding views, woodhens and unique vegetation. There are few better walks in the country.

Length: 8.5km

Time: 8km

Attraction Rating: ★ ★ ★ ★ ★

Fitness: ◼◼◼◼

Maps: LIC (CMA) Lord Howe Island 1:15 000 topographical. *Australian Geographic* has also released a Lord Howe Island map.

Access to Starting Point: To start this walk, it is best to use a bicycle or guesthouse transport to reach the southern end of Lagoon Road. If you have a mountain bike, cycle south parallel to Solomon Beach all the way to Little Island. The track deteriorates and you will have to push the bike some of the way, but it's still faster than walking the 1.4km. Bikes can be hired for about $5.00 a day and helmets are compulsory.

Facilities/Amenities: The closest accommodation is Capella South, (02) 9290 1922. Units 1 and 2 offer the best

views of Mt Lidgbird.

Recommended Equipment: Camera

Notes: Wait for a day that has no cloud over the summit. Typically this happens only once or twice a week. Leave very early to maximise your time at the lookout. A rope is installed for the final direct ascent to Mt Gower as well as on the Lower Road traverse.

Further Information:

www.wine.com.au/ ~ capella

Walk Description

Mt Gower is named after John Gower, Rear Admiral and First Captain to Lord Howe. Only experienced walkers prepared for a steep relentless uphill trek should attempt this climb. The cloud cover on the summit can make navigation confusing and the island has poor search and rescue facilities. Island authorities recommend that visitors use the local island guide, Jack Shick (Tel: (02) 6563 2218). He is available for hire once or twice each fortnight, weather permitting. While there is some advantage in using a guide on any walk in unfamiliar territory, there is a significant cost

involved and you are forced to walk in a group which may not be to every bushwalker's liking.

A section known as the Lower Road can be awkward. Here walkers must negotiate a 500m long ledge with a 150m sheer drop to the sea. The summit is the main breeding area for the endangered Lord Howe Island wooden, so there must be no irresponsible intrusion. Guides provide helmets on the tricky Lower Road section and assistance on the very steep final ascent near the summit where ropes have been installed. Despite all this, experienced walkers will still be able to complete the walk themselves. The track is well defined with a broad pad, but has no track markers.

Little Island, a large boulder close to the sea, is the accepted spot to meet guides for the climb. It also attracts painting classes and the providence petrel is abundant here. When the old vehicle track ends, rock-hop south along the boulder-strewn beach south for about 130m to locate the indistinct start of the track on the left. The track rises very steeply and ropes assist in the more difficult slippery sections. It heads directly up to the base of Mt Lidgbird's cliffs. Large rock overhangs act as potential shelters, and under one are the helmets the guides use. Head right, and shortly after, ropes are again provided where the pad leads on to a distinct narrow ledge. This is the Lower Road, which becomes quite breathtaking with a sheer 150m drop to the sea below. Inexperienced walkers may become nervous but ropes are provided for all the exposed section. The tricky part is about 400m long and is sometimes made more awkward by spider webs across the path. Once you reach the end of the ledge, the track heads left (east) around the side of Mt Lidgbird. After some minor scrambling here, as you ascend, the route basically contours along the side of Erskine Valley for about 600m until the creek. Cross this on the flat rocks—this is one of the few easy sections, but it can be very muddy and dark. Erskine Creek is a good spot for a break and a drink.

Continue on the far bank, swinging south-east and zigzagging up the crest of a spur to a high prominent ridge that joins Mt Lidgbird with Mt Gower. The slopes become more rocky and open as you ascend. Once on the ridge, attained well above and south of the Big Hill Saddle, there are great views across to Mt Lidgbird from some rocky outcrops, providing another good spot for a break. Follow the knife-edge spur up. Ropes are provided over numerous steep rocky sections. The rise in elevation is a further 350m in 500m, so exposure becomes acute as the plateau is reached. You can often see seabirds soaring in the updrafts. Views become spectacular and you can measure progress and judge your altitude relative to Mt Lidgbird, which you will eventually look down on.

The vegetation is heavily wind-pruned and stunted and goats may also be seen here. To the south, Balls Pyramid exudes a ghostly presence. As you near the top, the steep slope suddenly subsides and you enter a world of gnarled mossy trees, many of which grow nowhere else on earth. The sound of humans might attract the very tame woodhens. These

flightless birds almost became extinct in the late 1970s. In 1980, three pairs were taken into captivity and used for raising chicks. By 1984, 79 birds were released and now more than 250 birds live on the island. One colony at Transit Hill is so tame that they often come up to the residents' doors.

Follow the track to the right, down slightly and eventually through scrub to an open clearing that overlooks the entire island. This is a wonderful view with Mt Lidgbird in the foreground not looking half as imposing as from lower down, the aqua lagoon dominating the left and Mt Eliza in the background. Have lunch here and capture the views from this truly special place with your camera. If you are very lucky, some of the woodhen population might appear to complement the scene.

The rest of the walk involves retracing your steps and, no doubt, you will want to cool off in the lagoon on returning. After the walk, try to do a scenic flight that will give you another perspective on the two summits, while also allowing you a close-up look at Balls Pyramid.

The Goathouse Walk

Starting Point: The Airport, Lagoon Road, Lord Howe Island
Destination: The Goathouse (420m)
Summary: A circuit to the base of the north-facing cliffs of Mt Lidgbird
Attractions: Views over the lagoon, Boat Harbour
Length: 12km
Time: 6 hours
Options: This walk can be done in either direction

Attraction Rating: ★ ★ ★ ★
Fitness: ◨ ◨ ◨
Maps: LIC (CMA) Lord Howe Island 1:15 000 topographical or the *Australian Geographic* Lord Howe Island map
Access to Starting Point: Ride or walk to the airstrip from your accommodation via Lagoon Road
Facilities/Amenities: None on walk. The nearest accommodation is the Waimarie (Tel: 1800 671 546)
Recommended Equipment: Swimming gear, towel
Notes: Ropes installed along the ascent from Smoking Tree Ridge to the Goathouse

Walk Description

This reasonably strenuous climb involves little backtracking. Go to Cobbys Corner near the south-eastern end of the airstrip. Just opposite the turn-off into the airport, a signposted walking track leads over a stile and up into the forest. You are immediately presented with a junction.

For walkers short of time (or if poor weather makes the detour to Boat Harbour unpleasant), head right over Intermediate Hill direct to the Goathouse along Smoking Tree Ridge. But if you have the time, head left, contouring east through lovely palm-dominated rainforest around the base of Intermediate Hill. Along the way there are occasional glimpses north to Blinky Beach, one of Lord Howe Islands' few surf beaches.

The track climbs slightly as it swings east. There are many roots along this section and the track can get water-sodden, so wear good hiking boots. When you are level with Mutton Bird Point, a small side track leads down the slope and left to a viewing platform where you can observe masked boobies, the largest of Lord Howe Island's birds. Continue on the main track as it heads around a spur and then into the Rocky Run valley where water can be obtained. A junction at the track is signposted and you should head left to Boat Harbour noting this place for the return trip. From Rocky Run, Boat Harbour is about 15–20 minutes away. You emerge onto a rocky cove that has two streams feeding into it from the sides. In the background, Mt Lidgbird looms overhead with its distinct curvature. Boat Harbour is very rocky and unsuitable to sunbathing. Its protected water is pleasant for a swim, but not ideal for snorkelling. There's a picnic table on the far side of the cove among the trees. A small unofficial walking pad continues to Red Point.

Return to Rocky Run and head left, climbing 80m to Smoking Tree Ridge where there's another junction at a prominent saddle. You will be using the track opposite into Soldiers Creek Valley to exit the ridge. For now, head left along a well-formed track up to the Goathouse. The track is flat and easy at first but then climbs dramatically through more palm-dominated subtropical rainforest. It becomes increasingly rocky and ropes are needed over some slippery sections.

Near the base of the cliffs of Mt Lidgbird, veer left and climb up to a large overhang where red-tailed tropicbirds breed. In summer, their aerial aerobatics can be observed. If you continue along the overhang to the other side, you can round the prominent corner and see Balls Pyramid in the distance as well as the lesser-known eastern face of Mt Lidgbird with its curving cliffs and the upper Dinner Run Creek valley.

The Goathouse is an excellent spot for lunch with the lagoon forming a backdrop. Walk back to the saddle junction on Smoking Tree Ridge, head left and follow Lagoon Road north past Capella South back to the start.

Malabar Hill Circuit

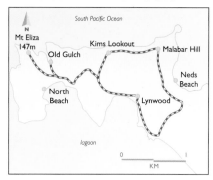

Starting Point: Neds Beach, Lord Howe Island National Park

Destination: Malabar Hill and Mt Eliza (147m)

Summary: A complete circuit of the northern hillocks of Lord Howe Island

Attractions: The views from Malabar Hill across Sugerloaf Passage to the Admiralty Islands

Length: 9km

Time: 4 hours

Options: This walk can be done in either direction

Attraction Rating: ★ ★ ★

Fitness: ◪ ◪ ◪ ◪

Maps: LIC (CMA) Lord Howe Island 1:15 000 topographical or the *Australian Geographic* Lord Howe Island map

Access to Starting Point: Neds Beach is at the end of Neds Beach Road. Turn off Lagoon Road at the post office.

Facilities/Amenities: Picnic shelters at North Beach. There is plenty of accommodation close by.

Recommended Equipment: Swimming gear, towel

Notes: Do not go to the very summit of Mt Eliza as this disturbs the sooty terns at their breeding grounds

Walk Description

The northern end of Lord Howe Island is comprised of several cliff-lined hills that provide views across the picturesque lagoon to the massive bulks of Mt Lidgbird and Mt Gower. Despite the distances being short, the walks are reasonably time-consuming as the track surface is often a tangle of tree roots. The highest vantage point is Malabar Hill, named after an Indian who died there while attempting to collect the red tail feathers from the tropicbirds that nest in the cliffs on the northern side.

The walk commences from Neds Beach, a beautiful swimming spot due to its sheltered cliffs. Fishing is prohibited here. Start walking by heading back along the sealed Neds Beach Road into palm forest and then turn immediately right onto a walking track that crosses a paddock via a stile. All around are mutton-bird burrows, especially under the palms. Head across the paddock (which can sometimes be quite boggy). The track then rises onto a prominent spur of Malabar Hill, 300m from Neds Beach Road. Another pad from the west joins in on the spur at a second stile. A climb, 800m long, follows the spur to the summit of Malabar Hill.

At first, the climb is within dense vegetation with a defined pad. Halfway up the hill is a plaque commemorating the 1948 crash of a Catalina flying boat, and near the summit the vegetation is heavily pruned by salt and wind. At several spots during the climb there are excellent views of Neds Beach and the centre of the island. Blackburn Island is prominent in the middle of the lagoon.

On top of Malabar Hill the high basalt sea cliffs of the north coast can be well appreciated, while offshore are the rocky Admiralty Islands. On a clear day most of Balls Pyramid can be seen to the south. West from Malabar

Looking to the north from the Goathouse, Lord Howe Island.

Looking south across the Lord Howe Island runway from Waimarie guest lodge.

Hill is a high ridge on what is known as the northern hills. A pad leads 800m along this ridge to Kims Lookout at about 200m elevation. The cliffs, however, are dangerous, so keep clear of them. The pad is well defined.

Seabirds frequent the cliffs and red-tailed tropicbirds can sometimes be seen soaring in updraughts. Views to the centre of the island are particularly good at Kims Lookout. By now you should be familiar with the horrid-looking golden orb spider. Large but harmless, it has a habit of spinning a strong web across all walking tracks on the island.

From Kims Lookout follow the pad west another 150m, then descend south 350m on the spur toward Dawson Point to link with the Max Nichols Walking Track. Head right over the crest toward North Beach and descend a gully among huge banyan trees and more palms for some 500m toward the coast. This section is very wet and water can be obtained from a small creek on the right. Still in forest at the bottom, it is then just 400m west to North Beach. Boats bring tourists to this secluded cove across the lagoon. At its northern end are some prominent volcanic rock outcrops. The sea here isn't as sheltered as the lagoon but is fine for a refreshing swim, if you can avoid the coral outcrops. If it

is not too windy, this would make a good spot for lunch. There are disused picnic shelters, toilets and tank water in trees just behind the beach. The area is subject to flooding after sustained heavy rain.

From the rear of the picnic shelters, a 250m-long flat pad leads off north of Old Gulch to a narrow rocky boulder cove. The cliff-line bulk of Mt Eliza is on the left and the Malabar–Kims headland on the right. Return to the picnic shelters, turn right and follow the pad across coral sands through thatch palms to Mt Eliza. The track is 700m long and rises almost immediately to 147m elevation. The vegetation suddenly becomes wind-swept as you emerge onto the tops. Sheer cliffs surround much of the summit and the views over the island are fantastic. A sign near the top asks visitors not to climb to the summit platforms as sooty terns have one of their primary breeding grounds here.

Return to North Beach and inspect the reef at the south-western end. Being frequently exposed at low tide, the coral is mostly dead, but rock pools provide interest. Retrace the route along the Max Nichols Memorial Track to the crest and down the other side. Head right at the junction to descend to Old Settlement Beach. The ridge traverse here is through a mass

of banyans, pandanus and palms dominated by vines.

Old Settlement Beach was the site of first settlement in the whaling days. Lord Howe Island was discovered on 17 February 1788, less than a month after settlement at Sydney Cove. For 100 years whalers and their Maori wives were the main inhabitants. Walk to the eastern end of Old Settlement Beach, the end of Lagoon Road, via a bridge and a tiny picnic area. The walk ends just 700m along the road at Neds Beach Road. You will pass the jetty on the way. It is no longer the centre of social activity on the island as it was from 1947 to 1974, when flying boats arrived from Rose Bay in Sydney. Small boats brought people from the plane in the lagoon to the jetty where they were welcomed with a necklace of flowers and the sounds of South Pacific island music. The present airstrip in the middle of the island was opened in 1974.

Other walks on Lord Howe Island

Several other smaller walks are possible on the island. Despite the distances being relatively short, you should allow plenty of time. These walks are: Transit Hill, Red Point, Valley of the Shadows, Hells Gates, and the Stevens Reserve Trail.

Australian Capital Territory

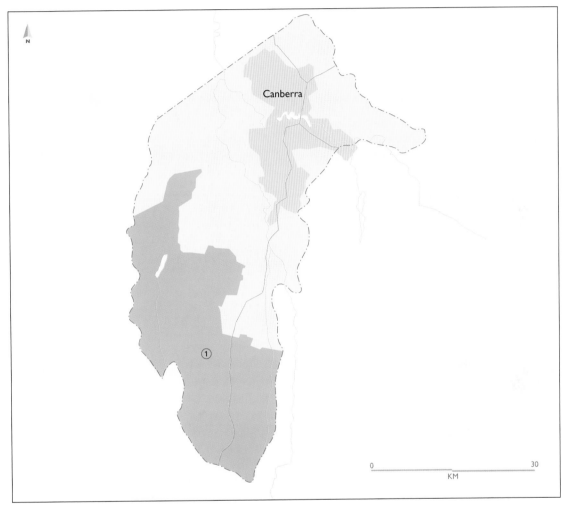

① Namadgi National Park   169

Introduction

Few people realise that about half of the Australian Capital Territory consists of national park and state forest. In particular, the southern and western halves of the territory are dominated by the wild Namadgi National Park. The most spectacular part of this is the Brindabella Range, a northern extension of Kosciuszko National Park. Canberra is a good place to live if you enjoy walking, with spectacular mountain ranges within an hour's drive from Parliament House. There are about 150km of formed walking trails in the national park.

Climate

Much of Namadgi National Park and the Brindabella Range are at considerable altitude and winter temperatures fall below freezing. In fact, the roads on the Brindabella Range are snowbound and closed in winter. Summer can be warm and dry, but above 1500m this is not a problem. Cold winds can blow across the ranges from Kosciuszko National Park so take windproof fleece clothing in all seasons. During the long dry periods Canberra experiences, carry water in the south of Namadgi National Park and on the peaks of Brindabella Range.

Transport

There is no public transport either south to Namadgi or west to the Brindabellas but, fortunately, the distances are small. The Brindabellas are best accessed via the Cotter Dam Road from Canberra and then Piccadilly Circus. No fuel at all is available once you leave Canberra in either direction. Cycling is an option too, given Canberra's many wonderful bikeways, but note that more than 1500m altitude must be gained if you wish to access the more remote peaks in the southern Brindabellas. To get to the southern area of the national park, drive to Tharwa and take Naas Road, then Boboyan Road to the Naas Valley.

Accommodation

Besides the usual hotels, motels, guesthouses and youth hostels in Canberra itself, there is little other private accommodation. The three camping grounds are:

Orroral Campground

Traditional tents-only sites for small parties, maximum six people. No provision for organised groups. Facilities include tables and wood BBQs at each site, firewood and flushing toilets. Walkers can proceed to the Orroral Heritage Track network. Access is by sealed road from Canberra.

Honeysuckle Campground

A camping area at the entrance to the former Honeysuckle Deep Space Tracking Station. Areas for organised groups, campervans and small parties. Facilities include covered shelter with seating, fireplace and gas BBQ, shared wood BBQs, firewood, rainwater tanks and composting toilets. There are walks to the historic Tracking Station site and track connections to Booroomba Rocks and Orroral Ridge. Access is by sealed road.

Mt Clear Campground

This is the park's smallest and most remote campground. Separate areas for small organised groups and small parties, maximum six people. Facilities include pit toilets, shared wood BBQs and firewood. Walkers can set out on trips to Naas Valley and Horse Gully Hut. The last 16km from Canberra are on an unsealed road.

Camping Permits

Camping permits are required for the park's three car-based campgrounds as well as overnight walking in the Bimberi wilderness. Bookings must be made in advance at the Namadgi Visitors' Centre, either in person or by phone or fax. Book early to secure a site, especially on long weekends. There is a maximum three-night stay at the campgrounds. No camping is permitted in the Corin Dam and Cotter Hut vicinities. A small fee is payable in advance at the Namadgi Visitors' Centre. The permit includes a sticker to attach to your tent or campervan.

- Pay by cash, cheque or credit card during open hours;
- or by cash or cheque using the after-hours facility at the front gate of the Namadgi Visitors' Centre.

Maps

The Land Information Centre (LIC) of New South Wales produces topographical maps covering the ACT, the most popular for bushwalking being Cotter Dam and Corin Dam 1:25 000 topographicals. The ACT Parks and Conservation Service produces a Namadgi National Park 1:100 000 map available from the visitors' centre on Naas Road. The LIC's headquarters and mail-order address is:

Map sales counter
Panorama Avenue
PO Box 143, Bathurst NSW 2795

Epic Walks

The Australian Capital Territory has only one formal long-distance walk:

Australian Alps Walking Trail
See New South Wales section, page 75

The view west from Mt Gingera, Brindabella Range, ACT.

Namadgi National Park

Namadgi National Park covers the mountainous area in the south-west of the Australian Capital Territory. It contains prehistoric sites and rare subalpine species of flora and wildlife. Popular recreations include camping, bushwalking, fishing, rock-climbing and cross-country skiing.

The pleasant bushland settings at Honeysuckle, Mt Clear and Orroral are ideal for low-key camping. The Cotter River is fed by rainwater and melting snow from the high peaks that rim the Australian Capital Territory. Camping is restricted in its catchment area, which supplies water for Canberra.

Namadgi is the Aboriginal name for the mountains that provide a backdrop to the city of Canberra. Namadgi has a rich human history, from the dawn of time to the space age, and contains the only Aboriginal art sites in the Australian Alps. The national park visitors' centre, 2km south of Tharwa on the Naas Road, features information displays, a wide-screen audiovisual documentary and guided tours. Telephone for information and bookings. Permits to enter the Bimberi Wilderness Area and Cotter River protected zone can be obtained here.

Facts and Figures

Name: Namadgi National Park
Size: 106 000ha
Enactment:
Gudgenby Nature Reserve, 1978
Namadgi National Park, 1984
Major extensions (12 000ha), 1991
(formerly called 'Gudgenby',
'Cotter' or 'Kelly' Wilderness)
Visitors: Unknown
Vegetation: Subalpine woodlands and heaths, wet sclerophyll forest, montane savannah woodland, and grassland swamps
Wildlife: Platypus, Bogong moth, koala, broad-toothed rat, river blackfish, gang-gang cockatoo
Camping: Official sites at Clear Hill, Orroral and Honeysuckle Creek
Adjoining Parks:
Kosciuszko National Park,
Tidbinbilla Nature Reserve,
Scabby Range Nature Reserve,
Brindabella National Park

Further Information:
Namadgi National Park
Visitors' Centre
Naas Rd, Tharwa ACT 2620
Tel: (02) 6207 2900
Fax: (02) 6207 2901
e-mail:
namadgi_national_park@dpa.act.gov.au
web site: www.act.gov.au/environ
Reception Hours:
9.00am–4.00pm weekdays
9.00am–4.30pm weekends and
public holidays

Mt Gingera Walk

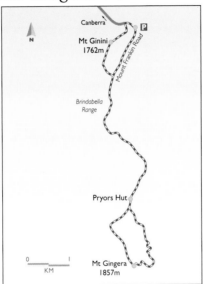

Starting Point: Mt Ginini (1762m), Namadgi National Park
Destination: Summit of Mt Gingera (1857m)
Summary: A walk along the spine of the Brindabella Range between two of the most prominent mountains
Attractions: Snow gums, panoramic views to Kosciuszko National Park from the summit
Length: 14.4km
Time: 4.5 hours
Options: To extend the walk, continue south along Mt Franklin Road to other peaks along the range
Attraction Rating: ★ ★ ★
Fitness: ◼ ◼ ◼
Maps: LIC (CMA) Corin Dam 1:25 000 topographical. For a general overview, consult the Namadgi National Park 1:100 000 map available from the ACT Parks and Conservation Service.
Access to Starting Point: From Canberra, take Cotter Road over the Murrumbidgee River. Turn right about

1km along Brindabella Road, then left when you reach a T-intersection with Uriarra Road. The road becomes unsealed as it ascends to Piccadilly Circus, where you turn left down the Mt Franklin road. Pass the Mt Franklin Chalet and, after 25.5km, take the Mt Ginini summit turn-off to the right and park at the top by the Civil Aviation Authority relay station.
Facilities/Amenities: Pryors Hut offers low-key overnight accommodation, but rats can be a problem
Recommended Equipment: Warm, windproof alpine clothing; water
Notes: The Mt Franklin road is closed and snowbound in winter. In late summer, alpine flowers are in bloom.
Further Information: See Facts and Figures, this page

Walk Description

Outstanding views over the Canberra hinterland, the northern hinterland of Kosciuszko National Park, Brindabella Range and Namadgi National Park from both starting and finishing summits. There are no higher peaks to the north on the Australian continent.

From the summit, walk straight down the southern slope over a field of alpine grass. Where the old ski run starts, veer to the right (west), then turn left and cut through bush to the Mt Franklin road. You must push through some thick undergrowth here and the last section is quite steep.

After about 2km you come to Stockyard Gap, and 1km farther on the Stockyard Spur Track comes in to your left. The minor track shown on the topographical map as paralleling Mt Franklin road through Cheyenne Flats is overgrown. It is fairly flat walking to Pryors Hut, built as part of the botanic gardens annexe. In the visitors' book are many accounts of expeditions by cross-country skiers. Opposite the wooden hut is a small arboretum of Scots pines planted in 1940. No water is available here.

Continue south along the road for another kilometre. After crossing a small creek near a sharp bend, follow a small track uphill to the right and climb over an old fence. As you approach the summit, notice how the snow gums become more stunted. From the boulder-strewn summit of

Mt Gingera, the waters of Tantangara Dam, Cave Creek and the Goodradigbee River valley can be seen. The best vantage point is the rock platform with the trig marker. There's a small camp clearing between the rare mountain plum pines. Scramble over some boulders to gain access to westerly views at the very highest point, This area is usually exposed to cold winds.

To leave the summit, head north over Brumby Flats by walking along the centre of the ridge. At the end, head right (north-west) and descend to the Pryors Hut saddle. Follow the Mt Franklin road all the way to the vehicle barrier. Some information signs here provide notes on walking and camping in the Brindabella Ranges. Head up the Mt Ginini summit road to the car. If you time it right, you can enjoy a memorable sunset watching the peaks turn red.

Bimberi Wilderness Walk

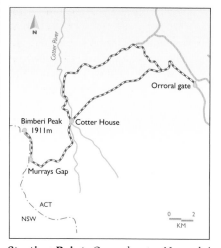

Starting Point: Orroral gate, Namadgi National Park

Destination: Summit of Mt Bimberi (1911m)

Summary: An extended walk through the remote western Bimberi Wilderness component of the Namadgi National Park, climbing to the highest point on the Brindabella Range from the Cotter River valley

Attractions: Wild remote camping and magnificent views over northern regions in the Australian Alps from Mt Bimberi

Length: Total distance, 68km

Day 1: Orroral Gate to Cotter River, 24km

Day 2: Cotter River to Mt Bimberi (return) 20km

Day 3: Cotter River to Orroral gate 24km

Time: 3 days

Options: A shorter route can be taken along the Australian Alps Walking Trail from the Orroral road to the Cotter River. Although not depicted on the map, it passes over Cotter Gap and proceeds to Pond Creek Flats.

Attraction Rating: ★ ★ ★

Fitness: ◩◩◩◩◩

Maps: LIC (CMA) Corin Dam and Rendezvous Creek 1:25 000 topographicals. An overview is given by the Namadgi National Park 1:100 000 map available from the ACT Parks and Conservation Service.

Access to Starting Point: Leaving from Canberra, drive south to Tharwa and along Naas Road, Boboyan Road and the Orroral road to a small car park close to the gate just past the former space tracking station.

Facilities/Amenities: There are a number of suitable camping spots back from the Cotter River. Water can be obtained from the Cotter River and many other creeks that flow off the Bimberi Range. The Orroral camping area provides car-camping facilities near the start of the walk.

Recommended Equipment: Warm alpine clothing and good-quality sleeping bags are essential

Notes: Camping permits are needed to camp anywhere in the 32 000ha Bimberi wilderness area and Cotter River catchment. There is no charge for the permit, but note only 24 campers are allowed within the area at any one time. No camping is allowed within 500m of the Cotter Hut vicinity or 100m of the Cotter River. The walk is best done in late spring, summer and early autumn as the peaks of the Brindabella Range are snowbound in winter.

Further Information: See Facts and Figures, page 169

Walk Description

This walk penetrates the heart of the most spectacular area of Namadgi National Park. Mt Bimberi is the highest mountain in the ACT and almost 1,000m of altitude must be gained to reach its fantastic summit. Consequently, walkers venturing here must be fit and experienced, with good-quality equipment. Navigation isn't a big issue as most of the way is along management trails; only the last section from Murrays Gap involves a steep trackless climb.

From Orroral gate near the former tracking station and just past the Orroral camping area, head north-west along the Orroral road (Smokers Trail) climbing out of the Orroral River valley and descending into the Cotter River valley via Cotter Hut Road. At this point, you officially enter the Bimberi Wilderness. Alternatively, use the Australian Alps Walking Trail (along an old bridle trail) to cut across from Orroral road to Cotter Gap and then Pond Creek, emerging at a ford about 50m north of Cotter Hut. Camp at any suitable place by the river, either to the north or south of Cotter Hut, but not within 500m of it. The building was once the residence of the Cotter family, but is now used as a temporary ranger station. One possible camping site is along Bimberi Creek, using the Murray Gap Trail. Another site is at the confluence of De Salis Creek and the Cotter River.

The next morning, leave the tent standing but secure and head up to Murrays Gap. Take plenty of water for this relentless and especially steep climb. At Murrays Gap, a yellow border marker (R1061) indicates that you are standing on the New South Wales state border. From here, head due north across country—always keeping to the highest ground. The thick forest gives way to open snow gum woodland and then finally to alpine grasses above the 1800m line.

The peak has long been popular with cross-country skiers. It was first climbed on skis in August 1932 by Bedford Osbourne and Bill Gordon. Walkers can also approach the summit from the north-east along the Mt Franklin road and from the west via Oldfields Hut. The trig marker is a large four-pronged contraption, designed to withstand the gales that blast the top during winter.

Have lunch on top, enjoying superb vistas all around. You can see north to Black Tower, Canberra and Tabletop Mountain. Cooleman Plains, Tantangara Reservoir, Mt Jagungal and the

Looking north-east from near the summit of Mt Gingera, Namadgi National Park.

Main Range are all visible in the south and west. Most of Namadgi National Park can be seen to the east. Retrace your steps to Cotter River valley and use the same campsite. On the third day, head back to the car either via Cotter Hut Road or the AAWT via Cotters Gap to make a circuit. The late afternoon view of Cotters Rocks from the gap is magnificent.

Mt Clear Circuit

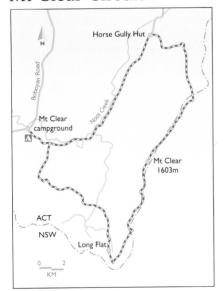

Starting Point: Mt Clear campground, Namadgi National Park
Destination: Long Flat, the summit of Mt Clear (1603m), and Horse Gully Hut
Summary: A circuit starting in the upper Naas River Valley, ascending the Clear Range to follow the ACT border south and returning to Mt Clear campground via Grassy Creek

Attractions: Views, a lovely river valley with black sallee and snow gum
Length: 35km
Time: 2 days
Options: This walk can be done in either direction. For a shorter 16km day walk, return to the Mt Clear campground from Horse Gully Hut.
Attraction Rating: ★ ★ ★
Fitness: ◪ ◪ ◪ ◪
Maps: LIC (CMA) Bredbo and Colinton 1:25 000 topographicals. For an overview consult the Namadgi National Park 1:100 000 map.
Access to Starting Point: Drive to Tharwa. Continue south on the Naas Road for 31km. After crossing the Gudgenby River for the second time, the road becomes unsealed. Continue 17km farther, passing Old Boboyan Road, Yerrabi Track, Shanahans Mountain track and 500m after crossing Naas Creek, turn left at the Mt Clear campground sign. Turn right at the Naas Valley walking track sign. The car park is 50m from this junction.
Facilities/Amenities: Rainwater tank at Horse Gully Hut. Overnight camping at Long Flat and Horse Gully Hut. Car-camping facilities at the Mt Clear campground include firewood and toilets. Note that the camping area is

structured specifically so that you can't camp right next to your car.
Recommended Equipment: Warm, windproof alpine clothing and good-quality overnight camping gear. Salt for combating leeches may be handy.
Notes: A mountain bike can also be used on this circuit
Further Information: See Facts and Figures, page 169

Walk Description

This is the ideal walk to explore the remote south of magnificent Namadgi National Park. The structure of the walk is flexible, although a little lopsided. Depending on what time you set out, most of the walk can be done on the first day or the second. If starting late, you can camp the first night at Horse Gully Hut, 8km from the Mt Clear campground. This entails a 27km walk along the Clear Range and down to Grassy Creek. If you begin the walk early you can walk the 27km in reverse on the first day and camp at Horse Gully Hut. Alternatively, camp at Long Flat.

The Mt Clear campground is on former private land in the far south of the Australian Capital Territory. To the east, the foreground is dominated by flat grassy fields in the Naas River Valley, first settled in the 1830s.

From Mt Clear campground, follow the Naas Valley fire trail east, crossing Grassy Creek and turning north-east through open fields. After 5km, the trail leaves Naas Creek and winds through alpine ash woodland to Horse Gully Hut. If the weather is hot and you prefer to camp by the river, head north for about 1km to Naas Creek. Beware of leeches in the reeds.

From the hut, head east up to Left Hand Creek, climbing until you reach the ACT border along Clear Range. Once you are on the summit of Mt Clear, views of Namadgi's granite mountain ranges capped by many rocky tors (stacks of boulders formed by freezing and erosion) become very spectacular. The beautiful upper Naas River Valley lies below you. Its headwaters are run-off rainfall from the southern slopes of Mt Gudgenby. The track then heads north and descends back down into the valley to rejoin the track from the campground.

Naas Valley Walk

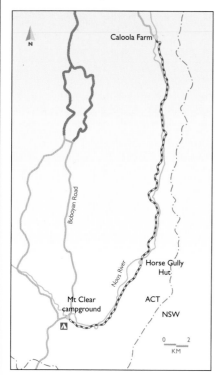

Starting Point: Mt Clear campground, Namadgi National Park

Destination: Caloola Farm

Summary: A one-way walk along the Naas River using the Naas River fire trail at the base of the Clear Range

Attractions: A pretty river valley with black sallee and snow gums

Length: 30km

Time: 2 days

Options: This walk can be done in either direction if you set up a car shuffle beforehand

Attraction Rating: ★ ★ ★

Fitness: ✕ ✕

Maps: LIC (CMA) Michelago and Colinton 1:25 000 topographicals. For an overview, consult the Namadgi National Park 1:100 000 map

Access to Starting Point: Drive to Tharwa. Continue south on Naas Road for 31km. After crossing the Gudgenby River for the second time, the road becomes unsealed. Continue 17km farther, passing the old Boboyan Road, Yerrabi track, Shanahans Mountain track and 500m after crossing the Naas creek, turn left at the Mt Clear campground sign. Turn right at the Naas valley walking track sign. The car park is 50m from this junction. Caloola Farm is best accessed by travelling south from the visitors' centre and turning left after you cross

the Gudgenby River. Follow this continuation of Naas Road to the end.

Facilities/Amenities: An overnight campsite at Horse Gully Hut. Water is available. Campsites also along Naas River Valley. Car-camping facilities at the Mt Clear campground include firewood and toilets. Again, the camping area is structured so that you can't camp right next to your car.

Recommended Equipment: Overnight gear suitable for river camping in alpine terrain

Notes: A mountain bike can also be used on this walk as it is entirely along fire trails

Further Information: See Facts and Figures, page 169

Walk Description

This is a simple low-altitude overnight walk in the south-eastern quadrant of the Namadgi National Park. There are no major uphills and camping sites are numerous along most of the route. The Mt Clear campground is on formerly private land in the far south of the Australian Capital Territory. To the east, the foreground is dominated by flat grassy fields in the Naas River valley, first settled in the 1830s.

From Mt Clear campground follow the Naas Valley fire trail east, crossing Grassy Creek and then turning northeast through open fields. After 5km, the trail leaves the Naas River and winds through alpine ash woodland to Horse Gully Hut.

Some of the following tracks do not appear on the Colinton topographical map, but are on the more recently printed Bredbo topographical. From the hut, head north along the Naas River through pleasant woodland. There are old stockyards here between the stands of black sallee and alpine grasses. Aim to camp near Reedy Creek to divide the distance about in half. Beware of leeches in the water.

Other walks in Namadgi National Park

Leaflets on some of the other walks may be available from the Namadgi National Park Visitors' Centre, located 3km south of Tharwa on Naas Road. Some of these walks, and others, are described in *70 Walks in Southern New South Wales and A.C.T.* by Tyrone

Thomas, and *Australian Mountains: The Best 100 Walks* by Tyrone Thomas and Sven Klinge.

Bendora Arboretum Walk (5km, 2 hours)

Park near the locked gate on the left side of the Mt Franklin road 4.5km past Bulls Head. Follow the fire trail through snow gum and mountain gum forest to Bendora arboretum, a 1940 trial planting of pines, spruces and larches.

Boboyan Forest Walk (5km, 2 hours)

From the car park at the locked gate at Boboyan Pine Forest, follow the Old Boboyan Road for 2.5km, then turn left to leave Bogong Creek. Continue around the signposted circuit through candlebark and snow gum woodland.

Booroomba Rocks Walk (4.5km, 2 hours)

These boulders are in the eastern half of the Namadgi National Park. To access the start, drive to Tharwa from Canberra. Continue south on the Naas Road for 11km past the Namadgi National Park Visitors' Centre, turning right at Honeysuckle Road. Drive a further 9.2km, turning off to the right at the Booroomba Rocks sign close to the Honeysuckle Creek camping area. Follow this unsealed road north and then east for 3km to a car park.

Booroomba Rocks, visible from southern Canberra, are one of Australia's premier rock-climbing sites. For the bushwalker, there are spectacular views and scenery. Start at the Booroomba Rocks walking track signpost and walk north along a small easy-to-follow track. It climbs through peppermint and mountain gum woodland, past two large boulders. After about 30 minutes and a climb of less than 200m, you reach a large bare area showing signs of campfires. Continue about 20m in the same direction up onto Middle Rocks. To the right is North Buttress. Be careful near the precipitous edges and be aware that there could be rock climbers in the vicinity.

Brandy Flat Walk (10km, 6 hours)

Start either at the northern end, 300m along Glendale Depot Road, or at the

Naas Creek valley from Clear Hill campground, Namadgi National Park.

southern end, at a locked gate 200m off Boboyan Road. Follow the fire trail, which is steep in parts and offers fine views of the Billy and Booth ranges. The hut at Brandy Flat has a rainwater tank and old stockyards nearby.

Cotter River Walk (5km, 2 hours)
This walk starts from Bendora Dam picnic area. The track crosses the Cotter River below the dam wall, then follows a fire trail through peppermint forest. Ford the river and pass through a ribbon gum gully to rejoin Bendora Road 300m from the picnic area.

Grassy Creek to Boboyan Valley via Sheep Station Creek Walk (20km, 1 day)
Start from the gate at the lower end of the Naas Creek valley, or from the gate beside the Boboyan Road just 100m north of the New South Wales border in the far south of the Namadgi National Park. Along the route are forested sections linking the open valleys of Grassy, Sheep Station and Naas creeks. The valleys feature ruins of old huts and homesteads that often have exotic species planted on them.

Mt Franklin Walk (3km, 1.5hours)
Start this walk from the car park at Mt Franklin and follow the track past the historic ski chalet through snow gum woodland to the summit of Mt Franklin. There are views of Canberra and Burrinjuck Dam in New South Wales.

Old Boboyan Road Walk (14km, 5 hours)
This walk follows the section of the Old Boboyan Road closed to vehicles between the Boboyan Pine Forest and the lower end of the Boboyan Valley. Highlights include the Boboyan homestead chimney, the sedgeland (or 'fen') stretching upstream from the Naas Creek crossing, and views of rugged Mt Gudgenby (1739m). The walk links up with the Grassy Creek track via the Sheep Station Creek property.

Square Rock Walk (10.5km, 4 hours)
From Smokers Gap car park, the track crosses Corin Road and climbs steeply through a maze of granite boulders. This first section is the most difficult of the walk. Halfway along, the open grassland at Smokers Flat appears through a stand of tall alpine ash. The track continues through snow gums to Square Rock (1400m). There is a short side trip to the Orroral Valley Lookout, almost 300m above the surrounding country. The sweeping views take in Brindabella Range, Cotter and Orroral River valleys and Canberra.

Yankee Hat Walk (5.4km, 2 hours)
This walk is to one of the few Aboriginal rock art sites in the alpine area. The track starts at the end of Old Boboyan Road. This road is best accessed by driving south from the visitors' centre along Boboyan Road. Turn right at the second crossing of the Gudgenby River. The walk heads across Bogong Swamp to approach the rock art site from the east. The shelter at Yankee Hat is a granite boulder that has been rounded off by erosion. This rounding (sometimes called 'onion-skin weathering') is caused by continual expansion and contraction through heating and cooling. Do not touch the painted surface as it can crumble. Dating suggests the art is about 800 years old.

The cream-coloured streaks on the rock are felspar deposits washed down by rain. The black to grey deposits are probably organic minerals, which may in the future allow more precise dating of the paintings. The white paint used at Yankee Hat is clay. The red paint is based on iron oxide or 'ochre'. The nearest known ochre quarries are at Michelago and Gungahim. The different shades of red in the paintings may be the result of paint weathering or they may have been mixed deliberately by adding some white clay to the ochre. Clay and ochre were usually mixed with a binding agent such as water, sap, blood or animal oils.

Yerrabi Track Walk (4km, 1.5 hours)
The highlights of this 160m climb through subalpine forest are some of the national park's dominant vegetation. The rocky summit of Boboyan Trig offers magnificent panoramic views across the ranges, including some of the most easily accessible views of the Bimberi Wilderness. The trackhead is on Boboyan Road in the far south of Namadgi National Park.

Other walks in the Australian Capital Territory
Black Mountain Nature Reserve offers some short tourist walks, including a walk for the blind with Braille information plaques. In the east of the Australian Capital Territory, Mt McDonald (788m), Mt Coree (1421m) and Mt Aggie (1496m) make reasonable destinations with great views. However, the wilderness atmosphere is partly marred by the existence of roads to their summits.

Victoria

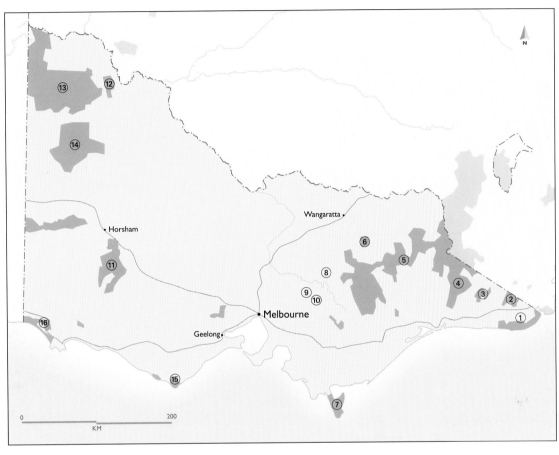

Introduction

With 17 people per square kilometre compared with a national average of two, Victoria is Australia's most densely populated state. By comparison, New South Wales and Tasmania have only six, and Queensland a lonesome 1.3. Fortunately for the bushwalker, most of Victoria's four million people live in one place—Melbourne. This leaves most of the state, especially the extreme west and eastern regions, relatively uninhabited.

The many reserves here are of outstanding quality. In addition to 36 national parks, the conservation system, one of Australia's oldest, includes numerous other state parks, wilderness areas, state forests, coastal parks, flora reserves and wildlife reserves. The last two decades have seen significant additions to national parks, not only in their quantity but also in their size. The supreme achievement is the 646 000ha Alpine National Park that links with Kosciuszko National Park in New South Wales to create a continuous reservation from Canberra to Mansfield. This rivals Kakadu as Australia's largest natural area. There is every indication that this area will increase as leasehold properties expire and state forests and uncommitted Crown Lands are reclassified.

Another mammoth conglomerate of parks occurs in the northwest corner of the state where the Murray–Sunset National Park (633 000ha) adjoins the Hattah–Kulkyne National Park (48 000ha). Just to the south, the Big Desert Wilderness Park (113 500ha) shares boundaries with the Wyperfeld National Park (356 800ha) and the Ngarkat Conservation Park in South Australia. Altogether, these parks total more than 1 000 000ha and represent the only sizeable pure wilderness in the state.

Generally, Parks Victoria's policy over the past decade has been to establish a system of national parks by creating new reservations in natural areas and extending existing reservations. The objective is to preserve a maximum of representative samples of the original landscapes, habitats, flora and wildlife from present-day remnants. In effect, these are 'islands' of nature in developed land. It is only in very recent times that we can say that most of what *can* be reserved has actually been reserved.

The view from Mt Cobbler, Alpine National Park.

Climate

Most of Victoria's parks can be enjoyed all year. However, the north-west semi-arid parks, such as Wyperfeld and Pink Lakes, are far too hot to visit from November to March. In addition they get almost no rainfall then and what little surface water is there is too salty to drink or has blue-green algae. Walkers can also experience bushfires in the summer months in the eastern forested areas, and campers must observe local fire regulations. Although a third of fires are caused by lightning strikes, about a quarter are preventable: they are either intentional or attributable to carelessness.

During winter months, the Alps are snow-covered and walking becomes impractical if not impossible. Rainfall is moderate compared to tropical areas of Australia, and wind is not half as prevalent as it is in Tasmania. Walkers intending to traverse the peaks and ridges of the Buller–Stirling and the Falls Creek–Mt Hotham regions must carry protective warm clothing and, if camping, a sheltered tent or fly and a good-quality down sleeping bag graded to three seasons or higher.

Transport

Victoria has an excellent public transport system. Rail and coach cover most areas while the highways are among the best in the country. Melbourne has trams in addition to its rail and bus network, giving visitors and locals a wide range of options and coverage. Over recent years, the far ends of the city have been interconnected with an innovative toll-based freeway system. Timetables for rail, bus and tram can all be found at the Victorian transport department's web site, www.victrip.gov.au

Accommodation

The State Office of the YHA Membership and Travel Centre is located close to trams and within walking distance of the Spencer St Railway Station, at:

205 King St (Corner King and Little Bourke Sts)
Melbourne VIC 3000
9.00am–5.30pm (weekdays)
9.00am–12.00pm (Saturday)

Postal address:

GPO Box 4793
Melbourne VIC 3001
Tel: (03) 9670 7991
Fax: (03) 9670 9840
e-mail: membership@yhavic.org.au

The range of services includes membership applications, general enquiries, advance hostel bookings for individuals, sale of sleeping sheets, handbooks, travel guides and accessories, badges and souvenirs. Membership is also available at Melbourne YHA hostels outside state office hours or at country hostels during hostel opening hours. Details of other membership-issuing agents are available on request from the office.

YHA Travel
Tel: (03) 9670 9611
Fax: (03) 9670 9840
e-mail: travel@yhavic.org.au

A small cascade in the Marysville State Forest near the Cathedral Range State Park.

Full travel service with member discounts is available. This includes overseas and domestic travel, bus, rail and ferry passes, hostel tour packages, and advice about visas. A range of tours depart from this hostel on a daily basis. For hostel accommodation in Melbourne, contact:

Queensberry Hill YHA

Tel: (03) 9329 8599

Maps

The main outlet for the state government's official maps is:

VICMAP–Information Victoria

356 Collins St, Melbourne VIC 3000

Tel: (03) 9603 9920

They have produced a series of recreational maps collectively called the *Outdoor Leisure Series*. These contain detailed topographical lines and information on places of interest, walks and tourist facilities. On the reverse side, many have close-up and location maps. Some are at scales that can be useful to walkers, primarily 1:50 000.

National Parks

The regulatory body that administers Victoria's 36 national parks is Parks Victoria, which was created in December 1996 by bringing together the management of:

- the former National Parks Service
- the former Melbourne Parks and Waterways, and
- other parks previously managed by a range of different authorities, committees of management and trusts.

Parks Victoria's charter is to manage parks and other assets on behalf of the state and it is empowered to do this under the *Parks Victoria Act 1998*. National, state and wilderness parks in Victoria are proclaimed under schedules to the *National Parks Act 1975* by the state parliament. Victoria's national parks have been expanded progressively from some 4 per cent of the state in the early 1970s to about 16 per cent today. Parks Victoria is committed to the protection of values that contribute to Victoria's world-class representative system. Legislation in the *Parks Victoria Act* formalised Parks Victoria's provision of services under a 'purchaser/provider' model, with the Department of Natural Resources and Environment purchasing Parks Victoria's services on behalf of the state government.

Entry Fees

The government has adopted a user-pays policy and has built toll booths at the main entrances to the most popular of the national parks. The small fees collected are used to defray running costs.

Epic Walks

Victoria has a variety of long walks to interest keen individuals. These are:

Australian Alps Walking Trail (AAWT)

See New South Wales section, page 75.

Bicentennial National Trail

This mammoth continent-spanning trail of interconnected vehicular tracks and stock-routes extends from Tom Groggin on the Murray River (NSW border) in the north to the Dandenongs near Melbourne, mainly following the western slopes of the Great Dividing Range, weaving between national parks and rural land. The trail is 5530km long, extending all the way to Cooktown in northern

Queensland. Because of its route and construction, it is not ideally suited to quality bushwalking and therefore is not covered in this book. The trail is more accessible to equestrians and cyclists, although walkers may find some sections suitable.

The Great South-west Walk

This 250km circuit passes through a mixture of rural land, the Lower Glenelg National Park and some minor coastal reserves. The Glenelg River contrasts with remote beaches and rocky headlands. The walk begins and ends at Portland.

McMillans Walking Track

Another historical route, this 200km walking track traverses the rugged eastern slopes of the Great Dividing Range from near Melbourne to Omeo. At time of writing, it is being re-routed to avoid developed areas and overgrown sections.

The Wilderness Coast Walk— Cape Conran (Victoria) to Pambula (New South Wales)

The beautiful Croajingolong National Park and Nadgee Nature Reserve are two of the least known coastal parks between Melbourne and Sydney. The area around Cape Howe in particular features beautiful wild coves and lagoons. The 151km walk can be done

The wild coastline of Croajingolong National Park, East Gippsland.

in stages and Mallacoota Inlet is crossed by boat. The most popular section is from Wingan Inlet to Mallacoota, although the Mallacoota to Newtons Beach walk is becoming increasingly popular as new guidebooks detail route descriptions.

Wilsons Promontory Circuit

The 40km circuit to Sealers Cove, the lighthouse and return via Oberon Bay is a great coastal walk, but avoid peak holiday times. The final section of this track was opened in 1999.

East Gippsland

Rainfall is high in this beautiful natural area. Fortunately, almost 90 per cent of it is public land, having survived the worst of the pioneering era because of its isolation from the urban centres of Sydney and Melbourne. The creation of some extensive wilderness parks now ensures that it will continue to survive. In recent times the area has been the focus of intense conservation protests over logging in the wet highland forests of the Errinundra Plateau and the upper Roger River Valley. While the controversy has largely subsided since the formation of national parks, many areas still remain unreserved.

The rugged topography of East Gippsland changes from elevated tablelands in the north to deeply dissected mountainous terrain along the west paralleling the Alps. Closer to the coast, undulating hilly foothills and broad plains contrast with extensive dune systems. The coast itself has broad sandy beaches with rocky headlands and coastal cliffs.

More than 20 different vegetation communities can be found in East Gippsland, from coastal heaths to tall mountain forests, with the most extensive type being lowland sclerophyll forest. Other communities include warm and cool temperate rainforest, rainshadow woodlands found on dry rocky hillsides in the Snowy River catchment, and the bloodwood forests.

The geology of East Gippsland reflects the extremes of earth's forces that have been sculpting the land for half a billion years.

About 140 million year ago, the land to the west uplifted to form what we refer to today as the Alps. Indirectly this resulted in rich volcanic soil deposits on the plains. The highlands are characterised by broad valleys and low divides generally at 1000m elevation. Tilting toward the north resulted in south-flowing rivers having steep gradients, numerous cascades and waterfalls, while north-flowing watercourses are characterised by broad winding shallow valleys and swampy areas of poor drainage.

Overnight walkers must be very well equipped and experienced. There are no railway lines and little other public transport to remote areas—you must be completely self-sufficient. Rainfall is high, ticks are common, terrain is largely steep, tracks are often in poor condition due to the wet climate and infrequent maintenance, and many areas are being classified as core wilderness areas with no right of access for cars.

The most extensive erosion in East Gippsland originates from gravel roads and earthen tracks. The problem is worse where roads have been constructed with grades that are too steep or where inadequate provision has been made for run-off. The typically high rainfall, especially on the Errinundra Plateau, can make camping conditions unpleasant and trails slippery and muddy. Note that on the plains it can lead to localised flooding, impassable river crossings and washed-out fords.

Croajingolong National Park is the most accessible and developed in East Gippsland with an extensive network of 2WD and 4WD trails and several fine camping areas amid picturesque mahogany gums, bloodwoods, paperbarks and stringybarks beside wide pristine river inlets. Because of the park's popularity, the local wildlife is quite used to humans. Animals can even become too friendly and food must not be left out at night. The beaches have beautiful white sand, drinking water is pure and the views along the rugged coast are stunning.

Climate

East Gippsland's climate is influenced by strong depressions off the coast

An approaching thunderstorm looms over Ninety-Mile Beach in East Gippsland.

and an inflow of warm, moist subtropical air from the Tasman Sea. It is more like conditions along the southern New South Wales coast than the rest of Victoria. The elevated tablelands experience wider variations in temperature and are subject to severe frosts during winter. Rainfall varies from below 700mm in the upper Snowy River valley to about 2000mm on the Errinundra Plateau, and there is no real distinguishable seasonal trend, precipitation being distributed fairly evenly throughout the year. The exception is snowfall that occurs above 600m elevation.

Droughts are relatively common on the tablelands and in rainshadow country, although severe droughts can affect the entire East Gippsland area.

Croajingolong National Park

The 87 500ha Croajingolong National Park extends for 100km along the wilderness coast of East Gippsland and comprises idyllic beaches, coastal heathland, old-growth forests, pockets of dense rainforest, river estuaries and granite peaks offering superb views.

A network of tracks allows bushwalkers to explore on short or long walks. Permits are necessary and can be obtained from the Parks Victoria office at Mallacoota. Rivers and inlets offer the safest swimming, but beware of strong currents near entrance areas.

History

Local Aborigines have strong links with the park and are thought to have lived in this area for 40 000 years. When Captain Cook discovered Australia, the very first land he saw, in April 1770, was Point Hicks. A plaque commemorates the event, with a list of the crew on the *Endeavour*. By the 1850s, pastoralists had occupied most of the better land. In 1902, two parks were set aside around Mallacoota and Wingan Inlet. These are now part of Croajingolong National Park.

Vegetation

Stands of warm temperate rainforest and coastal heathland support many threatened plant species. Indeed, the national park is one of the State's three Biosphere Reserves and its most significant conservation reserve.

Wildlife

About 50 mammal species have been recorded in the park along with 26 reptile species. The abundance of bats, possums and gliders is attributed to the presence of trees with hollows. More than 300 species of birds call Croajingolong home and these represent about a third of the species in the entire country. The wetlands attract 40 species of migratory seabirds and waders while the coastal heathlands and woodlands attract hawks, eagles and falcons. Six species of owl live in the forests. Threatened species include Australian fur seals, the grey-headed flying fox, smokey mouse, ground parrots and eastern bristlebirds.

Access

Croajingolong National Park is in the far-eastern corner of Victoria, about 450km east of Melbourne and 500km south of Sydney, via Eden. Access roads lead from the Princes Highway

The extensive wilderness beach south of Cape Howe, Croajingolong National Park.

Public boat-launching ramps are at Mallacoota, Gipsy Point, Bemm River and Furnell Landing.

Howe Wilderness Walk

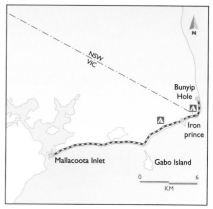

Starting Point: Mallacoota Inlet (VIC), adjacent to Croajingolong National Park

Destination: Bunyip Hole, Cape Howe (NSW)

Summary: A walk along remote beaches to the state border

Attractions: Coastal wilderness, the shipwrecks of the *Riverina* and *Iron Prince*, sand dunes

Length: 46km

Time: 4 days

Options: The track goes right through to Newtons Beach or Pambula in NSW, or you can do the trip in reverse, although this would make it more difficult to plan the timing of the boat across Mallacoota Inlet

Attraction Rating: ★ ★ ★

Fitness: ◨ ◨

Maps: VICMAP Outdoor Leisure and Topographical Map Series Mallacoota 1:50 000

Access to Starting Point: Mallacoota, 24km off the Princes Highway, equidistant from Sydney and Melbourne

Facilities/Amenities: None

Recommended Equipment: Fuel stove, full water containers

Notes: Beware of strong currents near entrances to rivers and inlets. Ocean beaches may be subject to rips and currents. Walkers must charter a boat to cross Mallacoota Inlet and arrange to be picked up at the same location.

Further Information:
Parks Victoria
Cnr of Allan & Buckland Drives
PO Box 179
Mallacoota VIC 3899

or from Mallacoota. All park roads have gravel surfaces—always check road conditions after heavy rain.

Facilities

There are four camping areas in the park and another nearby at Tamboon Inlet. Apply to the National Park Visitors' Centre for bookings during peak periods and year-round fees. All food, and in some cases water, must be carried in. Access to camping areas is by rough gravel roads that may be closed to all vehicles after heavy rain.

Camping is not permitted around the Mallacoota Lakes. Remote campsites on the coast are provided for walkers on overnight walks (permit required).

Facilities and accommodation are available in the townships of Cann River, Bemm River, Genoa and Mallacoota. Point Hicks lighthouse also offers up-market and out-of-the-way accommodation.

There are day-visitor picnic facilities in most of the coastal camping areas and around Mallacoota Inlet. Some are accessible by boat only.

Tel: (03) 5158 0219
Fax: (03) 5758 0583
Reference Guides: *70 Walks in New South Wales* by Tyrone Thomas, *Car Touring and Bush Walking in East Gippsland* by Grant Da Costa and *Walking the Wilderness Coast* by Peter Cook and Chris Dowd.

Walk Description

Boat operators at Mallacoota take walkers across the inlet and drop them behind Big Beach near Flathead in the Harrison Channel. Walkers will then have to scrub-bash through the heath to the beach. Navigation is straightforward as you head left (north-east) along the beach, hopefully finding a corridor of firm sand to make walking easier.

Fresh water can be obtained from Lake Barracoota and the small watercourse that flows south from Lake Wau Wauka. There's another camping area among the tea-tree here. Walking on sand will make it a surprisingly tiring day. Spend next day walking to Conference Point where the coast suddenly changes from open beaches to a series of coves and headlands.

Camp at the first beach (unnamed) in NSW, where water can be obtained from the Bunyip Hole at the northern end. This is extremely beautiful country and coastal camping does not get much more isolated in eastern Australia. Return to Mallacoota via the same route.

Wilderness Coast Walk

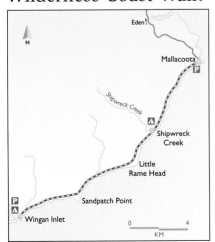

Starting Point: Wingan Inlet, adjacent to Croajingolong National Park
Destination: Mallacoota

Summary: A spectacular coastal walk through a terrific variety of scenery. The major part of the walk traverses the Sandpatch Wilderness Area.
Attractions: Secluded Seal Cove and various vantage points along the coast
Length: 41km
Time: 3 days
Options: Walkers can also set out from Point Hicks
Attraction Rating: ★ ★ ★ ★
Fitness: ◪ ◪ ◪
Maps: VICMAP Outdoor Leisure and Topographical Map Series Mallacoota 1:50 000 for the walk. The Cann–Point Hicks 1:50 000 topographical is useful for access.
Access to Starting Point: Wingen Inlet is 34km off the Princes Highway; the turn-off is 17km east of Cann River
Facilities/Amenities: Well-developed car-camping facilities at Wingan Inlet. Toilets and water are available and there are 24 sites.
Recommended Equipment: General overnight camping gear for complete self-sufficiency
Notes: A boat may be needed to ferry walkers across Wingan Inlet. Visitors to the area often have a variety of pleasure craft. Alternatively, it may be possible to wade across the outlet at low tide. Walkers should check the latest track conditions with the ranger before embarking.
Further Information:
Parks Victoria
Cnr of Allan & Buckland Drives
PO Box 179, Mallacoota VIC 3899
Tel: (03) 5158 0219
Fax: (03) 5758 0583
Reference guide: *Bushwalking in Australia* by John & Monica Chapman, to be published by Lonely Planet, 2001.

Walk Description

This walk alternates between forest and coast as it follows the Wilderness Coast Walk (formerly called the Benedore Walking Track) east from Wingan Inlet to Mallacoota. The route follows a combination of walking tracks and old fire trails and most of it is depicted in detail on the Mallacoota 1:50 000 topographical. Permanent fresh water can be obtained along the way from the Red River and from Shipwreck Creek; the trail also crosses other minor streams.

Sea cliffs and thick heath sometimes force walkers to detour inland, for example, to bypass Sandpatch Point. Seal Cove and Shipwreck Creek are great camping areas and the former might even be worthy of a rest day. Photographers will find the jagged rocky outcrops in the sand perfect foregrounds for coastal vistas.

Other walks in the Croajingolong National Park Area
Genoa Peak Walk
(3km return, 2 hours)
This walk uses steel ladders to access the granite peak (489m) for spectacular panoramic views over the eastern part of Croajingolong National Park. The final approach to the summit is very steep, passing through fantastic country dominated by boulders and rocky outcrops. Much of this area was burnt out by bushfires in 1983. The track starts at a picnic area and car park 8km from Princes Highway, just west of Genoa township.

Thurra Dunes Walk
(4km, 1.5 hours)
From the camping area at Thurra River, a walking track accesses the massive 150m-high sand dunes. The track starts near site 15. The Thurra River camping area is south of Cann River and can be accessed by the Tamboon and Point Hicks roads. Car campers can stay nearby at Mueller Inlet.

Point Hicks Walk
(4.5km, 1.5 hours)
Follow the road from the locked gate at the end of the Thurra Camping Area to access the lighthouse and the point where Captain Cook first saw Australia. This is a rocky, desolate and windy coast place for walking.

Cape Conran Nature Trail
(6km, 2 hours)
Unless you set up a car shuffle for this walk, you will have to backtrack the distance from West Cape. The walk starts at Sailors Grave, which can be accessed from Marlo, 19km along the Cape Conran road, and continues into Cape Conran Conservation Park, adjoining the Croajingolong National Park to the west.

Coopracambra National Park

Its remoteness from Melbourne, lack of facilities, publicity and public access are perhaps the main reasons for the absence of visitors in this wild, rugged 38 800ha national park. The scenery—steep escarpments and undisturbed vegetation—rivals any of the great sandstone national parks throughout south-eastern Australia. Savaged by fierce fires in 1983, the park is recovering reasonably well and the perimeter access points are slowly being developed and publicised. The national park's name is derived from an Aboriginal word for 'kookaburra'.

The park is bordered by New South Wales in the north (where it becomes Nungatta National Park), the Cann Valley Highway in the west and state forest to the south. Vegetation comprises dry sclerophyll forest dominated by silvertop, white stringybark, and silver wattle. The park is also the site of the famous Tetrapod footprints, believed to be the oldest fossil records of a land-dwelling vertebrate. This four-legged creature had a backbone between 50cm and 100cm long. The prints are similar to those of the earliest known amphibian, *Ichthyostegalia*, discovered in Greenland.

A fern leaf in the Genoa River Gorge near the New South Wales border.

Facts and Figures

Name: Coopracambra National Park
Size: 38 800ha
Enactment:
　State Park, 1979
　National Park, 1988
　(with significant extensions)
　Genoa Wilderness Zone, 1994
Visitors: 2500 a year
Vegetation: A good mix of species common to Tasmanian subalpine communities and south-eastern Australia. Includes warm temperate rainforest and open dry forests.
Wildlife: Possums, gliders, bats, owls, sea eagles

Genoa River Gorge Circuit

Starting Point: Beehive Falls car park, Coopracambra National Park
Destination: Genoa River Gorge
Summary: A triangular circuit walk using the WB Line Road, Genoa River and Yambulla Peak Track
Attractions: Wild sandstone gorge scenery, spectacular views of Mt Kaye, Mt Denmarsh, Yambulla Peak, and Mt Coopracambra
Length: Total distance, 84km
Day 1: Beehive Creek Falls car park to lower Genoa River, 31km
Days 2 & 3: Lower Genoa River to upper Genoa River, 29km
Day 4: Upper Genoa River to Beehive Creek Falls car park, 24km
Time: 4 days
Options: By organising a car shuffle with one car at Wangarabekk, hikers could walk down the gorge and save the long first day's ridge walk via Mealing Hill
Attraction Rating: ★ ★ ★ ★

Fitness: ◪ ◪ ◪ ◪
Maps: VICMAP Combienbar–Wangarabell 1:50 000 topographical. The NSW LIC Yambulla 1:25 000 topographical covers the river at a closer scale, but shows no topographical or other information.
Access to Starting Point: The start of the walk is accessed by travelling up the Cann Valley Highway from Cann River. Most of the highway parallels the Cann River (east). As you pass the 'township' signposted as Chandlers Creek, watch out for a turn-off on the right marked as WB Line Road (about 30km from Cann River). If you pass the signposted Buldah Road on the left, you've gone too far. The WB Line Road crosses the river immediately via a low bridge. Park at the Beehive Falls car park where a 500m walking track leads down to a view of the falls.
Facilities/Amenities: None
Recommended Equipment: Sandals for river walking—ensure they have good grip as there are numerous rock platforms; long tent pegs, useful for pitching camp on sandy river banks
Note: Walkers should lodge a record with the Cann River Parks Office on the Princes Highway. Don't forget to let the park authorities know that you've returned. Don't undertake the walk just after heavy rain as crossing the Genoa River will be impractical with overnight packs.
Further Information:
　Parks Victoria
　Princes Highway
　PO Box 79, Cann River VIC 3890
　Tel:　(03) 5158 6351
　Fax:　(03) 5158 6435
Reference Guide: *Car Touring and Bush Walking in East Gippsland*, by Grant Da Costa

Walk Description

Start walking east along the WB Line Road skirting the northern slopes of Mt Denmarsh (917m). Enter the Genoa Wilderness Zone and continue east all the way over Mealing Hill. Drop down to the Genoa River via the Ivor Track. This is, unfortunately, a 30km road-bash with a few obscured views, but it saves backtracking inside the gorge. Walk upstream along the banks of the Genoa River for the next two or more days. There are some spectacular sandstone cliffs along the gorge as it winds north-west. The soft red rocks here are officially classed as 'horizontally bedded Upper Devonian non-marine sediments'.

Narrow tributaries offer a sufficient level of protection to support small pockets of rich dense rainforest. Two kilometres before the border at the confluence with Black Jack Gully, the Yambulla Track heads steeply up to the left (west). It ascends more than 300m to several rocky knolls with great views before rejoining the WB Line Road. It is then simply a matter of heading west back to the car.

Errinundra National Park

Let us regard the forests as an inheritance, given to us by nature, not to be despoiled or devastated, but to be wisely used, reverently honoured, and carefully maintained. Let us regard the forests as a gift, entrusted to any of us only for transient care, to be surrendered to posterity... to pass as a sacred patrimony from generation to generation
  —Baron Ferdinand von Mueller
    Government botanist, 1854

The famous 'East Gippsland' poster distributed by the Wilderness Society portraying shining gums in the mist was photographed on the Coast Range of the Errinundra Plateau. People come here to breathe the oxygen-rich air and to experience the magnificent ancient wet forests for which the park is famous. It is the largest area of cool temperate rainforest in Victoria and dates from the ice ages. The dominant trees are mountain ash, shining gum, southern sassafras and messmate. The understorey comprises grey gums, peppermints and blackwood but, surprisingly, no myrtle beech.

In the 1980s, the plateau was the focus of some controversial logging protests that highlighted the economic and ecological values that governments place on natural areas. The Australian Heritage Commission declared the plateau 'a region of outstanding natural importance'. Logging was carried out on the plateau for almost 30 years

and about 50 per cent of the tall timber has been removed.

Errinundra National Park was named after the Aboriginal word *erraneen*, meaning 'to tattle'. The plateau is quite high but fairly flat. There are opportunities for short scenic walks and keen photographers can take classic shots of flowing waterfalls and white trunks in the mist. Some of the grandest eucalypts are between 250 and 400 years old. Other features are giant granite tors, clear pools and rare white waratahs.

Check with the parks office before doing any driving during autumn, winter and spring. During summer, tracks can also become very muddy. Another thing to watch for are logging trucks in the area—drive cautiously around blind corners.

Facts and Figures

Name: Errinundra National Park
Size: 25 600ha
Enactment: July 1988
Vegetation: Cool temperate rainforest, eucalypt wet forests with ancient shining gums, southern sassafras, black oliveberry and mountain plum pines
Wildlife: Rare frogs and native fish, large variety of birds
Camping: No campground within the park but several rest areas with basic facilities below the plateau: Ada River, the Gap Scenic Reserve, Goongerah and Delegate River
Attractions: Some of the oldest trees in Victoria, gums, lookouts, remote wilderness atmosphere, shining gums, mountain ash

Mt Ellery Walk

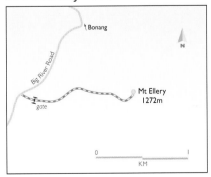

Starting Point: Ellery Saddle, Errinundra National Park
Destination: Mt Ellery (1272m)

Summary: A short steep walk to a high vantage point looking over the Errinundra Plateau
Attractions: Scenic views, granite outcrops
Length: 4km
Time: 2 hours
Options: None
Attraction Rating: ★ ★ ★
Fitness: ◪ ◪ ◪
Maps: VICMAP Goongerah–Ellery 1:50 000 topographical
Access to Starting Point: Access is north from Orbost along the Bonang Highway, about a 470km drive from Melbourne. Many of the park's trails and roads are subject to seasonal closure to vehicles because of the extremely wet conditions. All thoroughfares are unsealed and the unusually high rainfall causes the steep winding trails to become virtually impassable.

To access the start of the walk, drive to Ellery Saddle along Greens Road, which branches off Errinundra Road in the southern section of the park. Along here on the left is Ocean View Lookout. This is the first window where one has a glimpse of the rugged foothills surrounding the plateau. Pass the junction with B.A. Road. Drive slowly from here on as the road can get a little rough for conventional vehicles. One road follows the contour around the edge of the Errinundra Plateau turning left onto Big River Road through some wet but incredibly diverse forests dominated by messmate and shining gums. The start of the walking track is signposted on the left. There is a campsite clearing on the left just before a gate.
Facilities/Amenities: None
Recommended Equipment: Sturdy boots, because there are a significant number of snakes in the area
Notes: White-outs often occur with low cloud, so check the weather before you set off
Further Information:
  Parks Victoria
  Tel: (03) 6458 1456

Walk Description

From the locked gate, head straight up the steep track. About a kilometre up the old 4WD road, you'll encounter forest dominated by alpine ash with patches of silver wattle, montane wattle and blackwood. Also found here are Gippsland waratahs, pepper bushes and the red-fruited saw sedge. Farther up the steep track are outcrops of gigantic granite boulders. The track becomes flatter near the top and a narrow walking track left leads to the top of the main tor.

The summit is accessed by using installed chains and ladders, and by boulder-scrambling, although the climb is not of great technical difficulty. A sign at the bottom says climbing is not recommended for safety reasons and those afraid of heights should be wary of the exposure. The summit is named for the state astronomer who led a survey party into the area in 1870 to detail the New South Wales–Victorian border segment between Cape Howe and the headwaters of the Murray River. The Aboriginal word is more descriptive, *goongerah*, meaning 'egg-shaped'. Unfortunately, much of the limited summit area is taken up by radio antennae, transceivers, electrical cables, solar panels and windmills. If you're lucky enough not to have a

white-out (mist), you'll see fine views over the Errinundra foothills, most of the prominent peaks of East Gippsland and into New South Wales, and even to the coast. The eastern side has a 1km drop down to the Goolengook River, and immediately to the south are some of the best remote, prime core wilderness areas in the state. These zones are known to support the highest density of tree-dwelling mammals in the state. Return to the bottom via the same route.

Other walks on the Errinundra Plateau

There are a number of short day walks available throughout the plateau, most being of easy grade for tourists. Some are very new as the park is relatively young. The walks are best undertaken in summer, as the plateau can be inaccessible at other times of year. Ellery Saddle and Goonmirk Rocks are focal points for day visitors. The best reference for day walks is *Car Touring and Bush Walking in East Gippsland* by Grant Da Costa. This contains descriptions of walks around the plateau and surrounding foothills.

Snowy River National Park

The Snowy River National Park contains some of the state's most spectacular scenery, with a variety of environments from rainshadow woodlands and scrub on rocky outcrops to alpine ash and snow gum woodland.

The Gelantipy Plateau to the south of Deddick is one of the rugged foothill regions of the Great Divide that adjoins the north-eastern section of the Alpine National Park, helping to a create a huge undisturbed natural environment—a vast playground for adventurous bushwalkers. The Snowy River, which dominates the park with the huge gorge it has cut through the mountains, is not at full capacity as 50 per cent of its flow has been diverted over the Great Dividing Range into the Murray River by the Snowy Mountains hydro-electric/irrigation scheme.

A few trails dissect this wild country, so it presents a number of bushwalking opportunities for the reasonably fit. The area is remote with few facilities so experience in wild bush settings and self-sufficiency is

Mt Ellery on the Errinundra Plateau commands views over thousands of hectares of state forest.

necessary. Always carry enough extra food for one or two days in case of an emergency.

Facts and Figures

Name: Snowy River National Park
Size: 98 700ha
Enactment: 1979
Visitors: 22 000 a year
Aboriginal Sites: This was the last Victorian Aboriginal refuge. Access route for those travelling to Bogong moth feasts.
Vegetation: Red wattle 'dry rain-forest', cypress pines, white box
Wildlife: Brushtail rock wallaby and mammals, birds and marsupials common to south-eastern Australia
Facilities: Developed campground at McKillops Bridge for a small fee
Attractions: Wild river gorge country

Gelantipy Plateau Walk

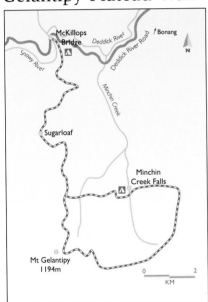

Starting Point: McKillops Bridge, Snowy River National Park
Destination: Gelantipy Plateau and Mt Gelantipy (1194m)
Summary: A high-level circuit walk in the Snowy River and Bowen wilderness zones
Attractions: Minchin Creek Falls, views over Snowy River National Park wilderness areas
Length: 51.4km
Time: 3 days
Options: Extensions are possible to the Snowy River at Campbell Knob
Attraction Rating: ★ ★ ★
Fitness: ☒☒☒☒

Maps: VICMAP Deception–Deddick 1:50 000 topographical
Access to Starting Point: McKillops Bridge is best approached from the east through Bonang, from the west through Buchan, or from the north via Jindabyne and Suggan Buggan
Facilities/Amenities: Well-developed car and camping facilities at McKillops Bridge, otherwise walkers must be completely self-sufficient
Recommended Equipment: General overnight backpacking gear for complete self-sufficiency. Because of the high altitude of the plateau, several litres of water should be carried, especially in summer.
Notes: Most of the route is along old fire trails so navigation is fairly straightforward
Further Information:
Parks Victoria
Main St, Bendoc VIC 3888
Tel: (03) 6458-0290

Walk Description

McKillops Bridge is one of only three bridges that span the Snowy River. It is 265m long and 30m above the river-bed—well out of range of floods. This area lies in a rainshadow and temperatures are surprisingly mild. The Snowy River is quite pleasant to swim in during summer. The Silvermine Walking Track heads downstream among native cypress pines along the river bank to old silver–lead mines that were worked briefly around the turn of the century. With discontinuous silver lodes, extreme isolation and lack of mining skills and technology, mining proved unviable and operations ceased in 1905.

The walk route leaves McKillops Bridge via the Deddick Track and climbs relentlessly to the junction with the Bowen Trail. Just before the top, there are some great views to the west. Turn left at the junction heading east. You are now on the Gelantipy Plateau, where the terrain levels out somewhat. The vegetation comprises magnificent blue gums (usually confined to much wetter environments), manna gums and alpine ash. Camp at Minchin Creek past the fire dams. Best waterfall access is from the left bank.

The next day, leave the tents at Minchin Creek while you make a 17km

circuit clockwise around the plateau via the Bowen Track, Waratah Flat Road and Deddick Track through magnificent stands of alpine ash forest. Remember to carry water. On the third day, simply head back down to McKillops Bridge by retracing the first day's route.

Little River Gorge Walk

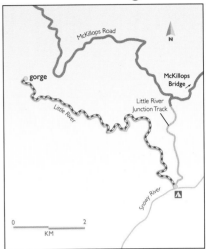

Starting Point: Little River Junction Track, Snowy River National Park
Destination: Little River Gorge
Summary: A walk up the Little River to access some of Victoria's most dynamic scenery
Attractions: Waterfalls, steep-sided canyon walls
Length: 30km
Time: 2–3 days
Options: It is possible to access the upper gorge directly from McKillops Road, but the terrain is extremely steep and ropes are almost essential
Attraction Rating: ★ ★ ★ ★
Fitness: ☒☒☒
Maps: VICMAP Deception–Deddick 1:50 000 topographical
Access to Starting Point: The turn-off to the Little River Junction Track is just west of McKillops Bridge, accessed through Buchan or Bonang. From the Upper Turnback, head from the Little River Junction Track to the western bank of the Snowy River.
Facilities/Amenities: An informal camping area lies at the confluence of the Little River and the Snowy River. Otherwise there are no facilities, not even walking tracks.
Recommended Equipment: A self-supporting tent for pitching on rock is

handy. If water levels are high after recent rain, there will be a lot of swimming required and pack contents must be waterproofed. Photographers will need a tripod to capture the upper falls as the centre of the narrow canyon does not get much sunlight.

Notes: Ropes and other climbing or abseiling equipment are needed to penetrate the upper part of the gorge where it becomes a canyon. The walk is best undertaken in summer when temperatures are warmer.

Further Information:
Parks Victoria
Main St, Bendoc VIC 3888
Tel: (03) 6458-0290

Walk Description

The route description of this walk is fairly simple—just head up the Little River as far as you want to go. The first half-day's walk is very straightforward. As the cliff walls start to close in and the terrain gets wilder, progress will slow. Bypass various obstacles, cascades and waterfalls by rock-scrambling; return the same way.

Other walks in East Gippsland
Mitchell River National Park
The Mitchell River Walking Track follows the western bank of the

The dramatic Little River Gorge near the Snowy River in East Gippsland.

Mitchell River within the 11 900ha Mitchell River National Park. One of the highlights is the Den of Nargun— a cavern beneath an overhanging rock ledge in the gorge of the Woolshed Creek. A waterfall usually masks the entrance to the cavern, falling to a pool below—a great spectacle.

The waterfall was formed because the sandstone overhead was much more erosion-resistant than the soft mudstone rock underneath. Flooding and the perpetual backwash spray from the waterfall have resulted in rapid weathering of the mudstone. This is the largest known example of this type of formation and is of particular significance for its decorative limestone stalactites. It was discovered by the explorer Alfred W. Howitt, who was told by local tribesmen that the den was inhabited by a fierce half-stone beast that could drag unwary visitors away and turn a spear or bullet's flight around.

Howitt, a geologist and naturalist, surveyed the Mitchell River in 1875, travelling downstream by bark canoe with two Aborigines from Tabberabbera. The rapids caught them and they exited the gorge via Woolshed Creek, happening upon the den. It has since been vandalised by fossil collectors and bat-hunters.

The national park is about 300km east of Melbourne, about 30km north of Bairnsdale. Access from Bairnsdale is via the Dargo road north. A car shuffle is handy to avoid backtracking. Options include short day strolls and a full three-day traverse.

The Alpine Region
Alpine National Park

Together with the Blue Mountains near Sydney, and the South West World Heritage Area of Tasmania, the Victorian Alps represent Australia's premier bushwalking country. Their rich pioneering history, commemorated in movies such as *The Man from Snowy River*, has left a legacy of trails that cover the mountains from their deep river gorges to their lofty snow-capped ridgetops. Being prohibited to 4WDs or too rough for them, many tracks are enjoyed solely by walkers.

Geology

More than 500 million years ago, eastern Australian lay in a huge trough known as the Tasman geosyncline. For several million years this filled up with marine sediments, such as mud, silt and sand, until eventually they were cemented together. The sediments became uplifted and were subjected to extremes of stress, heat and pressure. Consequently, they were severely tilted, folded and metamorphosed into sandstone, shale, gneiss and schist.

Some 70 million years later came a long period of violent volcanic activity while the newly formed rocks were being eroded. This created the igneous rocks present in the Alps: rhyolites, tuff, quartz and granite. A classic example of volcanic intrusion through the crust is the massive Mt Buffalo plateau. Granite is easily identified by its coarse crystal size, signifying its rapid cooling on exposure to air. By contrast, basalt cooled much more slowly, deep within the earth, and therefore has a much finer crystal structure.

The next 300 million years were relatively calm with little but erosion occurring. Then in the Tertiary period (only 60 million years ago) there was further uplifting of the range and more volcanic activity. This accelerated erosion during the Pliocene period (about six million years ago) and much of the early sedimentary layers were washed out to sea. Large deposits collected in the valleys of the Murray, Kiewa and Ovens rivers resulting in the rich farming land that exists there now.

The final natural effect on the landscape were the great ice ages of the Pleistocene period, which caused much fracturing of the rocks by freezing and thawing. Evidence of this is still obvious, with round granite boulders shedding layers of rock like onions. Unlike Kosciuszko to the north and Tasmania to the south, there was no permanent glaciation.

History

Aborigines have lived in the Alps for dozens of centuries with little impact. The most significant effects on the land were changes in vegetation brought about by their use of fire in hunting animals (herbivores were attracted to the subsequent regrowth). Possums provided a ready source of food, but the Bogong moth is perhaps the best-known part of the Aboriginal diet. During the summer, up to 700 Aborigines from local and friendly neighbouring tribes would gather on high plateaus to catch and roast great numbers of these insects.

With the advent of Europeans, Aborigines dwindled in number and the tribes virtually disappeared by the 1860s. The only remaining evidence of their occupation includes an axe quarry at Howqua, campsites around Omeo and implements found on the Bogong High Plains at Mt Buller.

The first recorded sighting of the Victorian Alps was by Hume and Hovell, who noted the peak of Mt Buller as they passed through the Mansfield district in 1824. Almost 20 years later, John Mitchell climbed up to the Bogong High Plains from the Kiewa Valley. However, it was the quest for grazing land that opened the Alps up during the 1830s and '40s. Stockmen Jim Brown and John Wells pioneered the route from Omeo to the Ovens Valley via Mt Hotham. Early settlers introduced domestic grazing animals wherever suitable forage occurred. The best land was cleared for pastoral purposes during the late 19th and early 20th centuries. Grazing of alpine meadows, woodlands and forests was practised from the very beginnings of settlement.

Mining activity followed, rapidly expanded and then slowly collapsed from the 1850s to the 1920s. This activity greatly added to the wealth of the young developing state and left a legacy of numerous access tracks to be exploited by walkers today. There are alluvial workings along many streams, and mine ruins at the sites of various gold-reefs.

The combined effects of grazing and mining helped blackberries to become established. They are a hardy pest that can severely scratch your legs along narrow tracks. Despite their sweet taste when ripe, it's not wise to eat blackberries in national parks as they're are often sprayed with poison.

Thunderstorm over the Alps, taken from Mt Hotham.

The State Electricity Commission began construction of the Kiewa Hydro-Electric Scheme in 1937. This has had a major impact on the area, providing vehicular access to the High Plains and SEC trails are still used by walkers. Other legacies of early Europeans include huts, cairns, fences, cattle yards, mineshafts and old machinery.

Because bushfires had destroyed mountain ash forests north of Melbourne in 1939, increasing demands for timber were made on the Alps after World War II. The Alps had not only mountain ash but the highly valued alpine ash. In addition, with increased leisure time and easier access, alpine areas became more popular for both summer and winter recreation. It was Myles Dunphy from Sydney, with the Town and Country Planning Association, who first formally proposed the idea of a Victorian national park centred on the Alps in 1949. The specific area was limited to the Bogong High Plains and part of the present-day Wonnangatta—Moroka section. Dunphy had been instrumental in having the Blue Mountains reserved after a long campaign during the inter-war years.

While the need was recognised, Victorian vested commercial interests, such as sawmillers, trail bike riders, ski-resort operators, cattlemen, miners and 4WD owners, were so deeply entrenched within the region that little was done for 30 years. In 1951, a special State Parliamentary Committee examined national parks and reported favourably on the Dunphy idea and also included an expansion in the Dartmouth region. That was ignored.

Some 20 years later the then-Premier Richard Hamer appointed the North-Eastern Alpine Area Working Group, composed of three conservationists and three representatives from the Forestry Commission and saw-milling operations. Predictably, issues relating to the inclusion of areas in a potential alpine reservation were split 3:3 and the chairman had to cast the deciding vote. Valuable attention was drawn to the lack of preservation with the publishing of *The Alps at the Crossroads* by the Victorian National Parks Association.

It was only after recommendations by the Land Conservation Council (LCC) in 1979 that four medium-size parks were established, a total half the size of today's Alpine National Park, or less than a third of public land available in the study area. Since it was government policy to accept all LCC recommendations without amendment, the parks were established—a total area of about 300 000ha.

By December 1989, the park had doubled in size and, at 646 200ha, it is now the 'jewel in the crown' of Victoria's park system. Commercial activities, such as cattle grazing, logging, beekeeping, mining, water production and tourism do continue, but operators are now required to adhere to strict guidelines and are subject to constant monitoring and review. Hundreds of kilometres of logging roads and fire-access tracks have been constructed, which means that few areas are more than 5km (or an hour's walk) from the nearest track. With the classification of official wilderness zones in recent times, many tracks are either being re-habilitated or are being allowed to degenerate of their own accord. National parks were once reserved for more utilitarian purposes: protection of water catchments, recreation, education and science, but wilderness is now recognised as an asset in its own right. The main elements of the appeal of pure wilderness are:

- Spiritual refreshment and an awareness of solitude arising from close contact with the uninhabited, undisturbed natural environment.
- Refuge from the pressures, sights and sounds of modern consumer-oriented urban life.
- The adventure and challenge of putting one's powers of endurance and self-reliance to the test against a rugged natural environment.

Climate

Most of the Alps are characterised by high precipitation, much of it falling as snow, often as low as 800m. Yet the rule of thumb is that the lower the altitude, the lower the annual rainfall. The average is between 40mm and 180mm per month and precipitation rain is not as seasonally erratic as in other areas. Temperatures are lower relative to other parts of the country— frosts may occur at any time and many peaks and ranges can be in the cloud for days at a time. The daily averages are about 6–19°C at low altitudes and minus 2–10°C at high altitudes. As a rule, air temperature decreases by one degree with every 100m increase in altitude. Walkers often experience this effect when descending from the tree line to the valley floor. Summer temperatures in high-altitude areas rarely get above 12°C so walkers need warm clothing.

Vegetation

The dynamic topography supports a diversity of habitats: wetlands, river-ine forests, alpine and subalpine woodlands, wet open forest, dry open forest and grasslands. The combination of this topography and predominant south-westerly winds has created dry rainshadow valleys contrasting with adjacent mountains covered by wet montane forests, and at higher elevations, subalpine woodlands and alpine herb and flower fields.

The mountains are a highly important source of water for Victoria, supplying about a quarter of the state's fresh water. Furthermore, this water is of very high quality and in most cases campers can safely drink from streams and creeks, as long as there is no development upstream. The forests of the Alps support an important segment of the Victorian woodproducts industry, generating a third of all hardwoods.

Wildlife

The fact that the Alps are largely national park and state forest has provided the native wildlife with relatively large blocks and corridors between habitats. There are recent records of 35 species of native mammals, 183 species of birds, 30 species of reptiles, 17 species of amphibians, 13 species of fish and countless species of invertebrates.

Since European occupation, a number of introduced species also live in the Alps—rabbits, hares, house mice, goats, black rats, dogs, foxes, cats, brumbies, sambar, red deer and cows. There are also many introduced plant species, the majority now being pests, for example blackberries.

Recreation

The first organised recreation in the Alps began with the establishment of a resort on Mt Buffalo in the late 1880s. Then, as now, Bright served as a centre for alpine activities. The local alpine club, using snowshoes, made the first winter ascent of Mt Feather-top in 1889. Skiing became a regular sport from the 1920s on and has never looked back. The high plains were used for ski-touring or cross-country. Cattlemen's huts were used for refuge and overnight accommodation, but new ones have since been built catering exclusively to bushwalkers and skiers. Alpine resorts followed, around Mt Buller, Falls Creek and, to some extent, Mt Hotham.

Another early pastime was fishing. Trout-acclimatisation societies were active in the 1870s, introducing sporting trout into mountain streams.

Further Information:

- Alpine High Country
  Visitors' Centre
  Bright VIC 3741
  Tel: (03) 5755 2275
- Australian High Country
  Visitors' Centre
  Mt Beauty VIC 3699
  Tel: (03) 5754 3172
- Bairnsdale Visitors' Centre
  Tel: (03) 5152 3444
- Orbost Visitors' Centre
  Tel: (03) 5154 2424

Looking south from Mt Clear, Alpine National Park.

- Mansfield Visitors' Centre
  Tel: (03) 5775 1464
- Omeo Visitors' Centre
  Tel: (03) 5159 1552

A lot of information about the Alpine National Park can be obtained from the Internet in the form of PDF files which you can download. The address is www.parks.vic.gov.au

Mt Tingaringy Walk

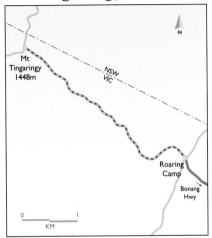

Starting Point: Roaring Camp, Alpine National Park
Destination: Mt Tingaringy (1448m)
Summary: A steep climb up Tingaringy Track to survey an awe-inspiring vista of the Cobberas–Tingaringy section of the Alpine National Park
Attractions: Views over East Gippsland and into New South Wales
Length: 20km
Time: 1 full day
Attraction Rating: ★ ★ ★
Fitness: ◪ ◪ ◪
Maps: LIC (CMA) Delegate and Tombong 1:50 000 topographicals
Access to Starting Point: Roaring Camp is accessed via Bonang Highway between Bogang in Victoria and Bombala in New South Wales. Just over 8km south of the New South Wales border, a turn-off west called Tingaringy Track leads to Roaring Camp by Dellicknora Creek. The car must be left here.
Facilities/Amenities: None
Recommended Equipment: Warm, windproof alpine clothing
Notes: Walkers should be prepared for sudden drops in temperature
Further Information:
  Parks Victoria
  Tel: (03) 6458 1456

Walk Description

Mt Tingaringy is situated very close to the state border but is not part of the Great Dividing Range. Like most alpine peaks, summer is the best time to walk here. Not only is the weather more comfortable and stable, but there is an abundance of alpine herbs and wildflowers to enjoy.

While it is possible to camp on the escarpment to marvel at the sunset and sunrise the next day, there is no water and the top is very exposed. The question is: is it better to carry an overnight pack up to more than 700m, or to complete the walk in one day?

There is a fire trail all the way to the summit, which passes through tall mountain ash forests that are representative of the foothills in the Snowy Mountains and Victoria's Alps. Once you cross Dellicknora Creek the track climbs relentlessly up a spur and then a ridge before it levels out slightly. Near the top, ignore a turn-off to the right leading to a small reservoir. Soon after is a junction where Tingaringy Track branches left, and the New South Wales border lies to the right. Head right and within a few minutes turn left on a short side track to reach the top of the escarpment set amid pleasant wind-pruned snow gums. This is a good spot for lunch before retracing your route back to Roaring Camp.

Cowombat Flat Circuit

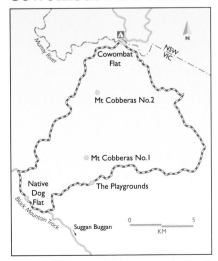

Starting Point: Black Mountain Track (near Native Dog Flat), Alpine National Park
Destination: Cowombat Flat (known, more correctly, as Quambat Flat)
Summary: A circuit in the remote and wild Cobberas–Tingaringy section of the Alpine National Park, accessing the upper headwaters of the Murray River on the state border
Attractions: Spectacular views and alpine scenery
Length: 57km
Time: 3–4 days
Options: This walk can be done in both directions. An extension to the summit of The Pilot in New South Wales is also possible.
Attraction Rating: ★ ★ ★ ★ ★
Fitness: ◪ ◪ ◪ ◪
Maps: LIC (CMA) Suggan Buggan 1:50 000 topographical
Access to Starting Point: Access to the starting point is via Bairnsdale and Buchan Caves following the Snowy River Road north. About 10 km before Suggan Buggan turn left onto Black Mountain Road, the only good 2WD access from East Gippsland to Omeo. If driving from Melbourne this will take most of the day: there is a well-developed official camping area at Buchan Caves. A more natural camp setting exists at Suggan Buggan as well as Native Dog Flat just before the staging area. Black Mountain Road is reasonably wide and well graded so there shouldn't be any problems with using a conventional vehicle. This area is quite popular for trail bike and mountain bike riding, shooting and 4WD excursions. Many tracks head off the road to the right. The start of Cowombat Flat Track is signposted on the right. Park the car here.
Facilities/Amenities: None provided. Camp beside any of the numerous creeks and rivers the trails cross.
Recommended Equipment: A Gore-Tex jacket, and at least one woollen or fleece jumper. Down sleeping bags or equivalent are essential. Wear gaiters and thick long pants for protection against tiger snakes, which are prevalent in the region.
Notes: This remote area of the Alps is very susceptible to sudden weather changes. Snow and frost in summer is not uncommon.
Further Information:
  Parks Victoria
  Tel: (03) 6458 1456

Walk Description

Start walking east along Cowombat Flat Track and then north passing through some excellent subalpine and montane forest dominated by mountain gums, snow gums, broad-leaved peppermints and candlebarks. Note that his route also coincides with the Australian Alps Walking Track. The only major uphill is about halfway along after crossing Bulley Creek when you have to gain 140m climbing up to the easterly ridge of the prominent Moscow Peak–Cobberas complex. Once over the saddle, walking is fairly easy down to Copperhead Creek, a small tributary of the Murray River that managed to cut a deep valley through the soft limestone common in this vicinity. One last uphill slog gets you to Cowombat Flat.

There are good campsites on the northern side of the Murray River, right on the border. After the junction of trails there is a fireplace on the right. This site is rarely crowded and the river provides clean drinking water. If you are quiet you have a very good chance of seeing the herds of brumbies that roam the region.

Next morning, investigate the wreckage of the plane that crashed here in 1954. Despite being marked on the map as *Southern Cloud*, park authorities say that it was an RAAF C-41 Dakota that ploughed into the ground during an unsuccessful emergency landing. One of the four crew-members was killed. Food was air-lifted in to the survivors until a ground-based search-and-rescue party located them. Most of what remained has been souvenired over the past few decades. Pieces of fuselage were once used to build a makeshift hut nearby. The crashsite of the *Southern Cloud* is in the north of Kosciuszko National Park.

To the east in the Great Dividing Range is Forest Hill (1370m), upon which a geodetic or trigonometrical control point marks the border switch from the irregular to the straight line. Return via the MacFarlane Flat Track and Cobberas Trail to the east flanking the Ramshead Range. Another good campsite lies on the Suggan Buggan River about halfway back to Black Mountain Road and Native Dog Flat.

Mt Bogong (from the north) Circuit

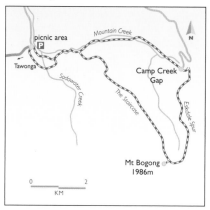

Starting Point: The Mountain Creek picnic area, Alpine National Park

Destination: The summit of Mt Bogong (1986m), climbing via Staircase Spur and descending via Eskdale Spur

Summary: A long steep walk through peppermint gums to the top of Victoria's highest mountain

Attractions: Alpine meadows and panoramic views

Length: 18.9km

Time: 1 full day

Options: Walkers can camp 3.7km south of the summit at the Cleve Cole Memorial Hut

Attraction Rating: ★ ★ ★ ★

Fitness: ☒ ☒ ☒ ☒

Maps: VICMAP Bogong Alpine Area 1:50 000 Outdoor Leisure Map or Trappers Creek 1:25,000 topographical. The start of the walk is on the Mt Beauty 1:25 000 topographical but this map is not really necessary for navigation purposes.

Access to Starting Point: Mountain Creek is best accessed from the Keiwa Valley Highway Tawonga, just north of the picturesque holiday township of Mt Beauty. The area is about 365km north-east of Melbourne via the Great Alpine Road.

Facilities/Amenities: None en route

Recommended Equipment: Windproof fleece jacket, warm clothes, Gore-tex jacket, water

Notes: Weather conditions can change rapidly and snow can fall at any time of the year. If cooking, remember that Mt Bogong is a fuel-stove-only area. Don't leave valuables in the car as theft has been common.

Further Information:
Parks Victoria
Australian High Country
Visitors' Centre
Mt Beauty
Tel: (03) 5754 3172

Walk Description

Mt Bogong isn't a dramatic peak by any stretch of the imagination; it is more a flat grandiorite dome with a broad summit. The name derives from *bugong* meaning 'big fella', the Aboriginal name for the large moths that occur in the area. The popular staging area for ascents is 10.6km along Mountain Creek Road from Tawonga. Here walkers from all over south-eastern Australia congregate to climb

Due to high altitude and close proximity to the coast, white-outs are common in the Mt Tingaringy region of the Alpine National Park, East Gippsland.

onto the Bogong High Plains and the Mt Bogong massif.

The summit tracks along the two main spurs, Staircase and Eskdale, are well signposted. The objective is to climb via Staircase Spur to the summit, just over 8km, and descend via Eskdale Spur, almost 11km long. In fine weather there are outstanding views over north-eastern Victoria.

Mt Bogong (from the south) Circuit

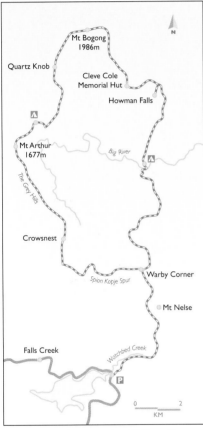

Starting Point: Rocky Valley Storage (Falls Creek), Alpine National Park
Destination: Mt Bogong (1986m)
Summary: A circuit of the best of Mt Bogong massif and its southern approaches
Attractions: Outstanding views, snow gum woodlands, alpine herbfields, etc
Length: Total distance, 55.5km
Day 1: Rocky Valley Storage to Big River, 15km
Day 2: Big River to Cleve Cole, 7.5km
Day 3: Cleve Cole to Bogong Creek Saddle, 12km
Day 4: Bogong Creek Saddle to Rocky Valley Storage, 21km
Time: 4 days

Cleft Peak in the Cobberas region of Alpine National Park.

Options: This circuit can be done in either direction. If time is available, two worthwhile side options are to Cairn Creek Hut by Big River, and to Howman Falls, near Cleve Cole.
Attraction Rating: ★ ★ ★ ★ ★
Fitness: ◪ ◪ ◪ ◪
Maps: VICMAP Bogong Alpine Area 1:50 000 Outdoor Leisure Map gives an excellent overview of the entire route. The detailed 1:25 000 topographical maps are Nelse and Trappers Creek, although the fourth edition is now rather out of date.
Access to Starting Point: To access Rocky Valley Storage, just south of Falls Creek, follow the Bogong High Plains road south of Mt Beauty. Also access Falls Creek directly from Omeo in the west. Park the car at the point where the Big River fire track meets the Bogong High Plains road.
Facilities/Amenities: None. A hut is provided at Cleve Cole.
Recommended Equipment: Windproof fleece jacket, warm clothes, Gore-Tex jacket, water, fuel stove, good-quality four-season sleeping bag
Notes: Weather conditions can change rapidly and snow can fall at any time of the year. If cooking, remember that Mt Bogong is a fuel-stove-only area.

Further Information:
Parks Victoria
Australian High Country
Visitors' Centre
Mt Beauty VIC 3699
Tel: (03) 5754 3172

Walk Description

This circuit approaches the summit of Mt Bogong from the south following part of the Australian Alps Walking Track. There's significant variation in the scenery and plenty to see and do. Fit parties could complete the walk in three days, but walking the middle days as half days to enjoy the area thoroughly is recommended.

Follow the Big River fire trail up the Watchbed Creek valley to join with a newly realigned section of the AAWT. Turn left and head north climbing Mt Nelse. It's fairly easy going along the flat grassy plains, although flies can be an annoying problem during late summer. Continue along the AAWT down Duane Spur before a final steep descent to the Big River for the first day's camp. Cross the river by means of the metal chain. Note that this might be very dangerous after heavy rain. The best campsites are on the northern bank.

On the second day, keep heading north to start a long, gruelling climb up the T-spur to the Mt Bogong massif. At the top, leave the AAWT and ford Camp Creek. Packs can be left at the turn-off to Howman Falls. These narrow falls are just a short walk south along Camp Creek. They drop in three main stages with some great swimming spots near the top. Some flat terraced rock platforms on the western side give an unobscured view. Spend the night at the Cleve Cole Memorial Hut. This stone hut was built in 1937 to honour Cleve Cole, who died from severe hypothermia and frostbite in a horrendous blizzard the previous year.

The third day is a pleasant amble to the summit of Mt Bogong and over the other side down Quartz Ridge to Bogong Creek Saddle and a popular camp clearing with westerly views to Mt Arthur. A partly overgrown side track to the confluence of Cairn Creek and Big River allows walkers to camp again by a good water source. The hut

Diamantina Creek and Razorback Ridge at Mt Feathertop.

here is called Cairn Creek (and has two bunks) even though it is marked as Survey Hut on older maps. When graziers were permitted to let their cattle roam here in the 1970s, these slopes below Mt Bogong used to accommodate more than 500 cows. They thrived on the alpine herbfields, heathlands and snow gum woodland.

Spend the last day walking over Mt Arthur and along the Grey Hills Track to the Spion Kopje fire track. Head left here to rejoin the Australian Alps Walking Trail north of Mt Nelse and retrace the first part of day one's route back to the Bogong High Plains road. If walkers wish to avoid the 300m climb over Mt Arthur, make a shorter but less attractive return along Timms Spur and the Big River fire trail.

Looking after Alpine Huts

Some huts, such as Wallace Hut, are more than 100 years old and are part of our national heritage. Some tips for staying in highland huts:

- Leave the hut cleaner than when you arrived and take your garbage with you.
- Cook with fuel stoves and keep fires to a minimum. This is not so much because of fire risk, but to maintain a supply of firewood for emergency situations. In several popular camping areas it can be a long walk to find firewood.
- Don't use all the matches in huts and replace any firewood you burn.

- Don't pollute the water supply. Observe standard camping toilet etiquette (dig a hole at least 50m from water, downstream from the camp, and cover it afterwards.) Collect water upstream from huts and always boil it, just in case.
- Use huts for shelter only, not for accommodation. Near most huts are flat grassy areas perfect for pitching a tent. Huts should never be relied upon.

Mt Feathertop Walk

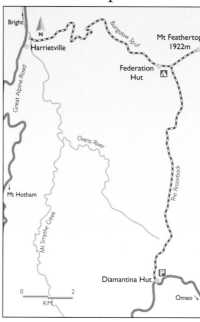

Starting Point: Diamantina Hut (Great Alpine Road), Alpine National Park
Destination: Harrietville via the summit of Mt Feathertop (1922m), the second-highest peak in the state
Summary: A high-level but easy southern approach to Australia's most rugged alpine mountain. Set up a car shuffle to avoid backtracking and allow a descent via Bungalow Spur.
Attractions: Superb panoramic views from the summit and scenic vistas for much of the walk
Length: 23km
Time: 1 long day
Options: Various spurs can be used to descend to the north and south, including the North-West Spur, but Bungalow is convenient and popular
Attraction Rating: ★ ★ ★ ★ ★
Fitness: ◪ ◪ ◪
Maps: VICMAP Bogong Alpine Area 1:50 000 Outdoor Leisure Map gives an excellent overview of the entire route. Detailed 1:25 000 topographical maps are Feathertop and Harrietville.
Access to Starting Point: The walk begins just west of the Mt Hotham ski resort, accessed via the Alpine Road south of Bright. Access to Harrietville, the walk's end, is via the same road.
Facilities/Amenities: Federation Hut lies just to the west near Little Mt Feathertop, while to the north lies the distinctive Melbourne University Mountaineering Club Hut, shaped like a geodesic dome.
Recommended Equipment: Wind-proof fleece jacket, warm clothes, Gore-Tex jacket, sunscreen, water
Notes: Weather conditions can change rapidly and snow can fall at any time of the year. Because of its prominence, the Feathertop massif is particularly prone to blizzards.
Further Information:
  Parks Victoria
  Australian High Country
  Visitors' Centre
  Mt Beauty VIC 3699
  Tel: (03) 5754 3172

Walk Description

Mt Feathertop, so-named because of the cloud wisps that form at the summit, is a most spectacular peak. At first glance, the mountain seems to be the only one in the area that is not eroded, but the opposite is true. Because of accelerated erosion caused by the steep tributaries of the West Kiewa River and the heavily tilted slate fracture systems of the massif, the peak became more alpine in appearance. It was first climbed by government botanist Baron von Mueller in 1854.

Most walkers have to backtrack but you could place a car at either end. Another convenient way of achieving the one-way walk is to drive to Harrietville and pay for a lift to Mt Hotham. Not only does one avoid backtracking, but there is the advantage of descending almost 1400m to the Ovens River valley.

From Diamantina Hut (1720m), at a prominent right-hand bend in the Alpine Road just west of the Mt Hotham ski resort, walk north to the Big Dipper and then along Razorback Ridge to a saddle just east of Little Mt Feathertop. From the memorial cross erected in memory of adventurers who have died on the massif it's about a 90-minute walk and a 200m gain in altitude to the top, well above the tree line. On a fine day, the top is a good place for lunch, with superb views of much of the alpine area, including the Bogong High Plains and Mt Buffalo.

When you're ready, head back down to Little Mt Feathertop to inspect the cosy Federation Hut (built in 1969) before commencing the very steep descent zigzagging down Bungalow Spur to Harrietville.

Returning from Mt Cobbler, Alpine National Park.

Mt Cobbler Walk

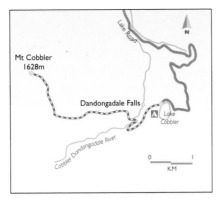

Starting Point: Lake Cobbler
Destination: Mt Cobbler (1628m), Alpine National Park
Summary: A fairly easy and straight-forward walk through snow gum woodland to climb one of the most prominent peaks in the central Alpine National Park
Attractions: Great 360-degree views
Length: 9km
Time: 4 hours
Options: None
Attraction Rating: ★ ★ ★
Fitness: ◪ ◪ ◪
Maps: VICMAP Howitt–Selwyn 1:50 000 topographical
Access to Starting Point: Access to Lake Cobbler is by 4WD or high-clearance 2WD from Mansfield via Tolmie and Whitfield, then Rose River Road (which becomes Lake Cobbler Road

Facilities/Amenities: None en route; good campground at Lake Cobbler
Recommended Equipment: Jumper, jacket and full water bottle
Notes: It is not wise to undertake the walk if inclement weather is imminent
Further Information:
Parks Victoria
Mansfield Visitors' Centre
33 Highett St, Mansfield VIC 3722
Tel: (03) 5733 0120
or (03) 5775 1464

Walk Description

The remote Cobbler Plateau is one of the less-visited areas in the Victorian Alps as the primary access road isn't as well graded as other entry routes. Camp by the lake. The simple shelter here contains a visitors' book and fireplace. If the primary camping area is full, follow the tracks around the shore for more campsites. Nearby are the Dandongadale Falls, the state's highest unbroken drop.

The walk starts just left of the hut and is signposted at an estimated 1.75 hours for a one-way trip. Once you cross the small brook at the back of the camping area, it's uphill on an old vehicular track through alpine ash forest to a turn-off. Veer right following orange triangular markers down to another creek. Fill water bottles, then from here it's uphill without reprieve through pleasant snow gum woodland. Generally, snow and mountain gums dominate with understoreys ranging from heath to grass. The vegetation becomes increasingly sparse and stunted until suddenly you are beyond the tree line. Keep to the rim of the escarpment until you come to a steep narrow saddle that leads to the summit, marked by a trigonometrical survey post. From the top, much of the best part of the Alps (including Mt Buller, Mt Howitt and the Buffalo Plateau) is visible as well as Lake Cobbler and the Cobbler Plateau.

The plateau is composed of sedimentary rock originating in the Lower Carboniferous age. The entire area is covered in snow during the winter months and summer falls are not uncommon. A small visitors' book below the post allows you to read others' experiences of the climb and views and to record your own.

The Man from Snowy River film set Walk

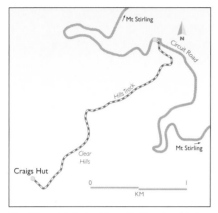

Starting Point: Circuit Road, Alpine National Park

Destination: Craig's Hut, Clear Hills

Summary: A short walk to one of the most picturesque scenes in the Alps

Attractions: Great views, particularly to the north

Length: 10km

Time: 3 hours

Options: The hut can also be approached via ski trails from Mt Stirling or from the north via the Cobbler Plateau. This latter option would entail an overnight walk, camping on the King River.

Attraction Rating: ★★★★

Fitness: ◨◨

Maps: VICMAP Buller–Stirling 1:25 000 Outdoor Leisure Series

Access to Starting Point: Mt Stirling and Circuit Road are best accessed from Mirimba via Mansfield on the approach to Mt Buller

Facilities/Amenities: None. In summer there are limited facilities at Mt Stirling.

Recommended Equipment: Camera

Notes: Circuit Road can be rough in places after rain. A 4WD vehicle might be necessary.

Further Information:
Parks Victoria
Mansfield Visitors' Centre
33 Highett St, Mansfield VIC 3722
Tel: (03) 5733 0120
or   (03) 5775 1464

Walk Description

Clear Hills is the very famous and often-photographed setting for the spectacular opening and closing footage of the film *The Man from Snowy River*. The hut, known as

Horse-riding is still popular in the Alpine National Park.

Craig's Hut (Craig was the character played by Tom Burlinson), is actually a facade, but it is on a particularly attractive knoll with unobstructed views of many beautiful alpine peaks.

From Circuit Road, simply follow the Clear Hills Track south, then south-west along Clear Hills Spur to the unmistakable hut site. As recently as the early 1990s, cattle grazed here. It is an ideal place for lunch before heading back to the car.

Mt Howitt Circuit

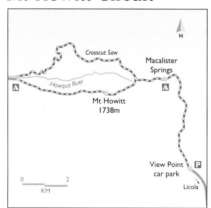

Starting Point: View Point car park (Mt Howitt Road), Alpine National Park

Destination: Mt Howitt (1738m)

Summary: A challenging but very rewarding two-day circuit centred on Mt Howitt and the dramatic Crosscut Saw, camping in the beautiful upper Howqua River valley

Attractions: Snow gum and alpine ash woodland, idyllic camping and rugged

alpine scenery with outstanding views

Length: Total distance is 31km

Day 1: View Point car park to Howqua River via Mt Howitt, 13km

Day 2: Howqua River to View Point car park via Crosscut Saw, 18km

Time: 2 days

Options: Walkers might enjoy an extra day to rest on the Howqua River before heading up again. Although the walk can start from the Howqua River, it is recommended that you start from View Point so you are descending with a lighter pack and camping by a good water source.

Attraction Rating: ★★★★

Fitness: ◨◨◨◨

Maps: VICMAP Howitt–Selwyn 1:50 000 topographical

Access to Starting Point: Access from Melbourne is via Traralgon and Heyfield to Licola. From Licola, it is about 81km of unsealed road to the View Point car park. Please note that the road is closed in winter.

Facilities/Amenities: The Vallejo Ganter Hut is at Macalister Springs. Otherwise self-sufficiency is essential.

Recommended Equipment: Complete self-sufficiency for alpine conditions, including waterproof jacket and four-season sleeping bag

Notes: Weather conditions can change rapidly and snow can fall at any time of the year on the Great Dividing Range.

Further Information:
Parks Victoria
Licola Road, Heyfield VIC 3858
Tel: (03) 5148 2355

Walk Description

This is a great introduction for walkers new to overnight walking in Victoria's Alps. There is plenty of variety and great views along the entire distance. Some degree of fitness is required as a substantial gain in elevation is made on the second day. Walkers should be well prepared with maps, compass and warm clothes.

From the View Point car park, follow the main walking track north to the pleasant Macalister Springs camp clearing. This follows an old vehicular track that has long since been closed to the public. Water can be obtained from the tiny flow just to the north of the hut. It is a good idea to boil it. Cross the narrow ridge of the Devils Staircase. Many campsites can be found here too, with superb views over the upper Wonnangatta River valley. Once on the other side, the track forks. Turn left, climbing up the open bulk of Mt Howitt. This is the Australian Alps Walking Track. The best and most wind-sheltered vantage points can be found in rocks to the north of the summit. First-class views, especially north to Mt Cobbler.

Continue south-west along the escarpment and to the West Peak before descending into the Howqua River via the steep Howitt Spur (marked on the map as the Howqua Feeder Track). The first part is especially steep and walkers must negotiate a series of rocky outcrops. Notice how distinct the tree line is. At the bottom, a delightful camp clearing is just to the east. The Howqua River is not very mature at this point but some rockpools will provide enough water to freshen up. It might be worthwhile to spend a rest day.

Exit the valley by heading along the river via the Queen Spur Road that rises to a saddle on Stanleys Name Spur (also known as Thorn Range). Turn right, leaving the main vehicular track and climbing east to Crosscut Saw via a pleasant saddle. Keep left when approaching the cliffs near the top. Once on the spectacular razor-edged ridge, head south (right) to rejoin the Devils Staircase, then follow the first part of day one's route back to View Point car park.

Wonnangatta River Circuit

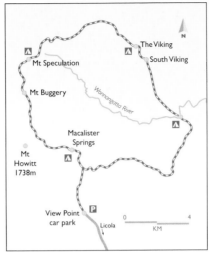

Starting Point: View Point car park (Mt Howitt Road), Alpine National Park

Destination: The upper Wonnangatta River

Summary: A very difficult four-day circuit through sometimes trackless terrain, centred on a spectacular section of the Great Dividing Range between Mt Howitt and The Viking

Attractions: Dramatic ridges, rugged alpine terrain, a remote river valley

Length: Total distance is 42km

Day 1: View Point car park to Mt Speculation (via Mt Howitt), 15.3km

Day 2: Mt Speculation to Viking Saddle, 7.5km

Day 3: Viking Saddle to Wonnangatta River, 6.2km

Day 4: Wonnangatta River to View Point car park, 13km

Time: 4 difficult days

Options: This track can be walked in either direction but, for ease of navigation, it is strongly recommended to take the clockwise option

Attraction Rating: ★ ★ ★ ★ ★

Fitness: ◪ ◪ ◪ ◪

Maps: VICMAP Howitt–Selwyn 1:50 000 topographical

Access to Starting Point: Access from Melbourne is via Traralgon and Heyfield to Licola. From Licola, it is about 81km of unsealed road to the View Point car park. Please note that the road is closed in winter.

Facilities/Amenities: The Vallejo Ganter Hut is at Macalister Springs. Otherwise self-sufficiency is essential.

Recommended Equipment: Complete self-sufficiency for alpine conditions, including waterproof jacket and four-season sleeping bag. Expert navigation skills are essential as many of the trails along the way are poorly defined. A GPS might also be handy.

Notes: Weather conditions can change rapidly and snow can fall at any time of the year on the Great Dividing Range.

Further Information:
Parks Victoria
Licola Road, Heyfield VIC 3858
Tel: (03) 5148 2355

Walk Description

This is one of the most challenging walks in the country. Not only does it centre on some of the most exposed ridges in south-eastern Australia, but expert navigation skills are needed to deal with numerous vague and

The Wonnangatta River from the Snowy Range, Alpine National Park.

obscure tracks, thick vegetation and false leads. But given the sheer number of highlights, from dramatic peaks such as Mt Howitt, Mt Speculation, The Razor and The Viking to beautiful riparian camping by the majestic upper Wonnangatta River, the circuit remains one of the 'must-do' walks for the serious bushwalker.

From the View Point car park, take the main walking track north to the pleasant Macalister Springs camp clearing. This follows an old vehicular track that has long since been closed to the public. Water can be obtained from the tiny flow just to the north of the hut. It is a good idea to boil it. Cross the narrow ridge of Devils Staircase. Many campsites can be found here too, with superb views over the upper Wonnangatta River valley.

Once on the other side, the track forks. Turn left, climbing up the open bulk of Mt Howitt. This is the Australian Alps Walking Track. The best and most wind-sheltered vantage points can be found in rocks to the north of the summit. There are first-rate views from here, particularly looking north to Mt Cobbler.

Backtrack to the junction and cross the dramatic Crosscut Saw ridge to the north. Some scrambling is necessary to negotiate more than a dozen knolls. Navigation is fairly easy here as you keep to the centre of the narrow crest on the approach to Mt Buggery. There are dramatic views to the east and west, before a long steep descent takes you to a saddle (Horrible Gap), and then a rise to Mt Speculation. More rock-scrambling is necessary to attain the summit, but it's not too exposed.

The first day's camp is on the north side of Mt Speculation, about half a kilometre from the summit. Water can be found by following the gully to the north from the clearing.

On the second day, keep on the AAWT as it heads north-east to Catherine Saddle and then onto Mt Despair. The area is well inside the Razor–Viking Wilderness Area and accordingly, all the AAWT markers have been removed, which confuses navigators in the area between Mt Despair and The Viking.

Progress is slow as you walk east, negotiating the rocky terrain via a series of large slabs. A gully provides

access left through cliffs to the crest of The Razor spur. If time is available, walkers might like to ascend The Razor to the north for yet more great views, otherwise proceed down to the Viking Saddle for the second day's camp. Be very wary of the navigational hazards occuring in the vegetation here. Water can be found in the upper headwaters of the west branch of Buffalo River to the left.

On the third day, head steeply up to The Viking, once again negotiating the cliffs though a gully, this time to the right. More outstanding views await you, before you should head south to South Viking and then follow an increasingly prominent spur due south down to the Wonnangatta River. There are plenty of misleading tracks in the vicinity, so keep to the centre of the spur wherever possible. Near the bottom, blackberries are a significant problem, slowing your progress even further. Watch out too for stinging nettles. Make camp at your discretion, upstream or downstream.

On the final day, locate the Zeka Spur Track, which ascends the southern side on the Wonnangatta Valley.

The beautiful Lake Tali Karng is a bushwalking mecca in the Alpine National Park.

It's a long uphill trudge along the track before you branch off left at a minor partly overgrown road to reach the Mt Howitt Walking Track situated between Macalister Springs and the View Point car park. Simply head left (south) along Clover Plain to complete what will be a memorable excursion.

Bryces Gorge Circuit

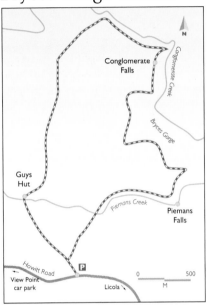

Starting Point: Bryces Gorge car park (Mt Howitt Road), Alpine National Park

Destination: Bryces Gorge and Piemans Falls

Summary: A very scenic short circuit walk in a rugged and popular part of the Alpine National Park

Attractions: Dynamic steep rocky terrain, great views over the gorge rim

Length: 7.6km

Time: 3 hours (plus whatever time you like for exploration)

Options: You can enter the gorge itself but progress is excruciatingly slow

Attraction Rating: ★ ★ ★ ★

Fitness: ☒ ☒

Maps: VICMAP Howitt–Selwyn 1:50 000 topographical

Access to Starting Point: Access from Melbourne is via Traralgon and Heyfield to Licola. From Licola, it is about 65km of unsealed road to the Bryces Gorge car park. Road closed in winter.

Facilities/Amenities: None

Recommended Equipment: A tripod would be useful for photographing the falls. Don't forget swimming gear for a swim in Piemans Creek.

Notes: Only plan to walk through the gorge if you have some experience on rock. Walkers must leave very early.

Further Information:

Parks Victoria
Licola Road, Heyfield VIC 3858
Tel: (03) 5148 2355

Walk Description

This is a simple but scenically very interesting walk in a remote section of the Alpine National Park. From the car park, head north to meet up with Piemans Creek which tumbles over the rim of an escarpment in a series of three giant leaps. There are good vantage points on the northern side. The track then continues to follow the rim around to survey Conglomerate Falls before heading west and back to the car park via Guys Hut.

Lake Tali Karng Circuit

Starting Point: McFarlane Saddle, Alpine National Park

Destination: Lake Tali Karng

Summary: A circuit centred on the Spion Kopje Range, approaching Lake Tali Karng via Mt Wellington and exiting the area via The Big Plain

Attractions: A beautiful natural lake set in stunning alpine scenery

Length: 45km

Time: 2 days (add an extra rest day in the middle if possible)

Options: If you don't mind backtracking, you can avoid the first day's road-bash by using the McFarlane Saddle Walking Track both to and from the lake. Ambitious walkers may want to set up a car shuffle to walk from McFarlane Saddle to Tamboritha Road via the Valley of Destruction and the Wellington River Walking Track or even the Mount Margaret Walking

Track to the south. There are many more approaches to the lake and experienced parties often plan their own custom route according to fitness and time.

Attraction Rating: ★ ★ ★ ★ ★

Fitness: ☒ ☒ ☒ ☒

Maps: VICMAP Howitt–Selwyn and Licola–Wellington 1:50 000 topographicals. The Lake Tali Karng 1:25 000 topographical is also very useful.

Access to Starting Point: McFarlane Saddle is on the Moroka Road about 59km from Licola via Tamboritha Road and Arbuckle Junction. A car park has been set aside.

Facilities/Amenities: Toilets are provided at Lake Tali Karng

Recommended Equipment: Fuel stoves. Insect repellent is crucial, as cattle flies can be vicious in this area.

Notes: As the walk destination is very popular it is best to plan your walk out of school holidays or summer weekends. Also note that snakes are a common sight.

Further Information:

Parks Victoria
Licola Road, Heyfield VIC 3858
Tel: (03) 5148 2355

Walk Description

This destination is an isolated natural lake of exquisite beauty. Lake Tali Karng is the only natural deep highland lake in Australia not of glacial or volcanic origin. It was formed when an ancient landslide from The Sentinels plateau dammed Nigothoruk Creek about 1500 years ago. The name 'Tali Karng' comes from two Welwenduk Aboriginal words; *talli*, meaning 'twilight', and *karn*, meaning 'snake'.

The walk follows a loop, so there's no backtracking. Along the way is a dramatic plateau escarpment on the boundary between the Alpine National Park and the Avon Wilderness Area. Not only are there spectacular views, but weird and wonderful rock outcrops, rugged folded valleys and massive alpine peaks and ridges. The Mt Wellington plateau and northern Avon Wilderness contain some important plant species endemic to the southern Alps and strangely concentrated in this one place. Examples are *Lomandra micrantha* and *Tetratheca pilosa*. There is also beautiful alpine vegetation, including the photogenic snow gums and mountain ash.

The area has long been popular so expect to share the tracks that run along the spine of the Wellington Plateau with other walkers, mountain-bikers and horse-riders. Estimates put visitors to the Wellington Plateau at in excess of 18 000 a year. Because of the region's popularity many of the roads that were here are now closed and are being rehabilitated or classified as walking tracks. Note that the lake's foreshore and surrounding area has been declared a fuel-stove-only zone.

Walk over Trapyard Hill to the Mt Wellington Track and then to Miller Gap. Along the way you cross the headwaters of the Avon River, one of the most pristine rivers in the state. It was named by Major Mitchell after William Shakespeare's birthplace.

Turn left at the gap, keeping on the Mt Wellington Track. As the road climbs, it swings north, then south again, rising out of the forests to the summit of Mt Wellington (1634m), the highest point of the walk. The peak was named after the Duke of Wellington by Angus McMillan in 1839 and offers superb panoramas of central and south Gippsland.

An easy walk along the ridge descends to Taylor Lookout. This point offers only limited obscured views to the south-west and is not worth investigating. Along the way are alpine meadows, snow gums and views over the rugged Avon Wilderness. The trail then kinks right and drops down to Millers Hut, where the vegetation becomes less stunted—snow gums, black sallee, spinning gums and candlebark trees. The area around the hut is a popular campsite, but the hut's interior is not pleasant.

From here, follow the disused fire trail north across Nigothoruk Creek to join with the McFarlane Saddle Walking Track near the site of the old Riggalls Hut. It is then a simple descent via the Gillios Track (left branch) to the lake. The campsites around the foreshore are very pleasant and the water temperature can be surprisingly mild for swimming, even in early autumn. The small Snowden Falls at the head of the lake are a photographic high-

Looking back over the Mt Buffalo Plateau from The Horn.

light, accessible by some boulder-scrambling. Just downstream of the lake, geologists have discovered a rich mineral site with chromium, lime-stone, nickel and corundum deposits.

Return to McFarlane Saddle via Riggalls Spur Track, which involves a hefty initial climb of about 600m, and then the McFarlane Saddle Walking Track along The Big Plain. Bush flies along this section can be annoying.

Mt Buffalo National Park

Referred to as an 'Island in the Sky', Mt Buffalo is not really a mountain but a dramatic 1km-high granite plateau 12km long by 7km wide, about 320km from Melbourne. It was one of the first national parks in Victoria and is still one of the most popular. The rock was extruded during the Devonian period (about 395 million years ago) and uplifted since then.

The plateau was once much higher (about 3000m), with a layer of softer sedimentary rock that has now been washed away. Watercourses following fracture lines cascade over the edge. In winter the plateau is blanketed in snow and two small ski fields cater for families, beginners and cross-country skiers. There are literally dozens of highlights and attractions. Visitors can spend days exploring the massive granite boulders, tors, waterfalls, summit lookouts and nature walks. A

well-developed campground (with hot showers) in the central part of the plateau makes an ideal base.

History

Aborigines made annual summer ascents to Mt Buffalo and other alpine areas to meet and hold ceremonies and to feast on the protein-rich Bogong moths that cluster in rock crevices. Surveyors Hume and Hovell named Mt Buffalo either after the wild cattle found in the area or some say because the plateau's profile from the Alps looks like a buffalo.

Goldminers and botanists began to find routes up to the plateau in the mid-19th century. With the beginning of tourism in the 1880s, an area around the spectacular gorge was reserved as a national park in 1898. The park has been enlarged several times since and now takes in all the plateau and surrounding slopes. The Mt Buffalo Chalet was built in 1910, soon after the construction of the first road. It replaced some earlier more 'rustic' accommodation. Despite it being declared a reservation, settlers brought their cattle to feed on the snow grasses and herb fields as they did in other alpine areas. The practice continued until 1958. The national park has long been a holiday destination for casual skiing and ice skating (the first ski tow in Australia was installed at Mt Buffalo), though summer is a popular time to visit too.

Vegetation

The park protects a diverse array of vegetation types and more than 550 native species. The most significant vegetation types are the alpine and subalpine communities. The ridges on the plateau's steep slopes are heavily forested with alpine ash and snow gum. Trees become sparse at the highest points and extensive granite outcrops are linked by expanses of subalpine grasslands and herb fields spotted with patches of stunted snow gum. Buffalo sallee, a eucalypt found only in the park, occurs mainly around the edges of the plateau.

The foothills below consist of undulating dissected terrain with valleys and low hills clothed mainly with peppermints and gums. As you ascend the mountain, the vegetation changes dramatically, from tall forests to snow gum woodlands and subalpine grasslands at the upper levels. During summer, carpets of silver snow daisies, yellow billy buttons and royal bluebells are in flower on the plateau.

Wildlife

Because of the range in altitude in the park, there is a variety of wildlife habitats. The foothill forests are home to kangaroos, wallabies and several species of possums and gliders. Smaller mammals, such as native rats and mice, inhabit the plateau and wombats occur everywhere. The alpine silver xenica is a species of butterfly found only here. Crimson rosellas are abundant and peregrine falcons sometimes nest on the granite rockfaces.

Facilities

Camping is best at Lake Catani during November–April. Bookings are necessary in busy periods. Lake Catani was named after Carlo Catani, who first reported on Kooweerup drainage plans and pioneered the original horse-track route up to the plateau. The 59 numbered sites are positioned in secluded areas to give privacy. A maximum of six persons are allowed on each place. Facilities include firewood, fireplaces, laundry, toilets, hot and cold showers, picnic areas and shelters. Fires are permitted only in designated communal places. Wood may not always be available and if it is, you might need to have an axe to split it. On the eastern bank of the lake is a jetty for canoe launching. To the north a popular walking track leads to the Chalet with its well-stocked kiosk.

Guesthouse-style accommodation is available at the Chalet. There is also Mt Buffalo Lodge and some motels. A wide range of accommodation is available in and around Bright. Useful phone numbers are:

- Mt Buffalo Chalet
  (03) 5755 1500
- Mt Buffalo Lodge
  (03) 5755 1988
- Lake Catani campground
  (03) 5756 2328

Mt Buffalo Walk

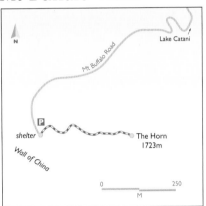

Starting Point: Mt Buffalo Road, Mt Buffalo National Park
Destination: The summit of The Horn (1723m)
Summary: A very short, but worthwhile, walk to the national park's highest point
Attractions: Fantastic views over the Mt Buffalo plateau and east towards the Victorian Alps
Length: 1.5km
Time: 30 minutes
Options: None, but walkers are encouraged to undertake any number of other walking tracks in the area
Attraction Rating: ★ ★ ★
Fitness: ⊠
Maps: VICMAP Buckland and Eurobin 1:25 000 topographicals cover the major part of the plateau, but maps are not necessary for this walk
Access to Starting Point: The Horn car park is at the end of Mt Buffalo Road at the southern end of the plateau. Mt Buffalo is best approached from Melbourne via Wangaratta. Take the Ovens Highway toward Bright and turn off at Porepunkah. The turn-offs are well signposted and the Mt Buffalo Tourist Road is sealed the entire length of its ascent.
Facilities/Amenities: Nearby, Tatra Inn provides limited services in summer. There is a picnic area at the end of Horn Road.
Recommended Equipment: Wind-jacket and camera
Notes: A small park entry fee applies per car. A comprehensive article on Mt Buffalo was featured in *WILD* magazine, Vol. 62 (Spring 1996, p 36).
Further Information:
Parks Victoria
Alpine High Country
Visitors' Centre
1A Delaney Ave, Bright VIC 3741
Tel: (03) 5755 2275

Walk Description

A number of short nature walks can be found south along Mt Buffalo Road. They total some 90km and many go to interesting granite tor formations. All walks are well graded, signposted and distanced. The best of the following walks are reasonably short, taking at most half a day: The

Eurobin Creek, below the cliff lines of Mt Buffalo National Park.

Cathedral; The Hump; The Castle; Dicksons Falls Lookout; Back Wall; Mt Dunn; Mt McLeod; Macs Point; South Buffalo (from Tatra Inn); View Point (and the cave at Underground River).

The most rewarding is the view from on top of the granite spire of The Horn (1720m) also known as Mt Buffalo, the highest point on the plateau. This can be seen from most summits in the western Alps.

On the way are the two small ski-fields of Dingo Dell and Cresta. Dingo Dell (1370m) is served by two poma lifts and a short mobile lift, while the larger Cresta field offers eight runs served by chairlifts. Rock climbers also frequent this stretch of road as the boulder stacks are especially large.

The final part to The Horn is on dirt but well graded and you can watch the symmetrical conical peak dominating the horizon in front of you. There is a car park at the end overlooking the steep Wall of China. Make your way up the short walking track (2km return). Access to the fenced lookout on top of the highest boulder is via some boards and stairs. On Mt Buffalo plateau the forests of snow gums all blend into matchstick shapes and are extremely stunted because of lack of protection. The plateau was raked by fires in 1926, 1939, 1972 and 1985. An obelisk gives directions and distances of prominent summits such as Mt Bogong and Mt Feathertop.

Why not spend the rest of the day undertaking some of the other short walks around the plateau, such as to The Monolith? Good tracknotes are available in *70 Walks in Victoria's Bright and Falls Creek Districts* by Tyrone Thomas.

Other walks in the Alpine National Park

There are hundreds of walking opportunities throughout the Alpine National Park. Obviously of prime interest to walkers is the rugged terrain of the Great Dividing Range, using the Australian Alps Walking Track. There are also many old forestry trails and cattle runs, creating unlimited potential for round trips that can last from a few hours to a week or more. Some of the main areas are:

Mt Bogong Area

Walks centred on the Mt Bogong massif include approaches from all directions. Some of the spurs and ridges have no formal tracks, but serious walkers have, over time, worn a fairly negotiable route. Guidebooks and *WILD* magazine recount expeditions using the Granny Spur, New Country Spur, Granite Flat Spur and the Long Spur.

Bogong High Plains

To the south of Falls Creek there are various walking destinations above the tree line along the open, flat Bogong High Plains. The rounded summits of Mt Fainter North, Mt Fainter South, Mt Niggerhead, Mt Jim and Mt Cope can all be strung together in a grand high-level circuit from Pretty Valley. An especially scenic destination is the historic Wallaces Hut, an easy 6km from the Bogong High Plains road.

Mt Feathertop

Victoria's second-highest mountain can be accessed from several directions.

Norman Bay and the popular Tidal River camping ground from Mt Oberon, Wilsons Promontory National Park.

From the north the approach is a continuation of the Razorback Ridge, the dramatic North West Spur, the Bon Accord Spur and the Champion Spur. From the east, the approach is via the Diamantina Spur that rises almost 1,000m in less than 4km.

Upper Kiewa River Valley (West Branch)

The Mt Hotham ski resort is a good staging area for walks to Mt Loch (1860m), Cobungra Gap and the Cobungra River valley. Challenging circuits incorporate Mt Feathertop and the Razorback, Swindlers Spur, Derrick Hut and the Australian Alps Walking Track. Old huts are common in the area. It is possible to connect walks in this region with those on the Bogong High Plains through routes on Paling Spur and Young Spur.

Mt Hotham (South and East)

The Dinner and Dargo plains as well as the Mother Johnson are settings for easy to medium graded walks to Mt Tabletop, Brandy Creek, and the Blue Rag Range. Waterfalls are common in the vicinity.

Mt Buller Region

A 7km tourist walk connects Mt Buller with Mt Stirling. Being within easy reach from Melbourne, the Mt Buller region is a popular area for walking. Destinations include the Cobbler Plateau via the King River valley in the north and the rugged Howqua River valley in the south. For longer, wilder expeditions, walk through to The Bluff and Mt Howitt areas.

Jamieson and Howqua River Valleys

The cliffs of the escarpment to the north of the Jamieson River valley provide the most dramatic backdrop in the Alpine National Park. The main section includes The Bluff, Mt Eadley Stoney, Mt Lovick, Mt Magdala and Mt Howitt. Walkers must be very experienced and well equipped in such exposed terrain. Another very high-level route lies along the range from Mt McDonald, Square Top, Mt Clear and King Billy 1 and 2. Shorter circuits centre on the Eagles Peaks from Sheepyard Flat.

Lake Tali Karng and the Wellington Plateau

The Avon wilderness has had the least impact from humans in the Alpine National Park. For walkers wanting a true wilderness experience, the Wellington Plateau south of the McFarlane Saddle is the ideal staging area. Lake Tali Karng can be approached from the west by walking up the Wellington River valley from the Tamboritha Road or over Mt Margaret. Other destinations include Mt Ligar (The Crinoline), Moroka Gorge and Snowy Bluff. There are few opportunities for day walks in the vicinity because of wild terrain, slow progress and the long distances involved. For more information, consult the Tamboritha–Moroka and Licola–Wellington 1:50 000 topographical maps.

Bowen Mountains

Outside the Alpine National Park, but still along the Great Dividing Range, are the Bowen Mountains. They are rarely visited and largely trackless, so appeal to walkers who enjoy pioneering new routes through uncharted territory. East of Omeo, you can follow the spine of the range over The Sisters (1231m), Mt Tambo (1431m) and Mt Leinster (1416m).

The South
Wilsons Promontory National Park

Wilsons Promontory is mainland Australia's southernmost extremity, and its entire area is reserved in a famous and popular national Park. Walkers come from all over Australia to explore the beautiful wild coastline. Named by Governor Hunter after an English merchant friend of Matthew Flinders, Wilsons Promontory (or 'the Prom') is undoubtably Victoria's most popular park. As the park is so close to Melbourne, the main camping ground at Tidal River is invariably full every holiday season. Tidal River has a cinema, police station, supermarket, telephones and laundries. Camp sites range from bush clearings to chalets.

The Prom has about 130km of coastline, framed by vast granite domes, mountains, forests and fern gullies. During the ice ages, the Prom extended right down to Tasmania. The Prom has a notorious reputation for inclement weather due to its protrusion into Bass Strait. Walkers should ensure they have specific forecasts before planning an extended camping trip.

Facts and Figures

Name: Wilsons Promontory National Park

Size: 50 300ha

Enactment: Wilsons Promontory National Park, 1905. Wilsons Promontory Marine Reserve and Marine Park, 1986.

Visitors: About 400 000 a year

Vegetation: 700 native plants. Most common are stringybark eucalypts, manna gum. Western extreme of warm temperate rainforest, cool temperate rainforest supporting myrtle beech and dry casuarina woodlands, grasstrees, banksia

Wildlife: Koalas, wallabies, kangaroos, wombats, fur seals

Aboriginal Sites: Middens from the Brataulong group of the Gippsland Kurani Aboriginal tribe have been found. The promontory was once called *Yiruk*.

Facilities: Highly developed campsite at Tidal River with shops, visitors' centre and police station. Many others are in remote bush settings by the coast and fresh water: Oberon Bay, Sealers Cove, Little Waterloo Bay, Refuge Cove, Five Mile Beach, Johnny Souey Cove, Tin Mine Cove, Roaring Meg, Half-Way Hut, Barry Creek, Lower Barry Creek. To book accommodation phone (03) 5680 9500.

Attractions: Contrasting vegetation, coastal atmosphere, beaches, tame wildlife, most southerly point of the mainland

Further Information: For further information about Wilsons Promontory National Park, call Parks Victoria on 13 1963

History

The Prom had (and still has) spiritual significance for different Aboriginal groups, who knew the area as Yiruk. They regarded the area as a valuable food source, particularly in summer.

George Bass 'discovered' the promontory in early 1798 and sailed around it with six men in a nine-metre open whaleboat after travelling all the way from Sydney. He named it Furneaux's Land. Soon after, it became a sealing and whaling base. During this period many of the geographical features were named. Since the Prom bordered what was a major maritime thoroughfare during the first half of the 19th century and because of the many islands, cliffs and reefs at the eastern entrance to Bass Strait, a lighthouse was built in 1859. Convicts constructed it from local granite. It was soon connected to Foster by means of a telegraph line via Mt Oberon (this is the peak that presides over the present-day Tidal River campground).

Timber extraction, tin mining, and grazing contributed to the development of the Prom. There were even plans to subdivide and build a township to be named Seaforth near Mt Singapore. Early Europeans recognised the Prom's commercial value, as the name Sealers Cove shows. The cattle grazing and the commercial exploitation of seals, whales and timber went on for nearly a century.

The history the conservation of the Prom began in 1853 when the well-known explorer and naturalist Baron Ferdinand von Mueller collected a variety of plant species during an extended excursion there. Some 30 years later, three members of the state's Field Naturalists' Club, John Gregory, Arthur Lucas and G. Robinson, conducted an extensive tour throughout the peninsula and came up with the idea of its reservation.

Official preservation occurred in 1898 when land was set aside for public recreation purposes and for the protection of wildlife. The proposed subdivision was repealed and, early in the 19th century, the peninsula officially became a national park with its first ranger, Charles McLennen. The area preserved has since shrunk to 50 300ha.

Throughout the latter half of the 20th century, fierce bushfires forced management to construct many fire trails. The army also contributed to road-making when they occupied the Prom for commando training during World War II. Army buildings at Tidal River formed the nucleus of a post-war holiday village that gradually developed as the Prom became increasingly popular. About 400 000 people now visit the park annually.

Controversy dogged the park throughout the 1990s with several radical development proposals being fiercely rejected by Prom supporters.

Vegetation

Wilsons Promontory National Park contains the largest coastal wilderness area in Victoria. The park contains many diverse vegetation communities, including both warm and cool temperate rainforest, open tall forests, coastal heathlands, and swamp and wetland communities.

The national park also has stands of white mangrove, which are the southernmost stands of mangroves in the world. Widespread heathlands are found in the park, and, influenced by the frequency and intensity of fires, they contain a near-perfect example of habitat succession, ranging from bare dunes along the coast to protected woodlands inland.

Looking across to Tidal River from Mt Bishop, Wilsons Promontory National Park.

Wildlife

More than 30 species of native mammals, not including marine mammals, have been recorded in the park. These include populations of the white-footed dunnart, broad-toothed rat, long-nosed potoroo, feather-tail glider and eastern pygmy-possum.

One of the most significant habitats of the New Holland mouse also occurs within the park, and a number of species of whale have been sighted off the coast. The grasslands are popular grazing venues for eastern grey kangaroos, wombats and emus.

Significant species of migratory wading birds feed on the tidal mudflats of Corner Inlet within and adjoining the park. Offshore islands provide roosting and breeding sites for seabirds, including a huge number of short-tailed shearwaters. Populations of the endangered damselfly, a 'living fossil', are found around freshwater swamps and lagoons in the park.

Access

The 200km drive from Melbourne via the South Gippsland Highway takes 2–3 hours. Turn south at Meeniyan and Fish Creek or Foster. Tidal River, where the main visitor facilities are, is 30km inside the park boundary. Very limited public transport is available. There is a small fee for each vehicle.

Facilities

Tidal River has some 450 camping and caravan sites, beautifully sited near beach and river. There are no powered sites and generators are not permitted. Campfires are not allowed at campsites; take a gas or fuel stove.

Tidal River has a general store, post office, camping gas supplies and a takeaway food shop. Meals are available on some nights. Petrol and diesel are available. Open-air cinema and doctor services are available during summer.

Tidal River also has self-contained flats and lodges (two to six beds), group lodges with 12, 24 and 30 beds, and motor huts (four and six beds) that offer compact and economical accommodation. To book accommodation or campsites at Tidal River call 1800 350 552 or (03) 5680 9555.

Permits

Park authorities have introduced a booking and permit system for overnight campers in Wilsons Promontory National Park. Bookings can be made up to 12 months in advance. To obtain a permit, either:

- complete an advance campsite booking form and fax it, with appropriate credit card details; or
- complete an advance campsite booking form and post it to the address listed on the form with a cheque for the camp and entry fees that apply. Cheques should be made payable to Wilsons Promontory National Park.

Upon arrival, call in at the park office in Tidal River or at the Park Entrance and take out a permit (there is a small charge). This is, however, subject to sufficient space being available at the time. The following conditions apply in respect of permits.

Southern campsites—except for Roaring Meg:

- 1 November–30 April, a maximum stay of one night at any campsite
- 1 May–31 October, a maximum stay of two consecutive nights at any particular campsite is permitted, excluding long weekends and school holidays.

Northern campsites—and Roaring Meg (southern):

- Year round, a maximum stay of two consecutive nights per camp site.

Maximum group sizes for southern section is 12 people and for the northern section six people. Larger groups must split, take out separate permits and camp at different locations.

Campsite limits

With the exception of Tidal River, campsites have a maximum number of campers allowed per night.

Campsite	Max. per night
Southern Section	
South Sealers Cove	60
Refuge Cove	60
Little Waterloo Bay	60
Half-Way Hut	30
Roaring Meg Creek	40
Oberon Bay	40
Northern Section	
Barry Creek	12
Lower Barry Creek	12
Five Mile Beach (Miranda Creek)	12
Johnny Souey Cove	12
Tin Mine Cove	12

For information on walks, consult *Discovering the Prom on Foot,* available from the park office at Tidal River.

Wilsons Promontory Northern Circuit

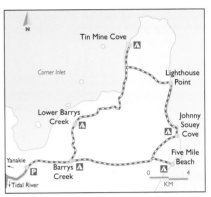

Starting Point: Five Mile Road car park (formerly known as Millers Landing car park), Wilsons Promontory National Park

Destination: Tin Mine Cove and Five Mile Beach

Summary: An easy circuit that incorporates all the major attractions of the northern half on the park

Attractions: Wild remote coastal scenery, isolated beaches and dramatic headlands

Length: Total distance is 68km

Day 1: Five Mile car park to Tin Mine Cove, 24km

Day 2: Tin Mine Cove to Johnny Souey Cove, 17km

Day 3: Johnny Souey Cove to Five Mile Beach, 9.8km

Day 4: Five Mile Beach to Five Mile car park, 17.2km

Time: 4 days

Options: This circuit can be done in either direction. For something different, walkers can ask boat operators at Port Welshpool to drop them at Tin Mine Cove during high tide, so that the walk has to be done in only one direction. A one-hour side trip to Vereker Lookout (300m) is recommended.

Attraction Rating: ★ ★ ★ ★

Fitness: ✗ ✗

Maps: VICMAP Wilsons Promontory Outdoor Leisure Map 1:50 000 topographical

VICTORIA

Access to Starting Point: Five Mile car park is on the Yanakie Isthmus about 11km south of the park entrance. A barrier prevents further vehicular access.

Facilities/Amenities: Toilets are provided at Tin Mine Cove, otherwise there are no facilities

Recommended Equipment: Fuel stove, several litres of water. Heavy-duty overtrousers might be handy for negotiating thick heath.

Notes: No camp fires are permitted in the national park

Further Information: Information can be sought from the ranger at the park entrance or the visitors' centre at Tidal River. Phone 131 963 for more details.

Walk Description

While most visitors stay at Tidal River and its immediate surrounds, walkers can escape the crowds by heading to the north of Wilsons Promontory National Park. While the terrain is flatter and the inland is dominated by poorly drained wetlands, the coastal scenery is still very pretty.

From the Five Mile Road car park, head east toward Vereker Range. The road skirts around to the north. If it is still relatively early, it is worthwhile to drop the packs and quickly scamper up the steep slope to Lookout Rock and Vereker Outlook to survey virtually the entire route of the walk.

Return to the road and continue east toward Barrys Creek. Turn left onto the Chinaman Creek Track, heading north to a small damp camping area at Barrys Creek. The next section is tough going, pushing through thick heath. Follow the fluorescent ribbon markers carefully. A further obstacle is Chinaman Creek and its three tributaries, which must usually be waded across.

Walking becomes noticeably easier once you approach Chinaman Beach. Simply walk north to the other side where a track traverses the headland to Tin Mine Cove for the first night's camp. Water can be found from Tin Mine Creek.

On the second night, head back down to Chinaman Beach and locate an old vehicular track about 500m south. Follow this road to the east of the prominent hill of Mt Margaret

where a turn-off heads left to Lighthouse Point. Walk south along Three Mile Beach and across a small headland for 1km to Johnny Souey Cove for the second night's camp. This is one of the best spots in the northern part of the park.

The third day is spent almost entirely on fire trails. Take the Johnny Souey Track south-west up and over to St Kilda Junction and then turn left again to Five Mile Beach. Don't get water from Miranda Creek, but from a spring just to the north. On the final day, simply head west along Five Mile Road back to the car park.

Wilsons Promontory Southern Circuit

Starting Point: Tidal River, Wilsons Promontory National Park

Destination: Sealers Cove, Little Waterloo Bay, South East Point

Summary: This outstanding coastal walks incorporates the best of the southern half of Wilsons Promontory National Park

Attractions: Great coastal scenery, wonderful views from granite outcrops and numerous boulders, great variety in terrain and no backtracking

Length: Total distance is 56.7km

Day 1: Tidal River to Sealers Cove, 13.1km

Day 2: Sealers Cove to Little Waterloo Bay, 13.7km

Day 3: Little Waterloo Bay to Roaring Meg, 15.1km

Day 4: Roaring Meg to Tidal River, 14.8km

Time: 4 days

Options: A half-day side trip to South

Point is possible from Roaring Meg; other camping areas at Refuge Cove, Half-Way Hut and Oberon Bay

Attraction Rating: ★ ★ ★ ★ ★

Fitness: ☒ ☒ ☒

Maps: VICMAP Wilsons Promontory Outdoor Leisure Map 1:50 000 topographical

Access to Starting Point: Tidal River is the main destination of visitors to the park. It is near the end of Wilsons Promontory Road. No directions are necessary as all turn-offs are well signposted. A bus shuttle operates from Tidal River to Telegraph Saddle every day in summer.

Facilities/Amenities: Toilets are provided at all major camping areas. Take toilet paper.

Recommended Equipment: Fuel stove, as no campfires are permitted

Notes: The walk is very popular. Permits must be obtained well in advance. Walkers should try to do the circuit out of school holidays. During high tide, Growler Creek may be impassable. Walkers may also have to wade across Sealers Creek if the tide is particularly high, although this presents no technical difficulty.

Further Information: Information can be sought from the ranger at the park entrance or at the visitors' centre at Tidal River. Or call Parks Victoria information line on 13 1963. Contact the ranger direct on:

    Tel: (03) 5680 9555

    Fax: (03) 5680 9516

or by mail:

    The Ranger

    Wilsons Promontory National Park

    Tidal River via Foster VIC 3960

Walk Description

For many Victorians, Wilsons Promontory National Park is their first backpacking or overnight camping experience. This walk is very popular and for good reason: it passes through an unparalleled number of attractions. Because of the number of camping areas, walkers can be flexible about planning their route. Depending on inclination and the time available, anything from three to seven days can be spent completing this beautiful circuit. The route incorporates much of what was known as the Eastern Coves Circuit, but adds in the newly constructed southern section to take in all the most common destinations frequented by walkers in one go, thus avoiding any backtracking.

From Tidal River, walk or catch the bus to the Mt Oberon car park. Once past the locked gate at Telegraph Saddle, leave the cars behind, heading due east to Black Fish Creek and photogenic Sealers Cove. Sections of the track are along duckboard and pass through fern glades and sassafras stands. The camping area is on the southern side of Sealers Creek. If you arrive early enough, you can spend the afternoon swimming in the turquoise waters.

The next day, head south to Refuge Cove. Several vantage points along here allow excellent photographic opportunities. Stands of lush green ferns make an excellent foreground. Refuge Cove can provide an ideal alternative campsite to Sealers Cove if the former is full. The swimming waters are just as protected. Once you have waded across Cove Creek, the track leaves Refuge Cove and climbs up over Kersop Peak, from which point the lighthouse is visible. Descend west to North Waterloo Bay and then Little Waterloo Bay for the second night's camp. Whales can sometimes be spotted from Kersop Peak on their annual migration north.

The nest day, walk south along the white sandy beach, ignoring the Waterloo Bay Track along Freshwater Creek. Instead, take the recently cons-tructed track from the southern corner of the beach across Boulder Range to the Lighthouse on South-East Cape (Australian Commonwealth property). There are views here to some of the many islands in Bass Strait with seal and penguin colonies.

Access to Roaring Meg camping area is via a combination of walking track and fire trails, crossing a number of creeks along the way. South Point, the most southerly point on the Australian mainland, is a two-hour return walk from here.

The final day is spent heading north along the Lighthouse Track. About a kilometre past Frasers Creek, turn left to Oberon Bay, nestled between the rugged rocky peaks of Mt Norgate (419m) and Mt Oberon (558m). Head north along the beach to ford the mouth of Growler Creek. A good-quality track leads around Little Oberon Bay and to Norman Point before contouring into Tidal River.

Other walks in Wilsons Promontory National Park
Northern Section

The many short walks here are well covered by leaflets and guidebooks. All overnight walks in the northern section of the park are within a Wilderness Zone that begins from the Five Mile Road car park.

Lilly Pilly Gully Nature Walk (5.1km, 2 hours)

Starting at the Lilly Pilly car park, this walk is an excellent introduction to the Prom's vegetation and wildlife. A separate leaflet is available from the visitors' centre.

Tongue Point Walk (6.3km, 2.5 hours)

The track starts at Darby Saddle (on the main road 6.7km from Tidal River) and leads out to Tongue Point. Short side tracks lead to Sparkes Lookout and Fairy Cove. A branch track to Darby River car park (3.5km) is recommended for the return trip. To avoid backtracking arrange for a car to be left at the Darby River car park.

Around Melbourne
Lake Eildon and Fraser National Park

The artificial reservoir of Lake Eildon is Victoria's largest. Its 500km shore-line is protected in a variety of reserves: Fraser National Park, the extensive Eildon State Park and various native state forests and pine plantations. The stored water is used by power boat enthusiasts, water-skiers, canoeists, houseboats and luxury yachts. The hills on the various peninsulas rise on average 300–500m higher than the water level and peak at Mt Torbreck (1516m). While most tracks follow ridges and the shore, many drop down dramatically steep spurs to lovely places on the water's edge, providing plenty of splendid walking opportunities.

Facts and Figures

Name: Lake Eildon State Park
Size: 24 000ha
Enactment: 1977
Aboriginal Sites: Inhabited by the Yauung Illam Baluk tribe, named the 'black devils'
Vegetation: Peppermint, stringybark, redbox, blue gums, ferns
Wildlife: Eastern grey kangaroos, water birds
Camping: Many dozens of sites on Lake Eildon's shore as well as in the hinterland. Bookings essential during holiday times, especially for the Jerusalem Creek Inlet, where fees apply. Ranger collects unpaid site-fees most mornings.

Lake Eildon dams several watercourses that flow from the Alps.

Further information:

Parks Victoria

Fraser National Park

46 Aitken St, Alexandra VIC 3714

Tel: (03) 5772 1293

Facts and Figures

Name: Fraser National Park

Size: 3750ha

Enactment: 1957

Aboriginal Sites Inhabited by the Yauung Illam Baluk tribe

Wildlife: Eastern grey kangaroos, water birds

Vegetation: Candlebark gums, red stringybark, redbox, blue gums

Camping: Developed areas in Fraser National Park. Bookings essential during holiday times. Fees apply.

History

Lake Eildon was named after the Eildon Hills in Scotland, the alleged burial place of King Arthur, by Dr James Dickson in 1838. The first settlers arrived in the area in 1839 and gold and timber extraction began in 1867. The dam, built in the mid-1950s, stores water from the Goulburn, Howqua, Jamieson, Big and Delatite rivers and services the lower Goulburn irrigation schemes. It has a catchment area of nearly 4000 square kilometres, of which about 30 per cent comes from the Alps.

Fraser National Park, reserved to protect the forested catchments of the lake, was named after the parliamentarian who steered the bill through the state chambers in the mid-1950s and became the chairman of the Victorian National Parks Authority, A.J. Fraser.

Access

Best access is from Melbourne via the Maroondah Highway through Healesville and Taggerty.

Facilities

Unlike other nearby reserves, the Lake Eildon State Park caters extensively for tourists with literally dozens of official facilitated camping areas and picnic places. It can be accessed by a variety of 2WD and 4WD roads. There is a Youth Hostel at Bonnie Doon, called the Lakeside Leisure Resort (which is really a caravan park), in Hutchinsons Road.

Fraser National Park Circuit

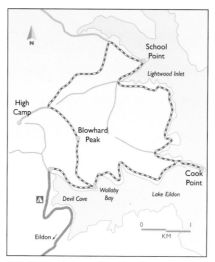

Starting Point: Devil Cove, Fraser National Park

Destination: Wallaby Bay and Lightwood Inlet

Summary: A medium-graded circuit incorporating Lake Eildon's foreshore as well as a good lookout

Attractions: Views, wildlife, swimming, recreation

Length: 15.3km

Time: 1 day

Options: Various tracks around Blowhard Spur allow flexibility in shortening or lengthening the walk

Attraction Rating: ★ ★ ★

Fitness: ☒ ☒ ☒

Maps: VICMAP Lake Eildon Outdoor Leisure Map 1:50 000 topographical or Coller Bay 1:25 000 topographical

Access to Starting Point: Devil Cove is on the main entrance road to the Fraser National Park via Alexandra, 145km north-east of Melbourne

Facilities/Amenities: Caravan park and ranger station at Devil Cove

Recommended Equipment: Swimming gear

Notes: Don't leave valuables in car

Further Information:

Parks Victoria

Fraser National Park

46 Aitken St, Alexandra VIC 3714

Tel: (03) 5772 1293

Walk Description

From Devil Cove, head along the road to Wallaby Bay where a walking path continues east along the shore to Italian Bay at the bottom of Blowhard Spur. Continue north, following the coast to Lightwood Inlet and School Point. An old road follows the water north-west to Aird Inlet. After 1km along this road, head left and ascend to Blowhard Spur. A lot of the Mt Buller region of the Alps can be seen from here. From the crest, turn left and climb to a lookout before descending to the south to Devil Cove.

Cathedral Range State Park

Facts and Figures

Name: Cathedral Range State Park

Size: 3577ha

Enactment: April 1979

Aboriginal Sites: Formerly inhabited by the Tuangurong tribe, but little evidence of occupation remains

Wildlife: Lyrebirds and mammals common to dry and wet sclerophyll forests

Vegetation: Many eucalypt communities, including snow gums

Cathedral Range Traverse Walk

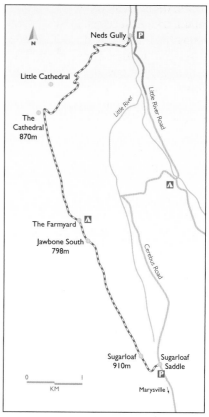

Starting Point: Sugarloaf Saddle, Cathedral Range State Park

Cloud sweeping in from the north over prominent Mt Sugarloaf in the Cathedral Range State Park, near Marysville.

Destination: Neds Gully

Summary: A spectacular walk, traversing the full length of the knife-edge ridge of Cathedral Range from south to north, thereby exploiting height differentials. Set up a car shuffle to avoid a three-hour, 9km road walk back to the starting point.

Attractions: Outstanding scenery for the entire route, especially over the Rubicon State Forest

Length: 11km

Time: 1 long day

Options: There are many different entry and exit approaches off the range, all to the east

Attraction Rating: ★ ★ ★ ★ ★

Fitness: ◪ ◪ ◪ ◪

Maps: VICMAP Cathedral Range Outdoor Leisure Map 1:25 000 topographical

Access to Starting Point: The nearest town, Marysville, is not more than 90 minutes from Melbourne via the Maroondah Highway. Keep on the highway to Buxton and turn right onto the Marysville road. Within 4km, turn left onto the Mount Margaret Road,

then left onto Cerberus Road. This leads north to Sugarloaf Saddle. To access the end of the walk, continue driving north to Cooks Mill, then take the Little River Road north to the Neds Gully camping area.

Facilities/Amenities: Basic picnic and camping areas at Blackwood Flat, Cooks Mill, Neds Gully and Sugarloaf Saddle. Backpack camping areas are located near The Farmyard and North Jawbone Peak, if you wish to make a two-day trip of the walk.

Recommended Equipment: A backpack is essential for all gear as both hands must be free.

Notes: Some degree of expertise on rock is necessary as there are numerous sections where you must scramble on steep slopes. Leave early to allow plenty of time as progress is quite slow on some sections.

Further Information:

Parks Victoria

Tel: (03) 5963 3306

Walk Description

....

The prominent Cathedral Range can

be traversed only by walking from Sugarloaf Saddle to mount the razorback ridge with spectacular views east and west. There are two approaches to the park's highest summit (923m): Well's Cave and The Canyon. The former is graded as hard and involves rock-scrambling; The Canyon takes a less-direct route (either can be done in less than half an hour). Mt Sugarloaf (named for its descriptive rock formation) is a challenge for rock climbers and quite a few have lost their lives on its flanks. The northerly view from the top is most spectacular and the entire day's journey can be surveyed. The razor-edge ridge caused by sharply sloping sedimentary rock is quite dramatic. The whole of the short Cathedral Range is visible from here, but it is only one uplifting in a vast geological phenomenon called the Cerberean Cauldron.

Keep to the centre of the Razorback as you head north following the painted track markers. Pass through The Farmyard, skirting the south and north Jawbone peaks on their western flanks. Continue north to Cathedral Peak (870m) and Neds Saddle before descending off the range via Neds Gully Walking Track.

Other walks in Cathedral Range State Park

Of several shorter circuit walks, the best is a circuit centred on The Cathedral and taking in Neds Saddle, Cathedral North and Little Cathedral. A smaller circuit can be found in the middle of the range between the two Jawbone peaks. This starts from the Jawbone car park and is popular with both walkers and rock climbers.

Lake Mountain Alpine Reserve

Lake Mountain Circuit

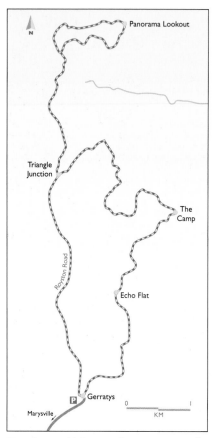

Starting Point: Gerratys, Lake Mountain Alpine Reserve
Destination: Panorama Lookout
Summary: An easy graded walk over flat open alpine plains with good views in all directions
Attractions: Snow gum woodland, alpine herbfields, views over the southern Alps
Length: 9.8km

Time: 3 hours
Options: Various side tracks such as the Boundary, Long Heath and Jubilee trails offer options for the energetic
Attraction Rating: ★ ★ ★
Fitness: ◪
Maps: VICMAP Marysville–Lake Mountain 1:10 000 Outdoor Leisure Series topographical
Access to Starting Point: Lake Mountain Alpine Reserve is either approached via the Maroondah Highway and then through Marysville, or via the Warburton Highway and then through McMahons Creek. Access to the small ski village of Gerratys is from Marysville via the Maroondah Highway, Marysville road, Marysville Woods Point Road and Lake Mountain Road. Park at Gerratys—public vehicles are not permitted to go any further.
Facilities/Amenities: Limited facilities at Gerratys in summer
Recommended Equipment: Warm, windproof clothing as most of the walk is in exposed terrain above 1400m altitude
Further Information:
Parks Victoria Information Centre
Tel: 131 963

Walk Description

Lake Mountain, just 100km from Melbourne, is slowly developing as a cross-country skiing venue. It lies just north of the Great Dividing Range at between 1300m–1400m elevation. The cross-country trails are perfect for walking in summer when the snow has melted. The distances are short and the gradients gentle, so even the most inexperienced walker can use Lake Mountain as an introductory training ground for alpine conditions. To add interest, the scenery is quite marvellous with the usual snow gums, wildflowers and views over mountain ash ranges.

From the wide turning circle and car park, take the Royston Gap Trail on the left and follow this north as it gently rises to 1440m at Triangle Junction. Continue north along the Panorama Trail that descends to a saddle then a short ascent to the turn-off to Panorama Lookout. This is an ideal place for lunch. Return via the same route to Triangle Junction,

where you turn left onto Royston Gap Trail to The Camp and right onto Echo Flat walking track. This winds south via Echo Flat to Gerratys.

Other walks in the Lake Mountain area

The Lake Mountain Alpine Reserve has many cross-country ski trails that allow for relatively easy scenic strolls (during the warmer months) through open woodland and grasslands. The site of the former Boundary Hut in the north of the reserve makes a good half-day destination. Full-day walks and overnight walks can be done by descending off the top to the west.

The West

Grampians (Gariwerd) National Park

A series of ridges 80km long by 50km wide, the Grampians mark the far end of the Great Dividing Range. Walking and camping opportunities are unlimited in this sandstone wonderland.

Facts and Figures

Name: Grampians (Gariwerd) National Park
Size: 167 000ha (1670 sq km)
Enactment: Land Conservation Council recommendation, 1982 Gazetted in parliament, 1984 Reservation as National Park, 1984
Visitors: at least three million a year
Vegetation: 20 endemic plant species, 1000 flowering plants in a variety of wet, dry and altitude-related communities. In total, about a third of Victoria's flora species occur throughout the park.
Wildlife: All common native mammals, including koalas, rock wallabies, the smokey mouse and a diverse birdlife. Many marsupials are campsite residents and are quite tame.
Aboriginal Sites: About 80 important rock-art sites originating from a tribe called the Koories. They referred to the western mountains as Gariwerd.
Attractions: Sandstone formations, waterfalls, lookouts, 50 individual short and long bushwalks totalling more than 150km. Any prospective

walkers are advised to carry a copy of *120 Walks in Victoria* or *50 Walks in the Grampians* by Tyrone Thomas, the definitive guides to the area. The park is also popular with rock climbers because of the sandstone escarpments.

Further Information: The Parks Victoria office is 2.5km south of Halls Gap shopping centre, along the Dunkeld road. It contains informative interactive displays about the natural and cultural features of the park. The centre is open daily from 9.00am to 4.45pm (except Christmas Day).

Geology

Almost half a billion years ago, uplifting caused sediments to fill depressions and lakes in the area. This continued for about 350 million years when further earth movement lifted, faulted and overturned strata. Volcanic activity during this time created several soft-granite outcrops near the present-day Zumsteins and Halls Gap. The landforms were eroded, then uplifted again and eroded again.

The reason the Grampians stand out from the surrounding plains is that their sandstone has a higher quartzite content making it relatively more erosion-resistant. Because of this quartz content, rock climbers find the Grampians one of the great Australian venues for their sport.

One of the distinguishing characteristics of the Grampians is that the western slopes have a gentle gradient while the eastern slopes are very steep. This effect is called the 'cuesta' landform and is most pronounced in the Wonderland Range in the central Grampians. Another characteristic is the unusual natural sculpting caused by weathering to rock of differing degrees of hardness. Some confusion arises about the rippling effect in some of the rock formations, especially on The Pinnacle walk in Wonderland Range, and around The Fortress area in the central Victorian range. Basalt sometimes looks like this because it was once molten rock, but sandstone? The answer is that the sediments were laid down in shallow, slow-flowing water.

The unusual geological formation, great variations in altitude and westerly position of the Grampians largely accounts for the huge variety of scenic interest. Features present include sandstone cliffs, rocky ravines, pristine watercourses, boulder-fields, plains and forests.

History

Evidence from excavations, archaeological deposits, surface scatters, scarred trees and artificial earthen mounds suggests that Aborigines occupied the Grampians for at least 3000 years. There is also a concentration of Aboriginal rock paintings. Most of the sites discovered to date have been found on the western side of the Grampians in the Victoria, Mt

Silverband Falls, near Halls Gap, is one of the more popular destinations in the Grampians National Park.

Zero, Black and Asses Ears ranges. More than half are grouped on the western slopes of the Victoria Range. The full extent and distribution of the art sites, however, is still unknown and sites continue to be found.

Glenisla shelter was the first site discovered about 1859, but by 1896 the art was much disfigured by graffiti. Even in those early days, the local Aborigines were not able (or willing) to relate anything about the meaning, functions or significance of the art. A few more sites were discovered over the next 60 years, but it was not until the 1960s that the importance of the area became apparent. In 1981 a major program was undertaken to record and evaluate the sites; this resulted in the number of known site doubling. Today, some 60 sites have been recorded within the national park, although only seven are publicised as tourist attractions. Nearly 4000 different motifs have been recorded. The Glenisla shelter has more than 2000, but most sites contain only a dozen or so motifs.

The range was first sighted by Europeans in 1836 when Major Thomas Mitchell climbed some of the peaks, such as Mt Zero and Mt William. Gold was discovered in the 1850s and settlement in the district commenced. For many decades, timber-felling was a major form of development. There were mills at Fyans Creek, Stoney Creek, Borough Huts, Zumsteins, Wartook, Cranages and Stachans. Relics of this pioneering age can still be found, but most mills were dismantled when they closed.

Tourism took off in the 1920s with the building of facilities and roads, and has never looked back. With this development came negatives: exotic plants, weeds and feral animals, such as foxes, pigs, goats, rabbits and cats. Visitor numbers increased after 1984 when the magic words 'national park' were attached to the Grampians. Before 1984, the area was state forest under the management of the Forestry Commission of Victoria, and most of it could have been logged. In fact, a large area was logged, with production peaking in the post-war period, and the park is still recovering. Grazing also damaged the Grampians; even

Beehive Falls beneath Briggs Bluff, Grampians National Park.

during the first years of their reservation, 24 grazing licences allowed livestock inside the park's boundaries. More-efficient heavy vehicles and an increased demand for timber then led to the rapid development of forestry roads in the area. Because of heavy winter rainfall and steep mountain slopes, soil erosion is quite severe, and many of these trails have since been closed to vehicular traffic.

Most people choose to access the Grampians by road via the Western Highway through Stawell. Halls Gap,

the tourist hub of the area, is about 270km from Melbourne (460km from Adelaide). This is only one of about 50 access points to the national park.

The popularity of the park ensures that walkers are well catered for, with a network of hundreds of kilometres of trails and well-developed campsites with abundant fresh water. Almost 90 per cent of visitors stay overnight, and the main recreational activities are walking, driving, rock climbing, painting, photography, fishing, boating and horse-riding. The most popular months to visit are January and April. If you want to avoid crowds, come in June or early December.

Some placenames and names of features, tracks and creeks might undergo revision as a push toward traditional tribal Aboriginal names continues. Also note that camping fees are applicable at most major camping areas within the Grampians.

Climate

The Grampian Ranges have a temperate climate with marked seasonal patterns. Winter and early spring are cool and wet while summer and autumn are warm and dry.

The mountain climate is considerably different to that on the surrounding plains. Being a region of high elevation, ranging from 200m to 1168m above sea level, the Grampians have a considerably higher rainfall than most areas in Western Victoria. Within the mountains, the complex topography produces various microclimates that contribute to a diverse array of plant communities.

In the national park, the average annual rainfall ranges from 220mm in the low-lying areas in the north to more than 1000mm on the slopes of the central region. Lying across the path of the prevailing westerly winds, the Grampians bring orographic rainfall by forcing air masses to rise, cool and, if sufficiently moist, condense and precipitate. These moist air masses collect mainly on the eastern side of the mountains.

Rainfall increases with altitude. Moving from south to north there is a general decrease in average annual rainfall coupled with an increase in the variability of this rainfall. This general pattern continues north through the Wimmera and Mallee, making this a region that is very dependent upon supplementary water supplies, largely from the Grampians.

Vegetation

Almost 1000 species of native plants have been recorded in the Grampians National Park, representing about one-third of Victoria's flora. The park also shelters 18 endemic species and many others occurring nowhere else in Victoria but found in other parts of Australia. The reasons for such a large species list include the wide variations in topography, soils and climate.

Wildlife

Varied habitats within the national park support a large and diverse assemblage of native and introduced wildlife, representing a high proportion of the known species in Victoria. There are six main habitats based on definable vegetation communities:

- **Woodlands** represent one of the most important areas of this habitat on public land in south-western Victoria for the 100 or so wildlife species that inhabit them. These include birds such as lorikeets and honeyeaters, which move into woodlands seasonally to feed on pollen, nectar and insects.
- **Heath communities** are widespread across the park and are inhabited by about 80 species of wildlife. The lowland forms the northern extremity of a coastal-type heath and, consequently, the northern limit of some species e.g. heath mouse and southern emu-wren.
- **Open and low open forests** form the most extensive habitat type in the park. At least 100 species commonly occur within them.
- **Sandstone ranges** with numerous cliffs and caves are an important habitat for species such as the brushtail rock wallaby and the peregrine falcon.
- **Tall open forest** occurs in scattered areas, the largest being near Silver-band Falls.
- **Aquatic habitats** include man-made reservoirs and permanent fast-flowing streams and canals. Most of the swamps remaining around the Grampians are outside the national park boundaries.

Facilities

There are many campgrounds in the park, in a variety of settings directly accessible by car. All have toilets, fireplaces and picnic tables. Not all campgrounds have water. Sites are available at these areas for most of the year, but some may be crowded at Easter, on long weekends and during summer holidays. Campers must pay a small fee for a site in the campgrounds, up to six people and one vehicle are allowed per site. Note that an extra fee applies for a second vehicle. Obtain a permit from the National Park Visitors' Centre at Halls Gap or at the campgrounds. This does not guarantee any particular site though and availability is always on a first-come, first-served basis. Leaders of large groups are asked to notify park staff at least four weeks ahead, giving details of number of people, length of stay and places to be visited.

Bush-camping is permitted in the national park, except in the Wonderland Range, in the watershed of Lake Wartook and as indicated by *No Camping* signs.

Northern Grampians

Stapylton: A large campground with sheltered and open sites. Tank water.
Troopers Creek: A medium campground in a forested valley. Water from a nearby creek.
Plantation: A large campground in an old pine forest just outside the park. Tapwater.
Smith Mill: A large campground in an old mill site among pines and native vegetation. Tap water.

Central Grampians

Boreang: A large campground with sheltered and open sites. Water from a creek (seasonal, usually dry in summer and autumn).
Borough Huts: A large campground in an open area near Fyans Creek (Barriyalcog Creek). Tank water.
Rosea: A small campground in a forested area at the foot of Mt Rosea. No water.

Southern Grampians

Bomunna: A small campground in a quiet wooded area. Creek (seasonal, usually dry in summer and autumn).
Wannon Crossing: Small campground by the Wannon River. Creek water.
Buandik: Large campground in forested area on Billimina Creek (Cultivation Creek) near Aboriginal art sites. Seasonal water, usually dry in summer and autumn.
Strachans: Small campground in a former mill site beside a creek (20 to 30 large sites; 10 to 15 medium sites; 4 to 8 small sites). Creek water.

Mt Difficult Walk

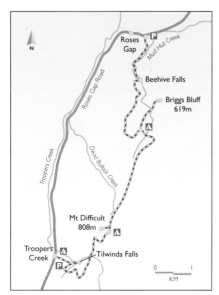

Starting Point: Troopers Creek campground, Grampians (Gariwerd) National Park

Destination: Roses Gap via Mt Difficult (808m) and Briggs Bluff (619m)

Summary: A traverse of a most spectacular section of Mt Difficult Range. Set up a car shuffle to avoid a 2-hour 7.5km road walk back to the start.

Attractions: Dramatic rocky terrain,

the summit of Mt Difficult

Length: 16km

Time: 1 long day

Options: A long, arduous 25km circuit walk can be undertaken by the adventurous. Instead of descending to Roses Gap, return to Troopers Creek by heading east using the Long Point Fire Line.

Attraction Rating: ★ ★ ★ ★ ★

Fitness: ☒ ☒ ☒ ☒

Maps: VICMAP Northern Grampians Outdoor Leisure Series 1:50 000 topographical and Mount Difficult 1:25 000 topographical

Access to Starting Point: Troopers Creek is in the western half of the national park, on Roses Gap Road. Roses Gap (also known as Barigar Gap) can be accessed by following the Mount Zero road north from Halls Gap. The Briggs Bluff ascent begins about 800m west of the intersection between the Halls Gap–Mt Zero road and Roses Gap Road.

Facilities/Amenities: Standard camping facilities at Troopers Creek

Recommended Equipment: Sturdy shoes with good tread as much of the way is along rock

Notes: Camping fees apply at Troopers Creek. Mt Difficult is also referred to by its traditional Koori name, Mt *Gar*. Some rock-scrambling is required.

Further Information:

Grampians National Park
Visitors' Centre
PO Box 18, Halls Gap VIC 3381
Tel:　(03) 5356 4381
Fax:　(03) 5356 4446

Walk Description

This spectacular walk requires a degree of fitness, skill and experience as it negotiates considerably wild terrain. Because of the variation and quality in the scenery, it is considered by many one of the best walks in the country. From Troopers Creek, head up to Tilwinda Falls and then to Wind Cave to begin a relentlessly steep ascent to the crest of the Mt Difficult Range. Head north over more rock, following painted arrows and small cairns to the awesome summit of Mt Difficult with its striking views along the crest of the range. This extraordinary vista is often featured on calendars and posters. Continue north along the range to Briggs Bluff (619m)

Looking south-east from near Boundary Gap on the Major Mitchell Plateau, Grampians National Park.

and its dramatic 400m northern cliff. Be very wary, especially in high winds. Backtrack and follow the signs down to Beehive Falls and then to Roses Gap to complete an eventful day's walking.

Major Mitchell Plateau Walk

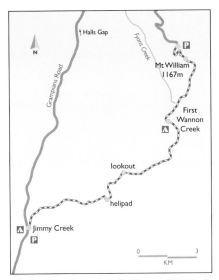

Starting Point: Mt William (1167m), Grampians (Gariwerd) National Park

Destination: Jimmy Creek picnic ground (Grampians Tourist Road) via the Major Mitchell Plateau

Summary: A long, challenging walk over a remote, rocky subalpine plateau. A car shuffle is necessary. By starting at Mt William, you avoid a considerable uphill of about 750m.

Attractions: Rugged mountainous terrain, expansive views, especially to the east, and one of the few genuine wilderness experiences possible in the Grampians

Length: 18.2km

Time: 1 full day or 2 medium days

Options: A longer extension can be done by walking up Mt William from Grampians Tourist Road in the Fyans Creek valley. This adds about 6km to the walk and virtually necessitates an overnight stay on the plateau. Camping areas are at First Wannon Creek or Boundary Gap. Mt William can also be approached from the east by starting from Bomjinna campground.

Attraction Rating: ★ ★ ★ ★

Fitness: ◪ ◪ ◪

Maps: VICMAP Southern Grampians Outdoor Leisure Series 1:50 000

topographical and Mount William 1:25 000 topographical

Access to Starting Point: The Grampians Tourist Road connects Halls Gap with Dunkeld south of the park. The turn-off to Mt William and Jimmy Creek are only 12km apart on the same road.

Facilities/Amenities: None

Recommended Equipment: Windjacket, warm clothes, fuel stove (no campfires), water (creeks may be dry)

Notes: Snow often falls on the Major Mitchell Plateau in winter. Recent closures and camping restrictions have been in force and walkers should check conditions with rangers before setting out. Permits are required to stay overnight on the plateau.

Further Information:
   Grampians National Park
   Visitors' Centre
   PO Box 18, Halls Gap VIC 3381
   Tel: (03) 5356 4381
   Fax: (03) 5356 4446

Walk Description

The Mt William Range is the highest and most dramatic in the Grampians National Park. Its relatively old sediments are about 1800m thick and slope upward at about 45 degrees, creating very impressive east-facing cliffs. The highest peak, Mt William (also referred to as Mt Duwill), was named by Major Mitchell in July 1836 in honour of King William IV, the then King of England.

The best time to walk in this spectacular area is autumn or spring. Summer can be extremely hot, dry and suffocating and winter is very cold. From the car park near the summit of Mt William, head past the gate up the road to the radio towers and enjoy the awesome view over the southern Grampians. Then head south following the line of cliffs to the Major Mitchell Plateau. The alpine terrain is extremely beautiful and walkers may want to capture the experience on film. With the exception of a short section immediately south of Boundary Gap, the track parallels the escarpment until the far southern end of the plateau. The best spot to obtain water is at First Wannon Creek, but sometimes Boundary Gap may have some after rain. At the southern edge

of the plateau, the track follows a narrow ridge to a scrubby knoll before descending to the Stockyard vehicular track and steeply down to the Jimmy Creek picnic ground.

The Fortress Walk

Starting Point: Buandik (Victoria Range, south-western Grampians), Grampians (Gariwerd) National Park

Destination: The Fortress (also known as Castle Rock)

Summary: A short but fascinating exploration of the most weathered portion of the remote Victoria Range

Attractions: Highly unusual rock formations, eroded by wind and water to astounding shapes

Length: 12km

Time: 1 long day

Options: The Fortress can also be approached from the east by parking on the Sawmill Track

Attraction Rating: ★ ★ ★ ★

Fitness: ◪ ◪ ◪

Maps: VICMAP Southern Grampians Outdoor Leisure Series 1:50 000 topographical and Victorian Range 1:25 000 topographical

Access to Starting Point: The approach to the Buandik region is from the south. Drive through Cavendish, Woohlpooer and Harrop Track. From the north, follow the Henty Highway from Horsham as far south as Billywing Road. The actual walk start is at a gate across the Deep Creek Track, just off Harrop Track.

Facilities/Amenities: A picnic area and camping ground at Buandik

Recommended Equipment: Sturdy shoes with lots of grip as most of the terrain is extremely rocky

Notes: Walkers are asked not to clamber over fragile formations or touch Aboriginal art in the vicinity

Further Information:
> Grampians National Park
> Visitors' Centre
> PO Box 18, Halls Gap VIC 3381
> Tel: (03) 5356 4381
> Fax: (03) 5356 4446

Walk Description

This short day walk packs a lot in a short space. The central Victoria Range is an outstanding gallery of sculpted rock and many hours can be spent marvelling at its pillars and stacks. Head east from the sandy road, then turn right onto a walking track, ascending the crest of a spur in a south-easterly direction.

The terrain becomes very wild as you approach The Fortress (or Castle Rock) with great sculpted rock formations dominating the scenery. The tiny footpad is sometimes difficult to discern over the rock, but generally head around the base of The Fortress until the cliff opens up. Then enter a long gully that runs through the central formation. There are giant chimney stacks, caves, cliffs, ravines, and overhangs and heavily weathered formations that puzzle geologists about how they were formed. You will no doubt be keen to explore this fascinating area for some time before backtracking to the car.

Other walks in the Grampians (Gariwerd) National Park

There are dozens of tracks, formal and informal, throughout the Grampians. Comprehensive route descriptions for all the major ones can be found in *50 Walks in the Grampians* by Tyrone Thomas. Some of the best are:

Northern Grampians

Mt Zero, Mt Hollow and Mt Stapylton are three interesting peaks within a few kilometres of each other near Horsham. Despite their summits being relatively low, they are very rugged and make interesting short day walks. Aboriginal paintings can be seen.

Wonderland Range

One of the central highlights of the Grampians is the Wonderland area

River red gums line the edge of Lake Mournpall, Hattah–Kulkyne National Park.

with its many rock features, such as Ladies Hat, the Cool Chamber and the Fallen Giant. The narrow canyon of Silent Street is also impressive. This was formed by a fault line in the sandstone, which allowed accelerated erosion to take place.

At the eastern end, walk out onto the tops of the Wonderland Range and follow the markers past strange rock outcrops to The Pinnacle lookout for views over Halls Gap and surrounds. Nearby to the right is The Nerve Tester, for people not afraid of heights. Even if you've no ambition to pass the test it's worth seeing.

Retrace your steps to the car park or continue on a circuit to Bellfield Peak and back down via the Garden of the Grampians. Another approach to the Wonderland Range is via Mackeys Peak from Halls Gap.

To the south of the range, Sundial Peak overlooks Lake Bellfield and several short day walks can be undertaken from the picnic ground at the end of Sundial Road. Nearby, Reeds Lookout and The Balconies near Mt Victory are one of the most photographed vistas in the Grampians.

Central Grampians

Mt Rosea (1009m) provides a challenging climb for walkers making the journey from the north or south. Other destinations in the central Grampians include Silverband Falls, Calectasia Falls and the Asses Ears.

Zumstein–Mackenzie Falls

These falls have one of the largest flow volumes in western Victoria. The direct walk is quite short, but extended walks along the Mackenzie River are an alternative if you wish to escape the crowds. Zumstein is a well-developed campground in the centre of the national park.

Southern Grampians

There are several caves and isolated formations in the Victoria Range near The Fortress, with approaches from east or west. One of the most popular is The Chimney Pots, a 3km walk through rocky, steep terrain from the Glenelg River Road. The central spine of the Serra Range leads south to Mt Abrupt (827m) and Mt Sturgeon (582m) and two short 7km walking tracks leads to their open summits.

The Mallee

Victoria's Mallee is also referred to as 'Sunset country', desert and GABA (Great Australian Bugger-All) country. The parks in this bleak open region contain Victoria's largest reserves and account for nearly all the state's prime wilderness area. Rainfall is very low, less than 200mm a year falls in places such as Pink Lakes, while the Little Desert National Park attracts only about 400mm. The mallee is labelled 'semiarid' rather than 'desert'. In fact, looking toward the flat horizon from any vantage point you can see quite a lot of scrub. While vegetation tends to look the same in all directions, communities are surprisingly diverse. Paperbarks grow around salt lakes, while grasslands contrast with pine woodland, dune systems alternate with the gypsum plains and river red gums line most of the major watercourses.

The chief attraction of these vast western parks (totalling about one million hectares) is that they are markedly different from the rest of Victoria. In stark contrast to the Alps, the rugged coast of Gippsland and the lush forests of the Otways, this region is almost perfectly flat with little open water. The great advantage of such semiarid regions is the visibility of the abundant wildlife. The forests of the Great Dividing Range are so dense that visibility is limited to a few metres, but in the open woodland of the mallee a great variety of species, such as emus, kangaroos, wedge-tailed eagles and parrots in particular, can easily be seen.

Hattah–Kulkyne National Park

One of the most accessible of the mallee parks, Hattah–Kulkyne allows you to experience a semiarid region in a not-too-remote area. The lakes were named after the original station property before their reservation in 1960. Hattah is probably of Scottish origin, but most of the park features are named in the Aboriginal language. The other name, Kulkyne, refers to a howling dingo in the native tongue.

This low-lying park contains sand dunes, mallee and magnificent giant red gums; the flat terrain makes for easy walking. Information leaflets describe the unique ways in which endemic flora and fauna adapt to the extremes in temperature. The camping area abounds with kangaroos—park authorities describe the population as an overabundance. The area is drained by the Murray River but floods are not uncommon, and in 1956 the area was 6m underwater. A sign warns not to camp under the river red gums as they have a curious habit of dropping seemingly healthy branches—quite a hazard to sleepers

in tents. These magnificent hardwood eucalypts grow to more than 25m and are found only near water. They are often found with the shorter black box (the two sometimes form hybrids called Deniliquin Box).

Facts and Figures

Name: Hattah–Kulkyne National Park
Size: 49 550ha
Enactment: National Park, 1960
  UNESCO World Biosphere Reserve, 1982
Aboriginal Sites: Surface campsites, scarred trees where canoes and coolamons have been cut out, burial sites, shell middens indicate that Aborigines occupied the lake areas for about 16 000 years
Vegetation: 700 species, including mallee eucalypts, river red gums, wattle, bull-oak gums, black box, hop bush, cypress pine, tea-tree
Wildlife: Grey and red kangaroos, emus, 200 bird species, including pelicans and spoonbills; reptiles, including tortoises and goannas
Attractions: Semiarid atmosphere, good wildlife viewing
Facilities: Campgrounds at Lake Hattah and Lake Mournpall. Several walking and cycling tracks as well as self-guided vehicle drives. A visitors' centre at the park entrance with a resident ranger. You will also find information boards and brochures here.

Bugle Ridge Circuit

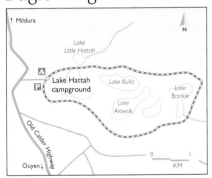

Starting Point: Lake Hattah camping area, Hattah–Kulkyne National Park
Destination: Lake Brockie
Summary: A short, easy circuit stroll through varied scenery
Attractions: Billabongs, wildlife and historic artefacts
Length: 10km

Time: 3 hours
Options: Longer overnight walks are possible by following old vehicular tracks all the way to the Murray River in the north. The Stockyard, Cantala and Kulkyne tracks traverse much of the most interesting sections of the park. Attempt this overnight walk only in cooler months and carry plenty of water.
Attraction Rating: ★★
Fitness: ✗✗
Maps: VICMAP Hattah Lakes Outdoor Leisure Series 1:25 000 topographical
Access to Starting Point: The national park is 50km south of Mildura, a full day's drive (450km) from Melbourne via Bendigo, Charlton and Ouyen
Facilities/Amenities: The camping grounds are on the lake shores and provide picnic facilities and toilets
Recommended Equipment: Water, sunscreen and a hat
Notes: Summer swimming is not safe because of blue-green algae from the Murray River. High levels of algae can cause eye irritation, throat problems, itchiness, skin rashes, and, if ingested, gastroenteritis and permanent liver damage. Fish and other invertebrates are able to survive in these waters, but their liver and digestive tracts accumulate toxins, so do not eat fish from waters where algae concentrations are high. When present at low levels the algae are not a serious health risk, but with high nutrient levels and summer heat they rapidly increase in numbers. Many algae have buoyancy sacs and can form a surface bloom. Boiling the water does not remove the toxins. In fact, it concentrates them. Check with park authorities at the ranger residence for the latest information on water quality.
Further Information:
  Parks Victoria
  Tel: (03) 5029 3253

Walk Description

From the weir across Lake Hattah, follow the signposted Bugle Ridge Walking Track east, skirting the north of Lake Bulla to Lake Brockie. Then either continue to Lake Nip Nip, around Lake Boich, or turn south along the Brockie Walking Track and west through sand dunes past Lake Arawak back to Lake Hattah.

The dry Lake Albacutya, just south of Wyperfeld National Park, fills very infrequently.

Murray Sunset National Park

Declared in 1991, this is the second largest park in Victoria at 633 000 ha. It contains four wilderness zones: mallee-covered dunes, saltbush flats, and pine woodlands to the south, and floodplains to the north. Despite the semiarid character of the park, wildflowers and wildlife are prolific.

Pink Lakes Nature Trail Walk

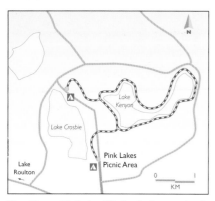

Starting Point: Pink Lakes picnic area, Murray Sunset National Park

Destination: Lake Crosbie
Summary: A very easy stroll around Lake Kenyon to reach Lake Crosbie
Attractions: The four pink salt lakes are one of the most accessible attractions in the massive Murray–Sunset National Park (633 000ha)
Length: 2.5km
Time: 1 hour
Options: Longer overnight extensions lead to Mopoke Hut and Mt Crozier. Circuit walks make use of Honeymoon Hut, Last Hope and Underbool tracks.
Attraction Rating: ★★
Fitness: ◪
Maps: VICMAP Boinka–Underbool 1:50 000 topographical (yet to be published at time of writing). This map is not necessary as the walk is well signposted.
Access to Starting Point: The closest town is Underbool, west of Ouyen on the Mallee Highway
Facilities/Amenities: A picnic ground and two camping areas at Pink Lakes provide toilets and water
Recommended Equipment: Water, sunscreen and a hat
Notes: Lake is most colourful in spring

Further Information:
Parks Victoria
Tel: (03) 5094 6267
or   (03) 5092 1322

Walk Description

From the picnic ground near Lake Crosbie, head north around Lake Kenyon. When you've completed the circuit, walk west across to Lake Crosbie (camping is permitted here). The four lakes here with their usually dry salt pans are a vibrant pink caused by the release of carotene from algae. The effect is best viewed in spring in diffused low light.

Wyperfeld National Park

In 1909, 4000ha of the present-day Wyperfeld National Park was set aside as a sanctuary for mallee fauna and flora. At that time there were 29 species of mammals in the vicinity. Since then, five have become extinct and 18 no longer occur in the mallee region. There were steady increases to the park size after its reclassification as a national park in 1921. Adjoining the park to the south is the Lake Albacutya Park, centred on a large dry lake that fills in 20-year cycles. Regulations are relaxed in this park, you can basically camp where you want.

Facts and Figures

Name: Wyperfeld National Park
Size: 1998, 356 800ha
Enactment: 1909
Vegetation: 450 species, including cypress pines, mallee eucalypts, porcupine grass, broom-brush
Wildlife: Wedge-tailed eagles, emus, grey kangaroos, mallee fowl, Major Mitchell parrot
Attractions: Sand dunes, wildlife, desert atmosphere
Facilities: Large camping area with shelters, water and toilets

Lake Brambruk Nature Walk

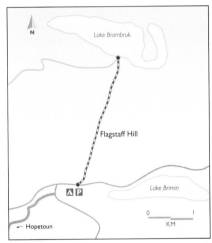

Starting Point: Main campground, Wyperfeld National Park
Destination: Lake Brambruk
Summary: A self-guided nature walk that passes through mallee scrub and river red gums
Attractions: Cypress-pine woodland, wildlife
Length: 6km
Time: 2 hours
Options: Longer overnight extensions to Lake Agnes in the north
Attraction Rating: ★ ★
Fitness: ✗ ✗
Maps: VICMAP Brambruk–Hopetoun 1:50 000 topographical (yet to be published at time of writing). The walk is well signposted.

Access to Starting Point: Wyperfeld National Park is best approached through Warracknabeal along the Sunraysia Highway, then Rainbow and Yaapeet. A 4WD is best, as sandy roads can be treacherous after rain.
Facilities/Amenities: Main camping ground has shelter, toilets and water
Recommended Equipment: Water, sunscreen and hat
Notes: Best to visit Wyperfeld National Park during the cooler months
Further Information:
Parks Victoria
Tel: (03) 5395 7221

Walk Description

From the northern end of the campground, head north toward Lake Brambruk, with Flagstaff Hill over on your right, and return via the same route. The track passes through mallee scrub and stands of river red rums. An information sheet available at the start has interesting numbered facts corresponding to small signposts that point out features of the semiarid vegetation communities. A telephoto lens is useful for capturing the wildlife abundant on the grassflats.

Other walks in the Mallee
Little Desert National Park

This is the closest of the desert parks to Melbourne and by far the most visited, with everyone from 4WD enthusiasts to school excursions coming here. Night temperatures can drop to −8°C, with frosts wiping out hundreds of trees. In summer, day temperatures of 40°C+ make conditions most unpleasant. The best time to come here is from April to October, but always carry plenty of water for any excursion into the core of the park. Unlike the more arid parks to the north, many of the trails in Little Desert can be quite sandy, making progress for bushwalkers difficult.

The main campground on the park's northern boundary has 2WD access, but little else in the park can be reached by conventional vehicles. Even 4WDs have trouble with the dunes, and only the serious 4WDs equipped with long-travel suspension and winches can tackle much of the terrain. The best camping areas are reached by travelling along the Western Highway from Melbourne through Horsham and Dimboola. At the small township of Kiata, turn left onto Kiata South Road following the signs into Little Desert National Park. The camping area is set amid yellow gums and stringybark, and offers standard facilities such as pit toilets, tables, fireplaces, etc. Birds to watch for include emu, grebes, pelicans, herons, ibis, Cape Barren geese, buzzards and a multitude of ducks and kites. The terrain is dominated by iron-rich sandstone ridges, bordering depressions where salt pools form.

Facts and Figures

Name: Little Desert National Park
Size: 132 000ha
Enactment: 1968
Aboriginal Sites: Scarred trees and very old campsite remains indicate Aboriginal occupation of the Wimmera, which they knew as *Tatyara*, 'the good country'
Vegetation: 600 species of flowering plants, mallee vegetation, orchids
Wildlife: Malleefowl, emus
Attractions: Semiarid atmosphere, visitors' centre, self-guided nature walks, wildflowers
Facilities: Some developed campsites line the boundaries of the park
Maps: A good map is the Westprint Little Desert National Park. The detailed VICMAP Nurcoung–Natimuk 1:50 000 topographical covers the southern half while the Natmap/Ausmap Nhill 1:100 000 covers the northern part.
Further Information:
Parks Victoria
Tel: (03) 5389 1204

The South-west
Otway National Park

The wet and dry forests that cover the Otway Ranges in south-west Victoria support an enormous variety of wildlife. The forests inland from the Great Ocean Road rank with Tasmania's south, East Gippsland and the Barrington Tops.

The magnificent mountain ash, one of the tallest trees in the world, is prolific in these forests. Reports from the 19th century of trees taller than

150m are unconfirmed. The tallest officially recorded was a 97m giant with its top broken off—before this it may have contested the world record. In addition to the ash, there are blackwood, myrtle beech and many rare endemic species.

Facts and Figures

Name: Otway National Park

Size: 12 900ha (Melba Gully State Park 65ha)

Aboriginal Sites: A few middens and campsite remains, especially east of Cape Otway. One significant site at Aire River mouth includes stone artefacts and grinding stones.

Wildlife: 250 bird species, 20 reptile species, 15 amphibian species, 50 fish species and the usual common marsupials. Glow-worms are also present.

Vegetation: 700 plant and fern species, including mountain ash, tree ferns, myrtle beech, messmate

Camping: Developed sites, and rough camping permitted

Attractions: Wet forests, rugged coastal scenery, river and marine fishing, waterfalls, lookouts, surf beaches and floating islands

Further Information:

Parks Victoria
Otway National Park
PO Box 63, Apollo Bay VIC 3233
Tel: (03) 5237 6889

or

Great Ocean Road Visitors'
Information Centre
Great Ocean Road
Apollo Bay VIC 3233
Tel: (03) 5237 6529

Geology

Originally, the Otway Ranges were a 3km-thick layer of sandstone. Surprisingly, this supported little plant or animal life. The area was folded and became uplifted from the surrounding land, accelerating erosion of the sandstone. Unlike other lush areas, the rich vegetation developed despite the absence of volcanic activity. During the ice ages, the Otways became an island and many marine fossil beds were laid down in the clays.

History

The extreme density of vegetation in the Otways possibly discouraged Aborigines from inhabiting the area as only a few midden piles have been found. The first European to see the Otways was explorer Lieutenant James Grant. Many years later, a convict, William Buckley, escaped from the Port Phillip Settlement and survived for 32 years living with the Aborigines in the ranges. This gave rise to the colloquial expression 'Buckley's chance' (meaning 'almost no chance'), as the odds were against him surviving in this region of the wild Australian bush.

In the mid-1870s white settlers rushed for the potential grazing land and clear-felled much of that magnificent, very dense forest. In response, the Minister for Lands set aside a timber reservation of nearly 80 000ha. Pressure for agricultural land continued, however, resulting in this land reserve being felled too. The state eventually bought back much of

The majestic Beauchamp Falls near the Aire River valley in the Otway Ranges, are a photographer's dream.

this land though it was destined to become a plantation of *radiata* pines.

The first permanent natural reserve was established here after a Royal Commission in 1899. Tourist access to the area grew after the installation of a railway line to Beech Forest in the early 20th century. The main route for tourists now is the 250km winding Great Ocean Road, built between 1916 and 1932 by 3000 World War I ex-servicemen. It closely follows the visually dramatic coastline. The mainland's highest coastal cliffs can be found at Moonlight Head near Lower Gellibrand.

Climate

Temperatures are generally mild, with maximum averages around 20°C and minimums around 10°C. The afternoons generally produce an on-shore sea breeze so swimming, surfing, and beach recreation is best done in the mornings. The climate is generally wet, with rainfall well above 1200mm a year, although the occasional dry conditions can produce devastating bushfires, such as in 1919 and 1939.

Lorne Waterfall Circuit

Starting Point: Sheoak picnic area, Angahook–Lorne State Park
Destination: Upper and Lower Kalimna Falls, Castle Rock, Swallow Cave, Sheoak Falls, Henderson Falls, The Canyon, Phantom Falls
Summary: An excellent three-part day walk consisting of smaller circuits of similar length
Attractions: Lush rainforest, an ocean lookout, cascades and waterfalls
Length: 25.6km
Time: 1 long day
Options: This walk comprises three

separate circuits all starting and ending at the Sheoak picnic area so walkers can do one, two or three
Attraction Rating: ★ ★ ★ ★
Fitness: ◪ ◪ ◪
Maps: VICMAP Otways and Shipwreck Coast Outdoor Leisure Series 1:50 000 topographicals and Lorne 1:25 000 topographical are helpful
Access to Starting Point: The Sheoak picnic area is just a short drive from Lorne via the Allenvale road
Facilities/Amenities: General picnic facilities at Sheoak picnic area: fireplaces, toilets, water, information. Walkers can leave food in the car as they will walk through the picnic area twice during the day.
Recommended Equipment: A tripod to photograph the many falls in low light. Swimming gear to take a dip in pools along the way if the weather is warm. Waterproof boots with good tread will be helpful on muddy tracks and for boulder-hopping.
Notes: After heavy rain, creeks and rivers might be too high to walk along. Leave very early as this lengthy walk will require the entire day.
Further Information: See Facts and Figures table for Otway National Park

Walk Description

This excellent day walk in the Angahook–Lorne State Park (21 340ha) is three walks rolled into one. From the Sheoak picnic area, three separate circuits lead to majestic waterfalls set in beautiful rainforest. Other attractions include canyons and caves.

i. The first circuit, to the west, is to Kalimna Falls on Sheoak Creek. There are actually two falls, Upper and Lower Kalimna Falls, and you can return via the Garvey Track.

ii. The second circuit, to the south, is to Sheoak Falls on the lower Sheoak Creek just near the mouth. The approach is via Sheoak Track (a short side trip to Castle Rock is worthwhile in good weather) and return to the picnic area via Sheoak Creek. A deep pool at the base of the falls makes an ideal spot for a break. Also found here is Swallow Cave, where welcome swallows nest in rock crevices each spring.

iii. The third circuit, to the north, is to Wonwondah and Henderson Falls,

The Canyon with its 8m-high walls and exit through a hole, and Fern Gully. Return to the picnic area via Phantom Falls and St George River.

Beauchamp Falls Walk

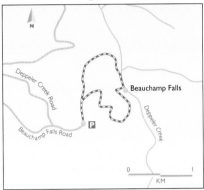

Starting Point: Beauchamp Falls Road, Aire Valley, Otway National Park
Destination: Beauchamp Falls
Summary: A short, steep walk to a beautiful waterfall
Attractions: Lush rainforest
Length: 2.9km
Time: 2 hours
Options: None
Attraction Rating: ★ ★ ★ ★
Fitness: ◪ ◪
Maps: VICMAP Otways and Shipwreck Coast Outdoor Leisure Series 1:50 000 topographicals and Aire Valley 1:25 000 topographical
Access to Starting Point: Aire Valley is best approached from the north via Colac and the Aire Valley road or from the south via Apollo Bay, the Great Ocean Road and Binns Road
Facilities/Amenities: None
Recommended Equipment: A tripod is essential to photograph the falls as the bottom of Deppeler Creek is very dark. Waterproof boots with good tread will be handy on the muddy tracks and for boulder-hopping.
Further Information: See Facts and Figures table for Otway National Park.

Walk Description

The route is fairly straightforward. From the car park, follow the old vehicle track through the pine forest until it becomes a walking track. The superb, lush rainforest vegetation closes in as you walk along the Deppeler Creek before finally descending steeply into the gully to the majestic Beauchamp Falls.

Lush vegetation grows along the banks of the Arve River in the Otway Ranges.

Other walks in the Otway Ranges

Many old logging and forestry trails provide countless opportunities for exploration in the region.

Angahook–Lorne State Park, Cumberland River Reserve Walk (9km, 4 hours)

Begin by heading upstream along the Cumberland River through spectacular cliff scenery to a series of cascades. This section requires some boulder-hopping and should not be attempted if it has been raining heavily. When returning, take the track that turns left from the river about a kilometre below the cascades and follow the ridge to Garvey Track. From there, follow Sheoak Track to Castle Rock. Continue to Sheoak Falls, then to the Great Ocean Road car park and back to the Cumberland Reserve.

Erskine Falls–Lorne Walk (7.5km, 3 hours)

Set up a car shuffle to avoid back-tracking. Start at Erskine Falls car park and follow the track past Straw Falls and Splitter Falls (named after the region's early timber splitters) and continue through the amphitheatre used in the 19th century for church services. Continue on to the bridge over the Erskine River in Lorne.

Central Otways
Hopetoun Falls Walk (1.5km, 1 hour)

From the Aire Valley road, a sign-posted track leads to a magnificent set of falls in the lush Aire Valley.

Mariners Falls Walk (4km, 2 hours)

From the end of the Barham River road, head up the Barham River and then Falls Creek to see these remote and seldom-visited falls.

Triplet Falls Walk (900m, 30 min)

From the car park near Lavers Hill, a good short trail leads to one of the most popular falls in the Otway Ranges. Signs give information.

Cape Otway
Cape Otway–Aire River Walk (11km, 3.5 hours)

From the lighthouse, follow the Great Ocean Walk north-west to the Aire River with fantastic coastal views and near Point Flinders, Rainbow Falls.

Western region
Mahogany Walking Track (22km, 6 hours)

This well-maintained walk links Warrnambool with Port Fairy and features numerous beaches, the odd shipwreck and often whales in winter.

Lower Glenelg River National Park
Lower Glenelg National Park and Discovery Bay Coastal Park

In the far south-west of Victoria are three parks that provide the setting for the 250km Great South-west Walk, first opened in November 1983. Lower Glenelg National Park (27 300ha) contains beautiful forest and the tranquil Glenelg River. The river rises in the Grampians and meanders for some 400km through western Victoria to the ocean at Nelson. A spectacular feature of this park is the limestone gorge that stretches 15km along the lower reaches of the river. In places, the cliffs are up to 50m high. Another important feature is Princess Margaret Rose Cave, noted for its beautiful calcite decorations.

Discovery Bay was named by Lieutenant Grant in 1800 during a voyage along the south-western coast. Discovery Bay Coastal Park (8590ha) takes in a broad range of coastal environments between Nelson and Portland. Attractions include seal colonies, magnificent coastal cliffs, sweeping ocean beaches, massive dune systems, freshwater lakes, blowholes, 'petrified forests' and volcanic features.

Cape Nelson State Park (210ha), the smallest of the three parks, is 11km south-west of Portland. The park was established to protect the rare soap mallee that occurs only here in Victoria. Other features are diverse birdlife, pleasant walking tracks, and the nearby Cape Nelson Lighthouse.

Vegetation

Lower Glenelg National Park has a very impressive array of native plants; some 700 species in all. The heath and fringing forest areas support about 50 species of orchids, while the tributaries at Moleside Creek support the most westerly tree fern gullies in Australia. At least 60 species of plants reach their westernmost occurrence in the park. The bushland is prone to fires, but regeneration from seeds, roots and epicormic buds shows the adaptation of many native species to fire. Discovery Bay features mainly low heath.

Wildlife

The area is rich in wildlife. Eastern grey kangaroos and red-necked wallabies, brushtail possums, koalas and echidnas are commonly seen. In heathy areas, many uncommon small mammals, including the heath rat, swamp antechinus and potoroo, can be found. A small colony of wombats in Lower Glenelg National Park and one or two colonies nearby form the only remnants of a once-widespread population in southwestern Victoria.

The park is also an important habitat for the endangered hooded plover and many other wader-birds migrating from overseas. Take care and watch for eggs when walking above the high tide line, as nests are often found in very exposed sites on the beach, especially between August and February. Take care not to disturb the birds, as they are easily scared away from nesting areas.

Facilities

Camping is permitted at several places along the Glenelg River and at Lake Mombeong and Swan Lake. Fireplaces, toilets and fresh water are available at all sites. All campsites must be booked in advance through the Parks Victoria office at Nelson. Walkers' camps are provided along the Great South-west Walk within a day's walk of each other.

Great South-west Walk

Starting Point: Portland, near Discovery Bay Coastal Park
Destination: Nelson

Summary: A massive circuit through three parks and some private property. The walk starts and finishes at Portland and passes through forests and heathland, along riversides and windswept coastal cliffs and beaches. The complete walk takes about 10 days, but there are a number of short walks leading from it.
Attractions: Magnificent coastal scenery contrasting with the serene Glenelg River
Length: 250km
Time: About 10 days (although extra rest days can be added)
Options: Many entry and exit points
Attraction Rating: ★ ★ ★
Fitness: ⚡⚡⚡
Maps: VICMAP Narrawong, Grant Bay, Chaucer, Cape Bridgewater, Hedditch, Lake Mombeong, Oxbow Lake, Wanwin, Keegan Bend, Wright and Portland 1:25 000 topographicals. A good information booklet is *A Walk on the Wild Side: The Great South-west Walk* by the friends of the Great South-west Walk. This contains all the maps you need and is a lot cheaper than buying all the topographicals.
Access to Starting Point: Portland is just off the Princes Highway in the far south-west about 365km from Melbourne via Geelong and Warrnambool
Facilities/Amenities: About 17 camping areas have been constructed along the route. Shops are at Nelson and a kiosk at Bridgewater Bay.
Recommended Equipment: Standard overnight camping gear, water. The best time is late spring when temperatures are just starting to warm up.
Notes: No permits are required. Some exposure to coastal breezes is possible so walkers may prefer to head inland from Portland in bad weather. Brochures are available covering the major walk and all the optional short walks leading from it.
Further Information:
　　Parks Victoria
　　Nelson VIC 3292
　　Tel:　(08) 8738 4051
or statewide hotline: 131 963

Walk Description

This epic 10-day circuit trek can be walked in either direction, but it is recommended that walkers head north from Portland, walking down the Glenelg River so as to have the wind at their backs when traversing the coast between Nelson and Portland. There are plenty of campsites and these are rarely full.

The most beautiful section is between Post and Rail Camp and Simons Camp on the Glenelg River, where swimming opportunities and fresh water are plentiful. The track is well marked by orange triangles and black emu symbols, even across those sections where access through private property has been secured, so there are generally no navigation problems.

Other walks in Victoria

Local author Tyrone Thomas has most of the state covered in a series of guidebooks focusing on the Alps, the goldfields and the Grampians. His larger *120 Walks in Victoria* outlines other walks on the Mornington Peninsula, the Dandenongs, Mt Macedon, and Mt Eccles. Additional walking areas are:

Baw Baw National Park
Like Lake Mountain, this alpine area is relatively close to Melbourne. A branch of the Australian Alps Walking Track connects it with the Great Dividing Range. Access is from Wahalla.

Kinglake National Park
The best walking is in the west of the park from Mt Sugarloaf to Running Creek and Masons Falls. Tracks range in distance from 500m to 12km.

Tarra-Bulga National Park
Several short day walks in this national park centre on the Strzelecki Ranges. Fern Gully Nature Walk, Lyrebird Ridge Walk and Ash Walk can all be connected to form a circuit from the Bulga Picnic Area and Tarra-Bulga Visitor Centre. Nearby the Tarra Valley Rainforest Walk to Cynthea Falls leaves from the Tarra Valley picnic area on the Tarra Valley road.

Burrowa–Pine Mountain National Park
The 4km (1.5 hour) Bluff Falls Nature Trail connects with Ross Lookout to form a varied excursion in the north-east of Victoria. The park is close to Shelley near the NSW border.

Tasmania

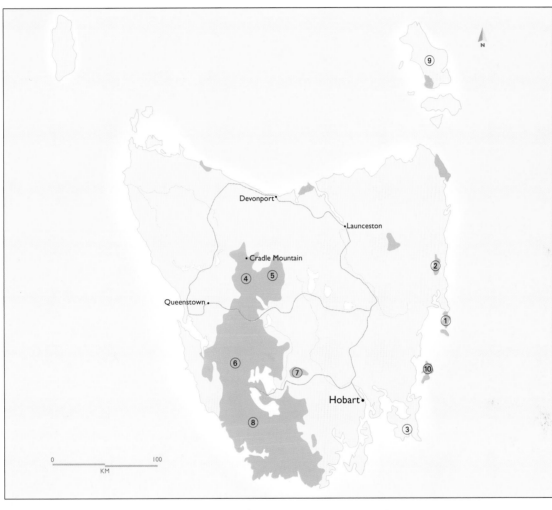

Introduction

Tasmania is Australia's smallest state, with just 68 331 square kilometres and only 455 000 people, equivalent to the population of Newcastle living in an area the size of Ireland. But it contains some of the most aesthetic wilderness areas in the world. The south-west region of the island, together with Fiordland in New Zealand, western Patagonia and Tierra del Fuego in South America, are the three major temperate wilderness areas of the southern hemisphere. If you stand on a peak on the Sentinel Range, which divides Lake Gordon from Lake Pedder, you can see nothing but rugged quartzite mountain ranges in all directions.

Mainland Australians and international visitors alike immediately notice the unique plant and wildlife characteristic of the island, the result of 12 000 years of isolation. In addition, there is a rich colonial history that is proudly promoted by local tourism. Indeed, it sometimes seems that anything more than a few decades old is automatically labelled an historic site and photographed on postcards for sale at the local milkbar.

Tasmania is recognised nationally and internationally as a haven for bushwalkers, regardless of their experience, skill level and aspirations. The natural and cultural landscape provides walkers with a diversity of walking tracks and high-quality recreational experiences within convenient reach of most townships and cities. In particular, the south-west is renowned for possessing some of the wildest terrain in the country and over the past three decades the area has become a mecca for serious bushwalkers. The slogan 'Discover Your Natural State' has been very successful in attracting tourists. In 1996, more than half of all visitors to the state (243 000 people) went walking during their stay. Even the locals walk regularly, which can result in excessive demand on some of the more popular tracks. However, within Tasmania's national parks, there are almost 1000 walking tracks, more than 3100km in total length, in addition to the many tracks managed by local councils, community organisations and other agencies. Despite these constructed tracks, many hardcore walkers prefer to venture into Tasmania's world heritage wilderness, away from the crowds.

Visitors will find roads generally of a high standard throughout Tasmania, as is the level of signposting. All major roads are labelled with a letter prefix signifying importance and grading. An 'A' with one number represents the sealed highways, a 'B' road with two numbers connects the secondary townships, while 'C' roads with three numbers are unsealed with less traffic and often lead to more scenic places. The RACT 1:600 000 Touring Map of Tasmania shows all major roads and the prefix codes.

Climate

In short—cold, wet and windy. The south-west is the second wettest place in Australia after the Queensland tropics, and is notorious for sudden and repeated weather transformations. It is plain to see by the tables presented on the opposite page that January to March are the warmest and driest months. Extended walking tours should be undertaken at this time, when the sky is most stable.

During winter, low-pressure systems cross Tasmania and mix with moist airstreams to produce clouds. In fact, there is so much cloud that the Lake Gordon area averages only two days of sunshine per month. The east coast is the driest

Approaching Cradle Mountain's dolerite summit from the south on the internationally renowned Overland Track.

at all times and the north-east is the only area that is comfortable to tour year-round. Wind is less of a problem because of the mountainous nature of the island, but walkers exploring the Tarkine area and the west coast will be guaranteed a constant strong crosswind that can make camping somewhat unpleasant if exposed sites are chosen. As a rule, walkers should bring plenty of warm clothing and a waterproof jacket, no matter what time of year it is. Be prepared for firewood that is damp and difficult to light. At the same time, watch for fire-danger periods where dry, windy conditions can whip flames into an inferno. The locals have seen this all too often in the past.

A big advantage with Tasmania's southerly latitude is that there are more daylight hours—around the summer solstice in late December, up to 16 hours of daylight.

The following is a summary of precipitation, rain days and temperatures for areas in three of the major parks:

Mean Precipitation (mm)

	Cradle Valley	Lake St Clair	Strathgordon
Jan	150	81	159
Mar	157	85	140
May	284	138	234
Jul	328	164	267
Sep	280	159	273
Nov	212	124	179

Rain Days per Month

	Cradle Valley	Lake St Clair	Strathgordon
Jan	16	14	18
Mar	18	15	17
May	21	21	22
Jul	24	22	24
Sep	22	21	24
Nov	19	19	20

Mean Daily Maximum Temperatures

	Cradle Valley	Lake St Clair	Strathgordon
Jan	17	19	19
Mar	14	16	17
May	8	10	12
Jul	5	7	9
Sep	8	10	11
Nov	13	14	16

Transport

To Tasmania

Getting to Tasmania is expensive, but fortunately there are several options.

1. A typical airfare to Hobart from Australia's east coast currently costs between $200.00 and $500.00 depending on the departure point. Launceston has the only other major airport. Flying is probably the cheapest option, but what you save in fares you will spend on car hire or other transport to get around. Contact Ansett Australia on 131515, or Qantas on 131313, for more details.

2. The slowest and most expensive option, despite a federal government subsidy, is the *Spirit of Tasmania* car and passenger ferry, operating between Port Melbourne and Devonport, taking about 15 hours. The advantages of the ferry are that it travels all year round and offers comfort and stability, which is especially appreciated when travelling on the mountainous seas of Bass Strait. There is also less chance that the *Spirit* will be delayed by storms, although this sometimes happens. Book your car and overnight accommodation ahead. There are special hostel-type accommodations (shared dormitories) for budget-conscious travellers.

3. The *Devilcat*. With its four 3.8-million-watt engines it takes about six hours to get from Port Melbourne to Georgetown, about 50km from Launceston. Cars can be transported, again with a federal government subsidy. The *Devilcat* travels only in peak holiday periods and you must book well in advance. While faster and cheaper, it is susceptible to delays during storms and the journey can be uncomfortable for passengers. Medication is advised for those prone to motion sickness. To minimise sway, move to the central longitudinal axis on the lower deck and lie horizontally on the floor.

Within Tasmania

Although there are 1000km of railway tracks on the island, there are no passenger services. The Tasmanian Wilderness Travel service is ideally suited for domestic and international visitors with no vehicle transport. It provides transport for bushwalkers in major cities, such as Devonport, Launceston and Hobart, to and from the most popular national parks. Many of the staging areas listed in this guide are specific destinations of Tasmanian Wilderness Travel, using their small bus service. Some of the destinations they offer are listed below. For details and information about costs, call 1300 300 520 or (03) 6234 4442.

Spirit of Tasmania: Backpackers' Value Pack

This package deal for backpackers includes return passage on the *Spirit of Tasmania*, complimentary evening buffet and continental breakfast, hostel accommodation for the two nights on the ship, and five days unlimited travel on scheduled services of Tasmanian Wilderness Travel. This package is available to full-time secondary and tertiary students, and YHA, VIP, and Z Card members. For details and bookings, telephone 1800 811 580. Tasmanian Wilderness Travel's Tasmanian Travel Pass offers flexible travel around Tasmania on all its timetabled services.

The following chart lists staging areas where Tasmanian Wilderness Travel drops off and picks up bushwalkers. Keep them in mind when you plan one-way thoroughfares. Examples of this include the Overland Track or the South Coast–Port Davey combination.

Mt Field National Park
to Florentine Concession state forests. Reserves in the Tyenna River valley.

Scotts Peak Dam
to Lake Pedder, Strathgordon, Gordon Dam, Scotts Peak Dam, Mt Anne, The Sentinels.

Dover–Lune River
to Hartz Mountains National Park, Thermal Pool, D'Entrecasteaux Historic Site, the southern state forests, Hastings Caves State Reserve, Esperance River Forest Reserve.

Lake St Clair
to Central Plateau Conservation Area, Franklin River, Lake King William, walking to southern part of Overland Track and The Labyrinth.

Strahan
to West coast, Ocean Beach, Henty Dunes, Queenstown, Huon Pine, rainforest, Gordon River cruises, scenic flights, Zeehan.

Cradle Mountain
to Cradle Valley, Waldheim, Lake Dove, Mt Roland Protected Area, King Solomons Cave State Reserve.

Walls of Jerusalem
to Mersey River, Forth River, Fish River, Lake McKenzie, Lake Parangana, Lake Rowallan, Central Plateau, Cradle Mountain National Park eastern perimeter state forests.

Burnie
to north-west state forests and forest reserves, Arthur River, Arthur Pieman Protected Area, The Nut, Rocky Cape National Park.

Ben Lomond
Only in winter (from 1 July), to north-east state forests and forest reserves, Hollybank, Mt William National Park, Ansons River, Mt Barrow State Reserve, Douglas–Apsley National Park.

Hobart
to Bruny Island, Seven Mile Beach, Tasman Peninsula (Port Arthur), Fortescue Forest Reserve, Maria Island, Freycinet Peninsula.

Launceston
to Asbestos Range National Park and surrounding state forests, Mt Barrow State Reserve, Bell Bay, northern beaches, Cataract Gorge.

Other bus services within Tasmania include:
Tasmanian Redline Coaches
Midland–North-west Coast Route
Hobart–Launceston–Devonport–Burnie–Wynyard–Smithton. Runs seven times a day weekdays, and three times a day weekends, in addition to return service.

East Coast
Hobart–Bicheno–Swansea–St Helens–St Marys–Derby–Launceston. Runs several times a day weekdays, once only night service on weekends. Return service also available.

West Coast
Hobart–Derwent Bridge–Queenstown–Burnie. One service daily Tuesday–Saturday. Return service same schedule. No service Sunday or Monday.

Metro
Various plane operators, such as Par Avion, fly walkers to and from Melaleuca so that walks along the South Coast Track can be done in just one direction.

Accommodation

Youth hostels are popular in Tasmania. Most are in convenient and scenic locations close to the parks. Lune River Youth Hostel, for example, is just around the corner from Hastings Caves, the Thermal Pool and the start of the South Coast Track in the far south-east of Tasmania. Membership is essential, but tariffs are low. Note that several hostels do not have permanent caretakers and you must pick up a key from the head office in Hobart, at:

1st Floor, 28 Criterion St
Hobart TAS 7000
Tel: (03) 6234 9617
Fax: (03) 6234 7422
e-mail: yhatas@yhatas.org.au
Reception hours: weekdays 9.00am–5.00pm

A booklet, *For Backpackers by Backpackers,* giving information on accommodation and travelling for domestic and international visitors, is available from the Hobart YHA.

There are also numerous caravan parks and official camping grounds. For example, the Cradle Mountain Camping Ground is run by P&O, who lease the site from the Parks and Wildlife Service. Naturally, fees apply. However, there is unlimited accommodation at no charge in the many natural campsites and huts in the national parks and state forests. The usual facilities provided are picnic tables and fireplaces. The more popular camping grounds have pit toilets, rubbish pits, shelters, fresh water and firewood or electric/gas BBQs.

Maps

TASMAP produces excellent coverage, very useful for bushwalkers, being accurate, up to date and well presented. Some special national parks maps have comprehensive information on the reverse side. TASMAP is located at the Government Information Building at:

134 Macquarie St
Hobart TAS 7000
To order by mail:
TASMAP
GPO Box 44A, Hobart TAS 7001
Tel: (03) 6233 3382

National Parks

Park passes provide entry to all Tasmania's national parks. For visitors to the state, a 'Holiday Pass' provides entry to all national parks for two months. These are available from:

1. The Tasmanian Parks and Wildlife Service web site at www.parks.tas.gov.au
2. Entry booths to Tasmanian National Parks
3. Tasmanian Travel Information Centres
4. Visitors' Centres
5. Service Tasmania Outlets
6. Aboard the *Spirit of Tasmania.*

To obtain an annual park pass, complete the application form. The money raised from these small park fees goes directly toward the upkeep of parks and reserves. It is used to maintain and upgrade visitor facilities, walking tracks and information booths.

The Acropolis stands over The Labyrinth in the Cradle Mountain–Lake St Clair National Park.

Epic Walks

The Overland Track

This internationally renowned 73km walk passes through outstanding scenery in the Cradle Mountain–Lake St Clair National Park. Although much of the walk is now duckboarded and can be done in three days, it is more common to take five or more days and include some of the many worthwhile side trips.

South Coast–Port Davey Track

This marathon track is a long and gruelling walk. Rain falls incessantly at any time of the year and walkers must also endure cold, howling winds and long sections of muddy button-grass plains. It is also one of the most remote walks, following the wild, desolate south coast of Tasmania. The two tracks run for a total distance of almost 160km and will take about two weeks. Walkers can order fresh supplies to be flown in to Melaleuca.

Penguin–Cradle Track

You can double the distance by walking from the coast straight through to the Overland Track and following this 76km walk south from the north-coast township of Penguin. There are no fuel stove restrictions as the track is outside the boundary of the World Heritage Area.

Tasman Coastal Trail

The spectacular and dramatic Tasman Peninsula is the setting of the Parks and Wildlife Service's most recent construction. The track passes through most of the rugged peninsula, alternating between high dolerite sea cliffs and secluded coves and forests.

The Tasmanian Trail

This is a 477km multi-purpose recreational trail extending from Devonport on the northern coast to Dover in the south. From its conception, it was intended for use by walkers, mountain bikers and horse-riders. The trail links existing forestry roads and fire trails, country roads and occasionally crosses private land. Up to 90 per cent of the trail is on some type of road. It passes through forests and farmlands, across highland plateaus and past the buildings and bridges of some of Australia's oldest towns.

The Tasmanian Trail is used by walkers not catered for in national parks or other reserves. It often passes through small towns, allowing walkers to use as little or as much of the trail as they wish and to take advantage of more up-market accommodation. It offers a variety of experiences for all, from enthusiastic long-distance travellers seeking a challenge to those interested in shorter, more relaxing day excursions. The experience provided by the trail is oriented to recreation, culture, history and nature. It is managed by the Tasmanian Trail Association, a nonprofit, state-wide incorporated body made up of representatives of user groups, landowners and government agencies.

For more information, contact:
Tasmanian Trail Association Inc
PO Box 99
Sandy Bay TAS 7005

The East
Freycinet National Park

The Freycinet Peninsula was originally named 'Vanderlyn Island' by Abel Tasman in 1642; he didn't realise it was part of the mainland. French explorer Thomas Baudin changed the name in 1802 to honour a member of his party. The national park is known for its clear water and white beaches, derived from eroded crystalline granite that dominates the local geology. Swimming conditions at Hazards Beach are ideal: if it weren't for the temperature, you could almost believe you were on the Great Barrier Reef.

Facilities

There are electric BBQs, picnic tables, water and toilets at Honeymoon Bay and Ranger Creek. The park has basic powered and unpowered campsites, none with showers. The Sand Dune and Honeymoon Bay campsites are open only over summer and Easter.

Freycinet Circuit

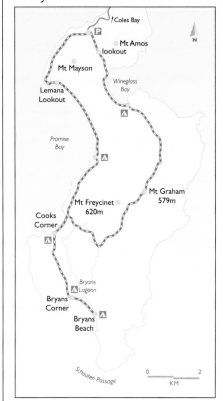

Starting Point: Coles Bay car park (near Parsons Cove), Freycinet National Park

Destination: Bryans Beach
Summary: A full circuit of Freycinet National Park, using the Peninsula Track, takes in all the park's major highlights. No backtracking required.
Attractions: Wineglass Bay, Hazards Beach, Mt Graham, Bryans Lagoon
Length: Total distance is 41.9km
Day 1: Coles Bay to Cooks Beach via Mt Graham, 18.4km
Day 2: Cooks Beach to Bryans Beach (return), 10.2km (day walk)
Day 3: Cooks Beach to Coles Bay via Hazards Beach, 13.3km
Time: 3 days
Options: The circuit can be walked in either direction. Extra rest days can be spent down in the picturesque southern section of the peninsula.
Attraction Rating: ★ ★ ★ ★
Fitness: ◼◼◼
Maps: TASMAP Freycinet National Park 1:50 000 topographical. The Coles Bay, Graham and Schouten 1:25 000 topographical sheets were unpublished as of early 2000.
Access to Starting Point: The Freycinet National Park is about three hours' drive from both Hobart and Launceston. Turn off the Tasman Highway (A3) onto the Coles Bay Road (C302) 12km south of Bicheno. The main park entrance is just after Coles Bay township about 30km from the highway on a good sealed road to the main car park/staging area.
Facilities/Amenities: For overnight walkers there are small campsites at Wineglass Bay, Hazards, Cooks and Bryans beaches. A quaint hut is available for campers at Cooks Beach. Apart from the main summer/Easter period, a self-registration system applies to camping. Booking details can be found on the display board outside the park entry ranger station.
Recommended Equipment: Swimming gear, sunscreen, towel, fuel stove
Notes: The park is a fuel-stove-only area. No campfires are allowed. Water can be scarce at Cooks Beach during long drought periods. Check with the ranger first. Be wary too of spreading dieback through the park.
Further Information:
Parks and Wildlife Service
Park Office, Freycinet National Park
Coles Bay TAS 7215
Tel: (03) 6257 0107

Walk Description

From the main car park, head up the track to Wineglass Bay Lookout. The path is very well signposted and constructed, and follows a gully up to a saddle between Mt Amos and Mt Mayson. From a lookout platform just to the left of the saddle, there are superb views to the south over one of Tasmania's most famous natural icons, Wineglass Bay. You might have to scramble around a little on the rock platforms here to get the best photographic composition.

Head down to the bay and along the beach. Some tame pademelons live here, but please resist the urge to feed them. From the far corner, pass though the camping area and steeply up Quartzite Ridge to cross Graham Creek on the approach to the rocky summit of Mt Graham. There are good views here south to Maria Island.

Descend to a saddle below Mt Freycinet, follow the contour around the steep eastern face of the mountain and turn west to Cooks Beach. You can either camp near the stone hut here or by the beach. Spend the next day without the overnight packs, walking 5km farther south to Bryans Beach to see Schouten Island and Bryans Lagoon. You would be unlucky indeed to find other people here.

Spend the last day returning to the car park. Follow the Peninsula Track north from Cooks Beach all the way along the western coast. From the north of Hazards Beach, head up onto the Hazards Beach Track, which contours around the base of Mt Mayson. There are some reasonable views here, one over Promise Bay, and several good vantage points that allow you to look over the boulder-strewn north-west slope of Mt Mayson.

Other walks in Freycinet National Park
Mt Amos Walk (3.5km, 2 hours)
Mt Amos (440m) is part of the range of granite mountains, known as 'the Hazards' that overlook Coles Bay. The track to the summit is steep and strenuous, but walkers are rewarded with some great panoramic views, especially of Wineglass Bay. Note that this walk is not recommended for the

The tranquil Wineglass Bay viewed from the lookout platform constructed in the saddle between Mt Mayson and Mt Amos, Freycinet National Park.

Douglas–Apsley National Park

This is one of Tasmania's less well-known national parks and it is not included in the famous World Heritage Area designation of the other larger more famous parks. It is not true wilderness as it is interlaced with mining tracks. Coal was extracted here for more than 100 years. Farmers and trappers also used parts of the area for much of that time, but loggers had only limited access because of the rugged terrain. Trappers used fire to bring on new growth and attract animals. This type of land-use favoured the drier eucalypt forest which can recover from all but the hottest fires, and is now typical of the area.

As a result of its mining history, Douglas–Apsley has one of the few dry sclerophyll forests in Tasmania. It is also the largest. Although superficially like other eucalypt forests of the south-east mainland, the Douglas-Apsley National Park shelters a considerable array of endemic vegetation and wildlife.

Leeaberra Track Walk

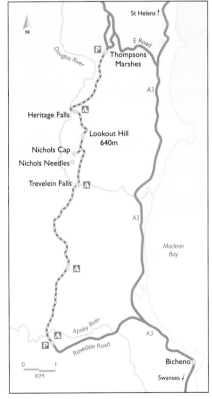

Starting Point: Thompsons Marshes, Douglas–Apsley National Park

elderly or young children. The track leaves from Parsons Cove car park.

Wineglass Bay–Hazards Beach Circuit (11km, 4.5 hours)

The Isthmus Track connects Wineglass Bay with Hazards Beach in an eventful but time-consuming circuit. From the car park, head up to Wineglass Bay Lookout and then down to the lovely white quartzite beach for a swim. To get to Hazards Beach, turn west at the far north of Wineglass Bay where the track starts to ascend. The junction is well signposted. After half an hour of relatively flat walking, you reach Hazards Beach, approaching through some sand dunes. Turn right and follow the beach to its northern end. Here you join up with another track that follows the coastline for about 5.5km farther around the rocky base of Mt Mayson before reaching the car park.

Destination: Apsley River
Summary: A fascinating and varied walk that traverses the park from north to south. A car shuffle is needed.
Attractions: Nichols Needles, Heritage Falls, Douglas River, Apsley Waterhole
Length: Total distance is 25km
Day 1: Thompsons Marshes to the Douglas River, 13km
Day 2: Douglas River to Apsley River, 12km
Time: 2–3 days
Options: A side trip to Leeaberra Falls is recommended. There are alternative campsites at Heritage Falls and Denison Rivulet.
Attraction Rating: ★ ★ ★
Fitness: ◪ ◪ ◪
Maps: TASMAP Douglas-Apsley Map and Notes 1:50 000 topographical
Access to Starting Point: Thompsons Marshes is best accessed via the forestry 'E' road, west off the Tasman Highway about 24km north of Bicheno, near the Chain of Lagoons. Follow the 'E' road for 4.5km to a left-hand turn-off clearly marked 'Douglas–Apsley National Park'. The road becomes steeper and rougher, and a 4WD or high-clearance vehicle may be required for the last 2km. You reach locked gates near the Thompsons Marshes car park. To reach the Apsley Waterhole at the southern end of the park, take Rosedale Road off the Tasman Highway (A3) about 3km north of Bicheno. Follow Rosedale Road for 7km to the car park.
Facilities/Amenities: None en route
Recommended Equipment: Water containers—not much water is encountered on the second day
Notes: No permits are needed. This is one of the few parks in Tasmania where campfires are permitted.
Further Information: A brochure called *The Leeaberra Track* is available from the Parks and Wildlife Service. There are basic track notes on the back of the park map.
Bicheno Park Office
Tel: (03) 6375 1236

Walk Description

From the car park and gate, head south, following the orange track markers through the upper Douglas River valley to the campsite on the Douglas River. Leave the overnight packs and follow the riverbank down to Heritage Falls. The terrain is pretty wild here, but you can scramble down to see the top of Leeaberra Falls.

Retrace your steps to the campsite, collect the packs and head up to Lookout Hill with its distant coastal views. The next stop is Nichols Cap with views over the awesome dolerite spires of Nichols Needles. Camp on the Douglas River to the south, preferably on the far bank.

Next day, the walking is easier. Continue south up to a saddle to meet an old road before crossing the Denison Rivulet. This last section through the marshes drags on for hours, but you will be rewarded with a wonderful swim at Apsley Waterhole.

Other walks in Douglas–Apsley National Park
Thompsons Marshes region
Heritage Falls/Rainforest Circuit (16km, 8 hours)

This walk combines the Rainforest Shelf Track and high coastal ridges with the northern section of the Leeaberra Track, making a long and fascinating day walk. Follow the orange markers to the Heritage Falls campsite and explore the falls downstream. From the campsite follow the orange markers steeply up to the Lookout Hill track junction. Check out the lookout before heading back down and east to follow signs and yellow markers down to the Rainforest Shelf that traverses dense wet sclerophyll forest to the north. Return to Thompsons Marshes on the Leeaberra Track.

Apsley Waterhole region
Lookout Track (300m, 10 min)

A short stroll from the Apsley Waterhole car park through open forest to the lookout platform above the Apsley Waterhole. There are good views both up and down stream. Return the same way or descend steeply to the waterhole via the campground.

Apsley Gorge Circuit (7.5km, 3 hours)

Walkers will enjoy the tranquil pools in spectacular Apsley Gorge. From the waterhole cross to the northern bank of the Apsley River and ascend the ridge track. Follow the yellow markers for about an hour north and then west. The track descends to the river near the gorge, where sheer dolerite cliffs line both sides of the river. Scramble down to the gorge, then follow the river downstream for about 10 minutes until the valley opens up. A rough track leads back to the waterhole via the bank. It is sometimes necessary to scramble up and down slopes to avoid rock outcrops.

Western region

Access is via the restricted-access 'MG logging road'. From St Marys, travel east toward Elephant Pass on the Tasman Highway for 4km. Turn south onto the gravelled MG road (not signposted). Continue south for about 30km to the Apsley–Myrtle Forest car park. You can also reach the 'MG' road via Old Coach Road at Cranbrook, or via the 'O' road at Cherry Tree Hill from the Tasman Highway. (Beware of logging trucks on these roads.) From here you can do the half-hour Apsley–Myrtle Rainforest Walk to follow Myrtle Creek through dense rainforest. Retrace your steps to the car park via the same route.

Tasman National Park

The Tasman Peninsula has a staggering variety of attractions, from the historic convict ruins of Port Arthur, to numerous coastal formations, such as the Tessellated Pavement and Tasman Arch.

Much of the natural scenery has recently been declared as part of Tasmania's newest national park, called Tasman. It protects the sea cliffs, eucalypt forests and a lot of wildlife kept relatively separate from the rest of Tasmania by the narrowness of Eaglehawk Neck, which connects the peninsula to the rest of Tasmania. The peninsula is in the far south-east of the state. Besides the Tasman Peninsula National Park, there are a number of other reserves worth visiting near here, such as Lime Bay.

Surrounding the peninsula is a rich marine environment. The Australian fur seal has hauling grounds at Cape Hauy, Hippolyte Rocks, Cape Pillar and Cape Raoul. Leopard and elephant seals have been observed in the waters and rocks off the park. Other common marine animals include cetaceans, such as the common and bottle-nosed dolphins and several species of whales (the pilot, southern right and humpback).

The national park is a mecca, not only for tourists and walkers, but marine enthusiasts and rock climbers too. Sea-kayakers take to the open ocean to explore the secluded coves between rocky ramparts, while climbers flock to the precipitous dolerite sea cliffs which line the Tasman Peninsula. Perhaps the two most famous landmarks in the park are the Candlestick and the Totem Pole, which are both located at the tip of Cape Hauy (see the Tasman Trail walk presented, right).

These two picture-postcard features are thin towering spires that provide superb hard-core freestyle sportsclimbing above a raging sea, in the most dramatic of settings. Posters of the Totem Pole adorn the walls of outdoor stores all over the country.

Tasman Trail Walk

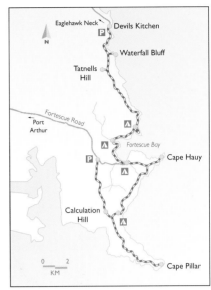

Starting Point: Devils Kitchen, Tasman National Park

Destination: Fortescue Road

Summary: An epic coastal walk passing dramatic dolerite cliffs with spectacular sculpting. Set up a car shuffle to avoid backtracking.

Attractions: The Totem Pole, The Candlestick, The Blade, waterfalls, sea cliffs, views from dozens of lookouts

Length: Total distance is 50.8km

Day 1: Devils Kitchen to Bivouac Bay, 12.6km

Day 2: Bivouac Bay to Lunchtime Creek via Cape Hauy, 18.8km

Day 3: Lunchtime Creek to Fortescue Road via Cape Pillar, 19.4km

Time: 3–4 days

Options: For a shorter trip, just walk from Waterfall Bay to Fortescue Bay, or do the southern Cape Hauy–Cape Pillar section. Along the way are various small side trips, such as to Waterfall Bluff and Tatnells Hill.

Attraction Rating: ★ ★ ★ ★

Fitness: ◪ ◪ ◪

Maps: TASMAP Taranna, Hippolyte, and Tasman 1:25 000 topographicals

Access to Starting Point: Tasman Peninsula National Park is on the Tasman Peninsula in south-eastern Tasmania. From Hobart, take the A3 to Sorell and then the Arthur Highway (A9) to Port Arthur. The park has several main access roads. The northern staging area can be accessed via the Blowhole Road (C338) turn-off just after Eaglehawk Neck. This leads to Tasman Arch and Devils Kitchen.

The dramatic top of The Candlestick, a tall dolerite spire, as seen from the end of Cape Hauy in the Tasman National Park—a popular rock-climbing site.

To access the southern staging area, continue along the A9 toward Port Arthur. Access to the Cape Pillar walking track is along Fortescue Road, a 12km gravel road.

Facilities/Amenities: Well-developed camping facilities at Fortescue Bay (fees apply). Bush-camping sites at Waterfall Bay, Bivouac Bay, Canoe Bay, Retakunna Creek and Lunchtime Creek. Some have pit toilets.

Recommended Equipment: water containers, Windproof jacket, overnight camping equipment

Notes: High winds can make sections of the track dangerous, especially close to the very high sea cliff edges

Further Information:

Tasman National Park Office
RA 5801, Arthur Highway
Taranna TAS 7180
Tel: (03) 6250 3497

or

South-East District Office
293 Surf Rd
Seven Mile Beach TAS 7170
Tel: (03) 6248 4053

Walk Description

There are attractions around every corner on this scenic coastal walk as you encounter wild coastal formations of the most spectacular kind. Despite the coast being wild and rugged, you are never far from civilisation and, in fact, you pass through the car-camping ground of Fortescue Bay along the way. Before starting the walk, leave a car parked at either end.

Leave the tourists behind at Tasman Arch and the Devils Kitchen and follow the Tasman Walking Track south to Waterfall Bay with its turquoise waters that really stand out when direct sun is on them. There's an out-of-the-way picnic ground with footpads around the clifftops to various vantage points.

A steep climb up past a series of waterfalls and cascades takes you to Clemes Peak and Tatnells Hill, which is the second-highest peak on the peninsula after Mt MacGregor. There are really good views here over the ocean and along the coast. Continue south, descending to Bivouac Bay for the first night's camp. There are numerous lookouts along here as you parallel the coast.

On the second day, keep following the coast as it heads west around Fortescue Bay. Until the early 1970s, Canoe Bay was the site of a fish-processing works and there is an old steel boat wreck there. From the main car-camping ground, a good-quality walking track heads out along a ridge through dry eucalypt forest to Cape Hauy. Cross a distinct saddle as you approach the end of the peninsula. The vegetation gets more wind-pruned as you near the end. Unfortunately the famous pillars of The Candlestick and the dramatic Totem Pole are difficult to see—the land is very steep and the rock is loose. You literally have to lie down and peer over the edge.

If you look closely at the 120m-high Candlestick, you'll notice climbing bolts in the stone. The two columns are popular sports-climbing destinations and have appeared on many posters, calendars and magazine front covers. Ideally, the two columns are seen and photographed from sea level, and there are few better places to sea-kayak than around the Tasman Peninsula.

Backtrack along Cape Hauy and left at the signposted junction to Mt Fortescue. As you once again walk along the top of cliffs approaching the 480m summit of Mt Fortescue, there are dramatic vistas across Munro Bight and directly below to pinnacles jutting out of the ocean. Descend the southern slope of Mt Fortescue, crossing Retakunna Creek, a possible campsite if you are running out of daylight hours. There is another waterfall downstream from here and a side option to another vantage point on the southern side of the creek.

Head up to Tornado Ridge and left along to Cape Pillar, camping at Lunchtime Creek for the second night. If time is available you can also continue south to camp by Perdition Ponds. Note that the water here can sometimes be slightly brackish or salty, depending on recent weather. Leave early next day, without the packs, and walk out to the end of Cape Pillar, almost 300m above the rough ocean. Be extremely wary of high winds when near the cliff edges. From Trident Bluff there are great views south to Tasman Island and its lighthouse. The dolerite formations of

The Blade and The Chasm make great photographic subjects.

Return for the packs and walk north to Fortescue Road via Calculation and Snake hills. This last section is a bit of a trudge through uninteresting forest. When more heritage funding is granted, the Tasman Walking Track will be upgraded and re-routed to take in even more highlights.

Other walks on the Tasman Peninsula

Cape Raoul Walk (14km, 5 hours)
This is another awe-inspiring cliff-lined peninsula at the far south of the Tasman Peninsula. A walking track begins at Stormlea Road, off Highcroft Road. The first section traverses private land before entering Tasman Peninsula National Park. There are excellent views from the trig point near the gulch at the end of the cape. Once again, dolerite cliffs dominate the foreground as you look across to Cape Pillar and Tasman Island.

The Cradle Mountain Region

Cradle Mountain–Lake St Clair National Park

One of the most famous reserves in Australia, this world heritage park covers a cross-section of Tasmania's best mountain scenery with countless lakes, tarns, rocky spires and pinnacles. The vegetation is equally impressive, with huon pines, pencil pines and King Billy pines contrasting with alpine moorlands. The park contains the state's highest mountain, Mt Ossa (1614m), and the famous 80km-long Overland Track.

Track guides are available from the two visitors' centres. Walkers will need sturdy waterproof footwear as many of the tracks are waterlogged. Note that the entire World Heritage Area has been declared a fuel-stove-only area and no campfires are permitted in the park. The northern region is centred on Cradle Mountain and the southern region on Lake St Clair. The centre can only be accessed by walkers prepared to carry overnight packs.

Facts and Figures

Name: Cradle Mountain–Lake St Clair National Park

Size: 161 000ha

Enactment:
Scenic Reserve, 1922
National Park, 1947
World Heritage, 1982

Vegetation: Antarctic beech, King Billy pine, huon pine, pencil pines, celery-top pine

Wildlife: at least 20 species of mammals, including pademelons, Bennetts wallaby, potoroos, possums and tiger cats

Attractions: Waldheim, Barn Bluff, Cradle Mountain, Overland Track

Facilities: P&O camping ground north of Cradle Lodge, numerous huts along the Overland Track

Further Information:
Cradle Mountain Park Office
Tel: (03) 6492 1133
Fax: (03) 6492 1120
Lake St Clair Park Office
Tel: (03) 6289 1172

Cradle Mountain

The distinctive dolerite summit of Cradle Mountain is seen on countless postcards, calendars and other tourist souvenirs. The main car park near Lake Dove in the north is the staging area for dozens of short and long day walks, including the classic Overland Track. There is accommodation for all budgets: rooms or cabins at Cradle Mountain Lodge or tent sites at the commercial campground to the north.

Gustav Weindorfer and Waldheim

Unique Waldheim, near Lake Dove, is a reconstruction of the picturesque Tyrolean hut built by Gustav Weindorfer. Born 23 February 1874, in Spittal, Austria, Gustav devoted his life to the preservation of Cradle Mountain. Educated as a botanist, he was fascinated with the mountain scenery, which reminded him of the Corinthian Alps. He first saw Cradle Mountain while camping on Mt Roland during his honeymoon in 1905, but he didn't visit Cradle Valley itself until a break in farming duties allowed him to undertake a walking expedition with his friend Charlie Sutton in 1909. On a later expedition, they climbed the summit with several more friends and the legendary vision was born.

Having witnessed the opening of the Mt Buffalo National Park in Victoria, he adopted a similar campaign strategy. The first step was to build an alpine chalet and petition the government for a road. They chose a site for the proposed chalet, to be called Waldheim (forest home), and purchased 600 acres of land classified as third-class Crown Land—today it's a World Heritage Area. Construction began in March 1912, using the slow-growing King Billy pine nearby. Most of the work was carried out by Weindorfer himself and by the end of the year the first visitors where arriving.

He commuted from Cradle Mountain to his farm in Roland Lea by bicycle on very rough roads. Improvements

The camping area by the Scott Kilvert Memorial Hut near Lake Rodway in the Cradle Mountain-Lake St Clair National Park.

were made to the area: a bathhouse, a chapel, an animal pen and further accommodation. Despite trouble with locals when Austria was fighting on the other side during World War I and the death of his wife, Weindorfer continued to promote Cradle Mountain throughout Australia and succeeded in establishing the northern part (64,000ha) as a national park in 1922. Improvements to the access road, transport and the blazing of walking trails led to hundreds of people enjoying the wilderness. Weindorfer named many of the local items after family, friends and visitors.

Waldheim was destroyed by the National Parks and Wildlife Service in 1976 but protests from all around Australia led to a hasty apology and reconstruction. Today the replica is a museum where you can learn about life in the 1920s' heyday of Cradle Valley. Weindorfer died in 1932 and is buried just outside the hut. A monument to him was erected in 1938. There is a short nature track where you can see the grand King Billy pines.

A small creek cascades into the wild Fury Gorge along the Overland Track, in the Cradle Mountain-Lake St Clair National Park.

The Overland Track

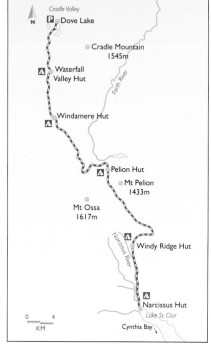

Starting Point: Dove Lake car park, Cradle Mountain–Lake St Clair National Park
Destination: Lake St Clair
Summary: An outstanding overnight walk, with wonderful varied scenery and a number of side trip options
Attractions: Many lookouts, enchanting forests, waterfalls, rivers, lakes and mountain summits. The quality of the constructed track is also a feature.
Length: 77–120km, depending on side options
Time: 4–6 days
Options: Numerous side trips form memorable highlights on the Overland Track. The best are to the summits of Barn Bluff, the Pelions, and Mt Ossa. A two-day excursion into Pine Valley to see The Labyrinth and/or The Acropolis is also very worthwhile. You can also do the Overland Track from south to north, but there are some disadvantages: (1) in this direction it is mostly uphill, and (2) you would be traversing the mountainous northern terrain at the end with no weather forecast available to you. It's safer to be in the protected Narcissus River valley if the weather deteriorates.
Attraction Rating: ★ ★ ★ ★ ★
Fitness: ☒☒☒☒
Maps: TASMAP Cradle, Will, Achilles, Cathedral, Du Cane, Olympus, Rufus 1:25 000 topographicals. An excellent overview of the entire route is given by the Cradle Mountain–Lake St Clair Map & Notes 1:100 000 topographical.
Access to Starting Point: Approach Cradle Valley from Launceston via Deloraine and Cethana using C132. From Devonport, head south-west to Forth, then to Wilmot. The turn-offs are well signposted. The roads are sealed but winding.
Facilities/Amenities: Several huts provide good shelter in blizzard conditions but don't rely on them as they are invariably crowded at peak times. They are Kitchen Hut, Waterfall Valley Hut, Windermere Hut, Old Pelion Hut, Pelion Hut, Kia Ora Hut, Du Cane Hut, Windy Ridge Hut, Pine Valley Hut (off the Overland Track), Narcissus Hut and Echo Point Hut.
Recommended Equipment: Many casual or first-time bushwalkers come ill-prepared for this track. The weather is very wet at any time of the year and a Gore-Tex jacket and over-trousers are highly recommended. It can even snow in summer. A good quality waterproof tent and ground-sheet are essential. A water-resistant sleeping bag liner is also handy. Chances are that you will encounter rain on at least a few days.
Notes: An entrance fee is payable and you must organise transport at both ends. Contact Tasmanian Wilderness Travel. In peak summer holidays, walkers intending to use the ferry across Cynthia Bay must book, tel: (03) 6289 1137. The cost is currently about $20.00 per person. Please note

the entire World Heritage Area is a fuel-stove-only area so no campfires are allowed. Even the use of coal-fed pot-belly stoves in the huts is discouraged, except in emergencies. Register at the station before setting out.

Further Information: If you are using the Tasmanian Wilderness Transport (TWT) service, allow about $70.00 for the return trip from Lake St Clair. In addition, walkers can opt to use the ferry across Lake St Clair for about $20.00. Two guidebooks give detailed tracknotes: *100 Walks in Tasmania* (5th Edition) by Tyrone Thomas, and *Cradle Mountain–Lake St Clair & Walls of Jerusalem National Parks* by John Siseman and John Chapman.

Cradle Mountain Park Office
Tel: (03) 6492 1133
Fax: (03) 6492 1120

Walk Description

Many backpackers come from Europe, New Zealand and the USA to experience the Overland Track. The route has been described in many published sources as well as in Tasmanian Parks and Wildlife Service brochures, but the signposting and track construction are so good that guidebooks and maps are not essential (although handy for the lesser-known side options and to plan each day's destination).

The official start of the track is at Waldheim, but it is recommended to begin at Dove Lake to allow more time in the particularly scenic Cradle Mountain area. Several variations are

possible in the opening section. For example, if you are fit and ambitious, walk around the eastern side of Dove Lake, over Hansons Peak and past the beautiful Artists Pool to join the Overland Track south of Cradle Mountain.

A more direct route is up Marions Lookout or through the Ballroom Forest. Possible side trips for the first day include an ascent of Cradle Mountain or Barn Bluff. Both involve some rock-scrambling but there is no real exposure or technical difficulty. Walkers should aim for Waterfall Valley Hut on the first night as no camping is allowed in the vicinity of Cradle Mountain.

Spend the second and third days walking south to Pelion Hut and Windy Ridge Hut with side trips to Lake Will and at least one of the Pelion summits. Packs can normally be dumped safely at various junctions for these side trips.

The numerous waterfalls in the upper Mersey River valley will please photographers. If the weather is stable, consider a side trip to Pine Valley where you can climb up to the fascinating Labyrinth alpine plateau. Glaciers have carved out hundreds of tiny tarns that look superb framed by pines with the mighty spire of Mt Geryon (1509m) in the distance.

The last day is easy walking down the Narcissus River valley to a jetty at the northern end of Lake St Clair. From here a ferry service takes you to Cynthia Bay. Alternatively, continue

walking south along the western shore. A campsite at Echo Point Hut is available if you are running out of time. At Cynthia Bay there's a bistro and a camping ground with showers.

Cradle Mountain Summit Walk

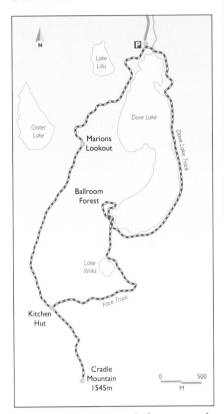

Starting Point: Dove Lake car park, Cradle Mountain–Lake St Clair National Park
Destination: The summit of Cradle Mountain (1545m)
Summary: A circuit of Dove Lake with an easy but steep climb to the summit of Cradle Mountain
Attractions: Great views over the northern Cradle Mountain–Lake St Clair National Park. Barn Bluff dominates the south while Black Bluff is clearly visible in the north.
Length: 13.6km
Time: 1 day
Options: Several approaches to the summit can be taken from Waldheim or Dove Lake, the most popular being the direct and shorter approach via Marions Lookout. Hansons Peak and Crater Peak are longer approaches.
Attraction Rating: ★★★
Fitness: ☒☒☒
Maps: TASMAP Cradle Mountain Day

The breath-taking summit of Cradle Mountain in north-eastern Tasmania.

Looking to the summit of Barn Bluff from the western flank of Cradle Mountain on the Overland Track, Cradle Mountain-Lake St Clair National Park.

Walk Map 1:20 000 topographical

Access to Starting Point: As for the Overland Track, page 234

Facilities/Amenities: Kitchen Hut has emergency shelter only

Recommended Equipment: Warm, windproof and waterproof clothing

Notes: Don't do this walk if the weather is deteriorating; the dolerite will be slippery and there will be no visibility from the summit.

Further Information:

Cradle Mountain Park Office

Tel: (03) 6492 1133

Fax: (03) 6492 1120

Walk Description

For an interesting and unusual approach to the summit, head left from Dove Lake car park walking along the eastern shore of the lake all the way to the Ballroom Forest. The track is flat and well graded. The track deteriorates at the turn-off to the Ballroom Forest and gets a little muddy as you ascend to Lake Wilks and the narrow Face Track. Turn right toward Kitchen Hut and take an obvious white gravelled track up the western spur of Cradle Mountain. Considerable height must be gained before the track levels out, passing through the top cliffs to the trig. Some boulder-hopping and scrambling will be necessary here. Snowdrifts are not uncommon on the southern face of Cradle Mountain, even in summer. The views to the south, where the terrain is most mountainous, are the best. The highest mountains in the state, Mt Ossa and the Pelons, can be seen on a clear day. To return to Dove Lake backtrack down to Kitchen Hut and walk across the exposed Cradle Plateau to Marions Lookout, then descend to Dove Lake (934m).

Cradle Mountain Circuit

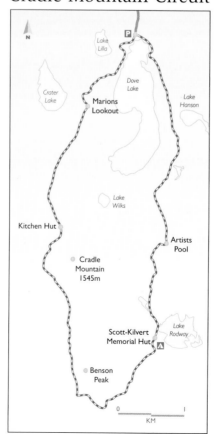

Starting Point: Dove Lake car park, Cradle Mountain-Lake St Clair National Park

Destination: Lake Rodway

Summary: A walk around Cradle Mountain via Hansons Peak, the Artists Pool and Marions Lookout

Attractions: Views from Hansons Peak and Marions Lookout, the Artists Pool surrounded by huon pines with Cradle Mountain in the background

Length: 16.8km

Time: 1 long day

Options: An overnight walk option can incorporate an ascent of Barn Bluff (1559m)

Attraction Rating: ★★★★

Fitness: ◪◪◪

Maps: TASMAP Cradle Mountain Day Walk Map 1:20 000 topographical

Access to Starting Point: As for the Overland Track, page 234

Facilities/Amenities: Scott-Kilvert Memorial Hut and Kitchen Hut on Cradle Plateau at Lake Rodway can provide emergency shelter

Recommended Equipment: Warm, windproof and waterproof clothing, camera—the Artists Pool is particularly photogenic

Notes: Snow can fall any time of year and winds can be fierce on the more exposed plateaus

Further Information:

Cradle Mountain Park Office

Tel: (03) 6492 1133

Fax: (03) 6492 1120

Walk Description

Most visitors to Cradle Valley walk around Dove Lake or between Waldheim and Cradle Mountain, but you can also do an interesting day walk behind Cradle Mountain that is a circuit of the entire area. Leave early as there is a long way to cover and walking can be slow in sections.

From Dove Lake head left on the Dove Lake Circuit and left again on the Lake Rodway Track. This ascends to rocky Hansons Peak and down to the Twisted Lakes, framed by huon pines. From here the track swings to the south-west. You will soon encounter a junction below Little Horn, with an adjacent rickety shelter. Head left (south) along a wet section contouring around Little Horn to the Artists Pool—one of the exquisite lakes in the area and in winter the scene can look very European. Continue south, descending gradually to Lake Rodway (919m).

The track then enters a forested section as you climb up to a prominent ridge below Benson Peak. Almost 300m altitude must be gained. From the open ridge, there are great views to Barn Bluff, although it can be extremely windy. Here you meet the Overland Track. Head right (north) contouring around the western flank of Cradle Mountain. There are some exceptional views over Fury Gorge.

You will probably meet overnight walkers embarking on the Overland Track along here. Turn right just after Kitchen Hut and cross over a bare alpine plateau to Marions Lookout before descending to Lake Dove again, a tiring section after a long day's walk.

Barn Bluff Walk

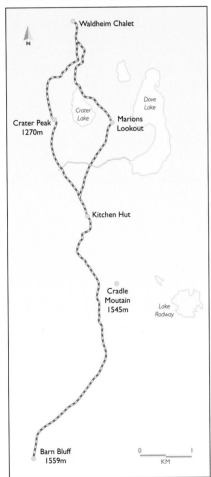

Starting Point: Waldheim Valley in the Cradle Mountain–Lake St Clair National Park
Destination: Barn Bluff (1559m)

Summary: A direct approach to Barn Bluff using the Overland Track, and returning via the Horse Track. The recommended overnight campsite is at Waterfall Valley.
Attractions: Views from the summit of Barn Bluff and Marions Lookout
Length: 13.5km each way, 27km circuit
Time: 2 days
Options: The walk can also be done by fit people in one long day from Dove Lake car park via Marions Lookout but no variation in the return is possible
Attraction Rating: ★ ★ ★
Fitness: ☒ ☒ ☒ ☒
Maps: TASMAP Cradle Mountain Day Walk Map 1:25 000 topographical
Access to Starting Point: Waldheim is just off the main Cradle Mountain Road at Cradle Valley between the visitors' centre and Dove Lake. It is the official start of the Overland Track.
Facilities/Amenities: Waterfall Valley Hut and Kitchen Hut provide emergency shelter
Recommended Equipment: As for Overland Track, page 234
Notes: No camping is allowed in the vicinity of Cradle Mountain
Further Information:
Cradle Mountain Park Office
Tel: (03) 6492 1133
Fax: (03) 6492 1120

Walk Description

Barn Bluff, in the north of Cradle Mountain–Lake St Clair National Park, is a very prominent dolerite knoll shaped like a volcanic plug. It is one of the highest peaks in northern Tasmania and from its open summit, 360-degree views are possible over most of north-east Tasmania. It is a popular side trip for walkers doing the Overland Track, but it also provides an interesting destination in its own right for people visiting the Cradle Valley area. The walk can be done as a day walk by fit people, but it is described here as an overnight walk to allow for a different route back to the walk start, to avoid some unecessary backtracking.

Start the walk by heading south along the Overland Track and going left (east) to Crater Falls and Crater Lake before climbing up to Marions Lookout (1223m). Head south-west

across the open plateau to Kitchen Hut and south along the western flank of Cradle Mountain. There are some great views over Fury Gorge from here. Camp at Waterfall Valley. If there is enough time (about 2–3 hours) to climb Barn Bluff, drop the packs at the junction. Some rock-scrambling is necessary to attain the summit, where dramatic southern views can be obtained. If there is no time on the first day, climb the peak in the morning. When returning to Waldheim, head left after passing Kitchen Hut. This is the Horse Track that passes over Crater Peak, providing an alternative route back.

Reynolds Falls Walk

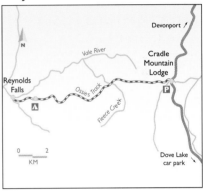

Starting Point: Cradle Mountain Lodge, Cradle Mountain–Lake St Clair National Park
Destination: Reynolds Falls via Ossies Track
Summary: A remote track outside the north-western park boundary that accesses an exquisite waterfall
Attractions: Reynolds Falls on the Vale River
Length: 24.4km (12.2km each way)
Time: 2 full days
Options: None
Attraction Rating: ★ ★ ★ ★
Fitness: ☒ ☒ ☒ ☒
Maps: TASMAP Cradle Mountain–Lake St Clair Map and Notes 1:100 000 topographical and the Pencil Pine 1:25 000 topographical
Access to Starting Point: Cradle Mountain Lodge is just outside the Cradle Mountain–Lake St Clair National Park entrance, close to the ranger station and visitors' centre. It's about 75km from Devonport, the last section being along alpine moorland using the C132 road.

Facilities/Amenities: A well-developed fully serviced campground to the north of Cradle Mountain Lodge. Up-market guesthouse accommodation is available at the Lodge, together with a restaurant and bistro. No facilities or huts at all along the route.

Recommended Equipment: Standard overnight camping equipment for complete self-sufficiency as well as waterproof clothing. Walking boots with good tread are recommended for the slippery rocks. The track traverses the poorly drained Speeler Plains so waterproof boots will be appreciated too. A tripod will be needed to capture the dark falls on film.

Notes: Several confusing logging roads to the west make navigating onto Ossies Track difficult

Further Information:

Cradle Mountain Park Office
Tel: (03) 6492 1133
Fax: (03) 6492 1120

Walk Description

From the lodge, head due west for 2.5km across Speeler Plains to a vehicular track. To the right lies the Cradle Mountain campground and the aerodrome, while straight head, the walking track continues all the way to Penguin via Black Bluff. You should head left (south-west) along the road to Fleece Creek and Pandani Creek, where it becomes a walking track. Continue west as it descends into and out of the Tumbling Creek valley. Fording can be difficult after recent rains. Campsites can be found closer to the Vale River. There is no problem with water at any time of the year. If you have time after setting up camp, head west down into a steep gully and into the Vale River valley. Reynolds Falls are just upstream, pouring out of a U-shaped gully in the cliffs. Return via the same route.

Lake St Clair

Discovered in 1826 by Jorgen Jorgensen, and named by Surveyor-General George Frankland in 1835 after the St Clair family of Loch Lomond, Lake St Clair (737m) is the source of the Derwent River. It was gouged out of a very deep crevice in the mountain-lined Narcissus River valley by a glacier. At 161m deep, it is Australia's deepest lake. Its Aboriginal name is Leeawuleena, meaning 'the sleeping water'. Mt Olympus (1430m) dominates the 17km western shore while the dramatic Du Cane Range presides over the area to the north.

Walks from Cynthia Bay are significantly longer and more difficult than around Cradle Mountain, so are less popular with day visitors. The terrain to the west and north of Lake St Clair is some of the most spectacular in all of the national park.

The Labyrinth with The Acropolis and Mt Geryon in the background, Cradle Mountain-Lake St Clair National Park.

The Acropolis and The Labyrinth Walk

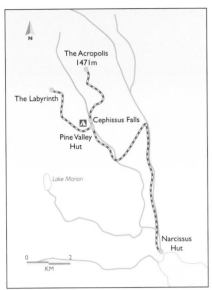

Starting Point: Narcissus Hut (on the shore of Narcissus Bay), Cradle Mountain–Lake St Clair National Park

Destination: The Acropolis (1471m) and The Labyrinth, via Pine Valley

Summary: Despite the exceptional nature of the scenery, this is a relatively easy walk. Two of the area's most remarkable destinations are included and accessed by day walks from Pine Valley. A popular hut located here should be used as a base camp.

Attractions: The Acropolis and The Labyrinth

Length: Total distance is 35km

Day 1: Narcissus Bay to Pine Valley Hut, 9km

Day 2: Pine Valley Hut to The Acropolis, 8.5km

Day 3: Pine Valley Hut to The Labyrinth (return) 8.5km

Day 4: Pine Valley Hut to Narcissus Bay, 9km

Time: 4 days

Options: You can also walk to Narcissus Bay from Cynthia Bay. It is 17.5km each way and takes the best part of a day. Alternatively, return along the western side of Mt Olympus and camp at the southern shore of Lake Petrach.

Attraction Rating: ★ ★ ★ ★ ★

Fitness: ◪ ◪ ◪ ◪

Maps: TASMAP Olympus and Du Cane 1:25 000 topographicals. An excellent overview of the entire route is given by the Cradle Mountain–Lake St Clair Map and Notes 1:100 000 topographical.

Access to Starting Point: To reach Lake St Clair, turn off the A10 at Derwent Bridge. From Hobart, head north-west to New Norfolk and Hamilton, about 172km.

Facilities/Amenities: Cynthia Bay at the southern end of the lake has visitor facilities including a ranger station, bistro and a very well-developed campground. A boat operator ferries walkers to Narcissus Bay at the other end of the lake. Pine Valley Hut (830m) is in good condition and sleeps about 20 people. However, it is very popular and even the tent sites near the hut can be full. You must then find flat ground toward Cephissus Falls up the valley.

Recommended Equipment: The weather is very wet at any time of the year so a Gore-Tex and fleece jacket and overtrousers are recommended. A good waterproof tent and groundsheet are essential. It would be wise to take a water-resistant sleeping-bag liner.

Notes: Book the boat across Lake St Clair by phoning (03) 6289 1137. The cost is currently about $20.00 each way. Bookings are essential to ensure a return berth and to check the time of departure. All walkers should register at Cynthia Bay before embarking.

Further Information:

Lake St Clair Park Office
Tel: (03) 6289 1172

Walk Description

The objective of this walk is to set up camp at Pine Valley Hut, an easy 3-hour walk north of Narcissus Bay, and then do two full-day walks: to The Acropolis and to The Labyrinth. They are two entirely different attractions but each is very worthwhile. The Acropolis is a prominent plateau commanding views over Lake St Clair and Narcissus River valley to the south as well as the Pelions and Mt Ossa to the north. By contrast, The Labyrinth is a wonderland of tarns and pines. Casual exploring here is a delight.

From the jetty at Narcissus Bay, head north on the Overland Track past Narcissus Hut and cross the Narcissus River suspension bridge. Continue north through pleasant woodland and turn left at the signposted junction less than 4km from the jetty. This leads to Pine Valley. The last section through a dark moss-covered forest of King Billy pines is enchanting, especially if there's mist.

Next day, head up past Cephissus Falls to The Acropolis. Rock cairns indicate the way as you ascend steeply over boulders to the flat summit. The columns that inspired the mountain's name are to the north-east. In fact, most of the nomenclature in the Du Cane Range area is derived from Greek mythology.

On the third day, take The Labyrinth Track up to the west. The ridge between The Parthenon and The Minotaur offers great views to Lake St Clair. The next section to the north is particularly wet as you follow track markers down to The Labyrinth, a small flat plateau gouged by ice, creating countless tarns. Walkers will want to wander around to get the best vantage points of Walled Mountain and Mt Geryon in particular. The place is a photographers' paradise and many of the great Peter Dombrovskis' best shots were taken here.

Spend the last day retracing your route to Narcissus Hut. Don't miss the boat, or a 17.5km walk around Lake St Clair's western shore awaits you.

Mt Olympus Circuit

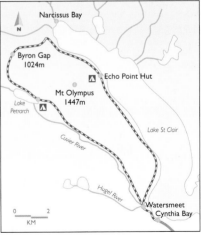

Starting Point: Cynthia Bay, Cradle Mountain–Lake St Clair National Park

Destination: Byron Gap (1024m) and Lake Petrach

Summary: A walk around Mt Olympus returning to Cynthia Bay via the Cuvier River valley

Attractions: Spectacular mountain

and lake scenery. A feature of this walk is that it is fairly easy with little climbing necessary.

Length: Total distance is 35km

Day 1: Cynthia Bay to Lake Petrach via the Cuvier River, 12km

Day 2: Lake Petrach to Cynthia Bay via Echo Point, 23km

Time: 2 days

Options: The walk can be done in either direction

Attraction Rating: ★ ★ ★

Fitness: ◪◪

Maps: TASMAP Olympus and Rufus 1:25 000 topographicals

Access to Starting Point: To reach Lake St Clair, turn off the A10 at Derwent Bridge. From Hobart, head north-west to New Norfolk and Hamilton, about 172km.

Facilities/Amenities: There is a hut at Echo Point, but it should be used only in emergencies

Recommended Equipment: The weather is very wet at any time of the year in this park, and a Gore-Tex and fleece jacket and overtrousers are highly recommended. A waterproof tent and groundsheet are essential and a water-resistant sleeping-bag liner is also wise.

Notes: All walkers should register at Cynthia Bay before setting out

Further Information:

Lake St Clair Park Office
Tel: (03) 6289 1172

Walk Description

One of the easier graded overnight walks in the Cradle Mountain–Lake St Clair National Park, but without sacrificing much in the way of views and attractions. From Cynthia Bay, head north along the Overland Track briefly before veering left at Watersmeet along the Cuvier Valley Track. The first day's distance is short, allowing either a late start or a lazy afternoon by the beautiful white sandy beach on the southern bank of Lake Petrach. Next day, leave early and head northwest between the lake and Mt Olympus, climbing about 150m to Byron Gap for great views over the upper Narcissus River valley and rugged Du Cane Range. Head north-east toward Lake St Clair to meet the Overland Track. Follow this southeast back to Cynthia Bay. There are

The Minotaur and Mt Gould tower over Narcissus Valley north of Lake St Clair.

occasional views to the rocky knolls on top of Mt Olympus as well as the prominent pinnacle of Mt Ida on the other side of the lake. This southern section of the Overland Track is less popular than the main track as most walkers prefer to use the ferry service.

Other walks in the Cradle Mountain–Lake St Clair National Park
Cradle Mountain section
Short Walks (less than an hour)

Several very short tourist walks are possible near Cradle Mountain. From the visitors' centre there's a rainforest walk with access for disabled people, and nearby, the Enchanted Walk follows both banks of Pencil Pine Creek. Near Waldheim, the Weindorfer Forest Walk enables casual walkers to experience the splendour of King Billy pines.

Medium Walks (less than half a day)

A westerly circuit walk from Waldheim follows the Hounslow Heath Track and the Maryland Track. This traverses a lot of pandani-based heath and can often be very muddy.

The Dove Canyon walk from the visitors' centre heads to Knyvet Falls before continuing downstream and returning to Cradle Mountain Road via the upper Dove River. From Dove Lake car park, lots of mini-circuits can be walked: Dove Lake, Lake Lilla,

Hansons Peak and Twisted Lakes, Lake Wilks and Marions Lookout. From Waldheim, mini-circuits include the Wombat Pool and Lake Lilla, and a walk around Crater Lake.

Long Walks (full day or overnight)

A different northern approach into the central section of Cradle Mountain–Lake St Clair National Park is from the east. Ambitious walkers can start from Lake MacKenzie on the northern rim of central tiers. The objective is to pass through the Walls of Jerusalem National Park, heading south-east to Lake Adelaide, Lake Meston and Junction Lake, then using the upper Mersey River valley to connect with the Overland Track, where you can head either north or south. If you wish, complete a circuit by using the River Forth to exit the area via Wolfram Mines. Only very experienced walkers adept at navigation should attempt extended walks such as this.

Another less wild approach to Cradle Mountain is from Penguin via Black Bluff (1339m).

Lake St Clair section
Short Walks (less than an hour)

Several short tourist walks have been constructed around Cynthia Bay: the Lake Walk, Watersmeet, Platypus Bay and the Woodland Nature Walk. Leaflets highlighting features of interest are available from the park office.

Medium Walks
(less than half a day)

A network of walking tracks to the west of Cynthia Bay allows circuit walks to be completed based on Mt Rufus (1416m), Shadow Lake and Little Hugel.

Long Walks
(full day or overnight)

Ambitious walkers can catch the ferry to Narcissus Bay and walk north-east to Mt Gould and Lake Marion. Rock climbers head up the Pine Valley to camp at the base of Mt Geryon (1509m) before tackling its sheer cliffs.

Walls of Jerusalem National Park

The nomenclature in this national park is derived from Biblical sources giving the park a certain enchanting mystique. Names of features include Ephraims Gate, Mt Ophel, Zion Vale, King Davids Peak, The Temple, Solomons Throne and the Wailing Wall. Most were named by naturalist and modern-day explorer Reg Hall in the 1950s. The park protects a remote alpine valley, encircled by mountains, to the east of the upper Mersey River Valley on Tasmania's central highland plateau, with an average altitude of about 1200m. It is particularly exposed to inclement weather and walkers must be very well prepared, even for day walks.

The Fish River, the starting point of the Walls of Jerusalem Walk, above.

Facts and Figures

Name: Walls of Jerusalem National Park

Size: 11,510ha

Enactment: 24 June 1981

Vegetation: Snow gums, yellow gums, swamp grass, heaths, huon pines and pencil pines

Wildlife: Eels, native and introduced fish in lakes

Attractions: Mt Jerusalem, Herods Gate, Lake Salome,

Camping: Dixons Kingdom Hut sleeps six. Other huts marked on the map are in disrepair. Tent camping by Lake Salome and Pool of Bethesda.

Walls of Jerusalem Walk

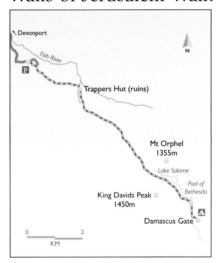

Starting Point: Fish River car park, Walls of Jerusalem National Park

Destination: Damascus Gate via Trappers Hut

Summary: An ascent to a valley enclosed by four mountains using the main walking track and returning the same way

Attractions: An eerie, desolate, open alpine setting, majestic tarns, the largest pencil pine forest in the world

Length: 18km

Time: 1 full day

Options: You can extend the walk to two days, leaving more time to explore, but this involves hauling an overnight pack up the long steep ascent. Trappers Hut (1050m) is in considerable disrepair, but several tarns along the way offer adequate campsites: Solomons Jewels, Lake Salome and the Pool of Bethesda.

Attraction Rating: ★ ★ ★

Fitness: ◩ ◩ ◩

Maps: TASMAP Walls of Jerusalem National Park 1:25 000 topographical

Access to Starting Point: Access from Launceston is via Deloraine and Mole Creek; those travelling from Devonport should pass through Sheffield. Head up the Mersey River valley to Lake Rowallan and turn left immediately after crossing Fish River. This road climbs up to a car park.

Facilities/Amenities: Limited car-camping tent sites are available at the Fish River crossing

Recommended Equipment: Warm, waterproof clothing

Notes: The Walls of Jerusalem are very exposed and snow can fall at any time. Retreat at the earliest warning that the weather is closing in.

Further Information:
Parks and Wildlife
Prospect Offices
Bass Highway
South Launceston TAS 7249
Tel: (03) 6363 5182
or   (03) 6336 5312

Walk Description

The only major route into the Walls of Jerusalem is from the Fish River car park up to Lake Laone via Trappers Hut. The first two hours involve steep climbing through eucalypt forest with limited views north to Clumner Bluff. Once over the rim of the escarpment, the track is considerably flatter. Head left at Lake Loane to Solomons Jewels and Herods Gate. The many tarns here were formed by glacial activity and are lined with pretty pines. The track passes through open moorland with wet muddy sections and occasional stands of pine forest. The parks and wildlife service has put duckboards through the most badly eroded parts.

Herods Gate (1250m) lies between Mt Ophel and King David Peak, where you get your first view of the amphitheatre formation. Most people camp at Lake Salome, but this is getting rather overused. The lake was named after the infamous daughter of King Herod who demanded the head of John the Baptist after performing the dance of the seven veils.

The West Wall, to the south as you venture farther into the amphitheatre, is particularly dramatic. All around are bright green cushion plants.

The main feature is the beautiful Pool of Bethesda at the base of The Temple on the far side. The huon pines around the shore are very photogenic, especially with the West Wall as a backdrop. Exit briefly to the south via Damascus Gate to see the largest pencil pine forest in the world. These trees grow very slowly. At about 1000 years of age, they are 20m tall; this area has some of the largest on record. The track is not marked on the original edition of the map, but it is well constructed. Wander a little farther along the track toward Dixons Kingdom Hut before backtracking all the way down to Fish River.

Other walks in the Walls of Jerusalem National Park

There are no other real walks possible in the national park, although you can always set up base camp in the Walls of Jerusalem and explore countless mountains and tarns in all directions. Rough footpads already lead up most of the main summits, such as Mt Jerusalem (1459m). The Walls can also be accessed from the east by driving to Lake Ada via Liawenee, or from the north via Lake Mackenzie, or from the south via the Overland Track and Junction Lake. Each of these three options involves up to a week of walking over sometimes trackless terrain—only for the very experienced and well equipped.

Franklin–Gordon Wild Rivers National Park

This is the least accessible of the World Heritage Area national parks. It adjoins Cradle Mountain–Lake St Clair National Park to the north and the Southwest National Park, forming a continuous chain of parks from the Dove River in the north to Southeast in the south. Much of this park is dissected by rugged gorges and dense vegetation, which deters all but the most determined and serious walkers. The primary activity is rafting or kayaking down the Franklin River gorge. The only walking track of any significance is to one of the country's great mountains, Frenchmans Cap.

The Franklin River, in the Franklin–Gordon Wild Rivers National Park.

Facts and Figures

Name: Franklin–Gordon Wild Rivers National Park

Size: 195,200ha

Enactment: 1981 (enlargement in 1982 when it was declared a World Heritage Area)

Aboriginal Sites: Archaeologically significant caves are located along the Franklin River

Vegetation: Horizontal, huon and King Billy pines, myrtles, snow gum

Wildlife: Wallabies, possums, devils, native cat, platypus

Attractions: Frenchmans Cap, rafting

Camping: Unrestricted (fuel-stove-only area, however)

Frenchmans Cap Walk

Starting Point: Lyell Highway (A10), Franklin–Gordon Wild Rivers National Park

Destination: Summit of Frenchmans Cap (1443m) via Lake Vera

Summary: A walk in two parts: the first along the sodden Loddon Plains and the second through sensational mountain scenery

Attractions: Views, Lake Tahune, the summit approach of Frenchmans Cap

Length: Total distance is 41.9km

Day 1: Lyell Highway to Lake Vera, 14.2km

Day 2: Lake Vera to Frenchmans Cap (return), 13.5km

Day 3: Lake Vera to Lyell Highway, 14.2km

Time: 3 days

Options: Frenchmans Cap can also be approached from Bubs Hill and Flat Bluff via the Franklin River

Attraction Rating: ★ ★ ★ ★ ★

Fitness: ☒ ☒ ☒ ☒

Maps: TASMAP Frenchmans Cap

Lake Gordon—a massive lake in the heart of Tasmania's south-west.

1:50 000 topographical

Access to Starting Point: The Lyell Highway (A10) connects Hobart with Queenstown in the west. It runs right through the Wild Rivers National Park and a signposted car park is on the left-hand side about 31km west of Derwent Bridge or just over 200km from Hobart. The best landmark is the Franklin River crossing—the walking track starts 3km farther up the road. Allow plenty of time as the road is particularly windy and by all means, avoid travelling at night because of the risk to wildlife.

Facilities/Amenities: Don't rely on the huts at Lake Vera and Lake Tahune, except in emergencies. A tent is essential.

Recommended Equipment: A fuel stove, as the entire national park is a fuel-stove-only area. Warm, waterproof clothing is essential because the weather can deteriorate suddenly. A change of dry socks for the evening will be welcome after walking in the mud all day.

Notes: Walkers leaving on the Frenchmans Cap track are asked to register their trip in logbooks at the Franklin River crossing. (Be sure to sign out on return.) Logbooks can provide important information for the proper management of a search and rescue operation if you become lost. Logbooks are not checked regularly and a search will be mounted only if

someone notifies the rangers that you are overdue. Be sure to leave details with someone reliable.

Further Information:
Lake St Clair Park Office
Tel: (03) 6289 1172
or Queenstown Park Office
Tel: (03) 6471 2511

Walk Description

Frenchmans Cap is flanked by cliffs almost 500m high and, from a distance, its white quartzite looks like a cap of snow. In the 1820s, the shape reminded surveyors of a French cook's hat. This walk will reward you with some unrivalled views of the south-west, including the Franklin River ravines all the way to Lake Gordon. The rock cairn on top was built by Surveyor-General Sprent in 1856.

After parking your car, walk 200m east along the highway to the start. A pleasant five-minute stroll along this good dry track will bring you to the Franklin River. Cross via a footbridge. About 1.5km past the southern bank, you will encounter a wash-down station used to reduce the spread of *Phytophthora* root rot (dieback). Scrub the undersides of your boots thoroughly with the brush provided.

It is then an uphill climb south over the Frankin Hills where great views of your destination can be obtained. Even from this distance, the mighty Frenchmans Cap dominates the lands-

cape. From here descend onto the Loddon Plains, which have become notorious among walkers for being permanently waterlogged. Cross the Loddon River via a suspension bridge and proceed along the button-grass plains. This part is not very pleasant and even with the best boots and gaiters mud will eventually get in.

Follow Philips Lead to the south-west, then west to Lake Vera. Camp near the hut, or the western bank of Vera Hut. Another option is 1km farther, on the far western shore of the lake. Fortunately, you can set up camp for two nights.

The next day is the highlight of the trip. Leave the overnight pack behind as you climb up to Barron Pass and contour around Sharlands Peak to enter Artichoke Valley. This is a bizarre highland with a blend of vegetation communities against a backdrop of dynamic spires.

More climbing is necessary to reach picturesque Lake Tahune framed by the majestic east-facing cliffs of Frenchmans Cap. Continue climbing to the North Col, then turn south for the final hair-raising ascent to the summit. Snowdrifts can often be found here. Have lunch on top of the summit and enjoy unsurpassed views in every direction.

A map of south-western Tasmania will be handy on a clear day to identify the host of jagged mountain ranges in every direction. Return to Lake Vera and next day retrace the first day's route to the Lyell Highway.

Other walks in the Franklin–Gordon Wild Rivers National Park
Franklin River Nature Trail (1km, 15 min)

From where the Lyell Highway (A10) crosses the Franklin River, an easy circuit meanders through cool temperate rainforest. Along the way is the wild Franklin River, the scene of a fierce conservation struggle in the early 1980s. The river flows through numerous deep gorges and some of the wildest country in Tasmania before being joined here by another river, the Surprise. Interpretive signs raise some issues about 'wilderness' and what it means to different people.

The trail is suitable for wheelchairs. Picnic tables and toilet facilities are provided, making it an ideal place to stop for lunch or a break.

Donaghys Hill Wilderness Lookout Walk (2km, 30 minutes)

The summit of Donaghys Hill offers a spectacular wilderness panorama that encompasses the Franklin River valley and Frenchmans Cap. It is a well-graded but steep track through forest. Once you emerge onto the rocky ridge, the views begin. Signs at the fenced lookout recite famous nature-appreciation poetry and quotes from some of the great thinkers of the conservation movement.

The South-west

There are no other landscapes in the world like the wilderness of south-west Tasmania. Dozens of jagged quartzite ranges with spectacular peaks share ridgetops with glacial lakes, valleys filled with rainforest, and button-grass plains to make this ideal terrain for the hard-core adventurer. Hydroelectric developments in the 1960s and 1970s have been responsible for the creation of roads penetrating areas previously accessible only by air or on foot. The two main roads to Strathgordon and Scotts Peak Dam have since become tourist roads. There are a number of maintenance trails around Lake Gordon and Lake Pedder, as well as a network of logging trails dating from 1932 throughout the Florentine River valley that offer excellent exploration opportunities and staging areas to less visited walking destinations.

For a truly rewarding experience of the south-west, do an overnight walk. Detailed tracknotes are beyond the scope of this book but some one-day walks are outlined. For fuller coverage, see books such as *100 Walks in Tasmania* (5th Edition) by Tyrone Thomas, or *South West Tasmania* by John Chapman, or any number of other field guides dealing exclusively with this region. Map coverage is limited and, because the terrain is so rugged, bushwalking, navigational, medical and survival expertise is crucial. Almost every year a few people venture into this huge wilderness never to be seen again.

Geology

How was it formed? A billion years ago, frequent crustal activity interrupted the deposition process in low-lying areas. The quartzite that dominates the texture of the present ranges is made of silicon oxide deposits laid down and cemented more than 200 million years ago. These Pre-Cambrian sedimentary layers became very tilted and folded and were subjected to high temperatures that caused them to metamorphose and fracture. Relatively recent events caused further turbulence: volcanic action injected molten rock up toward the surface, displacing large planes of rock. Glaciation and the inclement weather (howling winds and 3m of rain a year) accelerated the erosion process.

History

Our last great ice age, about 24,000 years ago, saw the sea level 100m lower than the present level, allowing Aborigines a 60km-wide corridor from the Australian mainland to Tasmania. Evidence of occupation remains in the form of middens, rock-art sites and cave deposits.

The Aborigines in the south-west occupied, at that time, the most southerly human habitat in the world, living mainly on the coast overlooking a sea of icebergs. Their diet included elephant seals, crayfish, muttonbirds (short-tailed shearwaters), shellfish, penguins and their eggs. Firelighting was a common practice, to aid hunting and travel). The present coastal sedge-lands are believed to be a product of this. The last Aboriginal inhabitants left the south-west in the 1840s.

European history is one of exploitation. The unique huon pine trees were logged, whaling and sealing was carried on from the bays along the coast, such as Port Davey, mining leases date back to 1890 for gold, coal, tin, copper, asbestos, limestone, lead, marble, nickel, osmiridium, antimony and silica. Trout were introduced into the rivers and convict road-builders began to penetrate from the east and north. Recently, forestry operations, tourism and, above all, hydroelectricity, have all had a major impact on the south-west. Management planning requires intense scrutiny and regulation of operations.

Originally labelled the 'jewel of the south-west', Lake Pedder was named after Sir John Pedder, Chief Justice of Van Diemen's Land Supreme Court when surveyor John Wedge discovered it in 1835. Its famous white quartz beach, 730m wide, which once served as a landing strip and provided the only non-foot access to the south-west, disappeared by 1973. Winter rains in 1972 began flooding the lake

Lake Pedder from the Sentinel Range, Southwest National Park

Russell Falls Creek downstream from the waterfall, Mt Field National Park.

Mt Field National Park

This national park serves as a gateway to Tasmania's south-west and is incorporated into the state's World Heritage Area. Originally known simply as 'National Park', the Mt Field plateau was a popular weekend cross-country skiing venue for Hobart folk in the late 1920s and early '30s. Winter excursions to the Hartz Mountains, Snowy Range, Mt King William, over Newdegate Pass to the Florentine Valley and even to Mt Anne. were common.

Nowadays, most visitors come to see Russell Falls, but there are many other great walking destinations in the park. Some of the tallest trees in the southern hemisphere can be found on the eastern slopes of the park, and the peaks to the west of Rodway Range command superb views over the sawback ranges in the Southwest National park. The park was renamed after its highest peak in honour of New South Wales Judge Barron Field who visited Hobart in 1819 and 1821.

Facts and Figures

Name: Mt Field National Park
Size: 16 977ha
Enactment: Scenic Reserve declared (22 024ha), 1885 National Park (first in Tasmania), 29 August 1916
Wildlife: Pademelons, wallabies, water rats, snakes, lizards, devils, wombats, frogs, potoroos, possums, robins
Vegetation: Pandani, King Billy pine, tanglefoot, pencil pines
Attractions: Russell Falls, Mt Field East and West, tall trees circuit, a waterfall circuit
Camping: A campground at base, accommodation huts on plateau

Mt Field West Walk

Starting Point: Lake Dobson car park, Mt Field National Park
Destination: Mt Field West (1,434m)
Summary: A high-altitude alpine walk along exposed plateau tops, returning via Lake Newdegate
Attractions: Great views, tarns, alpine meadows
Length: 21km

Time: 1 very long day
Options: If you are short of time, omit the Newgate Pass loop and retrace your outward route, which saves 5km
Attraction Rating: ★ ★ ★
Fitness: ☒ ☒ ☒ ☒
Maps: TASMAP Mount Field National Park Map and Notes 1:50 000 topographical
Access to Starting Point: Lake Dobson is at the end of Lake Dobson Road, 15km from Mt Field National Park, which is 80km from Hobart via New Norfolk and Westerway along B61 road
Facilities/Amenities: There are emergency shelters at Mt Rodway (Rodway Hut), K Col (Peterson Memorial Hut) and at Lake Newdegate
Recommended Equipment: Warm fleece jumpers, windproof and waterproof Gore-Tex jacket
Notes: Leave very early, preferably before 8.00am, to allow plenty of time to complete the trip. If there is any hint of bad weather approaching, abandon the walk immediately.
Further Information:
  Mt Field Park Office
  66 Lake Dobson Road
  Mt Field National Park TAS 7140
  Tel: (03) 6288 1149
  Fax: (03) 6288 1170

Walk Description

The open summit of Mt Field West lies on the western rim of an escarpment over the Florentine Valley and commands outstanding views to the highlights of Southwest National Park: Mt Anne, Wylds Crag and the Sentinel Range, as well Lake Gordon. This walk should be attempted only in good summer weather with relatively wind-free conditions. Much of the

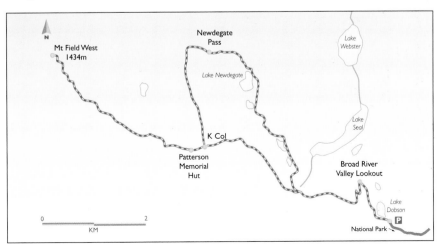

route is very exposed and there is little shelter should the temperature drop.

From the car park at Lake Dobson, head left around the southern shore of Lake Dobson and up the Urquhart Track. Zigzag up to Mawson Plateau and head north-west along the Rodway Range to the K Col. Boulders and small rocks make progress slow. Note the junction at the Col here for the return trip. Continue west, climbing intermittently to the summit of Mt Field West. It can be very windy at the edge so have lunch elsewhere.

Retrace your steps to K Col and head north to Newdegate Pass, descending to Lake Newdegate as the trail curves in a big loop. You pass a number of smaller tarns, all far too cold to swim in, even on the hottest days. The track eventually joins up with Mt Rodway again for hair-raising views down Lake Seal before the final zigzag down to Lake Dobson.

Mt Field Circuit

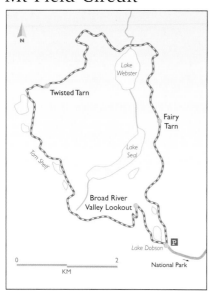

Starting Point: Lake Dobson, Mt Field National Park

Destination: Broad River

Summary: A high-altitude circuit along a series of glacial tarns. It goes clockwise from Lake Dobson to Johnston Tarn and Lake Newdegate before returning via Fairy Tarn and Lake Seal.

Attractions: Views, tarns, alpine meadows

Length: 12.5km

Time: 1 day

Options: An extension to the west is

possible, incorporating K Col and Newdegate Pass. An easterly extension to Lake Fenton is also possible but this involves returning to Lake Dobson via the road. Platypus Tarn and Lake Seal also provide short, interesting diversions.

Attraction Rating: ★ ★ ★

Fitness: ☒ ☒ ☒

Maps: TASMAP Mount Field National Park Map and Notes 1:50 000 topographical

Access to Starting Point: Lake Dobson is at the end of Lake Dobson Road, 15km from the park, which is 80km from Hobart via New Norfolk and Westerway along the B61 road

Facilities/Amenities: Emergency shelters at Mt Rodway (Rodway Hut), Lake Newdegate, Twilight Tarn and Broad River (aluminium shelter)

Recommended Equipment: Warm fleece jumpers and Gore-Tex jacket

Notes: Sections of the track are slowly being duckboarded for easier walking

Further Information:
Mt Field Park Office
66 Lake Dobson Road
Mt Field National Park TAS 7140
Tel: (03) 6288 1149
Fax: (03) 6288 1170

Walk Description

This easy and most pleasant circuit takes in both the upper and lower tarns east of the Rodway Range. On a good day, there will be plenty of photo opportunities. The area is quite poorly drained, so wear good-quality waterproof boots. From Lake Dobson, head up the Urquhart Track to the road that zigzags up to the Sitzmark Ski Lodge and the Broad River Valley Lookout. From here a walking track leads up to Tarn Shelf. Turn right walking through deciduous beech trees (*Nothofagus gunnii*). In autumn, their leaves turn a beautiful golden colour.

Head north to Robert Tarn with dramatic views straight down to Lake Seal more than 300m below. Many of the smaller lakes are frozen in winter, and as early as the 1920s ice-skating was popular here. At Lake Newdegate, head right to Twisted Tarn, then Twilight Tarn before descending from the alpine plateau to Lake Webster. Turn right about 15 minutes after crossing Broad River, head south and

uphill to Fairy Tarn. Turn left on the management road at Eagle Tarn and return to Lake Dobson.

Mt Field East Circuit

Starting Point: Lake Fenton, Mt Field National Park

Destination: Mt Field East (1270m)

Summary: A varied circuit with lakes and lookouts

Attractions: Seagers Lookout, Mt Field East, Lake Nicholls, Beatties Tarn

Length: 11.5km

Time: 4–5 hours

Options: This walk can be done in either direction. Set up a car shuffle to save 2.4km of road walking.

Attraction Rating: ★ ★

Fitness: ☒ ☒

Maps: TASMAP Mount Field National Park Map and Notes 1:50 000 topographical

Access to Starting Point: Lake Fenton is about 11.5km up Lake Dobson Road from Mt Field National Park entrance. The park is 80km from Hobart via New Norfolk and Westerway along the B61 road.

Facilities/Amenities: A hut at Lake Nicholls

Recommended Equipment: Warm fleece jumpers and Gore-Tex jacket

Notes: After rain, much of the track becomes waterlogged, making walking unpleasant and impractical

Further Information:
Mt Field Park Office
66 Lake Dobson Road
Mt Field National Park TAS 7140
Tel: (03) 6288 1149
Fax: (03) 6288 1170

Walk Description

This circuit can be done without any backtracking at all. Park your car at Lake Fenton and cross north over Lady Barron Creek. Then head up through twisted snow and cider gums and take the side option to Seagers Lookout, which looks down over Lake Fenton. This lake was dammed in the 1950s to supply water to Hobart's northern suburbs.

Once back on the track, proceed north to Mt Field East across Windy Moor. As the summit is so centrally located, there are great views along the Broad River valley to the north and the Derwent River to the east. This is a good spot for lunch if the weather is sunny and not too windy. Baron von Mueller climbed this peak in 1869 on a botanical expedition.

Descend from the summit and turn left to skirt Lake Nicholls' eastern shore. Continue south through alpine forest and take the short side trip to Beatties Tarn before descending to the Lake Dobson Road. Turn right, heading uphill back to Lake Fenton. This road was first opened in 1937.

Other walks in Mt Field National Park
Russell Falls–Tall Trees–Lady Barron Falls Circuit (5.5km, 2 hours)

These photogenic multilevel falls can be reached in an easy 10-minute stroll from the first car park. At first the track follows level ground and is sealed. Then you climb up to the right and cross the creek to see Horseshoe Falls. The track enters magnificent tall eucalypt scenery and many of the swamp gums are more than 70–80m tall. Signs give statistics on the tallest trees and in one spot a little game is presented where walkers have to guess how high a particular giant is. The track crosses the road and continues to Lady Barron Falls before returning to the car park.

Pandani Grove Nature Walk (1.2km, 30 minutes)

Leaving from the Lake Dobson car park, this short track follows the western and northern shore of the lake. In the colder months the track

Russell Falls can be reached with a short stroll in the Mt Field National Park.

can be covered with ice and snow. Even in dry conditions it's still often wet underfoot. It passes through pencil pine forest as well as a grove of exquisite pandani. Walkers can return directly to the car park via the road. A brochure is available from the park office giving information on the alpine environment. Another short walk through forest is the Lyrebird Nature Walk, halfway along Lake Dobson Road on the northern side.

Southwest Lookout Walk (5km, 2.5 hours)

From this vantage point on the Mawson Plateau, you'll have wonderful views to the jagged mountains of Southwest National Park. To reach the lookout, follow the Mawson ski tow uphill from the Belt Issue hut, adjacent to Sitzmark Ski Lodge.

Lake Belcher and Lake Belton Walk (16km, 5.5 hours)

The track to these two lakes leaves from Wombat Moor between Lake Fenton and Lake Dobson. It crosses open moorland before descending through subalpine forest. Sections in the Humbolt Valley can be wet and muddy. A hut is located between the lakes below Florentine Peak.

Marriotts Falls Walk (3km, 1 hour)

To reach these delightful falls just outside Mt Field National Park, follow the Gordon River Road south toward Maydena. Turn right at Tyenna.

Styx River Walk (10 min)

Some of the tallest trees in the world can be found in a stand of eucalypts in the Styx River valley. Surprisingly the area is not well known, nor is it developed or even signposted. Several specimens tower over the understorey, rising to between 90m and 100m. The valley can be reached by vehicle west of Maydena. About 3km west of the township, turn right at a cleared area and immediately right again, driving back under the Gordon River Road overpass. This is the Styx River Road, which climbs over Maydena Range and descends to the Styx River. Continue over the bridge, then east, following the river downstream. A small sign on the right here notes a particularly large eucalypt just off the road in the forest. This has had its crown broken, but is still 95m tall, with a tremendous girth at the base. Continue driving east. Once you pass under a set of powerlines, watch out for Jacques Road, the second on the right. Take this and drive up the hill (south) about a kilometre to the stand of trees on the left. The grid reference is 755605 on the Tyenna 1:100 000 topographical sheet. These few dozen trees are not only the tallest in the southern hemisphere, but the tallest flowering plants in the world. Only the California redwoods north of San Francisco are taller.

If the gate near Maydena on Styx River Road is locked, you can get a key from the ANM Forestry Office at

59 Hamilton Road, New Norfolk. Contact: (03) 6261 4055. A $50.00 deposit is required.

Southwest National Park

From a bushwalking, conservation, and aesthetic viewpoint, Southwest is one of the great national parks. Its gigantic size and first-priority classification preserves one of Australia's most beautiful wilderness areas. Only two roads penetrate this World Heritage Area: the Gordon River Road and Scotts Peak Road. They were built in the late 1960s and early 1970s as part of the controversial Middle Gordon hydro-electric power scheme that flooded Lake Pedder. Otherwise, most of the 4000 square kilometre region is wilderness of the purest quality.

The rugged quartzite and dolerite mountains contrast with lakes, glacial tarns and button-grass plains. The region lies directly in the path of the 'roaring forties', so it receives incessant precipitation for all but a few months in the year.

In winter, many of the ranges are snowbound and the tarns frozen. It is not uncommon for the southern regions around Bathurst Harbour to receive up to four months' continuous rain over this period. Precipitation is not of the heavy deluge variety, but more relentless sprinkling. For bushwalkers, the weather is most stable between December and March. This is the only time it is practical to venture into this magnificent region.

Walkers should be very well equipped with four-season down sleeping bags, good-quality waterproof tents and Gore-Tex jackets. Be prepared for blizzard conditions at any time of the year. Fuel stoves are essential as no fires are allowed anywhere in the national park.

Most of the walking is challenging not only from a fitness and endurance viewpoint, but also from a technical aspect. Climbing the peaks of the Arthur Ranges or completing the Mt Anne circuit requires an above-average level of competence on rocks. High exposed ledges and pack-hauling over awkward terrain can be quite unnerving for some, and inexperienced

walkers will not be able to complete the suggested alpine walks.

No tourist map has yet been published of the Southwest National Park. Furthermore, many of the 1:25 000 topographical maps are also unpublished, so walkers must take extreme care when venturing off the formed tracks. Register your route intentions at the installed booths at each staging area before setting out.

Facts and Figures

Name: Southwest National Park

Size: 800,000ha (about 20 per cent of Tasmania)

Enactment:
Lake Pedder National Park, 1955
Southwest Fauna district, 1962
Southwest National Park, 1976
World Heritage Area, 1982
Enlargements, 1989

Aboriginal Sites: Middens along the coast, but little else

Vegetation: Huon pines, King Billy pines, celery top pine, button grass, cushion plants, pandani, laurel, sassafras, waratah

Wildlife: Platypus, pademelons, possums, wallabies, tiger snakes

Attractions: Walking, rock climbing, fishing

Facilities: Camping grounds with toilets and water at Huon River and Edgar near Scotts Peak Dam. A camping ground is also provided at Teds Beach near Strathgordon. Picnic grounds are at the Wedge River near Sentinel Range, at Serpentine Dam and at the base of The Needles on the Gordon River Road near the Maydena entrance.

Further Reading

Several worthwhile publications give good background information and detailed route notes on many of the walks in the Southwest National Park. *Australian Mountains: The Best 100 Walks* by Tyrone Thomas and Sven Klinge contains many highlights of the southwest, while *South West Tasmania* by John Chapman has extensive coverage of major walks in the national park. For geological, botanical and historical information, it is difficult to go past *South-West Tasmania: A Natural History & Visitor's Guide* by Ken Collins.

Mt Anne Circuit

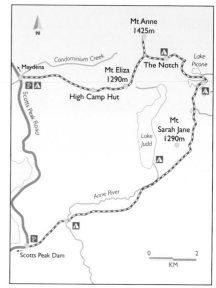

Starting Point: Condominium Creek (Scotts Peak Road), Southwest National Park

Destination: Mt Anne, Lake Judd and Scotts Peak Dam

Summary: An excellent action-packed but difficult circuit over awesome mountain and tarn scenery

Attractions: Views from Mt Eliza and Mt Anne (1425m), Lake Picone, Lonely Tarns, Lake Judd

Length: 36.2km

Time: 4 days

Options: A half-day side trip to Lots Wife, and a one-hour ascent of Mt Sarah Jane. Don't do the trip in reverse as you must have good weather on the Eliza Plateau, which can best be guaranteed by going there first.

Attraction Rating: ★ ★ ★ ★ ★

Fitness: ☒ ☒ ☒ ☒

Maps: TASMAP Anne 1:25 000 topographical

Access to Starting Point: To access Scotts Peak Road, turn off Gordon River Road at Frodshams Pass, 28km from the Maydena park entrance. The road is gravel but is well graded. A car park is on the left-hand side at Condominium Creek about 20km south from Gordon River Road.

Facilities/Amenities: A minor bush-camping area at Condominium Creek. Camping areas with facilities are located just a few minutes' drive south at Scotts Peak Dam. High Camp Memorial Hut is just before Mt Eliza at 1050m. Otherwise there are no facilities at all.

Recommended Equipment: Complete self-sufficiency. Warm, waterproof clothing. Fuel stove. Rope for pack-hauling. Waterproof walking boots with good tread. A self-supporting tent for pitching on rock is also handy.

Notes: The Notch area to the west of Mt Lot is technically challenging and calls for confidence over very steep exposed rock

Further Information:

Southwest National Park
Park Office (Maydena entrance)
Tel: (03) 6288 1283

Walk Description

Mt Anne is the highest peak in south-west Tasmania and on a clear day much of the spectacular ranges that extend south to the coast can be seen. While most people climb just to the Eliza Plateau and return, ambitious, experienced walkers can complete a challenging circuit and enjoy dramatic scenery to the south of Mt Anne. The exit off the Eliza Plateau to Mt Lot is very time-consuming, strenuous and awkward, and people who suffer from vertigo will find sections extremely hair-raising. In a ridge of soft dolomite (limestone rich in magnesium) to the north-east of Mt Anne is the entrance to Australia's deepest cave. Called The Anne-A-Kanada, its deepest survey point is at 373m and it includes a vertical pitch of 118m. So if abseiling dizzying heights and camping in total darkness appeals to you, this is the place to be. However, it's not open to the public and a permit is required.

From the car park on the southern side of Condominium Creek, head east through button grass and scrub with the massif looming in front of you. Start ascending immediately on the prominent spur. You are confronted with a relentless climb to the High Camp Memorial Hut and then to Mt Eliza. On the plateau the walking is noticeably flatter, but you'll notice the temperature is markedly colder. Button grass and pandani are the dominant vegetation. Cliffs to the east give awe-inspiring views straight down to Lake Judd 700m below. Be very careful of wind gusts when standing near the edge. Head north to a track junction and drop your overnight pack. If the weather is stable, head north to Mt Anne and scramble to the dolerite summit. This section can be quite treacherous and walkers must be extremely careful when boulder-hopping because ice and lichen makes rock surfaces very slippery. Snowdrifts are not uncommon here, even in summer. Quite a few fatalities have occurred in the vicinity. You'll find a visitors' logbook in the stone cairn at the top. Henry Judd walked from Huonville to Mt Anne in 1880 but it wasn't until 1929 that the summit was first climbed by W. Crookall and G. Chapman. It was named after Surveyor-General Frankland's wife. Enjoy the views before heading back down to the packs and camping at Shelf Camp just 20 minutes to the east.

This site has plenty of water from small tarns nearby and is protected from the predominant westerly winds. It also has good views to the east-facing columnar cliffs of Mt Anne and the karst area of North East Ridge down to Lake Timk. On the second day, continue east on an increasingly

The Mt Anne massif and the Eliza Plateau from the Sentinel Range, Southwest National Park.

narrow ridge. The exposure on the rock becomes acute as you approach The Notch. Descend into it from above on the northern side and exit to the south by following a gully down about 50–60m and scrambling east back up to the ridge. Generally stay on the southern side of the ridge leading up to Mt Lot as the crest is too difficult. A rope is very handy for pack-hauling along here. Once on the prominent summit of Mt Lot, enjoy the views before descending the very dramatic and sheer Lightning Ridge. This 'staircase' is not as bad as it looks because you lose about 300m of altitude quickly. Camp at the Lonely Tarns, or Judds Charm or Lake Picone to the north if there's time.

Spend the third day following the track south by Mt Sarah Jane where a one-hour detour leads up to the 1290m summit for great views over Lake Judd with the Eliza Plateau in the background. Join up with the Lake Judd track. If you have the time and inclination, you can drop the packs and walk north to inspect the lake, but you will have already seen it from every angle. Some wading across the Anne River will be required.

Continue south-east on the boggy button-grass plains to Anne River for the third day's camp. The final day is a relatively easy walk out to Red Tape Creek crossing a low range. Once back on Scotts Peak Road, head north for 9km back to Condominium Creek car park. To save effort, leave your packs at Red Tape Creek and pick them up in the car. If you are lucky, you might be able to hitch a ride to save the two-hour road walk.

Western Arthurs Walk

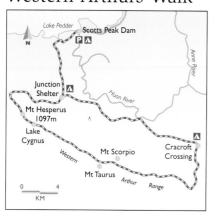

A moment of sunshine on the Arthur Plains, Southwest National Park.

Starting Point: Scotts Peak Dam (Huon campground and staging area), Southwest National Park

Destination: The Western Arthur Range, Lake Cygnus

Summary: An exhilarating epic traverse of a most dramatic mountain range returning via the Huon River at Cracroft Crossing and the Arthur Plains along McKays Track

Attractions: About 30 lakes that contrast with a host of high craggy peaks. Some of the most picturesque lakes are Lake Oberon, Lake Cygnus and Lake Roseanne. Some spectacular peaks are Mt Sirius, Mt Hesperus, Mt Hayes, Mt Scorpio, Mt Canopus and Mt Aldebaran.

Length: 78–86km (depending on side options). Distances are quite meaningless, though, because of the undulating nature of the terrain and because progress is slow.

Time: 8–12 days

Options: Numerous side options to lakes and mountains can extend this trip for several days. It can be shortened by exiting the range via spurs (called moraines) that descend to the north. These are Moraine E (Epsilon) and Moraine K (Kappa)

Attraction Rating: ★ ★ ★ ★ ★

Fitness: ✖ ✖ ✖ ✖ ✖

Maps: TASMAP Scotts, Razorback, Crossing and Glovers 1:25 000 topographicals. The Crossing map is still unpublished at time of writing. The AUSLIG (Ausmap/Natmap) Old River 1:100 000 topographical gives an overview of the entire walk as well as including all the tracks.

Access to Starting Point: From the Lyell Highway (A10) at New Norfolk take route B62 past Mt Field National Park to Maydena. Gordon River Road (B61) continues to Strathgordon. At Frodshams Pass on the Gordon River Road, a signposted winding gravel road (C607) turns off south to Scotts Peak and the Huon campground.

Facilities/Amenities: Car-camping facilities with toilets and water at Huon campground. Pit toilets and platforms are also provided at various spots in the Western Arthurs.

Recommended Equipment: Complete self-sufficiency is required for this major walk. Essentials include: warm, waterproof clothing, a fuel stove, rope for pack-hauling and waterproof walking boots with good tread. A self-supporting tent for pitching on rock could be useful. Reading material is recommended for days holed up in bad weather. Pack a few days' worth of spare food for tent-bound days.

Notes: Parts of the traverse are technically challenging and require a rope.

Further Information:
Southwest National Park
Park Office (Maydena entrance)
Tel: (03) 6288 1283
For detailed tracknotes see *Classic Wild Walks of Australia* by Robert Rankin and *South-West Tasmania* by Ken Collins.

Walk Description

Precipitous terrain, harsh weather, long distances and gruelling conditions all add up to a difficult circuit walk and an adventure of epic proportions. Walkers must be very experienced and particularly well equipped. Preferably a member of the party should have done some walking in south-west Tasmania so he or she can brief the others. Mainland walkers only used to the Blue Mountains or Victorian Alps will get quite a shock when confronted with the difficult conditions that south-west Tasmania presents. Under ideal conditions, a fit party could complete the circuit in a week, but in all probability bad weather will be encountered, forcing you to remain in your tent. If there are too many inclement days and you are running out of food, you should be prepared to exit the range prematurely by Moraine E or K.

This walk traverses the entire length of the Western Arthur Range. As the crow flies, it is not a very long range, only 23km from end to end. But the saw-tooth nature of the rugged topography forces walkers to descend and ascend constantly, effectively doubling the distance. The nomenclature is interesting: all the major lakes are named after planets in the solar system, while the mountains are named after constellations. It was during a photographic expedition here in the summer of 1996 that renowned Latvian wilderness photographer Peter Dombrovskis died. His funeral and wake were held on the slopes of Mt Wellington, near Hobart, his home city.

From the Scotts Peak Dam trackhead, register at the small information shelter and head south-west along a section with relatively new duckboards to enter the Arthur Plains. Please note that this first section has been realigned to what is printed on the 1:25 000 topographical map. The newer edition TASMAP 1:100 000 South Coast Walks map shows the correct alignment.

The track slowly gets wetter as you approach the western end of Arthur Range. A boot scrub-down station is installed here to prevent the spread of dieback disease. Ford Junction Creek

by wading or use the cable 'bridge' to the left if the watercourse is in flood. Just past the creek, you come to a major junction. Turn right onto Port Davey Track and follow this south. Turn left onto Moraine A (Alpha) and begin to ascend Mt Hesperus (1097m). A short side track leads to the summit, which is worth climbing if the weather is good.

Aim to camp at Lake Cygnus on the first day or Lake Oberon if you have enough time. Remember that even though distances are short on the map, progress will be slow; sometimes as little as 1km per hour can be maintained in such rugged terrain. Once past Square Lake you are onto the Razorback 1:25 000 topographical and navigation is a little easier.

Over the next 10 days, proceed along the crest of the range, aiming to camp at the various lakes. Some will be too low and made inaccessible by cliffs, but even so, drinking water is never a problem at any point. During good weather, try to make as much progress as possible and take the opportunity to enjoy the views from the summits. Where visibility is poor but walking is still practical, simply make your way to the next campsite. As there are so many peaks, it hardly matters if you miss out on a few.

The best campsites are at Lake Cygnus, Square Lake, Lake Oberon, High Moor, Haven Lake, Lake Sirona, Promontory Lake and Lake Roseanne,

but there are many other possibilities so walking times can be flexible.

Once you've reached the eastern end and negotiated the rocky Crags of Andromeda, descend by Lucifer Ridge to the open button-grass plains at Pass Creek. There's a camping area in the tea-tree scrub on the other side. From Pass Creek head north along a particularly boggy section, across the Razorback Range and down to Cracroft Crossing. There's a reasonably good camping area here also.

Spend the last day walking west along the permanently saturated Arthur Plains. The distance is about 30km back to Scotts Peak Dam and takes a full day. This can be broken into two smaller days by camping at Seven Mile Creek at the base of Moraine K.

Federation Peak Walk

Starting Point: Farmhouse Creek (near the Picton River), Southwest National Park

Destination: Scotts Peak Dam (Huon camping ground and staging area)

Summary: A high-level alpine traverse from east to west along the Eastern Arthur Range

Attractions: Federation Peak, a mecca for Australian bushwalkers, wilderness scenery of the first magnitude

Length: 64.6km

Time: 6–9 days

Options: Most people choose to walk

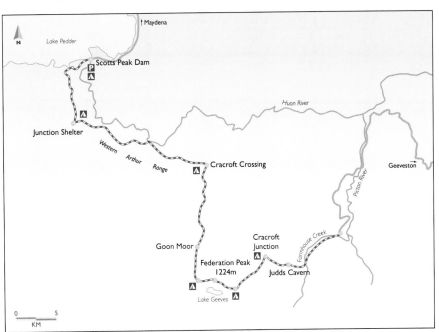

Federation Peak dominates the Eastern Arthur Range in south-west Tasmania.

to Federation Peak from Scotts Peak Dam and return by the same route. The advantage of this route is that it avoids a car shuffle or the necessity for public transport, but it is longer, involves backtracking, and entails walking more than 65km on sodden button-grass plains.

Attraction Rating: ★ ★ ★ ★ ★

Fitness: ◪ ◪ ◪ ◪ ◪

Maps: TASMAP Burgess, Bobbs, Federation, Glovers, Razorback and Scotts 1:25 000 topographicals, AUSLIG (Ausmap/Natmap) Lands Department Old River and Huon 1:100 000 topographicals, and Hobart Walking Club Eastern Arthur Range sketch sheet. At the time of writing, the Federation 1:25 000 topographical map is still unpublished.

Access to Starting Point:

• *To Farmhouse Creek (walk start):* Take the A6 from Hobart down to Huonville and then Geeveston. Turn right to the Arve River picnic area and

north-west (C631) to the Tahune Forest Reserve near the confluence of the Picton and Huon rivers. Then turn left on Picton Road, driving south through clear-felled state forest and plantations to Farmhouse Creek. A trackhead and walkers' registration are on the south side of the bridge.

• *To Scotts Peak Dam (walk end):* Take route B62 from the Lyell Highway (A10) at New Norfolk past Mt Field National Park to Maydena. Gordon River Road (B61) continues to Strathgordon. At Frodshams Pass on the Gordon River Road, a signposted winding gravel road (C607) turns off south to Scotts Peak and the Huon campground.

Facilities/Amenities: None en route. Complete self-sufficiency is essential.

Recommended Equipment: A 20m length of rope, a fuel stove, good waterproof walking boots with good grip, waterproof gaiters, four-season tent and sleeping bag, warm and

waterproof alpine clothing. Pack a few days' spare food, too.

Notes: A high level of competence is needed for several sections involving climbs over very exposed terrain

Further Information:

Park Office (Maydena entrance) Tel: (03) 6288 1283

or

Dover Park Office Tel: (03) 6298 1577

Detailed tracknotes for some of the route are given in *Australian Mountains: The Best 100 Walks* by Tyrone Thomas and Sven Klinge, *Classic Wild Walks of Australia* by Robert Rankin, and *South West Tasmania* by John Chapman. Another book, *South-West Tasmania* by Ken Collins, contains the full through-route as well as comprehensive background information. *WILD* magazine, 1992, No. 42, pp. 36–47 also has superb coverage of all aspects of Federation Peak, including the history of bushwalking there.

Walk Description

More has been written about Federation Peak than just about any other bushwalking destination in Australia. Since it was first conquered, the peak has earned a reputation as a most challenging destination and the bushwalking fraternity is divided between those who have done it and those who are going to do it. Its dramatic appearance, remote location, and difficulty of ascent make it irresistibly attractive to wilderness enthusiasts. It demands experience, fitness, perseverance and good-quality equipment, however.

The summit was not climbed until 27 January 1949, when John Bechervaise ended a run of failed attempts. As late as the 1960s, any assault on 'Feder' was of expedition proportions, involving weeks of scrub-bashing. Today, Scotts Peak Dam and Farmhouse Creek roads provide closer vehicular access and footpads have been developed and constructed, facilitating progress and navigation.

There are several obstacles, the first being the weather. Many walkers have been forced to turn back on the exposed Eastern Arthurs by inclement weather. It is virtually impossible to have fine weather throughout the trip so any party must be prepared for blizzard conditions at any time.

The second obstacle is the nature of the land—much of it is vertical. A traverse of the Eastern Arthurs involves some rock-ledge negotiation where pack-hauling is necessary and ropes are recommended. The greatest challenge is the Direct Ascent approach to the summit of Federation Peak. A number of fatalities have highlighted the extreme exposure of this climb. The exposure is bordering on technical rock climbing, and those fearful of heights will not be able to complete the walk. The cliffs are composed of quartzite and are therefore quite hard, but they are brittle and slippery after rain. The descent from the summit is by far the most dangerous part of the trip. Footholds are difficult to locate and any slip means a 600m fall and certain death.

The third obstacle is the poor quality of the walking tracks. More than 40km of this walk involves traversing the notorious button-grass plains. These are generally saturated with water and drain poorly. Walkers create depressions in the soft sand and clay soils that erode to gullies of mud. Park authorities recommend walking through the mud, rather than around, so as not to widen the tracks. This means you will often have your knees submerged and your feet will soften and swell and be very tender after you've walked from sunrise to sunset. Once off the plains the walking becomes very steep and many kilometres of tree roots and branches must be negotiated as you constantly ascend and descend. Only on Thwaites Plateau and the duck-boarded final 2km is the grade easy.

Despite (or perhaps because of) all these obstacles, the traverse is rewarding for those who can complete it. One of the unsurpassable experiences is looking over endless jagged peaks, wild river valleys and glacial lakes all the way to the horizon.

February and March are the best times to go. Get a forecast before setting off. There's no reason to wait for good weather before leaving as the first section is spent on the lowlands of the Cracroft River. Set up a car shuffle so there's transportation to and from either end, or you can use the Tasmania Wilderness Travel service for bushwalkers.

Start by registering at the small information shelter, then head along the south bank of Farmhouse Creek for several kilometres before leaving the beech rainforest. Cross the creek and head up to South Picton Saddle, climbing to 506m. Descend steeply on the western side, aiming to have lunch at Judds Cavern (also known as 'Wargata Mina'), a limestone cave containing Aboriginal stencil art. Continue down to the South Cracroft River and follow this to its junction with West Cracroft River. To ford the river, wade across a few hundred metres upstream from the Cracroft Junction and head up over a small knoll before descending back to the river. Continue upstream to Paperbark Camp for the first night's camp.

On the second day, continue up the West Cracroft River to the base of Moss Ridge. About 700m must be gained to reach the Bechervaise Plateau and progress is very slow. The terrain is extremely steep and treacherous, and walkers will be thwarted at every turn by fallen logs, dense horizontal vegetation (*Anodopetalum biglandulosum*) thickets and near-vertical slippery terrain. Camp up on the lower plateau where pools and soaks provide fresh drinking water.

The third day is even more hair-raising. If, and only if, the weather is fine, make your way back around the southern flank of Federation Peak via the Southern Traverse. There are good views down to Lake Geeves along this section. The Tasmanian Parks and Wildlife Service has been constructing a few steps and markers to reduce the risk of injury along here. Drop your packs at the start of the Direct Ascent, which is marked by a large cairn.

Climbing to the summit is not difficult technically—most rock climbers would regard it as a basic grade 10–12. But in conjunction with the extreme isolation (at least 2–3 days' walk to help in any direction), the tremendous psychological effect of Lake Geeves nearly a 600m sheer drop below, and the impracticality of carrying any safety equipment, bushwalkers are entitled to feel just a tad anxious. As you climb, keep in mind than the descent will be vastly more difficult. If you feel yourself hesitating or starting to panic, do not climb any farther. Most attempts on 'Feder' from either approach fail for various reasons and too many people have already died at this spot. It is doubtful whether park authorities will ever install ropes, ladders or other artificial aids, as wilderness lobby groups would be vehemently opposed. In fact everyone who has attained the summit agrees that this would seriously degrade the integrity of the region. If fatalities continue at a high rate, park authorities may consider that banning the ascent altogether is their best option.

A few small cairns mark the way to the summit about 200m higher. The first section involves a very tricky, slightly negative ledge about 3m high to attain a level platform. Then sidle left over an awkward rock to find a climbing gully and ascend for about 50m. Then again sidle up across more awkward rock to the right to a second gully. This one is covered with pine-apple grass and resembles a ramp between two rock walls. Scale this gully, known as Geeves Gully, to a ridge crest that leads left to the summit (1224m) marked by a large cairn. After three days of walking, you will now realise how worthwhile the effort has been. All of southern Tasmania seems to be in view and the wildest imaginable terrain envelops you. On all sides, almost sheer 600m cliffs drop down to dramatic lakes and deep abysses.

Prominent features include the Western Arthurs and the Four Peaks to the north-west. Mt Anne lies to the north, while Precipitous Bluff is dominant in the south. In the south-west, Bathurst Harbour can easily be made out on a clear day. Light aircraft frequent the region on scenic flights out of Hobart, much to the annoyance of those who want solitude.

It will be hard to leave the top, and extreme care is needed in descending back to the Southern Traverse, especially if the rock is wet, which it often is. Spend the rest of the day completing the Southern Traverse to the west and camp at the exposed but pretty Hanging Lake on Thwaites Plateau.

On the fourth day of walking, exit the Eastern Arthur Range. Proceed north along the range to Luckmans Lead and Pass Creek. Small signs recommend that parties spread out on the moorland to minimise erosion damage. The Four Peaks are the first obstacle after you walk across the open Thwaites Plateau. Walk around them on their western side by a slow, difficult and time-consuming section at the base of the cliffs. Further awkward ledge-negotiation is required at several points, especially the last, most northerly peak. It is then easier walking to Goon Moor where another time-consuming section through thick forest requires patience and perseverance to attain Stuarts Saddle. The saddle was named after Victorian, John Stuart who died of hypothermia there in January 1956, aged 23.

Continue down Luckmans Lead, losing more than 700m in altitude to re-enter button-grass plain territory. Camp at Pass Creek, where some reasonably dry tent sites can be found in the tea-tree scrub on the right.

On the fifth day, head north from Pass Creek along a particularly boggy section, cross the Razorback Range and descend to Cracroft Crossing, an ideal lunch spot. From here the McKay Track leads west back over the Razorback Range and to Seven Mile Creek where some small tent sites can be found. Alternatively, if time is still available, you could camp farther west at Wullyama Creek or Two Mile Creek. Scotts Peak Dam lies about two hours past Junction Creek, the last 2km being luxuriously duckboarded.

South Coast Track Walk

Starting Point: Scotts Peak Dam (Huon River staging area), Southwest National Park

Destination: Recherche Bay, Cockle Creek

Summary: By combining the Port Davey and South Coast tracks, walkers can complete a long and remote expedition traversing prime-quality wilderness from west to east

Attractions: Bathurst Harbour, the rare orange-bellied parrot, Cox Bight, New River Lagoon

Length: 149km

Time: 10–15 days, depending on weather, side options and rest days

Options: By contacting Par Avion, a private plane operator, walkers can opt to walk either the Port Davey or the South Coast Track. One option is to fly in to Melaleuca and walk out to the east via the South Coast Track. Of the two, the South Coast Track is the more scenic. For walkers wanting to get even farther away from it all, a walking track leads west along the coast from Melaleuca to Wilson Bight via New Harbour.

Attraction Rating: ★ ★ ★ ★ ★

Fitness: ☒ ☒ ☒ ☒ ☒

Maps: TASMAP South Coast Walks 1:100 000 topographical gives an excellent overview as well as detailed route notes. Detailed 1:25 000 topographical coverage is provided by the following maps: Recherche, Prion, Precipitous, De Witt, Louisa, Cox, Melaleuca, Rugby, Legge, Crossing, Razorback and Scotts. At time of writing, several of these from De Witt to Crossing were still unpublished. 1:100 000 coverage is given by South East Cape, South West Cape and Old River, but these maps are not necessary if you have the South Coast Walks map (cost is about $10.00).

Access to Starting Point:

To Scotts Peak Dam (walk start): From the Lyell Highway (A10) at New Norfolk take route B62 past Mt Field National Park to Maydena. Gordon River Road (B61) continues to Strathgordon. At Frodsham Pass on Gordon River Road, a signposted winding gravel road (C607) turns off south to Scotts Peak and Huon campground.

To Cockle Creek (walk end): Cockle Creek is about two hours' drive south from Hobart via the Huon Highway (A6) through Geeveston. Take the C635 past the Hastings Caves turn-off

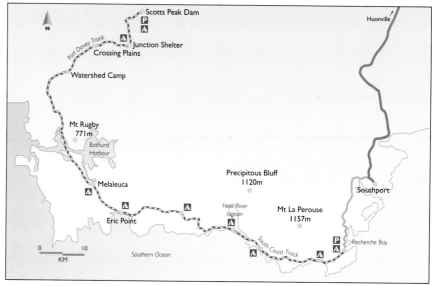

Looking across to South-East Cape—Australia's most southerly point—from the South Coast Track, Southwest National Park.

then follow C636, a gravel road, through Lune River to Cockle Creek.

Use the Tasmanian Wilderness Travel service to gain access to and be picked up from the two staging areas. See contact details at the beginning of this chapter. In addition, walkers can be resupplied by air about halfway along by contacting Par Avion scenic flights, who land daily (weather permitting) at the Melaleuca runway. They operate out of Cambridge Airport east of Hobart. Contact:

Par Avion
PO Box 324, Rosny Park TAS 7018
Tel: (03) 6248 5390
Fax: (03) 6248 5117
email: paravion@tassie.net.au
web site:
www.tassie.net.au/~paravion

Facilities/Amenities: Numerous campsites along the way, most with pit toilets. No commercial/retail facilities at Melaleuca. Boats are provided to cross New River Lagoon and Bathurst Narrows. Very basic accommodation for 20 people is provided in two huts at Melaleuca. Water and mattresses are available,

but there are no cooking facilities. The recommended campsites for the Port Davey Track are: Huon River campground at Scotts Peak Dam, Junction Creek, Crossing River, Spring River, Bathurst Narrows and Melaleuca. For the South Coast Track, the recommended sites are Cockle Creek, South Cape Rivulet, Granite Beach (east), Surprise Bay, New River Lagoon boat crossing, Deadmans Bay, Louisa River and Point Eric. There are also many more minor sites and water is never a problem. Campfires are permitted only at Surprise Bay and Little Deadmans Bay.

Recommended Equipment: Fuel stove, waterproof walking boots with good grip, waterproof gaiters, four-season tent and sleeping bag, warm and waterproof alpine clothing. Pack a few days' spare food and a book—it may well rain for most of the walk. Sandals for beach walking and wading will also be handy.

Notes: Good background information is given on both sides of the TASMAP South Coast Walks 1:100 000 topographical map. Several watercourse

crossings can be dangerous and sometimes walkers either have to retreat or wait for flood levels to subside. These are Crossing River, Spring River, South Cape Rivulet, Louisa River and Faraway Creek.

Further Information: Food drops to Melaleuca via the Par Avion service will incur a cost of around $150.00. Walkers using the TWT service between Hobart and Scotts Peak Dam and returning from Cockle Creek will need to allocate a further $100.00. For any further information on any aspect of the walk contact:

Dover Park Office
Tel: (03) 6298 1577
Fax: (03) 6298 1576
Maydena Park Office
Tel: (03) 6288 1283

Classic Wild Walks of Australia by Robert Rankin, *South West Tasmania* by John Chapman, and *South-West Tasmania* by Ken Collins both contain detailed track notes.

Walk Description

As the name suggests, this great walk follows the wild remote south coast of

The eastern end of the South Coast Track in Blowhole Valley, Southwest National Park.

Tasmania. Despite its epic proportions, about 2000 people attempt the second half (South Coast section) of the walk each year. Of these, three-quarters do it in the summer months from December to March. The first half (Port Davey section) receives only about a tenth of the traffic.

While it does not take in any alpine scenery, there are still plenty of highlights along the way, particularly the numerous isolated beaches and bays. It is suggested that you start inland at Scotts Peak Dam, following the historic Port Davey Track (formerly one of Australia's most remote mail runs) to Bathurst Harbour. Walkers may wish to organise a food drop with flight operators Par Avion, to avoid having to carry more than two weeks' food on their backs.

From the Scotts Peak Dam track-head, register at the small information shelter and head south-west along a relatively new duckboarded section to enter the Arthur Plains. Please note that this first section has been realigned to what is printed on the 1:25 000 topographical map. The newer edition of the TASMAP 1:100 000 South Coast Walks map shows the correct alignment.

The track slowly gets wetter as you approach the western end of the Arthur Range. A boot scrub-down station is installed here to prevent the spread of dieback disease. Wade across Ford Junction Creek or use the cable 'bridge' to the left if the watercourse is in flood. Just past the creek, you come to a major junction. Turn right here onto the Port Davey Track and follow this south across more button-grass plains. On the first night camp at Crossing River, past the Western Arthur Range. Be careful in the fast flow when wading across the river. If you've left early and/or made good progress, you can continue south to a tributary of the Spring River.

Next day, you pass through the low Lost World Plateau and camp on the Spring River with the Rugby Range looming ahead. The next day will feature the first of two boat crossings at Bathurst Narrows. If you leave early, you can make Melaleuca by dusk. The crossing is time-consuming because you have to do the trip three times to ensure that there's a boat at either end for the next party. When you've finished with them, turn the boats upside down and secure them against possible storms. Be careful when crossing with the boats in high wind or rough seas. You will have walked about 54km in total from Scotts Peak Dam to Melaleuca.

On the second half of the journey the scenery really improves. If you are lucky, you may spot the extremely rare orange-bellied parrot from a special hide constructed near Charles King Memorial Hut. These birds were almost extinct when a captive breeding program nursed their numbers back from fewer than 100 pairs.

Walk south along the wet button-grass plains of Moth Creek valley to reach Cox Bight. This section should take about half a day, giving you time to enjoy the water if the day is warm enough. The beach here is sometimes used as an airstrip, but hidden logs under the sand can make landing dangerous at times. Spend the next six days travelling east.

Many kilometres of the track have thankfully now been duckboarded to stabilise boggy sections. You must cross several ranges before you rejoin the coast, including the Red Point Hills and the mighty Ironbound Range. At New River Lagoon, more boats are provided to cross an estuary. Great views of Precipitous Bluff can be obtained here. Because of their orientation, some beaches here can be idyllic paradises while others are exposed to howling gales. Prion is probably the pick of the beaches.

Once at Turua Beach in Deadmans Bay, stick fairly close to the coast until you cross South Cape Range. Once past the distinctive sphinx-shaped outcrop of Lion Rock, you get a good view of the Three Hillocks on South East Cape, Australia's most southerly point. Be very careful during high tide along this part as you can be trapped between the coastal cliffs and the sea. The final section along the Blowhole Valley to Cockle Creek and Recherche Bay takes about two hours.

Other walks in the Southwest National Park
Tourist Walks
Creepy Crawly Nature Trail (15 min)

A short tourist stroll through cool temperate rainforest. Signs along the way give information on rainforest vegetation and invertebrates. The fully boarded track weaves around moss-covered trees and over giant fallen logs. There are 165 steps on the track, so it's not recommended for people who cannot climb a lot of stairs or who are unable to bend down and duck under branches. The start of the walk is 2.5km after you turn off at Frodshams Pass on the western side of Scotts Peak Road.

Jacks Track Walk (30 min)

Starting from Gordon Dam Road 200m west of the Huon Pine log, this short track leads through mixed rainforest varying between 100 and 200 years old. It is maintained by the Public Relations Department of the Hydro-Electric Commission and markers identify native species, such as mountain pepper and sassafras. At the end, cross the bridge and you're back on Gordon Dam Road. Walking time is half an hour (return).

Day Walks
Timbs Track Walk (8km, 3 hours)

From Gordon River Road, 13km west of Maydena, a walking track descends to the beautiful Florentine River, returning via the same route. It traverses a variety of forest vegetation indicative of much of the south-west region. Longer overnight expeditions extend from here north to the Lyell Highway near King William Saddle. Highlights are Denison Range, beautiful Lake Rhona with its white quartzite beach, The Spires and King William Range.

The Sentinel Range Walk (8–12km, 8 hours)

This unmarked wilderness walk is only for experienced bushwalkers familiar with the practice of minimal-impact walking. The Department of Parks, Wildlife and Heritage classifies its tracks on a scale of T1 to T4, with the T1 being the easiest. This is a T4, which implies that the track is largely unmarked. Fewer than 250 visitors use it each year.

The walk begins from the Wedge River picnic ground just off the Gordon River Road between Fordshams Pass and Strathgordon. Start by crossing the Wedge River to the south (carry plenty of water) and head straight up the slope through thick low scrub. When you can see the Sentinel Range ahead, walk toward a sheltered 'chimney' to the right of a massive block of sheer grey quartzite. It will take about an hour to reach the base but a track becomes apparent as the vegetation thins out. Look for the small white cloth markers. The track zigzags up over rock and provides relief from the thick scrub. Veer right off the track as it enters the gully because it's easier going over the rock. Watch out for foot and handholds that may come loose. About 600m of altitude must be gained. Keep heading right around outcrops until you eventually reach the razor-edged ridge crest with tremendous views over the other side to Lake Pedder and Frankland Range.

Continue west as close to the centre of the ridge as possible for 4–5 hours. Progress will be slow through occasional scrubby patches. The incredible 360-degree vistas include Frenchmans Cap, Mt Anne and a multitude of craggy peaks and saw-back ranges with the gigantic Pedder and Gordon lakes in the foreground. Head down to Gordon River Road. This takes about two hours through thick scrub. To make progress easier, keep to the crest of a spur when you are descending. Refer to topographical map: McPartlan 1:25 000.

The forests surrounding Lake Gordon from the Strathgordon Road.

The ascent of Precipitous Bluff is a strenuous side option for walkers undertaking the South Coast Track.

South Cape Bay Walk (16km, 5 hours)

From Cockle Creek, get a taste of the desolate south coast by walking up Blowhole Valley along the first section of the South Coast Track. An easy, well-graded walk with undulating stretches toward the end, walk along the beach to Lion Rock before returning.

Adamsons Peak Walk (1 day)

From Hastings Caves, follow a rough track ascending to the conical summit (1226m). Return via the same route.

Overnight Walks

Southwest National Park allows virtually unlimited walks if you are willing to explore uncharted territory. While there are none of the more officially managed tracks found in other parks, negotiable routes have been worn by walking parties and it is more by word of mouth that these walks become known. Would-be adventurers are warned that the nature of the terrain, in particular thick vegetation, can make progress very slow.

Truchanas Huon Pine Reserve Walk (28km, 4 days)

A rough, largely trackless walk to a remote reserve that protects 400ha of the largest remaining mature forests of the aromatic softwood, huon pine. The stand was discovered in 1928, miraculously unscathed by early convict timber-cutters because of its largely inaccessible location. The reserve was named posthumously for Olegas Truchanas, a Lithuanian migrant who was the first to canoe the Gordon River and who fought for its preservation. He died in a kayaking accident in the south-west while taking photographs for the 'Save Lake Pedder' campaign in 1972. The reserve is on the Denison River and is best accessed via the Hamilton Range. There are no facilities. You must have permission to walk up the steel ladder on the western side of the dam where the track quickly deteriorates.

To add a week-long extension, continue north along the remote Prince of Wales Range. The weather can be especially wet here as the north/south alignment of the peaks amplifies orographical precipitation. Topographical map: Olga 1:100 000.

Frankland Range Walk (1–2 weeks)

From Strathgordon, you can do a high level traverse of the distinctive Frankland Range that borders the southern shore of Lake Pedder. Access onto the range is via Mt Sprent and the Wilmot Range and the exit is via Scotts Peak Dam. Topographical maps: Olga, Wedge and Old River 1:100 000.

Southwest Cape Circuit (1 week)

From Melaleuca, walkers can access the most remote corner of the Southwest National Park by heading west along the coast to New Harbour. Follow the coast south-west past the sea cliffs at Ketchem Bay to Wilson Bight. It is not physically possible to go to South West Cape itself because of the large sea cliffs. Geologists have discovered extremely old outcrops here from the Pre-Cambrian and Devonian periods. Traverse the South West Cape Range to the north, descending to Window Plane Bay with its peculiar rock stack and follow the coast north-west to Noyhener Beach opposite Muttonbird Island. Return to Melaleuca by heading due east back over South West Cape Range. The last section will be particularly slow going because of thick vegetation and boggy ground. Topographical maps: South Coast Walks 1:100 000.

Precipitous Bluff Circuit (1 week)
From Ida Bay, follow the abandoned tram track past old quarry diggings to reach a track at Mystery Creek. This ascends to Moonlight Ridge and Mt La Perouse (1157m). From here walk along the high-level ridge to Knife Mountain and then Pandani Knob. Head across Leaning Tree Saddle to access the north side of Mt Wylly. A side track heads along the ridge crest north to Mt Victoria Cross, but you should aim for a saddle below Precipitous Bluff and climb it via a gully from the east. There are exposed campsites with outstanding views near the dolerite summit. Descend another gully on the western side to reach the shore of New River Lagoon. Some impressive tall forest grows here. Head down the lagoon shore to join up with the South Coast Track and exit via Cockle Creek.

Vanishing Falls Walk (1 week)
This remote waterfall plummets 50m into a limestone abyss on the Salisbury River about 10km to the north of Precipitous Bluff. You must walk through dense trackless terrain. The best approaches are from Lune River, Ida Bay or Cockle Creek. A GPS system is very useful here.

West Coast Trek (1 month)
Charter a boat or seaplane and attempt the ultimate wilderness experience: a full month's traverse of the wild west coast from Cape Sorell near Strahan to Melaleuca. This is one of the wettest places in Australia. Be prepared for the incessant wind. Few people have done this walk through trackless terrain and button-grass plains. Walkers must often wade through river estuaries, and must either wait or head inland when they the estuaries are in flood.

The Islands

Tasmania is surrounded by scenic islands on all sides, many of them sheltered in protective harbours. They often make idyllic settings for all kinds of walks, providing stunning coastal scenery without the crowds. Bruny Island in the south-east has the rugged Labillardiere Peninsula with topography like the sea cliffs near Cape Pillar on the Tasman Peninsula.

In Macquarie Harbour, on the west coast, Sarah Island is steeped in convict history. It was here that Alexander Pearce absconded in 1822 with seven other companions and survived by killing and eating all his accomplices. He was apprehended but no-one believed his story. After being sent back to Sarah Island and again escaping and eating his companion, his deed was discovered and he was finally sent to the Hobart gallows. A walking track allows you to tour the ruins of the penal settlement.

King Island to the north-west in Bass Strait provides some smaller reserves for easy, level walking. But the best walking conditions by far lie on two mountainous islands to the north-east and east: Flinders and Maria.

Flinders Island National Park

'There are few if any coastlines in Australia more beautiful and exciting than those of the Furneaux Group. And the mountains, particularly in the Strzelecki National Park, are often spectacular with great granite cliffs, rocky ridges, distinctive summits, and forests running down to sandy beaches. The coastal views from many of the peaks are superb. There are also heath lands, wetlands and lagoons, particularly on the east of Flinders Island.

There is something for everyone, from two-hour strolls to extended treks made by stringing together different combinations of the one-day walks, or by tackling the Cape Barren Island circuit.'

A Walker's Guide to Flinders and Cape Barren Island by Ted Lovegrove.

Flinders Island is the largest of a group of 46 granite islands named after Tobias Furneaux, captain of the *Adventure*, who first sighted them in 1773. Flinders is named after Matthew Flinders, who first charted it.

Like other islands off the Tasmanian coast, it's an adventurer's paradise. The roads have little traffic and the whole place has a unique tranquil atmosphere. Facilities outside of Whitemark and Lady Barron are limited, but regulations are relaxed and camp can be set up at public places along the coast. In fact the only complaints a walker might have are about the notorious 'roaring forties'—the relentless, harsh westerly winds that can blow up with little warning.

The islanders are friendly, but shy. A large contingent of the population is descended from early sealers and their Tasmanian Aboriginal partners. Today, the islanders are primarily engaged in agriculture, fishing and muttonbird harvesting.

Flinders Island is the site of the Wybalenna settlement, about 20km north of Whitemark, where 150 Aboriginal people of Tasmania were deported in 1831. By 1847, when Wybalenna was closed, only 46 people had survived the harsh treatment and neglect. The walker can explore the site as it stands today and see the graveyard where those who died there are buried. Truganini, the last survivor of the original group, died in 1876. Her body was buried at the old Female Factory in the Cascades, but was later exhumed and put in a vault at the Museum of the Royal Society of Tasmania. In the early part of the 20th century, her remains were toured as part of an exhibition and on display in the Museum until returned to the vault in 1947. In 1974, the local Aboriginal community petitioned for her reburial. Her remains were cremated and her ashes spread in the D'Entrecasteaux Channel. All graves at Wybalenna are believed to be empty now, as universities and academic physicians around the world offered up to £100 for the skeletons.

It takes about a week to explore the island adequately and if you stay that long, you should investigate the isolated east coast as well as Stanley Point. Remember that rainfall is generally very low and if you camp away from Whitemark and Lady Barron, you must carry plenty of water. The airport at Pats River was opened in 1934 and is the main route by which visitors can access the island. Regular flights leave from Launceston, Melbourne and Welshpool. Supplies are available just to the south of the airport at Whitemark.

Two booklets are available: *The Walks of Killercrankie and Environs* and *Flinders Island Scenic Walks*. Both of these are easily obtainable from almost all outlets on Flinders Island. With the TASMAP Flinders Island 1:100 000 topographic map and a little help from Jean Edgecombe's *Discovering Flinders Island*, you can easily plan a walking holiday. Talking with locals is a good way to get extra information for your trip.

Facts and Figures

Name: Flinders Island National Park
Population: 1200
Settlement: Late 19th century
Capital: Whitemark, tidal port to trading vessels
Area: 2000 square kilometres Strzelecki National Park is 4200ha (65km long x 40km wide)
Vegetation: The island includes both dry and wet sclerophyll forests containing species endemic to both mainland Australia and Tasmania. Mostly stunted heath and scrub on the west coast and exposed areas, allowing good visibility from any point a few metres high.
Wildlife: Muttonbirds, Cape Barren geese (the second-rarest goose in the world). The only two species of snakes are the copperhead and tiger, both of which are venomous. Fossils of the grey kangaroo have been found here.

Access

By Air

The Island is serviced by air both from mainland Australia and Tasmania. Aus-Air runs scheduled services from Melbourne (Moorabbin Airport), Latrobe Valley and Launceston, and will arrange holiday packages, tours

and car rentals. Book through travel agents or by phone on (03) 9580 6166. Dreamtime Flights specialise in charters to Flinders Island and elsewhere in Australia. Contact the company by phone on (03) 9329 1099. Island Airlines have regular scheduled services to Flinders Island from Melbourne, free shuttle service to Essendon Airport. Call 1800 818 455.

By Sea

Southern Shipping runs a small cargo vessel to the island from Bridport on Tasmania's north-east coast which takes passengers. It is an 8–9 hour journey, sometimes in quite turbulent seas. For more information, call (03) 6356 1753 or fax (03) 6356 1956.

Mt Strzelecki Walk

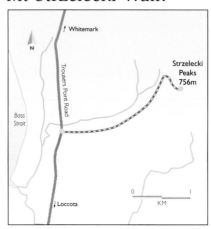

Starting Point: Trousers Point Road, Flinders Island
Destination: Summit of Mt Strzelecki (756m)
Summary: A direct, steep approach to the highest peak on Flinders Island
Attractions: Wind-sculpted rock formations and great views over minor Bass Strait islands and northern Tasmania
Length: 9km
Time: 5 hours
Options: None
Attraction Rating: ★ ★ ★
Fitness: ◪◪
Maps: AUSLIG (Ausmap/Natmap) Lady Barron 1:100 000 topographical or Flinders Island 1:100 000 land tenure (1985)
Access to Starting Point: The national park is 56km south of Whitemark
Facilities/Amenities: Pit toilets and picnic/camping area at the base

Recommended Equipment: A parka might be useful on the summit, as it is often very windy. Carry water—there is none en route.
Further Information: While there is no direct cost to do this walk, the airfare will cost about $300.00.
For further information on any other aspect of this walk contact:
The Ranger
Tasmanian Parks and Wildlife
Tel: (03) 6359 2217
Fax: (03) 6359 2210

Walk Description

Strzelecki Peaks are the highest points on Flinders Island and command views over Cape Barren Island, the Chappell Islands and north-eastern Tasmania, particularly Waterhouse Point. Take the signposted five-hour walk from Strzelecki Road north of Trousers Point to Mt Strzelecki. The route is fairly direct and steep, rapidly gaining height over the 4.5km walk. This peak marks the first leg of the three-peaks yacht race, in which two members from each boat must run to the summit before proceeding under sail to Freycinet Peninsula.

The trail passes through a small pocket of ferny rainforest, then through peppermint-based forest, alpine grasses and finally over open granite. As you ascend, the westerly views become spectacular, especially to the 200m bump of Chappell Island and the flat expanse of Badger Island behind it. Directly below is the prominent cove formed by Trousers Point. Mt Belstead dominates the foreground to the south. Near the top, large granite boulders, sculpted by prevailing winds and rain, look poised to tumble down. Rock climbers sometimes visit other parts of the Strzelecki Peaks, taking advantage of the hard granite cliffs. Return to the road via the same route after having lunch.

Maria Island National Park

Maria Island was named by Abel Tasman in honour of Maria Van Aelst, wife of Anthony Van Diemen. The island's European history dates from 1789, when Captain Cox stepped ashore at Shoal Bay. Contact with the resident Aborigines (who called the island 'Toarra Marra Monah') proved unsuccessful. When Hobart became a sealing and whaling port, and Maria Island was used as a base by ships from all around the world, hostility was inevitable. In one attack by Aborigines, 2000 seal skins were destroyed. Whaling settlements were established at Whalers Cove and Haunted Bay.

A convict colony was founded in 1825 with 50 'class six' convicts, one class away from the very worst offenders, who were sent to the notorious Sarah Island in Macquarie Harbour. Conditions on Maria Island were luxurious in comparison, and escape was relatively easy. The outpost slowly developed a reputation as more of a resort than a prison and soon convicts were misbehaving deliberately in order to be drafted to the island. Goods manufactured by interns here included cloth, shoes, blankets, wheelbarrows and pots.

Since escape was so easy, the settlement was closed in 1832, with most of the remaining convicts being sent to Port Arthur. For the next 10 years the island was leased by settlers, after which it became a probation station for about 800 convicts sent direct from England. The island was later leased again for £300 a year until the 1880s, when Angel Guilio Diego Bernacchi, an Italian silk merchant, arrived. He was granted a controversial lease for 10 years, paying just one shilling a year. Bernacchi prospered, spending and making thousands of pounds on wine and silk production. He hosted elaborate parties and Darlington became the thriving township of 'San Diego' with 250 employees and its own school, bank, post office and blacksmith. The Maria Island Company was floated in 1887 with capital of £250 000, to establish orchards, limestone quarries, fisheries, timber export and even a tourist resort. The island was then referred to as the 'Ceylon' of the South Pacific.

All this prosperity eventually came to an end. The company went into liquidation and it was discovered that the island's wealth potential had been somewhat exaggerated by Bernacchi. In the early 1900s, the island was opened once again to settlers. The population boomed in the 1920s as Bernacchi made another attempt to exploit Maria. Cement extraction reached 30 000 tons but double that was needed to be economically viable. The venture again went into debt and ceased business in 1930.

The island's population dwindled and it became known as the quiet place where it was 'always afternoon'. In 1972, the entire island was declared a national park, principally as a reserve for wildlife protection in dry sclerophyll forest. Between 1968 and 1971, endangered Cape Barren geese were released; these have now multiplied to many thousands. The waters north of the island are a 1500ha marine reserve where no fishing is permitted. The convict ruins have been restored and the island is now a highlight of any visit to Tasmania.

The summit of Mt Bishop and Mt Clerk—Maria Island, off the east coast of Tasmania.

Facts and Figures

Name: Maria Island National Park

Size: 9672ha (20km x 13km)

Enactment:
National Park, 1972
Marine Reserve, 1991

Vegetation: Blue, white and manna gums, stringybark, black and white peppermints

Wildlife: One of the last refuges for the 6000 remaining Cape Barren geese, one of 130 species of birds found on the island

Attractions: Unique tranquil island atmosphere and the old Darlington penal settlement. A geologists' paradise of dolerite, sandstone, granite and limestone formations.

Camping: Several campgrounds, two developed with standard facilities. Also basic accommodation units in the penitentiary.

Maria Island Circuit

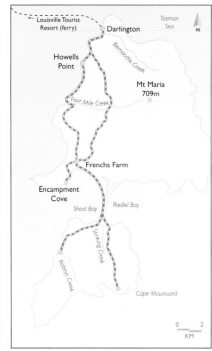

Starting Point: Darlington, Maria Island National Park

Destination: Robeys Creek

Summary: An extensive tour of all of the best features of the island

Attractions: Painted Cliffs, Hopground Beach, Encampment Cove, Robeys Creek, views from the summit of Mt Maria (709m)

Length: Total distance is 59.7km

Day 1: Darlington to Encampment Cove, 15.1km

Day 2: Encampment Cove to Robeys Creek, 12.3km

Day 3: Robeys Creek to Frenchs Farm, 9.8km

Day 4: Frenchs Farm to Darlington via Mt Maria, 22.5km

Time: 4 days

Options: Shorter options if time is limited. As the walking is easy, any two of the suggested days can be combined into one longer one. It is also possible to extend this circuit to include Big Hill, Mt Bishop and Clerk.

Attraction Rating: ★ ★ ★ ★ ★

Fitness: ◪◪

Maps: TASMAP Maria Island National Park 1:50 000 topographical

Access to Starting Point: A ferry leaves several times a day from Louisville Tourist Centre between Orford and Triabunna on the east coast. The departure point is about 88km from Hobart via the A3 through

Looking over the Fossil Cliffs, Maria Island, off the east coast of Tasmania.

Sorrell. The cost is about $40.00 return.

Facilities/Amenities: Firewood, pit toilets and water at Encampment Cove

Recommended Equipment: Water containers, overnight camping gear

Notes: A mountain bike, which can be hired at Darlington or brought across on the ferry, is particularly handy to get to the southern half of the island

Further Information: The ferry to Maria Island from Louisville Tourist Centre costs about $40.00 return. For further information on any other aspect of this walk contact:

Park Office

Maria Island National Park

Tel: (03) 6257 1420

Walk Description

Not much effort is required to get an excellent solitary atmosphere and outstanding scenery here. The variation and beauty on this walk is astonishing: coloured sea cliffs, exquisite beaches, a warm dry climate, an abundance of wildlife and commanding views from the highest point. The distances have been purposely kept short on the first three days allowing plenty of time to linger at the many wonderful places.

Purchase your camping permits at the ranger station/visitors' centre in the old Commissariat Store near the jetty in Darlington, and head south through the settlement to the Penitentiary. Ask the ranger about availability of water at Frenchs Farm, Encampment Cove and Robeys Creek. If it is early, drop the packs and spend some time exploring the old settlement buildings—many of them have been made into museums and the rangers give guided tours in peak season. Along the way you might spot Cape Barren Geese and kangaroos.

Head south past Mrs Hunts Cottage along the coast to Hopground Beach. On the far side are the fascinating Painted Cliffs, brilliantly stained by iron oxide deposits in percolating ground water. The best time to visit is at low tide; best photographs are taken when the afternoon sun is low.

Continue south to Howells Point and Four Mile Creek. Kangaroos can often be seen grazing here. It is fairly flat easy walking to Frenchs Farm, where you turn right to beautiful En-campment Cove. In the 1870s, Chinese abalone fishermen were based here. Secluded sites are on the right-hand side. Firewood and pit toilets are at the end and water is available from tanks by the shelter. Boats sometimes moor in the tranquil waters of Shoal Bay. For good views of the sunset, head up the hill past the shelter.

Next day head back to Frenchs Farm and turn right, walking south along the narrow isthmus to Robeys Creek. This is the site of an old sheep station, operated for 41 years before it was abandoned in 1965. It was owned by John Robey, one of the few settlers who remained after the closure of the Portland Cement works in 1930.

Spend the third day retracing the second day's route back towards Frenchs Farm. If you have the energy and inclination, go south and climb Big Hill for great views over Cape Maurouard and Barren Head. In the distance you can see Cape Frederick Hendrick on the northern Tasman Peninsula.

Leave early on the last day as there's a long slog up Ned Ryans Hill and Monah Hill to a track junction. Drop your packs and head up east to Mt Maria, where some boulder-scrambling is necessary to attain the dolerite summit. Have lunch at the top cairn enjoying expansive views. Remember to leave in plenty of time to catch the last ferry. Return to the packs and head north back to Hopground Beach, then to Darlington. Along the way is Howells Cottage, owned by one of the last families to leave the island.

Other walks on Maria Island
Bishop and Clerk
(9km, 3.5 hours)

At 630m this hill is not the highest point on the island but it certainly is the most spectacular. The views over Fossil Bay to the Freycinet Peninsula are truly awe-inspiring. The approach is moderately steep. From the Darlington Penitentiary head east past the rubble and standing chimneys of the 12 Apostles. These cottages, used to house Bernacchi's vineyard workers, were later moved to Maria Street, Hobart, in the inter-war years. It's easy walking, passing through pleas-ant forest. Cross a creek and head left at an intersection. The land opens up to a huge upward-sloping grassed area with the odd Forester kangaroo. On the right is the site of the old cement works dating from 1889.

Head east up a steady slope to the top of the cliffs, passing an old carboniferous limestone quarry on the right. This is claimed to be the first Portland Cement quarry in Australia and once boasted machinery imported from Copenhagen and London.

Once at the top, look out over the turquoise waters from the fantastic Fossil Cliffs. These contain many examples of marine fossils, the most common being mussel shells about 200 million years old. Turn right and head up the slope where the eucalypt forest closes in again. It gets progressively steeper as you ascend. The track then comes out on an unusual boulder-strewn field. There is no clear path, just head straight up and eventually left. At the base of some dolerite spires, scramble to the summit. The return is a simple backtrack.

Other walks on Tasmania's Islands
Bruny Island

Bruny Island was named after Admiral Bruni D'Entrecasteaux who, with Huon Kermandec, discovered the waterway separating the mainland and the island, now called D'Entre-casteaux Channel, in 1792. William Bligh anchored the *Bounty* here in 1788. In fact, a 'who's who' of maritime explorers landed here: Cook, Flinders, Bligh, Furneaux, Franklin, Bass and Baudin. Even Abel Tasman tried to land at Adventure Bay in 1642.

Like Maria Island to the north, Bruny Island actually consists of two islands with the sea accounting for the construction of the connecting sand isthmus, called a tombolo and named The Neck. The north is basically flat open pastoral land while the southern part, in stark contrast, is mountainous and heavily forested. The island's population totals about 500. The last Tasmanian Aborigine, Truganini, came from Bruny Island. There's a hostel at Quiet Corner, Main Road, Adventure Bay. There are 16 beds in three rooms.

Access

A passenger barge runs hourly between Kettering and Roberts Point. For timetable information, phone (03) 6273 6725. The timetable is also published in the white pages of the telephone book, listed under Bruny Island Ferry Service. During peak periods, the timetable may be ignored with the ferry sailing as often as necessary. To avoid the risk of being left behind, passengers should be at the ferry terminal at least 10 minutes before advertised departure times.

Walks

There are several reserves on the island, including the central isthmus and Cape Queen Elizabeth. At time of writing a South Bruny Island National Park consolidating several smaller reserves was proposed. This would protect the Labillardiere Peninsula and the Fluted Cape region.

A four-hour circuit of the Labillardiere Peninsula is possible from Old Jetty Road near Jetty Beach. Along the western coast you can climb Mt Bleak (142m). Another destination is East Cloudy Head and Pine Log Bight just north of Tasman Head. This is a full-day walk returning to Cloudy Bay Road. Mt Mangana behind Adventure Bay (571m) can be climbed from Coolangatta Road. The return time is 90 minutes. The Slide Track along the Bay of Islands connects Adventure Bay with Lockleys Road in the south. The route follows an old tramline through pleasant forest with occasional views,

but you will have to contend with leeches, snakes and mud. If you set up a car shuffle, it takes about 3.5 hours one way. Phone Parks and Wildlife on (03) 6293 1419 for more details.

King Island

Like Flinders Island, King Island also has a tragic history. Its western coast is a graveyard to many ships, and thousands of lives were lost between King Island and the Otway Coast in Victoria. Five lighthouses were built on this coast, one of them the tallest in Australia. There are no national parks and only one reserve of note but the aesthetic value is in the island as a whole. There is something about its character, people, scenery and lifestyle that make it a unique experience. It is even flatter than Flinders so walking is easy. Destinations are primarily isolated east-facing beaches with few camping restrictions. The west coast is subject to constant onshore winds.

Other walks in Tasmania

With so much of Tasmania being preserved in national parks and state reserves, there are great walking opportunities throughout. These range from short tourist strolls to fortnightlong expeditions through trackless rugged wilderness.

Tasmanian Trail
(477km, four weeks)

A publication called *The Tasmanian Trail Guide Book* gives walkers,

mountain bikers and equestrians all the information they need to travel all or part of the trail. In this book the trail has been divided into five sectors to correspond with the nature of the topography the trail passes through. Each sector has been further divided into stages that average 32km. At the end of each stage is a campsite. *The Guide* is in five parts:

• *Part One: Planning a Trip on the Tasmanian Trail* gives information about using the trail wisely and safely. A general code of conduct and guidelines are included, but there is a detailed code of conduct for individual user groups in Part Three if you are unsure of the generally accepted behaviour for particular user groups on multiple-use trails.

• *Part Two: Notes and Maps.* Each section provides an introduction to regions along the trail and a brief summary of the main townships and facilities. Each stage is presented as a journey from one campsite to the next and includes detailed trail notes and maps. The maps were accurate at time of printing but may require updating as features on the trail can change. For more information about townships, attractions and facilities along the trail, take along a copy of *Tasmania: A Visitor's Guide*, or *Travelways*, both excellent guides available at most Tasmanian tourist information centres.

• *Part Three: Further Information.* Relevant contacts are provided.

• *Part Four: Codes of Conduct for Individual User Groups.* Guidance for horse riders, mountain bikers and bushwalkers on conditions, general conduct and specific items to take along. Included are comprehensive checklists for the three groups.

• *Part Five:* Track Report Card, Membership Application, Key Request Form and Order for Merchandise. Forms that track users will find useful.

Asbestos Range National Park

Just east of Devonport is Asbestos Range National Park, featuring the massive Bakers Beach. A 10km circuit leads to Badger Head from Badger Beach, crossing over the low Asbestos Range. Another shorter walk leads from Bakers Beach to Archers Knob

Descending from the southern end of Mt Roland, Mt Roland Protected Area.

Arve Falls, in the Hartz Mountains National Park.

Cradle Mountain. At the summit (1339m) is a pretty glacial tarn. The 12km return walk is strenuous but not technically challenging. Access is via C129 through Upper Castra south of Ulverstone. Phone Parks and Wildlife on (03) 6429 1388 for more details.

Hartz Mountains National Park
Several day walks can be done to waterfalls and mountain summits from the end of Hartz Road (C632) south-west of Geeveston. Destinations include Lake Perry, Lake Osborne, Hartz Lake and Hartz Peak (1254m). Conditions are often wet, typical of the south-west. Consult the Hartz Mountains National Park Day Walk Map 1:50 000 topographical or phone (03) 6298 1577 for more details.

Mt Roland
A high-level circuit on this prominent isolated mountain 30km south of Devonport. From a car park at the end of O'Neills Road near the small township of Gowrie Park, head up the Roland Track to the summit (1233m). Backtrack to Reggies Falls and walk over Mt Vandyke and back down to O'Neills Road. A longer, full-day traverse runs from Round Mountain in the west to Kings Road in the east. Consult Mount Roland Day Walk Map.

Mt Wellington
The giant mountain (1270m) looming over Hobart attracts day walkers to numerous destinations on the eastern and southern slopes as well as the alpine plateau. Highlights include Wellington Falls, Smiths Monument and Collins Bonnet. Phone Parks and Wildlife on (03) 6233 6560 for details.

Queenstown area
The Eldon Range to the west of Lake St Clair provides an interesting but tough excursion away from the crowded Overland Track. Primary access is via Lake Burbury and the South Eildon and Eildon rivers. The objectives are the dolerite summits of Eldon Peak (1439m) and Eldon Bluff, but the terrain is extremely difficult and progress will be slow. An easier destination is the little-known and seldom-visited Tyndall Range, offering walks connecting a series of lakes.

(110m) in the centre of the park. Phone Parks and Wildlife on (03) 6428 6277 for more details. TASMAP has released a detailed 1:25 000 map of the national park.

Ben Lomond National Park
This lofty plateau east of Launceston is a focus for local skiers in winter, but walkers can still enjoy the alpine scenery with a walking track that connects Legges Tor (1575m) with Carr Villa (1230m) The 5.5km walk takes about 2 hours. Stacks Bluff (1527m) lies on the undeveloped southern end of the plateau. It can be climbed in a day from Storys Creek via Denison Crag. Nearby are several other high peaks worth exploring in summer: Mt Victoria (1213m), East Tower (1117m) and West Tower (1110m). Phone Parks and Wildlife on (03) 6390 6279 for more details.

Black Bluff
This little-known distinctive peak commands superb views over north-western Tasmania, including south to

South Australia

Introduction

South Australia evokes images of the picturesque Barossa vineyards, the Australia Day test match and the churches of Adelaide. Relatively few people from outside the state know much about its ancient geography. Two-thirds of the state, especially the north, is almost empty, occupied by just one percent of the population. Four deserts dominate the major part of the surface area: the Simpson, the Great Victorian, the Sturt Stony and the Strzelecki. Much of the remainder is also flat, dry, hot and uninteresting. For example, the limestone plateau of the Nullarbor Plain is featureless for thousands of kilometres. Accordingly, South Australia can hardly be considered a bushwalking icon.

However, there are rugged rocky hills that extend from Cape Jervis north to Mt Hopeless, a distance of about 800km, and several significant wild sections along these folded mountains have been preserved in national parks: the Gammon Ranges, Flinders Ranges and Mt Remarkable. Because of their isolation, their dynamic appearance and harsh terrain they provide settings for some unique walking experiences during the cooler months. Kangaroo Island and the Eyre Peninsula are other interesting coastal bushwalking escapes with good walking opportunities.

The capital, Adelaide, has 1.2 million people, three universities and a host of annual arts and cultural events. The city nestles between sheltered gulf waters and a range of low hills on the northern and southern banks of the Torrens River. Residents enjoy 12km of white sandy beaches and the coast at Glenelg can be accessed by tram. The northern part of Adelaide, in particular, is very cosmopolitan.

Climate

The summers of inland South Australia are notoriously hot and dry with frequent drought conditions. Rivers and creeks cease flowing, and walking and camping is uncomfortable at best. The only place worth visiting in summer is Kangaroo Island, with its cooler maritime temperatures.

The Flinders and Gammon ranges are much more pleasant to explore on foot during winter, when temperatures peak in the high teens. Rainfall is minimal at most times of year with most falling in winter. Rain falls on about 60 days a year in the Flinders, a total of about 400mm, while the Gammon Ranges have half this amount. Only the southern half of the state receives any significant rainfall and walkers can usually plan excursions without the need to consult weather forecasts. Forgetting your Gore-Tex jacket won't be a life-threatening mistake here.

Average temperatures for Adelaide are 29°C in summer and 15°C in winter. In the Flinders Ranges, temperatures fluctuate between winter lows of 3°C and summer highs of 31°C. Farther north at the Gammon Ranges, you can safely assume that temperatures will be about 5°C higher. Temperatures increase as you move inland, but rainfall is lower.

The Remarkable Rocks—eroded granite boulders in the Flinders Chase National Park.

Transport

Flights from all of Australia's other capitals land at Adelaide Airport. As the city is located between Australia's east and west coasts and largely surrounded by desert, most people fly there when visiting. There are no other major airports. Airline companies operating in and out of Adelaide are currently Qantas, Ansett, Airlink and Southern.

Drivers from Queensland must go through Nyngan and Broken Hill, NSW, as there is no practical direct route. Sydney residents can also take the inland way along the Barrier Highway, but may prefer to take the scenic Riverina route through Wagga Wagga and Mildura, a distance of about 1400km. From Melbourne, drive either by the coast and Mt Gambier (929km) or cut through the mallee to shave 200km off the distance. From the north, Adelaide is a 3000km drive from Darwin via the Stuart Highway and Alice Springs. From Perth, there is only one option: the Eyre Highway through Norseman (2700km).

A more romantic mode of transport is to take the Indian-Pacific, Australia's great trans-continental railway, but this is expensive because you will need a sleeping carriage.

Public Transport
Buses

All information and bookings can be done through Adelaide's Central Bus Station, tel: (08) 8415 5533.

A free bus circles the city and a tram service provides additional transport options, going all the way down to Glenelg by the sea. Stateliner buses also service the Flinders Ranges to the north, taking visitors to Wilpena Pound. A one-way ticket currently costs about $50.00. The terminal is in Flinders Street. Sealink coaches go to Kangaroo Island, using their new passenger ferry.

Trains

Interstate train information and timetables can be obtained by phoning 132 232, a direct inquiry line.

The local state YHA sells tickets for all services and can also give advice about timetables. For local bus and train information in Adelaide contact:

Trans Adelaide
75 King William St, Adelaide SA 5000
Tel: (08) 8210 1000

Accommodation

South Australian YHA Membership and Travel Agency is at:
38 Sturt St, Adelaide SA 5000
Tel: (08) 8231 5583
Fax: (08) 8231 4219
e-mail: yhasa@ozemail.com.au
Reception hours: 9.00am–5.00pm weekdays
The office staff provide the following services:
- Membership: new members and renewals.
- International Guest Cards.
- Stock sales of sleeping sheets, handbooks, etc.
- Forward bookings of hostels internationally (IBN) and throughout Australia.
- Fully accredited Travel Agency with special prices for

members, including discounts on coach tickets (most operators). The YHA is also an agent for Great Southern Rail Facility and can book and issue tickets on the spot for domestic and international airlines and make all travel arrangements.
- Tour bookings for places of local interest.
- 10 per cent YHA Member discount on Travel Insurance.
- Give advice on the Heysen Trail and on using the hostels along the way.

Maps

The South Australian Department of Environment and Natural Resources (DENR) has produced a series of Landsmap 1:50 000 topographical maps. These mainly cover the south-east of the state, including Eyre, Yorke and Fleurieu peninsulas. Kangaroo Island and the Flinders Ranges are covered by good-quality specific tourist maps. The DENR Resource Information Group's primary outlet is:

MAPLAND
300 Richmond Rd, Netley SA 5037
Tel: (08) 8226 4946 or (08) 8226 4919
Fax: (08) 8226 4900
The postal address is:
PO Box 550, Marleston SA 5033

Maps and information, including the Heysen Trail maps, can also be obtained from:

Land Information Centre
Colonel Light Centre
25 Pirie St, Adelaide SA 5000
Tel: (08) 8226 4230
Fax: (08) 8226 4223
Their postal address is:
GPO Box 1047, Adelaide SA 5001

National Parks

National Parks and Wildlife, a division of the Department of Environment, Heritage and Aboriginal Affairs, administers South Australia's 300 national parks and other reserves totalling more than 20 million hectares, or 20 per cent of the state's surface area. The department has published a series of information brochures for most of its national parks, recreation parks and conservation reserves. They are available at the comprehensive visitors' centre:

The Environment Shop
77 Grenfell St, Adelaide SA 5000
Tel: (08) 8204 1910
Fax: (08) 8204 1919
e-mail: Environmentshop@dehaa.sa.gov.au
Their postal address is:
GPO Box 1047, Adelaide SA 5001

Entry fees apply in many of South Australia's most popular parks, including Belair, Cleland, Flinders Chase, Flinders Ranges, Innes, Mt Remarkable, Lincoln and Seal Bay. The cost per vehicle is small. Annual passes to a particular region, such as Eyre Peninsula or the desert region, are available, and there is a statewide pass allowing entry into all parks (discounts for pensioners and motorcycles). A small camping fee also applies at designated campgrounds, the price depending on the level of development and facilities provided. These grounds have been divided into three types:

Category A: Toilets, showers, BBQs, rubbish collection, power, laundry, kiosk, water

Examples are Naracoorte Caves, Innes, Lincoln (Memory Cove), Witjira. The cost is currently $15.00 per vehicle and $4.00 per bushwalker.

Category B: Toilets, some showers, BBQs, rubbish disposal, water

Examples are Mt Remarkable, Deep Creek, Flinders Chase. The cost is currently $12.00 per vehicle and $3.00 per bushwalker.

Category C: Minimal facilities

The cost is currently $5.00 per vehicle and $3.00 per bushwalker. Some private campgrounds are leased from the National Parks and Wildlife Service and impose their own fees.

Some tips

- Always take plenty of water when venturing into any national park
- All wood fires are banned between 1 November to 30 April each year in all South Australian parks
- If walking in summer, avoid walking in the hottest hours of the day
- Always find out track conditions and water availability from the relevant park ranger prior to setting off for any of the remote desert or mountain reserves
- Do not camp in dry creek beds as local flash flooding can be a threat.

Epic Walks

Heysen Trail

Apart from the Bicentennial National Trail, the Heysen Trail is the longest constructed walking track in the country. It runs for 1500km from Cape Jervis south of Adelaide to Parachilna Gorge in the northern Flinders Ranges. Along the way is the south coast of the Fleurieu Peninsula, Mt Lofty Ranges, the Barossa vineyards, Tothill Range, Mt Remarkable, Wilpena Pound and Aroona Valley. The trail is closed during the hotter months (from 1 December–30 April) and water can be difficult to obtain at times. Much of the trail passes through rural land, but walkers often neglect these sections in favour of the far more spectacular northern route passing through the more dynamic scenery of the Flinders Ranges National Park.

The Department of Recreation and Sport is responsible for maintaining the trail's facilities. They have divided the Heysen Trail up into 15 segments, and published a detailed 1:50 000 topographical route map on each one. These cost about $8.00 each and are available from:

Department of Recreation
and Sport
27 Valetta Rd
Kidman Park SA 5025
Tel: (08) 8416 6677
Fax: (08) 8416 6753
The postal address is:
PO Box 219
Brooklyn Park SA 5032

Setting up camp on the Heysen Trail by Wilcolo Creek beneath the ABC Range.

The Flinders Ranges

These famous twisted and folded mountains begin about 450km north of Adelaide, aligned in a north/south direction. The Flinders Ranges are really a series of smaller ranges, some being quite prominent and distinct, such as Wilpena Pound and the Elders. There are three main sections:

Northern Flinders Ranges: Gammon Ranges National Park and Arkaroola Wildlife Sanctuary

Central Flinders Ranges: Flinders Ranges National Park

Southern Flinders Ranges: Mt Remarkable National Park

Gammon Ranges National Park

Remote, dry and dramatic, the Gammon Ranges are one of South Australia's least known, but most spectacular, bushwalking destinations. Located in the far north of the Flinders Ranges and west of Arkaroola, the Gammon Ranges National Park incorporates a rugged maze of mountains, gorges and inaccessible country. To the north it adjoins the Arkaroola Wildlife Sanctuary, an area dominated by the Mawson Plateau, the culmination of quality wilderness in the Flinders Ranges. In this terrain, only the most experienced walkers should attempt overnight excursions.

The main staging area for walks in the Gammon Ranges is the Arkaroola Village. From here, tracks head off in all directions to various highlights of the northern section of the park. Other access points include Paralana Hot Springs (Arkaroola Wildlife Sanctuary), Grindells Hut (central section), and Italowie Gorge (south-eastern section). Camping is allowed but a permit must first be obtained from ranger headquarters at Balcanoona. There are facilities at Italowie Camp, Weetootla Gorge, Wooturpa Spring and Arcoona Creek. Cars can normally be taken to the main staging areas, but a 4WD is recommended if you want to access any of the minor unsealed tracks through the area. For day visitors, one of the major highlights of the Gammon Ranges National Park is Italowie Gorge, where

the near-perpendicular cliff faces of red quartzite contrast with river red gums. Benbonyathe (1064m) is the peak of the range although many neighbouring peaks are of similar elevation.

Facts and Figures

Name: Gammon Ranges National Park

Size: 128 228ha

Enactment: 1970

Vegetation: Rasp fern, coolibah trees, silver wattle, hopbush, river red gum and northern cypress pine

Wildlife: 70 bird species including eagles and parrots, western grey and red kangaroos, rock wallabies, echidnas and bats. Large herds of feral goats are a major nuisance for park authorities and walkers.

Facilities: Rough bush-camping is permitted at Balcanoona Station, Arcoona Creek, Weetootla Gorge and Italowie Gorge. There's a caravan park at Arkaroola Village and some of the historic huts in the area are available for hire. Grindells Hut, for example, accommodates 10 people. There is no electricity so guests must provide their own lighting. Other huts are Nudlamutana Hut and the Balcanoona Shearer's Quarters. Book through the Parks and Wildlife Hawker Office on (08) 8648 4244.

Attractions: A sense of extreme isolation, red quartzite cliff-faces, buckled mountain ranges, wild gorges and deep narrow chasms. The Gammon Ranges are one of Australia's most seismically active areas. Frequent tremors occur.

Access: The park is about 750km north of Adelaide at the northern end of the Flinders Ranges. The main ranger office is at Balcanoona, 101km east of Copley or 272km north of Yunta. The main visitor accommodation is at Arkaroola, 30km north of Balcanoona.

Further Information:

National Parks and Wildlife
Gammon Ranges National Park
Tel: (08) 8648 5300 or
       (08) 8648 4829
or
National Parks and Wildlife
Post Office, Hawker SA 5434
Tel: (08) 8648 4244
Fax: (08) 8648 4242

An excellent booklet, *Explore the Flinders Ranges* by Sue Barker, Murray McCaskill and Brian Ward, gives comprehensive background information on flora, fauna, history and geology of the Gammon Ranges. Another more specific but harder to obtain guidebook is Adrian Heard's *Gammon Ranges and Arkaroola Sanctuary: A Walking Guide to the Northern Flinders*.

Bunyip Chasm Circuit

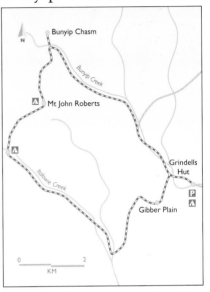

Starting Point: Grindells Hut, Gammon Ranges National Park

Destination: Bunyip Chasm, Mt John Roberts, Italowie Creek, Gibber Plain

Summary: A wild trackless circuit featuring deeply dissected ranges

Attractions: Bunyip Chasm, views of Mt John Roberts, remote isolated wilderness atmosphere

Length: Total distance is 28.1km
Day 1: Grindell Hut to Mt John Roberts, 13.9km
Day 2: Mt John Roberts to Grindells Hut, 14.2km

Time: 2 days

Options: Camp can also be set up in Italowie Creek

Grade: ★ ★ ★ ★

Fitness: ☒ ☒ ☒ ☒

Maps: Landsmap Illinawortina 1:50 000 topographical

Access to Starting Point: From Adelaide, drive north to Port Augusta. Just 7km before the port, turn right onto highway 47 to Quorn, Hawker, Parachilna and Leigh Creek. Continue north to Copley before turning right to

Near Arkaroola, Gammon Ranges National Park.

Balcanoona. From here, head north on the Arkaroola road but turn left 8km later and follow the road for 18km to Grindells Hut.

Facilities/Amenities: There is a basic car-camping area at Grindells Hut, otherwise none. The nearest supplies are to the north at Arkaroola.

Recommended Equipment: It is imperative that you carry sufficient water. A self-supporting tent for pitching on rock is handy as is a good-quality inflatable sleeping mattress because the ground is quite hard.

Notes: Some sections of the walk involve very steep climbs, so walkers should be accomplished on rock. Don't go in summer months.

Further Information:
National Parks and Wildlife
Gammon Ranges National Park
Tel: (08) 8648 4829

Walk Description

This is an excellent overnight walk featuring a spectacular chasm, outstanding sunset and sunrise views from camp and plenty of typical Gammon Ranges gorge scenery. Despite the short distances involved, the wild terrain between Bunyip Chasm and Mt John Roberts makes progress slow. Because of the dry location, several litres of water should be carried for each party member.

The walk starts and ends at the historic Grindells Hut staging area. The road deteriorates from here and cars should be left at the parking area.

There are several historic buildings and a windmill here, including the hut where cattle rustler George Snell was murdered in 1918. Head west along Balcanoona Creek. After 30 minutes, you pass a minor vehicular track that heads south to Mt McKinley Springs. Continue west on the main road to Loch Ness Well. Water can sometimes be found here but don't rely on it. Head up Balcanoona Creek, leaving the vehicular track behind.

About 1km past the well, fork left into Bunyip Creek, which gradually narrows into a cliff-lined gorge. After about 40 minutes of walking, the creek bed swings left and the entrance to Bunyip Chasm can be seen to the north. Leave your packs here.

Scramble up past several waterfalls and through a couple of amphitheatres. During the middle of the day when sunlight reaches down into the depths, the scenery is simply magnificent. Spend some time exploring and scrambling through here, although the nature of the topography makes it quite clear further progress past the chasm is virtually impossible without climbing equipment.

The afternoon involves more rock-scrambling to attain Steadman Ridge. If water is available from Bunyip Creek, fill any containers that are empty. Head west slightly from the junction with Bunyip Chasm and climb around a waterfall to a scrubby spur that leads to Steadman Ridge. Progress will be slow along this diffi-

cult section. Camp at Mt John Roberts, enjoying the panoramic spectacle. The sunset across the ranges is particularly serene as the wind usually stills and the birdlife quietens.

The second day is considerably easier as you keep following the crest of a ridge to the south-west of Mt John Roberts, descending into the northern branch of Italowie Creek via a small side gully to the left (south).

Once reaching the bottom, head downstream for several kilometres until you come to the Mt McKinley Springs track. Turn left, following this north-east over the Gibber Plain, back down to Balcanoona Creek and then due east to Grindells Hut.

Longer extensions to Cleft Peak, Fern Chasm, Mt McKinley Bluff, Prow Point and Shelf Chasm can be undertaken by very experienced, well-equipped and self-sufficient parties who are quite used to navigating in trackless terrain.

Italowie Gorge Walk

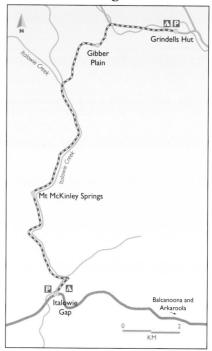

Starting Point: Grindells Hut, Gammon Ranges National Park
Destination: Italowie Gap
Summary: An easy walk along several creek beds that meander through fantastic gorge scenery. Set up a car shuffle (41km) to avoid backtracking.
Attractions: Mt McKinley Springs
Length: 16km

Time: 5 hours
Options: The route can be walked in either direction
Grade: ★ ★ ★
Fitness: ☒ ☒
Maps: Landsmap Illinawortina and Nepabunna 1:50 000 topographicals
Access to Starting Point: As for preceding walk
Facilities/Amenities: As for preceding walk
Recommended Equipment: It is imperative that you carry enough water
Notes: Not suitable for summer months
Further Information:
National Parks and Wildlife
Gammon Ranges National Park
Tel: (08) 8648 4829

Walk Description

The main focus of this walk is the outstanding tillite cliffs that Italowie Creek has carved through the Balcanoona Range in the eastern Gammon Ranges National Park. You will possibly also encounter feral goats that defy capture by park rangers.

From Grindells Hut, head west along Balcanoona Creek and left onto the old Mt McKinley Springs track. This climbs up to Gibber Plain (447m) where it's easy walking down to Italowie Creek (northern branch). Simply keep on the track as it meanders south to the springs. There are occasional good views, especially to the east, along here. From the spring, walk east to a gully before turning south and descending once again into Italowie Creek. Note the change in the rocks and general geological formations between the springs and the creek. Once you're in the Italowie Creek gorge, enjoy the scenery as you head south to the car park at Italowie Gap.

Other walks in the Gammon Ranges
Weetootla Gorge Circuit (12.6km, 4 hours)

Weetootla Camp is accessed by car just north of Balcanoona 2km off the Arkaroola road. From here, walk to Grindells Hut through Balcanoona Gorge, Hells Gates and the dramatic Weetootla Gorge. Take a longer return trip by following the main access road north and east all the way to Weetootla Creek before heading south along the creek back to Hells Gates.

Arkaroola Area

This tourist village was converted from a pastoral lease by geologist Reg Sprigg in 1968. From Arkaroola, day-walk destinations include:

Acacia Ridge (10km, 3.5 hours)

A walk to the summit of the ridge (566m), with superb views over the southern part of the park.

Bararranna Gorge (4.4km, 1.5 hours)

A return walk from the car park to Bararranna Waterhole, about 10km north of Arkaroola. The red quartzite here is about 900 million years old, making it the oldest in all the Flinders Ranges. For a longer circuit, follow Arkaroola Creek upstream and return via Spotted Schist Pass track.

Mawson Valley and the Pinnacles (8km, 3 hours)

A very interesting 8km circuit, returning via the Umberatana Road and a lookout on the Spriginna Track.

Mawson Plateau: This granite plateau is an almost intact wilderness area in the north of the Arkaroola Wildlife Sanctuary. A look at the Yudnamutana topographical map will highlight the extreme isolation you will encounter in the many gorges from Yudnamutana Creek north to Hamilton Creek. Ideally, walkers should have a GPS system to minimise the chance of getting lost. The main access is via the radioactive Paralana Hot Springs, 33km north of Arkaroola. A number of waterholes in the area make good, challenging destinations.

Terrapinna: At the far northern end of the Arkaroola Wildlife Sanctuary lies the ancient Terrapinna granite country. The landscape here dates from about 1.5 billion years ago. Take the Moolawatana road north from Balcanoona and the Lyndhurst Track west for 9km to the remote Terrapinna Spring on Hamilton Creek. Options include Mt Babbage (322m) just to the north and along Hamilton Creek to the south. This is the furthermost extent of the Flinders Ranges. The other end, is about 500km to the south.

Flinders Ranges National Park

Centred on Wilpena Pound, Flinders Ranges National Park occupies much of the central Flinders Ranges. It is very popular and takes in rugged mountain scenery interspersed with cliff-lined gorges. There is also plenty to delight geologists and historians.

Kangaroos grazing on the grassy flats of the remote Arcoona camping area, near the western boundary of the Gammon Ranges National Park.

Mt Ohlssen Bagge at Wilpena Pound, Flinders Ranges National Park.

The most visited features are Wilpena Pound, Edeowie gorge, Brachina gorge and the valleys of Aroona and Bunyeroo. Wildlife can be seen almost everywhere: wedge-tailed eagles, rock wallabies, western grey kangaroos and flocks of colourful birds. After the right rainfall, wildflowers bloom around springtime, transforming the otherwise arid country. Occasionally, visitors may encounter the historic ruins of a failed station property, such as at Aroona and in Wilpena Pound, reminders that this is a brutal continent. Several ranges are found within the Flinders

Ranges National Park: the Heysen, ABC, Trezona and the famous Wilpena Pound Range. Lying just outside the national park boundary are several other prominent ranges: Elder, Chace, Druid and The Bunkers. All of these destinations are a paradise for bushwalkers of all levels of experience. The longest track is the Heysen Trail, which enters Wilpena Pound from the Moralana Valley in the south-west and winds north to reach the Parachilna Gorge.

The best time for bushwalking in the Flinders Ranges is between May and October, when temperatures are

mild. As a safeguard, walkers must always be sure to carry plenty of water. All facilities can be found at Wilpena Chalet, upgraded in 1999 with a $6.4 million development.

Facts and Figures

Name: Flinders Ranges National Park

Size: 92 746ha

Enactment: 1971 (extensions in 1985)

Aboriginal Sites: Camp debris, ochre paintings and rock engravings are amongst the evidence of occupation by the Adnyamathanha tribes. The landscape was said to have been formed by the travels of Akurra, the Dreamtime serpent. Wilpena means 'place of bent fingers'.

Vegetation: The two most frequently encountered vegetation communities are cypress pine over the low hills and river red gums in the gorges. On the rocky mountain slopes, grasstrees are common.

Wildlife: About 23 mammal species remain from the 55 species that originally inhabited the area before Europeans arrived. The main surviving species are kangaroos and wallabies, including the rare yellow-footed rock wallaby. Almost 100 bird species have been recorded, including the spotted harrier, grey falcon and cinnamon quail-thrush. Reptiles here include snakes, goannas, geckos and skinks.

Attractions: Rugged rocky gorges with brilliant colours

Facilities: The only facilities in the park are found at the Wilpena Tourist Centre where there's a parks office, resort accommodation and small supermarket.

Further Information:

National Parks and Wildlife
Wilpena Pound
Tel: (08) 8648 0048 or
        (08) 8648 0049

or:

National Parks and Wildlife
Post Office, Hawker SA 5434
Tel: (08) 8648 4244
Fax: (08) 8648 4242

An excellent booklet, *Explore the Flinders Ranges* by Sue Barker, Murray McCaskill and Brian Ward, gives comprehensive background information on flora, fauna, history and geology of the Flinders Ranges.

Mt Ohlssen Bagge Walk

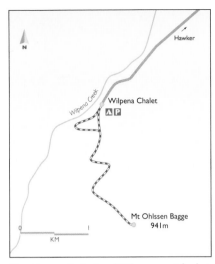

Starting Point: Wilpena Chalet, Flinders Ranges National Park

Destination: The summit of Mt Ohlssen Bagge (941m), also known as Mt John

Summary: A direct ascent from the resort to the summit of Mt Ohlssen Bagge, overlooking the Wilpena Pound formation. Return to the resort via Wilpena Creek.

Attractions: Views over Wilpena Pound and along the prominent range to the north and south

Length: 5.3km

Time: 3 hours

Options: None

Grade: ★ ★ ★

Fitness: ✗ ✗ ✗

Maps: Landsmap Wilpena 1:50 000 topographical. Heysen Trail map sheet #5 (Wilpena to Hawker) also contains the relevant topographical coverage.

Access to Starting Point: Wilpena Pound is about 450km north of Adelaide, through Wilmington and Quorn. The resort is about 55km north of Hawker and 4km off the main road. All turn-offs are signposted.

Facilities/Amenities: None en route. Resort facilities, camping area and visitors' centre at Wilpena Chalet.

Recommended Equipment: Water

Notes: If walking in summer, leave very early so you can complete the walk before 11.00am when the temperatures can become unbearable

Further Information:
National Parks and Wildlife
Wilpena Pound Office
Tel: (08) 8648 0048 or
        (08) 8648 0049

Walk Description

This short walk is the easiest, most accessible overview of the abruptly folded mountains that line Wilpena Pound. The only easier option is to charter a plane. The track leaves from the far side of the resort. Simply walk along Wilpena Creek until a sign-posted walking track heads up a hill on the left from a clearing amid tall eucalypts. The mountain was named in 1851 by Sinnett, the first surveyor to work in the Wilpena district. He named St Marys Peak at the same time. The track is initially of a high standard and the views to the east begin as soon as you reach the first small bluff. From then on it gets steeper, ascending to 900m, with some boulder-hopping necessary toward the end.

The views across the pound are spectacular, especially early in the morning when there is good contrast on the orange quartzite cliffs. The pound is about 16km long by 7km wide with a very even floor. It was once a cattle station with the cliffs making an ideal perimeter fence. The Elder Range in the distance is especially dramatic. Return to the bottom by the same route, but at the very end, why not take the Drought Busters nature trail loop along Wilpena Creek?

Wilpena Pound Circuit

Starting Point: Wilpena Chalet, Flinders Ranges National Park

Destination: Glenora Falls, Edeowie Gorge, Malloga Falls

Summary: A magnificent circuit walk connecting the best features of Wilpena Pound

Attractions: Outstanding views from St Marys Peak over the classic cupped-hands formation of Wilpena Pound. Other attractions are Edeowie Gorge, Malloga Falls and Glenora Falls.

Length: Total distance is 32.8km

Day 1: Wilpena Chalet to Cooinda Camp via St Marys Peak, 11.3km

Day 2: Cooinda Camp to Glenora Falls (return), 12.5km

Day 3: Cooinda Camp to Wilpena Pound via Pound Gap, 9km

Time: 3 days

Options: Optional 10km side trip to Pompey Pillar from Cooinda Camp

Grade: ★ ★ ★ ★ ★

Fitness: ✗ ✗ ✗ ✗

Maps: Landsmap Wilpena 1:50 000 topographical

Access to Starting Point: As for preceding walk

Facilities/Amenities: Resort facilities, camping area and visitors' centre at Wilpena Pound. There's a basic walk-in camping area at Cooinda Camp.

Recommended Equipment: Water containers

Notes: Check with the ranger at the visitors' centre about water at Cooinda Camp. Camping permits are required. The section past Malloga Falls is treacherous in parts and only experienced walkers should attempt it.

Further Information:
National Parks and Wildlife
Wilpena Pound Office
Tel: (08) 8648 0048 or
        (08) 8648 0049

Walk Description

St Marys Peak (1171m) is the highest mountain in the Flinders Range National Park, so provides an excellent vantage point. But the summit is only the first stop along a breathtaking circuit of the park's most interesting features. Begin at the pleasant campground on the northern side of Wilpena Creek and walk along the direct route to St Marys Peak. This section is part of the epic Heysen Trail marked by distinctive orange and white logos. Leave early to avoid the heat of the day. Initially you follow the base of the Attunga Bluff for 3km before beginning the strenuous ascent to Tanderra Saddle. About 400m of altitude must be gained and the views to the east toward the southern ABC Range are tremendous.

Looking north along the rim of Wilpena Pound, Flinders Ranges National Park.

At the top, a junction gives options to St Marys Peak and Cooinda Camp. Drop the packs and head up 1km and 220m higher along the range to the summit of St Marys Peak. The track keeps roughly to the centre of the ridge crest, but progress is slowed by the numerous rocky outcrops. It takes about 90 minutes to complete the return distance of just 2km. From the top, you can look down into Wilpena Pound to where you will be walking over the next two days. In the distance is the vast Lake Torrens. Collect the packs at Tanderra Saddle, head down the other side of the range to Cooinda Camp and set up your tents. Water can normally be found by following the Edeowie Track upstream to a rockhole. It's about 1.4km return.

The second day is a great day walk through the Edeowie Gorge to Glenora Falls. The gorge is an extraordinary example of the geological processes that formed Wilpena Pound about 500 million years ago. There's a lot to see and progress is slow, so leave early. Malloga Falls are at the beginning of the gorge on Edeowie Creek while Glenora Falls are 3km downstream. No progress is possible past Glenora Falls and walkers must backtrack to Cooinda Camp. The last day is the easiest as you simply walk south and west along the Wilpena Pound floor to the ruins of an old homestead by Wilpena Creek. The building was constructed in 1911 by John Hill, who grew crops of wheat in the pound. He was also responsible for most of the

clearing of vegetation on the pound floor. His wheat and grazing ventures failed because of the harsh weather and isolation. From the ruins, simply walk east over a footbridge and through the gap back to the resort and visitors' centre. An alternative way is to climb past Sliding Rock.

Heysen Trail (Flinders Ranges section) Walk

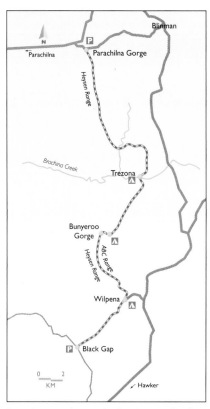

Starting Point: Black Gap, Flinders Ranges National Park

Destination: Parachilna Gorge
Summary: Many of the most attractive features of the 1500km Heysen Trail lie along this section in the Flinders Ranges
Attractions: Wilpena Pound, the ABC and Heysen ranges, excellent outback scenery, superb views
Length: Total distance is 90.5km
Day 1: Black Gap Lookout to Cooinda Camp, 12km
Day 2: Cooinda Camp to Wilpena Chalet, 9km
Day 3: Wilpena Chalet to Yanyanna Hut, 22.5km
Day 4: Yanyanna Hut to Aroona, 27km
Day 5: Aroona to Parachilna Gorge, 20km
Time: 5 days
Options: A side option down Edeowie Gorge is highly recommended. There's an alternative camping site on the Brachina Creek south of Aroona.
Grade: ★ ★ ★ ★
Fitness: ◪◪◪
Maps: Landsmap Wilpena, Oraparinna and Blinman 1:50 000 topographicals. Also Heysen Trail map sheets #4 (Parachilna Gorge to Wilpena) and #5 (Wilpena to Hawker).
Access to Starting Point: Black Gap Lookout is on the Moralana Scenic Drive, which turns off the main Wilpena road about 24km north of Hawker. Road access to the walk's end at Parachilna Gorge is via the Blinman–Parachilna road.
Facilities/Amenities: Resort facilities, camping area and visitors' centre at Wilpena Pound. Rough bush-camping at Cooinda Camp and various huts along the way. Water can be found at various creeks but don't rely on it.
Recommended Equipment: Water containers (carry at least four litres per person per day), warm sleeping bag for cold outback nights
Notes: The northern section of the trail is closed from 1 November to 1 March each year. The section to the south of Wilpena closes on 15 April. Walkers should check water availability with park rangers. Note that camping permits are required.
Further Information:
  National Parks and Wildlife
  Wilpena Pound Office
  Tel: (08) 8648 0048 or
         (08) 8648 0049

Walk Description

Although the Heysen Trail is 1500km long, a lot of the scenery it passes through is dry, flat, pastoral and un-interesting. As the trail passes through the central Flinders Ranges north of Hawker, it enters the rugged mountain scenery of the Wilpena Pound and the Heysen Range. This walk is only recommended for the winter months when temperatures are cooler. Set up a car shuffle to avoid backtracking. Shorter segments of this route can be done by parking a car at any of the suggested camping areas.

The trail was named after Sir Hans Heysen, a German painter whose outback art became internationally famous. He was born in Hamburg on 8 October 1877, and migrated to Australia in 1884, living most his life in Hahndorf in the Adelaide Hills. Heyson made frequent excursions to the Flinders Ranges, particularly the Aroona valley and Arkaba Range. One of his most famous paintings is of the majestic Cazneaux Tree just north of the turn-off to Wilpena Chalet. Many gum trees from the Mt Lofty Ranges were the subjects of his paintings. He won the prestigious Wynne Prize for landscapes nine times and was knighted at the age of 82 in recognition of his 'outstanding contribution to Australian art'. He died in 1968. The long-distance walking trail named in his honour was proposed by Warren Bonython in 1970 but political obstacles prevented its completion until 1992.

From Black Gap Lookout, head down the eastern side of the Bunbin-yunna Range to a minor creek. The sheer buttresses of Wilpena Pound dominate everything ahead. Climb up to Bridle Gap (690m), the highest point on the route. A short scramble up to the left leads to Dick Knob with great views over to the Elder Range. Grasstrees and boulders dominate the foreground. From Bridle Gap head down onto the flat pound floor and walk north-east to the other side. Mallee scrub, hopbush and native pine (*Callitris glaucophylla*) dominate the vegetation. Just before Wilpena Spring a track heads left to Cooinda Camp. While you could simply camp at the developed camping ground on the other side of Pound Gap, a detour to Cooinda Creek is recommended to explore Edeowie Gorge. Next day head to Wilpena Chalet either by Pound Gap or via Tanderra Saddle to climb St Marys Peak (1171m). The distance is not great so there's plenty of time to spend in the gorge or on the peak.

On the third day, rise early because there's a lot of territory to cover. From the camping ground head along the first section of the St Marys Peak ascent and walk along the main Wilpena Chalet access road for 800m before turning left. This leads all the way along the ABC Range with its series of small knolls. You will be more or less following this range until the end of the way.

The trail soon enters a pleasant valley between the towering 1000m peaks of Wilpena Pound on the left and the ABC Range on the right. Stay on the western bank of Wilcolo Creek, walking past magnificent river red gums and coolibah trees. Have lunch anywhere before turning right to climb over the ABC Range. It's a rocky scramble until you reach the crest and down again on the eastern side into the Bunyeroo Creek valley to join up with another vehicular trail. Keep north until you reach the open grounds of Yanyanna Hut. Don't rely on water from the spring just to the north.

Spend the next day continuing north to Aroona through open country dominated by cypress pines. At certain high points are great vistas to the ABC Range to the west. About 2 hours after leaving camp you should come to the old Elatina Hut site with a spring just downstream. The new Elatina Hut lies about 2.5km to the north. This is also called Middle Camp Hut and it too has a spring nearby. About 15 minutes after passing the hut, walking through wattle and hop-bush, you cross the Blinman road and soon after, the wide sandy bed of Brachina Creek. To the west, this watercourse has carved a fascinating gorge through the Heysen Range, exposing a wealth of geological and palaeontological features. While often dry, the creek is a shady spot for lunch under gum trees. Spend the afternoon continuing north, keeping the Trezona Range on your right. This mainly limestone range contains examples of rare stromatolite fossils, some of the oldest life forms on earth.

Turn left after 8km and check out Red Hill Lookout (550m) with views in all directions. Descend the western side, passing through the rocky quartz-based ABC Range once more to the ruins of historic Aroona. The homestead here was built by Frederick Hayward in May 1851. Here he ran sheep successfully for 11 years before

Overlooking the Bunyeroo Creek valley on the Heysen Trail en route to Aroona.

returning to England. Hans Heysen stayed here with friend and host Eddie Pumpa on some of his famous art expeditions, receiving inspiration from the surrounding hills. Koolaman Spring lies just to the north up a small hill, but it is boarded up. Water is available from a bore instead.

On the final day, head north along the Aroona Creek valley, following the rugged Heysen Range to the west. Iralbo and Kankana peaks are particularly dramatic. Porcupine grass is everywhere. The track eventually emerges on the Parachilna–Blinman road at the end of the Heysen Trail.

Other walks in the Central Flinders Ranges

As the Flinders Ranges National Park and neighbouring areas provide the best bushwalking country in the state, some more suggestions are warranted.

Blinman Pools Walk (8km, 3 hours)

A short track follows the Parachilna and Wockerawirra creeks to Blinman Pools in the far northern part of the central Flinders Ranges. Escape hot midday weather at this idyllic oasis.

Bunyeroo Gorge Walk (7km, 2 hours)

From the tourist road that crosses Bunyeroo Gorge, head west into the Heysen Range enjoying the solitude, pools and river red gums before backtracking.

Chambers Gorge Walk (upto 20km, 1 day)

About 70km north-east of Blinman Pools, a small but spectacular outlier of the Flinders Ranges has been carved by Mt Chambers Creek. When it flows, it empties into Lake Frome. Follow the normally dry bed for about 10km into the gorge. There are good views to the fortress of Mt Chambers.

Chace Range Walk (4km, 3 hours)

A difficult return climb up to Mt Havelock (800m) rewards walkers with grand views over the southern ramparts of Wilpena Pound, especially Rawnsley Bluff. Access is from Martins Well Road about 12km from the Hawker–Wilpena road.

The famous Cazneaux Tree at the entrance to Wilpena Pound.

Elder Range Walk (upto 9km, 1 day)

The Elders are one of the Flinders Ranges' more awe-inspiring outliers. Rising to Mt Aleck (1065m), they dominate the scenery to the west of Wilpena Pound, tempting hard-core walkers to tackle their steep bluffs. The range is best approached from the north using the Moralana Scenic Road as the nearest access point.

Heysen Range Walk (8km, 5 hours)

Mt Hayward, on the northern boundary of the national park, is a challenge.

Although the distance is only about 8km return via Walkandi Peak, progress is slow through trackless terrain from the Aroona homestead and over rocky topography on the ascent. Once on top, it is fairly easy walking.

Jarvis Hill Walk
(700m, 25 min)

Less than 7km to the west of Hawker, this very short circuit track leads to Jarvis Hill (540m) on the Yourambulla Range with views over similar but smaller geological formations to Wilpena Pound. The bronze plaque at the top points out prominent peaks.

Mt Sunderland Walk
(10.5km, 5 hours)

Leading up Mt Sunderland (790m) in the centre of the national park, with panoramic views over most of the vicinity, the track leaves the Wilpena–Oraparinna road about 2km south of Oraparinna. Vertical rise is only 190m.

Sacred Canyon Walk
(1km, 45 min)

Aboriginal engravings and paintings can be seen on this walk, accessed by a rough road to the south-east of Wilpena Chalet.

Wilkawillina Gorge Walk
(11.4km, 4.5 hours)

This walk follows Mt Billy Creek through the cliff-lined Wilkawillina Gorge in the far eastern part of the national park. Locked in the rocks here are fossils of *Archarocyatha*, the very first animals with skeletons. The gorge becomes reedy as you proceed south but you can walk all the way to Little Bunkers Trackhead and the Oraparinna–Wirrealpa road. For those unable to set up a car shuffle, simply walk in for about 7km, then backtrack to the Wilkawillina Gorge car park (Mt Billy Trailhead).

Other walks in Wilpena Pound

Several other walks to various vantage points around the rim of the pound are possible, including:

Arkaroo Rock Walk
(2.3km, 1 hour)

Some excellent examples of Aboriginal art can be seen at Arkaroo on the southern ramparts of Wilpena Pound. The walk to the rock shelter is easy, climbing just over 100m. The images are primarily of animals. Respect all painting and engravings. There are views across to the Chace Range.

Wangarra Lookout Walk
(6.9km, 2 hours)

Just inside Pound Gap, Wangarra Lookout offers reasonable views for walkers with insufficient time to ascend St Marys Peak or Mt Ohlssen Bagge. Reaching the lookout (806m) involves a 400m ascent. The walk can be shorter if the road to the Pound Gap car park is open. In this case, it's only 3.1km return.

Other Peaks

If you're willing to endure harsh trackless and often scrubby terrain, there are many other peaks around the pound, such as Binya Peak and Pompey Pillar. Perhaps the pick of them is the craggy quartzite and sandstone Rawnsley Bluff at the far south of the pound.

Mt Remarkable National Park

This small but geologically significant park lies between the shores of Spencer Gulf and the mountainous regions between Wilmington and Melrose. Its topography is varied, from temperate lowlands along the gulf, through the higher wheat country inland to the ranges. Being close to the coast, Mt Remarkable National Park receives a lot more rainfall than the other parks, usually averaging about 500mm a year, so flora and fauna are plentiful, in contrast with some of the drier inland parks.

Mt Remarkable (963m) was named by explorer Edward John Eyre for its sheer precipitous drop. The range is mainly composed of various forms of quartzite while the gorges are tillite. Being so close to Adelaide, the park attracts many bushwalkers, especially to Alligator Gorge, Hidden Gorge, Mt Cavern and Mt Remarkable.

There are three main access areas for Mt Remarkable:

• *Mambray Creek*, 45km north of Port Pirie on Highway Number One. The Stateliner bus service calls at park headquarters here.
• *Alligator Gorge*, which can be reached by following a tourist road south of Wilmington.
• *Mt Remarkable section*, directly north-east of Melrose.

Facts and Figures

Name: Mt Remarkable National Park

Size: 16 100ha

Aboriginal Sites: The Nukunu tribe inhabited the southern ranges before the coming of Europeans.

Vegetation: Primarily dry sclerophyll forest dominated by a mix of peppermint and grey box. Blue gums and white box are also common. Some drier sections contain stunted mallee heath.

Wildlife: The park is habitat to the death adder and lace goanna, among other reptiles. Marsupials such as the western grey and red kangaroos are common. Birdlife is plentiful, with many species having their northern limit here.

Attractions: Deeply dissected ranges have created superb gorges for walking. The mountains to the south command excellent views over the entire area.

Facilities: The main car-camping area is at Mambray Creek in the south. It has 53 sites, water, toilets and fireplaces. There is also a hut available for rent here.

Further information:

National Parks and Wildlife
Mt Remarkable National Park
PMB 7 Mambray Creek
via Port Pirie SA 5540
Tel: (08) 8634 7068
Fax: (08) 8634 7085

The nearest district offices are at Hawker (see information for Flinders Ranges National Park) and at Port Augusta:

Department of Environment, Heritage and Aboriginal Affairs
9 Mackay St, Port Augusta SA 5700
Tel: (08) 8648 5300

An excellent booklet is available entitled *Explore the Flinders Ranges* by Sue Barker, Murray McCaskill and Brian Ward. It gives comprehensive background information on the flora, fauna, history and geology of the Flinders Ranges.

Mt Cavern Circuit

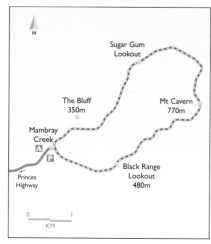

Starting Point: Mambray Creek, Mt Remarkable National Park

Destination: Mt Cavern (770m)

Summary: A loop track to the highest point on the Black Range

Attractions: Views over Spencer Gulf from Mt Cavern's conical peak

Length: 11.7km

Time: 5 hours

Options: Extensions can be added by connecting with Hidden Gorge Trail. The circuit can be walked in either direction, but park authorities recommend climbing the southern slope first so that the ascent is more gentle.

Grade: ★ ★ ★

Fitness: ☒☒☒☒

Maps: Landsmap Melrose 1:50 000 topographical

Access to Starting Point: Mambray Creek day-visitor area is just off the Princes Highway between Port Germein and Port Augusta

Facilities/Amenities: Well-developed camping facilities at Mambray Creek

Recommended Equipment: Water

Notes: The park can be closed during total fire bans

Further Information:
Mt Remarkable National Park
PMB 7 Mambray Creek
via Port Pirie SA 5540
Tel: (08) 8634 7068
Fax: (08) 8634 7085

Walk Description

Mt Cavern was named by Staff Commander Howard, a British naval officer who charted the Spencer Gulf in the 1860s. From the car park, head up the prominent, steep easterly spur to Black Range Lookout (480m) and follow the crest of the Black Range to the summit. Have lunch here in the shade while you enjoy the panorama. Unfortunately, much of the area was burnt out in 1988. Mt Remarkable dominates the horizon to the east. Return to the car park by descending to Mambray Creek via Sugar Gum Lookout to the north, and follow this pleasant watercourse lined by river red gums downstream to the car park.

Hidden Gorge Circuit

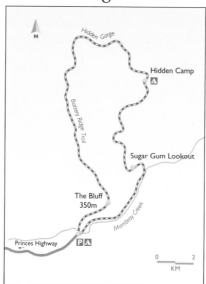

Starting Point: Mambray Creek, Mt Remarkable National Park

Destination: The Battery Ridge

Summary: A day circuit with both gorge scenery and ridgetop walking. It approaches Hidden Gorge from the east and returns by The Battery Ridge.

Attractions: Red quartzite cliffs in Hidden Gorge and coastal views

Length: 18km

Time: 1 full day

Options: The circuit can be walked in either direction, but it's best to leave the ridge walking until last, when the sun is lower in the west

Grade: ★ ★ ★ ★

Fitness: ☒☒☒

Maps: Landsmap Melrose 1:50 000 topographical

Access to Starting Point: Mambray Creek day-visitor area is just off the Princes Highway between Port Germein and Port Augusta

Facilities/Amenities: Well-developed camping facilities at Mambray Creek. There are also basic campsites at Hidden Camp for walkers wishing to make a leisurely two-day trip.

Recommended Equipment: Water

Notes: The park can be closed during total fire bans. Avoid peak periods, such as the school holidays at Easter.

Further Information:
Mt Remarkable National Park
PMB 7 Mambray Creek
via Port Pirie SA 5540
Tel: (08) 8634 7068
Fax: (08) 8634 7085
or refer to WILD magazine, issue 75 (Summer 2000).

Sturts desert pea is commonly found through outback South Australia.

Walk Description

The main attraction is the bright red cliffs of the narrow Hidden Gorge, worn through ancient quartzite. Walk along Mambray Creek and turn left at Sugar Gum Lookout. Turn left at Hidden Camp on Alligator Creek. Continue north and turn into Hidden Gorge, where the dynamic scenery is at its most spectacular. When you emerge from the western end, go south towards The Battery Ridge where sugar gums make a pleasant foreground to the outstanding views. Head south, returning to Mambray Creek day-visitor area via The Bluff.

Alligator Gorge Circuit

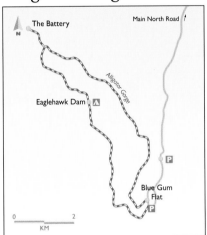

Starting Point: Blue Gum Flat, Mt Remarkable National Park

Destination: Alligator Gorge and The Battery Ridge

Summary: A circuit through a red quartzite-lined gorge in the north of Mt Remarkable National Park. The track enters the gorge from the car park and returns via the Ring Route

Attractions: Alligator Gorge, views from The Battery Ridge

Length: 12km

Time: Half a day

Options: Walk in either direction

Grade: ★ ★ ★

Fitness: ✗ ✗ ✗

Maps: Landsmap Wilmington 1:50 000 topographical

Access to Starting Point: Blue Gum Flat is 2.6km south past Alligator Lodge in the north of the park. Access is via Wilmington.

Facilities/Amenities: A developed car-camping and picnic area at Blue

Sunset from Battery Ridge, Mt Remarkable National Park.

Gum Flat. The nearest shops are at Wilmington.

Recommended Equipment: Water

Notes: The park may be closed in periods of high fire danger

Further Information:
Mt Remarkable National Park
PMB 7 Mambray Creek
via Port Pirie SA 5540
Tel: (08) 8634 7068
Fax: (08) 8634 7085

Walk Description

This less-frequented northern part of Mt Remarkable National Park centres on the stunning Alligator Gorge. A well-graded track enters the gorge where walkers can marvel at the towering formations. From the car park, follow the signs down to The Terraces, turn right into Alligator Gorge heading north-west. At one stage it is only 3m wide. When you emerge at the other side, turn right and head up onto The Battery, a razor-sharp ridge for good westerly views over Spencer Gulf. Sunset can be breathtaking here. Retrace your steps to the bottom and turn south onto the Ring Route Trail. Walk past the Eaglehawk Dam campground and follow the old fire trail to the car park to complete the circuit.

Other walks in the Mt Remarkable region
Alligator Creek Walk (35km, 2 days)
The best overnight walking route is through the middle of the western half

of the park, following Alligator Creek from south to north and returning via The Battery Ridge or the Black Range. The total distance is about 35km, and camping possibilities are at Kingfisher Flat and Fricks Dam.

Mt Remarkable Walk (9km, 4 hours)
Follow the Heysen Trail from a staging area just north of Melrose showground. It approaches the summit (960m) from the east. Return to Main North Road via a recently realigned (in 1999) track to the north.

Telowie Gorge
About 30km south of Mt Remarkable National Park, this is another wild segment of the Flinders Ranges. You will need to obtain the Pire topographical map to plan a great walk following Telowie Creek through the Telowie Gorge. The gorge is lined with Rhynie quartzite and is one of a few South Australian habitats of the harmless carpet python.

Black Range
There are several overnight options in the centre of the park. Follow Mambray Creek Trail north from Mambray Creek. The section from Suger Gum Lookout to Sugar Gum Dam and then to Alligator Lodge is all on old fire trails. From Sugar Gum Dam, you can head east to Mt Remarkable and follow the Heysen Trail north through the Willowie Forest.

A yacht anchored in the turquoise waters of the idyllic Western River Cove, northern Kangaroo Island.

Kangaroo Island

The third-largest island off the entire Australian coast (after Tasmania and Melville), Kangaroo Island is 4500 square kilometres in area. From shore to shore, it is 155km long and 55km wide. About 3000 people live there, half of them at Kingscote.

The island has marvellous rugged coastal scenery and secluded beaches of white sand and crystal turquoise water. There are more than 20 reserves, totalling about a third of the island. The two main ones are Flinders Chase National Park and Cape Gantheaume Conservation Park. The highest point, Easy Gosse in the north-west, is only 307m, so the walking is fairly flat and easy.

History

Kangaroo Island is steeped in European history, with many historical sites, including the first settlement in South Australia, at the place then known as Reeves Point, in July 1836. In 1854 John Buick arrived with his wife Frances, and the first home was built. South Australia's first fruit tree,

planted in 1836 at Reeves Point, still produces mulberries each year. The island was named by Matthew Flinders when he sailed around it in 1802 on board HMS *Investigator*. The first lighthouse in South Australia was built on Kangaroo Island, at Cape Willoughby, in 1852 to reduce the number of shipwrecks. Lighthouses were built at Cape Borda and Cape du Couedic in 1858 and 1906.

Climate

Kangaroo Island experiences a more temperate climate than the mainland, with summers not quite as hot and winters a little milder. (Average maximum temperature in Kingscote, January 23.5°C, June 15.2°C; minimum January 14.6°C, June 9.2°C.) Most rain falls in the cooler months, from about 450mm in the east to 1000mm in the west. The only complaint for walkers is the south-westerly wind blowing off the Southern Ocean.

Vegetation

There are more than 850 native plant species on the island, including wildflowers, orchids, eucalypts, mallee

and hakeas. Half of them are found in Flinders Chase National Park and among these are about 40 species found nowhere else in the world.

Wildlife

Kangaroo Island is renowned not only for a high density of wildlife, but also for having several species not commonly seen on the mainland. There are several reasons, the most important being that foxes and rabbits did not run amok and compete with native fauna. Furthermore, almost half the island remains in its natural state, never having been cleared of vegetation. Species recorded include Australian sea lions, tammar wallaby and the Kangaroo Island kangaroo.

Access

Kangaroo Island, 112km from Adelaide, is only 13km off the coast at Cape Jervis. Sealink operates a passenger and vehicle ferry service connecting Cape Jervis with Penneshaw on the island. There's on-board assistance with accommodation bookings and tourist information about the 1450km of roads on the island.

- *Reservations*—Sealink
  440 King William St
  Adelaide SA 5000
  Tel: 131 301
- *General Enquiries*
  Regional Office
  Government Office Building
  37 Dauncey St
  Kingscote SA 5223
  Tel: (08) 8553 2381
  Fax: (08) 8553 2531

Further Information:

- Cape Willoughby Lightstation
  PMB, via Penneshaw SA 5222
  Tel: (08) 8553 1191
  Fax: (08) 8553 1039
- Seal Bay Conservation Park
  PMB 203, via Kingscote SA 5223
  Tel: (08) 8559 4207
  Fax: (08) 8559 4295
- Kelly Hill Caves
  Kelly Hill Conservation Park
  PMB 38, via Kingscote SA 5223
  Tel: (08) 8559 7231
  Fax: (08) 8559 7373
- Cape Borda Lightstation
  via Kingscote SA 5223
  Tel: (08) 8559 3257
  Fax: (08) 8559 3298
- Kangaroo Island Gateway
  Information Centre
  Howard Drive
  Penneshaw SA 5222
  Tel: (08) 8553 1322
  Fax: (08) 8553 1355

Cape Gantheaume Conservation Park & Wilderness Protected Area

This 25 000ha undeveloped region is along the southern coast of Kangaroo Island about an hour's drive from Penneshaw. Most of the park is protected as wilderness area and there are no roads or tracks at all. The interior is covered with mallee, the largest undisturbed tract of vegetation on the island. This provides excellent habitats for kangaroos, bandicoots, pygmy possums and marsupial mice. The coastal regions, by contrast, are dominated by heath. To the west, there's a colony of sea lions living at Seal Bay; the rangers conduct extremely popular tours to see them.

Cape Gantheaume Wilderness Trail Walk

Starting Point: Bales Beach, Cape Gantheaume Conservation Park
Destination: D'Estrees Bay
Summary: An interesting coast walk
Attractions: Scenic, remote wilderness atmosphere, views from the top of sea cliffs, isolated coves and bays, a colony of New Zealand fur seals at Cape Gantheaume
Length: 34km
Time: 2 days
Options: None
Grade: ★ ★ ★
Fitness: ◪◪
Maps: Landsmap Kangaroo Island 1:200 000 Tourist Guide gives an overview of the island. Specific coverage is given by the D'Estrees and Seddon 1:50 000 topographicals.
Access to Starting Point: Bales Beach is at the end of Seal Bay Road in the south of the island
Facilities/Amenities: None. Very basic car-camping area near Point Tinline. Self-sufficiency required.
Recommended Equipment: Complete self-sufficiency. Take at least 4 litres of water per person per day for the entire journey. A windproof jacket is highly recommended as you are walking along the coast the entire time.
Notes: Bushwalkers entering the wilderness zone must register their route intention with the park ranger at Murray Lagoon. Set up a car shuffle to avoid backtracking.
Further Information:
  Murray Lagoon
  Cape Gantheaume
  Conservation Park
  PMB 203, via Kingscote SA 5223
  Tel: (08) 8553 8233
  Fax: (08) 8553 8273

Walk Description

The route description is simple—stick to the coast. From Bales Beach, head south-east over the headlands to Cape Gantheaume. If you walk in this direction you will keep the wind behind you. You are walking primarily on top of sea cliffs where the vegetation is dominated by wind-pruned coastal heath.

Cape Gantheaume is mainly a limestone plateau, so you will often encounter large caverns and sea caves in the cliffs. Be wary, as limestone crumbles very easily; be especially cautious near cliff edges. Off the coast just to the west of the cape is the wreck of the *You Yangs* from 1890.

When you reach D'Estrees Bay, you'll notice the ruins of the early whaling industry once based here. Operations ceased in 1851 when attention turned to slaughtering seals. Their skins were salted and stored in the limestone caves. Walkers are asked not to disturb sea lion colonies they encounter. Give them a wide berth, especially the big bulls. The New Zealand fur seals at the cape are smaller and darker than the Australia sea lions at Seal Bay to the west.

Flinders Chase National Park

Together with the adjoining Ravine des Casoars Wilderness Protection Area, this national park protects the western coast of Kangaroo Island. It contains a vegetation community found nowhere else on the island and rarely elsewhere in South Australia: tall, lush, wet forests.

In the north of the park is historic Cape Borda lighthouse, built in 1858. The cannon here was once used to warn ships of hazards. The lighthouse is perched on 155m-high sea cliffs and became automatic in 1989. A museum displays artefacts of a bygone maritime era. South of Cape Borda is the spectacular Ravine des Casoars with its beautiful beach and sea cliffs tunnelled by caves and overhangs. Perhaps the most scenically interesting features for day visitors are in the south of the park, near the lighthouse of Cape du Couedic: Admirals Arch and the famous and often-photographed Remarkable Rocks. However, 60 per cent of the island is wilderness and seldom visited.

Facts and Figures

Name: Flinders Chase National Park

Size: 73 920ha (including the Ravine des Casoars Wilderness Protection Area, 41 320ha)

Enactment: 1919: 53 000ha (after 30 years of lobbying by the Royal Society of South Australia). 1982: 73 920ha

Aboriginal Sites: Very few sites now remain

Visitors: About 90 000 a year

Vegetation: Mallee, scrub, tall sugar gum and paperbark forests

Wildlife: New Zealand fur seals, fairy penguins, kangaroos, koalas, emus, platypus and Cape Barren geese. Some species have been introduced because of the protective isolation the island offers. Many bird species roost in the limestone cliffs.

Attractions: Remarkable Rocks, West Bay beach, Admirals Arch, Ravine des Casoars and 70km of craggy coastline

Access: The main access is through the park headquarters at Rocky River in the south. Drive along Birchmore Road from Penneshaw, then take the South Coast Road. Much of the road is unsealed and the drive takes about 2.5 hours. A small daily entrance fee applies.

Facilities: There are limited facilities provided throughout the park. Car-camping is permitted at Harveys Return in the north (near Cape Borda). Other accommodation is also available at two lighthouse keepers' cottages situated at Cape du Couedic and Cape Borda. From the Rocky River entrance in the south, visitors can camp at West Bay, Snake Lagoon and Rocky River itself. This last site has toilets and showers. Camping fees apply. An excellent food outlet is located nearby at Tandanya.

Further Information:
Rocky River Headquarters
Flinders Chase National Park
PMB 246, via Kingscote SA 5223
Tel: (08) 8559 7235
Fax: (08) 8559 7268

Ravine des Casoars Circuit

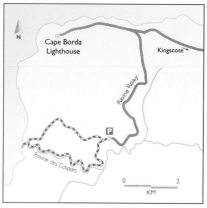

Starting Point: Ravine Road car park, Flinders Chase National Park

Destination: Ravine des Casoars

Summary: A short circuit in the northern part of the Ravine des Casoars Wilderness Protection Area

Attractions: Fairy penguins, sea cliffs, caves, a beautiful beach

Length: 8.9km

Time: 3.5 hours

Options: Longer overnight excursions can be done by walking south along the fire trail to West Bay and returning via the trackless coast

Grade: ★ ★ ★

Fitness: ◪ ◪

Maps: Landsmap Kangaroo Island 1:200 000 Tourist Guide gives a good overview of the island. Specific coverage of the area is given by the Borda 1:50 000 topographical.

Access to Starting Point: The car park at the end of Ravine Road is 7km south of the Playford Highway near Cape Borda. Access is via Parndana and Gosse.

Facilities/Amenities: None

Recommended Equipment: A torch to explore caves and limestone formations

Notes: Try to time the walk for low tide so you can explore the caverns

Further Information:
Rocky River Park Office
Tel: (08) 8559 7235

Walk Description

This is a concise but awe-inspiring walk in the north-west of Kangaroo Island. Despite the many attractions, not many people come here. The objective is to walk along a splendid ravine with impressive views of coastal formations. Some of the cliffs

are 150m high. From the staging area at the gate, the track passes through low mallee vegetation, eventually leading to the top of limestone cliffs. Scramble down to the beach where caves have been eroded in the limestone cliffs by strong seas.

The Ravine des Casoars was named by French explorer Nicolas Baudin, who sailed by on *Le Geographe* in 1802–1803. He mentions in his study notes that he observed many casso-waries near the ravine, but what he saw was more likely to have been the unique Kangaroo Island dwarf emu. This bird was hunted to extinction by sealers very shortly after—it remains one of Australia's most regrettable wildlife losses.

Shipwrecks nearby are the *Mermaid* (1905) and *Atalanta* (1860). Bring a torch and explore the caverns at low tide. If you sit still you will hear the little penguins moving around in their burrows. To return, head upstream to the fire trail and walk north.

Other walks on Kangaroo Island

A brochure entitled *Walking Tracks in Parks on Kangaroo Island*, giving full details, is available at the Rocky River park office in Flinders Chase and at the visitors' centre at Penneshaw. For information on coastal treks, contact a local ranger and complete a route-intention document.

Cape Borda
Coast to Coast Walk
(88km, 6 days)

The longest walk on the island leaves Harveys Return just east of the lighthouse. Head down to the Ravine des Casoars, then West Bay, Cape de Couedic, Hanson Bay and finally Kelly Hills Caves Visitors' Centre. Some sections are trackless.

Oval Historical Walk
(4km, 1.5 hours)

This walk route travels south of the lighthouse along the coast to a clearing used for grazing cattle.

Harveys Return Walk
(2km, 45 minutes)

An historically and geologically significant walk. Early in the 1930s, a tramway and capstan hauled goods up from the coast. The area is dominated by outcrops of folded schists.

Cape Gantheaume area

Two short tourist walks explore the wild area at Murray Lagoon in the north of Cape Gantheaume Conservation Park. At Seal Bay, pay a small fee to walk along a short boardwalk down to the beach to observe the sea lion colony. The skeleton of a southern right whale can be seen here too.

Flinders Chase National Park

This is the best walking area on the island, with wild and dazzling coastal scenery. The best map to have is the Vennachar 1:50 000 topographical, covering most of the main highlights of the national park.

Admirals Arch Walk
(300m, 15 min)

A short boarded tourist walk at Cape du Couedic leads to a dramatic limestone arch festooned with stalactites.

Black Swamp walk
(3km, 1 hour)

From Rocky River to a platypus pool. Walkers are asked to report sightings to the ranger via a form. The best time to visit is at dawn or dusk. Walkers must be still and quiet in order to glimpse these shy creatures.

Remarkable Rocks Walk
(500m, 10 min)

Explore the granite boulders sculpted by weather and time. Early morning or just before sunset is a lovely time.

Rocky River Mouth Walk
(3km, 1.5 hours)

From Snake Lagoon to the coast along the Rocky River. Progress is slow along the gully because of boulders and rocky outcrops.

Sandy Creek Walk (3km, 1 hour)

From the West Bay road to a remote spot on the coast.

Breakneck River Walk
(6km, 2.5 hours)

From the West Bay road to a remote spot on the coast.

Kelly Hill Conservation Park

This karst area is renowned among speleologists for its helictite-adorned caves, but it also offers several above-ground walking options.

Hanson Bay Walk
(9km one way, 3 hours)

From the visitors' centre, follow this walk south past freshwater lagoons and dunes to the coast. Either set up a car shuffle at Hanson Bay or return by the same route.

Mt Thisby

A very high sand dune just off the Hog Highway between Penneshaw and Kingscote. More than 500 steps lead up to a lookout over the narrowest point on the island. The views north to American River are especially good.

Western River Wilderness Protection Area

Exquisite Western River Cove on the remote north coast, is the setting for secluded beach-camping or walking through the 2375ha park.

Waterfall Creek Walk
(4km, 1.5 hours)

A short walk to a waterfall that flows mainly in winter.

Coast Walk (7km, 2.5 hours)

Long high sea cliffs give northerly ocean views over Investigator Strait and the Yorke Peninsula.

Looking from the Remarkable Rocks to Cape du Couedic, south-western Kangaroo Island.

Western Australia

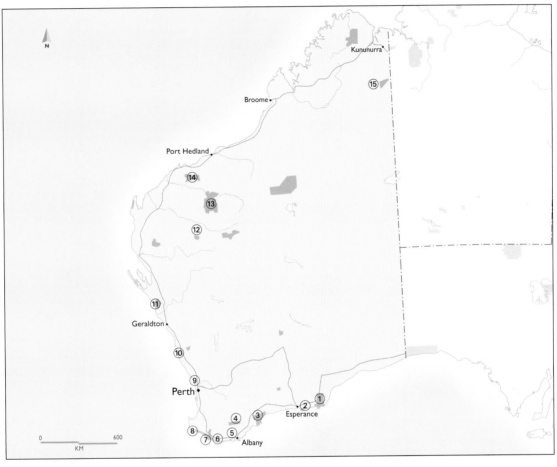

Introduction

At 2 529 875 square kilometres, Western Australia is larger than most countries of the world. It covers about a third of the Australian continent, but is largely unpopulated. Most residents live along the 12 889km of coastline in the state's major cities: Perth, Bunbury, Albany, Geraldton, Broome and Port Hedland. The only inland city of any significant size is Kalgoorlie. The state has many rugged and remote national parks of great beauty that can be accessed only by 4WD in the dry season. Walking is often the only way to explore them because of lack of roads, information and other visitor facilities. In this harsh terrain, walkers are encouraged to join a walking organisation, such as:

- Bushwalkers of WA, (08) 9457 1722
- Federation of WA Bushwalkers, (08) 9362 1614
- Orienteering Association of WA, (08) 9381 1727
- Over 55s Walking Association, (08) 9249 7316
- The Heart Foundation, (08) 9388 3343
- WA Rogaining Association Inc, (08) 9381 8608
- Walking for Fitness and Pleasure, (08) 9370 4209
- WA Family Bushwalking Club, (08) 9470 2707
- Western Walking Club, (08) 9384 4790.

Western Australia comprises some of the oldest terrain on earth, so much of the landscape has been greatly eroded and is very flat. The highest point is in the Pilbara, Mt Meharry, being just 1249m. But there are significant attractions for walkers looking for a different experience from what can be had in the national parks of eastern Australia. Instead of rainforests, alpine meadows and wild rivers, Western Australia offers rocky gorges, isolated wilderness atmosphere and 12 000 species of native vegetation, including some of the best wildflower displays to be seen anywhere in the world.

Perhaps the most popular bushwalking venue is the Stirling Range, rising from the fertile plains in the south-west corner. The range, a single chain of abrupt peaks, is 10km wide and 65km long and provides spectacular walking territory with awesome views. There are hundreds of species of wildflowers, and orchids are common in the sandy soils around the foothills.

The Nuyts Wilderness Area of Walpole–Nornalup National Park on the state's southern coast is also designated 'walkers only'. It contains thickly vegetated sand dunes, towering karri and jarrah forests, extensive heathlands, an abundance of wildflowers, and lonely beaches. A two-day 15km walk here follows a well-defined track and can be done at any time of the year.

In the far north, The Kimberley is a magnificent tropical wilderness of cliff-lined coast, rugged mountains, huge rivers and inland plateaus, offering unlimited pioneering bushwalking for self-reliant adventurers. Also within this region is the rather imposing Purnululu (Bungle Bungle) National Park, an expansive 350-million-year-old massif of giant beehive-like mounds or domes, gorges and palm-fringed rockpools.

Climate

Western Australia's climate falls into several zones. Many of the best national parks are concentrated in the wettest, coolest part, in the south-west. Despite frequent rainfall, rivers here can still be reduced to a series of stagnant pools. In fact, water is a problem in almost all of the state's national parks and walkers must always be aware of the need to carry spare supplies and filters in case natural watercourses have ceased to flow.

The Mediterranean climate in all the coastal parks between Kalbarri and Esperance is moderated by proximity to the Indian Ocean. Summer days are cooled in the afternoon by the arrival of the famous seabreeze called the 'Fremantle Doctor'. Temperatures in the northern half of the state and inland can be unbearable in summer, with maximums regularly in the 40s. The best seasons to visit are spring, when the magnificent wildflowers are on display, and autumn. Winter in the Pilbara and Kimberley is also pleasant, but water is very scarce. Cyclones are a problem in the tropics, and walkers should check weather warnings in summer. Phone 1900 155 366 for district forecasts.

Transport

To Western Australia

The only practical way of getting to Western Australia is by air. Qantas and Ansett have daily services to Perth from Sydney or Melbourne. To book, call Qantas on 131 131 or Ansett on 131 344. Airlink connects Adelaide and Darwin with Perth. For those with time and money, the Indian–Pacific Railway offers a romantic alternative. Allow at least a week to drive across the Nullarbor Plain from the east coast.

Within Western Australia

Air

The fastest, and often cheapest, way of getting from one end of the state to the other is by air. Airlink offers daily services to Kalgoorlie, Karratha, Port Hedland and Broome.

Rail

Westrail trains cover limited, mainly coastal, routes between Geraldton and Bunbury. Some infrequent inland services.

Bus

Coach transport is the most comprehensive. YHA Travel sells bus pass tickets for all companies, including Westrail, at a 10 per cent discount for members. Phone 131 053 or (08) 9326 2244 for details. Package tours are also available. Other coach services are:
- South-West Coachlines
  Coverage: Nannup, Bunbury, Manjimup, Bridgetown
  Tel: (08) 9324 2333
- Easyrider Backpackers
  Coverage: circuit of south-west region
  Tel: (08) 9226 0307
- Western Travel Bug
  Coverage: Pemberton to Northcliffe via the Gloucester Tree using an old tourist tram
  Tel: (08) 9561 5236 or 1800 627 488

Car

Book a car with an unlimited kilometre package from Avis, Budget, Hertz, or one of the smaller independent rental outlets, as the distances are enormous in this vast state. Most people travel more than 1000km north to Shark Bay, taking in Kalbarri National Park and Nambung with its famous pinnacles. South of Perth, the most popular destinations include Margaret River, Albany and Wave Rock. Fuel is expensive in the outback, so a fuel-efficient medium-sized car is recommended. Also note that driving at night can be dangerous because many of the roads are unfenced, allowing cattle and wildlife to stray on to them.

YHA Travel

The YHA's fully accredited travel agency can assist with your travel needs, including international and domestic flights; travel insurance; bus, rail and ferry passes; visas and domestic/international tours. Britannia YHA in Perth also has a specialist Domestic Travel Agency.

Around Perth

Public buses and trains service most parts of the Perth metropolitan area. Call Transperth on 132 213 for a timetable.

Accommodation

YHA Hostels

YHA hostels provide clean, comfortable and friendly accommodation for travellers. Hostels are open all day—most office hours are 8.00am–10.00am and 4.00pm–10.00pm.

The YHA Membership and Travel Centre state office is at:

236 William St, Northbridge WA 6003
Tel:　(08) 9227 5122
Tel:　(WA only) 1800 811 420
Fax:　(08) 9227 5123
Reception hours:
9.00am–5.00pm weekdays
9.00am–12.00pm Saturday

Staff can assist with new membership and renewal cards; Hostelling International Cards for overseas residents; advance bookings for Australian hostels; advance bookings for overseas hostels on the International Booking Network (IBN), and the sale of sleep sheets and travel accessories.

Families and Groups

Families can be accommodated at most West Australian hostels. Groups can book direct with individual hostel managers or YHA State Office.

Maps

Coverage of Western Australia's national parks is the responsibility of the Department of Land Administration (DOLA). Unfortunately, there is almost no 1:25 000 topographical coverage in national park areas and even colour maps are not available for much of the state. The Department of Conservation and Land Management (CALM) has produced a Land Management Series and is in the process of upgrading it. The entire Bibbulmun Track is covered by a series of eight 1:75 000 maps available from most tourist visitor centres in the south-west area. Please note that these are not topographical maps. The most detailed coverage is of the south-west, with an adequate 1:50 000 topographical scale. A free catalogue of maps is available from the DOLA head office. The most comprehensive land coverage is the Natmap/Ausmap series produced by AUSLIG. The principal DOLA outlet in Perth is:

Perth Map Centre
1st Floor, 884 Hay St
Perth WA 6000
Tel:　(08) 9322 5733
Fax:　(08) 9322 5673
e-mail: sales@perthmap.com.au
web site: www.perthmap.com.au

For mail orders, contact DOLA's Central Map Agency at:
PO Box 2222, Midland WA 6936

National Parks

There are about 65 national parks in Western Australia, the largest being the remote Rudall River at 1.3 million hectares (second in size only to Kakadu).

Most of the parks have fairly relaxed regulations in regard to camping, permits and walking, but entrance fees apply at some. These are paid into an honesty collection box at the park boundary. Motorists are required to deposit money (usually about $5.00–$8.00) in an envelope. Four-week holiday passes (about $20.00); annual passes (about $45.00).

Western Australia's national parks have few facilities and visitors must be self-reliant in all matters, particularly water. Sometimes just driving to a national park can be a serious undertaking, and dozens of people have died after experiencing mechanical problems and having insufficient emergency provisions.

Walkers in national parks should always take extra care to reduce the spread of dieback disease (*Phytophthora cinnamomi*). Clean your boots wherever scrub-down stations have been installed on walking tracks.

The Department of Conservation and Land Management (CALM) administers about 5 million hectares (equivalent to a quarter of France) of public land and produces a range of free brochures giving information about all major national parks. Their primary visitors' centre is:

On top of Wave Rock, near Hyden, in the remote outback of Western Australia.

WA Naturally
47 Henry St, Fremantle WA 6160
Tel: (08) 9430 8600
Fax: (08) 9430 8699
web site: www.calm.wa.gov.au
Hours: 10.00am–5.30pm daily
except Tuesday
CALM's Customer Service Centre is at:
50 Hayman Rd, Como WA 6152
Tel: (08) 9334 0333
Fax: (08) 9430 8699
More detailed park information can be best obtained from the various regional offices:
- South Coast
  120 Albany Hwy, Albany WA 6330
  Tel: (08) 9842 4500
  Fax: (08) 9841 3329
- Midwest
  193 Marine Tce, PO Box 72
  Geraldton WA 6530
  Tel: (08) 9921 5955
  Fax: (08) 9921 5713
- Pilbara
  SGIO Building, Welcome Rd
  PO Box 835, Karratha WA 6714
  Tel: (08) 9143 1488
  Fax: (08) 9144 1118
- Kimberley
  Messmate Way, PO Box 942
  Kununurra WA 6743
  Tel: (08) 9168 0200
  Fax: (08) 9168 2179
- Southern Forests
  Brain St, Manjimup WA 6258
  Tel: (08) 9771 7948
  Fax: (08) 9777 1363

Epic Walks

Bibbulmun Track

The 964km Bibbulmun Track is Western Australia's only true long-distance walking trail, stretching from Kalamunda (Perth hills) south to the centre of Albany. Refer to the Southwest section in this chapter.

The South Coast

Much of the south coast from Eucla near the South Australian border west to Cape Leeuwin, is protected in a series of wild national parks, many quite large and offering a true wilderness experience. Water can be scarce and walkers must be well prepared and informed of the conditions, especially when venturing overnight.

Cape Arid National Park

This huge (279 832ha) park, 120km east of Esperance, is a scenic coastal habitat for about 160 bird species, including a number of restricted and threatened species, and is important for their conservation.

Walkers will delight in the varied landscapes, from 20km of scenic beaches to the Thomas River estuary surrounded by banksia woodlands, swamps and heath. Farther inland, mallee dominates while mixed woodland surrounds the granite rocks and peaks of Russell Range, including Mt Ragged.

French Admiral D'Entrecasteaux named the cape 'Cap Arride' in 1792, and the name was later anglicised by Matthew Flinders. It's a fitting name because rainfall averages just 10mm a month in summer and peaks at 100mm a month in winter.

The park is bordered by the massive Nuytsland Nature Reserve, which protects more than 400km of coastline all the way to Red Rocks Point.

Tower Peak Walk

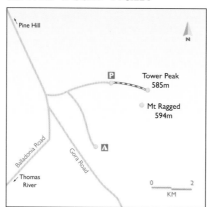

Starting Point: Mt Ragged car park (just off Balladonia Road), Cape Arid National park
Destination: The summit of Tower Peak (585m)
Summary: A climb to a central mountain peak with good views over the mallee interior of the park
Attractions: Ancient landscape from Pre-Cambrian period, panoramic views
Length: 3km
Time: 2 hours
Options: None
Attraction Rating: ★ ★ ★

Fitness: ⬕⬕
Maps: AUSLIG (Natmap/Ausmap) Sandy Bight 1:100 000 topographical
Access to Starting Point: Balladonia is 193km east of Norseman in the south-east. A rough unsealed 4WD track leads to the Mt Ragged car park, about 130km south of Balladonia. The car park can also be accessed directly from the Thomas River, Cape Arid and Seal Creek areas.
Facilities/Amenities: Low-key camping area with toilets, fireplaces and picnic tables nearby to the south
Recommended Equipment: As there is little tree cover, sunscreen is essential. Take a windjacket as the top is quite exposed.
Notes: The best time to visit is October to May
Further Information:
Cape Arid National Park Ranger
Tel: (08) 9075 0055
or
CALM District Office
Wallaceway Centre
Dempster St, Esperance WA 6450
Tel: (08) 9075 9022

Walk Description

Mt Ragged (594m) is the highest point of the Russel Range, which dominates the centre of the park. The walking track ascends nearby Tower Peak looking south to Mt Ragged. The range divides the mallee-dominated southern interior from the saltbush to the north. Birds found in the area include malleefowl, mulga parrot, chestnut quail-thrush and the shy heathwren. The world's oldest species of ant was discovered near here in 1930. Return via the same route.

Other walks in Cape Arid National Park

Other walks in the park do not require a 4WD to access the start and can be reached with a conventional vehicle. The most popular sector of the park is the south-west which is centred on the Thomas River and the camping areas near Cape Arid and at Jorndee Creek and Seal Creek. Some of the smaller tourist tracks include the Len Otte Nature Trail and the Boolenup Trail. Access to the national park from Esperance is via Condingup. More-challenging walks are:

Thomas River area

The 15km Tagon Coastal Trail Walk explores a deserted section of the coastline between the Thomas River and Tagon Bay. Beware of prolific ants along the trail. This walk takes about four hours.

Cape Arid area

A 2km walk heads straight up the granite slopes of Mt Arid to its 356m summit. Great views of the Recherche Archipelago, comprised of 105 islands and 1500 islets teeming with marine life. Whales are often seen from late winter to spring. Allow an hour.

Cape Le Grand National Park

Popular features of this 31 578ha park are its picturesque bays with wide sandy beaches separated by rocky headlands. Inland, the park protects an undulating sandy plain interspersed with swamps and occasional freshwater pools. Visually, the south-west of the park is the most interesting where an impressive chain of peaks, including Mt Le Grand (345m), Frenchman Peak (262m) and Mississippi Hill (180m), dominates the horizon. These peaks are the result of erosion and movements in the earth's crust over the past 600 million years. During the Eocene period, some 40 million years ago, sea levels were at least 300m above their present level and these peaks would have been largely submerged. Caves and tunnels found on their slopes are believed to have been formed from wave action and underwater currents.

The sand plains that cover much of the park support a great variety of vegetation, particularly of the heath community. In areas of deep sand, dense thickets of *Banksia speciosa* thrive, growing to three or four metres. Many species of small native marsupials rely on these plant communities for food and shelter. When in flower, banksias are a source of nectar and insects for the tiny honey-possum, while the quenda, or southern brown bandicoot, forages after dark in the understorey for grubs and worms.

History

The national park is named after Le Grand, an officer of *L'Esperance*, one of the ships in a French expedition commanded by Admiral D'Entrecasteaux in 1792. Matthew Flinders visited and named Lucky Bay in 1802, when taking shelter from a summer storm. Rossiter Bay was named by Edward John Eyre when his party, suffering from the rigours of crossing the Nullarbor, was relieved to find Captain Rossiter and his ship *Mississippi* anchored in the bay in June 1841. Mississippi Hill at Lucky Bay was named in honour of the ship.

Facilities

Two camping grounds have been constructed by park authorities, one at Lucky Bay and the other at Le Grand Beach. Facilities include septic toilets and showers. A camping fee is charged. Firewood is scarce, so bring a portable fuel stove.

Coastal Trail Walk

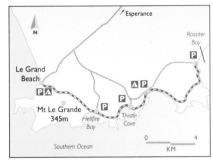

Starting Point: Le Grand Beach, Cape Le Grand National Park
Destination: Rossiter Bay via Hellfire Bay, Thistle Cove and Mississipi Hill
Summary: An excellent traverse of the national park, incorporating highlights of spectacular coastal scenery
Attractions: Hellfire Bay, Thistle Cove and Lucky Bay
Length: 15km
Time: 1 full day
Options: Leave a car at one of several access roads to shorten the track
Attraction Rating: ★ ★ ★
Fitness: ✖✖✖
Maps: AUSLIG (Natmap/Ausmap) Mondrain 1:100 000 topographical gives an overview of the cape region
Access to Starting Point: The park is 30km south-east of Esperance, 50km

The beautiful Royal Hakea.

by road. Approach via Fisheries, Merivale and Cape Le Grand roads. The route is well signposted from Fisheries Road. Travelling time is about 30 minutes from Esperance. The road to Rossiter Bay is unsealed but still negotiable by 2WD vehicles.
Facilities/Amenities: BBQs, toilets, tables, campsite, picnic areas, shade shelters, water and information at Lucky Bay and Le Grand Beach
Recommended Equipment: Protection from sun, sunscreen, wind jacket
Notes: The best time to visit is spring when the wildflowers are blooming. There are two resident rangers near the main entrance on Cape Le Grand Road, and a mobile ranger is based at Lucky Bay for much of the year.
Further Information:
CALM District Office
Wallaceway Centre
Dempster St, Esperance WA 6450
Tel: (08) 9075 9022

Walk Description

This excellent coastal trail connects all the premier coves in the Cape Le Grand National Park and features great inland scenery dominated by Mt Le Grand, Boulder Hill and Mississippi Hill. Park a car at either end of the walk but start from the west at Le Grand Beach. The walk can be broken into four shorter sections.

1. Le Grand Beach to Hellfire Bay (2–3 hours) This is the most difficult section as you skirt the northern flanks of Mt Le Grand. Some rock-scrambling is required.

2. Hellfire Bay to Thistle Cove (2 hours) Hellfire Bay, flanked by rounded granite-domed slopes, is quite spectacular. In bright sunshine, the water turns a brilliant turquoise.

3. Thistle Cove to Lucky Bay (30 minutes) Upgraded as a tourist nature trail with information signs, this is the easiest section of the trail.

4. Lucky Bay to Rossiter Bay (2–3 hours) This section climbs Mississippi Hill for views back towards Lucky Bay with its lovely turquoise waters. The bird sanctuary is also a feature here.

Other walks in Cape Le Grand National Park
Frenchman Peak Walk
(3km, 2 hours)

Follow the graded trail that ascends from the signposted car park near the Hellfire Bay turn-off. It climbs the bare east slope to the 262m rocky summit and gives good views of the coast, especially the many islands of Recherche Archipelago. There's a huge cavern to investigate just below the summit. Avoid leaving the track to access the peak directly as the rock is deceptively steep, especially on the descent. Don't do this walk in wet or windy weather as the slopes are very exposed to south-westerly winds.

Fitzgerald River National Park

This botanically significant 329 039ha reserve shelters about 20 per cent of Western Australia's plant species, including the magnificently colourful royal hakea, or Chinese lantern. It lies on the central south coast between Bremer Bay and Hopetoun, 420km southeast of Perth. Since 1970, the park has been an internationally recognised Biosphere Reserve under the UNESCO Man and the Biosphere Program, which means that it's a protected area large enough to serve as a base line for evaluating changes in the environment at both local and global levels.

The park has magnificent scenery and is one of the most flora-rich conservation areas in the state. So far, 1784 plant species have been identi-fied, 75 of which are found nowhere else. More wildlife species live in the park than in any other reserve in south-western Australia. These include 22 mammal species, 41 reptiles and 12 frogs. The 184 types of birds identified include rare species such as the ground parrot, western bristle bird and western whipbird.

Fortunately, the park is not yet severely affected by dieback disease and authorities hope to prevent its onset by strict regulation of access by visitors. Walkers should take the utmost care to clean their boots when entering the park. Because of its vast size, the best way to explore it is by setting up a car shuffle. Much of the park's interior is flat and featureless and it is the desolate, wild coast that holds the greatest attraction. Walks along the coast between the main access points are the most popular. Allow half a day to organise a car shuffle as the roads are unsealed and often corrugated. Beware of wildlife when driving at dusk.

Fitzgerald River Coastal Traverse Walk

Starting Point: Point Ann, Fitzgerald National park
Destination: Barrens Beach
Summary: An epic walk through wild and remote coastal scenery
Attractions: Fitzgerald Inlet, Quoin Head, Point Edwards
Length: 78km
Time: 4–6 days
Options: Shorter or longer options can be done by varying the staging areas
Attraction Rating: ★ ★ ★
Fitness: ☒ ☒ ☒ ☒
Maps: DOLA Whoogarup, Red Island and Dempster 1:50 000 topographicals
Access to Starting Point: Access is through Albany via the South Coast Highway. Turn right at Gairdner onto Devils Creek Road, then take Pabelup Drive past Mt Maxwell. The road surfaces are often heavily corrugated and sandy in patches. Point Ann Road is on the right. Travelling time is about 2.5 hours from Albany. To get to Barrens Beach, turn right at Ravensthorpe toward Hopetoun and follow the signs into the national park.
Facilities/Amenities: Picnic/camping facilities with gas BBQs at Point Ann. Campsites at Fitzgerald Inlet, St Mary Inlet, Four Mile Beach, Hamersley Inlet and Quoin Head. A water tank near a hut at Twin Bays should not be relied on—consult the rangers first.
Recommended Equipment: Complete self-sufficiency with overnight camping gear. is required. At least two days' worth of water is essential. In drought conditions, walkers may want to organise water dumps beforehand, using a 4WD vehicle. Insect repellent is essential because of high concentrations of mosquitoes. Fuel stove, as ground fires are not permitted.
Notes: There are three rangers resident in Fitzgerald River National Park and you should consult them when preparing to walk. All overnight walkers are strongly advised to register their route intention before setting out.

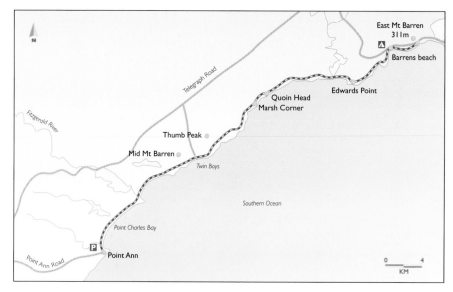

Further Information:
Ranger, Fitzgerald River
PO Box 33, Jerramungup WA 6337
Tel: (08) 9835 5043
Fax: (08) 9835 5045
Other rangers,
Eastern side: (08) 9838 3060
Western side: (08) 9837 1022

Walk Description

The core of this remote national park is so infrequently visited you are virtually guaranteed to have the entire coast for yourself. Not much has changed since 1841 when the explorer Edward Eyre trekked through from Adelaide—he found the arid country '...barren and worthless'. Walkers must be experienced, fit, self-reliant and well-equipped for this is extremely harsh country with no reliable water.

From the picnic area and whale-watching viewpoints at Point Ann, head north-east along the beach. Camp wherever you want, in bays and coves and on secluded beaches. Occasionally rough vehicular tracks just inland will make progress easier but a large component of the walking will be simply along beaches. Some trackless sections must be traversed through unrelenting scrub to avoid rocky cliff-lined headlands. Many dry ravines and gullies, often choked with thick bushes, must also be crossed. Tough overtrousers will be handy as the stunted heath can be quite abrasive. Check for ticks at the end of each day.

Note that the section between Point Charles and Quoin Head is classified as a dieback-prevention area, so walkers are not allowed to climb above the 150m contour lines on Woolbernup Hill, Mid Mt Barren and Thumb Peak (519m). Watch for quicksand when crossing the sandbars of Fitzgerald and Hamersley inlets and for strong rips when swimming.

On the last section between Quoin Head and Barrens Beach, you will encounter several car-camping sites accessible by 4WDs only. In contrast to much of the coast, Quoin Head slopes up as if tilted. On its eastern flank is an exquisite beach. Park authorities are in the process of upgrading facilities in the park and it is hoped that water availability will be improved so that walkers can carry less.

Looking south to Mt Bland and West Mt Barren, Fitzgerald River National Park.

Other walks in the Fitzgerald River National Park

The many quartzite peaks of the national park provide ideal vantage points from which to overview the extensive series of coastal headlands. The following summits can all be climbed via short walking tracks from the major access roads: Mt Maxwell, West Mt Barren, Sepucralis Hill, East Mt Barren, No Tree Hill. Walking times are between 30 minutes and 2 hours. Point Ann has an easy Heritage Trail featuring the endemic vegetation of the park. Allow about 40 minutes.

Other walks on the South Coast

Several other national parks protect Western Australia's south coast, most offering short walks for day visitors.

Eucla National Park

This small (3342ha) park in the far south-east of the state, adjoins the South Australian border. There are no facilities and access is very limited. Two attractions for walkers are Wilson Bluff, a massive limestone cliff, and the historic telegraph station that is now partly buried by a sand dune.

Stokes National Park

About 80km west of Esperance, this 8726ha park centres on Stokes Inlet and has several camping areas by the inlet waters and along the coast. The Stokes Heritage Trail is a 1.8km circuit with informative plaques and stunning views across the inlet. Allow 30 minutes. Access is from a car park near the end of Stokes Inlet Road.

Two Peoples Bay Nature Reserve

A 4639ha nature reserve protecting several very rare species of birds, including the noisy scrub-bird, considered extinct for more than 70 years. The endangered Gilberts potoroo also lives here, having been rediscovered only in 1994 after 120 years.

A shorter stroll to Little Beach takes just five minutes, while a longer 2km tourist walk starts at the visitors centre. It's called the Baie Des Deux Peuples Heritage Trail and has lookouts and signs explaining the vegetation. Allow 45 minutes to complete. Access is east of Albany via Lower King Road and Two Peoples Bay Road.

Torndrirrup National Park

Just 10km south of Albany, this spectacular 3936ha park protects the peninsula that forms King George Sound. Day visitors will find much to explore, including Western Australia's most southerly point. Walking destinations include Stony Hill lookout, The Blowholes and Salmon Holes (good swimming). The best walk is to prominent Bald Head at the end of Flinders Peninsula. Allow half a day for the 10km return trip. Several granite domes must be crossed. Other attractions include Natural Bridge and the 24m sea chasm of The Gap. Nearby, the Vancouver Peninsula is the setting for the Point Possession Heritage Trail, a 4km two-hour circuit leaving from Quaranup Road. Brambles Beach is a delightful swimming spot.

The South-west

The wettest part of Western Australia and scenically the most dynamic, this area has great variation in topography. Bluff Knoll (1073m) in the Stirling Ranges is the highest peak in the south-western quadrant of Australia. But the south-west is best known for its magnificent woodland. The karri tower more than 80m tall and several of the best specimens can be climbed by means of pegs installed in the trunks. The epic Bibbulmun Track meanders right through the heart of the south-west, allowing walkers to immerse themselves in the beauty of the many national parks and state forests it passes through.

Visitors will notice that many place names in the region end with 'up'. This was the Aboriginal way of referring to a place. For example *nornal* meant tiger snake, so Nornalup means 'place of the tiger snake'.

Bibbulmun Track Walk

Starting Point: Kalamunda (Perth)
Destination: Albany (South Coast)
Summary: One of the best long-distance trails in Australia
Attractions: Karri and jarrah forests, magnificent coastal scenery and rivers
Length: 964km

Sunset over Mt Maxwell, Fitzgerald River National Park.

Time: 7–8 weeks
Options: Literally hundreds of side branches, the best ones being in Nuyts Wilderness. Tracknotes are given in the Nuyts Wilderness Walk in the Walpole–Nornalup National Park section of this book.
Attraction Rating: ★ ★ ★ ★ ★
Fitness: ◪ ◪ ◪ ◪ ◪
Maps: CALM series of eight Bibbulmun Maps, each at 1:75 000 scale and costing about $6.00. Discounts on four-map packages.
Map 1: Kalamunda–North Bannister (Mundaring)
Map 2: North Bannister–Harvey-Quindanning Road (Dwellingup)
Map 3: Harvey-Quindanning Road–Mumballup (Collie)
Map 4: Mumballup–Brockman Highway (Blackwood)
Map 5: Brockman Highway to Middleton Road
Map 6: Middleton Road to Broke Inlet Road (Northcliffe)
Map 7: Broke Inlet Road–William Bay (Walpole)
Map 8: William Bay–Albany
Access to Starting Point: From Perth, pass the airport along the Great Eastern Highway and turn right onto the Great Eastern Bypass. Turn right at Hazelmere onto Roe Highway and head south for 3km to Kalamunda Road. Turn left onto this and follow it south-east to Kalamunda.
Facilities/Amenities: More than 50 campsites have been constructed using unique three-sided sleeping

shelters. They are about 20km apart but in the more difficult terrain around Walpole, camping areas are spaced only 10–15km apart. All sites have a pit toilet, rainwater tank and picnic table. Not every site can be relied on for water in summer. Fireplaces are provided along the first part of the trail to the Shannon River.
Recommended Equipment: Standard overnight camping equipment
Notes: You must cross Wilson Inlet by a ferry operated by the Wilson Inlet Holiday Park, phone (08) 9848 1267. Cross Irwin Inlet by canoe and wade across Parry Inlet. Walkers are encouraged to walk just to the left or right of the track to minimise erosion. Be careful not to disturb fox poison commonly found along the track as part of Operation Western Shield.
Further Information:
   CALM Bibbulmun Track Office
   Locked Bag 104
   Bentley Delivery Centre WA 6983
   Tel: (08) 9334 0265
   Fax: (08) 9334 0100
   e-mail: bibtrack@calm.wa.gov.au
   web site: www.calm.wa.gov.au
or
   Friends of the Bibbulmun Track
   PO Box 7605
   Cloisters Square WA 6850
   Tel: (08) 9481 0551
   Fax: (08) 9481 0546
   e-mail: friends@networx.net.au
   web site:
   www.bibbulmuntrack.org.au
Two comprehensive informative and

up-to-date guidebooks on the track are produced by CALM. To order by mail, contact the department at the address above. At time of writing, the cost is about $30.00 each: *A Guide to the Bibbulmun Track: Northern Half* and *A Guide to the Bibbulmun Track: Southern Half.*

Walk Description

The Bibbulmun Track stretches from Kalamunda south to Albany. Most walkers do only small sections of it at a time, the most popular area being from the karri forests of Pemberton to the inlets around Walpole. The Department of Conservation and Land Management (CALM) is responsible for the track and considerable funds have been devoted to maintaining it at a consistently high standard over the past 30 years.

In 1988 and 1998, the track underwent substantial realignments and extensions to avoid conflict with other land uses, such as logging and mining. Several government departments became involved and the track received a lot of publicity. For example, most of the camp shelters were built by prisoners through a Department of Justice work program.

Today, more than 10 000 people use the track each year, most doing day walks or short sections of less than three days' duration. But a select few undertake the entire distance. 'End to Enders' are entered in a register and receive a certificate from the Friends of the Bibbulmun Track association.

Government initiatives continue to improve the quality of the track and its facilities. Together with the Australian Alps Walking Track, it is one of the best long-distance walking tracks in the country. At time of writing, plans were underway through the government's Trailswest initiative to link the track with other walking tracks, such as the Coastal Plain Walk Trail to the north of Perth.

The Bibbulmun Track starts from the outskirts of Perth and heads north briefly before swinging south to North Bannister. Once past Dwellingup, the jarrah forests make the trail really interesting. This section south of the old timber-milling centre of Donnelly River Village is a good choice if you want to walk only part of the track. From here the Bibbulmun Track follows Donnelly River for almost 60km. On leaving Donnelly Valley, the track turns east and passes through Beedelup National Park, with its beautiful waterfalls, before skirting Big Brook Dam on the way to Pemberton. This tourist town is the gateway for tourists venturing into the beautiful tall karri forests of the south-west. Just south of Pemberton, the track passes the famous Gloucester Climbing Tree.

Another section popular with walkers is the area between Northcliffe and Albany where the track enters a succession of wild national parks alternating between the coast and the forests. Walkers are encouraged to buy the four southern maps (5–8) and plan their own route, according to available time and energy.

Throughout its entire distance, the Bibbulmun Track is marked with small triangular aluminium markers showing a black stylised 'Waugal' (rainbow serpent) on a reflective yellow background. These markers are nailed on trees (or on posts) in both directions, about 200m apart. They are placed vertically to indicate that the track continues straight ahead, and horizontally to indicate the direction of a turn.

Stirling Ranges National Park

From the flat plain of the state's southern agricultural district, the dramatic 65km-long Stirling Range rises abruptly to more than 1000m, the highest peaks even attracting snow occasionally in winter. The range forms an ecological island with a unique climate that harbours many species, such as orchids, heathland and tall gum trees. They are protected in the 115 661ha national park.

There are many craggy peaks, most offering unobscured views over the plains to the north and south and along the range. The level of walking is suitably challenging and a degree of experience and fitness is required. Furthermore, it is one of the few parks in the south-west where genuine overnight walking away from cars is necessary. Most of the peaks have rocky ramparts around their tops that provide walkers with interesting rock scrambling without being too dangerous or difficult. Walkers should avoid periods after heavy rain when muddy soils facilitate the spread of dieback disease. This is especially the case in the western half of the park where drainage is poor. In fact, some peaks may be closed at times, so walkers heading for the park are well advised to contact the ranger first.

The ideal time to visit is late spring and early summer (October–December) when days are warm and wildflowers are in bloom. More than 1500 species

The Bibbulmun Track at Peaceful Bay, Nornalup National Park.

of flowering plants occur naturally on the range, 87 of them endemic. Among the most unusual are the Darwinias, or mountain bells. Ten species have so far been identified in the park, only one of which is known to grow outside the Stirling Range. Mountain bells are usually found above the 300m contour level on acid, sandy, clay soil and they can be seen on the popular Bluff Knoll walk.

The range was formed more than 1000 million years ago when the area was a shallow sea and sediment was deposited on the granite lowland. After the sea receded, the range area sank and the surroundings were gradually eroded back to basic granite. The Stirling Range was slowly uplifted, eventually weathering to its present form. Both Chester and Red Gum passes mark the courses of rivers that flowed south during the initial stages of formation. Ripple marks can still be seen on the exposed rock near ridge crests in the west of the park.

From Perth, the national park is 350km south-east via the Albany Highway. From Albany, head north for 85km along the Chester Pass Road.

Bluff Knoll Walk

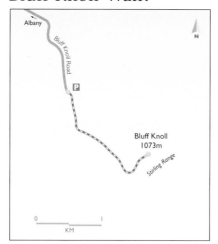

Starting Point: Bluff Knoll car park, Stirling Ranges National Park
Destination: The summit of Bluff Knoll (1073m) in the Stirling Range

Summary: This strenuous well-graded walking trail from the car-park approaches the peak from the west
Attractions: Superb views from south-western Australia's highest peak
Length: 7.5km
Time: 4 hours
Options: The peak can also be approached from the east via the North Isongerup Track, but this would entail camping overnight at the saddle near Moongoongoonderup Hill.
Attraction Rating: ★ ★ ★ ★
Fitness: ⊠ ⊠ ⊠
Maps: DOLA Ellen Peak 1:50 000 topographical (but this map is not detailed and is not necessary for the walk)
Access to Starting Point: Bluff Knoll car park is at the end of Bluff Knoll Road, which turns off Chester Pass Road at the northern boundary of the park. The turn-off is about 10km south of Amelup from where it's another 7km to the car park.
Facilities/Amenities: None en route. Bluff Knoll car park has water tanks.

Looking west to Mondrup Peak and Mt Gog in the Stirling Ranges National Park.

Descending from Bluff Knoll looking out to the western Stirling Ranges.

Recommended Equipment: Water bottle

Notes: Check that you will have fine weather before leaving, as Bluff Knoll can have white-outs in low cloud

Further Information:
CALM Park Office
Stirling Range National Park
Chester Pass Rd, c/- PO Box
Amelup via Borden WA 6338
Tel: (08) 9827 9230
or (08) 9827 9278

Walk Description

Begin from the Bluff Knoll car park at the end of Bluff Knoll Road. There are great views over the western Stirling Range, especially Mt Toolbrunup, from here. Behind the picnic shelter are water tanks where bottles can be filled. From the car park you can also see most of the initial walking track that heads up to the saddle between Coyanerup Peak and Bluff Knoll. Along the way on the left is a small waterfall, a good spot for a drink.

Approach the summit of Bluff Knoll from the south. Even though there are rocks and scrub all around, walking on the excellent track is fairly easy. The total height gained from the car park is 630m. Be careful when peering over the edge as wind gusts are frequent. Bluff Knoll attracts snow in winter and even during the rest of the year can form low clouds that cling to the tops.

While the views to the north and south over the flat plains are impressive,

the best vistas are looking east and west along the crest of the range. Some scrambling around to get the best vantage point will be necessary.

Stirling Ranges Traverse Walk

Starting Point: Bluff Knoll car park, Stirling Ranges National Park

Destination: Stirling Ridge including Ellen Peak (1012m)

Summary: A high-level traverse of the eastern Stirling Range, featuring trackless wilderness and great views. Walk from west to east along the range and return via the North East Track along the northern boundary fence.

Attractions: The cliff-lined summit of Bluff Knoll (1073m)

Length: 29.8km

Time: 3 days

Options: Set up a car shuffle to omit 18km of road walking. Even so, it is

still an overnight walk because of the difficult nature of the terrain. Or walk only half the ridge on the North Mirlpunda Track at the eastern end as an approach and descend via Ellen Peak. This would require only one overnight stop or could be done in a day walk if you leave early enough.

Attraction Rating: ★ ★ ★ ★

Fitness: ◩ ◩ ◩ ◩

Maps: DOLA Chester Pass and Ellen Peak 1:50 000 topographicals (little detail). DOLA has also released a detailed 1:15 000 map of the range. An overview is given by the AUSLIG (Natmap/Ausmap) Borden 1:100 000 topographical.

Access to Starting Point: Bluff Knoll car park is at the end of Bluff Knoll Road, which turns off Chester Pass Road at the northern boundary of the park. The turn-off is about 10km south of Amelup from where it's another 7km to the car park. If you are setting up a car shuffle, leave a vehicle at the north-eastern end near the Glenelg Estate, reached by driving north for 9km along Chester Pass Road and turning right onto Sandalwood Road. Follow this for 15km before turning right again and passing through the private property of the estate. Turn left at a gate. Some swampy ground is encountered before you come to the small parking area.

Facilities/Amenities: None en route. There is a well-developed car-camping area nearby at Moingup Springs and a caravan park at the intersection of Chester Pass and Bluff Knoll roads. For bookings, call (08) 9827 9229. Bluff Knoll Café, (08) 9827 9293, can assist (for a price) with pick-up and delivery of parties with only one vehicle. Bluff Knoll car park has water tanks.

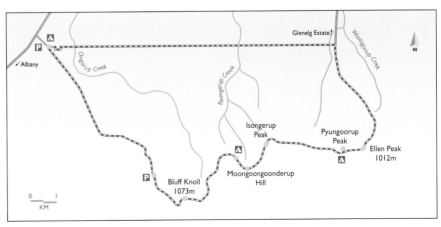

The lofty summit of Toolbrunup Peak is one of the highest in the Stirling Ranges.

Recommended Equipment: Water for the entire trip (some water may be available from near the Third Arrow camping cave). A fuel stove as no fires are permitted. A rain jacket is handy as the ranges can attract unexpected inclement weather.

Notes: Walkers are urged to register before and after a walk and leave details of water availability for the next party. Some rock-scrambling is necessary in parts, and this can be tricky during wet weather.

Further Information:

CALM Park Office
Stirling Range National Park
Chester Pass Rd, c/- PO Box
Amelup via Borden WA 6338
Tel: (08) 9827 9230
or   (08) 9827 9278

An excellent guide is A.T. Morphet's *Mountain Walks in the Stirling Range: Part 2—The peaks to the east of Chester Pass.*

Walk Description

The route is tough, following the crest of the range between the craggy peaks of the eastern Stirlings. Sections are scrubby and trackless and there is a chronic lack of water, so walkers must each drag at least eight litres along. Navigation has been made somewhat easier over recent years by the formation of footpads by previous walkers, but beware of several short false leads. Rock cairns also help mark the route in places. Follow the previous walk's tracknotes to the summit of Bluff Knoll. From here the walking gets a little harder as you continue east, not so much because of the terrain but more the absence of a good track. The ridge crosses over several lesser peaks and some scrub must be negotiated by means of a faint track. Aim to camp at the saddle before Moongoongoon-derup Hill as it will take about 6 hours to reach this point with heavy packs.

On the next day, head over Moon-goongoonderup Hill and onto the south Isongerup Peak, from where you get your first real look at the spectacular Arrows, a series of rocky crags west of Pyungoorup Peak (1060m). Head north along a well-defined ridge to a col dominated by she-oaks. From here, climb the First Arrow by going around all major outcrops to the north. The Second Arrow is easier and the Third Arrow is impossible—just skirt along its northern flanks. There are two alternatives: go around the left of the northern buttress via a camping cave, or head through the chasm between the northern and central buttresses. Another campsite and water can be found just to the right (south) of the western entrance to the chasm.

Once you've negotiated the Third Arrow, continue down to the Little Arrow and then over the broad dome of Bakers Knob (930m). The massive cliffs of Pyungoorup Peak loom ahead. Aim to camp in the overhang on the southern side of Pyungoorup Peak. The base of the cliffs must be skirted for quite some distance until you are almost at the eastern end. Campers who are familiar with the Budawangs in New South Wales will be used to this style of shelter.

Leave early on the third day, as a long road-bash is required to finish the circuit. Start by continuing along the cliffs, then climb up around the eastern flank of Pyungoorup Peak to a saddle. The summit can be easily climbed as a detour from here. This is the second-highest peak in the park and from the top, you can see that you are in the heart of the park's dynamic scenery. The wild cliffs of the Third Arrow make an excellent foreground.

Backtrack down to the saddle and head up east to Ellen Peak, the last of the peaks on the traverse. It is also one of the most rugged, being almost entirely surrounded by cliffs. If the time and inclination are there to tackle yet another summit, you can approach it directly via the western gully. Enjoy a mid-morning snack on the open summit with the bulk of Pyungoorup Peak dominating the foreground to the west. It is possible to go down the eastern side via a rock terrace and a gully but this is only for parties confident on exposed rock. Otherwise descend to the western gully and follow the base of the northern cliffs around to the eastern ridge.

From here it is fairly straightforward to descend off the range via a northerly spur until you come to a vehicular track near the northern perimeter fence of the national park. This is the North East Track. The car park at the Glenelg Estate is about 1km due north. If you have not arranged a car shuffle, follow the North East Track west for 11km back to Bluff Knoll Road and climb for 7km back up to the car park to complete the circuit. The overnight packs could be left at the Glenelg Estate to be collected by car later.

Toolbrunup Peak Walk

Starting Point: Toolbrunup Road car park (off Chester Pass Road), Stirling Ranges National Park

Destination: Toolbrunup Peak summit (1052m)
Summary: A challenging walk up the Stirling Range's third-highest peak
Attractions: Because of its central location, there are superb views along the Stirling Range in both directions
Length: 4km
Time: 4 hours
Options: The peak can also be approached from along the southern ridge and from the north via Mt Hassel, but park authorities discourage these routes because of rehabilitation work after a 1996 bushfire.
Attraction Rating: ★★★★
Fitness: ☒☒☒
Maps: DOLA Chester Pass 1:50 000 topographical
Access to Starting Point: Toolbrunup Road car park is 4km along Toolbrunup Road from Chester Pass Road. The turn-off is just north of the Moingup Springs camping area.
Facilities/Amenities: None. Nearby Moingup Springs has gas BBQs, toilets, tables and information boards.
Recommended Equipment: Water bottle
Notes: The final section of the track, marked by yellow-capped posts, is over rock but is easy to follow. Be prepared for a significant temperature variation between top and bottom, especially in windy conditions.
Further Information:
CALM Park Office
Stirling Range National Park
Chester Pass Rd, c/- PO Box
Amelup via Borden WA 6338
Tel: (08) 9827 9230
or   (08) 9827 9278

Walk Description

For walkers who have done Bluff Knoll and still want to explore further in the Stirling Ranges, this is the perfect challenge. Toolbrunup Peak is of similar height to Bluff Knoll, but because it stands on its own, as opposed to being part of a high-level ridge, the views are truly panoramic. It is also a far less popular peak and you often have it to yourself.

The route is pretty straightforward and you can see most of it from the car park at the end of the road. Some of the tallest trees in the park can be found near the beginning in the marri

stands around the creek on the right. Head straight up to a gully just left of the peak from where you must negotiate a boulder field to gain the summit. Some rock-scrambling is necessary but it's not too technically difficult. On a clear day, you can easily discern the coast to the south with the Porongurups to the southwest. The flat north is dominated by salt lakes and grazing land. The first recorded ascent of the peak was by Ensign Dale in 1832, looking for grain. Return via the same route.

Mt Magog to Talyuberlup Peak Walk

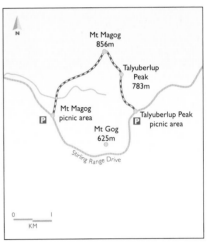

Starting Point: Mt Magog picnic area, Stirling Ranges National Park
Destination: Talyuberlup Peak picnic area
Summary: A ridge traverse between two peaks, Mt Magog (856m) and Talyupberlup Peak (783m), in the western Stirling Range
Attractions: Spectacular views over a less-frequented part of the park
Length: 8km
Time: 1 full day
Options: The traverse can be walked in either direction
Attraction Rating: ★★★
Fitness: ☒☒☒
Maps: DOLA Chester Pass and Mondurup 1:50 000 topographical (little detail)
Access to Starting Point: Stirling Range Drive is a scenic road that connects Red Gum Pass Road with Chester Pass Road. The two picnic areas are 6km apart, about halfway along the drive, (20km from Chester Pass Road).

Facilities/Amenities: Basic picnic facilities at each site. To the east, Moingup Springs has gas BBQs and toilets.
Recommended Equipment: Water bottle
Further Information:
  CALM Park Office
  Stirling Range National Park
  Chester Pass Rd, c/- PO Box
  Amelup via Borden WA 6338
  Tel: (08) 9827 9230
  or   (08) 9827 9278
An excellent guide is A.T. Morphet's *Mountain Walks in the Stirling Range: Part 1—The peaks to the west of Chester Pass.*

Walk Description

A continuous high-level traverse of the western range is not possible because of the isolated nature of the mountains, but the proximity of the two peaks, Mt Magog (856m) and Talyupberlup Peak (783m), allows a through-walk of sorts. If you are travelling to the area with only one car, you will have to walk a further 6km along the Stirling Range Drive between the picnic areas. The Magog picnic area is away from the main Stirling Range Drive in a thicket of impressive wandoo trees. Cross the creek, following an old vehicular trail up the base of Mt Magog. A walking track then heads straight up to a clearing in a saddle and from here you can access the twin peaks of Mt Magog. You encounter the south peak first, but the next one is slightly higher. If time is limited, just climb the first peak as the views are very similar.

Backtrack down to the saddle and head south along the ridge crest to Talyuberlup Peak. Although this is lower, its rocky summit comprises a series of pinnacles and offers a far more interesting climb. Negotiate a dramatic narrow pass between the pillars to join up with the main walking track from the Talyuberlup Peak car park before reaching the summit. An alternative is to use what is known as 'windy passage', a short tunnel that offers a more direct approach. There are great views to the east, dominated by the distinct slope of Bluff Knoll. Head down a steep gully on the southern flank, then it's a straightforward walk down the main summit track to the Talyuberlup Peak car park. If there is plenty of time, you can also reach the Stirling Range Road by wandering over Mt Gog (625m).

Other walks in the Stirling Ranges

The peaks of the Stirling Ranges are the primary attraction, and walking tracks of various grades allow access to the summits of most. The following mountains have graded trails and offer good 2–3 hour walks:

Moir Hill (457m) from Glenelg Estate (north-east boundary)
Mondurup Peak (817m) from Stirling Range Drive (west)
Mt Hassel (847m) from Stirling Range Drive (east)
Mt Trio (856m) from Formby South Road (north).

Peaks such as Yungermere Peak (753m), Little Mondurup Peak (640m) and Donnelly Peak have been closed because of measures to prevent the spread of dieback disease. Permits are required and these are granted only in very dry periods. One such area is the western end of the national park from Red Gum Pass on.

Other peaks have negotiable routes to the summits and tracknotes are provided in A.T. Morphet's *Mountain Walks in the Stirling Range*, Parts 1 and 2. These are Red Gum Hill (400m), Baby Barnett Hill (610m), Barnett Peak (765m), Henton Peak (777m), Twin Hills (625m), The Abbey (732m), Mt Success (750m), Kyanorup Eminence (500m) and Coyanarup Peak (1042m).

Porongurup National Park

The Porongurups are like a miniature version of the Stirling Range. They're just 12km long and rise to only 671m but nevertheless have a unique beauty derived from the contrast between rounded granite domes and forests of giant karri trees. The 2511ha national park is just 40km north of Albany. The most direct route is via Mt Barker on Albany Highway. The granite found throughout the Porongurups is more than 1100 million years old and has been exposed by the slow weathering of the softer rocks that surrounded the range, effectively isolating the mountains from other ecosystems.

The karri trees that cover the upper slopes of the range grow exclusively on a deep red soil known as karri loam. The trees need at least 700mm of rain a year and this is one of the most easterly remnants of the ancient karri forest that was once spread all over south-western Australia.

There are several walking opportunities in this park and all tracks are reasonably well marked and graded. Once again, the spread of dieback disease is of great concern and walkers are asked to stop at scrub-down stations to clean their boots. No camping facilities exist in the national park. The closest accommodation is at the Porongurup Caravan Park close to the Bolganup Road turn-off.

Nancys Peak Circuit

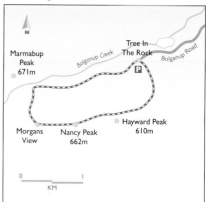

Starting Point: The Tree-in-the-Rock picnic area (Bolganup Road), Porongurup National Park
Destination: Hayward Peak (610m), Nancys Peak (662m), Morgans View
Summary: An eventful circuit in the centre of the park with many highlights and no backtracking
Attractions: Superb views to the south and west with massive boulders providing a photogenic foreground
Length: 5.5km
Time: 2.5 hours
Options: If time is available, you can extend the walk by climbing Marmabup Peak (671m) via the Devils Slide. This will add about 2 hours to your trip time.
Attraction Rating: ★ ★ ★
Fitness: ◨◨
Maps: DOLA Poronogurups 1:50 000 topographical (little detail)

Looking west to Marmabup Peak and the Devils Slide from Nancys Peak in the Porongurup Range.

Access to Starting Point: The Tree-in-the-Rock picnic area is at the end of Bolganup Road, which turns off the Mt Barker–Porongurup road about 20km east of Mt Barker

Facilities/Amenities: Picnic facilities at Tree-in-the-Rock include gas BBQs, toilets and tables. Comprehensive information billboards cover the park's geology, vegetation and wildlife.

Recommended Equipment: Water, especially if you are doing the Devils Slide option

Notes: The walk is best done early, when the Devils Slide is in the sun

Further Information:
CALM Park Office
Bolganup Rd, RMB 1310
Mt Barker WA 6324
Tel: (08) 9853 1095

Walk Description

This walk in the middle of the park offers a great overview of the Porongurup Range. The attractions begin almost immediately. From the car park head left to the fascinating tree-in-the-rock, a karri tree that has miraculously taken hold on a large boulder. From here the track zigzags steeply up past moss-covered boulders and wet forest of karri and marri trees that become progressively more stunted.

Eventually, you emerge on the bare granite dome of Hayward Peak. Use the boot scrub-down station to help prevent the spread of dieback. White-painted markers show the route over rock. Descend on the other side and proceed to Nancys Peak, the highest point on the walk at 662m. Large boulders dominate the foreground and there are good views here in most directions.

Continue west down to Morgans View, named after a politician who owned land just to the south. Drainage is poor and some sections can be boggy. If you are lucky, you may catch a glimpse of a quokka, a large ratlike native marsupial. This was one of the first Australian mammals ever seen by Europeans as they were prolific when Rottnest Island was visited in 1658 by Samuel Volckertzoon. From Morgans View, the track descends steeply through thick vegetation to a pleasant forested saddle called The Pass, where it intersects with the Wansbrough Walk. Another track heads up the Devils Slide to Marmabup Peak, the highest point in the park. Take this if time and energy permit. From the saddle follow the old fire trail east through the Bolganup Creek valley about 1.6km down to the car park. There are impressive stands of karri forest along this section. Near the end, the short Bolganup Heritage Trail heads left to the creek.

Other walks in Porongurup National Park
Castle Rock (4km, 2 hours)

This granite tor in the eastern end of the park is a great attraction. The walk starts at the car park at the end of Castle Road, which leaves the Mt Barker–Porongurup road about 3km west of Chester Pass Road and 40km north of Albany. Splendid karri specimens line the beginning of the walk as you climb gradually to Balancing Rock, a precarious boulder.

Climb Castle Rock via a steel ladder and gangway across the top of a jumbled mass of impressive boulders. There are fine views across the plains toward the Stirling Ranges.

Other walks

Two passes cross the Porongurup Range, Millinup Pass and Wansbrough Walk. The former ends at private property and you must backtrack; the latter makes a through-walk possible. Park one car at the Tree-in-the-Rock picnic area and another on the Millinup road. Consult the ranger if you want to traverse the entire range from Manyat Peak to Halls Rock as there are no tracks.

Walpole–Nornalup National Park

Dominated by tall pristine forests and wild coastal scenery, this beautiful 20 000ha park is truly a bushwalkers' paradise. It provides the setting for one of the best-loved sections of the Bibbulmun Track and a major side option leads into Nuyts Wilderness. Based on Nornalup Inlet, the park forms a continuous reserve that protects the coast from D'Entrecasteaux National Park east to Irwin Inlet. A great attraction are the giant 70m tingle trees that grow only within 15km of the Walpole area. These trees have thick red trunks. Access is from Walpole via the South Western Freeway, about 433km south of Perth and 121km west of Albany.

....

Nuyts Wilderness Walk

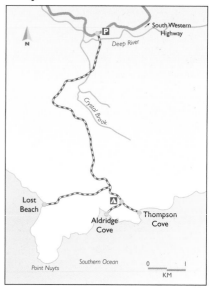

Starting Point: Nuyts car park, Shedley Drive, Walpole–Nornalup National Park

Destination: Thompson and Aldridge coves and Lost Beach

Summary: One of the best wilderness walks in the state is the traverse between Deep River and Point Nuyts

Attractions: A total wilderness atmosphere, secluded coves

Length: 19.4km

Time: 2 days

Options: Extend the walk by following the Bibbulmun Track to the west or by heading to Crystal Lake and Mt Hopkins (204m) to the east. This last option, discouraged by park authorities, is through thick trackless scrub.

Attraction Rating: ★ ★ ★ ★

Fitness: ☒ ☒ ☒

Maps: DOLA Saddle Island 1:50 000 topographical

Access to Starting Point: Shedley Drive is accessed by turning off the South Western Freeway about 8km west of Walpole onto Tinglewood Drive. Follow this unsealed road through forest, ignoring a turn-off to Mt Clare on the right. You pass Tinglewood Lodge as the road curves

Walking in Nuyts Wilderness, Walpole–Nornalup National Park.

Peaceful Bay in the eastern Walpole–Nornalup National Park.

to the right to enter the Deep River valley. Park your car at the signposted car park on the left. You will see markers for the Bibbulmun Track here. The road is one-way after this.

Facilities/Amenities: Tinglewood Lodge offers up-market accommodation, phone (08) 9840 1035 to book. There is a Bibbulmun Track campsite nearby at Mt Clare if you arrive late.

Recommended Equipment: Water and standard overnight camping gear. A fuel stove is essential as fires are not permitted in the park.

Notes: Tiger snakes are common in the area. Group size is limited to eight people (including the group leader). Organised groups wishing to camp are required to notify CALM at least four weeks in advance. During school holidays and long weekends, camping is limited to one night at each campsite. Organised groups are limited to one night at each campsite at all times. Only three tents are permitted at a campsite on any night.

Further Information:
Walpole District Office
South Western Highway
Walpole WA 6398
Tel: (08) 9840 1027
Fax: (08) 9840 1251

Walk Description

Since May 1976, the 4500ha Nuyts Wilderness (pronounced 'Newts') has been managed as a wilderness area. All mechanised transport is prohibited here, so the Nuyts area provides a superb bushwalking experience.

These days, controlled burning has been regularly undertaken by CALM in order to preserve the wilderness in a relatively intact state. In the mid-1900s, the area had been destroyed several times by bushfires. At the car park is a walkers' registration point that allows rangers to monitor visitor usage. It is not checked frequently though so as a safeguard, walkers should notify family or friends of their expected time of return.

The first 2km of the track winds through cool karri forest and peppermint groves interspersed with marri, jarrah and tingle. Soon after leaving the car park, you cross the Deep River via a footbridge. After 2km, walkers enter dry coastal heathland and continue south for a further 5km along an old vehicular track to the rugged coastline. Along the way is the Bibbulmun Track turn-off that heads west to Long Point and Mandalay Beach.

Walkers have several camping places to choose from, which reduces their impact. The main site is near the junction between Aldridge Cove and Thompson Cove. Other smaller sites can be found at other coves. Extreme caution is required on coastal areas as rogue waves, called king waves, have already washed five people to their deaths. Swimming is discouraged and is impractical at Lost Beach because of rocks. Spend some time exploring the three coves before returning via the same route. There are good views north along the desolate coast.

Other walks in the Walpole–Nornalup National Park

The national park provides several walking opportunities, from simple tourist walks suitable for families to longer overnight sections following the Bibbulmun Track. Serious walkers can even follow the coast to the west and east of Nornalup Inlet.

Coalmine Beach Walk (6km, 2 hours)

From Walpole's Pioneer Cottage, follow the Bibbulmun Track south to the beach via Collier Creek. The Knoll, covered by a mosaic of interesting vegetation, is also a highlight.

Giant Tingle Tree Trail (800m, 20 min)

Near Hilltop, 2km east of Walpole, a short walk has a massive burnt-out tingle tree as its main feature. With a girth of 24m, this is the widest eucalypt known world wide.

Valley of the Giants

This area gets its name from the large red tingle trees that grow here. The species is one of the largest of all eucalypts, with huge buttressed trunks. The valley is the easternmost occurrence of this species.

From Walpole, travel 13km east along the South Coast Highway past Nornalup to the Valley of Giants Road. A sealed road leads to the recreation area—all turn-offs are signposted. It is open from 8.00am to 6.00pm during summer holidays and 9.00am to 4.15pm at other times. Call (08) 9840 8263 for details.

The Tree Top Walk (600m, 15 min)

This raised gangway has become one of the main tourist attractions in the vicinity. The whole family can experience the excitement of exploring the canopy of the majestic tingle forest along a walkway that rises up to 38m above the forest. Some of the trees are more than 400 years old. A small admission fee is charged, and family passes are available.

Ancient Empire Walk (800m, 15 min)

The Valley of the Giants site includes a boardwalk through a grove of 20 veteran tingle trees known as the Ancient Empire. This area contains the 'Giants' for which the forest was named. There are three tingle species, the Red, Yellow and Rates.

Mt Frankland Walk (2km, 1 hour)

Although Mt Frankland is not in the Walpole–Nornalup National Park, this 411m peak overlooks the entire Walpole region. A spectacular view can be obtained from the granite-domed cap that rises abruptly out of the forest. Steps and ladders make the ascent quite safe. The car park and walk start is 27km north of Walpole via North Walpole Road and Mt Frankland Road. Another short walk around the base of the mountain wanders through stands of karris.

D'Entrecasteaux National Park

Isolation and unspoilt wilderness are features of D'Entrecasteaux National Park (pronounced don-truh-cast-oh, with a slight stress on the last syllable). The 118 000ha contains towering limestone cliffs, remote beaches, wildflowers and pockets of karri forest. More than 130km of the coastline is protected. Sand dunes have blocked most of the south-flowing watercourses, forming large freshwater lakes. One example is the 4000-year-old Lake Jasper in the west of the park, the largest body of fresh water in the south of Western Australia. First discovered in 1792 when Admiral Bruni D'Entrecasteaux sailed past looking for agricultural potential, much of the park area is now managed for its wilderness value, so few facilities are provided. Watch for wildlife when driving through.

Mt Chudalup Walk

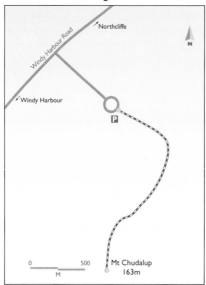

Starting Point: Windy Harbour Road, D'Entrecasteaux National Park
Destination: Mt Chudalup summit (163m)
Summary: A short steep walk up a granite-domed cap
Attractions: Views over the park
Length: 1km
Time: 25 minutes
Options: None
Attraction Rating: ★★
Fitness: ✖
Maps: DOLA Gardner River 1:50 000 topographical (not necessary)
Access to Starting Point: From Northcliffe, take Windy Harbour Road south for 15km to a car park on the left
Facilities/Amenities: None. The nearest facilities are in Northcliffe. A camping area is at Windy Harbour.
Recommended Equipment: Shoes with grip; wind jacket for windy days
Further Information:
  CALM Northcliffe Office
  Tel: (08) 9776 7095
or
  CALM Pemberton Office
  Tel: (08) 9776 1207

Walk Description

A broad expanse of coast can be seen from this great lookout, in particular the extensive Meerup and Doggerup sand dunes. From the car, head up the steep trail through wet karri and marri forest and turn right to approach the granite dome. Grasstrees have found shelter in a narrow gully, while lichen and stunted melaleuca create colourful 'rock gardens' on top. You have to walk to various parts of the dome to access the best vantage points. Be careful if the rock is wet. The views east to Broke Inlet are especially good. Return via the same route.

Other walks in D'Entrecasteaux National Park

At time of writing, a walking track was under construction from Salmon Beach (north-west of Point D'Entrecasteaux Lighthouse) to Windy Harbour (Cathedral Rock). It follows the 100m-high limestone cliffs with outstanding views along the coastal headlands and takes most of a day. Shorter tourist walks are based on the lighthouse and Mandalay Beach.

Leeuwin–Naturaliste National Park

Almost 20 000ha of Western Australia's wild south-west coast are protected in the limestone region between Cape Naturaliste and Cape

The D'Entrecasteaux coastline from Point D'Entrecasteaux.

Leeuwin. The Leeuwin–Naturaliste Ridge, up to 200m high in places and running roughly parallel to the coast, is a central feature of the park. It is composed of two very different rock types. Around the base is hard ancient granite, more than 600 million years old. Lying directly above, on much of the western side of the ridge, is the younger Tamala Limestone formation. As the Australian landmass drifted north-east away from Antarctica, the Leeuwin–Naturaliste Ridge became isolated from the main plateau of Western Australia. This south-western corner of the continent was left projecting into the Indian Ocean, to be eroded by wind and water and create spectacular scenery.

The granite was formed by the melting and reconstitution of the upper layers of the earth's crust through tremendous heat and pressure. Where there were joints and fault lines, erosive processes have been accelerated. The overlying limestone is derived from fragments of coral reef, shells and skeletons of sea-creatures that lived in the warm, shallow seas several million years ago. During the Pleistocene series of ice ages, the sea level was lower and this material was blown inland to form massive dune systems along the western side of the Leeuwin–Naturaliste Ridge. Calcium carbonate from these fragments dissolved in groundwater and was redeposited around the sand grains, cementing them together to form rock. In places, probably where a thin film of water trickled over a long period, a hard thin layer of almost pure calcium carbonate was formed. Sometimes known as cap-rock, this can often be seen exposed at or near the top of sea cliffs. Below this, the limestone may be much more fragile, consisting mainly of sand grains, tenuously held together by a lime-based cement and easily eroded by the sea.

The national park is famous for its cave systems as much of the drainage is underground. Only the larger streams, such as Margaret River and Willyabrup and Boodjidup brooks, have maintained their surface flow and cut deep valleys through to the sea. These streams flow only in

Sugarloaf Rock on the Cape to Cape Walking Track.

winter and sandbars form across their mouths in summer. Springs and seepages occur all along the coast at the point of contact between limestone and underlying impervious granite. Do not rely on drinking water from these springs, however, as most of them dry up over summer.

Cape to Cape Walking Track

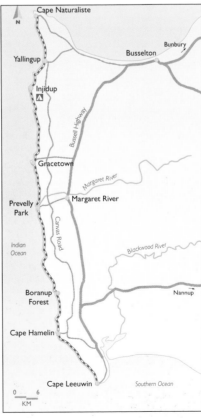

Starting Point: Cape Naturaliste, D'Entrecasteaux National Park

Destination: Cape Leeuwin
Summary: A walk that closely follows the rugged limestone coast in the Margaret River district
Attractions: Lookouts, coastal cliffs, rock formations, beaches and forest
Length: 140km
Time: 6–8 days
Options: Shorter sections are possible as there are numerous car access points. The main ones are Sugarloaf Rock, Yallingup, Canal Rocks, Moses Rock, Cowaramup Point, Prevelly Park, Black Rock, Hamelin Bay and Cosy Corner.
Attraction Rating: ★ ★ ★ ★
Fitness: ☒ ☒ ☒ ☒
Maps: DOLA Clairault, Yallingup, Mentelle, Leeuwin, Tooker, Karrdale and Cowaramup 1:50 000 topographicals. The track is also covered by a 1:25 000 series but these maps are not necessary.
Access to Starting Point: Cape Naturaliste is 36km from Busselton and 261km south of Perth via Bunbury. Cape Leeuwin is 9km from Augusta, which is 43km south of Margaret River via Bussell Highway.
Facilities/Amenities: Numerous camping areas along the way
Recommended Equipment: Water is essential as there are long sections between springs and water tanks
Notes: Consult with CALM rangers regarding water availability before setting out. Reliable springs are found near Ellenbrook Homestead (upstream from Meekadarabee Falls), at Bobs Hollow and near Contos campground near Cape Freycinet.

Further Information:

CALM Busselton Office
14 Queen St, Busselton WA 6280
Tel: (08) 9752 1677

or

Margaret River Office
Tel: (08) 9757 2322

Walk Description

This long-distance walk was started with a Bicentennial Grant and took about 10 years to construct. CALM has produced five helpful leaflets detailing the track, with maps, tracknotes and background information. These are:

Section 1: Cape Naturaliste to Wyadup, 18km

Section 2: Wyadup to Cowaramup Bay (Gracetown), 33km

Section 3: Cowaramup Bay to Redgate Beach, 31km

Section 4: Redgate Beach to Cape Hamelin, 29km

Section 5: Cape Hamelin to Cape Leeuwin, 29km

As the walking is fairly easy, aim to complete about 20km a day, which still allows plenty of time for the occasional swim and rest. This is, unfortunately, not a wild walk as you are in contact with people for most of the time because of numerous vehicle-access points along the coast. In summer, the region's popularity with tourists can lead to some of the lookouts and beaches being quite crowded. The best parts are in the southern section where the national park is at its wildest and water is more readily available.

Other walks in the Leeuwin–Naturaliste National Park

The guidebook *Bushwalks in the South-West*, published by CALM, has a chapter on the Limestone Coast detailing short tourist walks around Bunker Bay, Cape Naturaliste, Canal Rocks, Meekadarabee Falls, Hamelin Bay and Skippy Rock. Visitors can also walk underground in the many caves in the area. The best ones are Ngilgi, north of Margaret River, and Mammoth, Lake, Jewel and Moondyne Caves to the south.

Other walks in the south-west

As the south-west has the state's most aesthetic landscapes and a mild climate with water flowing all year, it offers a great number of walking opportunities, especially in the karri, jarrah and tingle forests.

Around Perth

The best guidebooks are CALM's *Family Walks in Perth Outdoors* and *More Family Walks in Perth Outdoors.* For example, many highlights of the John Forrest National Park are connected by the John Forrest Heritage Trail. Here, a pleasant walk can be done between Hovea Falls and Rocky Pool. Likewise, the Dryandra Woodland is the setting for some medium-distance walks through pleasant jarrah, paperbark, wandoo and she-oak forest. Here, the Ochre Trail visits a pit once used by local Aborigines. A 7km Heritage Trail at Jarrahdale follows an old railway line through jarrah forest. Mammoth specimens of these trees can be seen here.

The Cape to Cape limestone coast, Leeuwin–Naturaliste National Park.

Forests

There are several state forests and other reserves around Dwellingup. One of the best walks here is the King Jarrah Walk Trail, an 18km circuit in the Murray River valley. The Bibbulmun Track can also be used to form circuits with the Nanga Track to Scarp Pool. Near Manjimup, the Maxwell Trail follows Mylliup Pool for 7km, and walkers can admire flooded gum woodland that begins at Chindilup Pool. To the south, Pemberton is probably the pick of the forest areas with gorgeous attractions such as Beedelup Falls and Lane Poole Falls. In the Shannon National Park, the Great Forest Trees Walk is an 8km track centred on the beautiful Shannon River. Dozens more half-day walks are featured in CALM's *Bushwalks in the South-West*.

Trees

By means of about 150 rungs drilled into each trunk, visitors can climb three straight 50–70m karri trees that are open to the public and access lookout platforms constructed in the crowns. All situated in the Pemberton region, these trees were once used as fire-watch towers and now present one of the more unusual 'walking' experiences to be had. North of Pemberton is the Diamond Tree (51m); south is the famous Gloucester Tree (61m); and west is the Dave Evans Bicentennial Tree (65m).

Coast

The Yalorup National Park, south of Perth, has salt lakes and rare stromatolites. A 6km walking track goes from the Preston Beach road to Lake Pollard where you can watch birds from a hide. Another walk from the same road explores heath communities. Nearby, Martins Tank Lake camping area is a great place to relax.

Inland

Much-photographed Wave Rock is just east of the small outback town of Hyden (340km from Perth). This unique granite formation is the highlight of a short circuit that takes walkers on top of the rock for great views. Nearby, Hippos Yawn is another formation sculpted by wind and rain.

The West Coast

As you travel north of Perth, the landscape changes quite noticeably. The tall trees, rolling forested hills and pretty rivers are left behind as you enter more open, arid country. This section features four walks in the region between Perth and Shark Bay.

Yanchep National Park

Abundant wildlife is a feature of Yanchep National Park, north of Perth. Loch McNess (a freshwater lake), a koala sanctuary, visitor information centre, museum, limestone caves and a hotel are within the park boundaries and walkers can spot kangaroos and water fowl around the lake.

Coastal Plain Walk Trail

Starting Point: Loch McNess, Yanchep National Park
Destination: Yongka picnic area (Neaves Road, Wanneroo)
Summary: An easy overnight walk through Yanchep National Park and across the Swan coastal plain area to end at Melaleuca Conservation Park, north-east of Wanneroo
Attractions: Easy walking through flat country close to Perth
Length: 46.3km
Time: 2 days
Options: At time of writing, the trail was being extended west to Two Rocks at the Indian Ocean and south through the Melaleuca Conservation Park. Eventually, it will be connected with the Bibbulmun Track.
Attraction Rating: ★ ★
Fitness: ☒☒
Maps: DOLA Yanchep 1:25 000 topo-

A banksia on the Coastal Plain Walk Trail in Yanchep National Park.

graphical. The AUSLIG (Natmap/Ausmap) Perth 1:100 000 topographical
Access to Starting Point: Yanchep National Park is situated 50km north of Perth. Metropolitan train services run regularly to Joondalup with connecting public transport buses to Yanchep and Two Rocks in the morning and afternoon. There are no public transport services to or past the Yongka picnic area at the south-eastern end of the trail. Arrange with Swan taxis to be picked up from Yongka picnic area prior to starting the walk.
Facilities/Amenities: Three huts of similar construction to those of the Bibbulmun Track provide shelter along the trail. Shapcotts camping area (5km mark), Ridges (15.9km mark) and Moitch (35.8km mark) all have rainwater tanks, toilets, cleared tent sites and wood BBQ facilities. Some BBQs operate with free gas.

Other accommodation options are available in the Yanchep suburban area, including a small Flag Inn motel (adjacent to the Sun City Golf Club) and Bed-and-breakfast establishments. Accommodation can be arranged at Glendale Lodge, which is associated with a local horse-riding tourist attraction (The Stables). The largest facility in the area, Club Capricorn, provides campgrounds, resort-style

Limestone pinnacles form a fascinating landscape in the Nambung National Park.

accommodation and on-site caravans on the beachfront at Yanchep. The historic Yanchep Inn has a restaurant and serves counter meals; BBQ packs can be purchased at most times of the day. Several holiday units are part of the hotel accommodation.

Recommended Equipment: Because of ticks, insect repellent and gaiters are recommended

Notes: Pepper or kangaroo ticks are very common in the area. These are a nuisance only and are not dangerous. A small pair of tweezers, insect repellent or Vaseline can be used to remove any ticks easily. Dugite and tiger snakes are more dangerous, but these are not commonly encountered by walkers. The trail is well marked with small blue triangular signs on trees or posts every 200–250m.

Further Information:
Perth District Office
5 Dundebar Rd, Wanneroo WA 6065
Tel: (08) 9405 1222
Fax: (08) 9405 0777
or
Yanchep National Park
Tel: (08) 9561 1004
Fax: (08) 9561 2316

Walk Description

Leave your car in the car park just south of the Loch McNess Visitors' Centre and walk north for 5.6km to Shapcotts campsite via the Yandjidi Trail and Ghost House Trail around Loch McNess. The section between Shapcotts and Ridges campsites is the most scenic section of the trail. The Ridges site has nice views over broad valleys to the north. From here it is almost 20km south-east to Moitch camping area via Perry Road and a further 10.4km to the walk's end at Neaves Road. Fit walkers will be able to do this level section in a day with ease if they set out early enough.

Other walks in Yanchep National Park

A number of shorter walks within the park range in length from 400m to 7km. The 2km Yanjidi trail around Loch McNess is a pleasant stroll, as is the 2km Bunkers Trail to Cabaret Cave.

Nambung National Park

Thousands of huge limestone pillars, some up to 4m tall, stand in stark contrast to the surrounding sandy hills and low heathlands of Nambung National Park on the Swan Coastal Plain. The Pinnacles Desert features heavily in tourist guides to the state, but they are only a small part of the 17 491ha park. Serene beaches, coastal dune systems and wildflowers typical of the northern coastal plain are among its other features.

Geology

The first thing most people ask when seeing The Pinnacles is, 'How were they formed?' Many mistakenly believe they are fossilised trees, but they are, in fact, made of limestone, the same as stalagmites in a cave. The raw material for the limestone came from seashells broken down into lime-rich sands and carried inland by wind to form high mobile dunes.

Rain leached the lime from these sands, cementing grains of sand together in the lower levels of the dunes. Vegetation became established and stabilised the dunes, but created an acidic soil. This accelerated the leaching process and a hard layer of calcrete formed over the softer limestone below. Today this calcrete can be seen as a distinct lighter cap on many pinnacles and this has helped protect the softer limestone below.

Cracks in the calcrete layer were exploited by plant roots. Water seeped down along these channels to leach away the softer limestone beneath and the channels gradually filled with quartz sand. This subsurface erosion continued until only the most resilient columns remained. The Pinnacles were then gradually exposed by prevailing winds blowing away the overlying quartz sand.

Climate

Summer days between December and March are usually hot and dry, with afternoon sea breezes. During this time the fire danger is often extreme. Wildlife rests in the heat of the day, and appears only in the cooler hours of early morning and evening. Most of the annual 600mm of rain falls between May and September. From September on the weather warms up, but the days are still mild and native wildflowers throughout the area start their spring bloom. This is the best time of year to discover The Pinnacles and explore the park.

Vegetation

Three systems of sand dunes run parallel to the coast from Nambung to Busselton. These dunes, formed from wind-blown beach sand rich in lime, mark ancient shorelines on the Swan coastal plain. The dune systems become older and more gentle and undulating the farther they are from the sea. The shape and character of the sands determine which plants will grow on them. The Quindalup dune system of white, lime-rich sands is found immediately inland from the foredunes and is constantly being added to by sand from the foredunes and the beach. The vegetation here is strongly influenced by the shape of the dunes. Acacia thickets are common in the small valleys among the dunes and on the leeward slopes.

The older Spearwood dune system occurs farther inland. It is composed of yellow and brownish quartz sands, and often overlies limestone. The Pinnacles are the eroded remnants of what was once a thick bed of limestone beneath these sands. Tuart woodlands occur in the valleys, but it is the low exposed heaths of acacia and myrtles extending inland to the Pinnacles Desert that dominate the landscape. Scattered over these low heaths grow casuarinas and banksias, including the bright orange-flowered *Banksia prionotes*. In the silica-rich Bassendean dune system on the east of the park the vegetation is dominated by low, open banksia woodland.

Wildlife

Most of the mammals in the park are nocturnal, but during the day you may see emus or western grey kangaroos. Reptiles of many sorts are common, particularly bobtail skinks and snakes. More than 90 species of birds common to the Swan Coastal Plain have been recorded in Nambung National Park.

The Pinnacles Circuit

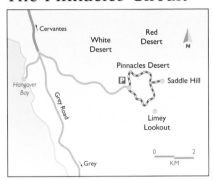

Starting Point: Pinnacles car park, Nambung National Park
Destination: The Pinnacles Desert and Saddle Hill
Summary: A walk around the main tourist drive and side trip to Saddle Hill
Attractions: The Pinnacles, views over the desert and coast
Length: 6km
Time: 2.5 hours
Options: Countless opportunities for wandering around exploring
Attraction Rating: ★ ★ ★ ★
Fitness: ☒
Maps: DOLA Cervantes 1:50 000 topographical (not needed for navigation)

Access to Starting Point: The Pinnacles are 245km north of Perth via the Brand Highway. Turn left 66km north of Cataby and follow the signs 70km west past Cervantes.
Facilities/Amenities: Toilets at the car park. No camping is allowed. The nearest accommodation is at Cervantes on the coast, 30km to the north.
Recommended Equipment: Camera
Notes: The only time to photograph The Pinnacles properly is at dawn and dusk when the sun is low, creating warm light and high contrast
Further Information:
CALM Office
PO Box 62, Cervantes WA 6511
Tel: (08) 9652 7043
or
Moora Office
Tel: (08) 9651 1424

Walk Description

Many people drive around the Pinnacles Desert stopping the car every few hundred metres to take photographs. It is actually more efficient and more interesting to leave your car at the car park and walk around the circuit, which allows you to move where you like. There are various types of Pinnacles, from thin sharp ones, to short stumpy ones and tall groups of several joined together. It's like being in a cave without the darkness. The road is clearly defined, but don't wander too far off as the formations can become disorienting.

From the top of Saddle Hill, you can view the entire region. Some of the tallest formations are found to the south and can be seen from a wooden lookout platform. A 500m circuit also leaves from the car park.

Kalbarri National Park

Kalbarri National Park, based on the Murchison River gorge, provides the type of landscapes you can normally see only in the Kimberley and Pilbara regions. Visitors can overview the rocky sandstone gorges from lookouts or go down to the river to swim and walk. Numerous banksias in bloom are a feature of the park in autumn.

Beneath this spectacular region, the bedrock consists of deep, horizontal bands of multicoloured sands that were deposited in layers some 400

View south to Castle Cove and Island Rock from the Kalbarri cliffs.

million years ago. The resultant distinctive formation is called the Tumblagooda Sandstone.

As the Murchison River carves its way to the sea, magnificent gorges, banded in red and white, have been cut by the water flow. The 186 096ha national park protects about 80km of these gorges. The park was proclaimed in 1963 to preserve the lower Murchinson River, but recent lease expirations and CALM land acquisitions extend protection upstream.

Along the coast, erosion has created awe-inspiring formations out of the dramatic sea cliffs, including a natural bridge and an island pinnacle.

Access

Kalbarri, just west of the national park and 586km north of Perth, is serviced by commercial aircraft and coaches. The road to the township is sealed, but those into the national park roads are dirt, although well-graded enough for conventional vehicles. Summer temperatures can reach 40°C and the weather is often dry and windy. Winter temperatures range from 10°C to 20°C, with most rain falling during June and July.

Kalbarri is famous for its wildflowers, which begin to bloom after July. The cooler months are the most comfortable time to visit. Located at the mouth of the Murchison River is the holiday township of Kalbarri, which supports a thriving fishing industry and provides the tourist base for visitors to the national park. The CALM office is on the left-hand side as you approach the town.

The Loop Circuit

Starting Point: Natures Window car park, Kalbarri National Park
Destination: Murchison River
Summary: An anti-clockwise circuit inside a particularly distinct loop in the river
Attractions: Shallow gorge scenery, Natures Window
Length: 7km
Time: 4 hours

Options: This walk can be done in either direction
Attraction Rating: ★ ★ ★
Fitness: ◩◩
Maps: AUSLIG (Natmap/Ausmap) Kalbarri 1:100 000 topographical
Access to Starting Point: The turn-off into the national park is at Ajana, 101km north of Geraldton. From here, it is 19km to the park boundary and then a further 36km to Natures Window/Z-Bend turn-off. Head right onto an unsealed road and follow this north-east for 20km to a T-intersection. Turn left and drive north for 6km to the car park.
Facilities/Amenities: Toilets, tables and fireplaces at Natures Window carpark. The nearest shops are at Kalbarri, 37km to the west.
Recommended Equipment: Broad hat and sunscreen, swimming gear if the day is hot
Notes: Some minor rock-scrambling is necessary, but not difficult
Further Information:
   CALM Office
   PO Box 37, Kalbarri WA 6536
   Tel: (08) 9937 1140 or
          (08) 9937 1192
   Fax: (08) 9937 1437
or
   Geraldton Office
   Tel: (08) 9921 5955

Walk Description

From the car park follow the broad well-graded walking track down a spur with great views to either side. In early morning or late afternoon, the colour of the cliffs seems to glow. Visit the sandstone arch called Natures Window, which frames the upstream gorge to perfection. A raised pedestal allows people to take photographs through it. Be careful when scampering around on the ledges as the rock is quite soft.

Head down the right-hand side and follow the Murchison River around a long loop, keeping the river to your right at all times. The water is reasonably shallow in parts, but fine for a dip in warm weather. Once you are back at Natures Window, the car park is only 400m up the hill. Take care when swimming as seasonal monsoon activity can keep the gorge dangerously flooded for weeks.

The Murchison River gorge at Z-Bend in Kalbarri National Park.

Murchison River Walk

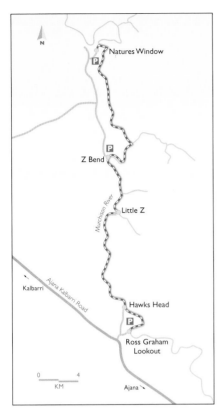

Starting Point: Ross Graham Lookout, Kalbarri National Park

Destination: Natures Window car park

Summary: A long walk following the Murchinson River downstream. A car shuffle is needed between staging areas.

Attractions: Rugged gorge scenery, beautiful pools and cascades

Length: 38km

Time: 3–4 days

Options: This walk can be done in either direction but it's always easier to walk downstream. One can also start or finish at the Z-Bend car park, about halfway. Longer extensions can be completed by following the gorge right through the national park from The Rapids and Hardabut Pool on the eastern boundary to Natures Window. Allow an extra day.

Attraction Rating: ★ ★ ★ ★

Fitness: ◪ ◪

Maps: AUSLIG (Natmap/Ausmap) Kalbarri 1:100 000 topographical

Access to Starting Point: The turn-off into the national park is at Ajana, 101km north of Geraldton. From here, it is 19km to the park boundary and then a further 12km to the Hawks Head/Ross Graham Lookout turn-off.

Looking over the Murchison River in Kalbarri National Park.

Head right onto an unsealed road and within a couple of hundred metres, turn right to Ross Graham. To reach the other end of the walk, see the directions given in the Loop Walk on the page opposite.

Facilities/Amenities: There are toilets, tables and fireplaces at Ross Graham Lookout and Natures Window car park. The nearest shops are at Kalbarri, 37km to the west.

Recommended Equipment: Broad hat and sunscreen, sturdy shoes for rock walking, and a self-supporting tent for pitching on rock platforms. A good-quality thick inflatable sleeping mat is also handy. A fuel stove is necessary as wood fires are banned.

Notes: Some rock-scrambling is necessary in the Z-Bend area where the gorge has steep-sided slopes that go right down to the water. Many crossings are necessary and walkers might like to wrap their gear in plastic bags. If the river is in flood because of recent cyclonic activity, the walk will not be possible. Overnight walkers are asked to register at the CALM office.

Further Information:

CALM Office
PO Box 37, Kalbarri WA 6536
Tel: (08) 9937 1140 or
(08) 9937 1192
Fax: (08) 9937 1437
or

Geraldton Office
Tel: (08) 9921 5955

Walk Description

The term 'bushwalking' is a bit of a misnomer when applied to Kalbarri National Park as there is no bush. The object of this extended overnight walk is to follow the Murchinson River downstream through spectacular gorge scenery for 38km, immersing yourself in the brilliant scenery. Only experienced, self-sufficient walkers should attempt this as the gorge can get fairly rugged at times.

The directions are simple—from the Ross Graham Lookout scamper down to the river, being careful on the loose rocky slopes. The gorge is fairly shallow and broad at this point and the walking is easy, but the section between Little Z and Natures Window is more rugged, with steep cliffs that often go right down to the water.

Swimming in the many tranquil pools here will be a long-remembered experience. However, make sure you are familiar with the Natures Window area so you don't miss the exit as there are no signs.

Other walks in Kalbarri National Park

The coast to the south of Kalbarri has an astonishing assortment of sandstone and limestone formations. The 8km Coastal Trail heads south from Eagle Gorge and overlooks such features as Castle Cove and Island Rock before terminating at the Natural Bridge car park. Some other colourful attractions to the north are Pot Alley, Rainbow Valley, Mushroom Rock and Red Bluff. This last feature contains a cairn commemorating what historians believe to be the first landing of Europeans on the Australian mainland when the trading vessel *Batavia* ran aground in 1629.

Other walks on the West Coast

Shark Bay is a wonderful World Heritage Area on the central western coast about 850km north of Perth. There are dozens of attractions, the most famous being the dolphins at Monkey Mia. Visitors can enjoy Shell Beach, a 10m-thick layer of tiny seashells, and the ancient stromatolites at Hamelin Pool. The small township of Denham is a good base from which to explore the area. Tours made by 4WD to Australia's most westerly point are very popular. Because of the hot, dry climate and absence of tree cover, there are no overnight walks available in this area, but short tourist walks of less than an hour can be found at Monkey Mia, Eagle Bluff and in the Francois Peron National Park.

The Pilbara

One of earth's oldest landmasses, the Pilbara is estimated to have been formed more than 2.5 billion years ago. Much of the most dynamic areas of the Pilbara have been protected in a series of outstanding national parks. The Pilbara also has a wealth of Aboriginal rock engravings, with the Burrup Peninsula alone having more than 10 000 examples.

Location: The Pilbara is located about 1500km north of Perth

Size: The region covers roughly 500 000 square kilometres and is bordered by the Gascoyne Region (south), the Kimberley (north), the Indian Ocean (west) and the Northern Territory (east).

Population: 50 000

Major Towns: Karratha and Port Hedland on the coast and Tom Price and Newman inland.

Climate

The Pilbara has a tropical, semi-desert climate with temperatures ranging from 0–45°C. A variable rainfall in summer, often associated with thunderstorms, is accompanied by temperatures often topping 40°C. In fact, the record for consecutive hot days in Australia remains with Marble Bar during 1923/24: 161 consecutive days above 37°C.

Visiting the Pilbara at various times of year offers different advantages. While autumn and spring are ideal, winter days are pleasantly warm and clear, though the nights can be cold and sometimes frosty. In the peak summer months, the refreshingly cool waters in the gorges compensate for the extreme heat.

As the Pilbara is in the cyclone belt of the country, conditions can change quite dramatically from day to day, particularly in late summer. In 1999, Exmouth and Onslow were hit by two ferocious cyclones that damaged much of their infrastructure. At other times, local thunderstorms can flood roads and watercourses. In winter, there is little rain and daytime temperatures are around 26°C. Nights can be cold as the skies are clear, so warm clothes will be handy.

Clothing is important in such a demanding climate as the Pilbara. A hat, comfortable, sturdy shoes and long pants are recommended to protect against both the sun and the native prickly plants.

Access

The Pilbara can be accessed by two major road arteries: the North West Coastal Highway and the Great Northern Highway, which passes through Newman. Small domestic air carriers, such as Skywest, fly from Perth to the main townships.

Mt Augustus (Burringurrah) National Park

The world's largest rock, Mt Augustus, is twice the size of Uluru, but as it is clad in low scrub it does not look nearly as spectacular. The 1650-million-year-old sandstone and quartz monolith constantly changes colour from bright red at sunrise through shades of green, blue then orange and gold at sunset. The massif is protected in a 9170ha national park and has a 49km scenic drive around its circumference allowing visitors to view it from all angles.

More than 100 bird species were recorded at nearby Edithanna Pool in this park in just two days. The vegetation is tall, open mulga shrubland. Several rare plants are known to grow only on the mountains in this area, including a hibiscus, a mulla-mulla and a native foxglove. To the Wadjari Aborigines, the rock is a slain ancestral figure known as 'Burringurrah'.

Mt Augustus Walk

Starting Point: Beedoboondu car park, Mt Augustus (Burringurrah) National Park

Destination: The summit of Mt Augustus (1106m)

Summary: A long, arduous and steep ascent to the summit

Attractions: Commanding views over the Pilbara plateau

Length: 12km

Time: 6 hours

Options: None

Attraction Rating: ★ ★ ★ ★

Fitness: ◪ ◪ ◪

Maps: CALM produces a brochure entitled Mt Augustus National Park with a reasonably good map in it

Access to Starting Point: The park boundary is 465km from Carnarvon via Gascoyne Junction and Dairy Creek or the Lyons River. The roads are unsealed but of reasonably good quality when dry. Turn right as you enter the park. The Beedoboondu car park is on the left about 7km along the scenic drive.

Facilities/Amenities: The Beedoboondu car park has toilets, picnic tables and visitor information. The

Many Western Australian wildflowers bloom in the spring months.

nearest facilities are at the Mt Augustus Outback Tourist Resort, 5km from the base of the rock at the junction of Mt Augustus Woodlands Road and Dooley Downs Road.

Recommended Equipment: Carry plenty of water when climbing
Notes: The best time to walk is April to October when it's cooler. It is strongly advised not to attempt the climb in summer. Leave early so you are not climbing in the hottest part of the day.
Further Information:

CALM Denham Office
67 Knight Terrace
Denham WA 6537
Tel: (08) 9948 1208
Fax: (08) 9948 1024

or

Gascoyne Junction Office
Tel: (08) 9943 0988

Walk Description

From the Beedoboondu car park, head straight up the south-western flank of the mountain and follow the track to the right along the tops to the east. The best views are on the south-eastern side from the top of sheer red cliffs overlooking the Lyons River valley. Here flocks of parrots and waterbirds gather at permanent pools shaded by river red gums. Shrubby mulga, gidgee and myall wattles provide sparse cover over the red

sandplains and rocky foothills. After summer deluges, ephemeral flowers, such as mulla-mulla, everlasting daisies and native foxglove, bloom.

Other walks in the Mt Augustus National Park
Edneys Lookout Walk (6km, 2.5 hours)

A shorter walk from the Oorambu car park, leading a third of the way up the southern face and affording impressive views over the Lyons River valley to the Godfrey Range escarpment. A good walk for those who don't have time to do the full summit ascent.

Kotka Gorge Walk (2km, 1 hour)

Rock-hopping and boulder-scrambling is necessary if you wish to do this walk up the northern side at Warrarla to a small usually dry gorge that is a delight to explore.

Aboriginal Sites

Several short tourist walks access the sites of engravings and paintings around the base of Mt Augustus. One such walk is the Petroglyph Trail, which leaves from Mundee car park.

Karijini National Park

The park lies about 1400km north of Perth, accessed via Meekatharra and the Great Northern Highway, in the Hamersley Range in the heart of the Pilbara. The second-largest national park (627 445ha) in Western Australia, it takes in a high plateau dissected by breathtaking gorges.

Karijini offers some spectacular rugged scenery, ancient geological formations, a variety of arid-land ecosystems and a range of recreational experiences. Rocky, tree-lined watercourses wind over the dusty plain and mountains dominate the horizon, including Mt Meharry (1249m) and Mt Bruce (1235m).

Most of the southern half of the park is largely inaccessible. About 60 000 visitors a year concentrate on the 20 spectacular gorges in the north. The chief attractions are rockpools, waterfalls and the narrow cliffs.

Geology

The banded iron formations exposed in many of the rocks in and around

the gorges originated more than 2500 million years ago as iron- and silica-rich sediment deposits on an ancient sea-floor. Over millions of years, these deposits were transformed by the pressure of further sediments laid down over them, forcing trapped water to be driven out and gradually turning the sediments into tough, well-bedded rock. Horizontal compression later caused the rocks to buckle and develop numerous vertical cracks, before they were lifted to the surface to form dry land. A sharp drop in sea level caused rivers to cut rapidly through the soft land, creating sheer-sided gorges. This, combined with millions of years of erosion, has sculpted the present landscape.

Climate

Being just north of the Tropic of Capricorn, the park's climate can best be described as tropical semi-desert. A highly variable, mainly summer rainfall of 250–350mm, often associated with thunderstorms and cyclones, is accompanied by temperatures often topping 40°C. The ideal times to visit are winter and spring. Winter days are warm and clear, but nights are cold and sometimes frosty.

Vegetation

Wildflowers vary in abundance with the seasons and from year to year, but there is always something interesting in flower. Many of the 480 flowering species in the park bloom profusely after rains. During cooler months, the land is covered with yellow-flowering sennas (cassias) and acacias, northern bluebells and purple mulla-mullas.

Wildlife

Birds are many and varied, especially in fringing vegetation beside pools and streams. Walkers may also encounter red kangaroos, euros, Rothschild's rock wallaby, bats and dingoes. The many species of native rodents and marsupial carnivores (such as the Pilbara ninguai) are nocturnal and shy. Reptiles, such as frogs, geckoes, goannas, dragons, legless lizards, pythons and other snakes, can also be found here. Interesting wildlife habitats include huge termite nests and the rock piles of the pebble-mound mouse.

Asbestos Danger

Unfortunately, carcinogenic asbestos is still common in the Pilbara region, where it is present even in the roads. Wittenoom has been gradually closed by the state government as it is deemed residentially unsafe. For traffic passing through, however, the risk is thought to be acceptable. On the Wittenoom side of Karijini National Park lies a historic asbestos mine that has been the subject of major legal actions.

Avoiding exposure to very large amounts of very fine dust over long periods of time is the key. The risks relate to particle size and exposure times. Keep the air-conditioning on in the car to pressurise the interior cabin and set the air-conditioning to recycle.

Traditional Owners

The traditional owners, the Panyjima, Innawonga and Kurrama tribes, call the Hamersley Range Karijini. The park's name recognises the historic and continuing significance of the area to these people, and their involvement in park management. Evidence of their ancestors' occupation dates back more than 20 000 years. During that period, Aboriginal land management practices such as 'firestick farming' resulted in a diversity of vegetation types that determined the nature of the plants and animals found in the park today.

Karijini Gorges Walk

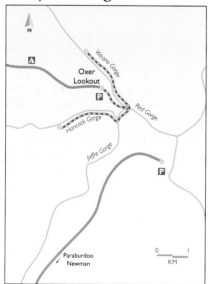

Starting Point: Oxer Lookout, Karajini National Park

Destination: Hancock Gorge and Weano Gorge

Summary: Explore two gorges and see four more from the spectacular Oxer Lookout: Weano, Red, Knox and Joffre gorges

Attractions: The primary attractions of Karijini National Park are the spectacular gorges and the contrast they provide with the typical semi-arid environment of the surrounding landscape

Length: 3km

Time: 3 hours

Options: There are many walks and accommodation alternatives in the park. Select the combination that most adequately fits your abilities.

Attraction Rating: ★ ★ ★

Fitness: ▨▨

Maps: Mt Bruce 1:250 000 topographical gives an overview of the park. CALM has produced a leaflet with a more detailed sketch map.

Access to Starting Point: Access to Karijini is by road from Newman (200km south-east), Tom Price (80km west), Paraburdoo/Marandoo (west), or Port Hedland (300km north-east). Daily domestic airline services to Newman, Paraburdoo, Karratha and Port Hedland from Perth. Newman and Paraburdoo are the closest airports to Karijini while Tom Price is the closest town (bus transfers from Paraburdoo to Tom Price are available at the airport).

Vehicles can be hired in each of the major Pilbara towns and various companies run guided tours from Newman, Tom Price and Karratha. Most tour operators are extremely flexible and you should find it relatively easy to organise a tour that meets your requirements.

Facilities/Amenities: Camping is permitted at several places within the park adjacent to the gorges. The closest is Weano camping area on the Oxer Lookout road. Others are Joffre camping area and Fortescue camping area. The nearest commercial facilities are in Tom Price and Newman.

Recommended Equipment: Sturdy shoes for rock walking. An inflatable lilo or air mattress would be handy to float on the many pools in the gorge and to access more remote parts.

Notes: Pools within the gorges can be extremely cold in comparison with the typical ambient plain temperatures, which often reach 40°C in summer. While it is very tempting to dive straight into the water after a strenuous walk, take time to adjust gradually to the water temperature. In winter, hypothermia is a real danger, so a wetsuit is recommended.

Further Information:
CALM Office
PO Box 29, Tom Price WA 6751
Tel: (08) 9189 8157
Fax: (08) 9189 8104
or
Karratha Office
Tel: (08) 9143 1488
Fax: (08) 9144 1118
Also:
The West Australian Tourist Centre
1300 361 351 (local call costs)
Newman Tourist Bureau
PO Box 303, Newman WA 6753
Tel: (08) 9175 2888
Fax: (08) 9175 2964
Tom Price Tourist Bureau
PO Box 567, Tom Price WA 6751
Tel: (08) 9188 1112
Fax: (08) 9188 1441
Karratha Tourist Bureau
PO Box 1234, Karratha WA 6714
Tel: (08) 9144 4600
Fax: (08) 9144 4620

The Wittenoom Gem Shop is an excellent source of local information and its display is well worth a look. The Gem Shop's web site is:
www.holidaywa.net/gemacom.htm
The Wittenoom Gem Shop
Sixth Avenue, Wittenoom WA 6752
Tel: (08) 9189 7096

Walk Description

Oxer Lookout provides a staging area into a very scenic part of the park. Being at the junction of four gorges, it is the ideal first-stop area for visitors. From the lookout, head down into Weano Gorge to Handrail Pool, which is enclosed by high narrow cliffs colourfully banded by iron oxide. Then walk down Hancock Gorge to beautiful Kermits Pool between polished walls before returning to Oxer Lookout and the car park. If you want to explore further, such as in Red Gorge, you must swim or use a lilo. Be wary of deceptively cold temperatures in the deep recesses of these canyons.

Other walks in Karijini National Park

Many of the walking trails within the gorges take less than one hour to complete at a relatively easy pace and most take a maximum of three hours. You should be prepared to swim across pools and navigate narrow passes and steep climbs if you intend to explore farther than the concrete steps provided at most of the tourist stops.

Kalamina Gorge Walk (3km, 3 hours)

Leaves from car park to an open gorge in the centre of the northern section. Features a waterfall and Rock Arch Pool.

Hamersley Gorge Walk (1km, 3 hours)

This gorge on the south branch of the Fortescue River is away from the main gorges. The car park is in the far northwest of the park, just off the Nanutarra–Munjina road about 78km from Tom Price. Attractions include The Spa Pool, a waterfall and 'The Grotto', a lush amphitheatre.

Dale Gorge Walk (upto 10km each way, 1 day)

The car park is only 10km east of the visitors' centre and the gorge features lookouts, Fortescue Falls and Circular Pool, framed by green ferns. Fern Pool, 10 minutes' walk upstream from Fortescue Falls in Dale Gorge, is one of the prettiest spots in the park. A rock ledge, crystal-clear pool and waterfall makes it virtually impossible to leave for several hours, but few visitors make the effort to walk there. It is possible to get behind the waterfall to photograph it with a backdrop of ferns.

Joffre Gorge Walk (upto 20km, 1 long day)

From this car park it is possible to walk through the fantastic Wittenoom Gorge, with a host of wonderful pools, to the old township of Wittenoom. Other attractions are Joffre Falls, in an impressive amphitheatre, as well as Red Gorge and Knox Gorge.

Mt Bruce Walk (9km, 6 hours)

If you've seen all the gorges, why not climb the other way—upwards? A track ascends steeply to the summit (1235m), similar in appearance to Mt Augustus. The car park is just south of the Hamersley Mt Bruce road. Leave early to avoid the heat of the day.

Millstream–Chichester National Park

A landscape of rolling spinifex hills contrasts with spectacular escarpments and tree-lined watercourses in the Millstream–Chichester National Park (200 000ha). The lush oasis of Millstream wetlands, centred on Fortescue River, are another attraction. There's remote rugged outback scenery, no crowds and no development.

Chichester Range Camel Trail Walk

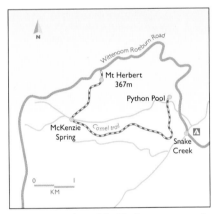

Starting Point: Mt Herbert car park, Millstream–Chichester National Park
Destination: Python Pool
Summary: This eventful walk follows a Heritage Trail that was part of an old camel road built in the 1870s. Walkers must backtrack if a car shuffle is not possible. Alternatively, follow the Wittenoom–Roebourne road back to the Mt Herbert car park.
Attractions: McKenzie Spring, red sandstone cliffs and views over the Chichester Range from Mt Herbert (367m). A swim in the magnificent Python Pool is a must.
Length: 8km
Time: 2.5 hours
Options: None
Attraction Rating: ★ ★ ★
Fitness: ◼◼◼
Maps: CALM has produced a leaflet on the park with maps and background information
Access to Starting Point: The most direct road access is to drive 90km south of Karratha via the Wittenoom–Roebourne road
Facilities/Amenities: Camping areas are nearby at Snake Creek, Crossing Pool and Deep Reach Pool
Recommended Equipment: Wide-brimmed hat, sunscreen and water as there is little tree cover
Notes: Autumn and spring are the best seasons to undertake the walk
Further Information:
CALM Karratha Office
Welcome Rd, PO Box 835
Karratha WA 6714
Tel: (08) 9143 1488 or
     (08) 9184 5144
Fax: (08) 9144 1118 or
     (08) 9184 5146

Walk Description

This is the longest official walk in the park and takes in some of its best scenery, including the wonderful Python Pool. From the car park, head up over Mt Herbert for great views, then south down to McKenzie Spring. Cameleers used the road to deliver stores from the coast to outback cattle and sheep stations as well as mining towns. From the old McKenzie Spring waterhole head down to Python Pool where you can relax in the water and admire the red cliffs above. Unless you have set up a car shuffle, allow a good three hours to return to Mt Herbert car park.

Other walks in the Millstream–Chichester National Park

The Millstream area in the south of the park is an oasis in the arid outback. The Murlunmunyjurna Track links Millstream Homestead Visitors' Centre with the Crossing Pool camping area. Along the way is a variety of vegetation communities, including the grand Millstream palm. Allow 2 hours to complete the 6.8km return route. Signs along the way explain matters of significance to local Jindjibanji tribes. Access via the Millstream–Yarraloola road, just south of the Wittenoom–Roebourne road.

Other walks in the Pilbara

The Kennedy Range National Park, just north of Gascoyne Junction, is another eroded plateau with high waterfalls and gorges lined by 100m cliffs. Much of Kennedy Range is inaccessible and is yet to be explored fully. A central area of the park has been opened up and walks are possible to The Temple and various waterfalls and rockpools. Walkers must be reasonably experienced and well equipped if venturing farther into the range's escarpment. Phone the CALM Office at Denham for more details on (08) 9948 1208.

The Kimberley

Regarded as the last frontier in Australian exploration, much of The Kimberley is completely undeveloped and inaccessible. Extreme tropical climatic fluctuations and the presence of estuarine crocodiles make this a somewhat unpleasant and difficult place for walkers to venture. Some of the parks here can be reached only by boat or plane at certain seasons. Extreme tidal fluctuations are another problem. The major parks are Purnululu, Drysdale River, Mirima (Hidden Valley), Geikie Gorge, Wolfe Creek, Meteorite Crater, Tunnel Creek and Windjana Gorge. Phone Kununurra office on (08) 9168 0200 for details.

Purnululu (Bungle Bungle) National Park

The striking sandstone domes striped with orange and grey bands in the Bungle Bungle Range are widely known. Purnululu, the Aboriginal name for this sandstone area, is thought to be a corruption of the local word for bundle bundle grass, found throughout the Kimberley. The 209 000ha park was declared in 1987 with an adjoining 110 000ha as a conservation reserve. The dissected plateau of the Bungle Bungle Range rises to about 250m above the surrounding plain in the north-west, 600m above sea level.

Geology

The sandstone and conglomerate that formed the beehive domes was deposited about 360 million years ago in the Devonian period. Erosion by creeks and rivers over the past 20 million years carved out steep, narrow gorges. The banding is caused by differences in clay content and porosity of the sandstone layers. The dark grey banding on the domes is where dark cyanobacteria (or blue-green algae) has grown on layers where moisture accumulates. The orange bands are oxidised iron compounds in layers that dry out too quickly for the cyanobacteria to grow.

The beehives, occupying about a fifth of the total area of the park, are the best examples of this landform found anywhere in the world.

Bushwalkers delight in the deep chasms of the north-west. Examples include sheer-sided Echidna Chasm and Mini Palms Gorge, which extend for several kilometres and are often only a couple of metres wide. High cliffs of the western escarpment mark the western edge of the Bungle Bungle Range. Cliffs up to 200m high are cut by several deep gorges. The escarpment dominates the landscape along the gorge track and the view from Walanginjdji Lookout. Broad valleys up to 500m wide occur in the southwestern and north-western parts of the range. The longest valley, Piccaninny Creek, probes many kilometres into the centre of the range.

Facilities

A shop at the ranger station sells cool drinks, film, books and souvenirs. There's also a pay phone. Food, fuel, and mechanical services are not available in the park. Camping areas are at Walardi, Bellburn and Kurrajong.

Piccaninny Gorge Walk

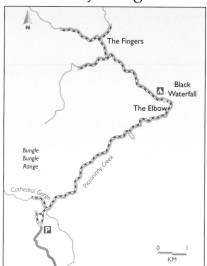

Starting Point: Piccaninny Creek car park, Purnululu National Park
Destination: The Fingers
Summary: One of the best walks in Western Australia with never-ending attractions and outstanding gorge scenery. Set up camp in Piccaninny Gorge and explore the Fingers region on the second day, returning via the Domes Trail.
Attractions: Cathedral Gorge, groves of *Livistona* palms, sandstone beehive-shaped domes (one with a hole in it)
Length: 34km
Time: 2–3 days
Options: Many side gorges and chasms to explore in The Fingers

Beehive rock formations in the Bungle Bungle Range, Purnululu National Park.

Dry rocky terrain along Didbagirring Trail, Mirima National Park.

Attraction Rating: ★ ★ ★ ★ ★
Fitness: ◩ ◩ ◩
Maps: The CALM office has produced a series of informative leaflets on Purnululu National Park with maps

Access to Starting Point: Piccaninny car park is in the south of the Bungle Bungle Range. The park is about 160km south of Kununurra and 100km north-east of Halls Creek by air. Vehicle access from the Great Northern Highway is signposted 250km south of Kununurra or 109km north of Halls Creek. From the highway the 53km Spring Creek Track leads to the ranger station and information bay at Three Ways. Spring Creek Track suits only 4WDs with good clearance. There is no vehicular access to the park during the wet season from 1 January to 31 March. At this time roads and tracks may be impassable and are extremely susceptible to damage from vehicles. Unseasonal rains may also result in temporary closure of the park at other times.

Facilities/Amenities: Toilets and shelters at the car park. The nearest camping area, with toilets and water, is at Walardi about 20km away. The nearest shop is at Three Ways. No facilities once you are in the gorge.

Recommended Equipment: Allow 5–8 litres of water per person per day. There is no running water. All water pools have stagnant water from wet season rains which occur December to March. Don't drink water from the pools, but if you have to, use water purifiers and iodine tablets. Sturdy shoes with good grip are essential on the slippery rocks. Take plenty of film.

Notes: Register your party in the registration book at the 'Verandah Shop'. Don't forget to sign out on your return. Flash flooding can occur around the wet season.

Further Information:
   Kimberley Regional Office
   PO Box 942
   Cnr of Messmate Way and
   Konkerberry Drive
   Kununurra WA 6743
   Tel: (08) 9168 0200
   Fax: (08) 9168 2179
or
   The Ranger Base at Three Ways
   (only during the dry season)
   Tel: (08) 9168 7300
An excellent reference book is Dean Hoatson's *Bungle Bungle Range*.

Walk Description

Walkers must be self-reliant in this remote terrain but the effort to do this fantastic overnight walk deep into the heart of the Bungle Bungle Range is well worth while. From the car park, it is 15km to the upper reaches of Piccaninny Gorge, passing Cathedral Gorge, a worth while side trip with its peaceful waterholes and awesome amphitheatre. Allow one day to walk into the gorge and one day out. The Elbow, about 7km from the car park along the firm and usually dry Piccaninny Creek bed, is deemed the official entrance to the gorge.

Set up a base camp around Black Waterfall. Spend a third day exploring The Fingers upstream carrying only a day pack or bumbag. Each Finger has numerous cold pools and rocky climbs and the walking is fairly slow and difficult. Some of the cliffs tower to 200m high. Return the same way.

Other walks in the Bungle Bungles

There are several great day walks, exploring picturesque chasms, pools and gorges. The best of the rest are:

Echidna Chasm Walk
(2km, 1 hour)
This extremely narrow, tall chasm in the northern part of the range at the end of the road must be seen to be believed. Time your entry for midday when sunlight reaches the bottom for just a few minutes.

Froghole Gorge Walk
(1km, 1 hour)
This wide, open gorge is bordered by towering ramparts. It contains beautiful stands of *Livistona* palms and a sheer waterfall. There is an imposing series of cliffs at the far eastern end.

Mini Palms Gorge Walk
(5km, 3 hours)
Accessed from the same car park as Froghole Gorge, this is another oasis of astonishing beauty. A narrow amphitheatre is formed by sloping red cliffs and stunted *Livistona* palms.

Other walks in The Kimberley

Mirima (Hidden Valley) National Park
This small park (2068ha) is only 3km east of Kununurra. The sandstone ranges, cliffs and valleys found in Mirima look similar to parts of the Bungle Bungle Range. The 350-million-year-old sandstone formed at the same time and has been subjected to similar weathering conditions as the Bungle Bungle Range. Mirima is the name given to the area by the Miriwoong people who live in the East Kimberley. There is much evidence of past Aboriginal use of Mirima and areas of the park are important for traditional Aboriginal law.

Didbagirring Trail Walk
(800m, 15 min)
Climb the steep slopes to a lookout with views over the Ord Valley and the sandstone range of Mirima. Much of the rock in Mirima is unstable. Stay on the walk trails and don't stand on or walk close to cliff edges.

Wuttuwutubin Trail Walk
(500m, 10 min)
An easy return walk through a narrow valley with interesting rock formations and view through to Kununurra.

Northern Territory

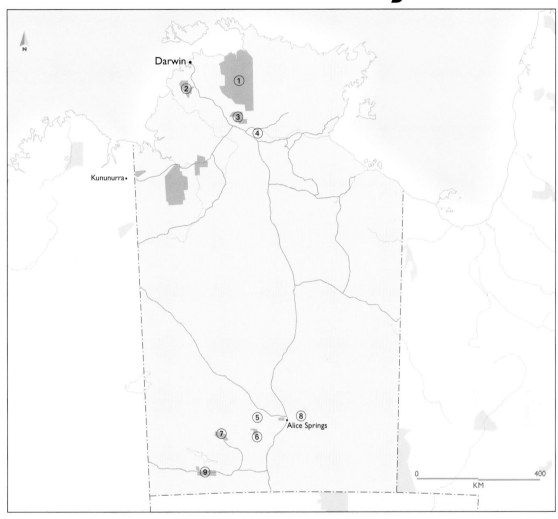

Introduction

In many ways, the landscapes of the Northern Territory typify the quintessential Australian outback. Uluru (Ayers Rock), Kata Tjuta (The Olgas), Katherine Gorge and Kakadu are all internationally recognised tourist icons and some have World Heritage status. Only 150 000 residents occupy the Northern Territory, concentrated mainly in two population centres, Darwin and Alice Springs. That leaves most of the state's 1 346 200 square kilometres for vast Aboriginal reserves, cattle ranches and national parks.

Climate dictates most activity in the Top End and Red Centre. Because of extreme fluctuations in precipitation and temperature, walking is practical only in the cooler months. In summer, oppressive heat, floods, cyclones and impassable roads all present major obstacles. The most scenic areas are well distributed throughout the Territory, with Australia's largest national park, Kakadu, more than 1500km to the north of Uluru. In the middle, the Katherine River has carved a spectacular gorge rich in vegetation and wildlife. The parks preserve the outstanding rugged scenery of this ancient and eroded land, where bushwalkers can experience solitude, wilderness and the sheer contrast with anything they may be used to in eastern Australia.

Because of the difficulty in planning and undertaking many of the more remote walks, there are specialised tour operators who conduct bushwalking holidays. This style of package tour is not for everybody, but it does alleviate many problems caused by distance. Destinations include Kakadu, the East and West MacDonnell Ranges, Gregory National Park, Nitmiluk National Park (Katherine Gorge), Finke Gorge and Watarrka. The largest such operator, Willis' Walkabouts, can be contacted on (08) 8985 2134.

Crocodiles are a problem in most of the river estuaries of the Top End. The Northern Territory Parks and Wildlife Commission regularly monitors their movements and relocates any that might constitute a threat to humans—more than 100 are removed from Darwin Harbour each year.

Climate

There are two distinct seasons in the Northern Territory: Wet and Dry. During the Dry (May to September) temperatures are significantly lower and access along unsealed roads is more reliable. However, water is more difficult to obtain from rivers and waterholes. On the other hand, the Wet (October to April) can be extremely hot and humid, with frequent and regular deluges, and many unsealed roads become too boggy even for 4WDs.

The Red Centre, containing some of the same attractions as the West MacDonnell Ranges, the Finke Gorge and Uluru, is best visited during the cooler months, April to September. Despite being winter, temperatures regularly exceed 30°C in the middle of the day and walkers should plan to rest then to prevent heat stroke, exhaustion and dehydration. The ideal time to climb

Ormiston Gorge, West MacDonnell National Park.

Uluru, for example, is in the early morning and park authorities have actually closed the climb from 10.00am–3.00pm. By contrast, nights are cool and temperatures can fall below freezing, so campers should be suitably prepared with warm sleeping bags. Average minimums for July are only 4°C. Generally, annual rainfall is low in the Centre, but quite variable, which makes planning a bushwalking expedition a little difficult. The lowest recorded annual rainfall for Alice Springs was 60mm in 1928 and the highest was 782mm in 1974. Drought is common and sometimes prolonged.

The Top End usually has more predictable weather, with its pronounced pattern of summer rain in the form of afternoon thunderstorm activity. Humidity is also higher, so walkers will perspire a lot more. Maximum temperatures fluctuate little, averaging around 33°C in summer and 30°C in winter. In contrast to the Red Centre, it rarely falls below 20°C near Darwin and Kakadu, even in winter. As it is close to the equator, there is also little variation in daylight hours between seasons.

Transport

To the Northern Territory

With a population of about 80 000, Darwin has the Territory's main airport. Both Qantas (131 313) and Ansett (131 344) operate daily services from all state capitals. Alice Springs also has services from Sydney, Adelaide and Melbourne. A shuttle bus connects the airport and CBD. Airlink, Australia's largest regional airline, runs services connecting both Darwin and Alice Springs with Perth, Broome and Cairns. Some direct services also to the Yulara Tourist Village at Uluru from Perth, Sydney and Cairns.

The only train service to the Northern Territory is the historic Ghan service connecting Adelaide with Alice Springs. It runs on Tuesdays and Fridays and has optional sleeper-carriage accommodation.

Driving to either the Red Centre or the Top End is difficult as there are no direct roads from the east coast of Australia. Motorists must travel either via Adelaide from Melbourne (3931km) or through Mt Isa in Queensland from Sydney (4006km) or Brisbane (3258km). From Perth, you must drive all the way up the west coast via Broome (4166km), which takes about a week. Drivers should be well prepared with plenty of reserve fuel, water, emergency provisions and driving lights for the lonely desert roads.

Within the Northern Territory

Numerous coach operators shuttle people down the Stuart Highway between Darwin and Alice Springs and then to the Yulara Tourist Village at Uluru, stopping at such places as Tennant Creek. Call Greyhound–Pioneer on 132 030. There are also many package tours available that include accommodation and day excursions, such as a boat trip down Katherine Gorge. Special off-road buses are used in parks such as Kakadu and Watarrka. There's also a range of transport services that cater specifically for backpackers.

Hiring a campervan is a popular way of getting around and most outlets, such as Hertz, Avis, Budget and Britz, have depots in Darwin and Alice Springs. To access the more remote national parks, a 4WD is essential because most of the roads are unsealed and infrequently graded. These can be hired, but insurance costs make them very expensive. Drive slowly and carefully on outback roads as fatalities are common. Collisions with wildlife result in overturns and loss of control. Distances are long and you must allow plenty of time for rough roads. For example, most people think Uluru is very close to Alice Springs but it is actually a five-hour, 450km drive. Also be aware of road trains and bulldust on Northern Territory roads.

Around Darwin, a shuttle bus operates seven days a week connecting major attractions within 4km of the CBD. Buses also cover all suburbs as far out as Tiwi and Karama. For information about internal transport, call the Tourism Commission on 1800 621 336.

Accommodation

The main YHA in Darwin is at:
69 Mitchell St, Darwin NT 0801
Tel: (08) 8981 3995
Fax: (08) 8981 6674
The YHA Travel bureau can organise tours, travel and accommodation throughout the Northern Territory. Call:
Tel: (08) 8981 2560
Fax: (08) 8981 7222
In Alice Springs:
Alice Springs Pioneer YHA/YHA Travel
Cnr Parsons St and Leichhardt Tce
Central Alice Springs NT 0870
Tel: (08) 8952 8855
Fax: (08) 8952 4144
e-mail: yhant@yhant.org.au

Yulara Tourist Village (Ayers Rock Resort)

All visitors to Uluru–Kata Tjuta National Park must stay at Yulara. Built in 1983, this is now the fifth-largest town in the Northern Territory with about 2200 people. It has its own airport and is one of the busiest tourist resorts in the southern hemisphere. It offers a range of accommodation, from camping to hostels to up-market luxury suites. Phone (08) 8956 2737 or 1800 089 622 for bookings.

Maps

The Department of Land, Planning and the Environment produces only a limited range of topographical maps for the Territory. The 1:50 000 coverage is confined to the Top End, from Darwin south to Daly Waters and from Wadeye east to Mataranka. Mt Compton is also covered.

Maps can be ordered at:
Maps NT
PO Box 1680, Darwin NT 0821
Tel: (08) 8999 7032
Fax: (08) 8999 7750
AUSLIG also covers the Top End down to Newcastle Waters with 1:100 000 maps. Phone 1800 800 173 to order. Farther south toward the Red Centre, only 1:250 000 scale maps are available. This scale is generally not detailed enough for walking navigation. Furthermore, many

interior maps remain unpublished and only rough dyelines can be ordered.

The Northern Territory Parks and Wildlife Commission, in conjunction with the Department of Land, Planning and the Environment, produce some fantastic colour maps of their own national parks, including Nitmiluk and the West MacDonnell national parks, while the Australian Nature Conservation Agency produces maps of Kakadu and Uluru–Kata Tjuta national parks through AUSLIG's Ausmap series.

National Parks

There are nearly 100 national parks and reserves in the Northern Territory, most of them managed by the Parks and Wildlife Commission, which can be contacted at:

Goyder Centre
25 Chung Way Tce (PO Box 496)
Palmerston NT 0831
Tel: (08) 8999 5511 or (08) 8999 4555
Fax: (08) 8999 4558
web site: www.nt.gov.au/paw/parks

Regional Offices are in Katherine and Alice Springs:

PO Box 344
Katherine NT 0851
Tel: (08) 8973 8888
Fax: (08) 8973 8899 and
PO Box 1046
Alice Springs NT 0871
Tel: (08) 8951 8211
Fax: (08) 8951 8268

Small camping fees apply in all Northern Territory national parks, whether you are at car-camping areas, at developed grounds or backpacking with a tent in the wilderness. Overnight walkers must have a permit from the park office, district office or Commission headquarters. Permits are not needed for day walks. Entry fees also apply to the Territory Wildlife Park, Alice Springs Desert Park and Alice Springs Telegraph Station Historical Reserve.

Two of the World Heritage national parks, Kakadu and Uluru–Kata Tjuta, are managed by Environment Australia. A small entry fees applies to these national parks, as well as camping fees. Contact:

GPO Box 787, Canberra ACT 2601
Tel: (02) 6274 1111

or

PO Box 1260, Darwin NT 0801
Tel: (08) 8946 4300
Fax: (08) 8981 3497

There are many Aboriginal reserves in the Northern Territory and you must cross some to access more remote national parks. For permits for the Top End, apply to:

Northern Land Council
PO Box 42921, Casuarina NT 0811
Tel: (08) 8920 5178
Fax: (08) 8945 2633

For permits for the Red Centre, apply to:

Aboriginal Land Council & Pitjantjatjara Land Council
PO Box 3321, Alice Springs NT 0871
Tel: (08) 8953 4400

Epic Walks

Jatbula Trail (Edith Falls walk)

This spectacular five-day walk from Nitmiluk Visitors' Centre and Leliyn (Edith Falls) is best undertaken in the cooler winter months. The total distance is 66.1km and the trail is walked only one-way, to the west, to minimise contact with other walkers. Along the way are exquisite pools to camp by as well as dramatic waterfalls. For more information, consult the walk entry in this chapter (p. 326).

Larapinta Trail

At 220km, this is the longest constructed walk in the northern half of the continent. Routed recently through the best of the West MacDonnell National Park, the trail extends from Alice Springs west to Mt Razorback. The Parks and Wildlife Commission of the Northern Territory has published a series of brochures, each describing a section of the route. There are 13 stages, some completed as recently as 2000. For more information, refer to the walk entry in this chapter (p. 329).

Kakadu National Park is steeped in Aboriginal tradition.

The Far North
Kakadu National Park

About 170km east of Darwin lies the famous World Heritage Area of Kakadu National Park—a unique region with wetlands rich in wildlife, bordered by the truly breathtaking Arnhem Land escarpment. It includes almost the entire catchment area of the South Alligator River, which drains most of the region. At 20 000 square kilometres, it is Australia's largest national park by far, but it isn't just this vastness that astounds visitors. It's also the timeless nature of the land. Kakadu is leased by the traditional Aboriginal owners to the Australian Nature Conservation Agency, and many representatives of local tribes are employed as park rangers. The name Kakadu is derived from one of the languages of the area known as Gagudju. Indeed, this was the main language spoken in the northern section of the park until early in the 20th century.

Geology

The wetlands lie only about 20m above sea level, but the escarpment plateau is about 300–350m above sea level and 200km inland. Creation of this 600km escarpment began about two billion years ago, when layers of sandstone built up a plateau that was once a coastal shoreline. It later became dissected by high-volume watercourses, creating rugged gorges filled with rainforest. The combination of escarpment and tropical weather created massive waterfalls of which Twin Falls and Jim Jim Falls are the most famous.

Climate

From November to March, during the wet season, waterfalls appear everywhere, pouring from the top of the escarpment. Cyclonic activity is also a risk during summer. The best time to visit is the dry season between May and September when the roads are open and temperatures are cooler. Average minimums are in the low 20s and average maximums are in the low to mid-30s. Rainfall and humidity are also very low.

Vegetation

With abundant water and sunlight, about 1000 species of plants thrive here. The various communities—woodland, sedgeland, tidal mangroves, grasslands, rainforests and wetlands—have been largely undisturbed by humans, although Aborigines did engage in fire-management practices to facilitate hunting. Up on the plateau, heathland and sandstone-based scrub are prevalent and walkers have little protection from the sun, but views are largely unobscured.

Wildlife

An astounding range of species includes 25 frogs, 75 reptiles (lizards, turtles, goannas, skinks and snakes), 50 types of fish, 30 mammals and 1500 butterflies. It is estimated that up to 3 million waterbirds inhabit the park (mostly magpie geese).

Crocodiles, the world's largest reptiles, are among the most respected of inhabitants. In the early 20th century, they were hunted close to extinction, but today are completely protected. Occasionally, aggressive ones that intrude in public areas will be captured and relocated.

There are two distinct types, the saltwater (*Crocodylus porosus*) and the freshwater (*Crocodylus johnstoni*). Only the saltwater or estuarine crocodile has been known to kill humans. Both species can remain underwater for as long as one hour, reducing their heartbeats to just two or three per minute to conserve energy. The temperature in the nest determines the sex of baby crocodiles. Many fail to reach maturity, falling prey to other crocs, feral pigs and other animals.

The cane toad, a recent intruder from Queensland, is becoming a menace. It breeds well in the wetlands below the escarpment.

Aboriginal Sites

About 2000 Aborigines, from seven tribes, once inhabited the region. Kakadu is a very special place from a heritage perspective and there are numerous examples of rock art scattered throughout the park. The most famous are at Nourlangie and Ubirr (also known as Obiri) Rocks, with their distinct X-ray paintings of wildlife. The age of this ancient art is unknown, but it is believed that some could be 25 000 years old. There are even depictions of the thylacine (Tasmanian tiger), now extinct. Most of the 5000 recorded sites are closed to the public.

Conservation

The conservation history of Kakadu National Park has been controversial, plagued by the construction of the Ranger and Jabiluka uranium mines. Another controversy over the Coronation Hill development proposal in the early 1990s led to it being abandoned. One of the primary considerations was the interests of the Aboriginal people. Aboriginal elders are opposed to mining because it desecrates sacred sites associated with the Dreamtime figure Bulla. Most of the local Jawoynese tribe supported this view, being fearful of disturbing the Bulla at Coronation Hill.

The struggle for Kakadu continued throughout the 1990s when Energy Resources Australia won the Howard Government's support for another uranium mine at Jabiluka. An international contingent from the World Heritage Bureau (UNESCO) visited the park in October 1998 at the invitation of the traditional owners. The Federal Government downplayed the ecological value of Kakadu, and spent more than $1 million lobbying other nations not to classify the area as 'in danger'. Although it was formally concluded that the area was in fact 'in danger', preparation for mining commenced regardless.

Access

From Darwin, head south on the Stuart Highway and turn left onto the Arnhem Highway to Jabiru. The entrance station is about 170km from Darwin and the drive takes about three hours. The main entrance road and the Kakadu Highway to Yellow Water and Mardukal are sealed, but all other roads are unsealed and closed in the wet season. A daily bus service connects Darwin with Kakadu; it goes to the visitors' centre, Ubirr Rock, Nourlangie Rock, Cooinda and

Yellow Water. It currently costs $15.00 per adult to enter the park (children under 16 are free). A pass is valid for two weeks. You need at least three or four days to see the major sites.

Facilities

Visitor facilities in the main section of the park around Jabiru include motels, caravan parks and camping grounds with hot water, showers, flushing toilets and drinking water. The major grounds are at Merl, Mulrella Park, Mardugal and Gunlom. Almost all are closed in the wet season. Permits are required and a small camping fee applies. Fuel, food and provisions are available from Jabiru, Frontier Kakadu Village, and Border Store. The Bowali Visitors' Centre, 5km south of Arnhem Highway on the Kakadu Highway, is open 8.00am–5.00pm daily.

Further Information:
Bowali Visitor Centre
Kakadu National Park
PO Box 71, Jabiru NT 0886
Tel: (08) 8938 1120
Fax: (08) 8938 1123

East Alligator River Circuit

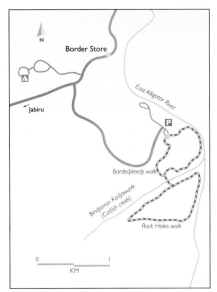

Starting Point: East Alligator River (3km from Border Store), Kakadu National Park

Destination: Bindjarran Kadjawurrk (Catfish Creek)

Summary: This walk combines two of the longer constructed tracks, the Bardedjileedji Walk and the Rock Holes

Walk. Both are circuits and can be done as a figure-8, returning to the car park without backtracking.

Attractions: Sandstone outcrops, the East Alligator River, Catfish Creek

Length: 9km

Time: 3 hours

Options: The tracks can be walked in either direction

Attraction Rating: ★ ★ ★

Fitness: ◩ ◩

Maps: The Kakadu National Park Visitor Guide provides a close-up map of the Border Store area

Access to Starting Point: The car park at the start of the Bardedjileedji Walk is 3km south of Border Store and 46km north-east of Jabiru

Facilities/Amenities: Provisions are available from Border Store, phone (08) 8979 2474. The Merl camping area is just west of Border Store. Information at the East Alligator Ranger Station 3km to the west.

Recommended Equipment: Hat, sunscreen, insect repellent

Walk Description

From the car park, head south to Bindjarran Kadjawurrk (Catfish Creek) along the Bardedjileedji Track and cross over to do the Rock Holes extension. On this track you'll see all sorts of vegetation: waterlilies, screw palm, bombax and paperbark trees, and a whole host of birdlife—pied herons, magpie geese and jabirus. Return to the car park via the East Alligator River. Another circuit, the Manngarre track, leaves Border Store just to the north and follows the East Alligator River farther downstream.

Other walks in Kakadu National Park
Day Walks

There are short, constructed walking tracks through the park, leading to Aboriginal rock art sites, waterholes and waterfalls. From the Ubirr car park, 3km north of Border Store, a 1km circuit takes you past a lookout point on the rock over the Nardab wetlands, featured in the movie *Crocodile Dundee*. The other public rock art site is at Nourlangie, 7km east off the Kakadu Highway. A 1.5km circuit leads past the Anbangbang Gallery, Shelter and another lookout.

Among the art figures you will see are Namondjok, a dangerous spirit, Namarrgon, the lightning man, and his wife Barrginj.

The Buba Wetlands Walk, accessed from Mulrella Park, goes through creek beds, forest and woodland to the Buba. Here you will encounter billabongs and swamps with long-necked turtles, countless birds, ghost gums, bloodwoods and paperbark trees just some of the attractions.

The Iligajarr Wetlands Walk, accessed from the Malabanbandju camping ground, covers a small area of the South Alligator River wetlands. The track winds through forests, past billabongs and over a grassy flood-plain. From Iligadjarr Point there's an outstanding view of the Mt Brockman massif. Burdulba Billabong forms a part of the Burdulba Creek and flows west to the South Alligator River.

Farther east, the Kubarra Track (3km return) leads between sandstone massifs up the Burdulba Creek catchment area. In the south, short walking tracks lead from car parks to plunge pools at the base of Twin Falls and Jim Jim Falls.

The Kakadu Highway leads south to Mary River and side options will take you to Gunlom and Yurmikmik where there are good day walks to lookouts, pools and waterfalls. Watch for crocodiles in the lagoons at the base of the escarpment.

Overnight Walks

A camping permit is required within the park and applications must be accompanied by a map showing your intended walking route. Most of the best destinations are centred on the Arnhem Land escarpment between Jim Jim Falls and Coronation Hill. Attractions include Kooinda Creek and the view from the top of Twin Falls. Rough tracks ascend the escarpment from both of the falls' car parks. Set up a car shuffle so that a vehicle is left either at Makuk or Gunlom (Waterfall Creek). The walk-through takes about a week but the remote wilderness atmosphere and terrific scenery make it rewarding. Walking can be quite difficult along the top of the escarpment, even for the most experienced parties. With few detailed

Tolmer Falls, one of the many pleasant sights in Litchfield National Park.

For the large secluded falls and plunge pool, take the 3.5km return walking track from Sandy Creek campground.

Tolmer Falls Walk
(1.6km, 45 min)

A two-tiered waterfall and natural rock arch are the main attractions of this gorge. A short 400m walk from the car park to the lookout offers views of the gorge and falls. Walkers with more time may wish to do the 1.6km loop track. Entry into the gorge itself is prohibited, as a cave here houses a large colony of rare orange horseshoe bats. Only six colonies of this insect-eating bat are known.

Wangi Falls Walk
(approx. 2.5km, 1 hour)

This picturesque pool has easy access for swimming and is very popular with locals and visitors. A track leads from the pool to a lookout above the 80m falls, returning to the picnic area via a rainforest boardwalk. Drinking water, toilet and camping facilities are available near these falls.

Overnight Walks

Most of the national park is inaccessible to vehicles. From Surprise Creek in the south, venture out to the east, following numerous creeks and gorges. Walker Creek is another great wild destination. If you are planning an extended walk, you will need either the Reynolds River 1:100 000 or 1:50 000 topographical. Contact the Batchelor Office at (08) 8976 0282.

Nitmiluk (Katherine Gorge) National Park

Nitmiluk National Park (292 008ha) stretches 32km north-east from Katherine. The two major attractions are Edith Falls and the gorges.

1. Edith Falls

Beautiful Edith Falls, in the northwestern corner of the national park, tumble into a natural waterhole that is suitable and safe for swimming for most of the year, except at the height of the wet season when park authorities may close it. A short walk with spectacular views of the surrounding country will take you along the Edith

topographical maps and constructed tracks, navigation is a problem. Consult the ranger before beginning any walk.

Litchfield National Park

Just two hours from Darwin via Batchelor, Litchfield has spectacular waterfalls, patches of rainforest and unusual 'magnetic' termite mounds. The 146 118ha park, declared in 1986, offers a host of half-day walks.

Florence Falls Walk
(approx. 5km, 2 hours)

A lookout high above Florence Falls offers a view over rainforest trees to the gorge's plunge pool. Access to the pool is via a short, steep path. There are camping and toilet facilities. A network of short walking trails connects the camping area with the plunge pool, falls and Buley Rockhole.

Tjaetaba Falls Walk
(2.7km, 1 hour)

From Greenant Creek picnic area, near Tolmer Falls, a walk follows the creek to view the falls (2.7km return).

Tjaynera Falls Walk (Sandy Creek)
(3.5km, 1.5 hours)

Tjaynera Falls are accessible by 4WD vehicles only. The track often becomes inaccessible after wet-season rains.

River to more rockpools and water-holes. Facilities for overnight camping are available. Access is by a 20km sealed road that branches off the Stuart Highway, 40km north of Katherine.

2. The Gorges

Where the Katherine River cuts through the Arnhem Land plateau, there are 13 spectacular gorges. This southern section of the park is owned by the local Aboriginal people, the Jawoyn, and there are a number of well-preserved Aboriginal rock art sites within the park, along with several natural features of cultural significance.

Visitors can choose from a range of walks, including one- and two-hour short walks, half-day walks and overnight walks along the southern tops to Eighth Gorge. The best walk is the five-day walk to Edith Falls. For overnight walks, visitors must obtain permits from the main visitors' centre.

The sealed road to the gorge ensures year-round access, but flooding during the wet season may cause temporary closures. The gorge is closed to swimming in the wet season because of debris and crocodiles.

Facilities

A commercially operated caravan park with powered sites at the Gorges section of the national park. Diesel and petrol are available here and at Katherine on the Stuart Highway.

Jatbula Trail (Edith Falls) Walk

Starting Point: Nitmiluk Visitor Centre, Nitmiluk National Park

Destination: Edith Falls (Leliyn)
Summary: An overland walk from Katherine Gorge north-west to the park boundary via the Edith River
Attractions: Northern Rockhole, Biddlecombe Cascades, Crystal Falls, 17 Mile Falls, Sandy Camp Pool, Sweetwater Pool
Length: Total distance is 66.1km
Day 1: Nitmiluk Visitor Centre to Biddlecombe Cascades, 11.5km
Day 2: Biddlecombe Cascades to 17 Mile Falls, 23.5km
Day 4: 17 Mile Falls to Sandy Camp Pool, 16.5km
Day 5: Sandy Camp Pool to Edith Falls (Leliyn), 14.6km
Time: 5 days
Options: There are several alternative campsites to choose from, for example, at Crystal Falls and Edith River Crossing, if you wish to avoid contact with other campers (the day distances will then be somewhat different). Rest days are recommended at some of these idyllic places.
Attraction Rating: ★ ★ ★ ★ ★
Fitness: ◪ ◪ ◪ ◪
Maps: Maps NT Nitmiluk National Park 1:50 000 topographical has colour-coded information and photographs of the major campsites
Access to Starting Point: Edith Falls are 60km from Katherine (19km off the Stuart Highway); the Nitmiluk Visitor Centre is 30km from Katherine, which is 321km south of Darwin
Facilities/Amenities: Commercial campground at walk start. Some campgrounds en route have toilets, fresh water and emergency communication devices.
Recommended Equipment: Fuel stoves are recommended
Notes: A registration and deposit system applies. Walkers are asked to check-out at Leliyn. Permits can be obtained from the visitors' centre. The best time to walk is in winter. Take full water containers—some waterholes are more than 10km (3 hours) apart.
Further Information:
> Nitmiluk Visitor Centre
> Tel: (08) 8972 1886 or
>   (08) 8972 3150
or
> Katherine Regional Office
> PO Box 344, Katherine NT 0851
> Tel: (08) 8972 1886

Walk Description

Although it may get hot along the open plateau tops, there are dozens of tranquil pools to swim in, most with their own cascade. While this walk can be completed within four days, most groups deliberately take it at a more leisurely pace to enjoy the fantastic scenery. From the visitor centre, the trail first heads south before crossing the Katherine River and heading north up the 17 Mile Valley. After about 7km, a side track leads east to the Northern Rockhole, the first of the many highlights. This peaceful spot is framed by high cliffs but unfortunately the falls do not flow in the dry season. This is also the farthest point you can reach if you wish to return in one day.

The Jatbula Trail then heads north to 17 Mile Creek via Crystal Falls before curving west to the Edith River. It is then simply a matter of following the river downstream to the car park. Near the end are some minor options to the Upper Falls, Bemang Pool and Leliyn Lookout. The main pool at Edith Falls is a delight but can be crowded in holiday periods.

Eighth Gorge Walk

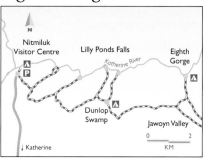

Starting Point: Nitmiluk Visitors' Centre, Nitmiluk National Park
Destination: Eighth Gorge
Summary: This is the most extensive walk in the southern part of the national park. Follow a network of walking trails on the southern side of the Katherine River all the way downstream to the Eighth Gorge. Along the way is a 5.8km circuit into the Jawoyn Valley with 7000-year-old rock art.
Attractions: Idyllic swimming pools, waterfalls, lookouts, Aboriginal art
Length: 45–57.8km (depending on side trips)

Time: 3–5 days

Options: Numerous side trips to gorges along the Katherine River. The best are to the Lily Ponds (4.8km) and the Southern Rockhole (4.6km). Cool, narrow Butterfly Gorge is also worth a side trip (3.4km). Allow plenty of time to investigate these places fully and to swim in the pools.

Attraction Rating: ★ ★ ★ ★ ★

Fitness: ✖ ✖ ✖ ✖

Maps: Maps NT Nitmiluk National Park 1:25 000 (this is on the reverse side of the Jatbula Trail 1:50 000 map)

Access to Starting Point: The Nitmiluk Visitor Centre is 30km east from Katherine along a sealed road. Watch for wildlife when driving at night.

Facilities/Amenities: Basic camping areas are at Dunlop Swamp and Eighth Gorge. Emergency communication devices are installed at intervals along the route.

Recommended Equipment: Fuel stoves are recommended; a lilo would be handy for exploring the gorges

Notes: Permits are required for all overnight camping

Further Information:
  Nitmiluk Visitors' Centre
  Tel: (08) 8972 1886 or
          (08) 8972 1222
or
  Katherine Regional Office
  PO Box 344, Katherine NT 0851
  Tel: (08) 8973 8888

Walk Description

This great walk visits all the main attractions of the Katherine Gorge part of the park. Allow at least four days to enjoy some of the beautiful swimming holes, for example, the Southern Rockhole and the Lily Ponds, and various lookouts and waterfalls. From the visitors' centre, take the Lookout Loop along the rim of the gorge. It soon turns south and inland before the first turn-off presents itself. This is the Windolf Walk leading to Southern Rockhole. Some Aboriginal paintings can be seen on the other side of the Katherine River when the river is low.

Return toward the Lookout Loop and turn left toward Butterfly Gorge via an old 4WD track. Keep heading east all the way to Eighth Gorge, where you can camp at Dunlop Swamp on the first night. Some of the side options on offer can be done on the approach to Eighth Gorge, while others can be done on the return. This will depend on time available, the temperature, your fitness and inclinations. You can leave the heavy overnight packs at the track intersections when doing the side options. Allow about three hours for each one.

Avoid walking in the hottest part of the day, especially in the exposed section east of Dunlop Swamp. Spend the second night at Eighth Gorge, having done the 5.8km loop along the Jawoyn Valley. Spend the third night at Smitt Rock. Unfortunately, you must backtrack all the way to the Nitmiluk Visitor Centre.

Other walks in Nitmiluk National Park

The two suggested walks cover virtually all of the 100km of walking tracks in the park. Day visitors using the two main camping grounds as a base can do small loops of one or two hours' duration, along the main walking trails. Access to Southern Rockhole and Bemang Lookout is easy.

If you have an air mattress, do this great variation with no backtracking: complete a half-day circuit by walking via Butterfly Gorge to the Katherine River, then float back down to the first gorge on the mattress. From the jetty, the visitor centre is only 500m to the south. Some rapids are encountered on the way but these are not too difficult.

The famous cliff-lined Katherine Gorge in Nitmiluk National Park.

The beautiful Mataranka Pool, a popular thermal spring in Elsey National Park.

If there's too much white water because of recent rain, walk along the portage tracks between the gorges.

Elsey National Park

The spring-fed Waterhouse River and the Little Roper River combine to form the Roper River, which begins its life within the 13 840ha Elsey National Park, just 4km off the Stuart Highway at Mataranka. In the dry season the placid Roper River flows sleepily through large waterholes and tumbles over a series of rocks known as Mataranka Falls.

The thermal pool sector, a picture-perfect oasis, is a major attraction. Here, 30.5 million litres of 34°C water rise from an underground spring each day to create a relaxing swimming pool surrounded by a forest of *Livistona rigida* palms, paperbarks and pandanus. A well-used campsite and a number of day-use areas have been developed along the river.

Along the 1.5km Botanical Walk is a host of interesting plants to enjoy. Ferns, shrubs, vines and many trees provide a pleasant, shady habitat for countless bird species; watch for them, particularly early in the morning. If you enjoy fishing, be aware that barramundi-fishing controls apply within the park. There is a boat ramp, ideal for boats and canoes, at 12 Mile Yards and at Mataranka Homestead.

Climate

The most comfortable months to visit are from May to September. The Roper River floods in the wet season imposing restrictions on some activities.

Mataranka Falls Walk

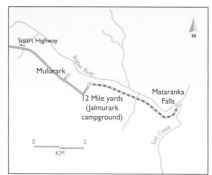

Starting Point: 12 Mile Yards (Jalmurark camping area), Elsey National Park
Destination: Mataranka Falls
Summary: A pleasant stroll along the Roper River
Attractions: The Roper River and Mataranka Falls
Length: 8km
Time: 2.5 hours
Attraction Rating: ★ ★ ★
Fitness: ✗ ✗
Maps: The best available map is on the reverse side of the Elsey National Park Fact Sheet available from the District Office at Katherine

Access to Starting Point: The main access road is via Homestead Road, about 1.5km south of the town of Mataranka along the Stuart Highway. To reach the Roper River sector, proceed along John Hauser Drive to Mulurark, 12 Mile Yards and the Jalmurark camping area. The Thermal Pool sector lies at the end of Homestead Road. Note that access roads may be cut for short periods during the wet season.

Facilities/Amenities: An established campground at the 12 Mile Yards is suitable for tents or caravans. It has grassed areas, hot water and washing facilities but there are no powered sites and generators are not permitted. Alternative accommodation and camping facilities are available from commercial establishments. Day-use areas, complete with picnic furniture, wood BBQs and toilet facilities, are available at the 12 Mile Yards, Mulurark and 4 Mile.

Recommended Equipment: Hat, sunscreen and insect repellent
Further Information:
The District Office, Mataranka
Tel: (08) 8975 4560
or
Katherine Regional Office
PO Box 344, Katherine NT 0851
Tel: (08) 8973 8888
Fax: (08) 8973 8899

Walk Description

From the Jalmurark camping area, head east along the well-defined track that parallels the southern bank of the Roper River until its confluence with Salt Creek to see Mataranka Falls. They are especially spectacular after a deluge. Return via the same route. Why not spend the remainder of the afternoon relaxing in the nearby Mataranka Thermal Pool, where the temperature is always perfect?

Other walks in Elsey National Park

Walking tracks are still being developed at Elsey so ask the ranger at Mataranka what walks are available. From the thermal pool, a track heads downstream for 1.2km to Stevies Hole, which connects to a short Botanic Walk and emerges at John Hauser Drive.

The MacDonnell Ranges

From a distance the MacDonnell Range looks like a convoluted mass of folded and twisted red hills aligned east/west. Its tallest peak, Mt Zeil (1531m), is the highest mountain west of the Great Dividing Range. The range was formed about half a billion years ago when a colossal push from the north forced the rocks of the Amadeus Basin into a series of east/west wave-like folds that can be seen distinctly from the air. The largest of the folds formed a very high range, the precursor to the present MacDonnell Range.

A long period of erosion reduced the mountains to low, rounded rises surrounded by a flat plain. For the past 20 million years, the land surface has been rising, competing with the erosive processes of wind and water, and giving the MacDonnell Range its very rugged appearance. Since 1992, the West MacDonnell National Park (210 000ha) has protected the hills. Within its boundaries are precipitous cliffs and narrow gorges. Precipitation quickly streams off the slopes and is channelled into gullies to form pools in the valleys. Here, protected from annual evaporation rates of up to 3400mm, oases of plants and animals thrive. The most spectacular, Palm Valley in Finke Gorge National Park, shelters ancient endemic red cabbage palms and relict aquatic invertebrates.

Several endemic snails here are more closely related to tropical and temperate species than to anything in the desert. In fact, the entire range can be seen as an oasis with two-thirds (about 1300 species) of the vegetation of the entire arid zone represented. Nearby, Kings Canyon in Watarrka National Park boasts gigantic sandstone cliffs of the deepest reds. Trephine Gorge in the east is another striking example of how the landscape has been shaped by time. Some other attractions include Standley Chasm, Ormiston Gorge, Ellery Creek Big Hole and Simpsons Gap. Due to a plethora of scenic sights here, allow at least a week to explore the West MacDonnell Ranges adequately. Many visitors budget for too little time.

West MacDonnell Ranges National Park

Larapinta Trail Walk

Starting Point: Alice Springs, The West MacDonnell Ranges National Park
Destination: Redbank Gorge
Summary: A classic long-distance walk along the spine of the West MacDonnell Range
Attractions: Superb rugged outback scenery, many small gorges with rockholes
Length: 220km
Time: 2 weeks
Options: Numerous side options exploring Simpsons Gap, Standley Chasm, Hugh Gorge, Ellery Creek Big Hole, and Serpentine, Ormiston and Redbank gorges
Attraction Rating: ★ ★ ★ ★
Fitness: ⬛ ⬛ ⬛ ⬛
Maps: The Northern Territory West MacDonnell National Park 1:250 000 map gives an overview of the walk. The Parks and Wildlife Commission has produced a series of 13 leaflets covering the entire route with comprehensive background information on flora, fauna and history as well as route notes and maps.
Access to Starting Point: The Alice Springs Telegraph Station is beside the Todd River just to the north of Alice Springs. Access is by the Stuart Highway. To reach Red Bank Gorge, the other end of the walk, follow Larapinta Drive and Namatjira Drive west from Alice Springs.
Facilities/Amenities: Camping areas have been constructed along the way. Most have drinking water; some are shared with car visitors as the trail intersects roads.
Recommended Equipment: Complete self-sufficiency is essential. Water for two days must be carried. A fuel stove is recommended as firewood is very scarce. A jumper and warm sleeping bag are required for winter nights as temperatures can drop to freezing.
Notes: The Larapinta Trail is closed in summer because of oppressive heat
Further Information:
Parks and Wildlife Commission
Stuart Highway
PO Box 1046, Alice Springs NT 0871
Tel: (08) 8951 8211
or
Alice Springs Telegraph Station Historical Reserve
Tel: (08) 8952 1013
or
Simpsons Gap Ranger Station
Tel: (08) 8955 0310
or
Ormiston Gorge Ranger Station
Tel: (08) 8956 7799

Walk Description

The Larapinta Trail was constructed during the late 1990s in 13 stages:
1. Alice Springs Telegraph Station to Simpsons Gap
2. Simpsons Gap to Jay Creek
3. Jay Creek to Standley Chasm
4. Standley Chasm to Brinkley Bluff
5. Brinkley Bluff to Hugh Gorge
6. Hugh Gorge to Ellery Creek Big Hole
7. Ellery Creek Big Hole to Serpentine Gorge
8. Serpentine Gorge to Inarlanga Pass (Ochre Pits)
9. Inarlanga Pass (Ochre Pits) to Ormiston Gorge
10. Ormiston Gorge to Glen Helen Lodge
11. Glen Helen Lodge to Redbank Gorge
12. Redbank Gorge to Mt Sonder (return)
13. Redbank Gorge to Mt Razorback

A leaflet on each section gives basic map and background information. At time of writing, sections 6 and 7 were being constructed and the Parks and

The mighty Ormiston Gorge is one of the best sights to be seen in the West MacDonnell National Park.

Wildlife Commission was negotiating with local Aboriginal land owners to secure access from Hugh Gorge to Ellery Creek Big Hole. These sections lie outside the park boundary but are expected to be completed by 2002.

Most people do only small sections of the trail at any one time, but with food drops and vehicular support it is possible to do the entire journey within two weeks. Walkers should seek the advice of park authorities before starting, especially checking on the availability of water.

Mt Sonder Walk

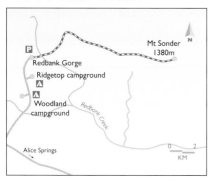

Starting Point: Redbank Gorge, West MacDonnell Ranges National Park

Destination: Summit of Mt Sonder (1380m)
Summary: A steep climb
Attractions: Tremendous unobscured views over West MacDonnell Range from Mt Giles to Mt Razorback and Mt Zeil. Soaring wedge-tailed eagles and peregrine falcons are often sighted.
Length: 8km
Time: 4.5 hours
Options: None
Attraction Rating: ★ ★ ★
Fitness: ◪ ◪ ◪
Maps: Northern Territory Parks and Wildlife Commission Larapinta Trail, Section 12
Access to Starting Point: Redback Gorge is about 160km west of Alice Springs via Larapinta Drive and Namatjira Drive
Facilities/Amenities: Redbank Gorge has a picnic area. Two camping areas, Ridgetop and Woodland, both with toilets, are just a couple of kilometres to the south.
Recommended Equipment: Hat and sunscreen; plenty of water
Notes: The peak is also known as Rwetyepme. Leave early before the hottest part of the day.

Further Information:
Parks and Wildlife Commission
Stuart Highway
PO Box 1046, Alice Springs NT 0871
Tel: (08) 8951 8211

Walk Description

The rocky summit of Mt Sonder commands views over the entire western half of the park. You can see as far west as Haasts Bluff, more than 60km away. In fact, the views are so good that some people haul a tent up so they can watch the sun set and rise again next day. The mountain was named in the 1870s by Baron Ferdinand von Mueller, a patron of explorer Ernest Giles, after a fellow German botanist. On 10 August 1997, Tim Fischer, then Deputy Prime Minister, climbed it to commemorate the opening of Stage 12 of the Larapinta Trail.

The start of the trail is signposted from Redbank Gorge and there are track markers for some of the way. Cross Redbank Creek, lined by wonderful river red gums, and start climbing the elongated Mt Sonder massif from its western end. Once you attain the crest of the ridge, head east on the relentless climb. Track markers stop here but there's no difficulty in navigation. Try to reach the summit before the heat of midday. Return to the creek the same way. Spend the afternoon exploring the cool, narrow crevice of the 550m-long Redbank Gorge before returning to the car.

Ambitious walkers can set up a car shuffle and continue east from Mt Sonder's summit, descending to Ormiston Gorge along the range. This is an overnight walk and you must carry plenty of water.

Ormiston Pound Circuit

Starting Point: Ormiston Gorge car park, West MacDonnell Ranges National Park

Destination: Ormiston Pound

Summary: A circuit through a fascinating geological formation

Attractions: Ormiston Gorge, waterhole, views to towering cliffs

Length: 7km

Time: 2–3 hours

Options: Overnight extensions to Bowmans Gap and Mt Giles (1389m) are possible from the far side of the pound. The circuit can be walked in either direction.

Attraction Rating: ★ ★ ★ ★

Fitness: ◩ ◩ ◩

Maps: An adequate map with fact sheet is produced by the Northern Territory Parks and Wildlife Commission

Access to Starting Point: From Alice Springs, head west along Namatjira Drive for 135km and then turn right at the signpost for Ormiston Gorge. The car park lies at the end of this road.

Facilities/Amenities: Well-developed campground at the gorge with gas BBQs, toilets, showers and drinking water. Fees apply.

Recommended Equipment: Water bottles, hat, sunscreen

Notes: Walkers must register with the park authorities and obtain a permit to do the longer extensions to Mt Giles

Further Information:
   Parks and Wildlife Commission
   Stuart Highway
   PO Box 1046, Alice Springs NT 0871
   Tel: (08) 8951 8211

Tracknotes for the Mt Giles ascent are given in *Bushwalking in Australia* by John Chapman.

Walk Description

This short, good-value day walk passes through Ormiston Gorge and enters the wild Ormiston Pound. From the car park, head north through the gorge and past the main waterhole. The track swings around to the east as you enter the natural open amphitheatre of the pound. The relatively flat floor of the pound was formed by violent movements in the earth's crust that separated the bowl's quartzite walls. The colours in early morning or late afternoon are extraordinary and photographers will have lots to capture. The track then swings to the west after climbing onto the range. There are fine views before you descend back to Ormiston Creek and rejoin the Larapinta Trail. A swim in the waterhole will be most welcome.

Fit, ambitious walkers can continue east from the pound (at the confluence of Ormiston Creek with another dry creek) to reach either Bowmans Gap to the north or the lofty summit of Mt Giles to the east. Both destinations entail overnight camping as progress is slow in this largely trackless territory. From Ormiston Gorge, the summit cairn and trig point of Mt Giles is 16km return and involves a 600m vertical ascent. This is another peak where some walkers like to camp to see an unsurpassable sunset and sunrise. From the top, the cliff-lined fortress of Mt Sonder looms over the cliffs of Ormiston Gorge in the foreground. Both east-facing walls glow deep red in the early morning.

Other walks in the West MacDonnell Ranges

Areas such as Standley Chasm, Simpsons Gap, Serpentine Gorge, the Ochre Pits, Ellery Creek Big Hole and Glen Helen Gorge all offer short tourist walks of between one and three hours' duration. For longer extensions, connect them by using the Larapinta Trail. There are pioneering bushwalks in the more rugged and remote western half of the park. Mt Razorback and Mt Zeil beckon to all latent explorers.

Finke Gorge National Park

Just south of the small Aboriginal mission settlement of Hermannsburg is the Finke Gorge National Park, which protects about 46 000ha of the Finke River and surrounds. It is claimed to be the oldest river in the world and a casual dig in the riverbed will turn up a handful of seashells. But its most distinguished feature is an isolated grove of tall cabbage palms that contrast with the red cliffs. Remnants from a wetter era, these palms and other rare plants are found nowhere else. Large waterholes along the Finke River are important refuges for waterbirds during long droughts. Vehicle access along the last 13km of the sandy riverbed is by 4WD only.

Mpaara Track Circuit

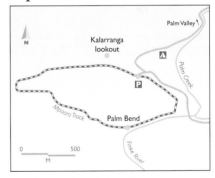

Starting Point: Palm Creek car park, Finke Gorge National Park

Destination: Palm Bend, Finke River, The Amphitheatre

Summary: A circuit walk that focuses on Aboriginal mythology

Attractions: Impressive square amphitheatre surrounded by tall cliffs

Length: 5km

Time: 2 hours

Options: Conclude the walk by heading up to Kalarranga Lookout. This is an extra 1.5km return, 45 minutes,

Ancient palms by the Finke River, one of the oldest water courses in the world.

Walk Description

The Arrernte tribe once occupied the region and remnants of their culture are evident everywhere. This walk has been specifically designed to outline aspects of Dreamtime mythology by means of information signs. From the car park, follow the track out to Palm Creek and down to the Finke River. It flows only sporadically, often in flood times, sometimes peaking at 7m. The Mpaara Track follows the river for 1km before turning right at Palm Bend and heading up a side creek into The Amphitheatre. The track then heads north and back to the car park.

Other walks in the Finke Gorge National Park
**Mpulungkinya Walk
(5km, 2 hours)**
Leads from the car park at the end of Cycad Gorge and returns to the car park via the top of a dry hot plateau. The name Mpulungkinya means Palm Valley. A shorter option to see the red cabbage palms is the 2km Arankaia Walk, taking just 50 minutes.

Watarrka National Park

The main highlight of this 71 720ha park is Kings Canyon, a stunning part of the remote George Gill Range with enormous sheer red cliffs. Permanent waterholes, Desert Oak woodlands, striking rock formations and dozens of rare species of plant and wildlife provide excellent bushwalking. The park is about 310km south-west of Alice Springs and can be reached by high-clearance 2WD vehicle.

but gives a splendid overview of the Amphitheatre formation.
Attraction Rating: ★ ★ ★
Fitness: ◪◪
Maps: A Northern Territory Parks and Wildlife Commission leaflet has a rough sketch map of the walk route, but as it is well signposted, walkers don't need to navigate in detail
Access to Starting Point: The car park is in the Cycad Gorge near the end of the only public-access road. Follow Larapinta Drive west and south-west from Alice Springs. Ignore

the turn-off to Namatjira Drive. At Hermannsburg, turn left to Palm Valley. A 4WD is required on the rough road.
Facilities/Amenities: Campground at Palm Valley near the walk start, but provisions can only be obtained at Hermannsburg.
Recommended Equipment: Hat and sunscreen
Further Information:
Parks and Wildlife Commission
Stuart Highway
PO Box 1046, Alice Springs NT 0871
Tel: (08) 8951 8211

Giles Track Walk

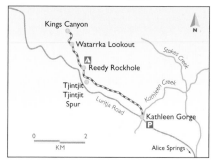

Starting Point: Kings Canyon, Watarrka National Park

Destination: Kathleen Gorge

Summary: A high-level walk from Kings Canyon, following George Gill Range south-east to Kathleen Gorge

Attractions: A maze of weathered sandstone domes, Watarrka Lookout, wilderness atmosphere and great open scenery all the way

Length: 22km

Time: 2 days

Options: If you wish, take an early exit from the range via the Tjintjit Tjintjit Spur. This would shorten the distance to about 12km, taking one day. Fit walkers who leave very early should be able to do the entire walk in one day, with just a small day pack.

Attraction Rating: ★ ★ ★ ★

Fitness: ✗ ✗ ✗

Maps: A Northern Territory Parks and Wildlife Commission leaflet has a rough sketch map of the walk route, but as it is well signposted, walkers don't need to navigate in detail

Access to Starting Point: There are three main approaches to the park. From the north via Larapinta Drive and Mereenle Loop Road; from the east via the Sturt Highway and Ernest Giles Road; and from the south (Yulara) via Luritja Road and Lassetters Highway.

Facilities/Amenities: Accommodation and camping facilities at Frontier Kings Canyon and Kings Creek Station. No camping facilities en route—you must be completely self-sufficient.

Recommended Equipment: Water for the entire distance and warm clothing as night temperatures can be chilly

Further Information:

Parks and Wildlife Commission
Stuart Highway
PO Box 1046
Alice Springs NT 0871
Tel: (08) 8951 8211

Walk Description

While most park visitors only see the main cliff formation, there is much more spectacular scenery available to the wilderness walker. From Kings Canyon, Giles Track leads to Watarrka Lookout and south to Reedy Rockhole. Camp at Reedy Creek, a distance of only 8km, which allows you plenty of time to explore the Kings Canyon area via Canyon Walk, King Creek Walk and Garden of Eden. On the second day, continue south for 14km via Rocky Creek, Hill Mulga Creek, Warru Creek and Wanga Creek. Then it's a scramble down to Luritja Road. The shady waterhole at Kathleen Spring will be a relief after the open tops.

Trephina Gorge Nature Park

In the east of the MacDonnell Ranges, about 85km from Alice Springs, Trephina Gorge Nature Park (1800ha) is noted for sheer quartzite cliffs and watercourses lined with river red gums. Two gorges dissect the range: Trephina, with wide views and a sandy creek bed, and a narrow one at John Hayes Rockhole. Waterholes in this area attract animal and bird life.

Lost City, near Kings Canyon, Watarrka National Park.

Trephina Ridge Top Walk

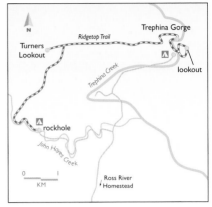

Starting Point: John Hayes Rockhole, Trephina Gorge Nature Park

Destination: Trephina Gorge

Summary: Several short walks combine into a day walk through rugged isolated terrain in a less-frequented part of the MacDonnell Ranges

Attractions: Chain of Ponds, Turners Lookout

Length: 16.5km

Time: 7.5 hours

Options: Shorter versions of this walk are possible by omitting the Chain of Ponds loop, Turners Lookout, or Trephina Gorge

Attraction Rating: ★ ★ ★ ★

Fitness: ✗ ✗ ✗

Maps: A Northern Territory Parks and Wildlife Commission leaflet has just a rough sketch map of the walk route. The route is well signposted so a detailed navigation map isn't necessary.

Access to Starting Point: Access from Alice Springs is south, then east, via the sealed Ross Highway, then a 9km drive north into Trephina Gorge. The last 5km is on a gravel road suitable for 2WD vehicles, but a 4WD vehicle is necessary on the John Hayes Rockhole track. Infrequent heavy rains can make all roads impassable here.

Facilities/Amenities: Campgrounds with pit toilets, drinking water, picnic tables, BBQs (wood and free gas) are provided at Trephina Bluff and Trephina Gorge. No water at the John Hayes campground.

Recommended Equipment: Sturdy footwear, a hat, sunscreen and water

Notes: If a car shuffle is not possible, you must return to the John Hayes Rockhole via Trephina Creek

Further Information:
Parks and Wildlife Commission
PO Box 1046,
Alice Springs NT 0871
Tel: (08) 8951 8211

Walk Description

For a fantastic out-of-the-way walk that takes in many different types of terrain, head for Trephina Gorge. A network of cleverly interconnected tracks allows ambitious walkers to do many walks without backtracking. This walk begins from the John Hayes Rockhole, a popular swimming spot. Be aware that most swimming holes are extremely cold. Prolonged exposure, even during summer, can result in hypothermia. Beware of submerged logs and rocks when diving. During prolonged dry periods Trephina Gorge Waterhole dries up. Walk through the gorge and take the Chain of Ponds walk (yellow markers) up the northern slope to meet with the Ridgetop Trail.

Turn left (north) and ascend to Turners Lookout (blue markers). Mallee, spinifex and white cypress pine dominate the vegetation. The track doubles back to Trephina Gorge. Turn left (orange markers) and descend into the northern end of the gorge. Walk south through the gorge and climb up to Panorama Lookout (red markers), another circuit, before descending to the car park and campground.

The Red Centre
Uluru–Kata Tjuta National Park

About 450km south-west of Alice Springs, Uluru (formerly Ayers Rock) is one of the world's largest monoliths (the largest is Mt Augustus in Western Australia). An Aboriginal sacred site, it is arguably Australia's most famous natural landmark. The sandstone glows bright red at sunset (a wonderful time for photographs). Visitors are discouraged from climbing the rock (863m above sea level) out of respect for its Aboriginal significance, but they cannot be prohibited from doing so. Many instead opt to take the Circumference Walk around Uluru, learning about its importance in Dreamtime legends.

A host of Aboriginal sacred sites are found in this enormous national park, as well as spectacular scenery and famous rock formations. Nearby, the Kata Tjuta (The Olgas) consist of a dramatic series of 36 dome-like rock formations that stand up to 546m above the plain and cover an area of 35 square kilometres. Uluru–Kata Tjuta National Park covers an area of 126 132ha and is leased by the traditional owners to the Australian Nature Conservation Agency (formerly the Australian Parks and Wildlife Service). Uluru, an Aboriginal word, means 'great pebble'.

Glowing red in the sunset, the sloping sandstone buttresses of Uluru in Uluru–Kata Tjuta National Park.

Circumference Circuit

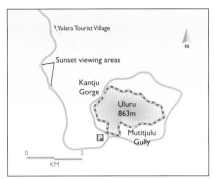

Starting Point: Main car park, Uluru–Kata Tjuta National Park

Destination: Kantju Gorge and Mutitjulu Gully

Summary: A walk around the base of Uluru

Attractions: Various overhangs

Length: 8km

Time: 3 hours

Options: Some small side options lead to overhangs and crevices. The Mutitjulu (formerly known as Maggie Springs) gully is a very photogenic place, especially after a downpour.

Attraction Rating: ★ ★ ★

Fitness: ◪

Maps: There are literally dozens of tourist brochures with maps of the area available from the tourist visitors centre at the Yulara Resort

Access to Starting Point: Access is via Lasseter Highway, 450km south, then west from Alice Springs. Allow 5 hours.

Facilities/Amenities: Accommodation and camping facilities are available at Yulara. No camping is allowed in the national park.

Recommended Equipment: Hat, sunscreen and water

Notes: Signs erected by tribal owners discourage visitors from climbing Uluru, but many people still do it. It is 348m above the plain and very steep. The walk is closed in the hottest part of the day to prevent heat stroke.

Further Information:
Park Office
PO Box 119
Yulara NT 0872
Tel: (08) 8956 2299

Walk Description

The base of Uluru is every bit as awe-inspiring as the summit. From the main car park, head around in either direction, exploring the many over-hangs, gorges and gullies along the way. Not every cave is accessible—some have been fenced off because they are sacred sites. Information leaflets and signs explain the significance and purpose of various rock art.

Valley of The Winds Circuit

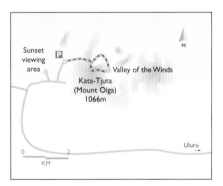

Starting Point: The Valley of the Winds car park, Uluru–Kata Tjuta National Park

Destination: The Valley of the Winds

Summary: A short circuit through several of the narrow gorges that separate the domes of Kata Tjuta

Attractions: Cool gorges, high domes, views over the plain

Length: 5.5km

Time: 2.5 hours

Options: If you set up a car shuffle, you can walk through to the southern side via the Link Track and Kata Tjuta Lookout

Attraction Rating: ★ ★ ★ ★

Fitness: ◪ ◪

The Valley of the Winds lies between two massive sandstone domes in The Olgas.

Maps: There are literally dozens of tourist brochures with maps of the area available from the tourist visitors' centre at Yulara Resort

Access to Starting Point: Access is via Lasseter Highway, 450km south, then west from Alice Springs. Allow 5 hours.

Facilities/Amenities: Accommodation and camping facilities available at Yulara. No camping is allowed in the national park.

Recommended Equipment: Hat, sunscreen, water, shoes with good tread

Further Information:
Park Office
PO Box 119
Yulara NT 0872
Tel: (08) 8956 2299

Walk Description

With its multiple domes, Kata Tjuta is, in many ways, more fascinating than Uluru. It is also higher, standing 546m above the plain (or 1066m above sea level). This walk is the only loop track in the Kata Tjuta part of the park. From the car park on the northern side of Kata Tjuta head south, following the signs into the first of the gorges between the domes. Some get so narrow that you can literally touch both sides at the same time. It is always cool here, despite oppressive desert temperatures out on the plain. To add a longer extension, continue on the Link Track to Kata Tjuta Lookout which lies in the centre of the dome formation. Be careful on the steep sandstone slopes.

Appendices

Useful Addresses

National Park administrators

Federal
Parks Australia—Wildlife Australia
GPO Box 636, Canberra ACT 2601
Tel: (02) 6250 0221

Australian Capital Territory
Environment Information Centre
Level 2, Macarthur House, 12 Wattle St
PO Box 144, Lyneham ACT 2602
Tel: (02) 6207 9777

New South Wales
Level 1, 43 Bridge St
PO Box 1967, Hurstville NSW 2220
Tel: 1300 361 967 or (02) 9585 6333

Northern Territory
Darwin Region (Headquarters)
Goyder Centre, 25 Chung Wah Tce
PO Box 496, Palmerston NT 0831
Tel: (08) 8999 5511

Queensland
Department of Environment
Ground floor, 160 Ann St
Brisbane Qld 4000
Tel: (07) 3227 8187

Tasmania
Parks and Wildlife Service
GPO Box 44A, Hobart Tas 7001
Tel: (03) 6233 6191

Victoria
Parks Victoria
Head Office, 8 Nicholson St
East Melbourne Vic 3002
Tel: (03) 9637 8000

Western Australia
Department of Land Administration
1 Midland Square, Midland WA 6056
Tel: (08) 9273 7373

Other useful addresses

The Wilderness Society
130 Davey St, Hobart TAS 7000
Tel: (03) 6234 9799

Australian Conservation Foundation
Melbourne
Head Office, 340 Gore St
Fitzroy VIC 3065
Tel: (03) 9416 1166 or 1800 332 510

Internet Resources

The Internet is an outstanding source of up-to-date information on bushwalking throughout Australia. Resources include links to equipment manufacturers, on-line shopping for camping equipment, information about walking permits, the latest national park policy amendments, and more. The Newsgroup is a discussion forum for walkers interested in sharing information and ideas.

National park administrators all have web pages where resources include up-to-date contact details, weather forecasts, changes in administration policy, new track construction details, management plans and frequently asked questions. As department titles often change, especially after elections, check the relevant government's home page first.

Commonwealth:
www.fed.gov.au
Queensland:
www.qld.gov.au
New South Wales:
www.nsw.gov.au
Australia Capital Territory:
www.act.gov.au
Victoria: www.vic.gov.au
South Australia: www.sa.gov.au
Western Australia:
www.wa.gov.au
Northern Territory:
www.nt.gov.au

Bushwalking sites

These usually have links to National Parks web sites, outdoor equipment manufacturers, other bushwalking sites and weather forecasts.
Australian Bushwalking Web:
www.bushwalking.org.au
Australian Bushwalking Reference Site: www.galactic.net.au/ bushwalking/main.html
Queensland Bushwalking:
www.qldwalking.bit.net.au/ index.html
Tyrone T. Thomas—author of several guidebooks: www.ozemail.com. au/ ~ tyronet
Australias National Parks:
www.atn.com.au/parks/index.html
David Noble's Bushwalking and Canyoning site: www.lisp. com.au/ ~ daven/index.html

The Wilderness Society:
www.wilderness.org.au
Australian Conservation Foundation:
www.acfonline.org.au
Wilderness Australia:
www.zeta.org.au/ ~ avatar
Wildsports:
www.wildsports.com.au
John Chapman Home Page:
www.ozemail.com.au/ ~ johnchapm an/index.html
Confederation of Bushwalking Clubs NSW:
www.bushwalking.org.au
Federation of Victoria Walking Clubs:
avoca.vicnet.net.au/ ~ vicwalk
Richard Merry's Bushwalking and Camping Web Site:
www.users.fl.net.au/ ~ merry/bushw alking.html
The Bushwalker's Guide to the Galaxy:
www.ix.net.au/ ~ als/impnav.htm
Sydney University Bushwalkers:
www.chem.usyd.edu.au/ ~ hynes_r/ subw/
Danny Yee's Bushwalking and Travel: www.anatomy.su.oz.au/ danny/bushwalking/index.html

Equipment Sites

Bogong on-line shopping: outdoor equipment:
www.bogong.com.au
Macpac Wilderness Equipment:
www.macpac.co.nz
Mountain Designs:
www.mountaindesign.com.au
Salomon Boots:
www.salomonsports.com/
Spelean (Petzel):
www.spelean.com.au
Teva sandals: www.teva.com

Other sites:

The Youth Hostel Association of Australia: www.yha.gov.au
Australian Bureau of Meteorology (Weather Forecasts):
www.bom.gov.au/weather

Newsgroups

aus.bushwalking

Reserve Classifications

National Parks

The definition of the International Union for the Conservation of Nature and Natural Resources (IUCN) in classifying a national park is:

a relatively large area where one or several ecosystems are not materially altered by human exploitation and occupation ... and where visitors are allowed to enter under special conditions, for inspiration, education, cultural, and recreative purposes.

Another simpler definition is, 'an extensive area of public land of nation-wide significance because of its outstanding natural features and diverse land types, set aside primarily to provide public enjoyment, education, and inspiration in natural environments'. These reserves have high conservation, scenic and recreational values and are usually larger than 4000ha. Despite the prefix 'national', they are state-managed. The 'special conditions' referred to include the prohibition of pets, firearms and cutting equipment, fire regulations, and the requirement of vehicle registration. Rangers have the authority to evict people and impose penalties on those who do not observe the regulations. An example is the spectacular Kalbarri National Park in Western Australia.

World Heritage Areas

These are areas of exceptional natural and/or cultural significance that are registered with UNESCO in Paris. About 500 sites are registered worldwide. Kinchega National Park/Willandra Lakes in western NSW was Australia's first World Heritage Area, although Uluru (Ayers Rock) and the Great Barrier Reef are the most famous. Tasmania has 20 per cent of its area (some 1.38 million hectares) classified as world heritage. State legislation determines land tenure, but international agreements and commonwealth legislation regulate management frameworks. These are Australia's World Heritage Area properties:

1981 Willandra Lakes Region
1981 Great Barrier Reef
1981 Kakadu National Park
1982 Tasmanian Wilderness
1982 Lord Howe Island Group
1987 Uluru–Kata Tjuta National Park
1987 Central Eastern Rainforest Reserves (Australia)
1988 Wet Tropics of Queensland
1991 Shark Bay, Western Australia
1992 Fraser Island
1994 Australian Fossil Mammal Sites (Riversleigh/Naracoorte)
1997 Heard and McDonald Islands
1997 Macquarie Island
2001 Greater Blue Mountains (nominated)

A related reservation status is the UNESCO Biosphere Reserve, which monitors human impact on pristine areas. Kosciuszko National Park in New South Wales is an example of this type of reserve.

State Recreation Areas (SRAs)

These are smaller reserves that often protect only a particular feature, rather than a self-sustained ecosystem. They are part of the NSW reserve system and similar in tenure to Victoria's state parks. Regulations are less restrictive than in national parks with the emphasis more on public recreation than conservation. A good example is Bungonia, near Goulburn.

Nature Reserves

These reserves entail the highest level of protection that can be awarded in the state. Usually a particular type of rare environment is preserved: for example, coastal rainforest in Broken Head Nature Reserve. Facilities are very limited—in many, camping is prohibited. One of the suggested walks in this guide is through the Pantoneys Crown Nature Reserve in the Capertee Valley, NSW.

State Forests

These are managed by the Forestry Commission of NSW for timber production, which generates about $100 million annual income. The forests can be either softwood radiata pine plantations or native eucalypt hard-woods. There are just over 3.5 million hectares of state forest in the state, 95 per cent being native. Recreation activities are well catered for in state forests, with more and better roads than in national parks. There is an abundance of picnic and camping areas in popular regions, and restrictions are usually less severe. While the scenery may not be as aesthetic as in national parks, the sheer scale and relative ease of access make state forests ideal for extended exploration.

Flora, Fauna, Forest Reserves

These small reserves, often with picnic and camping facilities, are found along tourist drives in state forests and pre-serve particularly sensitive or aesthetic areas for conservation and recreational purposes. Primarily, they act as a con-trol against which to judge the effects of logging elsewhere. Despite popular belief, these have full legislation-backed protection and can be revoked only by parliament. There are a number of such reserves on Kangaroo Island.

Catchment Authority/Water Board territory

Since the contamination debacle with Sydney's drinking water in 1998, there is an even greater emphasis on maintaining the purity of urban water-supply catchment areas. The states' various water utilities jointly administer large portions of natural land surrounding state capitals. In the Blue Mountains, the construction of Warragamba Dam in 1960 blocked the Coxs and Wollondilly River valleys, forming a massive stored water build-up in Lake Burragorang. A 3km margin around this 7500ha lake is totally prohibited to bushwalkers. Other water authorities, such as the Tasmanian Hydro-Electric Commission, are more relaxed, even allowing canoeing and powerboating on stored water.

State Reserves

Generally smaller than 4000ha, these preserve a particular feature or site, such as Hastings Caves in Tasmania.

Game Reserves

Areas where habitats and animals are protected to the same level as in state reserves but where certain species may be hunted by permit. An example is Bruny Island Neck.

Conservation Areas

These provide protection from the actions of the public but not from actions undertaken in pursuance of a right granted under other legislation, whether this be forestry or mining. The level of protection of a conservation area can be expanded by the implementation of a statutory management plan of the area. Two examples of such areas are the Central Plateau and Cape Direction in Tasmania.

Protected Areas

These offer a degree of protection similar to conservation areas, but allow controlled use of resources. They are reserved under the Crown Lands Act (Tasmania) 1976. An example is Mt Roland, in northern Tasmania.

State Parks

Generally smaller than 4000ha, preserving a particular feature or site, such as Lake Eildon in Victoria. Recreational facilities are common, but management is conducted according to the same principles as national parks.

Coastal Parks/Marine Reserves/Lakeside Reserves

Because of the popularity of water-based recreation, these are managed on a multi-use basis where the aquatic and marine natural environment is protected as well as access and facilities being provided for public enjoyment. About 90 per cent of Victoria's 2000km coast-line is publicly owned, with two-thirds being managed by Parks Victoria in more than 300 reserves totalling an area of 47 000ha. Good examples include the Phillip Island Penguin Reserve in Victoria and the Jervis Bay Marine Park in New South Wales.

Historic Sites

These are prehistoric, historic and cultural features on public land managed within national, state, regional and coastal parks as well as within state forests.

Other Reserves

Bushland Reserves, Flora and Fauna Reserves (an example is Wychitella in Victoria), Flora Reserves, Historic Parks (such as Pirianda Garden in Victoria), Public Purpose Reserves, Scenic Lookout Reserves, Wilderness Areas and vacant Crown Land.

Glossary

algae: simple aquatic plants consisting of hair-like filaments or green slime in water or on damp soil.

alluvial soil: sand, silt and clay deposited in riverbeds, flood plains and lakes.

amphibolite: a metamorphic rock consisting mainly of iron and magnesium-rich silicate.

andalusite: a mineral, aluminium silicate, generally found in metamorphosed terrain in rocks such as schist and gneiss.

basalt: a hard, dark-coloured rock of volcanic origin.

basement: complex deposits of chiefly metamorphic and igneous rocks under the stratified rocks and sedimentary deposits of a region.

batholith: a great mass of granite or other igneous rock intruded below the surface, commonly along the axis of a mountain range. This is sometimes exposed by erosion.

bora ground: normally, a circular arrangement of rocks marking an Aboriginal site of special spiritual significance, usually to do with burial.

brachiopod: a marine animal similar to a mussel, common and widespread in the Cambrian period.

breccia: a coarse-grained rock composed of broken rock fragments held together by mineral cement or in a finer-grained matrix.

bush: any uncleared area, and the native vegetation found there.

bushbash: to walk through trackless terrain, especially when it is heavily vegetated.

buttress: pillar-like stone projection from a hillside.

cairn: mound of rocks, erected as a marker in trackless terrain or to claim a summit. Erecting them is discouraged by national park authorities.

calcareous: a substance that contains calcium carbonate (limestone).

canyon: a narrow cliff-lined valley, smaller than a gorge but larger than a chasm. Australia's premier canyon country lies in a sandstone belt that runs north from the Grose River in the Blue Mountains to Nullo Mountain in Wollemi National Park.

car shuffle: a walking party arranges beforehand to leave a car at the end of a walk.

cascade: small waterfall. Cascading is to swim across a waterhole rather than to scramble around it.

cataract: a large, steep waterfall.

chimney: vertical rock fissure large enough for a person to climb.

circuit: walk that ends back at its starting point.

cirque: rounded high precipice formed by past glacial action in the alpine zone.

col: mountain pass.

confluence: the junction of two watercourses.

conglomerate: a sedimentary rock consisting of very coarse particles, up to river rock size, cemented together.

contour: to sidle around a hill at about the same altitude (or contour level).

cornice: overhanging ledge, usually of snow.

coppice: a tree that has been cut near ground level, encouraging the growth of several new trunks.

creek: small stream that may be dry in hot weather.

Cretaceous: the last geological period of the Mesozoic era, characterised by the formation of chalk deposits, dinosaurs

becoming extinct and the development of flowering plants.

cyanobacteria: a group of organisms without a cell nucleus, formerly called blue-green algae. They release oxygen during photosynthesis and were responsible hundreds of millions of years ago for increasing the oxygen level in the atmosphere to a point that can support higher forms of life. They are the main organisms responsible for the formation of stromatolites.

desert varnish: dark shiny coating on the surface of stones exposed for thousands of years to the sun.

dingo fence: the world's longest fence, erected to keep dingoes out of south-eastern Australia.

Diprotodon: a large, herbivorous mammal, often described as a giant wombat weighing one to two tonnes.

divide: (or watershed) a relatively high point in the land surface separating one river or creek system from another.

dolerite: coarse-grained type of basalt.

dolomite: calcium-magnesium carbonate. As a rock name, it refers to a sedimentary rock with at least 90 per cent mineral dolomite and less than 10 per cent calcium carbonate (calcite).

Dry: the dry season in northern Australia, where rainfall is least during late winter.

endemic: found only within a particular localised area.

erosion: the constant wearing away of land and rock formations by the action of wind, water, ice and gravity.

erratic: piece of rock that differs in composition, etc, from rocks surrounding it, having been transported, usually by glacial action, from its place of origin.

estuary: the seaward end of a river valley where fresh water runs into the sea and is affected by the tides.

fault: a fracture along which a sliding movement has taken place, so that rock is displaced on either side of the fracture for a few centimetres or up to many kilometres.

faultline: a line marking the intersection of a fault plane with the earth's surface.

feldspar: a group of very abundant silicate minerals, containing mainly calcium, sodium, potassium and aluminium in various proportions; commonly white, cream, pale grey or reddish.

fire trail: vehicle track cut to provide access during bushfires.

folded mountains: mountains with bends and flexures formed by tremendous pressures after their stratification. The MacDonnell Ranges in the Northern Territory are a prime example.

food chain: a series of organisms interrelated by the fact that each member feeds on another and in turn forms food for another organism in the series.

food web: a group of interrelated food chains.

ford: to cross a watercourse. It is also a point on a river or creek where this is possible.

fuel-stove-only area: a region where campfires are totally banned.

geophyte: a plant that survives winter by storing food in subterranean buds.

geosyncline: a broad, elongated depression in the earth's crust in which layers of sediment accumulate to thicknesses of thousands of metres.

gibber plain: stony plain; from *gibber*, an Aboriginal word for stone or boulder.

gneiss: a coarse-grained, metamorphic rock. It is distinguished from granite by its foliated or laminated structure.

Gondwanaland: one of two ancient supercontinents produced by the first splitting of the larger supercontinent Pangaea about 200 million years ago. Gondwanaland later split into Africa, South America, Australia, Antarctica and the Indian subcontinent.

gorge: large, steep-sided valley, usually bounded by cliffs.

GPS: Global Positioning System; a device that uses Einstein's theory of relativity to calculate position and elevation by reading and decoding signals from satellites.

granite: light-coloured, coarse-grained lava rock.

gulch: narrow ravine cut by a fast stream or the ocean.

gully: small, steep-sided valley.

igneous: a rock formed by intense heat or volcanic action, usually hardened from the molten state.

indigenous: native to, or originating in, a particular country or region.

inlet: narrow entrance or opening to a watercourse.

intrusion: the process by which material has been injected into preexisting rocks.

isohyet: a line on a map joining all places having the same rainfall within a prescribed period.

isthmus: narrow stretch of land connecting two relatively large land areas.

karst area: a region dominated by limestone, usually with caves and sinkholes.

land bridge: a connecting tract of land between two large bodies of water; *see also* isthmus.

lead: narrow opening in the scrub.

limestone: a sedimentary rock comprising at least 50 per cent calcium carbonate (usually in excess of 95 per cent), generally in the form of the mineral calcite, with or without magnesium carbonate.

magnesite: magnesium carbonate, a white, grey, yellow or brown mineral commonly formed by the alteration of other rocks (e.g. dolomite and certain types of igneous rocks).

mallee: a low, scrubby, multistemmed eucalypt generally growing from a swollen rootstock known as a lignotuber. There are many species, ranging from shrubs of 3m, to some with a single trunk up to 15m tall. The term also refers to the bush mangrove, a hardy coastal tree genus that grows in salt water.

matrilineal: kinship and relationship between generations carried through the female line, rather than the male line (patrilineal).

Mesozoic: an era in earth's history that began 245 million years ago and finished 65 million years ago; it includes the Triassic, Jurassic and Cretaceous periods.

metamorphic rock: derived from pre-existing rock by changes in structure, mineral composition and/or chemical composition due generally to marked changes in temperatures and pressure, most commonly caused by deep burial in the earth's crust.

metazoans: the large group of multi-celled organisms that includes all true animals. The Ediacara animals are the oldest known metazoan fossils.

midden: a domestic refuse site, usually comprised of shells, indicating pre-historic Aboriginal occupation.

minimal-impact camping: a set of principles governing campers' behaviour and choice of equipment.

monolith: a mountain-size rock, such as Mt Augustus in Western Australia.

moraine: ridges and mounds of glacial debris, along a glacier's margins (lateral moraine), in its centre (medial moraine), or at its mouth (terminal moraine).

mylonite: a rock with a streaky or banded structure produced by shearing, often associated with intense faulting.

orographic: clouds formed by mountains or ridges pushing moisture-laden air up into colder temperatures and causing condensation.

outlet: of a lake, an opening that permits water to flow away.

pad: a faint track, usually not officially developed or maintained.

pass: gap between peaks in a mountain range; also a route through such a gap.

pinnacle: towering peak.

phyllite: a metamorphic rock, largely of mica crystals, with a silvery sheen.

plateau(s): elevated, almost level area(s) of land.

Pleistocene: the geological epoch commonly called the ice age, characterised by vast glaciation of the northern hemisphere and the evolution of homo sapiens. It ended 10 000 years ago.

porphyry: an igneous rock that contains conspicuous large mineral crystals in a finer-grained matrix.

pound: a geological formation created by the uplifting and sinking of land leaving broad-basin valleys.

Pre-Cambrian: the earliest geological division of time. It began before the Palaeozoic era and accounts for nearly 90 per cent of earth's history.

quartzite: white or grey sandstone composed of quartz grains.

rain shadow: a dry area on the lee side of high ground that intercepts rain-bearing winds causing them to drop the water they are carrying.

Red Centre: central Northern Territory.

saddle: a low place in a ridge resembling a horse saddle in profile.

sand blow: large, unstable sand dune.

sandstone: a sedimentary rock in which sand grains are cemented by a mineral, e.g. quartz or calcium carbonate.

schist: a crystalline metamorphic rock composed mainly of mica. It splits easily into thin flakes or slabs.

scintillometer: an instrument used to measure ionising radiation.

sclerophyll: an evergreen tough-leaved plant usually growing where rainfall is low; the leaf structure reduces water loss.

scramble: to climb a steep slope with the help of your hands.

scree: weathered boulders at the foot of a cliff or on a hillside; also called talus.

scrub: term used for areas of thick, low vegetation, often difficult to walk in.

sedimentary rock: a rock resulting from consolidation of loose fragments of older rock accumulated in layers after transport by water, ice or wind. The definition also includes chemically precipitated rocks such as limestone and dolomite.

shale: a fine-grained sedimentary rock formed by the consolidation of clay, and characterised by a finely laminated structure along which the rock separates readily into thin layers.

sidle: to walk around or along the side of a hill.

siltstone: a sedimentary rock formed by the consolidation of silt-sized rock and mineral fragments.

sinkhole: depression in the ground where a surface stream disappears.

slate: a fine-grained, bluish-grey metamorphic rock formed from shale. It flakes easily into thin, smooth layers.

snowline: level below which snow seldom falls and does not remain on the ground.

snow plain: open grassy area above the tree line.

snow poles: a series of distinctive coloured markers enabling a route to be found even in difficult conditions.

Snowy Mountains: the unofficial term used to describe the skiing resorts of the Australian Alps.

spur: small sloping ridge that leads up from a valley to a main ridge.

stage: a single section of a longer walk.

staging area: a place from which walking tracks radiate, usually at the end of a national park road.

stalactite: a cave formation that grows from the roof.

stalagmite: a cave formation that grows from the floor.

stromatolite: a sedimentary fossil structure commonly produced by cyanobacteria trapping, binding and precipitating sediment (commonly calcium carbonate) to form layered, domed or columnar structures such as those seen in Shark Bay, Western Australia.

switchback: a route that follows a zigzag course up or down a steep grade.

syncline: a downfold in rock strata.

tarn: small alpine lake, usually of glacial origin.

tech-head: a bushwalker who enjoys using state-of-the-art hi-tech gadgets when in the bush.

temperature inversion: an atmospheric condition in which a layer of warm air develops above a layer of cool air.

Tertiary: a period of earth's history from 65 million years to 1.6 million years ago.

thylacine: a dog-like carnivorous marsupial, now believed to be extinct on the Australian mainland; it has tapered hindquarters and a striped back.

Top End: northern section of the Northern Territory.

topocadastral map: a map that indicates both surface features of a region and the extent and ownership of land.

topographical map: map with lines joining all places of equal height.

tor: pile of boulders, usually rounded by erosion.

trackhead: the starting point of a walking track, usually at a car park.

traverse: to move horizontally across a slope.

tree line: uppermost (natural) level to which tree cover extends on a mountainside.

trig point/trig marker: the term for a triangulation point, used in triangulation as a basis for trigonometrical survey mapping. These markers are normally at the summit of prominent peaks throughout Australia.

Wet: late summer in Australia's north, the time of peak rainfall.

Wet season watershed: a ridge that divides two watercourses, especially if they flow in opposite directions. The Great Dividing Range is the longest watershed in Australia.

Xerophyte: a plant that loses little water.

Glossary of karst terms

blind valley: a valley in which a stream sinks underground.

cave coral: speleothem formed by splashing, or diffuse capillary flow.

cave sediments: material washed into a cave.

doline: a closed depression produced by solution, subsidence and/or collapse.

flowstone: speleothem produced by degassing of thin films of water flowing over cave walls.

helictite: horizontal stalactite formed in stable cave environment where the rates of water percolation are so slow that drops do not form.

karst: landforms, above and below ground, produced by chemical solution of the bedrock.

solution form: small-scale features, such as pits and ripples in rock surface, produced by water dissolving limestone.

speleothem: cave decoration such as stalactites etc.

tufa: a porous deposit often containing organic material.

Rock formations in the Gardens of Stone National Park, New South Wales.

Further Reading

General Reading

Alcorta, Frank, *Explore Australia's Northern Territory*, New Holland, 1997

Andrews, Bill, *Explore Australia's Great Inland*, New Holland, 1997

Australian Alps Liaison Committee, *Explore the Australian Alps*, New Holland, 1998

Baxter, Nick, *Getting Started*, Wild Publications, 1992

Carter, Simon, *Rock Climbing in Australia*, New Holland, 1998

Colls, Keith, and Whitaker, Richard, *The Australian Weather Book*, New Holland, 1996

Cronin, Leonard, *Key Guide to Australia's National Parks*, New Holland, 1998

Klinge, Sven, and Hart, Adrian, *Don't Die in the Bush*, New Holland, 2000

Land Information Centre, *CMA Map Reading Guide*, Land Information Centre, 1984

Mirtschin, Peter, and Davis, Richard, *Snakes of Australia—Dangerous and Harmless*, Hill of Content, 1992

Pallin, Paddy, *Bushwalking and Camping*, self-published, 1995

Swan, Gerry, *Snakes and Other Reptiles of Australia*, New Holland, 1996

Toghill, Jeff, *Knots and Splices*, New Holland, 1997

Wilson, Sally, *Some Plants are Poisonous*, New Holland, 1997

Guidebooks

Queensland

Buchanan, Ross, *Bushwalking in South East Queensland*, Hema Maps, 1996

Buchanan, Ross, and Buchanan, Heather, *Fraser Island and Cooloola Visitors Guide*, Hema Maps, 1996

Islands of Australia's Great Barrier Reef, Lonely Planet, 1998

Jarrott, Keith J., *History of Lamington National Park*, J.K. Jarrott and the National Parks Association of Queensland, 1990

Sinclair, John (with Peter Corris), *Fighting for Fraser Island*, Kerr Publishing, 1994

Thomas, Tyrone, *50 Walks in North Queensland*, Hill of Content, 2000

New South Wales

Cameron, Bruce, *A History of the Blue Labyrinth, Blue Mountains National Park*, B. Cameron, 1992

Chapman, John, *Classic New South Wales Walks*, Wild Publications, 1997

Doughton, Ron, *Bushwalking in the Budawangs*, Envirobook, 1989

Dunk, Anthony, *Discovering the Colo Wilderness on Foot*, Envirobook, 1999

Fitzroy Falls and Beyond, Budawang Committee, 1988

Hill, Harry, *Hume and Hovell Walking Track Guidebook*, 1993

Klinge, Sven, *Cycling the Bush, 100 Rides in NSW*, Hill of Content, 1994

McDougall, Garry, and Shearer-Heriot, Leigh, *The Great North Walk*, Kangaroo Press, 1998

National Parks Association, *Volumes 1 and 2, Bushwalks in the Sydney Region*, NPA, 1997

Noble, David, *Blue Mountains Canyons*, Wild Publications, 1996

Noble, David, *Classic Blue Mountains Walks*, Wild Publications, 1996

Paton, Neil, *Sydney Bushwalks*, Kangaroo Press, 1986

Paton, Neil, *Treks in New South Wales*, Kangaroo Press, 1986

Paton, Neil, *Walks in the Blue Mountains*, Kangaroo Press, 1987

Pigeon House and Beyond, Budawang Committee, 1982

Prineas, Peter, and Gold, Henry, *Wild Places, Wilderness in Eastern New South Wales*, Colong Foundation, 1997

Sloss, Robert William, *Mittagong Nattai—Walking Tracks for the Southern Highlands*, self-published, 1992

Thomas, Tyrone, *120 Walks in New South Wales*, Hill of Content, 2000

Thomas, Tyrone, *70 Walks in Southern New South Wales and A.C.T.*, Hill of Content, 1998

UNE Mountaineering Club, *A Guide to North-Eastern New South Wales*, UNE Mountaineering Club, 1984

Warner, Charles, *Bushwalking in Kosciuszko National Park*, Warner, 1989

Australian Capital Territory

ACT Parks and Conservation Service, *Namadgi National Park (Map and Guide)*, Environment ACT, 1999

Siseman, John, *Alpine Walking Track*, Pindari Publications, 1998

Thomas, Tyrone, *70 Walks in Southern New South Wales and A.C.T.*, Hill of Content, 1998

Victoria

A Walk on the Wild side—The Great South-West Walk (Ed. Bennett, Gwen), Friends of the Great South West Walk, 1996

Cook, Peter, and Dowd, Chris, *Walking the Wilderness Coast*, Wildcoast Publications, 1996

Chapman, John, *Classic Victorian Alpine Walks*, Wild Publications, 1999

Da Costa, Grant, *Car Touring and Bush walking in East Gippsland*, Australian Conservation Foundation, 1998

Geelong Bushwalking Club, *Walking the Otways*, Geelong Bushwalking Club, 1996

Klinge, Sven, *Cycling the Bush, 100 Rides in Victoria*, Hill of Content, 1994

Siseman, John, *Victoria's Alpine National Park*, Macstyle Media, 1997

Thomas, Tyrone, *120 Walks in Victoria*, Hill of Content, 2000

Thomas, Tyrone, *50 Walks in the Grampians*, Hill of Content, 1991

Thomas, Tyrone, *60 Walks in Central Victoria's Gold Fields and Spa Country*, Hill of Content, 2000

Thomas, Tyrone, *70 Walks in Victoria's Bright and Falls Creek Districts*, Hill of Content, 2000

van der Knijff, Glenn, *Extended Walks In The Victorian Alps*, Wild Publications, 1992

Tasmania

Brand, Ian, *Sarah Island: An Account of the penal settlements of Sarah Island, Tasmania, from 1822 to 1833 and 1846 to 1847*, Regal Publications, 1984

Chapman, John, *Cradle Mountain–Lake St Clair and Walls of Jerusalem National Park*, John Chapman and Pindari Publications, 1998

Chapman, John, *South West Tasmania*, J. Chapman, 1998

Chapman, John, *Wild Alternative Tasmania*, Wild Publications, 1994

Collins, Ken, *South-West Tasmania*, Heritage Books, 1990

Klinge, Sven, *Cycling the Bush: 100 Rides in Tasmania*, Hill of Content, 1993

Siseman, John, and Chapman, John, *Cradle Mountain–Lake St Clair National Park*, John Chapman and Pindari Publications, 1998

Storey, Peter, and Storey, Shirley, *Tasman Tracks*, Koonya Press, 1996

Thomas, Tyrone, *100 Walks in Tasmania*, Hill of Content, 2000

South Australia

Bird, Peter, and Fisher, David, *Walks with Nature: 20 Nature Walks in the Mount Lofty Ranges*, Nature Conservation Society of South Australia, 1995

Conservation Council of South Australia, *Flinders Ranges Walks*, Federation of South Australian Walking Clubs, 1997

Heard, Adrian, *Gammon Ranges and Arkaroola Sanctuary: A Walking Guide to the Northern Flinders Ranges*, State Publishing, 1990

Explore the Flinders Ranges (Ed. Barker, Sue), Royal Geographical Society of Australasia (SA Branch), 1995

Western Australia

Dept of Conservation and Land Manage ment (CALM), *A Guide to the Bibbul mun Track, Northern Half*, CALM, 1998

Dept of Conservation and Land Manage ment (CALM), *A Guide to the Bibbul mun Track, Southern Half*, CALM, 1998

Department of Conservation and Land Management (CALM), *Bushwalks in the South-West*, CALM, 1997

Department of Conservation and Land Management (CALM), *Family Walks in the Perth Outdoors*, CALM, 1996

Department of Conservation and Land Management (CALM), *More Family Walks in Perth Outdoors*, CALM, 1997

Morphet, A.T., *Mountain Walks in the Stirling Range, A pictorial guide: Part 1: The peaks to the west of Chester Pass*, Torridon Publications, 1996

Morphet, A.T., *Mountain Walks in the Stirling Range, A pictorial guide: Part 2: The peaks to the east of Chester Pass*, Torridon Publications, 1996

Northern Territory

Breiter, Mattias, *Kakadu and The Top End*, Kangaroo Press, 1996

Conservation Commission of NT, *Explore Australia's Northern Territory*, Conservation Commission of NT, 1995

Australia-wide

Chapman, John, and Chapman, Monica, *Bushwalking in Australia*, Lonely Planet, 1997

Chapman, John, *Gorge Walks*, Wild Publications, 1991

Chapman, John, *Wild Peak Bagging*, Wild Publications, 1994

Chapman, John, *Wild Waterfalls*, Wild Publications, 1992

Dunphy, Myles, *Myles Dunphy: Selected Writings* (annotated by Patrick Thompson), Ballagirin, 1986

Hermes, Neil, *Explore Wilderness Australia*, New Holland, 1997

Klinge, Sven, *Cycling the Bush: The Best Rides in Australia*, Hill of Content, 1996

Meredith, Peter, *Myles and Milo*, Allen & Unwin, 1999

Rankin, Robert, *Classic Wild Walks of Australia* (also available on CD-ROM), Rankin Publishers, 1996

Thomas, Tyrone, *20 Best Walks in Australia*, Hill of Content, 2000

Thomas, Tyrone, and Klinge, Sven, *Australian Mountains: The Best 100 Walks*, Hill of Content, 1998

Periodicals

Australian Geographic, Expanse, Outdoor Australia, Rock and *Wild*

Bibliography

Angel, G., and Bell, M., *Wilderness In Danger*, Colong Committee, Sydney, 1978

Carron, L.T., *A History of Forestry in Australia*, ANU Press, Canberra, 1985

Coper, M., *The Franklin Dam Case*, Butterworths, Sydney, 1984

Corkhill, J., *Tourism And The Environ ment*, North Coast Environment Centre, Sydney, 1987

Dargavel, John, *The Allocation of Australian Forest Resources*, Cres D-189, ANU, 1986

Davis, B., *The Struggle for South-West Tasmania*, Macmillan, Hobart, 1980

Division of Recreation/Education Dep artment of Tasmania, *Recreation And Tourism Land Use Planning In Australia*, Hobart, 1982

Elliot, R., and Gare, A. (Eds), *Environ mental Philosophy: A Collection of Readings*, University of Queensland Press, St Lucia, 1983

Fowler, R., *Environmental Impact Assess ment, Planning, and Pollution Meas ures in Australia*, AGPS, Canberra, 1982

Frith, H.J. *Wildlife Conservation*, Angus and Robertson, 1979

Frawley, Kevin J., *Forest And Land Management In North-East Queensland: 1859-1960*, PhD thesis, Department Of Geography, ANU, 1983

Frawley, Kevin J., *Exploring Some Aus tralian Images of Environment*, Working Paper 1987/1, Department of Geography and Oceanography, University College, Australian Defence Force Academy

Gilpin, Alan, *Environment Policy In Australia*, University Of Queensland Press, St Lucia, 1980

Green, R., *Battle for the Franklin*, Fontana/Australian Conservation Foundation, Sydney, 1983

Haye, P., *Environmental Politics in Australia and New Zealand*, Centre For Environmental Studies, Hobart, 1989

Hutton, Drew (Ed.), *Green Politics In Australia: Working Towards A Peaceful, Sustainable, and Achieveable Future*, Angus & Robertson, Sydney, 1987

Kendell, J., and Buivids, E. (Eds), *Earth First; The Struggle to Save Australia's Rainforest*, ABC Enterprises, Sydney, 1987

Mathews, R.L. (Ed), *Federalism and The Environment*, Centre For Research On Federal Financial Relations, ANU, Canberra, 1985

McCombe, A., and Lake, P. (Eds), *The Conservation of Australian Wetlands*, Surrey Beatty, Sydney, 1988

McHenry, K., *Recreation, Wilderness, and the Public*, Department of Youth, Sport, and Recreation, Melbourne, 1976

Meyer, A., *The Forestors*, Institute of Foresters, Hobart, 1985

Mosley, J.G., and Messer, J. (Eds), *Fighting For Wilderness: Papers From The ACF's Third National Wilderness Conference*, Fontana/ACF, Sydney, 1984

Figgis, P., *Out of the Wilderness for the Wilderness Issue?*, National Conser vation Strategy For Australia, National Conference held in Canberra in June, 1983, Chaired by Sir Rupert Myers.

Parv, V., *The Changing Face Of Aus tralia*, Bay Books, Sydney, 1984

Recher, H.F., and Lunney, D., *A Natural Legacy—Ecology In Australia*, Pergamon Press, Sydney, 1979

Rich, D.C., and Young, R.W., *Environment and Development in Australia*, Geo graphic Society of NSW, Sydney, 1988

Robertson, R.W., Helman, P., and Davey, A. (Eds), *Wilderness Manage ment in Australia*, Canberra College of Advanced Education, Canberra, 1980

Thompson, Peter, and Brown, Bob, *Of the Franklin River*, Allen & Unwin, Sydney, 1984

Wilderness Society, *The Franklin Block ade*, Wilderness Society, Hobart, 1983

Lilly Pilly Gully, Wilsons Promontory National Park, Victoria.

Index of walks

	Distance (km)	Time (days)	Height Variation (m)	Attraction Rating	Fitness	Alpine	Coast	River	Lake	Wilderness	Geological	Aboriginal	Historical	Wildlife	Vegetation	Waterfalls	Circuit Walk	Public Transport	Page Number
QUEENSLAND																			
Cape York																			
Mt Cook Walk	8	1	350	2	2										•				22
Mossman River Circuit	3.2	1	40	1	1			•							•		•		24
The Islands																			
Dunk Island Circuit	10.4	1	271	2	1		•						•		•		•	•	26
Thorsborne Trail	32	4-5	263	5	3		•	•		•				•	•		•	•	27
Forest-Lakes Circuit	38.1	3-5	180	3	2		•		•		•			•	•		•		33
The Coast & Mountains																			
Mt Bartle Frere Walk	15	1	1544	3	5	•				•	•				•	•			35
Clarke Range Track	8.3	1	U/A	2	2										•				38
Broken River Trail	8.4	1	U/A	2	2			•							•	•			38
Finch Hatton Gorge Falls Walk	9	1	U/A	3	2			•							•	•			39
Cooloola Wilderness Trail Walk	46.2	3	85	3	2			•	•					•					41
Inland Parks																			
Upper Gorge Circuit	7	1	110	3	2			•			•						•		44
Island Stack Circuit	6.5	1	105	3	2			•			•	•					•		44
Carnarvon Gorge Walk	19.2	1	130	5	2			•		•	•	•			•	•			45
Battleship Spur Walk	10.4	1	210	3	4						•								46
The South-east																			
Westcott Plains Track	11.3	1	U/A	2	2										•		•		53
Barker Creek and Lookout Circuit	14.4	1	U/A	3	2			•		•					•	•	•		54
Ships Stern Circuit	19	1	460	4	3			•		•					•	•	•		56
Coomera Circuit	21.6	1	270	4	4			•		•					•	•	•		56
Border Track Link Walk	21.4	1	560	5	3					•					•				57
Canungra Creek Circuit	13.9	1	470	3	3			•		•					•				59
Albert River Circuit	20.6	1	490	4	4			•		•					•		•		59
Mt Barney Walk	16	1	1200	5	4	•		•		•				•	•				61
Gap Creek Falls Walk	9.4	1	379	3	3			•							•	•			64
Bare Rock Walk	12.4	1	416	4	3					•					•				65
Mt Mitchell Walk	10.3	1	414	3	3					•					•				65
The Pyramids Walk	3.5	1	180	2	1						•								67
Mt Norman Walk	10.4	1	367	3	2					•	•								67
Red Rocks Gorge Walk	16	1	245	2	2			•			•		•	•		•	•		68
NEW SOUTH WALES																			
The Northern Rainforests																			
Mt Warning Walk	8.8	1	757	4	3						•				•				77
Washpool Rainforest Circuit	8	1	250	3	3			•		•			•		•	•	•		78
Gibraltar Range Highlights Walk	18	1	300	4	3			•		•	•				•	•			80
Inland Parks																			
South Bald Rock Walk	11	1	200	3	3						•			•					82
Scutts Hut Walk	19	1	620	4	4			•		•	•		•			•			83
Grand High Tops Walk	14.5	1	305	5	3						•			•			•		86
Mt Exmouth Walk	20	1	746	3	4						•								86
Gunneemooroo Camp Walk	39	2	400	4	3									•					87
The New England Tableland																			
Lucifers Thumb Walk	13	1	160	3	3										•	•			89
Woolpack Rocks Walk	7.4	1	180	3	2	•					•								90
Cathedral Rock Walk	5.8	1	190	3	2	•					•								91
Point Lookout Circuit	9	1	265	3	3	•								•	•		•		94
Wright Plateau and Cascades Walk	9	1	200	4	3			•		•				•	•	•			94
Platypus Creek Walk	26	2	950	3	5			•		•			•		•				95
Wonga Walk	6.6	1	160	4	2			•							•	•	•		97
Cedar Falls Circuit	8.2	1	200	3	3			•							•	•	•		97
The Hunter Valley Region																			
Barrington Tops Circuit	53	2	155	5	3			•	•	•				•	•		•		99

NEW SOUTH WALES

	Distance (km)	Time (days)	Height Variation (m)	Attraction Rating	Fitness	Alpine	Coast	River	Lake	Wilderness	Geological	Aboriginal	Historical	Wildlife	Vegetation	Waterfalls	Circuit Walk	Public Transport	Page Number
The Sandstone Parks																			
Gospers Mountain Walk	76	3	340	4	4					•	•		•						103
Pantoneys Crown Walk	24	1-2	532	4	5			•			•			•					105
Wolgan River-Capertee River Circuit	68	4-6	615	5	4			•		•	•		•	•	•		•		106
Glen Davis to Culoul Range Walk	49	5-7	450	5	3			•		•	•		•	•	•				108
Glow Worm Tunnel Circuit	7.5	1	335	3	2						•		•	•			•		109
Wollemi Creek Circuit	12	1	430	4	4			•		•	•						•		111
Canoe Creek Circuit	7	1	400	4	3			•		•	•				•		•		112
The Lower Colo River Walk	19	1-2	550	3	2			•		•	•			•	•				113
Grose Gorge (Victoria Falls-Lochleys Pylon)	19	1	630	5	4			•			•				•	•			116
Grose Gorge (Pierces Pass-Evans Lookout)	18	1	660	4	4			•			•				•	•			117
Grand Canyon Circuit	7	1	310	4	3			•			•				•	•	•		118
Mt Banks Circuit	14	1	222	3	2						•				•				118
Hanging Rock Walk	1.1	1	110	4	1						•								120
Mt Solitary Circuit	22	2	870	3	4			•			•		•	•	•				120
Katoomba cliffs and falls Circuit	14	1	220	4	3						•				•	•	•	•	121
National Pass Circuit	5	1	160	5	2			•			•				•	•	•	•	122
Lower Grose River Walk	15	2	430	4	4			•		•									122
Six Foot Track Walk	42	3	950	3	4			•			•	•	•		•			•	125
Upper Kowmung River Circuit	34	3-4	880	5	4			•		•	•			•	•		•		126
Mt Cloudmaker Walk	28	2	350	3	4	•				•	•				•				127
Colong Caves Walk	8	1	300	3	3			•		•	•				•				128
Middle Nattai River Walk	19	1	442	4	4			•		•	•				•		•		129
Upper Nattai River Walk	24	1-2	495	3	4			•		•	•				•				130
Fitzroy Falls Walk	9.5	1	250	3	3			•			•				•	•			132
Shoalhaven River Walk	16	1-2	535	4	4			•		•	•			•					133
Bungonia Canyon Circuit	9.8	1	420	5	4			•			•						•		135
Ettrema Gorge Circuit	15.7	2	510	5	4			•		•	•			•	•	•	•		136
Northern Budawang Circuit	64.5	5	780	5	5			•		•	•	•	•	•	•	•	•		137
The Castle Walk	12	1	770	5	4			•		•	•				•				139
Mt Owen Walk	17	2-3	810	5	5			•		•	•				•				141
Pigeon House Mountain Walk	19	1	484	4	4						•								142
Around Sydney																			
The Great North Walk	250	14	495	4	4		•	•	•		•	•	•	•	•	•		•	145
The Coast Walk	27	1-2	260	5	3		•	•	•		•		•	•	•	•		•	147
Heathcote Creek Circuit	13	1	110	3	3			•									•	•	148
The South Coast																			
Bendethera Caves Walk	7	1	220	3	3			•			•		•	•	•				149
Mother Woila Circuit	48.6	4	1105	3	5	•		•		•	•				•				150
Nadgee Beach	42	4	240	4	3		•		•	•		•		•	•				152
The Snowy Mountains																			
Cooleman Caves Walk	7	1	135	4	4	•		•		•	•			•		•	•		154
Mt Jagungal Circuit	42.6	2-3	760	4	4	•		•		•	•		•		•				155
Valentines Hut Walk	54	3	710	4	4	•		•		•	•		•		•	•	•		156
Main Range Circuit	24.5	1-2	510	5	3	•		•	•	•	•		•			•	•		157
Mt Kosciuszko Walk	12.2	1	265	4	2	•			•		•							•	158
Pilot Wilderness Walk	89	4	700	5	5	•		•		•	•		•	•	•	•			158
The Islands																			
Mt Gower Walk	8.5	1	875	5	4	•	•	•			•			•	•			•	161
The Goathouse Walk	12	1	420	4	3		•				•			•	•	•		•	163
Malabar Hill Circuit	9	1	209	4	4		•								•	•		•	164
Namadgi National Park																			
Mt Gingera	14.5	1	312	3	3	•					•		•		•				169
Bimberi Wilderness	68	3	965	3	5	•		•		•				•			•		170
Mt Clear Circuit	35	2	760	3	4	•		•					•	•	•		•		171
Naas Valley Walk	30	2	440	3	2			•					•	•	•				172
East Gippsland																			
Howe Wilderness Walk	46	4	50	3	2		•		•	•					•				180
Wilderness Coast Walk	41	3	95	4	3		•			•				•	•				181
Genoa River Gorge Circuit	84	4	536	4	4			•		•	•			•	•	•	•		182
Mt Ellery Walk	4	1	420	3	3						•				•				183
Gelantipy Plateau Walk	51.4	3	1016	3	4	•				•					•	•	•		185
Little River Gorge Walk	30	2-3	240	4	3			•			•					•			185
The Alpine Region																			
Mt Tingaringy Walk	20	1	710	3	3	•				•					•				189
Cowombat Flat Circuit	57	3-4	290	5	4	•		•		•			•	•	•		•		189

ACT

VICTORIA

VICTORIA · TASMANIA · SOUTH AUSTRALIA

Walk	Distance (km)	Time (days)	Height Variation (m)	Attraction Rating	Fitness	Alpine	Coast	River	Lake	Wilderness	Geological	Aboriginal	Historical	Wildlife	Vegetation	Waterfalls	Circuit Walk	Public Transport	Page Number
Mt Bogong (from the north) Circuit	18.9	1	1400	4	5	•		•		•				•	•		•		190
Mt Bogong (from the south) Circuit	55.5	4	950	5	4	•		•	•	•			•	•	•	•	•		191
Mt Feathertop Walk	23	1	1372	5	3	•					•	•	•	•	•				192
Mt Cobbler Walk	9	1	530	3	3	•			•	•	•				•				193
Man From Snowy River film set Walk	10	1	110	4	2	•							•						194
Mt Howitt Circuit	31	2	858	4	4	•		•		•	•			•	•		•		194
Wonnangatta River Circuit	42	4	1160	5	4	•		•		•	•			•	•		•		195
Bryces Gorge Circuit	7.6	1	160	4	2	•		•		•	•			•	•	•	•		197
Lake Tali Karng Circuit	45	2	755	5	4	•		•	•	•	•			•	•	•	•		197
Mt Buffalo Walk	1.5	1	105	3	1	•					•								199
South Gippsland																			
Wilsons Promontory Northern Circuit	68	4	220	4	2		•			•	•			•	•		•		203
Wilsons Promontory Southern Circuit	56.7	4	430	5	3		•	•		•			•	•	•		•		204
Around Melbourne																			
Fraser National Park Circuit	15.3	1	295	3	3				•								•		206
Cathedral Range Traverse Walk	11	1	630	5	4						•								206
Lake Mountain Walk	9.8	1	160	3	1	•									•		•		208
The West																			
Mt Difficult Walk	16	1	630	5	4						•					•			212
Major Mitchell Plateau Walk	18.2	1	865	4	3	•				•	•			•	•				213
The Fortress Walk	12	1	620	4	3					•	•								213
The Mallee																			
Bugle Ridge Circuit	10	1	10	2	2								•	•	•		•		215
Pink Lakes Nature Trail Walk	2.5	1	10	2	1				•										216
Lake Brambruk Nature Walk	6	1	40	2	2				•										217
South-west																			
Lorne waterfall Circuit	25.6	1	185	4	3			•							•	•	•		218
Beauchamp Falls Walk	2.9	1	140	4	2			•								•			219
Great South-west Walk	250	10	180	3	3		•	•						•	•		•	•	221
The East																			
Freycinet Circuit	41.9	3	579	4	3		•				•	•		•	•		•		228
Leeaberra Track Walk	25	2-3	465	3	3						•			•	•		•		229
Tasman Trail Walk	50.8	3-4	560	4	3		•				•			•		•	•		231
The Cradle Mountain Region																			
The Overland Track	77	4-6	877	5	4	•		•	•	•	•		•	•	•		•		234
Cradle Mountain Summit Walk	13.6	1	660	3	3	•		•	•	•				•	•	•	•		235
Cradle Mountain Circuit	16.8	1	330	3	3	•		•	•	•				•		•	•		236
Barn Bluff Walk	27	2	680	3	4	•			•	•				•	•	•	•		237
Reynolds Falls Walk	24.4	2	755	4	4			•		•				•	•		•		237
The Acropolis and The Labyrinth Walk	35	4	735	5	4	•		•	•	•	•			•	•		•		239
Mt Olympus Circuit	35	2	287	3	2				•	•	•			•		•	•		239
Walls of Jerusalem Walk	18	1	660	3	3	•			•	•	•			•			•		241
Frenchmans Cap Walk	41.9	3	1090	5	4	•		•	•	•	•			•			•		242
The South-west																			
Mt Field West Walk	21	1	400	3	5	•			•	•	•			•					245
Mt Field Circuit	12.5	1	495	3	3	•		•	•	•	•			•		•			246
Mt Field East Circuit	11.5	1	450	2	2	•		•	•	•	•			•		•			246
Mt Anne Circuit	36.2	4	1105	5	4	•		•	•	•	•			•			•		248
Western Arthurs Walk	78	8-12	810	5	5	•		•	•	•	•			•			•		250
Federation Peak Walk	64.6	6-9	1085	5	5	•		•	•	•	•			•			•		251
South Coast Track Walk	149	10-15	920	5	5		•			•		•	•	•			•		254
The Islands																			
Mt Strzelecki Walk	9	1	751	3	2		•				•				•				260
Maria Island Circuit	59.7	4	709	5	2		•				•		•	•	•	•	•		262
The Flinders Ranges																			
Bunyip Chasm Circuit	28.1	2	520	4	4			•			•		•	•	•	•	•		271
Italowie Gorge Walk	16	1	160	3	2						•			•	•				272
Mt Ohlssen Bagge Walk	5.3	1	480	3	3						•								275
Wilpena Pound Circuit	32.8	3	635	5	4			•			•		•	•		•	•		275
Heysen Trail (Flinders Ranges section) Walk	90.5	5	450	4	3			•			•		•	•	•				276
Mt Cavern Circuit	11.7	1	640	3	4			•			•						•		280
Hidden Gorge Circuit	18	1	350	4	3			•			•						•		280
Alligator Gorge Circuit	12	1	320	3	3			•			•						•		281
Kangaroo Island																			
Cape Gantheaume Wilderness Trail	34	2	110	3	2		•			•			•	•					283
Ravine des Casoars Circuit	8.9	1	175	3	2		•	•		•	•		•	•			•		284

	Distance (km)	Time (days)	Height Variation (m)	Attraction Rating	Fitness	Alpine	Coast	River	Lake	Wilderness	Geological	Aboriginal	Historical	Wildlife	Vegetation	Waterfalls	Circuit Walk	Public Transport	Page Number
The South Coast																			
Tower Peak Walk	3	1	390	3	2						•			•					290
Coastal Trail Walk	15	1	200	3	3		•				•			•	•				291
Fitzgerald River Coastal Traverse Walk	78	4-6	360	3	5		•	•	•	•	•			•	•				292
South-west																			
Bibbulmun Track Walk	964	49-56	500	5	5		•	•	•	•	•	•	•	•	•	•		•	294
Bluff Knoll Walk	7.5	1	630	4	3	•					•				•				296
Stirling Ranges Traverse Walk	29.8	3	795	4	4	•					•			•	•		•		297
Toolbrunup Peak Walk	4	1	630	4	3						•				•				299
Mt Magog to Talyuberlup Peak Walk	8	1	500	3	3						•						•		299
Nancys Peak Circuit	5.5	1	300	3	2						•			•	•		•		300
Nuyts Wilderness Walk	19.4	2	170	4	3		•	•		•	•			•	•				302
Mt Chudalup Walk	1	1	110	2	1						•				•				304
Cape to Cape Walking Track	140	6-8	190	4	4		•	•			•		•	•	•	•		•	305
The West Coast																			
Coastal Plain Walk Trail	46.3	2	75	2	2		•		•				•	•					307
The Pinnacles Circuit	6	1	40	4	1						•						•		309
The Loop Circuit	7	1	140	3	2			•			•			•	•		•		310
Murchison River Walk	38	3-4	210	4	2			•			•	•		•	•	•			311
The Pilbara																			
Mt Augustus Walk	12	1	850	4	3						•								312
Karijini Gorges Walk	3	1	170	3	2			•			•					•			314
Chichester Range Camel Trail Walk	8	1	200	3	3			•			•		•	•	•	•			315
The Kimberley																			
Piccaninny Gorge Walk	34	2-3	60	5	3			•			•	•	•	•	•	•			316
The Far North																			
East Alligator River Circuit	9	1	40	3	2			•				•		•	•		•		324
Jatbula Trail (Edith Falls Walk)	66.1	5	180	5	4			•		•	•	•		•	•	•			326
Eighth Gorge Walk	45-58	3-5	230	5	4			•		•	•	•		•	•	•			326
Mataranka Falls Walk	8	1	50	3	2			•						•	•	•			328
The MacDonnell Ranges																			
Larapinta Trail Walk	220	14	780	4	4			•		•	•	•	•	•	•	•			329
Mt Sonder Walk	8	1	650	3	3						•								330
Ormiston Pound Circuit	7	1	120	4	3			•			•	•		•	•		•		331
Mpaara Track Circuit	5	1	90	3	2			•			•	•		•			•		331
Giles Track Walk	22	2	380	4	3			•	•	•	•	•		•	•				332
Trephina Ridge Top Walk	16.5	1	200	4	3			•			•	•		•	•		•		333
The Red Centre																			
Circumference Circuit	8	1	5	3	1						•	•		•			•		335
The Valley of the Winds Circuit	5.5	1	200	4	2						•	•					•		335

Index

CLASSIC WALKS OF AUSTRALIA

833